The Complete Works of
E. M. Bounds
on Prayer

The Complete Works of
E. M. Bounds
on Prayer

Baker Books

A Division of Baker Book House Co.
Grand Rapids, Michigan 49516

Compilation copyright © 1990 by Baker Books
a division of Baker Book House Company
P.O. Box 6287, Grand Rapids, MI 49516-6287

ISBN: 0-8010-0985-5

Seventeenth printing, March 2003

Original publication dates of the books in this compilation
are as follows: *Power Through Prayer,* 1912 (originally
published as *Preacher and Prayer* in 1907); *Purpose in
Prayer,* 1920; *Prayer and Praying Men,* 1921; *Possibilities
of Prayer,* 1923; *The Reality of Prayer,* 1924; *The
Essentials of Prayer,* 1925; *The Necessity of Prayer,* 1929;
The Weapon of Prayer, 1931.

Printed in the United States of America

For information about academic books, resources for
Christian leaders, and all new releases available from
Baker Book House, visit our web site:
http://www.bakerbooks.com/

Contents

5

Publisher's Preface

FOR almost a century Edward McKendree Bounds's books on prayer have been classic works, stimulating and inspiring Christians to become prayer warriors. A forceful writer and very deep thinker, Bounds spent the last seventeen years of his life reading, writing, and praying. He rose at 4 A.M. daily for many years, and was indefatigable in his study of the Bible.

As breathing is a physical reality to us, so prayer was a reality for Bounds. He took the command, "Pray without ceasing," almost as literally as animate nature takes the law of the reflex nervous system, which controls our breathing.

Because Bounds so diligently practiced what he preached, he was able to capture the essence of prayer, and his works live on to call today's Christians to higher discipleship and an energetic prayer life.

Baker Book House is pleased to present this new compilation of Bounds's exquisite works on prayer.

Book seven in this compilation, *Power Through Prayer*, was first published in 1907 with the title *Preacher and Prayer*. All type has been reset, and archaic words have been modernized, but we have been careful not to dim the intense spirit and clear challenges of this godly man who lived to pray and write about prayer.

Introduction

EDWARD MCKENDREE BOUNDS was born in northeastern Missouri on August 15, 1835. His father was instrumental in organizing Shelby County, Missouri, and was an original landholder in the county seat, Shelbyville. Bounds attended the Shelbyville one-room school, where he quickly learned to read and write. Because his father served as county clerk, the Bounds home was used for court sessions. This likely motivated Edward to study law, and he passed the bar exam shortly before he turned nineteen. He practiced law until he was twenty-four and then, somewhat suddenly, felt and answered the call to preach. He ardently read Scripture, savored John Wesley's sermons, and began preaching in a small church in the nearby town of Monticello.

During this time the Missouri populace was torn by dissension over slavery and preservation of the Union. Because Bounds was pastor of a congregation in the recently formed Methodist Episcopal Church, South (resulting from the North-South polarity), he was arrested in 1861 by Union troops in Brunswick, Missouri, and charged as a Confederate sympathizer. He was held (with other noncombatants) in a Federal prison in St. Louis for a year and a half. He then was transferred to Memphis and released in a prisoner exchange between the Union and the Confederacy. Shortly afterward he was sworn in as a Confederate chaplain and served concurrently in the Third Missouri Volunteer Infantry Regiment and the Missouri Fifth Infantry (the units had combined after the fighting at Atlanta).

Bounds comforted and prayed with troops under General John Bell Hood just before one of the most severe encounters in the Civil War erupted in the Battle of Franklin (the last great charge mounted by the Confederates). After General Hood's second defeat at Nashville, Bounds was among Confederate prisoners who were released upon the taking of an oath of loyalty to the United States. He returned to the site of the battle to pastor the Franklin Methodist Episcopal Church, South.

Bounds later was assigned to a pastorate in Selma, Alabama. There he met Emma Elizabeth Barnett from Washington, Georgia. In 1874 Bounds was transferred to St. Louis; he and Emma married in 1876. From this union two daughters, Celeste and Corneille, and a son, Edward, were born. Emma died eight years after they were married. About two years after Emma's death, Bounds married her cousin, Harriet Elizabeth Barnett. To them were born three sons (Samuel, Charles, and Osborne) and three daughters (Elizabeth, Mary, and Emmie). Two children died within a year, Edward, at the age of six, and Charles, shortly after his first birthday.

While in St. Louis, Bounds accepted the position of associate editor of the *St. Louis Advocate*, a regional Methodist journal. After nineteen months in this position he moved to Nashville to become the associate editor of the *Christian Advocate*, the official weekly paper for the entire Methodist Episcopal Church, South, denomination.

In 1894 E. M. Bounds concluded his duties in Nashville. He and his family moved to Washington, Georgia, to live in the Barnett House. Here he spent the final nineteen years of his life engaged in intercessory prayer, writing, and itinerant revival ministry. He typically arose at four o'clock every morning to be alone with God in prayer, usually praying until seven o'clock. E. M. Bounds died in 1913 with only two of his books published, *Preacher and Prayer* and *The Resurrection*. Homer W. Hodge, with some help from another friend of Bounds, Claude L. Chilton, assumed the task of bringing to publication nine more books written by E. M. Bounds.

Claude Chilton captured the essence of the books on prayer by Bounds when he said:

> These books are unfailing wells for a
> lifetime of spiritual water-drawing.
> They are hidden treasures,
> wrought in the darkness of dawn
> and the heat of the noon
> on the anvil of experience,
> and beaten into wondrous form
> by the mighty stroke of the divine.
> They are living voices
> whereby he, being dead,
> yet speaketh!

BOOK

◆1◆

The Necessity of Prayer

1

Prayer and Faith

IN any study of the principles and procedure of prayer, of its activities and enterprises, first place, must, of necessity, be given to faith. It is the initial quality in the heart of any man who essays to talk to the unseen. He must, out of sheer helplessness, stretch forth hands of faith. He *must* believe, where he cannot prove. In the ultimate issue, prayer is simply faith, claiming its natural yet marvelous prerogatives—faith taking possession of its illimitable inheritance. True godliness is just as true, steady, and persevering in the realm of faith as it is in the province of prayer. Moreover: when faith ceases to pray, it ceases to live.

Faith does the impossible because it brings God to undertake for us, and nothing is impossible with God. How great—without qualification or limitation—is the power of faith! If doubt be banished from the heart, and unbelief made stranger there, what we ask of God shall surely come to pass, and a believer hath vouchsafed to him "whatsoever he saith."

Prayer projects faith on God, and God on the world. Only God can move mountains, but faith and prayer move God. In his cursing of the fig tree our Lord demonstrated his power. Following that, he proceeded to declare, that large powers were committed to faith and prayer, not in order to kill but to make alive, not to blast but to bless.

At this point in our study, we turn to a saying of our Lord, which there is need to emphasize, since it is the very keystone of the arch of faith and prayer.

> Therefore I say unto you, What things soever ye desire when ye pray, believe that ye receive them, and ye shall have them.

We should ponder well that statement—"Believe that ye receive them, and ye shall have them." Here is described a faith which realizes, which appropriates, which *takes*. Such faith is a consciousness of the divine, an experienced communion, a realized certainty.

Is faith growing or declining as the years go by? Does faith stand strong and foursquare, these days, as iniquity abounds and the love of many grows cold? Does faith maintain its hold, as religion tends to become a mere formality and worldliness increasingly prevails? The inquiry of our Lord, may, with great appropriateness, be ours. "When the Son of Man cometh," he asks, "shall he find faith on the earth?" We believe that he will, and it is ours, in this our day, to see to it that the lamp of faith is trimmed and burning, lest he come who *shall* come, and that right early.

Faith is the foundation of Christian character and the security of the soul. When Jesus was looking forward to Peter's denial, and cautioning him against it, he said unto his disciple:

> Simon, Simon, behold, Satan hath desired to have you, to sift you as wheat; but I have prayed for thee, that thy faith fail not.

Our Lord was declaring a central truth; it was Peter's faith he was seeking to guard; for well he knew that when faith is broken down, the foundations of spiritual life give way, and the entire structure of religious experience falls. It was Peter's faith which needed guarding. Hence Christ's solicitude for the welfare of his disciple's soul and his determination to fortify Peter's faith by his own all-prevailing prayer.

In his second epistle, Peter has this idea in mind when speaking of growth in grace as a measure of safety in the Christian life, and as implying fruitfulness.

> And besides this, giving diligence, add to your faith virtue; and to virtue knowledge; and to knowledge temperance; and to temperance patience; and to patience godliness.

Of this additive process, faith was the starting point—the basis of the other graces of the Spirit. Faith was the foundation on which other things were to be built. Peter does not enjoin his readers to add to works or gifts or virtues but to *faith*. Much depends on starting right in this business of growing in grace. There is a divine order, of which Peter was aware; and so he goes on to declare that we are to give diligence to making our calling and election sure, which election is rendered certain adding to faith which, in turn, is done by constant, earnest praying. Thus faith is kept alive by prayer, and every step taken, in this adding of grace to grace, is accompanied by prayer.

The faith which creates powerful praying is the faith which centers itself on a powerful person. Faith in Christ's ability to *do* and to do *greatly*, is the faith which prays greatly. Thus the leper lay hold upon the power of Christ. "Lord, if thou wilt," he cried, "Thou canst make me clean." In this instance, we are shown how faith centered in Christ's ability to *do*, and how it secured the healing power.

It was concerning this very point, that Jesus questioned the blind men who came to him for healing:

> "Believe ye that I am able to do this?" They said unto him, "Yea, Lord." Then touched he their eyes, saying, "According to your faith be it unto you."

It was to inspire faith in his ability to *do* that Jesus left behind him, that last, great statement, which, in the final analysis, is a ringing challenge to faith. "All power," he declared, "is given unto me in heaven and in earth."

Again: faith is obedient; it goes when commanded, as did the nobleman, who came to Jesus, in the day of his flesh, and whose son was grievously sick.

Moreover: such faith acts. Like the man who was born blind, it goes to wash in the pool of Siloam when *told* to wash. Like Peter on Gennesaret it casts the net where Jesus commands, instantly, without question or doubt. Such faith takes away the stone from the grave of Lazarus promptly. A praying faith keeps the commandments of God and does those things which are well pleasing in his sight. It asks, "Lord, what wilt thou have me to do?" and answers quickly, "Speak, Lord, thy servant heareth." Obedience helps faith, and faith, in turn, helps obedience. To do God's will is essential to true faith, and faith is necessary to implicit obedience.

Yet faith is called upon, and that right often to wait in patience before God, and is prepared for God's seeming delays in answering prayer. Faith does not grow disheartened because prayer is not immediately honored; it takes God at his Word, and lets him take what time he chooses in fulfilling his purposes, and in carrying on his work. There is bound to be much delay and long days of waiting for true faith, but faith accepts the conditions—knows there will be delays in answering prayer, and regards such delays as times of testing, in the which, it is privileged to show its mettle, and the stern stuff of which it is made.

The case of Lazarus was an instance of where there was delay, where the faith of two good women was sorely tried: Lazarus was critically ill, and his sisters sent for Jesus. But, without any known reason, our Lord delayed his going to the relief of his sick friend. The plea was urgent and touching—"Lord, behold, he whom thou lovest is sick"—but the master is not moved by it, and the women's earnest request seemed to fall on deaf ears. What a trial to faith! Furthermore: our Lord's tardiness appeared to bring about hopeless disaster. While Jesus tarried, Lazarus died.

But the delay of Jesus was exercised in the interests of a greater good. Finally, he makes his way to the home in Bethany.

> Then said Jesus unto them plainly, "Lazarus is dead. And I am glad for your sakes, that I was not there, to the intent ye may believe; nevertheless let us go unto him."

Fear not, O tempted and tried believer, Jesus *will* come, if patience is exercised, and faith holds fast. His delay will serve to make his coming the more richly blessed. Pray on. Wait on. You cannot fail. If Christ delay, wait for him. In his own good time, he *will* come, and will not tarry.

Delay is often the test and the strength of faith. How much patience is required when these times of testing come! Yet faith gathers strength by waiting and praying. Patience has its perfect work in the school of delay. In some instances, delay is of the very essence of the prayer. God has to do many things, antecedent to giving the final answer—things which are essential to the lasting good of him who is requesting favor at his hands.

Jacob prayed, with point and ardor, to be delivered from Esau. But before that prayer could be answered, there was much to be done with, and for Jacob. He must be changed, as well as Esau. Jacob had to be made into a new man, before Esau could be. Jacob had to be converted to God, before Esau could be converted to Jacob.

Among the large and luminous utterances of Jesus concerning prayer, none is more arresting than this:

> Verily, verily, I say unto you, he that believeth on me, the works that I do shall he do also; and greater works than these shall he do; because I go unto my Father. And whatsoever ye shall ask in my name, that will I do, that the Father may be glorified in the Son. If ye shall ask anything in my name, I will do it.

How wonderful are these statements of what God will do in answer to prayer! Of how great importance these ringing words, prefaced, as they are, with the most solemn verity! Faith in Christ is the basis of all working, and of all praying. All wonderful works depend on wonderful praying, and all praying is done in the name of Jesus Christ. Amazing lesson, of wondrous simplicity, is this praying in the name of the Lord Jesus! All other conditions are depreciated, everything else is renounced, save Jesus only. The name of Christ—the person of our Lord and Savior Jesus Christ—must be supremely sovereign, in the hour and article of prayer.

If Jesus dwells at the fountain of my life; if the currents of his life have displaced and superseded all self-currents; if implicit obedience to him is the inspiration and force of every movement of my life, then he can safely commit the praying to my will, and pledge himself, by an obligation as profound as his own nature, that whatsoever is asked shall be granted. Nothing can be clearer, more distinct, more unlimited both in application and extent, than the exhortation and urgency of Christ, "Have faith in God."

Faith covers temporal as well as spiritual needs. Faith dispels all undue anxiety and needless care about what shall be eaten, what shall be drunk, what shall be worn. Faith lives in the present, and regards the day as being sufficient unto the evil thereof. It lives day by day, and dispels all fears for the morrow. Faith brings great ease of mind and perfect peace of heart.

> Thou wilt keep him in perfect peace whose mind is stayed on thee: because he trusted in thee.

When we pray, "Give us this day our daily bread," we are, in a measure, shutting tomorrow out of our prayer. We do not live in tomorrow but in today. We do not seek tomorrow's grace or tomorrow's bread. They thrive best, and get most out of life, who live in the living present. They pray best who pray for today's needs, not for tomorrow's, which may render our prayers unnecessary and redundant by not existing at all!

True prayers are born of present trials and present needs. Bread, for today, is bread enough. Bread given for today is the strongest sort of pledge that there will be bread tomorrow. Victory today, is the assurance of victory tomorrow. Our prayers need to be focused upon the present. We must trust God today, and leave the morrow entirely with him. The present is ours; the future belongs to God. Prayer is the task and duty of each recurring day—daily prayer for daily needs.

As every day demands its bread, so every day demands its prayer. No amount of praying, done today, will suffice for tomorrow's praying. On the other hand, no praying for tomorrow is of any great value to us today. Today's manna is what we need; tomorrow God will see that our needs are supplied. This is the faith which God seeks to inspire. So leave tomorrow, with its cares, its needs, its troubles, in God's hands. There is no storing tomorrow's grace or tomorrow's praying; neither is there any laying-up of today's grace, to meet tomorrow's necessities. We cannot have tomorrow's grace, we cannot eat tomorrow's bread, we cannot do tomorrow's praying. Sufficient unto the day is the evil thereof; and, most assuredly, if we possess faith, sufficient also, will be the good.

2

Prayer and Faith
(*Continued*)

GENUINE, authentic faith must be definite and free of doubt. Not simply general in character; not a mere belief in the being, goodness, and power of God, but a faith which believes that the things which "he saith, shall come to pass." As the faith is specific, so the answer likewise will be definite: "He shall have whatsoever he saith." Faith and prayer select the things, and God commits himself to do the very things which faith and persevering prayer nominate, and petition him to accomplish.

The American Revised Version renders the twenty-fourth verse of the eleventh chapter of Mark, thus: "Therefore I say unto you, All things whatsoever ye pray and ask for, believe that ye receive them, and ye shall have them." Perfect faith has always in its keeping what perfect prayer asks for. How large and unqualified is the area of operation—the "All things whatsoever!" How definite and specific the promise—"Ye shall have them!"

Our chief concern is with our faith—the problems of its growth, and the activities of its vigorous maturity. A faith which grasps and holds in its keeping the very things it asks for, without wavering, doubt or fear—that is the faith we need—faith, such as is a pearl of great price, in the process and practice of prayer.

The statement of our Lord about faith and prayer quoted above is of supreme importance. Faith must be definite, specific; an unqualified, unmistakable request for the things asked for. It is not to be a vague, indefinite, shadowy thing; it must be something more than an abstract belief in God's willingness and ability to do for us. It is to be a definite, specific, asking for, and expecting the things for which we ask. Note the reading of Mark 11:23:

> And shall not doubt in his heart, but shall believe that those things which he saith shall come to pass; he shall have whatever he saith.

Just so far as the faith and the asking is definite, so also will the answer be. The giving is not to be something other than the things prayed for, but the actual things sought and named. "He shall have whatsoever he saith." It is all imperative, "He shall have." The granting is to be unlimited, both in quality and in quantity.

18

Faith and prayer select the subjects for petition, thereby determining what God is to do. "He shall have whatsoever he saith." Christ holds himself ready to supply exactly, and fully, all the demands of faith and prayer. If the order on God is made clear, specific and definite, God will fill it, exactly in accordance with the presented terms.

Faith is not an abstract belief in the Word of God, nor a mere mental credence, nor a simple assent of the understanding and will; nor is it a passive acceptance of facts, however sacred or thorough. Faith is an operation of God, a divine illumination, a holy energy implanted by the Word of God and the Spirit in the human soul—a spiritual, divine principle which takes of the supernatural and makes it a thing apprehendable by the faculties of time and sense.

Faith deals with God, and is conscious of God. It deals with the Lord Jesus Christ and sees in him a savior; it deals with God's Word, and lays hold of the truth; it deals with the Spirit of God, and is energized and inspired by its holy fire. God is the great objective of faith; for faith rests its whole weight on his Word. Faith is not an aimless act of the soul, but a looking to God and a resting upon his promises. Just as love and hope have always an objective so, also, has faith. Faith is not believing just *anything;* it is believing God, resting in him, trusting his Word.

Faith gives birth to prayer, and grows stronger, strikes deeper, rises higher, in the struggles and wrestlings of mighty petitioning. Faith is the substance of things hoped for, the assurance and realization of the inheritance of the saints. Faith, too, is humble and persevering. It can wait and pray; it can stay on its knees, or lie in the dust. It is the one great condition of prayer; the lack of it lies at the root of all poor praying, feeble praying, little praying, unanswered praying.

The nature and meaning of faith is more demonstrable in what it does, than it is by reason of any definition given it. Thus, if we turn to the record of faith given us in that great honor roll, which constitutes the eleventh chapter of Hebrews, we see something of the wonderful results of faith. What a glorious list it is—that of these men and women of faith! What marvelous achievements are there recorded, and set to the credit of faith! The inspired writer, exhausting his resources in cataloguing the Old Testament saints, who were such notable examples of wonderful faith, finally exclaims:

> And what more shall I say? For the time would fail me to tell of Gideon and Barak, and of Samson, and of Jephthah; of David also, and Samuel, and of the prophets.

And then the writer of Hebrews goes on again, in a wonderful strain, telling of the unrecorded exploits wrought through the faith of the men of old, "of whom the world was not worthy." "All these," he says, "obtained a good report through faith."

What an era of glorious achievements would dawn for the church and the world, if only there could be reproduced a race of saints of like mighty faith, of like wonderful praying! It is not the intellectually great that the church needs; nor is it men of wealth that the times demand. It is not people of great social influence that this day requires. Above everybody and everything else, it is men of faith, men of mighty prayer, men and women after the fashion of the saints and heroes enumerated in Hebrews, who "obtained a good report through faith," that the church and the whole wide world of humanity needs.

Many men, of this day, obtain a good report because of their money-giving, their great mental gifts and talents, but few there be who obtain a "good report" because of their great faith in God, or because of the wonderful things which are being wrought through their great praying. Today, as much as at any time, we need men of great faith and men who are great in prayer. These are the two cardinal virtues which make men great in the eyes of God, the two things which create conditions of real spiritual success in the life and work of the church. It is our chief concern to see that we maintain a faith of such quality and texture, as counts before God; which grasps, and holds in its keeping, the things for which it asks, without doubt and without fear.

Doubt and fear are the twin foes of faith. Sometimes, they actually usurp the place of faith, and although we pray, it is a restless, disquieted prayer that we offer, uneasy and often complaining. Peter failed to walk on Gennesaret because he permitted the waves to break over him and swamp the power of his faith. Taking his eyes from the Lord and regarding the water all about him, he began to sink and had to cry for succor—"Lord, save, or I perish!"

Doubts should never be cherished, nor fears harbored. Let none cherish the delusion that he is a martyr to fear and doubt. It is no credit to any man's mental capacity to cherish doubt of God, and no comfort can possibly derive from such a thought. Our eyes should be taken off self, removed from our own weakness and allowed to rest implicitly upon God's strength. "Cast not away therefore your confidence, which hath great recompence of reward." A simple, confiding faith, living day by day, and casting its burden on the Lord, each hour of the day, will dissipate fear, drive away misgiving and deliver from doubt:

> Be careful for nothing, but in everything, by supplication and prayer, with thanksgiving, let your requests be made known unto God.

That is the divine cure for all fear, anxiety, and undue concern of soul, all of which are closely akin to doubt and unbelief. This is the divine prescription for securing the peace which passeth all understanding, and keeps the heart and mind in quietness and peace.

All of us need to mark well and heed the caution given in Hebrews: "Take heed, brethren, lest there be in any of you an evil heart of unbelief, in departing from the living God."

We need, also, to guard against unbelief as we would against an enemy. Faith needs to be cultivated. We need to keep on praying, "Lord, increase our faith," for faith is susceptible of increase. Paul's tribute to the Thessalonians was, that their faith grew exceedingly. Faith is increased by exercise, by being put into use. It is nourished by sore trials.

> That the trial of your faith, being much more precious than of gold that perisheth, though it be tried with fire, might be found unto praise and honor and glory at the appearing of Jesus Christ.

Faith grows by reading and meditating upon the Word of God. Most, and best of all, faith thrives in an atmosphere of prayer.

It would be well, if all of us were to stop, and inquire personally of ourselves: "Have I faith in God? Have I *real* faith—faith which keeps me in perfect peace, about the things of earth and the things of heaven?" This is the most important question a man can propound and expect to be answered. And there is another question, closely akin to it in significance and importance—"Do I really pray to God so that he hears me and answers my prayers? And do I truly pray unto God so that I get direct from God the things I ask of him?"

It was claimed for Augustus Cæsar that he found Rome a city of wood, and left it a city of marble. The pastor who succeeds in changing his people from a prayerless to a prayerful people, has done a greater work than did Augustus in changing a city from wood to marble. And after all, this is the prime work of the preacher. Primarily, he is dealing with prayerless people—with people of whom it is said, "God is not in all their thoughts." Such people he meets everywhere, and all the time. His main business is to turn them from being forgetful of God, from being devoid of faith, from being prayerless, so that they become people who habitually pray, who believe in God, remember him, and do his will. The preacher is not sent to merely induce men to join the church, nor merely to get them to do better. It is to get them to pray, to trust God, and to keep God ever before their eyes, that they may not sin against him.

The work of the ministry is to change unbelieving sinners into praying and believing saints. The call goes forth by divine authority, "Believe on the Lord Jesus Christ, and thou shalt be saved." We catch a glimpse of the tremendous importance of faith and of the great value God has set upon it, when we remember that he has made it the one indispensable condition of being saved. "By grace are ye saved, through faith." Thus, when we contemplate the great importance of prayer, we find faith standing immediately by its side. By faith are we saved, and by faith we *stay* saved. Prayer introduces us to a life of faith. Paul declared that the life he lived, he lived by faith in the Son of God, who loved him and gave himself for him—that he walked by faith and not by sight.

Prayer is absolutely dependent upon faith. Virtually, it has no existence apart from it, and accomplishes nothing unless it is its inseparable companion. Faith makes prayer effectual, and in a certain important sense, must precede it.

> For he that cometh to God must believe that he is, and that he is a rewarder of them that diligently seek him.

Before prayer ever starts toward God; before its petition is preferred, before its requests are made known—faith must have gone on ahead; must have asserted its belief in the existence of God; must have given its assent to the gracious truth that "God is a rewarder of those that diligently seek his face." This is the primary step in praying. In this regard, while faith does not bring the blessing, yet it puts prayer in a position to ask for it, and leads to another step toward realization, by aiding the petitioner to believe that God is able and willing to bless.

Faith starts prayer to work—clears the way to the mercy seat. It gives assurance, first of all, that there is a mercy seat, and that there the high priest awaits the pray-ers and the prayers. Faith opens the way for prayer to approach God. But it does more. It accompanies prayer at every step she takes. It is her inseparable companion and when requests are made unto God, it is faith which turns the asking into obtaining. And faith follows prayer, since the spiritual life into which a believer is led by prayer, is a life of faith. The one prominent characteristic of the experience into which believers are brought through prayer, is not a life of works, but of faith.

Faith makes prayer strong, and gives it patience to wait on God. Faith believes that God is a rewarder. No truth is more clearly revealed in the Scriptures than this, while none is more encouraging. Even the closet has its promised reward, "He that seeth in secret, shall reward thee openly," while the most insignificant service rendered to a disciple in the name of the Lord, surely receives its reward. And to this precious truth faith gives its hearty assent.

Yet faith is narrowed down to one particular thing—it does not believe that God will reward everybody, nor that he is a rewarder of all who pray, but that he is a rewarder of them that *diligently seek him*. Faith rests its case on diligence in prayer, and gives assurance and encouragement to diligent seekers after God, for it is they, alone, who are richly rewarded when they pray.

We need constantly to be reminded that faith is the one inseparable condition of successful praying. There are other considerations entering into the exercise, but faith is the final, the one indispensable condition of true praying. As it is written in a familiar, primary declaration: "Without faith, it is impossible to please him."

James puts this truth very plainly.

If any of you lack wisdom, let him ask of God, that giveth to all men liberally, and upbraideth not, and it shall be given him. But let him ask in faith, nothing wavering. For he that wavereth [or doubteth] is like a wave of the sea, driven with the wind and tossed. For let not that man think that he shall receive any thing of the Lord.

Doubting is always put under the ban, because it stands as a foe to faith and hinders effectual praying. In the First Epistle to Timothy Paul gives us an invaluable truth relative to the conditions of successful praying, which he thus lays down: "I will therefore that men pray everywhere, lifting up holy hands, without wrath and doubting."

All questioning must be watched against and eschewed. Fear and peradventure have no place in true praying. Faith must assert itself and bid these foes to prayer depart.

Too much authority cannot be attributed to faith; but prayer is the scepter by which it signalizes its power. How much of spiritual wisdom there is in the following advice written by an eminent old divine.

Would you be freed from the bondage to corruption? Would you grow in grace in general and grow in grace in particular? If you would, your way is plain. Ask of God more faith. Beg of him morning, and noon and night, while you walk by the way, while you sit in the house, when you lie down and when you rise up; beg of him simply to impress divine things more deeply on your heart, to give you more and more of the substance of things hoped for and of the evidence of things not seen.

Great incentives to pray are furnished in Holy Scriptures, and our Lord closes his teaching about prayer, with the assurance and promise of heaven. The presence of Jesus Christ in heaven, the preparation for his saints which he is making there, and the assurance that he will come again to receive them—how all this helps the weariness of praying, strengthens its conflicts, sweetens its arduous toil! These things are the star of hope to prayer, the wiping away of its tears, the putting of the odor of heaven into the bitterness of its cry. The spirit of a pilgrim greatly facilitates praying. An earthbound, earth-satisfied spirit cannot pray. In such a heart, the flame of spiritual desire is either gone out or smoldering in faintest glow. The wings of its faith are clipped, its eyes are filmed, its tongue silenced. But they, who in unswerving faith and unceasing prayer, wait continually upon the Lord, *do* renew their strength, *do* mount up with wings as eagles, *do* run, and are not weary, *do* walk, and not faint.

3
Prayer and Trust

PRAYER does not stand alone. It is not an isolated duty and independent principle. It lives in association with other Christian duties, is wedded to other principles, is a partner with other graces. But to faith, prayer is indissolubly joined. Faith gives it color and tone, shapes its character, and secures its results.

Trust is faith become absolute, ratified, consummated. There is, when all is said and done, a sort of venture in faith and its exercise. But trust *is firm belief,* it is faith in full flower. Trust is a conscious act, a fact of which we are sensible. According to the Scriptural concept it is the eye of the newborn soul, and the ear of the renewed soul. It is the feeling of the soul, the spiritual eye, the ear, the taste, the feeling—these one and all have to do with trust. How luminous, how distinct, how conscious, how powerful, and more than all, how Scriptural is such a trust! How different from many forms of modern belief, so feeble, dry, and cold! These new phases of belief bring no consciousness of their presence, no "joy unspeakable and full of glory" results from their exercise. They are, for the most part, adventures in the peradventures of the soul. There is no safe, sure trust in anything. The whole transaction takes place in the realm of maybe and perhaps.

Trust like life, is feeling, though much more than feeling. An unfelt life is a contradiction; an unfelt trust is a misnomer, a delusion, a contradiction. Trust is the most felt of all attributes. It is *all* feeling, and it works only by love. An unfelt love is as impossible as an unfelt trust. The trust of which we are now speaking is a conviction. An unfelt conviction? How absurd!

Trust sees God doing things here and now. Yea, more. It rises to a lofty eminence, and looking into the invisible and the eternal, realizes that God has done things, and regards them as being already done. Trust brings eternity into the annals and happenings of time, transmutes the substance of hope into the reality of fruition, and changes promise into present possession. We know when we trust just as we know when we see, just as we are conscious of our sense of touch. Trust sees, receives, holds. Trust is its own witness.

Yet, quite often, faith is too weak to obtain God's greatest good, immediately; so it has to wait in loving, strong, prayerful, pressing obedience, until it grows in strength, and is able to bring down the eternal, into the realms of experience and time.

To this point, trust masses all its forces. Here it holds. And in the struggle, trust's grasp becomes mightier, and grasps, for itself, all that God has done for it in his eternal wisdom and plenitude of grace.

In the matter of waiting in prayer, mightiest prayer, faith rises to its highest plane and becomes indeed the gift of God. It becomes the blessed disposition and expression of the soul which is secured by a constant communicating with, and unwearied application to God.

Jesus Christ clearly taught that faith was the condition on which prayer was answered. When our Lord had cursed the fig tree, the disciples were much surprised that its withering had actually taken place, and their remarks indicated their incredulity. It was then that Jesus said to them, "Have faith in God."

> For verily I say unto you, that whosoever shall say unto this mountain, "Be thou removed and be thou cast into the sea", and shall not doubt in his heart, but shall believe that those things which he saith shall come to pass, he shall have whatsoever he saith. Therefore, I say unto you, what things soever ye desire, when ye pray, believe that ye receive them, and ye shall have them.

Trust grows nowhere so readily and richly as in the prayer chamber. Its unfolding and development are rapid and wholesome when they are regularly and well kept. When these engagements are hearty and full and free, trust flourishes exceedingly. The eye and presence of God give vigorous life to trust, just as the eye and the presence of the sun make fruit and flower to grow, and all things glad and bright with fuller life.

"Have faith in God," "Trust in the Lord" form the keynote and foundation of prayer. Primarily, it is not trust in the Word of God, but rather trust in the person of God. For trust in the person of God must precede trust in the Word of God. "Ye believe in God, believe also in me," is the demand our Lord makes on the personal trust of his disciples. The person of Jesus Christ must be central, to the eye of trust. This great truth Jesus sought to impress upon Martha, when her brother lay dead, in the tomb at Bethany. Martha asserted her belief in the fact of the resurrection of her brother:

> Martha saith unto him, "I know that he shall rise again in the resurrection at the last day."

Jesus lifts her trust clear above the mere fact of the resurrection, to his own person, by saying:

> "I am the resurrection and the life: he that believeth in me, though he were dead, yet shall he live: and whosoever liveth and believeth in me, shall never die. Believest thou this?" She saith unto him, "Yea, Lord: I believe that thou art the Christ, the Son of God, which should come into the world."

Trust, in an historical fact or in a mere record may be a very passive thing, but trust in a person vitalizes the quality, fructifies it, informs it with love. The trust which informs prayer centers in a person.

Trust goes even further than this. The trust which inspires our prayer must be not only trust in the person of God, and of Christ, but in their ability and willingness to grant the thing prayed for. It is not only, "Trust, ye, in the Lord," but, also, "for in the Lord Jehovah, is everlasting strength."

The trust which our Lord taught as a condition of effectual prayer, is not of the head but of the heart. It is trust which "doubteth not in his heart." Such trust has the divine assurance that it shall be honored with large and satisfying answers. The strong promise of our Lord brings faith down to the present, and counts on a present answer.

Do we believe, without a doubt? When we pray, do we believe, not that we shall receive the things for which we ask on a future day, but that we receive them, then and there? Such is the teaching of this inspiring Scripture. How we need to pray, "Lord, increase our faith," until doubt be gone, and implicit trust claims the promised blessings, as its very own.

This is no easy condition. It is reached only after many a failure, after much praying, after many waitings, after much trial of faith. May our faith so increase until we realize and receive all the fulness there is in that name which guarantees to do so much.

Our Lord puts trust as the very foundation of praying. The background of prayer is trust. The whole issuance of Christ's ministry and work was dependent on implicit trust in his Father. The center of trust is God. Mountains of difficulties, and all other hindrances to prayer are moved out of the way by trust and his virile henchman, faith. When trust is perfect and without doubt, prayer is simply the outstretched hand, ready to receive. Trust perfected, is prayer perfected. Trust looks to receive the thing asked for—and gets it. Trust is not a belief that God *can* bless, that he *will* bless, but that he *does* bless, here and now. Trust always operates in the present tense. Hope looks toward the future. Trust looks to the present. Hope expects. Trust possesses. Trust receives what prayer acquires. So that what prayer needs, at all times, is abiding and abundant trust.

Their lamentable lack of trust and resultant failure of the disciples to do what they were sent out to do, is seen in the case of the lunatic son, who was brought by his father to nine of them while their master was on the Mount of Transfiguration. A boy, sadly afflicted, was brought to these men to be cured of his malady. They had been commissioned to do this very kind of work. This was a part of their mission. They attempted to cast out the devil from the boy, but had signally failed. The devil was too much for them. They were humiliated at their failure, and filled with shame, while their enemies were in triumph. Amid the confusion incident to failure Jesus draws near. He is informed of the circumstances, and told of the conditions connected therewith. Here is the succeeding account:

Then Jesus answered and said, "O faithless and perverse generation, how long shall I be with you? How long shall I suffer you? Bring him hither to me." And Jesus rebuked the devil, and he departed out of him and the child was cured from that very hour. And when he was come into the house, his disciples asked him privately, "Why could not we cast him out?" And he said unto them, "This kind can come forth by nothing but by prayer and fasting."

Wherein lay the difficulty with these men? They had been lax in cultivating their faith by prayer and, as a consequence, their trust utterly failed. They trusted not God, nor Christ, nor the authenticity of his mission, or their own. So has it been many a time since, in many a crisis in the church of God. Failure has resulted from a lack of trust, or from a weakness of faith, and this, in turn, from a lack of prayerfulness. Many a failure in revival efforts has been traceable to the same cause. Faith had not been nurtured and made powerful by prayer. Neglect of the inner chamber is the solution of most spiritual failure. And this is as true of our personal struggles with the devil as was the case when we went forth to attempt to cast *out* devils. To be much on our knees in private communion with God is the only surety that we shall have him with us either in our personal struggles, or in our efforts to convert sinners.

Everywhere, in the approaches of the people to him, our Lord put trust in him, and the divinity of his mission, in the forefront. He gave no definition of trust, and he furnishes no theological discussion of, or analysis of it; for he knew that men would see what faith was by what faith *did*; and from its free exercise trust grew up, spontaneously, in his presence. It was the product of his work, his power, and his person. These furnished and created an atmosphere most favorable for its exercise and development. Trust is altogether too splendidly simple for verbal definition; too hearty and spontaneous for theological terminology. The very simplicity of trust is that which staggers many people. They look away for some great thing to come to pass, while all the time "the word is nigh thee, even in thy mouth, and in thy heart."

When the saddening news of his daughter's death was brought to Jairus our Lord interposed: "Be not afraid," he said calmly, "only believe." To the woman with the issue of blood, who stood trembling before him, he said:

Daughter, thy faith hath made thee whole; go in peace, and be whole of thy plague.

As the two blind men followed him, pressing their way into the house, he said:

According to your faith be it unto you. And their eyes were opened.

When the paralytic was let down through the roof of the house, where Jesus was teaching, and placed before him by four of his friends, it is recorded after this fashion:

And Jesus seeing their faith, said unto the sick of the palsy: "Son, be of good
cheer; thy sins be forgiven thee."

When Jesus dismissed the centurion whose servant was seriously ill, and
who had come to Jesus with the prayer that he speak the healing word, without even going to his house, he did it in the manner following:

And Jesus said unto the centurion, "Go thy way; and as thou hast believed,
so be it done unto thee. And his servant was healed in the selfsame hour."

When the poor leper fell at the feet of Jesus and cried out for relief, "Lord,
if thou wilt, thou canst make me clean," Jesus immediately granted his
request, and the man glorified him with a loud voice. Then Jesus said unto
him, "Arise, go thy way; thy faith hath made thee whole."

The Syrophoenician woman came to Jesus with the case of her afflicted
daughter, making the case her own, with the prayer, "Lord, help me," making
a fearful and heroic struggle. Jesus honors her faith and prayer, saying:

"O woman, great is thy faith: be it unto thee even as thou wilt." And her
daughter was made whole from that very hour.

After the disciples had utterly failed to cast the devil out of the epileptic
boy, the father of the stricken lad came to Jesus with the plaintive and almost
despairing cry, "If thou canst do anything, have compassion on us and help
us." But Jesus replied, "If thou canst believe, all things are possible to him
that believeth."

Blind Bartimæus sitting by the wayside, hears our Lord as he passes by, and
cries out pitifully and almost despairingly, "Jesus, thou son of David, have
mercy on me." The keen ears of our Lord immediately catch the sound of
prayer, and he says to the beggar:

"Go thy way; thy faith hath made thee whole." And immediately he received
his sight, and followed Jesus in the way.

To the weeping, penitent woman, washing his feet with her tears and wiping them with the hair of her head, Jesus speaks cheering, soul-comforting
words: "Thy faith hath saved thee; go in peace."

One day Jesus healed ten lepers at one time, in answer to their united
prayer, Jesus, master, have mercy on us," and he told them to go and show
themselves to the priests. "And it came to pass as they went, they were
cleansed."

4

Prayer and Desire

DESIRE is not merely a simple wish; it is a deep seated craving; an intense longing, for attainment. In the realm of spiritual affairs, it is an important adjunct to prayer. So important is it, that one might say, almost, that desire is an absolute essential of prayer. Desire precedes prayer, accompanies it, is followed by it. Desire goes before prayer, and by it, created and intensified. Prayer is the oral expression of desire. If prayer is asking God for something, then prayer must be expressed. Prayer comes out into the open. Desire is silent. Prayer is heard; desire, unheard. The deeper the desire, the stronger the prayer. Without desire, prayer is a meaningless mumble of words. Such perfunctory, formal praying, with no heart, no feeling, no real desire accompanying it, is to be shunned like a pestilence. Its exercise is a waste of precious time, and from it, no real blessing accrues.

And yet even if it be discovered that desire is *honestly* absent, we should pray, anyway. We *ought* to pray. The "ought" comes in, in order that both desire and expression be cultivated. God's Word commands it. Our judgment tells us we ought to pray—to pray whether we feel like it or not—and not to allow our feelings to determine our habits of prayer. In such circumstance, we ought to pray for the *desire* to pray; for such a desire is God-given and heaven-born. We should pray for desire; then, when desire has been given, we should pray according to its dictates. Lack of spiritual desire should grieve us, and lead us to lament its absence, to seek earnestly for its bestowal, so that our praying, henceforth, should be an expression of "the soul's sincere desire."

A sense of need creates or should create, earnest desire. The stronger the sense of need, before God, the greater should be the desire, the more earnest the praying. The "poor in spirit" are eminently competent to pray.

Hunger is an active sense of physical need. It prompts the request for bread. In like manner, the inward consciousness of spiritual need creates desire, and desire breaks forth in prayer. Desire is an inward longing for something of which we are not possessed, of which we stand in need—something which God has promised, and which may be secured by an earnest supplication of his throne of grace.

Spiritual desire, carried to a higher degree, is the evidence of the new birth. It is born in the renewed soul:

> As newborn babes, desire the sincere milk of the word, that ye may grow thereby.

The absence of this holy desire in the heart is presumptive proof, either of a decline in spiritual ecstasy, or, that the new birth has never taken place.

> Blessed are they which do hunger and thirst after righteousness: for they shall be filled.

These heaven-given appetites are the proof of a renewed heart, the evidence of a stirring spiritual life. Physical appetites are the attributes of a living body, not of a corpse, and spiritual desires belong to a soul made alive to God. And as the renewed soul hungers and thirsts after righteousness, these holy inward desires break out into earnest, supplicating prayer.

In prayer, we are shut up to the name, merit and intercessory virtue of Jesus Christ, our great high priest. Probing down, below the accompanying conditions and forces in prayer, we come to its vital basis, which is seated in the human heart. It is not simply our need; it is the heart's yearning for what we need, and for which we feel impelled to pray. Desire is the will in action; a strong, conscious longing, excited in the inner nature, for some great good. Desire exalts the object of its longing, and fixes the mind on it. It has choice, and fixedness, and flame in it, and prayer, based thereon, is explicit and specific. It knows its need, feels and sees the thing that will meet it, and hastens to acquire it.

Holy desire is much helped by devout contemplation. Meditation on our spiritual need, and on God's readiness and ability to correct it, aids desire to grow. Serious thought engaged in before praying, increases desire, makes it more insistent, and tends to save us from the menace of private prayer—wandering thought. We fail much more in desire, than in its outward expression. We retain the form, while the inner life fades and almost dies.

One might well ask, whether the feebleness of our desires for God, the Holy Spirit, and for all the fulness of Christ, is not the cause of our so little praying, and of our languishing in the exercise of prayer? Do we really *feel* these inward pantings of desire after heavenly treasures? Do the inbred groanings of desire stir our souls to mighty wrestlings? Alas for us! The fire burns altogether too low. The flaming heat of soul has been tempered down to a tepid lukewarmness. This, it should be remembered, was the central cause of the sad and desperate condition of the Laodicean Christians, of whom the awful condemnation is written that they were "rich, and increased in goods and *had need of nothing*," and knew not that they "were wretched, and miserable, and poor, and blind."

Again: we might well inquire—have we that desire which presses us to close communion with God, which is filled with unutterable burnings, and holds us there through the agony of an intense and soul-stirred supplication? Our hearts need much to be worked over, not only to get the evil out of them, but to get the good into them. And the foundation and inspiration to the incoming good, is strong, propelling desire. This holy and fervent flame in the soul awakens the interest of heaven, attracts the attention of God, and places at the disposal of those who exercise it, the exhaustless riches of divine grace.

The dampening of the flame of holy desire is destructive of the vital and aggressive forces in church life. God requires to be represented by a fiery church, or he is not in any proper sense, represented at all. God, himself, is all on fire, and his church, if it is to be like him, must also be at white heat. The great and eternal interests of heaven-born, God-given religion are the only things about which his church can afford to be on fire. Yet holy zeal need not to be fussy in order to be consuming. Our Lord was the incarnate antithesis of nervous excitability, the absolute opposite of intolerant or clamorous declamation, yet the zeal of God's house consumed him; and the world is still feeling the glow of his fierce, consuming flame and responding to it, with an ever-increasing readiness and an ever-enlarging response.

A lack of ardor in prayer, is the sure sign of a lack of depth and of intensity of desire; and the absence of intense desire is a sure sign of God's absence from the heart! To abate fervor is to retire from God. He can, and does, tolerate many things in the way of infirmity and error in his children. He can, and will pardon sin when the penitent prays, but two things are intolerable to him—insincerity and lukewarmness. Lack of heart and lack of heat are two things he loathes, and to the Laodiceans he said, in terms of unmistakable severity and condemnation:

> I would thou wert cold or hot. So then because thou art lukewarm, and neither cold nor hot, I will spue thee out of my mouth.

This was God's expressed judgment on the lack of fire in one of the seven churches, and it is his indictment against individual Christians for the fatal want of sacred zeal. In prayer, fire is the motive power. Religious principles which do not emerge in flame, have neither force nor effect. Flame is the wing on which faith ascends; fervency is the soul of prayer. It was the "fervent, effectual prayer" which availed much. Love is kindled in a flame, and ardency is its life. Flame is the air which true Christian experience breathes. It feeds on fire; it can withstand anything, rather than a feeble flame; and it dies, chilled and starved to its vitals, when the surrounding atmosphere is frigid or lukewarm.

True prayer *must* be aflame. Christian life and character need to be all on fire. Lack of spiritual heat creates more infidelity than lack of faith. Not to be consumingly interested about the things of heaven, is not to be interested in them at all. The fiery souls are those who conquer in the day of battle, from whom the kingdom of heaven suffereth violence, and who take it by force. The citadel of God is taken only by those, who storm it in dreadful earnestness, who besiege it, with fiery, unabated zeal.

Nothing short of being red hot for God, can keep the glow of heaven in our hearts, these chilly days. The early Methodists had no heating apparatus in their churches. They declared that the flame in the pew and the fire in the pulpit must suffice to keep them warm. And we, of this hour, have need to have the live coal from God's altar and the consuming flame from heaven glowing in our hearts. This flame is not mental vehemence nor fleshly energy. It is divine fire in the soul, intense, dross-consuming—the very essence of the Spirit of God.

No erudition, no purity of diction, no width of mental outlook, no flowers of eloquence, no grace of person, can atone for lack of fire. Prayer ascends by fire. Flame gives prayer access as well as wings, acceptance as well as energy. There is no incense without fire; no prayer without flame.

Ardent desire is the basis of unceasing prayer. It is not a shallow, fickle inclination, but a strong yearning, an unquenchable ardor, which impregnates, glows, burns, and fixes the heart. It is the flame of a present and active principle mounting up to God. It is ardor propelled by desire, that burns its way to the throne of mercy, and gains its plea. It is the pertinacity of desire that gives triumph to the conflict, in a great struggle of prayer. It is the burden of a weighty desire that sobers, makes restless, and reduces to quietness the soul just emerged from its mighty wrestlings. It is the embracing character of desire which arms prayer with a thousand pleas, and robes it with an invincible courage and an all-conquering power.

The Syrophenician woman is an object lesson of desire, settled to its consistency, but invulnerable in its intensity and pertinacious boldness. The importunate widow represents desire gaining its end, through obstacles insuperable to feebler impulses.

Prayer is not the rehearsal of a mere performance; nor is it an indefinite, widespread clamor. Desire, while it kindles the soul, holds it to the object sought. Prayer is an indispensable phase of spiritual habit, but it ceases to be prayer when carried on by habit alone. It is depth and intensity of spiritual desire which give intensity and depth to prayer. The soul cannot be listless when some great desire fires and inflames it. The urgency of our desire holds us to the thing desired with a tenacity which refuses to be lessened or loosened; it stays and pleads and persists, and refuses to let go until the blessing has been given.

> Lord, I cannot let thee go,
> Till a blessing thou bestow;
> Do not turn away thy face;
> Mine's an urgent, pressing case.

The secret of faintheartedness, lack of importunity, want of courage and strength in prayer, lies in the weakness of spiritual desire, while the nonobservance of prayer is the fearful token of that desire having ceased to live. That soul has turned from God whose desire after him no longer presses it to the inner chamber. There can be no successful praying without consuming desire. Of course there can be much *seeming* to pray, without desire of any kind.

Many things may be catalogued and much ground covered. But does desire compile the catalogue? Does desire map out the region to be covered? On the answer, hangs the issue of whether our petitioning be prating or prayer. Desire is intense, but narrow; it cannot spread itself over a wide area. It wants a few things, and wants them badly, so badly, that nothing but God's willingness to answer, can bring it easement or content.

Desire single-shots at its objective. There may be many things desired, but they are specifically and individually felt and expressed. David did not yearn for everything; nor did he allow his desires to spread out everywhere and hit nothing. Here is the way his desires ran and found expression:

> One thing have I desired of the Lord, that will I seek after; that I may dwell in the house of the Lord all the days of my life, to behold the beauty of the Lord, and to enquire in his temple.

It is this singleness of desire, this definiteness of yearning, which counts in praying, and which drives prayer directly to the core and center of supply.

In the Beatitudes Jesus voiced the words which directly bear upon the innate desires of a renewed soul, and the promise that they will be granted: "Blessed are they that do hunger and thirst after righteousness, for they shall be filled."

This, then, is the basis of prayer which compels an answer—that strong inward desire has entered into the spiritual appetite, and clamors to be satisfied. Alas for us! It is altogether too true and frequent, that our prayers operate in the arid region of a mere wish, or in the leafless area of a memorized prayer. Sometimes, indeed, our prayers are merely stereotyped expressions of set phrases, and conventional proportions, the freshness and life of which have departed long years ago.

Without desire, there is no burden of soul, no sense of need, no ardency, no vision, no strength, no glow of faith. There is no mighty pressure, no holding on to God, with a deathless, despairing grasp—"I will not let thee go, except thou bless me." There is no utter self-abandonment, as there was with Moses, when, lost in the throes of a desperate, pertinacious, and all-consuming plea he cried: "Yet now, if thou wilt forgive their sin; if not, blot me, I pray thee, out of thy book." Or, as there was with John Knox when he pleaded: "Give me Scotland, or I die!"

God draws mightily near to the praying soul. To see God, to know God,

and to live for God—these form the objective of all true praying. Thus praying is, after all, inspired to seek after God. Prayer-desire is inflamed to see
God, to have clearer, fuller, sweeter, and richer revelation of God. So to those
who thus pray, the Bible becomes a new Bible, and Christ a new savior, by the
light and revelation of the inner chamber.

We stress and emphasize that burning desire—enlarged and ever enlarging—for the best, and most powerful gifts and graces of the Spirit of God, is
the legitimate heritage of true and effectual praying. Self and service cannot
be divorced—cannot possibly be separated. More than that: desire must be
made intensely personal, must be centered on God with an insatiable hungering and thirsting after him and his righteousness. "My soul thirsteth for God,
the living God." The indispensable requisite for all true praying is a deeply
seated desire which seeks after God himself, and remains unappeased, until
the choicest gifts in heaven's bestowal, have been richly and abundantly
granted.

5

Prayer and Fervency

PRAYER, without fervor, stakes nothing on the issue, because it has nothing to stake. It comes with empty hands. Hands, too, which are listless, as well as empty, which have never learned the lesson of clinging to the cross.

Fervorless prayer has no heart in it; it is an empty thing, an unfit vessel. Heart, soul, and life, must find place in all real praying. Heaven must be made to feel the force of this crying unto God.

Paul was a notable example of the man who possessed a fervent spirit of prayer. His petitioning was all-consuming, centered immovably upon the object of his desire, and the God who was able to meet it.

Prayers must be red hot. It is the fervent prayer that is effectual and that availeth. Coldness of spirit hinders praying; prayer cannot live in a wintry atmosphere. Chilly surroundings freeze out petitioning; and dry up the springs of supplication. It takes fire to make prayers go. Warmth of soul creates an atmosphere favorable to prayer, because it is favorable to fervency. By flame, prayer ascends to heaven. Yet fire is not fuss, nor heat, noise. Heat is intensity—something that glows and burns. Heaven is a mighty poor market for ice.

God wants warmhearted servants. The Holy Spirit comes *as a fire,* to dwell in us; we are to be baptized, with the Holy Spirit and with fire. Fervency is warmth of soul. A phlegmatic temperament is abhorrent to vital experience. If our religion does not set us on fire, it is because we have frozen hearts. God dwells in a flame; the Holy Spirit descends in fire. To be absorbed in God's will, to be so greatly in earnest about doing it that our whole being takes fire, is the qualifying condition of the man who would engage in effectual prayer.

Our Lord warns us against feeble praying. "Men ought always to pray," he declares, "and not to faint." That means, that we are to possess sufficient fervency to carry us through the severe and long periods of pleading prayer. Fire makes one alert and vigilant, and brings him off, more than conqueror. The atmosphere about us is too heavily charged with resisting forces for limp or languid prayers to make headway. It takes heat, and fervency and meteoric fire, to push through, to the upper heavens, where God dwells with his saints, in light.

Many of the great Bible characters were notable examples of fervency of spirit when seeking God. The psalmist declares with great earnestness:

My soul breaketh for the longing that it hath unto thy judgments at all times.

What strong desires of heart are here! What earnest soul longings for the Word of the living God!

An even greater fervency is expressed by him in another place:

As the hart panteth after the water brooks, so panteth my soul after thee, O God. My soul thirsteth for God, for the living God: when shall I come and appear before God?

That is the word of a man who lived in a state of grace, which had been deeply and supernaturally wrought in his soul.

Fervency before God counts in the hour of prayer, and finds a speedy and rich reward at his hands. The psalmist gives us this statement of what God had done for the king, as his heart turned toward his Lord:

Thou hast given him his heart's desire, and hast not withholden the request of his lips.

At another time, he thus expresses himself directly to God in preferring his request:

Lord, all my desire is before thee; and my groaning is not hid from thee.

What a cheering thought! Our inward groanings, our secret desires, our heart-longings, are not hidden from the eyes of him with whom we have to deal in prayer.

The incentive to fervency of spirit before God, is precisely the same as it is for continued and earnest prayer. While fervency is not prayer, yet it derives from an earnest soul, and is precious in the sight of God. Fervency in prayer is the precursor of what God will do by way of answer. God stands pledged to give us the desire of our hearts in proportion to the fervency of spirit we exhibit, when seeking his face in prayer. *you think so?*

Fervency has its seat in the heart, not in the brain, nor in the intellectual faculties of the mind. Fervency therefore, is not an expression of the intellect. Fervency of spirit is something far transcending poetical fancy or sentimental imagery. It is something else besides mere preference, the contrasting of like with dislike. Fervency is the throb and gesture of the emotional nature.

It is not in our power, perhaps, to create fervency of spirit at will, but we can pray God to implant it. It is ours, then, to nourish and cherish it, to guard it against extinction, to prevent its abatement or decline. The process of personal salvation is not only to pray, to express our desires to God, but to acquire a fervent spirit and seek, by all proper means, to cultivate it. It is never out of place to pray God to beget within us, and to keep alive the spirit of fervent prayer.

Fervency has to do with God, just as prayer has to do with him. Desire has always an objective. If we desire at all, we desire *something*. The degree of fervency with which we fashion our spiritual desires, will always serve to determine the earnestness of our praying. In this relation, Adoniram Judson says:

> A travailing spirit, the throes of a great burdened desire, belongs to prayer. A fervency strong enough to drive away sleep, which devotes and inflames the spirit, and which retires all earthly ties, all this belongs to wrestling, prevailing prayer. The Spirit, the power, the air, and food of prayer is in such a spirit.

Prayer must be clothed with fervency, strength and power. It is the force which, centered on God, determines the outlay of himself for earthly good. Men who are fervent in spirit are bent on attaining to righteousness, truth, grace, and all other sublime and powerful graces which adorn the character of the authentic, unquestioned child of God.

God once declared, by the mouth of a brave prophet, to a king who, at one time, had been true to God, but, by the incoming of success and material prosperity, had lost his faith, the following message:

> The eyes of the Lord run to and fro throughout the whole earth, to shew himself strong in the behalf of them whose heart is perfect toward him. Herein hast thou done foolishly; therefore, from henceforth thou shalt have wars.

God had heard Asa's prayer in early life, but disaster came and trouble was sent, because he had given up the life of prayer and simple faith.

In Romans 15:30, we have the word *strive* occurring in the request which Paul made for prayerful cooperation.

In Colossians 4:12, we have the same word, but translated differently: "Epaphras always laboring fervently for you in prayer." Paul charged the Romans to "strive together with him in prayer," that is, to help him in his struggle of prayer. The word means to enter into a contest, to fight against adversaries. It means, moreover, to engage with fervent zeal to endeavor to obtain.

These recorded instances of the exercise and reward of faith, give us easily to see that, in almost every instance, faith was blended with trust until it is not too much to say that the former was swallowed up in the latter. It is hard to properly distinguish the specific activities of these two qualities, faith and trust. But there is a point, beyond all peradventure, at which faith is relieved of its burden, so to speak; where trust comes along and says: "You have done your part, the rest is mine!"

In the incident of the barren fig tree, our Lord transfers the marvelous power of faith to his disciples. To their exclamation, "How soon is the fig tree withered away!" He said:

> If ye have faith, and doubt not, ye shall not only do this which is done to the fig tree, but also if ye shall say unto this mountain, "Be thou removed, and be

thou cast into the sea"; it shall be done. And all things, whatsoever ye shall ask in prayer, believing, ye shall receive.

When a Christian believer attains to faith of such magnificent proportions as these, he steps into the realm of implicit trust. He stands without a tremor on the apex of his spiritual outreaching. He has attained faith's veritable top stone which is unswerving, unalterable, unalienable trust in the power of the living God.

6

Prayer and Importunity

OUR Lord Jesus declared that "men ought always to pray and not to faint," and the parable in which his words occur, was taught with the intention of saving men from faintheartedness and weakness in prayer. Our Lord was seeking to teach that laxity must be guarded against, and persistence fostered and encouraged. There can be no two opinions regarding the importance of the exercise of this indispensable quality in our praying.

Importunate prayer is a mighty movement of the soul toward God. It is a stirring of the deepest forces of the soul, toward the throne of heavenly grace. It is the ability to hold on, press on, and wait. Restless desire, restful patience, and strength of grasp are all embraced in it. It is not an incident, or a performance, but a passion of soul. It is not a want, half-needed, but a sheer necessity.

The wrestling quality in importunate prayer, does not spring from physical vehemence or fleshly energy. It is not an impulse of energy, not a mere earnestness of soul; it is an inwrought force, a faculty implanted and aroused by the Holy Spirit. Virtually, it is the intercession of the Spirit of God, in us; it is, moreover, "the effectual, fervent prayer, which availeth much." The divine Spirit informing every element within us, with the energy of his own striving, is the essence of the importunity which urges our praying at the mercy seat, to continue until the fire falls and the blessing descends. This wrestling in prayer may not be boisterous nor vehement, but quiet, tenacious, and urgent. Silent, it may be, when there are no visible outlets for its mighty forces.

Nothing distinguishes the children of God so clearly and strongly as prayer. It is the one infallible mark and test of being a Christian. Christian people are prayerful, the worldly-minded, prayerless. Christians call on God; worldlings ignore God, and call not on his name. But even the Christian had need to cultivate *continual* prayer. Prayer must be habitual, but much more than a habit. It is duty, yet one which rises far above, and goes beyond the ordinary implications of the term. It is the expression of a relation to God, a yearning for divine communion. It is the outward and upward flow of the inward life toward its original fountain. It is an assertion of the soul's paternity, a claiming of the sonship, which links man to the eternal.

Prayer has everything to do with molding the soul into the image of God, and has everything to do with enhancing and enlarging the measure of divine grace. It has everything to do with bringing the soul into complete communion with God. It has everything to do with enriching, broadening and maturing the soul's experience of God. That man cannot possibly be called a Christian, who does not pray. By no possible pretext can he claim any right to the term, nor its implied significance. If he does not pray, he is a sinner, pure and simple, for prayer is the only way in which the soul of man can enter into fellowship and communion with the source of all Christlike spirit and energy. Hence, if he prays not, he is not of the household of faith.

In this study however, we turn our thought to one phase of prayer—that of importunity; the pressing of our desires upon God with urgency and perseverance; the praying with that tenacity and tension which neither relaxes nor ceases until its plea is heard, and its cause is won.

He who has clear views of God, and scriptural conceptions of the divine character; who appreciates his privilege of approach unto God; who understands his inward need of all that God has for him—that man will be solicitous, outspoken, and importunate. In Scripture the duty of prayer, itself, is advocated in terms which are only barely stronger than those in which the necessity for its importunity is set forth. The praying which influences God is declared to be that of the fervent, effectual outpouring of a righteous man. That is to say, it is prayer on fire, having no feeble, flickering flame, no momentary flash, but shining with a vigorous and steady glow.

The repeated intercessions of Abraham for the salvation of Sodom and Gomorrah present an early example of the necessity for, and benefit deriving from importunate praying. Jacob, wrestling all night with the angel, gives significant emphasis to the power of a dogged perseverance in praying, and shows how, in things spiritual, importunity succeeds, just as effectively as it does in matters relating to time and sense.

As we have noted, elsewhere, Moses prayed forty days and forty nights, seeking to stay the wrath of God against Israel, and his example and success are a stimulus to present-day faith in its darkest hour. Elijah repeated and urged his prayer seven times ere the raincloud appeared above the horizon, heralding the success of his prayer and the victory of his faith. On one occasion Daniel though faint and weak, pressed his case three weeks, ere the answer and the blessing came.

Many nights during his earthly life did the blessed Savior spend in prayer. In Gethsemane he presented the same petition, three times, with unabated, urgent, yet submissive importunity, which involved every element of his soul, and issued in tears and bloody sweat. His life crises were distinctly marked, his life victories all won, in hours of importunate prayer. And the servant is not greater than his Lord.

The Parable of the Importunate Widow is a classic of insistent prayer. We shall do well to refresh our remembrance of it, at this point in our study:

> And he spake a parable unto them to this end, that men ought always to
> pray, and not to faint; saying, There was in a city a judge, which feared not God,

neither regarded man; and there was a widow in that city; and she came unto him, saying, "Avenge me of my adversary." And he would not for a while; but afterward he said within himself, Though I fear not God nor regard man; yet because this widow troubleth me, I will avenge her, lest by her continual coming she weary me. And the Lord said, Hear what the unjust judge saith. And shall not God avenge his own elect, which cry day and night unto him, though he bear long with them? I tell you he will avenge them speedily.

This parable stresses the central truth of importunate prayer. The widow presses her case till the unjust judge yields. If this parable does not teach the necessity for importunity, it has neither point nor instruction in it. Take this one thought away, and you have nothing left worth recording. Beyond all cavil, Christ intended it to stand as an evidence of the need that exists, for insistent prayer.

We have the same teaching emphasized in the incident of the Syrophoenician woman, who came to Jesus on behalf of her daughter. Here, importunity is demonstrated, not as a stark impertinence, but as with the persuasive characteristics of humility, sincerity, and fervency. We are given a glimpse of a woman's clinging faith, a woman's bitter grief, and a woman's spiritual insight. The master went over into that Sidonian country in order that this truth might be mirrored for all time—there is no plea so efficacious as importunate prayer, and none to which God surrenders himself so fully and so freely.

The importunity of this distressed mother, won her the victory, and materialized her request. Yet instead of being an offense to the Savior, it drew from him a word of wonder, and glad surprise. "O woman, great is thy faith! Be it unto thee, even as thou wilt."

He prays not at all, who does not press his plea. Cold prayers have no claim on heaven, and no hearing in the courts above. Fire is the life of prayer, and heaven is reached by flaming importunity rising in an ascending scale.

Reverting to the case of the importunate widow, we see that her widowhood, her friendlessness, and her weakness counted for nothing with the unjust judge. Importunity was everything. "Because this widow *troubleth* me," he said, "I will avenge her speedily, lest she weary me." Solely because the widow imposed upon the time and attention of the unjust judge, her case was won.

God waits patiently as, day and night, his elect cry unto him. He is moved by their requests a thousand times more than was this unjust judge. A limit is set to his tarrying, by the importunate praying of his people, and the answer richly given. God finds faith in his praying child—the faith which stays and cries—and he honors it by permitting its further exercise, to the end that it is strengthened and enriched. Then he rewards it by granting the burden of its plea, in plenitude and finality.

The case of the Syrophoenician woman previously referred to is a notable instance of successful importunity, one which is eminently encouraging to all who would pray successfully. It was a remarkable instance of insistence and perseverance to ultimate victory, in the face of almost insuperable obstacles and hindrances. But the woman surmounted them all by heroic faith and persistent spirit that were as remarkable as they were successful. Jesus had gone over into her country, "and would have no man know it." But she breaks through his purpose, violates his privacy, attracts his attention, and pours out to him a poignant appeal of need and faith. Her heart was in her prayer.

At first, Jesus appears to pay no attention to her agony, and ignores her cry for relief. He gives her neither eye, nor ear, nor word. Silence, deep and chilling, greets her impassioned cry. But she is not turned aside, nor disheartened. She holds on. The disciples, offended at her unseemly clamor, intercede for her, but are silenced by the Lord's declaring that the woman is entirely outside the scope of his mission and his ministry.

But neither the failure of the disciples to gain her a hearing nor the knowledge—despairing in its very nature—that she is barred from the benefits of his mission, daunt her, and serve only to lend intensity and increased boldness to her approach to Christ. She came closer, cutting her prayer in twain, and falling at his feet, worshiping him, and making her daughter's case her own cries, with pointed brevity—"Lord, help me!" This last cry won her case; her daughter was healed in the self-same hour. Hopeful, urgent, and unwearied, she stays near the master, insisting and praying until the answer is given. What a study in importunity, in earnestness, in persistence, promoted and propelled under conditions which would have disheartened any but an heroic, a constant soul.

In these parables of importunate praying, our Lord sets forth, for our information and encouragement, the serious difficulties which stand in the way of prayer. At the same time he teaches that importunity conquers all untoward circumstances and gets to itself a victory over a whole host of hindrances. He teaches, moreover, that an answer to prayer is conditional upon the amount of faith that goes to the petition. To test this, he delays the answer. The superficial pray-er subsides into silence, when the answer is delayed. But the man of prayer hangs on, and on. The Lord recognizes and honors his faith, and gives him a rich and abundant answer to his faith-evidencing, importunate prayer.

7

Prayer and Importunity
(Continued)

THE tenor of Christ's teachings, is to declare that men are to pray earnestly—to pray with an earnestness that cannot be denied. Heaven has harkening ears only for the wholehearted, and the deeply earnest. Energy, courage, and persistent perseverance must back the prayers which heaven respects, and God hears.

All these qualities of soul, so essential to effectual praying, are brought out in the parable of the man who went to his friend for bread, at midnight. This man entered on his errand with confidence. Friendship promised him success. His plea was pressing: of a truth, he could not go back empty-handed. The flat refusal chagrined and surprised him. Here even friendship failed! But there was something to be tried yet—stern resolution, set, fixed determination. He would stay and press his demand until the door was opened, and the request granted. This he proceeded to do, and by dint of importunity secured what ordinary solicitation had failed to obtain.

The success of this man, achieved in the face of a flat denial, was used by the Savior to illustrate the necessity for insistence in supplicating the throne of heavenly grace. When the answer is not immediately given, the praying Christian must gather courage at each delay, and advance in urgency till the answer comes which is assured, if he have but the faith to press his petition with vigorous faith.

Laxity, faintheartedness, impatience, timidity will be fatal to our prayers. Awaiting the onset of our importunity and insistence, is the Father's heart, the Father's hand, the Father's infinite power, the Father's infinite willingness to hear and give to his children.

Importunate praying is the earnest, inward movement of the heart toward God. It is the throwing of the entire force of the spiritual man into the exercise of prayer. Isaiah lamented that no one stirred himself, to take hold of God. Much praying was done in Isaiah's time, but it was too easy, indifferent and complacent. There were no mighty movements of souls toward God. There was no array of sanctified energies bent on reaching and grappling with God, to draw from him the treasures of his grace. Forceless prayers have no power to overcome difficulties, no power to win marked results, or to gain complete victories. We must win God, ere we can win our plea.

Isaiah looked forward with hopeful eyes to the day when religion would flourish, when there would be times of real praying. When those times came, the watchmen would not abate their vigilance, but cry day and night, and those, who were the Lord's remembrancers, would give him no rest. Their urgent, persistent efforts would keep all spiritual interests engaged, and make increasing demands on God's exhaustless treasures.

Importunate praying never faints nor grows weary; it is never discouraged; it never yields to cowardice, but is buoyed up and sustained by a hope that knows no despair, and a faith which will not let go. Importunate praying has patience to wait and strength to continue. It never prepares itself to quit praying, and declines to rise from its knees until an answer is received.

The familiar, yet heartening words of that great missionary, Adoniram Judson, are the testimony of a man who was importunate at prayer. He says:

> I was never deeply interested in any object, never prayed sincerely and earnestly for it, but that it came at some time, no matter how distant the day. Somehow, in some shape, probably the last I would have devised, it came.

"Ask, and ye shall receive. Seek, and ye shall find. Knock, and it shall be opened unto you." These are the ringing challenges of our Lord in regard to prayer, and his intimation that true praying must stay, and advance in effort and urgency, till the prayer is answered, and the blessing sought, received.

In the three words *ask, seek, knock,* in the order in which he places them, Jesus urges the necessity of importunity in prayer. Asking, seeking, knocking, are ascending rounds in the ladder of successful prayer. No principle is more definitely enforced by Christ than that prevailing prayer must have in it the quality which waits and perseveres, the courage that never surrenders, the patience which never grows tired, the resolution that never wavers.

In the parable preceding the one of the friend at midnight, a most significant and instructive lesson in this respect is outlined. Indomitable courage, ceaseless pertinacity, fixity of purpose, are chief among the qualities included in Christ's estimate of the highest and most successful form of praying.

Importunity is made up of intensity, perseverance, patience, and persistence. The seeming delay in answering prayer is the ground and the demand of importunity. In the first recorded instance of a miracle being wrought upon one who was blind, as given by Matthew, we have an illustration of the way in which our Lord appeared not to hearken at once to those who sought him. But the two blind men continue their crying, and follow him with their continual petition, saying, "Thou Son of David, have mercy on us." But he answered them not, and passed into the house. Yet the needy ones followed him, and, finally, gained their eyesight and their plea.

The case of blind Bartimæus is a notable one in many ways. Especially is it remarkable for the show of persistence which this blind man exhibited in appealing to our Lord. If it be—as it seems—that his first crying was done as

Jesus entered into Jericho, and that he continued it until Jesus came out of the place, it is all the stronger an illustration of the necessity of importunate prayer and the success which comes to those who stake their all on Christ, and give him no peace until he grants them their hearts' desire.

Mark puts the whole incident graphically before us. At first, Jesus seems not to hear. The crowd rebukes the noisy clamor of Bartimæus. Despite the seeming unconcern of our Lord, however, and despite the rebuke of an impatient and quick-tempered crowd, the blind beggar still cries, and increases the loudness of his cry, until Jesus is impressed and moved. Finally, the crowd, as well as Jesus, hearkens to the beggar's plea and declare in favor of his cause. He gains his case. His importunity avails even in the face of apparent neglect on the part of Jesus, and despite opposition and rebuke from the surrounding populace. His persistence won where half-hearted indifference would surely have failed.

Faith has its province, in connection with prayer, and, of course, has its inseparable association with importunity. But the latter quality drives the prayer to the believing point. A persistent spirit brings a man to the place where faith takes hold, claims and appropriates the blessing.

The imperative necessity of importunate prayer is plainly set forth in the Word of God, and needs to be stated and restated today. We are apt to overlook this vital truth. Love of ease, spiritual indolence, religious slothfulness, all operate against this type of petitioning. Our praying, however, needs to be pressed and pursued with an energy that never tires, a persistency which will not be denied, and a courage which never fails.

We have need, too, to give thought to that mysterious fact of prayer—the certainty that there will be delays, denials, and seeming failures, in connection with its exercise. We are to prepare for these, to brook them, and cease not in our urgent praying. Like a brave soldier, who, as the conflict grows more stern, exhibits a superior courage than in the earlier stages of the battle; so does the praying Christian, when delay and denial face him, increase his earnest asking, and ceases not until prayer prevail. Moses furnishes an illustrious example of importunity in prayer. Instead of allowing his nearness to God and his intimacy with him to dispense with the necessity for importunity, he regards them as the better fitting him for its exercise. When Israel set up the golden calf, the wrath of God waxed fierce against them, and Jehovah, bent on executing justice, said to Moses when divulging what he purposed doing, "Let me alone!" But Moses would *not* let him alone. He threw himself down before the Lord in an agony of intercession in behalf of the sinning Israelites, and for forty days and nights, fasted and prayed. What a season of importunate prayer was that!

Jehovah was wroth with Aaron, also, who had acted as leader in this idolatrous business of the golden calf. But Moses prayed for Aaron as well as for the Israelites; had he not, both Israel and Aaron had perished, under the consuming fire of God's wrath.

That long season of pleading before God, left its mighty impress on Moses. He had been in close relation with God aforetime, but never did his character attain the greatness that marked it in the days and years following this long season of importunate intercession.

There can be no question but that importunate prayer moves God, and heightens human character! If we were more with God in this great ordinance of intercession, more brightly would our faces shine, more richly endowed would life and service be, with the qualities which earn the goodwill of humanity, and bring glory to the name of God.

8

Prayer and Character and Conduct

PRAYER governs conduct, and conduct makes character. Conduct is what we do; character is what we are. Conduct is the outward life. Character is the life unseen, hidden within, yet evidenced by that which is seen. Conduct is external, seen from without; character is internal—operating within. In the economy of grace conduct is the offspring of character. Character is the state of the heart, conduct its outward expression. Character is the root of the tree, conduct, the fruit it bears.

Prayer is related to all the gifts of grace. To character and conduct its relation is that of a helper. Prayer helps to establish character and fashion conduct, and both for their successful continuance depend on prayer. There may be a certain degree of moral character and conduct independent of prayer, but there cannot be anything like distinctive religious character and Christian conduct without it. Prayer helps, where all other aids fail. The more we pray, the better we are, the purer and better our lives.

The very end and purpose of the atoning work of Christ is to create religious character and to make Christian conduct.

> Who gave himself for us, that he might redeem us from all iniquity, and purify unto himself a peculiar people, zealous of good works.

In Christ's teaching, it is not simply works of charity and deeds of mercy upon which he insists, but inward spiritual character. This much is demanded, and nothing short of it, will suffice.

In the study of Paul's Epistles, there is one thing which stands out, clearly and unmistakably—the insistence on holiness of heart, and righteousness of life. Paul does not seek, so much, to promote what is termed "personal work," nor is the leading theme of his letters deeds of charity. It is the condition of the human heart and the blamelessness of the personal life, which form the burden of the writings of Paul.

Elsewhere in the Scriptures, too, it is character and conduct which are made preeminent. The Christian religion deals with men who are devoid of spiritual character, and unholy in life, and aims so to change them, that they become holy in heart and righteous in life. It aims to change bad men into good men; it deals with inward badness, and works to change it into inward goodness. And it is just here where prayer enters and demonstrates its wonderful power and fruit. Prayer drives toward this specific end. In fact, without prayer, no such supernatural change in moral character, can ever be effected. For the change from badness to goodness is not wrought "by works of righteousness which we have done," but according to God's mercy, which saves us "by the washing of regeneration." And this marvelous change is brought to pass through earnest, persistent, faithful prayer. Any alleged form of Christianity which does not effect this change in the hearts of men is a delusion and a snare.

The office of prayer is to change the character and conduct of men, and in countless instances, has been wrought by prayer. At this point, prayer, by its credentials, has proved its divinity. And just as it is the office of prayer to effect this, so it is the prime work of the church to take hold of evil men and make them good. Its mission is to change human nature, to change character, influence behavior, to revolutionize conduct. The church is presumed to be righteous, and should be engaged in turning men to righteousness. The church is God's manufactory on earth, and its primary duty is to create and foster righteousness of character. This is its very first business. Primarily, its work is not to acquire members, nor amass numbers, nor aim at money-getting, nor engage in deeds of charity and works of mercy, but to produce righteousness of character, and purity of the outward life.

A product reflects and partakes of the character of the manufactory which makes it. A righteous church with a righteous purpose makes righteous men. Prayer produces cleanliness of heart and purity of life. It can produce nothing else. Unrighteous conduct is born of prayerlessness; the two go hand-in-hand. Prayer and sinning cannot keep company with each other. One or the other must of necessity stop. Get men to pray, and they will quit sinning, because prayer creates a distaste for sinning, and so works upon the heart, that evil-doing becomes repugnant, and the entire nature is lifted to a reverent contemplation of high and holy things.

Prayer is based on character. What we are with God gauges our influence with him. It was the inner character, not the outward bearing, of such men as Abraham, Job, David, Moses, and all others, who had such great influence with God in the days of old. And, today, it is not so much our words, as what we really are, which weighs with God. Conduct affects character, of course, and counts for much in our praying. At the same time, character affects conduct to a far greater extent, and has a superior influence over prayer. Our inner life not only gives color to our praying, but body, as well. Bad living means bad praying and, in the end, no praying at all. We pray feebly because we live feebly. The stream of prayer cannot rise higher than the fountain of living. The force of the inner chamber is made up of the energy which flows from the confluent streams of living. And the weakness of living grows out of the shallowness and shoddiness of character.

Feebleness of living reflects its debility and languor in the praying hours. We simply cannot talk to God, strongly, intimately, and confidently unless we are living for him, faithfully and truly. The prayer-closet cannot become sanctified unto God, when the life is alien to his precepts and purpose. We must learn this lesson well—that righteous character and Christlike conduct give us a peculiar and preferential standing in prayer before God. His holy Word gives special emphasis to the part conduct has in imparting value to our praying when it declares:

> Then shalt thou call and the Lord shall answer; thou shalt cry, and he shall say, Here I am; if thou take away from the midst of thee the yoke, the putting forth the finger, and speaking vanity.

The wickedness of Israel and their heinous practices were definitely cited by Isaiah, as the reason why God would turn his ears away from their prayers:

> And when ye spread forth your hands, I will hide mine eyes from you: yea, when ye make many prayers, I will not hear: your hands are full of blood.

The same sad truth was declared by the Lord through the mouth of Jeremiah:

> Therefore, pray not thou for this people, neither lift up a cry or prayer for them; for I will not hear them in the time that they cry unto me for their trouble.

Here, it is plainly stated, that unholy conduct is a bar to successful praying, just as it is clearly intimated that, in order to have full access to God in prayer, there must be a total abandonment of conscious and premeditated sin.

We are enjoined to pray, "lifting up holy hands, without wrath and doubting," and must pass the time of our sojourning here, in a rigorous abstaining from evil if we are to retain our privilege of calling upon the Father. We cannot, by any process, divorce praying from conduct.

> Whatsoever we ask, we receive of him, because we keep his commandments, and do those things which are pleasing in his sight.

And James declares roundly that men ask and receive not, because they ask amiss, and seek only the gratification of selfish desires.

Our Lord's injunction, "Watch ye, and pray always," is to cover and guard all our conduct, so that we may come to our inner chamber with all its force secured by a vigilant guard kept over our lives.

> And take heed to yourselves, lest at any time your hearts be overcharged with surfeiting, and drunkenness, and cares of this life, and so that day come upon you unawares.

Quite often, Christian experience founders on the rock of conduct. Beautiful theories are marred by ugly lives. The most difficult thing about piety, as it is the most impressive, is to be able to live it. It is the life which counts, and our praying suffers, as do other phases of our religious experience, from bad living.

In primitive times preachers were charged to preach by their lives, or not to preach at all. So, today, Christians, everywhere, ought to be charged to pray by their lives, or not to pray at all. The most effective preaching, is not that which is heard from the pulpit, but that which is proclaimed quietly, humbly, and consistently; which exhibits its excellencies in the home, and in the community. Example preaches a far more effective sermon than precept. The best preaching, even in the pulpit, is that which is fortified by godly living, in the preacher himself. The most effective work done by the pew is preceded by, and accompanied with, holiness of life, separation from the world, severance from sin. Some of the strongest appeals are made with mute lips—by godly fathers and saintly mothers who, around the fireside, feared God, loved his cause, and daily exhibited to their children and others about them, the beauties and excellencies of Christian life and conduct.

The best-prepared, most eloquent sermon can be marred and rendered ineffective, by questionable practices in the preacher. The most active church worker can have the labor of his hands neutralized by worldliness of spirit and inconsistency of life. Men preach by their lives, not by their words, and sermons are delivered, not so much in, and from a pulpit, as in tempers, actions, and the thousand and one incidents which crowd the pathway of daily life.

Of course, the prayer of repentance is acceptable to God. He delights in hearing the cries of penitent sinners. But repentance involves not only sorrow for sin, but the turning away from wrong-doing, and the learning to do well. A repentance which does not produce a change in character and conduct, is a mere sham, which should deceive nobody. Old things *must* pass away, all things *must* become new.

Praying, which does not result in right thinking and right living, is a farce. We have missed the whole office of prayer if it fail to purge character and rectify conduct. We have failed entirely to apprehend the virtue of prayer, if it bring not about the revolutionizing of the life. In the very nature of things, we must quit praying, or our bad conduct. Cold, formal praying may exist side by side, with bad conduct, but such praying, in the estimation of God, is no praying at all. Our praying advances in power, just insofar, as it rectifies the life. Growing in purity and devotion to God will be a more prayerful life.

The character of the inner life is a condition of effectual praying. As is the life, so will the praying be. An inconsistent life obstructs praying and neutralizes what little praying we may do. Always, it is "the prayer of the righteous man which availeth much." Indeed, one may go further and assert, that it is only the prayer of the righteous which avails anything at all—at any time. To have an eye to God's glory; to be possessed by an earnest desire to please him in all our ways; to possess hands busy in his service; to have feet swift to run in the way of his commandments—these give weight and influence and power to prayer, and secure an audience with God. The wordly spirit of our lives often breaks the force of our praying, and, not infrequently, acts as a door of brass in the face of prayer.

Praying must come out of a cleansed heart and be presented and urged with the "lifting up of holy hands." It must be fortified by a life aiming, unceasingly, to obey God, to attain conformity to the divine law, and to come into submission to the divine will.

Let it not be forgotten, that, while life is a condition of prayer, prayer is also the condition of righteous living. Prayer promotes righteous living, and is the one great aid to uprightness of heart and life. The fruit of real praying is right living. Praying sets him who prays to the great business of "working out his salvation with fear and trembling"; puts him to watching his temper, conversation and conduct; causes him to "walk circumspectly, redeeming the time"; enables him to "walk worthy of the vocation wherewith he is called, with all lowliness and meekness"; gives him a high incentive to pursue his pilgrimage consistently by "shunning every evil way, and walking in the good."

9

Prayer and Obedience

UNDER the Mosaic law, obedience was looked upon as being "better than sacrifice, and to harken, than the fat of lambs." In Deuteronomy 5:29, Moses represents Almighty God declaring himself as to this very quality in a manner which left no doubt as to the importance he laid upon its exercise. Referring to the waywardness of his people he cries:

> O that there were such a heart in them, that they would fear me, and keep all my commandments always, that it might be well with them, and with their children after them.

Unquestionably obedience is a high virtue, a soldier quality. To obey belongs, preeminently, to the soldier. It is his first and last lesson, and he must learn how to practice it all the time, without question, uncomplainingly. Obedience, moreover, is faith in action, and is the outflow as it is the very test of love. "He that hath my commandments and keepeth them, he it is that loveth me."

Furthermore: obedience is the conserver and the life of love.

> If ye keep my commandments, ye shall abide in my love, even as I have kept my Father's commandments and abide in his love.

What a marvelous statement of the relationship created and maintained by obedience! The Son of God is held in the bosom of the Father's love, by virtue of his obedience! And the factor which enables the Son of God to ever abide in his Father's love is revealed in his own statement, "For I do, always, those things that please him."

The gift of the Holy Spirit in full measure and in richer experience, depends upon loving obedience:

> If ye love me, keep my commandments, is the master's word. And I will pray the Father, and he shall give you another Comforter, that he may abide with you for ever.

Obedience to God is a condition of spiritual thrift, inward satisfaction, stability of heart. "If ye be willing and obedient, ye shall eat the fruit of the

52

land." Obedience opens the gates of the holy city, and gives access to the tree
of life.

> Blessed are they that do his commandments, that they may have right to the
> tree of life, and may enter in through the gates, into the city.

What is obedience? It is doing God's will: it is keeping his commandments.
How many of the commandments constitute obedience? To keep half of them,
and to break the other half—is that real obedience? To keep all the commandments but one—is that obedience? On this point, James the apostle is most
explicit: "Whosoever shall keep the whole law," he declares, "and yet offend
in one point, he is guilty of all."

The spirit which prompts a man to break one commandment is the spirit
which may move him to break them all. God's commandments are a unit, and
to break one strikes at the principle which underlies and runs through the
whole. He who hesitates not to break a single commandment, would—it is
more than probable—under the same stress, and surrounded by the same circumstances, break them all.

Universal obedience of the race is demanded. Nothing short of implicit
obedience will satisfy God, and the keeping of all his commandments is the
demonstration of it that God requires. But can we keep all of God's commandments? Can a man receive moral ability such as enables him to obey every
one of them? Certainly he can. By every token, man can, through prayer,
obtain ability to do this very thing.

Does God give commandments which men cannot obey? Is he so arbitrary,
so severe, so unloving, as to issue commandments which cannot be obeyed?
The answer is that in all the annals of Holy Scripture, not a single instance is
recorded of God having commanded any man to do a thing, which was
beyond his power. Is God so unjust and so inconsiderate as to require of man
that which he is unable to render? Surely not. To infer it is to slander the
character of God.

Let us ponder this thought, a moment: Do earthly parents require of their
children duties which they cannot perform? Where is the father who would
think, even, of being so unjust, and so tyrannical? Is God less kind and just
than faulty, earthly parents? Are they better and more just than a perfect God?
How utterly foolish and untenable a thought!

In principle, obedience to God is the same quality as obedience to earthly
parents. It implies, in general effect, the giving up of one's own way, and following that of another; the surrendering of the will to the will of another; the
submission of oneself to the authority and requirements of a parent.
Commands, either from our heavenly Father or from our earthly father, are
love-directing, and all such commands are in the best interests of those who
are commanded. God's commands are issued neither in severity nor tyranny.
They are always issued in love and in our interests, and so it behooves us to

heed and obey them. In other words, and appraised at its lowest value—God having issued his commands to us, in order to promote our good, it pays, therefore, to be obedient. Obedience brings its own reward. God has ordained it so, and since he has, even human reason can realize that he would never demand that which is out of our power to render.

Obedience is love, fulfilling every command, love expressing itself. Obedience, therefore, is not a hard demand made upon us, any more than is the service a husband renders his wife, or a wife renders her husband. Love delights to obey, and please whom it loves. There are no hardships in love. There may be exactions, but no irk. There are no impossible tasks for love.

With what simplicity and in what a matter-of-fact way does the apostle John say: "And whatsoever we ask, we receive of him, because we keep his commandments, and do those things which are pleasing in his sight."

This is obedience, running ahead of all and every command. It is love, obeying by anticipation. They greatly err, and even sin, who declare that men are bound to commit iniquity, either because of environment, or heredity, or tendency. God's commands are not grievous. Their ways are ways of pleasantness, and their paths peace. The task which falls to obedience is not a hard one. "For my yoke is easy, and my burden is light."

Far be it from our heavenly Father, to demand impossibilities of his children. It is possible to please him in all things, for he is not hard to please. He is neither a hard master, nor an austere lord, "taking up that which he lays not down, and reaping that which he did not sow." Thank God, it is possible for every child of God to please his heavenly Father! It is really much easier to please him than to please men. Moreover, we may *know* when we please him. This is the witness of the Spirit—the inward divine assurance, given to all the children of God that they are doing their Father's will, and that their ways are well-pleasing in his sight.

God's commandments are righteous and founded in justice and wisdom. "Wherefore the law is holy, and the commandment holy and just and good." "Just and true are thy ways, thou king of saints." God's commandments, then, can be obeyed by all who seek supplies of grace which enable them to obey. These commandments *must* be obeyed. God's government is at stake. God's children are under obligation to obey him; disobedience cannot be permitted. The spirit of rebellion is the very essence of sin. It is repudiation of God's authority, which God cannot tolerate. He never has done so, and a declaration of his attitude was part of the reason the Son of the highest was made manifest among men:

> For what the law could not do, in that it was weak through the flesh, God sending his own Son in the likeness of sinful flesh, and for sin, condemned sin in the flesh: that the righteousness of the law might be fulfilled in us, who walk not after the flesh, but after the Spirit.

If any should complain that humanity, under the fall, is too weak and helpless to obey these high commands of God, the reply is in order that, through the atonement of Christ, man is enabled to obey. The atonement is God's enabling act. That which God works in us, in regeneration and through the agency of the Holy Spirit, bestows enabling grace sufficient for all that is required of us, under the atonement. This grace is furnished without measure, in answer to prayer. So that, while God commands, he at the same time stands pledged to give us all necessary strength of will and grace of soul to meet his demands. This being true, man is without excuse for his disobedience and eminently censurable for refusing or failing to secure requisite grace, whereby he may serve the Lord with reverence, and with godly fear.

There is one important consideration those who declare it to be impossible to keep God's commandments strangely overlook, and that is the vital truth, which declares that through prayer and faith, man's nature is changed, and made partaker of the divine nature; that there is taken out of him all reluctance to obey God, and that his natural inability to keep God's commandments, growing out of his fallen and helpless state, is gloriously removed. By this radical change which is wrought in his moral nature, a man receives power to obey God in every way, and to yield full and glad allegiance. Then he can say, "I delight to do thy will, O my God." Not only is the rebellion incident to the natural man removed, but a heart which gladly obeys God's Word, blessedly received.

If it be claimed that the unrenewed man, with all the disabilities of the fall upon him, cannot obey God, there will be no denial. But to declare that, after one is renewed by the Holy Spirit, has received a new nature, and become a child of the king, he cannot obey God, is to assume a ridiculous attitude, and to display, moreover, a lamentable ignorance of the work and implications of the atonement.

Implicit and perfect obedience is the state to which the man of prayer is called. "Lifting up holy hands, without wrath and doubting," is the condition of obedient praying. Here inward fidelity and love, together with outward cleanness are put down as concomitants of acceptable praying.

John gives the reason for answered prayer in the passage previously quoted: "And whatsoever we ask we receive of him because we keep his commandments and do those things which are pleasing in his sight."

Seeing that the keeping of God's commandments is here set forth as the reason why he answers prayer, it is to be reasonably assumed that we *can* keep God's commandments, *can* do those things which are pleasing to him. Would God make the keeping of his commandments a condition of effectual prayer, think you, if he knew we could not keep his statutes? Surely, surely not!

Obedience can ask with boldness at the throne of grace, and those who exercise it are the only ones who *can* ask, after that fashion. The disobedient folk are timid in their approach and hesitant in their supplication. They are halted by reason of their wrong-doing. The requesting yet obedient child comes into the presence of his father with confidence and boldness. His very consciousness of obedience gives him courage and frees him from the dread born of disobedience.

To do God's will without demur, is the joy as it is the privilege of the successful praying man. It is he who has clean hands and a pure heart, that can pray with confidence. In the Sermon on the Mount, Jesus said:

> Not every one that saith unto me, Lord, Lord, shall enter into the kingdom of heaven, but he that doeth the will of my Father which is in heaven.

To this great deliverance may be added another:

> If ye keep my commandments ye shall abide in my love, even as I have kept my Father's commandments, and abide in his love.

"The Christian's trade," says Luther, "is prayer." But the Christian has another trade to learn, before he proceeds to learn the secrets of the trade of prayer. He must learn well the trade of perfect obedience to the Father's will. Obedience follows love, and prayer follows obedience. The business of *real* observance of God's commandments inseparably accompanies the business of *real* praying.

One who has been disobedient may pray. He may pray for pardoning mercy and the peace of his soul. He may come to God's footstool with tears, with confession, with penitent heart, and God will hear him and answer his prayer. But this kind of praying does not belong to the child of God, but to the penitent sinner, who has no other way by which to approach God. It is the possession of the unjustified soul, not of him who has been saved and reconciled to God.

An obedient life helps prayer. It speeds prayer to the throne. God cannot help hearing the prayer of an obedient child. He always has heard his obedient children when they have prayed. Unquestioning obedience counts much in the sight of God, at the throne of heavenly grace. It acts like the confluent tides of many rivers, and gives volume and fulness of flow as well as power to the prayer chamber. An obedient life is not simply a reformed life. It is not the old life primed and painted anew nor a churchgoing life, nor a good veneering of activities. Neither is it an external conformation to the dictates of public morality. Far more than all this is combined in a truly obedient Christian, God-fearing life.

A life of full obedience; a life settled on the most intimate terms with God; where the will is in full conformity to God's will; where the outward life shows the fruit of righteousness—such a life offers no bar to the inner chamber but rather, like Aaron and Hur, it lifts up and sustains the hands of prayer.

If you have an earnest desire to pray well, you must learn how to obey well. If you have a desire to learn to pray, then you must have an earnest desire to learn how to do God's will. If you desire to pray to God, you must first have a consuming desire to obey him. If you would have free access to God in prayer, then every obstacle in the nature of sin or disobedience must be removed. God delights in the prayers of obedient children. Requests coming from the lips of those who delight to do his will reach his ears with great rapidity, and incline him to answer them with promptitude and abundance. In themselves, tears are not meritorious. Yet they have their uses in prayer. Tears should baptize our place of supplication. He who has never wept concerning his sins, has never really *prayed* over his sins. Tears, sometimes, is a penitent's only plea. But tears are for the past, for the sin and the wrongdoing. There is another step and stage, waiting to be taken. It is that of unquestioning obedience, and until it is taken, prayer for blessing and continued sustenance, will be of no avail.

Everywhere in Holy Scripture God is represented as disapproving of disobedience and condemning sin, and this is as true in the lives of his elect as it is in the lives of sinners. Nowhere does he countenance sin, or excuse disobedience. Always, God puts the emphasis upon obedience to his commands. Obedience to them brings blessing, disobedience meets with disaster. This is true, in the Word of God, from its beginning to its close. It is because of this, that the men of prayer, in Scripture, had such influence with God. Obedient men always have been the closest to God. These are they who have prayed well and have received great things from God, who have brought great things to pass.

Obedience to God counts tremendously in the realm of prayer. This fact cannot be emphasized too much or too often. To plead for a religious faith which tolerates sinning is to cut the ground from under the feet of effectual praying. To excuse sinning by the plea that obedience to God is not possible to unregenerate men is to discount the character of the new birth, and to place men where effective praying is not possible. At one time Jesus broke out with a very pertinent and personal question, striking right to the core of disobedience, when he said: "Why call ye me, Lord, Lord, and do not the things I say?"

He who would pray, must obey. He who would get anything out of his prayers, must be in perfect harmony with God. Prayer puts into those who sincerely pray a spirit of obedience, for the spirit of disobedience is not of God and belongs not to God's praying hosts.

An obedient life is a great help to prayer. In fact, an obedient life is a necessity to prayer, to the sort which accomplishes things. The absence of an obedient life makes prayer an empty performance, a mere misnomer. A penitent sinner seeks pardon and salvation and has an answer to his prayers even with a life stained and debauched with sin. But God's *royal* intercessors come before him with royal lives. Holy living promotes holy praying. God's intercessors "lift up holy hands," the symbols of righteous, obedient lives.

10

Prayer and Obedience

(Continued)

IT is worthy of note that the praying to which such transcendent position is given and from which great results are attributable, is not simply the saying of prayers, but holy praying. It is the "prayers of the saints," the prayers of the holy men of God. Behind such praying, giving to it energy and flame are the men and women who are wholly devoted to God, who are entirely separated from sin, and fully separated unto God. These are they who always give energy, force, and strength to praying.

Our Lord Jesus Christ was preeminent in praying, because he was preeminent in saintliness. An entire dedication to God, a full surrender, which carries with it the whole being, in a flame of holy consecration—all this gives wings to faith and energy to prayer. It opens the door to the throne of grace, and brings strong influence to bear on Almighty God.

The "lifting up of holy hands" is essential to Christlike praying. It is not, however, a holiness which only dedicates a closet to God, which sets apart merely an hour to him, but a consecration which takes hold of the entire man, which dedicates the whole life to God.

Our Lord Jesus Christ, "holy, harmless, undefiled, separate from sinners," had full liberty of approach and ready access to God in prayer. And he had this free and full access because of his unquestioning obedience to his Father. Right through his earthly life his supreme care and desire was to do the will of his Father. And this fact, coupled with another—the consciousness of having so ordered his life—gave him confidence and assurance, which enabled him to draw near to the throne of grace with unbounded confidence, born of obedience, and promising acceptance, audience, and answer.

Loving obedience puts us where we can "ask anything in his name," with the assurance, that "He will do it." Loving obedience brings us into the prayer realm, and makes us beneficiaries of the wealth of Christ, and of the riches of his grace, through the coming of the Holy Spirit who will abide with us, and be in us. Cheerful obedience to God, qualifies us to pray effectually.

This obedience which not only qualifies but foreruns prayer, must be loving, constant, always doing the Father's will, and cheerfully following the path of God's commands.

In the instance of King Hezekiah, it was a potent plea which changed God's decree that he should die and not live. The stricken ruler called upon God to remember how he had walked before him in truth, and with a perfect heart. With God, this counted. He hearkened to the petition and as a result death found his approach to Hezekiah barred for fifteen years.

Jesus learned obedience in the school of suffering, and, at the same time, he learned prayer in the school of obedience. Just as it is the prayer of a righteous man which availeth much, so it is righteousness which is obedience to God. A righteous man is an obedient man, and he it is, who can pray effectually, who can accomplish great things when he betakes himself to his knees.

True praying, be it remembered, is not mere sentiment, nor poetry, nor eloquent utterance. Nor does it consist of saying in honeyed cadences, "Lord, Lord." Prayer is not a mere form of words; it is not just calling upon a name. Prayer is obedience. It is founded on the adamantine rock of obedience to God. Only those who obey have the right to pray. Behind the praying must be the doing; and it is the constant doing of God's will in daily life which gives prayer its potency, as our Lord plainly taught:

> Not every one which saith unto me, Lord, Lord, shall enter into the kingdom of heaven, but he that doeth the will of my Father which is in heaven. Many will say unto me in that day, "Lord, have we not prophesied in thy name, and in thy name have cast out devils? And in thy name done many wonderful works?" And then will I profess unto them, "I never knew you; depart from me, ye that worketh iniquity."

No name, however precious and powerful, can protect and give efficiency to prayer which is unaccompanied by the doing of God's will. Neither can the doing, without the praying, protect from divine disapproval. If the will of God does not master the life, the praying will be nothing but sickly sentiment. If prayer does not inspire, sanctify and direct our work, then self-will enters, to ruin both work and worker.

How great and manifold are the misconceptions of the true elements and functionings of prayer! There are many who earnestly desire to obtain an answer to their prayers but who go unrewarded and unblessed. They fix their minds on some promise of God and then endeavor by dint of dogged perseverance, to summon faith sufficient to lay hold upon, and claim it. This fixing of the mind on some great promise may avail in *strengthening* faith, but, to this holding on to the promise must be added the persistent and importunate prayer that expects and waits till faith grows exceedingly. And who is there that is able and competent to do such praying save the man who readily, cheerfully, and continually *obeys God?*

Faith, in its highest form, is the attitude as well as the act of a soul surrendered to God, in whom his Word and his Spirit dwells. It is true that faith must exist in some form, or another, in order to prompt praying; but in its strongest form, and in its largest results, faith is the fruit of prayer. That faith increases the ability and the efficiency of prayer is true; but it is likewise true that prayer increases the ability and efficiency of faith. Prayer and faith, work, act and react, one upon the other.

Obedience to God helps faith as no other attribute possibly can. When obedience exists,—implicit recognition of the validity, the paramountcy of the divine commands—faith ceases to be an almost superhuman task. It requires no straining to exercise it. Obedience to God makes it easy to believe and trust God. Where the spirit of obedience fully impregnates the soul; where the will is perfectly surrendered to God; where there is a fixed, unalterable purpose to obey God, faith almost believes itself. Faith then becomes almost involuntary. After obedience it is, naturally, the next step, and it is easily and readily taken. The difficulty in prayer is not with faith, but with obedience, which is faith's foundation.

We must look well to our obedience, to the secret springs of action, to the loyalty of our heart to God, if we would pray well, and desire to get the most out of our praying. Obedience is the groundwork of effectual praying; this it is, which brings us nigh to God.

The lack of obedience in our lives breaks down our praying. Quite often, the life is in revolt and this places us where praying is almost impossible, except it be for pardoning mercy. Disobedient living produces mighty poor praying. Disobedience shuts the door of the inner chamber, and bars the way to the Holy of Holies. No man can pray—really *pray*—who does not obey.

The will must be surrendered to God as a primary condition of all successful praying. Everything about us gets its coloring from our inmost character. The secret will makes character and controls conduct. The will, therefore, plays an important part in all successful praying. There can be no praying in its richest implication and truest sense, where the will is not wholly and fully surrendered to God. This unswerving loyalty to God is an utterly indispensable condition of the best, the truest, the most effectual praying. We have "simply *got* to trust and obey; *there's no other way,* to be happy in Jesus—but to trust, and *obey!*"

11

Prayer and Vigilance

THE description of the Christian soldier given by Paul in the sixth chapter of the Epistle to the Ephesians is compact and comprehensive. He is depicted as being ever in the conflict, which has many fluctuating seasons—seasons of prosperity and adversity, light and darkness, victory and defeat. He is to pray at all seasons, and with all prayer, this to be added to the armor in which he is to fare forth to battle. At all times, he is to have the full panoply of prayer. The Christian soldier, if he fights to win, must pray much. By this means, only, is he enabled to defeat his inveterate enemy, the devil, together with the evil one's manifold emissaries.

"Praying always, with all prayer," is the divine direction given him. This covers all seasons, and embraces all manner of praying.

Christian soldiers, fighting the good fight of faith, have access to a place of retreat, to which they continually repair for prayer. "Praying always, with all prayer," is a clear statement of the imperative need of much praying, and of many kinds of praying, by him who, fighting the good fight of faith, would win out, in the end, over all his foes.

The Revised Version puts it this way:

> With all prayer and supplication, praying at all seasons in the Spirit, and watching thereunto in all perseverance and supplications, for all saints, and on my behalf, that utterance may be given unto me, in opening my mouth to make known with boldness the mystery of the gospel, for which I am in bonds.

It cannot be stated too frequently that the life of a Christian is a warfare, an intense conflict, a lifelong contest. It is a battle, moreover, waged against invisible foes, who are ever alert, and ever seeking to entrap, deceive, and ruin the souls of men. The life to which Holy Scripture calls men is no picnic, or holiday junketing. It is no pastime, no pleasure jaunt. It entails effort, wrestling, struggling; it demands the putting forth of the full energy of the spirit in order to frustrate the foe and to come off, at the last, more than conqueror. It is no primrose path, no rose-scented dalliance. From start to finish, it is war. From the hour in which he first draws sword, to that in which he doffs his harness, the Christian warrior is compelled to "endure hardness like a good soldier."

What a misconception many people have of the Christian life! How little the average church member appears to know of the character of the conflict, and of its demands upon him! How ignorant he seems to be of the enemies he must encounter, if he engage to serve God faithfully and so succeed in getting to heaven and receive the crown of life! He seems scarcely to realize that the world, the flesh and the devil will oppose his onward march, and will defeat him utterly; unless he give himself to constant vigilance and unceasing prayer.

The Christian soldier wrestles not against flesh and blood, but against spiritual wickedness in high places. Or, as the scriptural margin reads, "wicked spirits in high places." What a fearful array of forces are set against him who would make his way through the wilderness of this world to the portals of the celestial city! It is no surprise, therefore, to find Paul, who understood the character of the Christian life so well, and who was so thoroughly informed as to the malignity and number of the foes, which the disciple of the Lord must encounter, carefully and plainly urging him to "put on the whole armor of God," and "to pray with all prayer and supplication in the Spirit." Wise, with a great wisdom, would the present generation be if all professors of our faith could be induced to realize this all-important and vital truth, which is so absolutely indispensable to a successful Christian life.

It is just at this point in much present-day Christian profession, that one may find its greatest defect. There is little, or nothing, of the soldier element in it. The discipline, self-denial, spirit of hardship, determination, so prominent in, and belonging to the military life, are, one and all, largely wanting. Yet the Christian life is *warfare,* all the way.

How comprehensive, pointed, and striking are all Paul's directions to the Christian soldier, who is bent on thwarting the devil and saving his soul alive! First of all, he must possess a clear idea of the character of the life on which he has entered. Then, he must know something of his foes—the adversaries of his immortal soul—their strength, their skill, their malignity. Knowing, therefore, something of the character of the enemy, and realizing the need of preparation to overcome them, he is prepared to hear the apostle's decisive conclusion:

> Finally, my brethren, be strong in the Lord, and in the power of his might. Put on the whole armor of God, that ye may be able to stand against the wiles of the devil. Wherefore, take unto you the whole armor of God, that ye may be able to stand in the evil day, and having done all, to stand.

All these directions end in a climax; and that climax is prayer. How can the brave warrior for Christ be made braver still? How can the strong soldier be made stronger still? How can the victorious battler be made still more victorious? Here are Paul's explicit directions to that end:

> Praying always with all prayer and supplication in the Spirit, and watching thereunto with all perseverance and supplication for all saints.

Prayer, and more prayer, adds to the fighting qualities and the more certain victories of God's good fighting men. The power of prayer is most forceful on the battlefield amid the din and strife of the conflict. Paul was preeminently a soldier of the cross. For him, life was no flowery bed of ease. He was no dress-parade, holiday soldier, whose only business was to don a uniform on set occasions. His was a life of intense conflict, the facing of many adversaries, the exercise of nonsleeping vigilance and constant effort. And, at its close—in sight of the end—we hear him chanting his final song of victory, "I have fought a good fight," and reading between the lines, we see that he is more than conqueror!

In his epistle to the Romans, Paul indicates the nature of his soldier-life, giving us some views of the kind of praying needed for such a career. He writes:

> Now I beseech you, brethren, for the Lord Jesus Christ's sake, and for the love of the Spirit, that ye strive together with me in your prayers to God for me, that I may be delivered from them that do not believe in Judæa.

Paul *had* foes in Judæa—foes who beset and opposed him in the form of "unbelieving men" and this, added to other weighty reasons, led him to urge the Roman Christians to "strive with him in prayer." That word *strive* indicated wrestling, the putting forth of great effort. This is the kind of effort, and this the sort of spirit, which must possess the Christian soldier.

Here is a great soldier, a captain-general, in the great struggle, faced by malignant forces who seek his ruin. His force is well-nigh spent. What reinforcements can he count on? What can give help and bring success to a warrior in such a pressing emergency? It is a critical moment in the conflict. What force can be added to the energy of his own prayers? The answer is—in the prayers of others, even the prayers of his brethren who were at Rome. These, he believes, will bring him additional aid, so that he can win his fight, overcome his adversaries, and, ultimately, prevail.

The Christian soldier is to pray at all seasons, and under all circumstances. His praying must be arranged so as to cover his times of peace as well as his hours of active conflict. It must be available in his marching and his fighting. Prayer must diffuse all effort, impregnate all ventures, decide all issues. The Christian soldier must be as intense in his praying as in his fighting, for his victories will depend very much more on his praying than on his fighting. Fervent supplication must be added to steady resolve, prayer and supplication must supplement the armor of God. The Holy Spirit must aid the supplication with his own strenuous plea. And the soldier must pray in the Spirit. In this, as in other forms of warfare, eternal vigilance is the price of victory; and thus, watchfulness and persistent perseverance must mark every activity of the Christian warrior.

The soldier-prayer must reflect its profound concern for the success and well-being of the whole army. The battle is not altogether a personal matter; victory cannot be achieved for self, alone. There is a sense, in which the entire army of Christ is involved. The cause of God, his saints, their woes and trials, their duties and crosses, all should find a voice and a pleader in the Christian soldier, when he prays. He dare not limit his praying to himself. Nothing dries up spiritual secretions so certainly and completely; nothing poisons the fountain of spiritual life so effectively; nothing acts in such deadly fashion, as selfish praying.

Note carefully that the Christian's armor will avail him nothing, unless prayer be added. This is the pivot, the connecting link of the armor of God. This holds it together, and renders it effective. God's true soldier plans his campaigns, arranges his battle-forces, and conducts his conflicts, with prayer. It is all important and absolutely essential to victory, that prayer should so impregnate the life that every breath will be a petition, every sigh a supplication. The Christian soldier must needs be always fighting. He should, of sheer necessity, be always praying.

The Christian soldier is compelled to constant picket duty. He must always be on his guard. He is faced by a foe who never sleeps, who is always alert, and ever prepared to take advantage of the fortunes of war. Watchfulness is a cardinal principle with Christ's warrior, "watch and pray," forever sounding in his ears. He cannot dare to be asleep at his post. Such a lapse brings him not only under the displeasure of the captain of his salvation, but exposes him to added danger. Watchfulness, therefore, imperatively constitutes the duty of the soldier of the Lord.

In the New Testament, there are three different words, which are translated "watch." The first means "absence of sleep," and implies a wakeful frame of mind, as opposed to listlessness; it is an enjoinder to keep awake, circumspect, attentive, constant, vigilant. The second word means "fully awake"—a state induced by some rousing effort, which faculty excited to attention and interest, active, cautious, lest through carelessness or indolence, some destructive calamity should suddenly evolve. The third word means "to be calm and collected in spirit," dispassionate, untouched by slumberous or beclouding influences, a wariness against all pitfalls and beguilements.

All three definitions are used by St. Paul. Two of them are employed in connection with prayer. Watchfulness intensified, is a requisite for prayer. Watchfulness must guard and cover the whole spiritual man, and fit him for prayer. Everything resembling unpreparedness or nonvigilance, is death to prayer.

In Ephesians, Paul gives prominence to the duty of constant watchfulness, "Watching thereunto with all perseverance and supplication." Watch, he says, watch, WATCH! "And what I say unto you, I say unto all, Watch."

Sleepless wakefulness is the price one must pay for victory over his spiritual foes. Rest assured that the devil never falls asleep. He is ever "walking about, seeking whom he may devour." Just as a shepherd must never be careless and unwatchful lest the wolf devour his sheep, so the Christian soldier must ever have his eyes wide open, implying his possession of a spirit which neither slumbers nor grows careless. The inseparable companions and safeguards of prayer are vigilance, watchfulness, and a mounted guard. In writing to the Colossians Paul brackets these inseparable qualities together: "Continue in prayer," he enjoins, "and watch in the same, with thanksgiving."

When will Christians more thoroughly learn the twofold lesson, that they are called to a great warfare, and that in order to get the victory they must give themselves to nonsleeping watchfulness and unceasing prayer?

> Be sober, be vigilant because your adversary, the devil, walketh about seeking whom he may devour.

God's church is a militant host. Its warfare is with unseen forces of evil. God's people compose an army fighting to establish his kingdom in the earth. Their aim is to destroy the sovereignty of Satan, and over its ruins, erect the kingdom of God, which is "righteousness and peace and joy in the Holy Spirit." This militant army is composed of individual soldiers of the cross, and the armor of God is needed for its defense. Prayer must be added as that which crowns the whole.

> Stand then in his great might,
>   With all his strength endued;
> But take, to arm you for the fight,
>   The panoply of God.

Prayer is too simple, too evident a duty, to need definition. Necessity gives being and shape to prayer. Its importance is so absolute, that the Christian soldier's life, in all the breadth and intensity of it, should be one of prayer. The entire life of a Christian soldier—its being, intention, implication, and action—are all dependent on its being a life of prayer. Without prayer—no matter what else he has—the Christian soldier's life will be feeble, and ineffective, and constitute him an easy prey for his spiritual enemies.

Christian experience will be sapless, and Christian influence will be dry and arid, unless prayer has a high place in the life. Without prayer the Christian graces will wither and die. Without prayer, we may add, preaching is edgeless and a vain thing, and the gospel loses its wings and its loins. Christ is the lawgiver of prayer, and Paul is his apostle of prayer. Both declare its primacy and importance, and demonstrate the fact of its indispensability. Their prayer-directions cover all places, include all times, and comprehend all things. How, then, can the Christian soldier hope or dream of victory, unless he be fortified by its power? How can he fail, if in addition to putting on the armor of God he is, at all times and seasons, "watching unto prayer"?

12

Prayer and the Word of God

GOD'S Word is a record of prayer—of praying men and their achievements, of the divine warrant of prayer and of the encouragement given to those who pray. No one can read the instances, commands, examples, multiform statements which concern themselves with prayer, without realizing that the cause of God, and the success of his work in this world, is committed to prayer; that praying men have been God's deputies on earth; that prayerless men have never been used of him.

A reverence for God's holy name is closely related to a high regard for his Word. This hallowing of God's name; the ability to do his will on earth, as it is done in heaven; the establishment and glory of God's kingdom, are as much involved in prayer, as when Jesus taught men the universal prayer. That "men ought always to pray and not to faint," is as fundamental to God's cause, today, as when Jesus Christ enshrined that great truth in the immortal setting of the Parable of the Importunate Widow.

As God's house is called "the house of prayer," because prayer is the most important of its holy offices; so by the same token, the Bible may be called the book of prayer. Prayer is the great theme and content of its message to mankind.

God's Word is the basis, as it is the directory of the prayer of faith. "Let the word of Christ dwell in you richly in all wisdom," says Paul, "teaching and admonishing one another in psalms and hymns and spiritual songs, singing with grace in your hearts to the Lord."

As this word of Christ dwelling in us richly is transmuted and assimilated, it issues in praying. Faith is constructed of the Word and the Spirit, and faith is the body and substance of prayer.

In many of its aspects, prayer is dependent upon the Word of God. Jesus says:

> If ye abide in me, and my words abide in you, ye shall ask what ye will, and it shall be done unto you.

The Word of God is the fulcrum upon which the lever of prayer is placed, and by which things are mightily moved. God has committed himself, his purpose, and his promise to prayer. His Word becomes the basis, the inspiration of our praying, and there are circumstances under which, by importunate prayer, we may obtain an addition, or an enlargement of his promises. It is said of the old saints that they, "through faith obtained promises." There would seem to be in prayer the capacity for going even beyond the Word, of getting even beyond his promise, into the very presence of God, himself.

Jacob wrestled, not so much with a promise, as with the promiser. We must take hold of the promiser, lest the promise prove inoperative. Prayer may well be defined as that force which vitalizes and energizes the Word of God, by taking hold of God, himself. By taking hold of the promiser, prayer reissues, and makes personal the promise. "There is none that stirreth up himself to take hold of me," is God's sad lament. "Let him take hold of my strength, that he may make peace with me," is God's recipe for prayer.

By scriptural warrant, prayer may be divided into the petition of faith and that of submission. The prayer of faith is based on the written Word, for "faith cometh by hearing, and hearing by the Word of God." It receives its answer, inevitably—the very thing for which it prays.

The prayer of submission is without a definite word of promise, so to speak, but takes hold of God with a lowly and contrite spirit, and asks and pleads with him, for that which the soul desires. Abraham had no definite promise that God would spare Sodom. Moses had no definite promise that God would spare Israel; on the contrary, there was the declaration of his wrath, and of his purpose to destroy. But the devoted leader gained his plea with God, when he interceded for the Israelites with incessant prayers and many tears. Daniel had no definite promise that God would reveal to him the meaning of the king's dream, but he prayed specifically, and God answered definitely.

The Word of God is made effectual and operative by the process and practice of prayer. The Word of the Lord came to Elijah, "Go show thyself to Ahab, and I will send rain on the earth." Elijah showed himself to Ahab; but the answer to his prayer did not come, until he had pressed his fiery prayer upon the Lord seven times.

Paul had the definite promise from Christ, that he "would be delivered from the people and the Gentiles," but we find him exhorting the Romans in the urgent and solemn manner concerning this very matter:

> Now I beseech you, brethren, for the Lord Jesus Christ's sake, and for the love of the Spirit, that ye strive together with me in your prayers to God for me; that I may be delivered from them that do not believe in Judæa, and that my service which I have for Jerusalem may be accepted of the saints.

The Word of God is a great help in prayer. If it be lodged and written in our hearts, it will form an outflowing current of prayer, full and irresistible. Promises, stored in the heart, are to be the fuel from which prayer receives life and warmth, just as the coal, stored in the earth, ministers to our comfort on stormy days and wintry nights. The Word of God is the food, by which prayer is nourished and made strong. Prayer, like man, cannot live by bread alone, "but by every word which proceedeth out of the mouth of the Lord."

Unless the vital forces of prayer are supplied by God's Word, prayer, though earnest even vociferous in its urgency, is in reality flabby, vapid, and void. The absence of vital force in praying can be traced to the absence of a constant supply of God's Word by which to repair the waste, and renew the life. He who would learn to pray well, must first study God's Word, and store it in his memory and thought.

When we consult God's Word, we find that no duty is more binding, more exacting, than that of prayer. On the other hand, we discover that no privilege is more exalted, no habit more richly owned of God. No promises are more radiant, more abounding, more explicit, more often reiterated, than those which are attached to prayer. "All things, whatsoever" are received by prayer, because "all things whatsoever" are promised. There is no limit to the provisions, included in the promises to prayer, and no exclusion from its promises. "Every one that asketh, receiveth." The word of our Lord is to this all-embracing effect: "If ye shall ask anything in my name, I will do it."

Here are some of the comprehensive, and exhaustive statements of the Word of God *about* prayer, the things to be taken in *by* prayer, the strong promise made in answer *to* prayer:

> Pray without ceasing; continue in prayer; continuing instant in prayer; in everything by prayer, let your request be made known unto God; pray always, pray and not faint; men should pray everywhere; praying always, with all prayer and supplication.

What clear and strong statements are those which are put in the divine record, to furnish us with a sure basis of faith, and to urge, constrain and encourage us to pray! How wide the range of prayer, as given us, in the divine revelation! How these Scriptures incite us to seek the God of prayer, with all our wants, with all our burdens!

In addition to these statements left on record for our encouragement, the sacred pages teem with facts, examples, incidents, and observations, stressing the importance and the absolute necessity of prayer, and putting emphasis on its all-prevailing power.

The utmost reach and full benefit of the rich promises of the Word of God, should humbly be received by us, and put to the test. The world will never receive the full benefits of the gospel until this is done. Neither Christian experience nor Christian living will be what they ought to be till these divine promises have been fully tested by those who pray. By prayer, we bring these promises of God's holy will into the realm of the actual and the real. Prayer is the philosopher's stone which transmutes them into gold.

If it is asked, what is to be done in order to render God's promises real, the answer is, that we must *pray*, until the words of the promise are clothed with the rich raiment of fulfillment.

God's promises are altogether too large to be mastered by desultory praying. When we examine ourselves, all too often, we discover that our praying does not rise to the demands of the situation; is so limited that it is little more than a mere oasis amid the waste and desert of the world's sin. Who of us, in our praying, measures up to this promise of our Lord:

> Verily, verily, I say unto you, he that believeth on me, the works that I do shall he do also, and greater works than these shall he do, because I go to my Father.

How comprehensive, how far reaching, how all-embracing! How much is here, for the glory of God, how much for the good of man! How much for the manifestation of Christ's enthroned power, how much for the reward of abundant faith! And how great and gracious are the results which can be made to accrue from the exercise of commensurate, believing prayer!

Look, for a moment, at another of God's great promises, and discover how we may be undergirded by the Word as we pray, and on what firm ground we may stand on which to make our petitions to our God:

> "If ye abide in me, and my words abide in you, ye shall ask what ye will, and it shall be done unto you."

In these comprehensive words, God turns himself over to the will of his people. When Christ becomes our all-in-all, prayer lays God's treasures at our feet. Primitive Christianity had an easy and practical solution of the situation, and got all which God had to give. That simple and terse solution is recorded in John's first epistle:

> Whatsoever we ask, we receive of him, because we keep his commandments, and do those things which are pleasing in his sight.

Prayer, coupled with loving obedience, is the way to put God to the test, and to make prayer answer all ends and all things. Prayer, joined to the Word of God, hallows and makes sacred all God's gifts. Prayer is not simply to get things from God, but to make those things holy, which already have been received from him. It is not merely to get a blessing, but also to be able to give a blessing. Prayer makes common things holy and secular things, sacred. It receives things from God with thanksgiving and hallows them with thankful hearts, and devoted service.

In the First Epistle to Timothy, Paul gives us these words:

> For every creature of God is good, and nothing to be refused, if it be received with thanksgiving. For it is sanctified by the word of God and prayer.

That is a statement which gives a negative to mere asceticism. God's good gifts are to be holy, not only by God's creative power, but, also, because they are made holy to us by prayer. We receive them, appropriate them and sanctify them by prayer.

Doing God's will, and having his Word abiding in us, is an imperative of effectual praying. But, it may be asked, how are we to know what God's will is? The answer is, by studying his Word, by hiding it in our hearts, and by letting the Word dwell in us richly. "The entrance of thy word, giveth light."

To know God's will in prayer, we must be filled with God's Spirit, who makes intercession for the saints, and in the saints, according to the will of God. To be filled with God's Spirit, to be filled with God's Word, is to know God's will. It is to be put in such a frame of mind, to be found in such a state of heart, as will enable us to read and interpret aright the purposes of the infinite. Such filling of the heart, with the Word and the Spirit, gives us an insight into the will of the Father, and enables us to rightly discern his will, and puts within us, a disposition of mind and heart to make it the guide and compass of our lives.

Epaphras prayed that the Colossians might stand "perfect and complete in all the will of God." This is proof positive that, not only may we know the will of God, but that we may know *all* the will of God. And not only may we know all the will of God, but we may *do* all the will of God. We may, moreover, do all the will of God, not occasionally, or by a mere impulse, but with a settled habit of conduct. Still further, it shows us that we may not only do the will of God externally, but from the heart, doing it cheerfully, without reluctance, or secret disinclination, or any drawing or holding back from the intimate presence of the Lord.

13

Prayer and the Word of God
(Continued)

PRAYER has all to do with the success of the preaching of the Word. This, Paul clearly teaches in that familiar and pressing request he made to the Thessalonians:

> Finally, brethren, pray for us that the Word of the Lord may have free course, and be glorified.

Prayer opens the way for the Word of God to run without let or hindrance, and creates the atmosphere which is favorable to the Word accomplishing its purpose. Prayer puts wheels under God's Word, and gives wings to the angel of the Lord "having the everlasting gospel to preach unto them that dwell on the earth, and to every nation, and kindred, and tongue, and people." Prayer greatly helps the Word of the Lord.

The Parable of the Sower is a notable study of preaching, showing its differing effects and describing the diversity of hearers. The wayside hearers are legion. The soil lies all unprepared either by previous thought or prayer; as a consequence, the devil easily takes away the seed (which is the Word of God) and dissipating all good impressions, renders the work of the sower futile. No one for a moment believes, that so much of present-day sowing would go fruitless if only the hearers would prepare the ground of their hearts beforehand by prayer and meditation.

Similarly with the stony-ground hearers, and the thorny-ground hearers. Although the word lodges in their hearts and begins to sprout, yet all is lost, chiefly because there is no prayer or watchfulness or cultivation following. The good-ground hearers are profited by the sowing, simply because their minds have been prepared for the reception of the seed, and that, after hearing, they have cultivated the seed sown in their hearts, by the exercise of prayer. All this gives peculiar emphasis to the conclusion of this striking parable: "Take heed, therefore, how ye hear." And in order that we *may* take heed how we hear, it is needful to give ourselves continually to prayer.

We have *got* to believe that underlying God's Word is prayer, and upon prayer, its final success will depend. In the Book of Isaiah we read:

So shall my word be that goeth out of my mouth; it shall not return unto me void, but it shall accomplish that which I please, and it shall prosper in the thing whereto I sent it.

In Psalm 19, David magnifies the Word of God in six statements concerning it. It converts the soul, makes wise the simple, rejoices the heart, enlightens the eyes, endures eternally, and is true and righteous altogether. The Word of God is perfect, sure, right, pure. It is heart-searching, and at the same time purifying, in its effect. It is no surprise therefore that after considering the deep spirituality of the Word of God, its power to search the inner nature of man, and its deep purity, the psalmist should close his dissertation with this passage:

Who can understand his errors? Cleanse thou me from secret faults. Keep back thy servant also from presumptuous sins. Let them not have dominion over me. Let the words of my mouth, and the meditations of my heart be acceptable in thy sight, O Lord, my strength and my redeemer.

James recognizes the deep spirituality of the Word, and its inherent saving power, in the following exhortation:

Wherefore, lay apart all filthiness and superfluity of naughtiness, and receive with meekness the engrafted word, which is able to save your souls.

And Peter talks along the same line, when describing the saving power of the Word of God:

Being born again, not of corruptible seed, but of incorruptible, by the word of God, which liveth and abideth forever.

Not only does Peter speak of being born again, by the incorruptible Word of God, but he also informs us that to grow in grace we must be like newborn babes, desiring or feeding upon the "sincere milk of the Word."

That is not to say, however, that the mere form of words as they occur in the Bible have in them any saving power. But the Word of God, be it remembered, is impregnated with the Holy Spirit. And just as there is a divine element in the words of Scripture, so also is the same divine element to be found in all true preaching of the Word, which is able to save and convert the soul.

Prayer invariably begets a love for the Word of God, and sets people to the reading of it. Prayer leads people to obey the Word of God, and puts into the heart which obeys a joy unspeakable. Praying people and Bible-reading people are the same sort of folk. The God of the Bible and the God of prayer are one. God speaks to man in the Bible; man speaks to God in prayer. One reads the Bible to discover God's will; he prays in order that he may receive power to do that will. Bible-reading and praying are the distinguishing traits of those who strive to know and please God. And just as prayer begets a love for the

Scriptures, and sets people to reading the Bible, so, also, does prayer cause men and women to visit the house of God, to hear the Scriptures expounded. Church-going is closely connected with the Bible, not so much because the Bible cautions us against "forsaking the assembling of ourselves together as the manner of some is," but because in God's house, God's chosen minister declares his Word to dying men, explains the Scriptures, and enforces their teachings upon his hearers. And prayer germinates a resolve in those who practice it not to forsake the house of God.

Prayer begets a church-going conscience, a church-loving heart, a church-supporting spirit. It is the praying people who make it a matter of conscience, to attend the preaching of the Word; who delight in its reading; exposition; who support it with their influence and their means. Prayer exalts the Word of God and gives it preeminence in the estimation of those who faithfully and wholeheartedly call upon the name of the Lord.

Prayer draws its very life from the Bible, and has no standing ground outside of the warrant of the Scriptures. Its very existence and character is dependent on revelation made by God to man in his holy Word. Prayer, in turn, exalts this same revelation, and turns men toward that Word. The nature, necessity and all-comprehending character of prayer, is based on the Word of God.

Psalm 119 is a directory of God's Word. With three or four exceptions, each verse contains a word which identifies, or locates, the Word of God. Quite often, the writer breaks out into supplication, several times praying, "Teach me thy statutes." So deeply impressed is he with the wonders of God's Word, and of the need for divine illumination wherewith to see and understand the wonderful things recorded therein, that he fervently prays:

Open thou mine eyes, that I may behold wondrous things out of thy law.

From the opening of this wonderful psalm to its close, prayer and God's Word are intertwined. Almost every phase of God's Word is touched upon by this inspired writer. So thoroughly convinced was the psalmist of the deep spiritual power of the Word of God that he makes this declaration:

Thy word have I hid in my heart that I might not sin against thee.

Here the psalmist found his protection against sinning. By having God's Word hidden in his heart; in having his whole being thoroughly impregnated with that Word; in being brought completely under its benign and gracious influence, he was enabled to walk to and fro in the earth, safe from the attack of the evil one, and fortified against a proneness to wander out of the way.

We find, furthermore, the power of prayer to create a real love for the Scriptures, and to put within men a nature which will take pleasure in the Word. In holy ecstasy he cries, "O, how I love thy law! It is my meditation all the day." And again: "How sweet are thy words to my taste! Yea, sweeter than honey to my taste."

Would we have a relish for God's Word? Then let us give ourselves continually to prayer. He who would have a heart for the reading of the Bible must not—dare not—forget to pray. The man of whom it can be said, "His delight is in the law of the Lord," is the man who can truly say, "I delight to visit the place of prayer." No man loves the Bible, who does not love to pray. No man loves to pray, who does not delight in the law of the Lord.

Our Lord was a man of prayer, and he magnified the Word of God, quoting often from the Scriptures. Right through his earthly life Jesus observed Sabbath-keeping, church-going, and the reading of the Word of God, and had prayer intermingled with them all:

> And he came to Nazareth where he had been brought up, and as his custom was, he went into the synagogue on the Sabbath day, and stood up to read.

Here, let it be said, that no two things are more essential to a spirit-filled life than Bible-reading and secret prayer; no two things more helpful to growth in grace; to getting the largest joy out of a Christian life; toward establishing one in the ways of eternal peace. The neglect of these all-important duties, presages leanness of soul, loss of joy, absence of peace, dryness of spirit, decay in all that pertains to spiritual life. Neglecting these things paves the way for apostasy, and gives the evil one an advantage such as he is not likely to ignore. Reading God's Word regularly, and praying habitually in the secret place of the most high puts one where he is absolutely safe from the attacks of the enemy of souls, and guarantees him salvation and final victory, through the overcoming power of the lamb.

14

Prayer and the House of God

PRAYER stands related to places, times, occasions and circumstances. It has to do with God and with everything which is related to God, and it has an intimate and special relationship to his house. A church is a sacred place, set apart from all unhallowed and secular uses, for the worship of God. As worship is prayer, the house of God is a place set apart for worship. It is no common place; it is where God dwells, where he meets with his people, and he delights in the worship of his saints.

Prayer is always in place in the house of God. When prayer is a stranger there, then it ceases to be God's house at all. Our Lord put peculiar emphasis upon what the church was when he cast out the buyers and sellers in the temple, repeating the words from Isaiah, "It is written, my house shall be called the house of prayer." He makes prayer preeminent, that which stands out above all else in the house of God. They, who sidetrack prayer or seek to minimize it, and give it a secondary place, pervert the church of God, and make it something less and other than it is ordained to be.

Prayer is perfectly at home in the house of God. It is no stranger, no mere guest, it belongs there. It has a peculiar affinity for the place, and has, moreover, a divine right there, being set therein by divine appointment and approval.

The inner chamber is a sacred place for personal worship. The house of God is a holy place for united worship. The prayer closet is for individual prayer. The house of God is for mutual prayer, concerted prayer, united prayer. Yet even in the house of God, there is the element of private worship, since God's people are to worship him and pray to him, personally, even in public worship. The church is for the united prayer of kindred, yet individual believers.

The life, power, and glory of the church is prayer. The life of its members is dependent on prayer and the presence of God is secured and retained by prayer. The very place is made sacred by its ministry. Without it, the church is lifeless and powerless. Without it, even the building itself is nothing, more or other, than any other structure. Prayer converts even the bricks, and mortar, and lumber, into a sanctuary, a Holy of Holies, where the Shekinah dwells. It separates it in spirit and in purpose from all other edifices. Prayer gives a peculiar sacredness to the building, sanctifies it, sets it apart for God, conserves it from all common and mundane affairs.

With prayer, though the house of God might be supposed to lack everything else, it becomes a divine sanctuary. So the tabernacle, moving about from place to place, became the Holy of Holies, because prayer was there. Without prayer the building may be costly, perfect in all its appointments, beautiful for situation, and attractive to the eye, but it comes down to the human, with nothing divine in it, and is on a level with all other buildings.

Without prayer, a church is like a body without spirit; it is a dead, inanimate thing. A church with prayer in it, has God in it. When prayer is set aside, God is outlawed. When prayer becomes an unfamiliar exercise, then God himself is a stranger there.

As God's house is a house of prayer, the divine intention is that people should leave their homes and go to meet him in his own house. The building is set apart for prayer especially, and as God has made special promise to meet his people there, it is their duty to go there, and for that specific end. Prayer should be the chief attraction for all spiritually minded churchgoers. While it is conceded that the preaching of the Word has an important place in the house of God, yet prayer is its predominating, distinguishing feature. Not that all other places are sinful, or evil, in themselves or in their uses. But they are secular and human, having no special conception of God in them. The church is, essentially, religious and divine. The work belonging to other places is done without special reference to God. He is not specifically recognized, nor called upon. In the church, however, God is acknowledged, and nothing is done without him. Prayer is the one distinguishing mark of the house of God. As prayer distinguishes Christian from non-Christian people, so prayer distinguishes God's house from all other houses. It is a place where faithful believers meet with their Lord.

As God's house is, preeminently, a house of prayer, prayer should enter into and underlie everything that is undertaken there. Prayer belongs to every sort of work pertaining to the church of God. As God's house is a house where the business of praying is carried on, so is it a place where the business of making praying people out of prayerless people is done. The house of God is a divine workshop, and there the work of prayer goes on. Or the house of God is a divine schoolhouse, in which the lesson of prayer is taught; where men and women learn to pray, and where they are graduated in the school of prayer.

Any church calling itself the house of God, and failing to magnify prayer; which does not put prayer in the forefront of its activities; which does not teach the great lesson of prayer, should change its teaching to conform to the divine pattern or change the name of its building to something other than a house of prayer.

On an earlier page, we made reference to the finding of the book of the law of the Lord given to Moses. How long that book had been there, we do not know. But when tidings of its discovery were carried to Josiah, he rent his clothes and was greatly disturbed. He lamented the neglect of God's Word and saw, as a natural result, the iniquity which abounded throughout the land.

And then, Josiah thought of God, and commanded Hilkiah, the priest, to go and make inquiry of the Lord. Such neglect of the Word of the law was too serious a matter to be treated lightly, and God must be inquired of, and repentance shown, by himself, and the nation:

> Go inquire of the Lord for me, and for them that are left in Israel and in Judah, concerning the words of the book that is found; for great is the wrath of the Lord that is poured out upon us, because our fathers have not kept the word of the Lord, to do after all that is written in this book.

But that was not all. Josiah was bent on promoting a revival of religion in his kingdom, so we find him gathering all the elders of Jerusalem and Judah together, for that purpose. When they had come together, the king went into the house of the Lord, and himself read in all the words of the book of the covenant that was found in the house of the Lord.

With this righteous king, God's Word was of great importance. He esteemed it at its proper worth, and counted a knowledge of it to be of such grave importance, as to demand his consulting God in prayer about it, and to warrant the gathering together of the notables of his kingdom, so that they, together with himself, should be instructed out of God's book concerning God's law.

When Ezra, returned from Babylon, was seeking the reconstruction of his nation, the people, themselves, were alive to the situation, and, on one occasion, the priests, Levites, and people assembled themselves together as one man before the water gate.

> And they spake unto Ezra the scribe, to bring the book of the law of Moses, which the Lord had commanded to Israel. And Ezra the priest brought the law before the congregation, both of men and women, and all that could hear with understanding. And he read therein before the street that was before the water gate from the morning until midday; and the ears of all the people were attentive unto the book of the law.

This was Bible-reading day in Judah—a real revival of Scripture-study. The leaders read the law before the people, whose ears were keen to hear what God had to say to them out of the book of the law. But it was not only a Bible-reading day. It was a time when real preaching was done, as the following passage indicates:

> So they read in the book in the law of God distinctly and gave the sense, and caused them to understand the reading.

Here then is the scriptural definition of preaching. No better definition can
be given. To read the Word of God distinctly—to read it so that the people
could hear and understand the words read; not to mumble out the words, nor
read it in an undertone or with indistinctness, but boldly and clearly—that
was the method followed in Jerusalem, on this auspicious day. Moreover: the
sense of the words was made clear in the meeting held before the water gate;
the people were treated to a high type of expository preaching. That was *true*
preaching—preaching of a sort which is sorely needed, today, in order that
God's Word may have due effect on the hearts of the people. This meeting in
Jerusalem surely contains a lesson which all present-day preachers should
learn and heed.

No one having any knowledge of the existing facts, will deny the compara-
tive lack of expository preaching in the pulpit effort of today. And none, we
should, at least, imagine, will do other than lament the lack. Topical preaching, polemical preaching, historical preaching, and other forms of sermonic
output have, one supposes, their rightful and opportune uses. But expository
preaching—the prayerful expounding of the Word of God is preaching that *is*
preaching—pulpit effort *par excellence.*

For its successful accomplishment, however, a preacher needs must be a
man of prayer. For every hour spent in his study-chair, he will have to spend
two upon his knees. For every hour he devotes to wrestling with an obscure
passage of Scripture, he must have two in which to be found wrestling with
God. Prayer and preaching: preaching and prayer! They cannot be separated.
The ancient cry was: "To your tents, O Israel!" The modern cry should be:
"To your knees, O preachers, to your knees!"

◆2◆

The Essentials of Prayer

1

Prayer Takes In the Whole Man

PRAYER has to do with the entire man. Prayer takes in man in his whole being, mind, soul and body. It takes the whole man to pray, and prayer affects the entire man in its gracious results. As the whole nature of man enters into prayer, so also all that belongs to man is the beneficiary of prayer. All of man receives benefits in prayer. The whole man must be given to God in praying. The largest results in praying come to him who gives himself, all of himself, all that belongs to himself, to God. This is the secret of full consecration, and this is a condition of successful praying, and the sort of praying which brings the largest fruits.

The men of olden times who wrought well in prayer, who brought the largest things to pass, who moved God to do great things, were those who were entirely given over to God in their praying. God wants, and must have, all that there is in man in answering his prayers. He must have wholehearted men through whom to work out his purposes and plans concerning men. God must have men in their entirety. No double-minded man need apply. No vacillating man can be used. No man with a divided allegiance to God, and the world and self, can do the praying that is needed.

Holiness is wholeness, and so God wants holy men, men whole-hearted and true, for his service and for the work of praying. "And the very God of peace sanctify you wholly; and I pray God your whole spirit and soul and body be preserved blameless unto the coming of our Lord Jesus Christ." These are the sort of men God wants for leaders of the hosts of Israel, and these are the kind out of which the praying class is formed. Man is a trinity in one, and yet man is neither a trinity nor a dual creature when he prays, but a unit. Man is one in all the essentials and acts and attitudes of piety. Soul, spirit and body are to unite in all things pertaining to life and godliness. The body, first of all, engages in prayer, since it assumes the praying attitude in prayer. Prostration of the body becomes us in praying as well as prostration of the soul. The attitude of the body counts much in prayer, although it is true that the heart may be haughty and lifted up, and the mind listless and wandering, and the praying a mere form, even while the knees are bent in prayer.

Daniel kneeled three times a day in prayer. Solomon kneeled in prayer at the dedication of the temple. Our Lord in Gethsemane prostrated himself in

81

that memorable season of praying just before his betrayal. Where there is earnest and faithful praying the body always takes on the form most suited to the state of the soul at the time. The body, that far, joins the soul in praying.

The entire man must pray. The whole man, life, heart, temper, mind, are in it. Each and all join in the prayer exercise. Doubt, double-mindedness, division of the affections, are all foreign to the closet. Character and conduct, undefiled, made whiter than snow, are mighty potencies, and are the most seemly beauties for the closet hour, and for the struggles of prayer.

A loyal intellect must conspire and add the energy and fire of its undoubting and undivided faith to that kind of an hour, the hour of prayer. Necessarily the mind enters into the praying. First of all, it takes thought to pray. The intellect teaches us we ought to pray. By serious thinking beforehand the mind prepares itself for approaching a throne of grace. Thought goes before entrance into the closet and prepares the way for true praying. It considers what will be asked for in the closet hour. True praying does not leave to the inspiration of the hour what will be the requests of that hour. As praying is asking for something definite of God, so, beforehand, the thought arises—"What shall I ask for at this hour?" All vain and evil and frivolous thoughts are eliminated, and the mind is given over entirely to God, thinking of him, of what is needed, and what has been received in the past. By every token, prayer, in taking hold of the entire man, does not leave out the mind. The very first step in prayer is a mental one. The disciples took that first step when they said unto Jesus at one time, "Lord, teach us to pray." We must be taught through the intellect, and just in so far as the intellect is given up to God in prayer, will we be able to learn well and readily the lesson of prayer.

Paul spreads the nature of prayer over the whole man. It must be so. It takes the whole man to embrace in its godlike sympathies the entire race of man—the sorrows, the sins and the death of Adam's fallen race. It takes the whole man to run parallel with God's high and sublime will in saving mankind. It takes the whole man to stand with our Lord Jesus Christ as the one mediator between God and sinful man. This is the doctrine Paul teaches in his prayer-directory in the second chapter of his first epistle to Timothy.

Nowhere does it appear so clearly that it requires the entire man in all departments of his being, to pray than in this teaching of Paul. It takes the whole man to pray till all the storms which agitate his soul are calmed to a great calm, till the stormy winds and waves cease as by a godlike spell. It takes the whole man to pray till cruel tyrants and unjust rulers are changed in their natures and lives, as well as in their governing qualities, or till they cease to rule. It requires the entire man in praying till high and proud and unspiritual ecclesiastics become gentle, lowly and religious, till godliness and gravity bear rule in church and in state, in home and in business, in public as well as in private life.

It is man's business to pray; and it takes manly men to do it. It is godly business to pray and it takes godly men to do it. And it is godly men who give over themselves entirely to prayer. Prayer is far-reaching in its influence and in its gracious effects. It is intense and profound business which deals with God and his plans and purposes, and it takes whole-hearted men to do it. No half-hearted, half-brained, half-spirited effort will do for this serious, all-important, heavenly business. The whole heart, the whole brain, the whole spirit, must be in the matter of praying, which is so mightily to affect the characters and destinies of men. The answer of Jesus to the scribe as to what was the first and greatest commandment was as follows:

> The Lord our God is one Lord; And thou shalt love the Lord thy God with all thy heart, and with thy soul, and with all thy mind, and with all thy strength.

In one word, the entire man without reservation must love God. So it takes the same entire man to do the praying which God requires of men. All the powers of man must be engaged in it. God cannot tolerate a divided heart in the love he requires of men, neither can he bear with a divided man in praying.

In the one hundred and nineteenth Psalm the psalmist teaches this very truth in these words:

> Blessed are they that keep his testimonies, and seek him with the whole heart.

It takes whole-hearted men to keep God's commandments and it demands the same sort of men to seek God. These are they who are counted "blessed." Upon these whole-hearted ones God's approval rests.

Bringing the case closer home to himself the psalmist makes this declaration as to his practice: "With my whole heart have I sought thee; O let me not wander from thy commandments."

And further on, giving us his prayer for a wise and understanding heart, he tells us his purposes concerning the keeping of God's law:

> Give me understanding and I shall keep thy law; Yea, I shall observe it with my whole heart.

Just as it requires a whole heart given to God to gladly and fully obey God's commandments, so it takes a whole heart to do effectual praying.

Because it requires the whole man to pray, praying is no easy task. Praying is far more than simply bending the knee and saying a few words by rote.

> Tis not enough to bend the knee,
> And words of prayer to say;
> The heart must with the lips agree,
> Or else we do not pray.

Praying is no light and trifling exercise. While children should be taught early to pray, praying is no child's task. Prayer draws upon the whole nature of man. Prayer engages all the powers of man's moral and spiritual nature. It is this which explains somewhat the praying of our Lord as described in Hebrews 5:7:

> Who in the days of his flesh, when he had offered up prayers and supplications, with strong crying and tears, unto him that was able to save him from death, and was heard in that he feared.

It takes only a moment's thought to see how such praying of our Lord drew mightily upon all the powers of his being, and called into exercise every part of his nature. This is the praying which brings the soul close to God and which brings God down to earth.

Body, soul and spirit are taxed and brought under tribute to prayer. David Brainerd makes this record of his praying:

> God enabled me to agonize in prayer till I was wet with perspiration, though in the shade and in a cool place.

The Son of God in Gethsemane was in an agony of prayer, which engaged his whole being:

> And when he was at the place, he said unto them, Pray ye that ye enter not into temptation. And he was withdrawn from them about a stone's cast, and kneeled down and prayed, saying, Father, if thou be willing, remove this cup from me; nevertheless, not my will, but thine, be done. And there appeared an angel unto him from heaven, strengthening him. And being in an agony, he prayed more earnestly: and his sweat was as it were great drops of blood falling down to the ground. (Luke 22:40–44).

Here was praying which laid its hands on every part of our Lord's nature, which called forth all the powers of his soul, his mind and his body. This was praying which took in the entire man.

Paul was acquainted with this kind of praying. In writing to the Roman Christians, he urges them to pray with him after this fashion:

> Now I beseech you, brethren, for the Lord Jesus Christ's sake, and for the love of the Spirit, that ye strive together with me in your prayers to God for me.

The words, "strive together with me," tells of Paul's praying, and how much he put into it. It is not a docile request, not a little thing, this sort of praying, this "striving with me." It is of the nature of a great battle, a conflict to win, a great battle to be fought. The praying Christian, as the soldier, fights a life-and-death struggle. His honor, his immortality, and eternal life are all in it. This is praying as the athlete struggles for the mastery, and for the crown, and as he wrestles or runs a race. Everything depends on the strength he puts in it. Energy, ardor, swiftness, every power of his nature is in it. Every power is quickened and strained to its very utmost. Littleness, half-heartedness, weakness and laziness are all absent.

Just as it takes the whole man to pray successfully, so in turn the whole man receives the benefits of such praying. As every part of man's complex being enters into true praying, so every part of that same nature receives blessings from God in answer to such praying. This kind of praying engages our undivided hearts, our full consent to be the Lord's, our whole desires.

God sees to it that when the whole man prays, in turn the whole man shall be blessed. His body takes in the good of praying, for much praying is done specifically for the body. Food and raiment, health and bodily vigor, come in answer to praying. Clear mental action, right thinking, an enlightened understanding, and safe reasoning powers, come from praying. Divine guidance means God so moving and impressing the mind, that we shall make wise and safe decisions. "The meek will he guide in judgment."

Many a praying preacher has been greatly helped just at this point. The unction of the Holy One which comes upon the preacher invigorates the mind, loosens up thought and gives utterance. This is the explanation of former days when men of very limited education had such wonderful liberty of the Spirit in praying and in preaching. Their thoughts flowed as a stream of water. Their entire intellectual machinery felt the impulse of the divine Spirit's gracious influences.

And, of course, the soul receives large benefits in this sort of praying. Thousands can testify to this statement. So we repeat, that as the entire man comes into play in true, earnest effectual praying, so the entire man, soul, mind and body, receives the benefits of prayer.

2

Prayer and Humility

To be humble is to have a low estimate of one's self. It is to be modest, lowly, with a disposition to seek obscurity. Humility retires itself from the public gaze. It does not seek publicity nor hunt for high places, neither does it care for prominence. Humility is retiring in its nature. Self-abasement belongs to humility. It is given to self-depreciation. It never exalts itself in the eyes of others nor even in the eyes of itself. Modesty is one of its most prominent characteristics.

In humility there is the total absence of pride, and it is at the very farthest distance from anything like self-conceit. There is no self-praise in humility, Rather it has the disposition to praise others. "In honor preferring one another." It is not given to self-exaltation. Humility does not love the uppermost seats and aspire to the high places. It is willing to take the lowliest seat and prefers those places where it will be unnoticed. The prayer of humility is after this fashion:

> Never let the world break in,
> Fix a mighty gulf between;
> Keep me humble and unknown,
> Prized and loved by God alone.

Humility does not have its eyes on self, but rather on God and others. It is poor in spirit, meek in behavior, lowly in heart. "With all lowliness and meekness, with long-suffering, forbearing one another in love."

The parable of the Pharisee and publican is a sermon in brief on humility and self-praise. The Pharisee, given over to self-conceit, wrapped up in himself, seeing only his own self-righteous deeds, catalogues his virtues before God, despising the poor publican who stands afar off. He exalts himself, gives himself over to self-praise, is self-centered, and goes away unjustified, condemned and rejected by God.

The publican sees no good in himself, is overwhelmed with self-depreciation, far removed from anything which would take any credit for any good in himself, does not presume to lift his eyes to heaven, but with downcast countenance smites himself on his breast, and cries out, "God be merciful to me, a sinner."

Our Lord with great preciseness gives us the sequel of the story of these two men, one utterly devoid of humility, the other utterly submerged in the spirit of self-depreciation and lowliness of mind.

> I tell you this man went down to his house justified rather than the other; for every one that exalteth himself shall be abased; and he that humbleth himself shall be exalted. (Luke 18:14).

God puts a great price on humility of heart. It is good to be clothed with humility as with a garment. It is written, "God resisteth the proud, but giveth grace to the humble." That which brings the praying soul near to God is humility of heart. That which gives wings to prayer is lowliness of mind. That which gives ready access to the throne of grace is self-depreciation. Pride, self-esteem, and self-praise effectually shut the door of prayer. He who would come to God must approach him with self hid from his own eyes. He must not be puffed-up with self-conceit, nor be possessed with an over-estimate of his virtues and good works.

Humility is a rare Christian grace, of great price in the courts of heaven, entering into and being an inseparable condition of effectual praying. It gives access to God when other qualities fail. It takes many descriptions to describe it, and many definitions to define it. It is a rare and retiring grace. Its full portrait is found only in the Lord Jesus Christ. Our prayers must be set low before they can ever rise high. Our prayers must have much of the dust on them before they can ever have much of the glory of the skies in them. In our Lord's teaching, humility has such prominence in his system of religion, and is such a distinguishing feature of his character, that to leave it out of his lesson on prayer would be very unseemly, would not comport with his character, and would not fit into his religious system.

The parable of the Pharisee and publican stands out in such bold relief that we must again refer to it. The Pharisee seemed to be inured to prayer. Certainly he should have known by that time how to pray, but alas! like many others, he seemed never to have learned this invaluable lesson. He leaves business and business hours and walks with steady and fixed steps up to the house of prayer. The position and place are well chosen by him. There is the sacred place, the sacred hour, and the sacred name, each and all invoked by this seemingly praying man. But this praying ecclesiastic, though schooled to prayer, by training and by habit, prays not. Words are uttered by him, but words are not prayer. God hears his words only to condemn him. A death-chill has come from those formal lips of prayer—a death-curse from God is on his words of prayer. A solution of pride has entirely poisoned the prayer offering of that hour. His entire praying has been impregnated with self-praise, self-congratulation, and self-exaltation. That season of temple going has had no worship whatever in it.

On the other hand, the publican, smitten with a deep sense of his sins and his inward sinfulness, realizing how poor in spirit he is, how utterly devoid of anything like righteousness, goodness, or any quality which would commend him to God, his pride within utterly blasted and dead, falls down with humiliation and despair before God, while he utters a sharp cry for mercy for his sins and his guilt. A sense of sin and a realization of utter unworthiness has fixed the roots of humility deep down in his soul, and has oppressed self and eye and heart, downward to the dust. This is the picture of humility against pride in praying. Here we see by sharp contrast the utter worthlessness of self-righteousness, self-exaltation, and self-praise in praying, and the great value, the beauty and the divine commendation which comes to humility of heart, self-depreciation, and self-condemnation when a soul comes before God in prayer.

Happy are they who have no righteousness of their own to plead and no goodness of their own of which to boast. Humility flourishes in the soil of a true and deep sense of our sinfulness and our nothingness. Nowhere does humility grow so rankly and so rapidly and shine so brilliantly, as when it feels all guilty, confesses all sin, and trusts all grace. "I the chief of sinners am, but Jesus died for me." That is praying ground, the ground of humility, low down, far away seemingly, but in reality brought nigh by the blood of the Lord Jesus Christ. God dwells in the lowly places. He makes such lowly places really the high places to the praying soul.

> Let the world their virtue boast,
> Their works of righteousness;
> I, a wretch undone and lost,
> Am freely saved by grace;
> Other title I disclaim,
> This, only this, is all my plea,
> I the chief of sinners am,
> But Jesus died for me.

Humility is an indispensable requisite of true prayer. It must be an attribute, a characteristic of prayer. Humility must be in the praying character as light is in the sun. Prayer has no beginning, no ending, no being, without humility. As a ship is made for the sea, so prayer is made for humility, and so humility is made for prayer.

Humility is not abstraction from self, nor does it ignore thought about self. It is a many-phased principle. Humility is born by looking at God, and his holiness, and then looking at self and man's unholiness. Humility loves obscurity and silence, dreads applause, esteems the virtues of others, excuses their faults with mildness, easily pardons injuries, fears contempt less and less, and sees baseness and falsehood in pride. A true nobleness and greatness are in humility. It knows and reveres the inestimable riches of the cross, and the humiliations of Jesus Christ. It fears the luster of those virtues admired by men, and loves those that are more secret and which are prized by God. It draws comfort even from its own defects, through the abasement which they occasion. It prefers any degree of compunction before all light in the world.

Somewhat after this order of description is that definable grace of humility, so perfectly drawn in the publican's prayer, and so entirely absent from the prayer of the Pharisee. It takes many sittings to make a good picture of it.

Humility holds in its keeping the very life of prayer. Neither pride nor vanity can pray. Humility, though, is much more than the absence of vanity and pride. It is a positive quality, a substantial force, which energizes prayer. There is no power in prayer to ascend without it. Humility springs from a lowly estimate of ourselves and of our deservings. The Pharisee prayed not, though well schooled and accustomed to pray, because there was no humility in his praying. The publican prayed, though banned by the public and receiving no encouragement from church sentiment, because he prayed in humility. To be clothed with humility is to be clothed with a praying garment. Humility is just feeling little because we *are* little. Humility is realizing our unworthiness because we *are* unworthy, the feeling and declaring ourselves sinners because we *are* sinners. Kneeling well becomes us as the attitude of prayer, because it betokens humility.

The Pharisee's proud estimate of himself and his supreme contempt for his neighbor closed the gates of prayer to him, while humility opened wide those gates to the defamed and reviled publican.

That fearful saying of our Lord about the works of big, religious workers in the latter part of the Sermon on the Mount, is called out by proud estimates of work and wrong estimates of prayer:

> Many shall say unto me in that day, Lord, Lord, have we not prophesied in thy name? and in thy name cast out devils and in thy name done many wonderful works? And then will I profess unto them, I never knew you: depart from me, ye that work iniquity.

Humility is the first and last attribute of Christlike religion, and the first and last attribute of Christlike praying. There is no Christ without humility. There is no praying without humility. If you would learn well the art of praying, then learn well the lesson of humility.

How graceful and imperative does the attitude of humility become to us! Humility is one of the unchanging and exacting attitudes of prayer. Dust, ashes, earth upon the head, sackcloth for the body, and fasting for the appetites, were the symbols of humility for the Old Testament saints. Sackcloth, fasting and ashes brought Daniel a lowliness before God, and brought Gabriel to him. The angels are fond of the sackcloth-and-ashes men.

How lowly the attitude of Abraham, the friend of God, when pleading for God to stay his wrath against Sodom! "Which am but sackcloth and ashes." With what humility does Solomon appear before God! His grandeur is abased, and his glow and majesty are retired as he assumes the rightful attitude before God: "I am but a little child, and know not how to go out or to come in."

The pride of doing sends its poison all through our praying. The same pride of being infects our prayers, no matter how well-worded they may be. It was this lack of humility, this self-applauding, this self-exaltation, which kept the most religious man of Christ's day from being accepted of God. And the same thing will keep us in this day from being accepted of him.

> O that now I might decrease!
> O that all I am might cease!
> Let me into nothing fall!
> Let my Lord be all in all.

3

Prayer and Devotion

DEVOTION has a religious signification. The root of devotion is to devote to a sacred use. So that devotion in its true sense has to do with religious worship. It stands intimately connected with true prayer. Devotion is the particular frame of mind found in one entirely devoted to God. It is the spirit of reverence, of awe, of godly fear. It is a state of heart which appears before God in prayer and worship. It is foreign to everything like lightness of spirit, and is opposed to levity and noise and bluster. Devotion dwells in the realm of quietness and is still before God. It is serious, thoughtful, meditative.

Devotion belongs to the inner life and lives in the closet, but also appears in the public services of the sanctuary. It is a part of the very spirit of true worship, and is of the nature of the spirit of prayer.

Devotion belongs to the devout man, whose thoughts and feelings are devoted to God. Such a man has a mind given up wholly to religion, and possesses a strong affection for God and an ardent love for his house. Cornelius was "a devout man, one that feared God with all his house, which gave much alms to the people, and prayed always." "Devout men carried Stephen to his burial." "One Ananias, a devout man, according to the law," was sent unto Saul when he was blind, to tell him what the Lord would have him do. God can wonderfully use such men, for devout men are his chosen agents in carrying forward his plans.

Prayer promotes the spirit of devotion, while devotion is favorable to the best praying. Devotion furthers prayer and helps to drive prayer home to the object which it seeks. Prayer thrives in the atmosphere of true devotion. It is easy to pray when in the spirit of devotion. The attitude of mind and the state of heart implied in devotion make prayer effectual in reaching the throne of grace. God dwells where the spirit of devotion resides. All the graces of the Spirit are nourished and grow well in the environment created by devotion. Indeed, these graces grow nowhere else but here. The absence of a devotional spirit means death to the graces born in a renewed heart. True worship finds congeniality in the atmosphere made by a spirit of devotion. While prayer is helpful to devotion, at the same time devotion reacts on prayer, and helps us to pray.

Devotion engages the heart in prayer. It is not an easy task for the lips to try to pray while the heart is absent from it. The charge which God at one time made against his ancient Israel was, that they honored him with their lips while their hearts were far from him.

The very essence of prayer is the spirit of devotion. Without devotion prayer is an empty form, a vain round of words. Sad to say, much of this kind of prayer prevails, today, in the church. This is a busy age, bustling and active, and this bustling spirit has invaded the church of God. Its religious performances are many. The church works at religion with the order, precision and force of real machinery. But too often it works with the heartlessness of the machine. There is much of the treadmill movement in our ceaseless round and routine of religious doings. We pray without praying. We sing without singing with the Spirit and the understanding. We have music without the praise of God being in it, or near it. We go to church by habit, and come home all too gladly when the benediction is pronounced. We read our accustomed chapter in the Bible, and feel quite relieved when the task is done. We say our prayers by rote, as a schoolboy recites his lesson, and are not sorry when the Amen is uttered.

Religion has to do with everything but our hearts. It engages our hands and feet, it takes hold of our voices, it lays its hands on our money, it affects even the postures of our bodies, but it does not take hold of our affections, our desires, our zeal, and make us serious, desperately in earnest, and cause us to be quiet and worshipful in the presence of God. Social affinities attract us to the house of God, not the spirit of the occasion. Church membership keeps us after a fashion decent in outward conduct and with some shadow of loyalty to our baptismal vows, but the heart is not in the thing. It remains cold, formal, and unimpressed amid all this outward performance, while we give ourselves over to self-congratulation that we are doing wonderfully well religiously.

Why all these sad defects in our piety? Why this modern perversion of the true nature of the religion of Jesus Christ? Why is the modern type of religion so much like a jewel-case with the precious jewels gone? Why so much of this handling religion with the hands, often not too clean or unsoiled, and so little of it felt in the heart and witnessed in the life?

The great lack of modern religion is the spirit of devotion. We hear sermons in the same spirit with which we listen to a lecture or hear a speech. We visit the house of God just as if it were a common place, on a level with the theater, the lecture-room or the forum. We look upon the minister of God not as the divinely-called man of God, but merely as a sort of public speaker, on a plane with the politician, the lawyer, or the average speech maker, or the lecturer. Oh, how the spirit of true and genuine devotion would radically change all this for the better! We handle sacred things just as if they were the things of the world. Even the sacrament of the Lord's Supper becomes a mere religious performance, no preparation for it beforehand, and no meditation and prayer afterward. Even the sacrament of Baptism has lost much of its solemnity, and degenerated into a mere form, with nothing specially in it.

We need the spirit of devotion, not only to salt our secularities, but to make praying real prayers. We need to put the spirit of devotion into Monday's business as well as in Sunday's worship. We need the spirit of devotion, to recollect always the presence of God, to be always doing the will of God, to direct all things always to the glory of God.

The spirit of devotion puts God in all things. It puts God not merely in our praying and church-going, but in all the concerns of life. Whether, therefore, ye eat or drink, or whatsoever ye do, do all to the glory of God." The spirit of devotion makes the common things of earth sacred, and the little things great. With this spirit of devotion, we go to business on Monday directed by the very same influence, and inspired by the same influences by which we went to church on Sunday. The spirit of devotion makes a Sabbath out of Saturday, and transforms the shop and the office into a temple of God.

The spirit of devotion removes religion from being a thin veneer, and puts it into the very life and being of our souls. With it religion ceases to be doing a mere work, and becomes a heart, sending its rich blood through every artery and beating with the pulsations of vigorous and radiant life.

The spirit of devotion is not merely the aroma of religion, but the stalk and stem on which religion grows. It is the salt which penetrates and makes savory all religious acts. It is the sugar which sweetens duty, self-denial and sacrifice. It is the bright coloring which relieves the dullness of religious performances. It dispels frivolity and drives away all skin-deep forms of worship, and makes worship a serious and deep-seated service, impregnating body, soul and spirit with its heavenly infusion. Let us ask in all seriousness, has this highest angel of heaven, this heavenly spirit of devotion, this brightest and best angel of earth, left us? When the angel of devotion has gone, the angel of prayer has lost its wings, and it becomes a deformed and loveless thing.

The ardor of devotion is in prayer. In the fourth chapter of Revelation, verse eight, we read: "And they rest not day nor night, saying, Holy, Holy, Holy, Lord God Almighty, which was, and is, and is to come." The inspiration and center of their rapturous devotion is the holiness of God. That holiness of God claims their attention, inflames their devotion. There is nothing cold, nothing dull, nothing wearisome about them or their heavenly worship. "They rest not day nor night." What zeal! What unfainting ardor and ceaseless rapture! The ministry of prayer, if it be anything worthy of the name, is a ministry of ardor, a ministry of unwearied and intense longing after God and after his holiness.

The spirit of devotion pervades the saints in heaven and characterizes the worship of heaven's angelic intelligences. No devotionless creatures are in that heavenly world. God is there, and his very presence begets the spirit of reverence, of awe, and of real fear. If we would be partakers with them after death, we must first learn the spirit of devotion on earth before we get there.

These living creatures in their restless, tireless, attitude after God, and their rapt devotion to his holiness, are the perfect symbols and manifestations of true prayer and its ardor. Prayer must be aflame. Its ardor must consume. Prayer without fervor is as a sun without light or heat, or as a flower without beauty or fragrance. A soul devoted to God is a fervent soul, and prayer is the creature of that flame. He only can truly pray who is all aglow for holiness, for God, and for heaven.

Activity is not strength. Work is not zeal. Moving about is not devotion. Activity often is the unrecognized symptom of spiritual weakness. It may be hurtful to piety when made the substitute for real devotion in worship, The colt is much more active than its mother, but she is the wheel-horse of the team, pulling the load without noise or bluster or show. The child is more active than the father, who may be bearing the rule and burdens of an empire on his heart and shoulders. Enthusiasm is more active than faith, though it cannot remove mountains nor call into action any of the omnipotent forces which faith can command.

A feeble, lively, showy religious activity may spring from many causes. There is much running around, much stirring about, much going here and there, in present-day church life, but sad to say, the spirit of genuine, heartfelt devotion is strangely lacking. If there be real spiritual life, a deep-toned activity will spring from it. But it is an activity springing from strength and not from weakness. It is an activity which has deep roots, many and strong.

In the nature of things, religion must show much of its growth above ground. Much will be seen and be evident to the eye. The flower and fruit of a holy life, abounding in good works, must be seen. It cannot be otherwise. But the surface growth must be based on a vigorous growth of unseen life and hidden roots. Deep down in the renewed nature must the roots of religion go which is seen on the outside. The external must have a deep internal groundwork. There must be much of the invisible and the underground growth, or else the life will be feeble and short-lived, and the external growth sickly and fruitless.

In the Book of Isaiah these words are written:

> They that wait on the Lord shall renew their strength; they shall mount up with wings as eagles; they shall run and not be weary; and they shall walk and not faint (40:31).

This is the genesis of the whole matter of activity and strength of the most energetic, exhaustless and untiring nature. All this is the result of waiting on God.

There may be much of activity induced by drill, created by enthusiasm, the product of the weakness of the flesh, the inspiration of volatile, short-lived forces. Activity is often at the expense of more solid, useful elements, and generally to the total neglect of prayer. To be too busy with God's work to commune with God, to be busy with doing church work without taking time to talk to God about his work, is the highway to backsliding, and many people have walked therein to the hurt of their immortal souls.

Notwithstanding great activity, great enthusiasm, and much hurrah for the work, the work and the activity will be but blindness without the cultivation and the maturity of the graces of prayer.

4

Prayer, Praise, and Thanksgiving

PRAYER, praise and thanksgiving all go in company. A close relationship exists between them. Praise and thanksgiving are so near alike that it is not easy to distinguish between them or define them separately. The Scriptures join these three things together. Many are the causes for thanksgiving and praise. The Psalms are filled with many songs of praise and hymns of thanksgiving, all pointing back to the results of prayer. Thanksgiving includes gratitude. In fact thanksgiving is but the expression of an inward conscious gratitude to God for mercies received. Gratitude is an inward emotion of the soul, involuntarily arising therein, while thanksgiving is the voluntary expression of gratitude.

Thanksgiving is oral, positive, active. It is the giving out of something to God. Thanksgiving comes out into the open. Gratitude is secret, silent, negative, passive, not showing its being till expressed in praise and thanksgiving. Gratitude is felt in the heart. Thanksgiving is the expression of that inward feeling.

Thanksgiving is just what the word itself signifies—the giving of thanks to God. It is giving something to God in words which we feel at heart for blessings received. Gratitude arises from a contemplation of the goodness of God. It is bred by serious meditation on what God has done for us. Both gratitude and thanksgiving point to, and have to do with God and his mercies. The heart is consciously grateful to God. The soul gives expression to that heartfelt gratitude to God in words or acts.

Gratitude is born of meditation on God's grace and mercy. "The Lord hath done great things for us, whereof we are glad." Herein we see the value of serious meditation. "My meditation of him shall be sweet." Praise is begotten by gratitude and a conscious obligation to God for mercies given. As we think of mercies past, the heart is inwardly moved to gratitude.

> I love to think on mercies past,
> And future good implore;
> And all my cares and sorrows cast
> On him whom I adore.

Love is the child of gratitude. Love grows as gratitude is felt, and then breaks out into praise and thanksgiving to God: "I love the Lord because he hath heard my voice and my supplication." Answered prayers cause gratitude, and gratitude brings forth a love that declares it will not cease praying: "Because he hath inclined his ear unto me, therefore will I call upon him as long as I live." Gratitude and love move to larger and increased praying.

Paul appeals to the Romans to dedicate themselves wholly to God, a living sacrifice, and the constraining motive is the mercies of God:

> I beseech you, therefore, brethren, by the mercies of God, that ye present your bodies a living sacrifice, holy, acceptable unto God, which is your reasonable service.

Consideration of God's mercies not only begets gratitude, but induces a large consecration to God of all we have and are. So that prayer, giving and consecration are all linked together inseparably.

Gratitude and thanksgiving always looks back at the past though it may also take in the present. But prayer always looks to the future. Thanksgiving deals with things already received. Prayer deals with things desired, asked for and expected. Prayer turns to gratitude and praise when the things asked for have been granted by God.

As prayer brings things to us which beget gratitude and thanksgiving, so praise and gratitude promote prayer, and induce more praying and better praying.

Gratitude and thanksgiving forever stand opposed to all murmurings at God's dealings with us, and all complainings at our lot. Gratitude and murmuring never abide in the same heart at the same time. An unappreciative spirit has no standing beside gratitude and praise. And true prayer corrects complaining and promotes gratitude and thanksgiving. Dissatisfaction at one's lot, and a disposition to be discontented with things which come to us in the providence of God, are foes to gratitude and enemies to thanksgiving.

The murmurers are ungrateful people. Appreciative men and women have neither the time nor disposition to stop and complain. The bane of the wilderness journey of the Israelites on their way to Canaan was their proneness to murmur and complain against God and Moses. For this, God was several times greatly grieved, and it took the strong praying of Moses to avert God's wrath because of these murmurings. The absence of gratitude left no room nor disposition for praise and thanksgiving, just as it is so always. But when these same Israelites were brought through the Red Sea dry shod, while their enemies were destroyed, there was a song of praise led by Miriam, the sister of Moses. One of the leading sins of these Israelites was forgetfulness of God and his mercies, and ingratitude of soul. This brought forth murmurings and lack of praise, as it always does.

When Paul wrote to the Colossians to let the word of Christ dwell in their hearts richly and to let the peace of God rule therein, he said to them, "and be ye thankful," and adds, "admonishing yourselves in psalms and hymns and spiritual songs, singing with grace in your hearts unto the Lord."

Further on, in writing to these same Christians, he joins prayer and thanksgiving together: "Continue in prayer, and watch in the same with thanksgiving."

And writing to the Thessalonians, he again joins them in union: "Rejoice evermore. Pray without ceasing. In everything give thanks, for this is the will of God concerning you."

> We thank thee, Lord of heaven and earth,
> Who hast preserved us from our birth;
> Redeemed us oft from death and dread,
> And with thy gifts our table spread.

Wherever there is true prayer, there thanksgiving and gratitude stand hard by, ready to respond to the answer when it comes. For as prayer brings the answer, so the answer brings forth gratitude and praise. As prayer sets God to work, so answered prayer sets thanksgiving to work. Thanksgiving follows answered prayer just as day succeeds night.

True prayer and gratitude lead to full consecration, and consecration leads to more praying and better praying. A consecrated life is both a prayer life and a thanksgiving life.

The spirit of praise was once the boast of the primitive church. This spirit abode on the tabernacles of these early Christians, as a cloud of glory out of which God shined and spoke. It filled their temples with the perfume of costly, flaming incense. That this spirit of praise is sadly deficient in our present-day congregations must be evident to every careful observer. That it is a mighty force in projecting the gospel, and its body of vital forces, must be equally evident. To restore the spirit of praise to our congregations should be one of the main points with every true pastor. The normal state of the church is set forth in the declaration made to God in Psalm 65: "Praise waiteth for thee, O Lord, and unto thee shall the vow be performed."

Praise is so distinctly and definitely wedded to prayer, so inseparably joined, that they cannot be divorced. Praise is dependent on prayer for its full volume and its sweetest melody.

Singing is one method of praise, not the highest it is true, but it is the ordinary and usual form. The singing service in our churches has much to do with praise, for according to the character of the singing will be the genuineness or the measure of praise. The singing may be so directed as to have in it elements which deprave and debauch prayer. It may be so directed as to drive away everything like thanksgiving and praise. Much of modern singing in our churches is entirely foreign to anything like hearty, sincere praise to God.

The spirit of prayer and of true praise go hand in hand. Both are often entirely dissipated by the flippant, thoughtless, light singing in our congregations. Much of the singing lacks serious thought and is devoid of everything like a devotional spirit. Its lustiness and sparkle may not only dissipate all the essential features of worship, but may substitute the flesh for the spirit.

Giving thanks is the very life of prayer. It is its fragrance and music, its poetry and its crown. Prayer bringing the desired answer breaks out into praise and thanksgiving. So that whatever interferes with and injures the spirit of prayer necessarily hurts and dissipates the spirit of praise.

The heart must have in it the grace of prayer to sing the praise of God. Spiritual singing is not to be done by musical taste or talent, but by the grace of God in the heart. Nothing helps praise so mightily as a gracious revival of true religion in the church. The conscious presence of God inspires song. The angels and the glorified ones in heaven do not need artistic directors to lead them, nor do they care for paid choirs to chime in with their heavenly doxologies of praise and worship. They are not dependent on singing schools to teach them the notes and scale of singing. Their singing involuntarily breaks forth from the heart.

God is immediately present in the heavenly assemblies of the angels and the spirits of just men made perfect. His glorious presence creates the song, teaches the singing, and impregnates their notes of praise. It is so on earth. God's presence begets singing and thanksgiving, while the absence of God from our congregations is the death of song, or, which amounts to the same, makes the singing lifeless, cold and formal. His conscious presence in our churches would bring back the days of praise and would restore the full chorus of song.

Where grace abounds, song abounds. When God is in the heart, heaven is present and melody is there, and the lips overflow out of the abundance of the heart. This is as true in the private life of the believer as it is so in the congregations of the saints. The decay of singing, the dying down and out of the spirit of praise in song, means the decline of grace in the heart and the absence of God's presence from the people.

The main design of all singing is for God's ear and to attract his attention and to please him. It is "to the Lord," for his glory, and to his honor. Certainly it is not for the glorification of the paid choir, to exalt the wonderful musical powers of the singers, nor is it to draw the people to the church, but it is for the glory of God and the good of the souls of the congregation. Alas! How far has the singing of choirs of churches of modern times departed from this idea! It is no surprise that there is no life, no power, no unction, no spirit, in much of the church singing heard in this day. It is sacrilege for any but sanctified hearts and holy lips to direct the singing part of the service of God's house of prayer. Much of the singing in churches would do credit to the opera house, and might satisfy as mere entertainments, pleasing the ear, but as a part of real worship, having in it the spirit of praise and prayer, it is a fraud, an imposition on spiritually minded people, and entirely unacceptable to God. The cry should go out afresh, "Let all the people praise the Lord," for "it is good to sing praises unto our God; for it is pleasant; and praise is comely."

The music of praise, for there is real music of soul in praise, is too hopeful and happy to be denied. All these are in the "giving of thanks." In Philippians, prayer is called "requests." "Let your requests be made known unto God," which describes prayer as an asking for a gift, giving prominence to the thing asked for, making it emphatic, something to be given by God and received by us, and not something to be done by us. And all this is closely connected with gratitude to God, "with thanksgiving, let your requests be made known unto God."

God does much for us in answer to prayer, but we need from him many gifts, and for them we are to make special prayer. According to our special needs, so must our praying be. We are to be special and particular and bring to the knowledge of God by prayer, supplication and thanksgiving, our particular requests, the things we need, the things we greatly desire. And with it all, accompanying all these requests, there must be thanksgiving.

It is indeed a pleasing thought that what we are called upon to do on earth, to praise and give thanks, the angels in heaven and the redeemed disembodied spirits of the saints are doing also. It is still further pleasing to contemplate the glorious hope that what God wants us to do on earth, we will be engaged in doing throughout an unending eternity. Praise and thanksgiving will be our blessed employment while we remain in heaven. Nor will we ever grow weary of this pleasing task.

Joseph Addison sets before us, in verse, this pleasing prospect:

> Through every period of my life
> Thy goodness I'll pursue;
> And after death, in distant worlds,
> The pleasing theme renew.
>
> Through all eternity to thee
> A grateful song I'll raise;
> But Oh! eternity's too short
> To utter all thy praise.

5

Prayer and Trouble

TROUBLE and prayer are closely related to other. Prayer is of great value to trouble. Trouble often drives men to God in prayer, while prayer is but the voice of men in trouble. There is great value in prayer in the time of trouble. Prayer often delivers out of trouble, and still oftener gives strength to bear trouble, ministers comfort in trouble, and begets patience in the midst of trouble. Wise is he in the day of trouble who knows his true source of strength and who fails not to pray.

Trouble belongs to the present state of man on earth. "Man that is born of a woman is of few days and full of trouble." Trouble is common to man. There is no exception in any age or clime or station. Rich and poor alike, the learned and the ignorant, one and all are partakers of this sad and painful inheritance of the fall of man. "There hath no temptation taken you but such as is common to man." The "day of trouble" dawns on every one at some time in his life. "The evil days come and the years draw nigh" when the heart feels its heavy pressure.

That is an entirely false view of life and shows supreme ignorance that expects nothing but sunshine and looks only for ease, pleasure and flowers. It is this class who are so sadly disappointed and surprised when trouble breaks into their lives. These are the ones who know not God, who know nothing of his disciplinary dealings with his people and who are prayerless.

What an infinite variety there is in the troubles of life! How diversified the experiences of men in the school of trouble! No two people have the same troubles under like environments. God deals with no two of his children in the same way. And as God varies his treatment of his children, so trouble is varied. God does not repeat himself. He does not run in a rut. He has not one pattern for every child. Each trouble is proportioned to each child. Each one is dealt with according to his own peculiar case.

Trouble is God's servant, doing his will unless he is defeated in the execution of that will. Trouble is under the control of Almighty God, and is one of his most efficient agents in fulfilling his purposes and in perfecting his saints. God's hand is in every trouble which breaks into the lives of men. Not that he directly and arbitrarily orders every unpleasant experience of life. Not that he is personally responsible for every painful and afflicting thing which comes into the lives of his people. But no trouble is ever turned loose in this world and comes into the life of saint or sinner, but comes with divine permission, and is allowed to exist and do its painful work with God's hand in it or on it, carrying out his gracious designs of redemption.

All things are under divine control. Trouble is neither above God nor beyond his control. It is not something in life independent of God. No matter from what source it springs nor whence it arises, God is sufficiently wise and able to lay his hand upon it without assuming responsibility for its origin, and work it into his plans and purposes concerning the highest welfare of his saints. This is the explanation of that gracious statement in Romans, so often quoted, but the depth of whose meaning has rarely been sounded, "And we know that all things work together for good to them that love God."

Even the evils brought about by the forces of nature are his servants, carrying out his will and fulfilling his designs. God even claims the locusts, the earthworm, the caterpillar are his servants, "My great army," used by him to correct his people and discipline them.

Trouble belongs to the disciplinary part of the moral government of God. This is a life of probation, where the human race is on probation. It is a season of trial. Trouble is not penal in its nature. It belongs to what the Scriptures call "chastening." "Whom the lord loveth he chasteneth, and scourgeth every son whom he receiveth." Speaking accurately, punishment does not belong to this life. Punishment for sin will take place in the next world. God's dealings with people in this world are of the nature of discipline. They are corrective processes in his plans concerning man. It is because of this that prayer comes in when trouble arises. Prayer belongs to the discipline of life.

As trouble is not sinful in itself, neither is it the evidence of sin. Good and bad alike experience trouble. As the rain falls alike on the just and unjust, so drought likewise comes to the righteous and the wicked. Trouble is no evidence whatever of the divine displeasure. Scripture instances without number disprove any such idea. Job is a case in point, where God bore explicit testimony to his deep piety, and yet God permitted Satan to afflict him beyond any other man for wise and beneficent purposes. Trouble has no power in itself to interfere with the relations of a saint to God. "Who shall separate us from the love of Christ? Shall tribulation, or distress, or persecution, or famine, or nakedness, or peril, or sword ?"

Three words practically the same in the processes of divine discipline are found, temptation, trial and trouble, and yet there is a difference between them. Temptation is really a solicitation to evil arising from the devil or born in the carnal nature of man. Trial is testing. It is that which proves us, tests us, and makes us stronger and better when we submit to the trial and work together with God in it. "My brethren, count it all joy when ye fall into temptations; knowing this, that the trying of your faith worketh patience."

Peter speaks along the same line:

Wherein ye greatly rejoice, now for a season, if need be, ye are in heaviness through manifold temptations; that the trial of your faith being much more precious than that of gold that perisheth, though it be tried with fire, might be found unto praise, and honor and glory at the appearing of Jesus Christ.

The third word is trouble itself, which covers all the painful, sorrowing, and grievous events of life. And yet temptations and trials might really become troubles. So that all evil days in life might well be classed under the head of the "time of trouble." And such days of trouble are the lot of all men. Enough to know that trouble, no matter from what source it comes, becomes in God's hand his own agent to accomplish his gracious work concerning those who submit patiently to him, who recognize him in prayer, and who work together with God.

Let us settle down at once to the idea that trouble arises not by chance, and neither occurs by what men call accident. "Although affliction cometh not forth of the dust, neither doth trouble spring out of the ground, yet man is born unto trouble as the sparks fly upward." Trouble naturally belongs to God's moral government, and is one of his invaluable agents in governing the world.

When we realize this, we can the better understand much that is recorded in the Scriptures, and can have a clearer conception of God's dealings with his ancient Israel. In God's dealings with them, we find what is called a history of divine providence, and providence always embraces trouble. No one can understand the story of Joseph and his old father Jacob unless he takes into the account trouble and its varied offices. God takes account of trouble when he urges his prophet Isaiah on this wise:

Comfort ye, comfort ye my people, saith your God. Speak ye comfortably to Jerusalem, and cry unto her that her warfare is accomplished, that her iniquity is pardoned.

There is a distinct note of comfort in the gospel for the praying saints of the Lord, and he is a wise scribe in divine things who knows how to minister this comfort to the broken-hearted and sad ones of earth. Jesus himself said to his sad disciples, "I will not leave you comfortless."

All the foregoing has been said that we may rightly appreciate the relationship of prayer to trouble. In the time of trouble, where does prayer come in? The psalmist tells us: Call upon me in the day of trouble; I will deliver thee, and thou shalt glorify me." Prayer is the most appropriate thing for a soul to do in the "time of trouble." Prayer recognizes God in the day of trouble. "It is the Lord; let him do what seemeth him good." Prayer sees God's hand in trouble, and prays about it. Nothing more truly shows us our helplessness than when trouble comes. It brings the strong man low, it discloses our weakness, it brings a sense of helplessness. Blessed is he who knows how to turn to God in "the time of trouble." If trouble is of the Lord, then the most natural thing to do is to carry the trouble to the Lord, and seek grace and patience and submission. It is the time to inquire in the trouble, "Lord, what wilt thou have me to do?" How natural and reasonable for the soul, oppressed, broken, and bruised, to bow low at the footstool of mercy and seek the face of God? Where could a soul in trouble more likely find solace than in the closet?

Alas! trouble does not always drive men to God in prayer. Sad is the case of him who, when trouble bends his spirit down and grieves his heart, yet knows not whence the trouble comes nor knows how to pray about it. Blessed is the man who is driven by trouble to his knees in prayer!

> Trials must and will befall;
> But with humble faith to see
> Love inscribed upon them all—
> This is happiness to me.
>
> Trials make the promise sweet
> Trials give new life to prayer;
> Bring me to my savior's feet
> Lay me low, and keep me there.

Prayer in the time of trouble beings comfort, help, hope, and blessings, which, while not removing the trouble, enable the saint the better to bear it and to submit to the will of God. Prayer opens the eyes to see God's hand in trouble. Prayer does not interpret God's providences, but it does justify them and recognize God in them. Prayer enables us to see wise ends in trouble. Prayer in trouble drives us away from unbelief, saves us from doubt, and delivers from all vain and foolish questionings because of our painful experiences. Let us not lose sight of the tribute paid to Job when all his troubles came to the culminating point: "In all this Job sinned not, nor charged God foolishly."

Alas! for vain, ignorant men, without faith in God and knowing nothing of God's disciplinary processes in dealing with men, who charge God foolishly when troubles come, and who are tempted to "curse God." How silly and vain are the complainings, the murmurings and the rebellion of men in the time of trouble! What need to read again the story of the children of Israel in the wilderness! And how useless is all our fretting, our worrying over trouble, as if such unhappy doings on our part could change things! "And which of you with taking thought, can add to his stature one cubit?" How much wiser, how much better, how much easier to bear life's troubles when we take everything to God in prayer?

Trouble has wise ends for the praying ones, and these find it so. Happy is he who, like the psalmist, finds that his troubles have been blessings in disguise. "It is good for me that I have been afflicted, that I might learn thy statutes. I know, O Lord, that thy judgments are right, and that thou in faithfulness hast afflicted me."

O who could bear life's stormy doom,
Did not thy wing of love
Come brightly wafting through the gloom
Our peace branch from above.

Then sorrow, touched by thee, grows bright,
With more than rapture's ray;
As darkness shows us worlds of light
We never saw by day.

Of course, it may be conceded that some troubles are really imaginary. They have no existence other than in the mind. Some are anticipated troubles, which never arrive at our door. Others are past troubles, and there is much folly in worrying over them. Present troubles are the ones requiring attention and demanding prayer. "Sufficient unto the day is the evil thereof." Some troubles are self-originated. We are their authors. Some of these originate involuntarily with us, some arise from our ignorance, some come from our carelessness. All this can be readily admitted without breaking the force of the statement that they are the subjects of prayer, and should drive us to prayer. What father casts off his child who cries to him when the little one from its own carelessness has stumbled and fallen and hurt itself? Does not the cry of the child attract the ears of the father even though the child be to blame for the accident? "Whatever things ye desire" takes in every event of life, even though we are responsible for some events.

Some troubles are human in their origin. They arise from second causes. They originate with others and we are the sufferers. This is a world where often the innocent suffer the consequences of the acts of others. This is a part of life's incidents. Who has not at some time suffered at the hands of others? But even these are allowed to come in the order of God's providence, are permitted to break into our lives for beneficent ends, and may be prayed over. Why should we not carry our hurts, our wrongs and our privations, caused by the acts of others, to God in prayer? Are such things outside of the realm of prayer? Are they exceptions to the rule of prayer? Not at all. And God can and will lay his hand upon all such events in answer to prayer, and cause them to work for us "a far more exceeding and eternal weight of glory."

Nearly all of Paul's troubles arose from wicked and unreasonable men. Read the story as he gives it in 2 Corinthians 11:23–33.

So also some troubles are directly of Satanic origin. Quite all of Job's troubles were the offspring of the devil's scheme to break down Job's integrity, to make him charge God foolishly and to curse God. But are these not to be recognized in prayer? Are they to be excluded from God's disciplinary processes? Job did not do so. Hear him in those familiar words. "The Lord gave, and the Lord hath taken away. Blessed be the name of the Lord."

O what a comfort to see God in all of life's events! What a relief to a broken, sorrowing heart to see God's hand in sorrow! What a source of relief is prayer in unburdening the heart in grief!

> O thou who driest the mourner's tear,
> How dark this world would be,
> If, when deceived and wounded here,
> We could not fly to thee?
>
> The friends who in our sunshine live,
> When winter comes are flown,
> And he who has but tears to give,
> Must weep those tears alone.
>
> But thou wilt heal the broken heart,
> Which, like the plants that throw
> Their fragrance from the wounded part,
> Breathes sweetness out of woe.

But when we survey all the sources from which trouble comes, it all resolves itself into two invaluable truths: First, that our troubles at last are of the Lord. They come with his consent. He is in all of them, and is interested in us when they press and bruise us. And secondly, that our troubles, no matter what the cause, whether of ourselves, or men or devils, or even God himself, we are warranted in taking them to God in prayer, in praying over them, and in seeking to get the greatest spiritual benefits out of them.

Prayer in the time of trouble tends to bring the spirit into perfect subjection to the will of God, to cause the will to be conformed to God's will, and saves from all murmurings over our lot, and delivers from everything like a rebellious heart or a spirit critical of the Lord. Prayer sanctifies trouble to our highest good. Prayer so prepares the heart that it softens under the disciplining hand of God. Prayer places us where God can bring to us the greatest good, spiritual and eternal. Prayer allows God to freely work with us and in us in the day of trouble. Prayer removes everything in the way of trouble, bringing to us the sweetest, the highest and greatest good. Prayer permits God's servant, trouble, to accomplish its mission in us, with us and for us.

The end of trouble is always good in the mind of God. If trouble fails in its mission, it is either because of prayerlessness or unbelief, or both. Being in harmony with God in the dispensations of his providence, always makes trouble a blessing. The good or evil of trouble is always determined by the spirit in which it is received. Trouble proves a blessing or a curse, just according as it is received and treated by us. It either softens or hardens us. It either draws us to prayer and to God or it drives us from God and from the closet. Trouble hardened Pharaoh till finally it had no effect on him, only to make him more desperate and to drive him farther from God. The same sun softens the wax and hardens the clay. The same sun melts the ice and dries out the moisture from the earth.

As is the infinite variety of trouble, so also is there infinite variety in the relations of prayer to other things. How many are the things which are the subject of prayer! It has to do with everything which concerns us, with everybody with whom we have to do, and has to do with all times. But especially does prayer have to do with trouble. "This poor man cried and the Lord heard him, and saved him out of all his troubles." O the blessedness, the help, the comfort of prayer in the day of trouble! And how marvelous the promises of God to us in the time of trouble!

> Because he hath set his love upon me, therefore will I deliver him; I will set him on high because he hath known my name. He shall call upon me, and I will answer him; I will be with him in trouble; I will deliver him and honor him.

> If pain afflict, or wrongs oppress,
> If cares distract, or fears dismay;
> If guilt deject, if sin distress,
> In every case, still watch and pray.

How rich in its sweetness, how far-reaching in the realm of trouble, and how cheering to faith, are the words of promise which God delivers to his believing, praying ones, by the mouth of Isaiah:

> But now, thus saith the Lord that created thee, O Jacob, and he that formed thee, O Israel, Fear not: for I have redeemed thee, I have called thee by thy name; thou art mine. When thou passest through the waters, I will be with thee; and through the rivers, they shall not overflow thee: when thou walkest through the fire, thou shalt not be burned: neither shall the flame kindle upon thee. For I am the Lord thy God, the Holy One of Israel, thy savior.

6

Prayer and Trouble
(*Continued*)

IN the New Testament there are three words used which embrace trouble. These are tribulation, suffering and affliction, words differing somewhat, and yet each of them practically meaning trouble of some kind. Our Lord put his disciples on notice that they might expect tribulation in this life, teaching them that tribulation belonged to this world, and they could not hope to escape it; that they would not be carried through this life on flowery beds of ease. How hard to learn this plain and patent lesson! "In the world ye shall have tribulation; but be of good cheer; I have overcome the world." There is the encouragement. As he had overcome the world and its tribulations, so might they do the same. Paul taught the same lesson throughout his ministry, when in confirming the souls of the brethren, and exhorting them to continue in the faith, he told them that "we must, through much tribulation, enter into the kingdom of God." He himself knew this by his own experience, for his pathway was anything but smooth and flowery.

He it is who uses the word "suffering" to describe the troubles of life, in that comforting passage in which he contrasts life's troubles with the final glory of heaven, which shall be the reward of all who patiently endure the ills of divine providence:

> For I reckon that the sufferings of this present time are not worthy to be compared with the glory which shall be revealed in us.

And he it is who speaks of the afflictions which come to the people of God in this world, and regards them as light as compared with the weight of glory awaiting all who are submissive, patient and faithful in all their troubles:

> For our light affliction, which is but for a moment, worketh for us a far more exceeding and eternal weight of glory.

But these present afflictions can work for us only as we cooperate with God in prayer. As God works through prayer, it is only through this means he can accomplish his highest ends for us. His providence works with greatest effect with his praying ones. These know the uses of trouble and its gracious

108

designs. The greatest value in trouble comes to those who bow lowest before the throne.

Paul, in urging patience in tribulation, connects it directly with prayer, as if prayer alone would place us where we could be patient when tribulation comes. "Rejoicing in hope, patient in tribulation, continuing instant in prayer." He here couples up tribulation and prayer, showing their close relationship and the worth of prayer in begetting and culturing patience in tribulation. In fact there can be no patience exemplified when trouble comes, only as it is secured through instant and continued prayer. In the school of prayer is where patience is learned and practiced.

Prayer brings us into that state of grace where tribulation is not only endured, but where there is under it a spirit of rejoicing. In showing the gracious benefits of justification, in Romans 5:3, Paul says:

> And not only so, but we glory in tribulation also: knowing that tribulation worketh patience; and patience, experience; and experience, hope; and hope maketh not ashamed; because the love of God is shed abroad in our hearts by the Holy Spirit which is given unto us.

What a chain of graces are here set forth as flowing from tribulation! What successive steps to a high state of religious experience! And what rich fruits result from even painful tribulation!

To the same effect are the words of Peter in his first epistle, in his strong prayer for those Christians to whom he writes; thus showing that suffering and the highest state of grace are closely connected; and intimating that it is through suffering we are to be brought to those higher regions of Christian experience:

> But the God of all grace, who hath called us into his eternal glory, by Christ Jesus, after that ye have suffered awhile, make you perfect, stablish, strengthen and settle you.

It is in the fires of suffering that God purifies his saints and brings them to the highest things. It is in the furnace their faith is tested, their patience is tried, and they are developed in all those rich virtues which make up Christian character. It is while they are passing through deep waters that he shows how close he can come to his praying, believing saints.

It takes faith of a high order and a Christian experience far above the average religion of this day, to count it joy when we are called to pass through tribulation. God's highest aim in dealing with his people is in developing Christian character. He is after begetting in us those rich virtues which belong to our Lord Jesus Christ. He is seeking to make us like himself. It is not so much work that he wants in us. It is not greatness. It is the presence in us of patience, meekness, submission to the divine will, prayerfulness which brings everything to him. He seeks to beget his own image in it. And trouble in some form tends to do this very thing, for this is the end and aim of trouble. This is its work. This is the task it is called to perform. It is not a chance incident in life, but has a design in view, just as it has an all-wise designer back of it, who makes trouble his agent to bring forth the largest results.

The writer of the Epistle to the Hebrews gives us a perfect directory of trouble, comprehensive, clear and worthwhile to be studied. Here is "chastisement," another word for trouble, coming from a Father's hand, showing God is in all the sad and afflictive events of life. Here is its nature and its gracious design. It is not punishment in the accurate meaning of that word, but the means God employs to correct and discipline his children in dealing with them on earth. Then we have the fact of the evidence of being his people, namely, the presence of chastisement. The ultimate end is "that we may be partakers of his holiness," which is but another way of saying that all this disciplinary process is to the end that God may make us like himself. What an encouragement, too, that, chastisement is no evidence of anger or displeasure on God's part, but is the strong proof of his love. Let us read the entire directory on this important subject:

> And ye have forgotten the exhortation which speaketh unto you as unto children, My son, despise not thou the chastening of the Lord, nor faint when thou art rebuked of him: For whom the Lord loveth he chasteneth, and scourgeth every son whom he receiveth. If ye endure chastening, God dealeth with you as with sons; for what son is he whom the father chasteneth not? But if ye are without chastisement, whereof all are partakers, then are ye bastards and not sons.
>
> Furthermore, we have had fathers of our flesh which corrected us, and we gave them reverence: shall we not much rather be in subjection to the Father of spirits and live? For they verily for a few days chastened us after their own pleasure; but he for our profit, that we might be partakers of his holiness. Now no chastening for the present seemeth to be joyous, but grievous; nevertheless, afterward it yieldeth the peaceable fruit of righteousness to them which are exercised thereby.

Just as prayer is wide in its range, taking in everything, so trouble is infinitely varied in its uses and designs. It takes trouble sometimes to arrest attention, to stop men in the busy rush of life, and to awaken them to a sense of their helplessness and their need and sinfulness. Not till King Manasseh was bound with thorns and carried away into a foreign land and got into deep trouble, was he awakened and brought back to God. It was then he humbled himself and began to call upon God.

The Prodigal was independent and self-sufficient when in prosperity, but when money and friends departed, and he began to be in want, then it was he "came to himself," and decided to return to his father's house, with prayer and confession on his lips. Many a man who has forgotten God has been arrested, caused to consider his ways, and brought to remember God and pray by trouble. Blessed is trouble when it accomplishes this in men!

It is for this among other reasons that Job says:

> Behold, happy is the man whom God correcteth. Therefore, despise not thou the chastening of the Almighty. For he maketh sore, and bindeth up; he woundeth, and his hands maketh whole. He shall deliver thee in six troubles; yea, in seven there shall no evil touch thee.

One thing more might be named. Trouble makes earth undesirable and causes heaven to loom up large in the horizon of hope. There is a world where trouble never comes. But the path of tribulation leads to that world. Those who are there went there through tribulation. What a world set before our longing eyes which appeals to our hopes, as sorrows like a cyclone sweep over us! Hear John, as he talks about it and those who are there:

> What are these which are arrayed in white robes? and whence came they? . . . And he said to me, These are they which came out of great tribulation, and have washed their robes and made them white in the blood of the Lamb. . . . And God shall wipe away all tears from their eyes.

> There I shall bathe my weary soul,
> In seas of heavenly rest,
> And not a wave of trouble roll,
> Across my peaceful breast.

Oh, children of God, ye who have suffered, who have been sorely tried, whose sad experiences have often brought broken spirits and bleeding hearts, cheer up! God is in all your troubles, and he will see that all shall "work together for good," if you will but be patient, submissive and prayerful.

7

Prayer and God's Work

GOD has a great work on hand in this world. This work is involved in the plan of salvation. It embraces redemption and providence. God is governing this world, with its intelligent beings, for his own glory and for their good. What, then, is God's work in this world? Rather what is the end he seeks in his great work? It is nothing short of holiness of heart and life in the children of fallen Adam. Man is a fallen creature, born with an evil nature, with an evil bent, unholy propensities, sinful desires, wicked inclinations. Man is unholy by nature, born so. "They go astray as soon as they be born, speaking lies." God's entire plan is to take hold of fallen man and to seek to change him and make him holy. God's work is to make holy men out of unholy men. This is the very end of Christ coming into the world:

> For this purpose was the Son of God manifested that he might destroy the works of the devil.

God is holy in nature and in all his ways, and he wants to make man like himself.

> As he who hath called you is holy, so be ye holy in all manner of living; because it is written, Be ye holy, for I am holy.

This is being Christlike. This is following Jesus Christ. This is the aim of all Christian effort. This is the earnest, heartfelt desire of every truly regenerated soul. This is what is to be constantly and earnestly prayed for. It is that we may be made holy. Not that we must make ourselves holy, but we must be cleansed from all sin by the precious atoning blood of Christ, and be made holy by the direct agency of the Holy Spirit. Not that we are to *do* holy, but rather to *be* holy. Being must precede doing. First be, then do. First, obtain a holy heart, then live a holy life. And for this high and gracious end God has made the most ample provisions in the atoning work of our Lord and through the agency of the Holy Spirit.

The work of God in the world is the implantation, the growth and the perfection of holiness in his people. Keep this ever in mind. But we might ask

112

just now, Is this work advancing in the church? Are men and women being made holy? Is the present-day church engaged in the business of making holy men and women? This is not a vain and speculative question. It is practical, pertinent and all important.

The present-day church has vast machinery. Her activities are great, and her material prosperity is unparalleled. The name of religion is widespread and well-known. Much money comes into the Lord's treasury and is paid out. But here is the question: Does the work of holiness keep pace with all this? Is the burden of the prayers of church people to be made holy? Are our preachers really holy men? Or to go back a little further, are they hungering and thirsting after righteousness, desiring the sincere milk of the Word that they may grow thereby? Are they really seeking to be holy men? Of course men of intelligence are greatly needed in the pulpit, but prior to that, and primary to it, is the fact that we need holy men to stand before dying men and proclaim the salvation of God to them.

Ministers, like laymen, and no more so than laymen, must be holy men in life, in conversation and in temper. They must be examples to the flock of God in all things. By their lives they are to preach as well as to speak. Men in the pulpit are needed who are spotless in life, circumspect in behavior, "without rebuke and blameless in the midst of a crooked and perverse nation, among whom they are to shine in the world." Are our preachers of this type of men? We are simply asking the question. Let the reader make up his own judgment. Is the work of holiness making progress among our preachers?

Again let us ask: Are our leading laymen examples of holiness? Are they seeking holiness of heart and life? Are they praying men, ever praying that God would fashion them according to his pattern of holiness? Are their business ways without stain of sin, and their gains free from the taint of wrongdoing? Have they the foundation of solid honesty, and does uprightness bring them into elevation and influence? Does business integrity and probity run parallel with religious activity, and with churchly observance?

Then, while we are pursuing our investigation, seeking light as to whether the work of God among his people is making progress, let us ask further as to our women. Are the leading women of our churches dead to the fashions of this world, separated from the world, not conformed to the world's maxims and customs? Are they in behavior as becometh holiness, teaching the young women by word and life the lessons of soberness, obedience, and home-keeping? Are our women noted for their praying habits? Are they patterns of prayer?

How searching are all these questions? And will anyone dare say they are impertinent and out of place? If God's work be to make men and women holy, and he has made ample provisions in the law of prayer of doing this very thing, why should it be thought impertinent and useless to propound such personal and pointed questions as these? They have to do directly with the work and with its progress and its perfection. They go to the very seat of the disease. They hit the spot.

We might as well face the situation first as last. There is no use to shut our eyes to real facts. If the church does not do this sort of work—if the church does not advance its members in holiness of heart and life—then all our show of activities and all our display of church work are a delusion and a snare.

But let us ask as to another large and important class of people in our churches. They are the hope of the future church. To them all eyes are turned. Are our young men and women growing in sobermindedness and reverence, and in all those graces which have their root in the renewed heart, which mark solid and permanent advance in the divine life? If we are not growing in holiness, then we are doing nothing religious nor abiding.

Material prosperity is not the infallible sign of spiritual prosperity. The former may exist while the latter is significantly absent. Material prosperity may easily blind the eyes of church leaders, so much so that they will make it a substitute for spiritual prosperity. How great the need to watch at that point! Prosperity in money matters does not signify growth in holiness. The seasons of material prosperity are rarely seasons of spiritual advance, either to the individual or to the church. It is so easy to lose sight of God when goods increase. It so easy to lean on human agencies and cease praying and relying upon God when material prosperity comes to the church.

If it be contended that the work of God is progressing, and that we are growing in holiness, then some perplexing questions arise which will be hard to answer. If the church is making advances on the lines of deep spirituality—if we are a praying people, noted for our prayer habits—if our people are hungering after holiness—then let us ask, why do we now have so few mighty outpourings of the Holy Spirit on our chief churches and our principal appointments? Why is it that so few of our revivals spring from the life of the pastor, who is noted for his deep spirituality, or the life of our church? Is the Lord's hand shortened that he cannot save? Is his ear heavy that he cannot hear? Why is it that in order to have so-called revivals, we must have outside pressure, by the reputation and sensation of some renowned evangelist? This is largely true in our larger charges and with our leading men. Why is it that the pastor is not sufficiently spiritual, holy, and in communion with God, that he cannot hold his own revival services, and have large outpourings of the Holy Spirit on the church, the community and upon himself? There can be but one solution for all this state of things. We have cultivated other things to the neglect of the work of holiness. We have permitted our minds to be preoccupied with material things in the church. Unfortunately, whether designedly or not, we have substituted the external for the internal. We have put that which is seen to the front and shut out that which is unseen. It is all too true as to the church, that we are much further advanced in material matters than in matters spiritual.

But the cause of this sad state of things may be traced further back. It is largely due to the decay of prayer. For with the decline of the work of holiness there has come the decline of the business of praying. As praying and holiness go together, so the decline of one, means the decay of the other.

Excuse it if we may, justify the present state of things if we will, yet it is all too patent that the emphasis in the work of the present-day church is not put on prayer. And just as this has occurred, the emphasis has been taken from the great work of God set on foot in the atonement, holiness of heart and life. The church is not turning out praying men and women, because the church is not intently engaged in the one great work of holiness.

At one time, John Wesley saw that there was a perceptible decline in the work of holiness, and he stopped short to inquire into the cause, and if we are as honest and spiritual as he was, we will now see the same causes operating to stay God's work among us. In a letter to his brother, Charles, at one time, he comes directly to the point, and makes short, incisive work of it. Here is how he begins his letter:

> What has hindered the work? I want to consider this. And must we not first say, we are the chief. If we were more holy in heart and life, thoroughly devoted to God, would not all the preachers catch fire, and carry it with them, throughout the land?
>
> Is not the next hindrance the littleness of grace (rather than of gifts) in a considerable part of our preachers? They have not the whole mind that was in Christ. They do not steadily walk as he walked. And, therefore, the hand of the Lord is stayed, though not altogether; though he does work still. But it is not in such a degree as he surely would, were they holy as he that hath sent them is holy.
>
> Is not the third hindrance the littleness of grace in the generality of our people? Therefore, they pray little, and with little fervency for a general blessing. And, therefore, their prayer has little power with God. It does not, as once, shut and open heaven.
>
> Add to this, that as there is much of the spirit of the world in their hearts, so there is much conformity to the world in their lives. They ought to be bright and shining lights, but they neither burn nor shine. They are not true to the rules they profess to observe. They are not holy in all manner of conversation. Nay, many of them are salt that has lost its savor, the little savor they once had. Wherewith then shall the rest of the land be seasoned? What wonder that their neighbors are as unholy as ever?

He strikes the spot. He hits the center. He grades the cause. He freely confesses that he and Charles are the first cause, in this decline of holiness. The chief ones occupy positions of responsibility. As they go, so goes the church. They give color to the church. They largely determine its character and its work. What holiness should mark these chief men? What zeal should ever characterize them? What prayerfulness should be seen in them! How influential they ought to be with God! If the head be weak, then the whole body will feel the stroke.

The pastors come next in his catalogue. When the chief shepherds and those who are under them, the immediate pastors, stay their advance in holiness, the panic will reach to the end of the line. As are the pastors, so will the people be as a rule. If the pastors are prayerless, then will the people follow in their footsteps. If the preacher be silent upon the work of holiness, then will there be no hungering and thirsting after holiness in the laymen. If the preacher be careless about obtaining the highest and best God has for him in religious experience, then will the people take after him.

One statement of Wesley needs to be repeated with emphasis. The littleness of grace, rather than the smallness of gifts,—this is largely the case with the preachers. It may be stated as an axiom: That the work of God fails as a general rule, more for the lack of grace, than for the want of gifts. It is more than this. It is more than this, for a full supply of grace brings an increase of gifts. It may be repeated that small results, a low experience, a low religious life, and pointless, powerless preaching always flow from a lack of grace. And a lack of grace flows from a lack of praying. Great grace comes from great praying.

> What is our calling's glorious hope
> But inward holiness?
> For this to Jesus I look up,
> I calmly wait for this.
>
> I wait till he shall touch me clean,
> Shall life and power impart;
> Give me the faith that casts out sin,
> And purifies the heart.

In carrying on his great work in the world, God works through human agents. He works through his church collectively and through his people individually. In order that they may be effective agents, they must be "vessels unto honor, sanctified, and meet for the master's use, and prepared unto every good work." God works most effectively through holy men. His work makes progress in the hands of praying men. Peter tells us that husbands who might not be reached by the Word of God, might be won by the conduct of their wives. It is those who are "blameless and harmless, the sons of God," who can hold forth the word of life "in the midst of a crooked and perverse nation."

The world judges religion not by what the Bible says, but by how Christians live. Christians are the Bible which sinners read. These are the epistles to be read of all men. "By their fruits ye shall know them." The emphasis, then, is to be placed upon holiness of life. But unfortunately in the present-day church, emphasis has been placed elsewhere. In selecting church workers and choosing ecclesiastical officers, the quality of holiness is not considered. The praying fitness seems not to be taken into account, when it was just otherwise in all of God's movements and in all of his plans. He looked for holy men, those noted for their praying habits. Prayer leaders are scarce. Prayer conduct is not counted as the highest qualification for offices in the church.

We cannot wonder that so little is accomplished in the great work in the world which God has in hand. The fact is that it is surprising so much has been done with such feeble, defective agents. "Holiness to the Lord" needs again to be written on the banners of the church. Once more it needs to be sounded out in the ears of modern Christians. "Follow peace with all men, and holiness, without which no man shall see the Lord."

Let it be emphasized and reemphasized that this is the divine standard of religion. Nothing short of this will satisfy the divine requirement. O the danger of deception at this point! How near one can come to being right and yet be wrong! Some men can come very near to pronouncing the test word, "Shibboleth," but they miss it. "Many will say unto me, Lord, Lord, in that day," says Jesus Christ, but he further states that then will he say unto them, "I never knew you; depart from me, ye that work iniquity."

Men can do many good things and yet not be holy in heart and righteous in conduct. They can do many good things and lack that spiritual quality of heart called holiness. How great the need of hearing the words of Paul guarding us against self-deception in the great work of personal salvation:

> Be not deceived; God is not mocked: for whatsoever a man soweth, that shall he also reap.

O may I still from sin depart;
A wise and understanding heart,
Jesus, to me to be given;
And let me through thy Spirit know
To glorify my God below,
And find my way to heaven.

8

Prayer and Consecration

WHEN we study the many-sidedness of prayer, we are surprised at the number of things with which it is connected. There is no phase of human life which it does not affect, and it has to do with everything affecting human salvation. Prayer and consecration are closely related. Prayer leads up to, and governs consecration. Prayer is precedent to consecration, accompanies it, and is a direct result of it. Much goes under the name of consecration which has no consecration in it. Much consecration of the present day is defective, superficial and spurious, worth nothing so far as the office and ends of consecration are concerned. Popular consecration is sadly at fault because it has little or no prayer in it. No consecration is worth a thought which is not the direct fruit of much praying, and which fails to bring one into a life of prayer. Prayer is the one thing prominent in a consecrated life.

Consecration is much more than a life of so-called service. It is a life of personal holiness, first of all. It is that which brings spiritual power into the heart and enlivens the entire inner man. It is a life which ever recognizes God, and a life given up to true prayer.

Full consecration is the highest type of a Christian life. It is the one divine standard of experience, of living and of service. It is the one thing at which the believer should aim. Nothing short of entire consecration must satisfy him.

Never is he to be contented till he is fully, entirely the Lord's by his own consent. His praying naturally and voluntarily leads up to this one act of his.

Consecration is the voluntary set dedication of one's self to God, an offering definitely made, and made without any reservation whatever. It is the setting apart of all we are, all we have, and all we expect to have or be, to God first of all. It is not so much the giving of ourselves to the church, or the mere engaging in some one line of church work. Almighty God is in view and he is the end of all consecration. It is a separation of one's self to God, a devotement of all that he is and has to a sacred use. Some things may be devoted to a special purpose, but it is not consecration in the true sense. Consecration has a sacred nature. It is devoted to holy ends. It is the voluntary putting of one's self in God's hands to be used sacredly, holily, with sanctifying ends in view.

118

Consecration is not so much the setting one's self apart from sinful things and wicked ends, but rather it is the separation from worldly, secular and even legitimate things, if they come in conflict with God's plans, to holy uses. It is the devoting of all we have to God for his own specific use. It is a separation from things questionable, or even legitimate, when the choice is to be made between the things of this life and the claims of God.

The consecration which meets God's demands and which he accepts is to be full, complete, with no mental reservation, with nothing withheld. It cannot be partial, any more than a whole burnt offering in Old Testament times could have been partial. The whole animal had to be offered in sacrifice. To reserve any part of the animal would have seriously vitiated the offering. So to make a half-hearted, partial consecration is to make no consecration at all, and is to fail utterly in securing the divine acceptance. It involves our whole being, all we have and all that we are. Everything is definitely and voluntarily placed in God's hands for his supreme use.

Consecration is not all there is in holiness. Many make serious mistakes at this point. Consecration makes us relatively holy. We are holy only in the sense that we are now closely related to God, in which we were not related heretofore. Consecration is the human side of holiness. In this sense, it is self-sanctification, and only in this sense. Sanctification or holiness in its truest and highest sense is divine, the act of the Holy Spirit working in the heart, making it clean and putting therein in a higher degree the fruits of the Spirit.

This distinction is clearly set forth and kept in view by Moses in Leviticus, wherein he shows the human and the divine side of sanctification or holiness:

> Sanctify yourselves, therefore, and be ye holy, for I am the Lord your God.
> And ye shall keep my statutes and do them; I am the Lord which sanctify you.

Here we are to sanctify ourselves, and then in the next word we are taught that it is the Lord which sanctifies us. God does not consecrate us to his service. We do not sanctify ourselves in this highest sense. Here is the twofold meaning of sanctification, and a distinction which needs to be always kept in mind.

Consecration being the intelligent, voluntary act of the believer, this act is the direct result of praying. No prayerless man ever conceives the idea of a full consecration. Prayerlessness and consecration have nothing whatever in common. A life of prayer naturally leads up to full consecration. It leads nowhere else. In fact, a life of prayer is satisfied with nothing else but an entire dedication of one's self to God. Consecration recognizes fully God's ownership of us. It cheerfully assents to the truth set forth by Paul:

> Ye are not your own. For ye are bought with a price. Therefore, glorify God
> in your body and spirit, which are God's.

And true praying leads that way. It cannot reach any other destination. It is bound to run into this depot. This is its natural result. This is the sort of work which praying turns out. Praying makes consecrated people. It cannot make any other sort. It drives to this end. It aims at this very purpose.

As prayer leads up to and brings forth full consecration, so prayer entirely impregnates a consecrated life. The prayer life and the consecrated life are intimate companions. They are Siamese twins, inseparable. Prayer enters into every phase of a consecrated life. A prayerless life which claims consecration is a misnomer, false, counterfeit.

Consecration is really the setting apart of one's self to a life of prayer. It means not only to pray, but to pray habitually, and to pray more effectually. It is the consecrated man who accomplishes most by his praying. God must hear the man wholly given up to God. God cannot deny the requests of him who has renounced all claims to himself, and who has wholly dedicated himself to God and his service. This act of the consecrated man puts him "on praying ground and pleading terms" with God. It puts him in reach of God in prayer. It places him where he can get hold of God, and where he can influence God to do things which he would not otherwise do. Consecration brings answers to prayer. God can depend upon consecrated men. God can afford to commit himself in prayer to those who have fully committed themselves to God. He who gives all to God will get all from God. Having given all to God, he can claim all that God has for him.

As prayer is the condition of full consecration, so prayer is the habit, the rule, of him who has dedicated himself wholly to God. Prayer is becoming in the consecrated life. Prayer is no strange thing in such a life. There is a peculiar affinity between prayer and consecration, for both recognize God, both submit to God, and both have their aim and end in God. Prayer is part and parcel of the consecrated life. Prayer is the constant, the inseparable, the intimate companion of consecration. They walk and talk together.

There is much talk today of consecration, and many are termed consecrated people who know not the alphabet of it. Much modern consecration falls far below the scriptural standard. There is really no real consecration in it. Just as there is much praying without any real prayer in it, so there is much so-called consecration current, today, in the church which has no real consecration in it. Much passes for consecration in the church which receives the praise and plaudits of superficial, formal professors, but which is wide of the mark. There is much hurrying to and fro, here and there, much fuss and feathers, much going about and doing many things, and those who busy themselves after this fashion are called consecrated men and women. The central trouble with all this false consecration is that there is no prayer in it, nor is it in any sense the direct result of praying. People can do many excellent and commendable things in the church and be utter strangers to a life of consecration, just as they can do many things and be prayerless.

Here is the true test of consecration. It is a life of prayer. Unless prayer is preeminent, unless prayer is to the front, the consecration is faulty, deceptive, falsely named. Does he pray? That is the test. A question of every so-called consecrated man. Is he a man of prayer? No consecration is worth a thought if it be devoid of prayer. Yea, more—if it be not preeminently and primarily a life of prayer.

God wants consecrated men because they can pray and will pray. He can use consecrated men because he can use praying men. As prayerless men are in his way, hinder him, and prevent the success of his cause, so likewise unconsecrated men are useless to him, and hinder him in carrying out his gracious plans, and in executing his noble purposes in redemption. God wants consecrated men because he wants praying men. Consecration and prayer meet in the same man. Prayer is the tool with which the consecrated man works. Consecrated men are the agents through whom prayer works. Prayer helps the consecrated man in maintaining his attitude of consecration, keeps him alive to God, and aids him in doing the work to which he is called and to which he has given himself. Consecration helps to effectual praying. Consecration enables one to get the most out of his praying.

> Let him to whom we now belong
> His sovereign right assert;
> And take up every thankful song,
> And every loving heart.
>
> He justly claims us for his own,
> Who bought us with a price;
> The Christian lives to Christ alone,
> To Christ alone he dies.

We must insist upon it that the prime purpose of consecration is not service in the ordinary sense of that word. Service in the minds of not a few means nothing more than engaging in some of the many forms of modern church activities. There are a multitude of such activities, enough to engage the time and mind of any one, yea, even more than enough. Some of these may be good, others not so good. The present-day church is filled with machinery, organizations, committees and societies, so much so that the power it has is altogether insufficient to run the machinery, or to furnish life sufficient to do all this external work. Consecration has a much higher and nobler end than merely to expend itself in these external things.

Consecration aims at the right sort of service—the scriptural kind. It seeks to serve God, but in entirely a different sphere than that which is in the minds of present-day church leaders and workers. The very first sort of service mentioned by Zachariah, father of John the Baptist, in his wonderful prophecy and statement in Luke 1:74, was thus:

> That he would grant unto us, that we, being delivered out of the hand of our enemies, might serve him without fear, in holiness and righteousness, all the days of our life.

Here we have the idea of "serving God in holiness and righteousness all the days of our life."

And the same kind of service is mentioned in Luke's strong tribute to the father and mother of John the Baptist before the latter's birth:

> And they were both righteous before God, walking in all the commandments and ordinances of the Lord blameless.

And Paul, in writing to the Philippians, strikes the same keynote in putting the emphasis on blamelessness of life:

> Do all things without murmurings and disputings, that ye may be blameless and harmless, the sons of God without rebuke, in the midst of a crooked and perverse nation, among whom ye shine as lights in the world; holding forth the word of life.

We must mention a truth which is strangely overlooked in these days by what are called personal workers, that in the Epistles of Paul and others, it is not what are called church activities which are brought to the front, but rather the personal life. It is good behavior, righteous conduct, holy living, godly conversation, right tempers—things which belong primarily to the personal life in religion. Everywhere this is emphasized, put in the forefront, made much of and insisted on. Religion first of all puts one to living right. Religion shows itself in the life. Thus is religion to prove its reality, its sincerity and its divinity.

> So let our lips and lives express
> The holy gospel we profess;
> So let our works and virtues shine
> To prove the doctrine all divine.
>
> Thus shall we best proclaim abroad
> The honors of our Savior God;
> When the salvation reigns within
> And grace subdues the power of sin.

The first great end of consecration is holiness of heart and of life. It is to glorify God, and this can be done in no more effectual way than by a holy life flowing from a heart cleansed from all sin. The great burden of heart pressed on every one who becomes a Christian lies right here. This he is to ever keep in mind, and to further this kind of life and this kind of heart, he is to watch, to pray, and to bend all his diligence in using all the means of grace. He who is truly and fully consecrated, lives a holy life. He seeks after holiness of heart. Is not satisfied without it. For this very purpose he consecrates himself to God. He gives himself entirely over to God in order to be holy in heart and in life.

As holiness of heart and of life is thoroughly impregnated with prayer, so consecration and prayer are closely allied in personal religion. It takes prayer to bring one into such a consecrated life of holiness to the Lord, and it takes prayer to maintain such a life. Without much prayer, such a life of holiness will break down. Holy people are praying people. Holiness of heart and life puts people to praying. Consecration puts people to praying in earnest.

Prayerless people are strangers to anything like holiness of heart and cleanness of heart. Those who are unfamiliar with the closet are not at all interested in consecration and holiness. Holiness thrives in the place of secret prayer. The environments of the closet of prayer are favorable to its being and its culture. In the closet holiness is found. Consecration brings one into holiness of heart, and prayer stands hard by when it is done.

The spirit of consecration is the spirit of prayer. The law of consecration is the law of prayer. Both laws work in perfect harmony without the slightest jar or discord. Consecration is the practical expression of true prayer. People who are consecrated are known by their praying habits. Consecration thus expresses itself in prayer. He who is not interested in prayer has no interest in consecration. Prayer creates an interest in consecration, then prayer brings one into a state of heart where consecration is a subject of delight, bringing joy of heart, satisfaction of soul, contentment of spirit. The consecrated soul is the happiest soul. There is no friction whatever between him who is fully given over to God and God's will. There is perfect harmony between the will of such a man and God, and his will. And the two wills being in perfect accord, this brings rest of soul, absence of friction, and the presence of perfect peace.

> Lord, in the strength of grace,
> With a glad heart and free,
> Myself, my residue of days,
> I consecrate to thee.
>
> Thy ransomed servant, I
> Restore to thee thy own;
> And from this moment, live or die,
> To serve my God alone.

9

Prayer and a Definite Religious Standard

MUCH of the feebleness, barrenness and paucity of religion results from the failure to have a scriptural and reasonable standard in religion, by which to shape character and measure results; and this largely results from the omission of prayer or the failure to put prayer in the standard. We cannot possibly mark our advances in religion if there is no point to which we are definitely advancing. Always there must be something definite before the mind's eye at which we are aiming and to which we are driving. We cannot contrast shapeliness with unshapeliness if there be no pattern after which to model. Neither can there be inspiration if there be no high end to stimulate us.

Many Christians are disjointed and aimless because they have no pattern before them after which conduct and character are to be shaped. They just move on aimlessly, their minds in a cloudy state, no pattern in view, no point in sight, no standard after which they are striving. There is no standard by which to value and gauge their efforts. No magnet is there to fill their eyes, quicken their steps, and to draw them and keep them steady.

All this vague idea of religion grows out of loose notions about prayer. That which helps to make the standard of religion clear and definite is prayer. That which aids in placing that standard high is prayer. The praying ones are those who have something definite in view. In fact prayer itself is a very definite thing, aims at something specific, and has a mark at which it aims. Prayer aims at the most definite, the highest and the sweetest religious experience. The praying ones want all that God has in store for them. They are not satisfied with anything like a low religious life, superficial, vague and indefinite. The praying ones are not only after a "deeper work of grace," but want the very deepest work of grace possible and promised. They are not after being saved from some sin, but saved from all sin, both inward and outward. They are after not only deliverance from sinning, but from sin itself, from its being, its power and its pollution. They are after holiness of heart and life.

Prayer believes in, and seeks for the very highest religious life set before us in the Word of God. Prayer is the condition of that life. Prayer points out the only pathway to such a life. The standard of a religious life is the standard of prayer. Prayer is so vital, so essential, so far-reaching, that it enters into all religion, and sets the standard clear and definite before the eye. The degree of

124

our estimate of prayer fixes our ideas of the standard of a religious life. The standard of biblical religion is the standard of prayer. The more there is of prayer in the life, the more definite and the higher our notions of religion.

The Scriptures alone make the standard of life and experience. When we make our own standard, there is delusion and falsity for our desires, convenience and pleasure form the rule, and that is always a fleshly and a low rule. From it, all the fundamental principles of a Christlike religion are left out. Whatever standard of religion which makes in it provision for the flesh, is unscriptural and hurtful.

Nor will it do to leave it to others to fix the standard of religion for us. When we allow others to make our standard of religion, it is generally deficient because in imitation, defects are transferred to the imitator more readily than virtues, and a second edition of a man is marred by its defects.

The most serious damage in thus determining what religion is by what others say, is in allowing current opinion, the contagion of example, the grade of religion current among us, to shape our religious opinions and characters. Adoniram Judson once wrote to a friend, "Let me beg you, not to rest contented with the commonplace religion that is now so prevalent."

Commonplace religion is pleasing to flesh and blood. There is no self-denial in it, no cross bearing, no self-crucifixion. It is good enough for our neighbors. Why should we be singular and straight-laced? Others are living on a low plane, on a compromising level, living as the world lives. Why should we be peculiar, zealous of good works? Why should we fight to win heaven while so many are sailing there on "flowery beds of ease"? Are the easy-going, careless, sauntering crowd, living prayerless lives, going to heaven? Is heaven a fit place for non-praying, loose living, ease loving people? That is the supreme question.

Paul gives the following caution about making for ourselves the jolly, pleasure-seeking religious company all about us the standard of our measurement:

> For we dare not make ourselves of the number, or compare ourselves with some that commend themselves; but they, measuring themselves by themselves, and comparing themselves among themselves, are not wise. But we will not boast of things without our measure, but according to the measure of the rule which God hath distributed to us, a measure to reach even unto you.

No standard of religion is worth a moment's consideration which leaves prayer out of the account. No standard is worth any thought which does not make prayer the main thing in religion. So necessary is prayer, so fundamental in God's plan, so all important to everything like a religious life, that it enters into all biblical religion. Prayer itself is a standard, definite, emphatic, scriptural. A life of prayer is the divine rule. This is the pattern, just as our Lord, being a man of prayer, is the one pattern for us after whom to copy.

Prayer fashions the pattern of a religious life. Prayer is the measure. Prayer molds the life.

The vague, indefinite, popular view of religion has no prayer in it. In its program, prayer is entirely left out or put so low down and made so insignificant, that it hardly is worth mentioning. Man's standard of religion has no prayer about it.

It is God's standard at which we are to aim, not man's. It is not the opinions of men, not what they say, but what the Scriptures say. Loose notions of religion grow out of low notions of prayer. Prayerlessness begets loose, cloudy and indefinite views of what religion is. Aimless living and prayerlessness go hand in hand. Prayer sets something definite in the mind. Prayer seeks after something specific. The more definite our views as to the nature and need of prayer, the more definite will be our views of Christian experience and right living, and the less vague our views of religion. A low standard of religion lives hard by a low standard of praying.

Everything in a religious life depends upon being definite. The definiteness of our religious experiences and of our living will depend upon the definiteness of our views of what religion is and of the things of which it consists.

The Scriptures ever set before us the one standard of full consecration to God. This is the divine rule. This is the human side of this standard. The sacrifice acceptable to God must be a complete one, entire, a whole burnt offering. This is the measure laid down in God's Word. Nothing less than this can be pleasing to God. Nothing half-hearted can please him. "A living sacrifice," holy, and perfect in all its parts, is the measurement of our service to God. A full renunciation of self, a free recognition of God's right to us, and a sincere offering of all to him—this is the divine requirement. Nothing indefinite in that. Nothing is in that which is governed by the opinions of others or affected by how men live about us.

And while a life of prayer is embraced in such a full consecration, at the same time prayer leads up to the point where a complete consecration is made to God. Consecration is but the silent expression of prayer. And the highest religious standard is the measure of prayer and self-dedication to God. The prayer life and the consecrated life are partners in religion. They are so closely allied they are never separated. The prayer life is the direct fruit of entire consecration to God. Prayer is the natural outflow of a really consecrated life. The measure of consecration is the measure of real prayer. No consecration is pleasing to God which is not perfect in all its parts, just as no burnt offering of a Jew was ever acceptable to God unless it was a "whole burnt offering." And a consecration of this sort, after this divine measurement; has in it as a basic principle, the business of praying. Consecration is made to God. Prayer has to do with God. Consecration is putting one's self entirely at the disposal of God. And God wants and commands all his consecrated ones to be praying ones. This is the one definite standard at which we must aim. Lower than this we cannot afford to seek.

A scriptural standard of religion includes a clear religious experience. Religion is nothing if not experiential. Religion appeals to the inner consciousness. It is an experience if anything at all, and an experience in addition to a religious life. There is the internal part of religion as well as the external. Not only are we to "work out our salvation with fear and trembling," but "it is God that worketh in us to will and do of his good pleasure." There is a "good work in you," as well as a life outside to be lived. The new birth is a definite Christian experience, proved by infallible marks, appealing to the inner consciousness. The witness of the Spirit is not an indefinite, vague something, but is a definite, clear inward assurance given by the Holy Spirit that we are the children of God. In fact everything belonging to religious experience is clear and definite, bringing conscious joy, peace and love. And this is the divine standard of religion, a standard attained by earnest, constant prayer, and a religious experience kept alive and enlarged by the same means of prayer.

An end to be gained, to which effort is to be directed, is important in every pursuit in order to give unity, energy and steadiness to it. In the Christian life, such an end is all important. Without a high standard before us to be gained, for which we are earnestly seeking, lassitude will unnerve effort, and past experience will taint or exhale into mere sentiment, or be hardened into cold, loveless principle.

We must go on. "Therefore, leaving the principles of the doctrine of Christ, let us go on unto perfection." The present ground we occupy must be held by making advances, and all the future must be covered and brightened by it. In religion, we must not only go on. We must know where we are going. This is all important. It is essential that in going on in religious experience, we have something definite in view, and strike out for that one point. To ever go on and not to know to which place we are going, is altogether too vague and indefinite, and is like a man who starts out on a journey and does not have any destination in view. It is important that we not lose sight of the starting point in a religious life, and that we measure the steps already trod. But it is likewise necessary that the end be kept in view and that the steps necessary to reach the standard be always in sight.

10

Prayer Born of Compassion

WE speak here more particularly of spiritual compassion, that which is born in a renewed heart, and which finds hospitality there. This compassion has in it the quality of mercy, is of the nature of pity, and moves the soul with tenderness of feeling for others. Compassion is moved at the sight of sin, sorrow and suffering. It stands at the other extreme to indifference of spirit to the wants and woes of others, and is far removed from insensibility and hardness of heart, in the midst of want and trouble and wretchedness. Compassion stands beside sympathy for others, is interested in them, and is concerned about them.

That which excites and develops compassion and puts it to work, is the sight of multitudes in want and distress, and helpless to relieve themselves. Helplessness especially appeals to compassion. Compassion is silent but does not remain secluded. It goes out at the sight of trouble, sin and need. Compassion runs out in earnest prayer, first of all, for those for whom it feels, and has a sympathy for them. Prayer for others is born of a sympathetic heart. Prayer is natural and almost spontaneous when compassion is begotten in the heart. Prayer belongs to the compassionate man.

There is a certain compassion which belongs to the natural man, which expends its force in simple gifts to those in need, not to be despised. But spiritual compassion, the kind born in a renewed heart, which is Christlike in its nature, is deeper, broader and more prayerlike. Christlike compassion always moves to prayer. This sort of compassion goes beyond the relief of mere bodily wants, and saying, "Be ye warmed—be ye clothed." It reaches deeper down and goes much farther.

Compassion is not blind. Rather we should say, that compassion is not born of blindness. He who has compassion of soul has eyes, first of all, to see the things which excite compassion. He who has no eyes to see the exceeding sinfulness of sin, the wants and woes of humanity, will never have compassion for humanity. It is written of our Lord that "when he saw the multitudes, he was moved with compassion on them." First, seeing the multitudes, with their hunger, their woes and their helpless condition, then compassion. Then prayer for the multitudes. Hard is he, and far from being Christlike, who sees the multitudes, and is unmoved at the sight of their sad state, their unhappiness and their peril. He has no heart of prayer for men.

Compassion may not always move men, but is always moved toward men. Compassion may not always turn men to God, but it will, and does, turn God to man. And where it is most helpless to relieve the needs of others, it can at least break out into prayer to God for others. Compassion is never indifferent, selfish, and forgetful of others. Compassion has alone to do with others. The fact that the multitudes were as sheep having no shepherd, was the one thing which appealed to our Lord's compassionate nature. Then their hunger moved him, and the sight of the sufferings and diseases of these multitudes stirred the pity of his heart.

> Father of mercies, send thy grace
> All powerful from above,
> To form in our obedient souls
> The image of thy love.
>
> O may our sympathizing breasts
> That generous pleasure know;
> Kindly to share in others' joy,
> And weep for others' woe.

But compassion has not alone to do with the body and its disabilities and needs. The soul's distressing state, its needs and danger all appeal to compassion. The highest state of grace is known by the infallible mark of compassion for poor sinners. This sort of compassion belongs to grace, and sees not alone the bodies of men, but their immortal spirits, soiled by sin, unhappy in their condition without God, and in imminent peril of being forever lost. When compassion beholds this sight of dying men hurrying to the bar of God, then it is that it breaks out into intercessions for sinful men. Then it is that compassion speaks out after this fashion:

> But feeble my compassion proves,
> And can but weep where most it loves;
> Thy own all saving arm employ,
> And turn these drops of grief to joy.

The prophet Jeremiah declares this about God, giving the reason why sinners are not consumed by his wrath:

> It is of the Lord's mercies we are not consumed, because his compassions fail not.

And it is this divine quality in us which makes us so much like God. So we find the psalmist describing the righteous man who is pronounced blessed by God: "He is gracious and full of compassion, and righteous."

And as giving great encouragement to penitent praying sinners, the psalmist thus records some of the striking attributes of the divine character: "The Lord is gracious and full of compassion, slow to anger, and of great mercy."

It is no wonder, then, that we find it recorded several times of our Lord while on earth that "he was moved with compassion." Can any one doubt that his compassion moved him to pray for those suffering, sorrowing ones who came across his pathway?

Paul was wonderfully interested in the religious welfare of his Jewish brethren, was concerned over them, and his heart was strangely warmed with tender compassion for their salvation, even though mistreated and sorely persecuted by them. In writing to the Romans, we hear him thus express himself:

> I say the truth in Christ, I lie not, my conscience also bearing me witness in the Holy Spirit, that I have great heaviness and continual sorrow in my heart; for I could wish that myself were accursed for my brethren, my kinsmen according to the flesh.

What marvelous compassion is here described for Paul's own nation! What wonder that a little later on he records his desire and prayer:

> Brethren, my heart's desire and prayer to God for Israel is that they might be saved.

We have an interesting case in Matthew which gives us an account of what excited so largely the compassion of our Lord at one time:

> But when he saw the multitudes, he was moved with compassion on them, because they fainted, and were scattered abroad, as sheep having no shepherd. Then saith he unto his disciples, The harvest truly is plenteous, but the laborers are few. Pray ye therefore the Lord of the harvest, that he will send forth laborers into his harvest.

It seems from parallel statements that our Lord had called his disciples aside to rest awhile, exhausted as he and they were by the excessive demands on them, by the ceaseless contact with the persons who were ever coming and going, and by their exhaustive toil in ministering to the immense multitudes. But the multitudes precede him, and instead of finding wilderness solitude, quiet and repose, he finds great multitudes eager to see and hear, and to be healed. His compassions are moved. The ripened harvests need laborers. He did not call these laborers at once, by sovereign authority, but charges the disciples to betake themselves to God in prayer, asking him to send forth laborers into his harvest.

Here is the urgency of prayer enforced by the compassions of our Lord. It is prayer born of compassion for perishing humanity. Prayer is pressed on the church for laborers to be sent into the harvest of the Lord. The harvest will go to waste and perish without the laborers, while the laborers must be God-chosen, God-sent, and God-commissioned. But God does not send these laborers into his harvest without prayer. The failure of the laborers is owing to the failure of prayer. The scarcity of laborers in the harvest is due to the fact that the church fails to pray for laborers according to his command.

The ingathering of the harvests of earth for the granaries of heaven is dependent on the prayers of God's people. Prayer secures the laborers sufficient in quantity and in quality for all the needs of the harvest. God's chosen laborers, God's endowed laborers, and God's thrust-forth laborers, are the only ones who will truly go, filled with Christlike compassion and endued with Christlike power, whose going will avail, and these are secured by prayer. Christ's people on their knees with Christ's compassion in their hearts for dying men and for needy souls, exposed to eternal peril, is the pledge of laborers in numbers and character to meet the wants of earth and the purposes of heaven.

God is sovereign of the earth and of heaven, and the choice of laborers in his harvest he delegates to no one else. Prayer honors him as sovereign and moves him to his wise and holy selection. We will have to put prayer to the front ere the fields of paganism will be successfully tilled for Christ. God knows his men, and he likewise knows full well his work. Prayer gets God to send forth the best men and the most fit men and the men best qualified to work in the harvest. Moving the missionary cause by forces this side of God has been its bane, its weakness and its failure. Compassion for the world of sinners, fallen in Adam, but redeemed in Christ will move the church to pray for them and stir the church to pray the Lord of the harvest to send forth laborers into the harvest.

> Lord of the harvest, hear
> Thy needy servants' cry;
> Answer our faith's effectual prayer,
> And all our wants supply.
>
> Convert and send forth more
> Into thy church abroad;
> And let them speak thy word of power,
> As workers with their God.

What a comfort and what hope there is to fill our breasts when we think of one in heaven who ever lives to intercede for us, because "His compassion fails not!" Above everything else, we have a compassionate savior, one "who can have compassion on the ignorant, and on them who are out of the way, for that he himself is compassed about with infirmity." The compassion of our Lord well fits him for being the great high priest of Adam's fallen, lost and helpless race.

And if he is filled with such compassion that it moves him at the Father's right hand to intercede for us, then by every token we should have the same compassion on the ignorant and those out of the way, exposed to divine wrath, as would move us to pray for them. Just in so far as we are compassionate will we be prayerful for others. Compassion does not expend its force in simply saying, "Be ye warmed; be ye clothed," but drives us to our knees in prayer for those who need Christ and his grace.

> The Son of God in tears
> The wondering angels see;
> Be thou astonished, O my soul!
> He shed those tears for thee.
>
> He wept that we might weep;
> Each sin demands a tear;
> In heaven alone no sin is found,
> And there's no weeping there.

Jesus Christ was altogether man. While he was the divine Son of God yet at the same time, he was the human Son of God. Christ had a preeminently human side, and, here, compassion reigned. He was tempted in all points as we are, yet without sin. At one time how the flesh seems to have weakened under the fearful strain upon him, and how he must have inwardly shrunk under the pain and pull! Looking up to heaven, he prays, "Father, save me from this hour." How the spirit nerves and holds —"but for this cause came I to this hour." Only he can solve this mystery who has followed his Lord in straits and gloom and pain, and realized that the "spirit is willing but the flesh is weak."

All this but fitted our Lord to be a compassionate savior. It is no sin to feel the pain and realize the darkness on the path into which God leads. It is only human to cry out against the pain, the terror, and desolation of that hour. It is divine to cry out to God in that hour, even while shrinking and sinking down, "For this cause came I unto this hour." Shall I fail through the weakness of the flesh? No. "Father, glorify thy name." How strong it makes us, and how true, to have one pole star to guide us to the glory of God!

11

Concerted Prayer

THE pious Quesnel says that "God is found in union and agreement. Nothing is more efficacious than this in prayer." Intercessions combine with prayers and supplications. The word does not mean necessarily prayer in relation to others. It means a coming together, a falling in with a most intimate friend for free, unrestrained communion. It implies prayer, free, familiar and bold.

Our Lord deals with this question of the concert of prayer in the eighteenth chapter of Matthew. He deals with the benefit and energy resulting from the aggregation of prayer forces. The prayer principle and the prayer promise will be best understood in the connection in which it was made by our Lord:

> Moreover, if thy brother shall trespass against thee, go and tell him his fault between thee and him alone: if he shall hear thee, thou hast gained thy brother. But if he will not hear thee, then take with thee one or two more, that in the mouth of two or three witnesses, every word may be established.

> And if he shall neglect to hear them, tell it unto the church; but if he neglect to hear the church, let him be unto thee as an heathen and a publican.

> Verily I say unto you, Whatsoever ye shall bind on earth, shall be bound in heaven; and whatsoever ye shall loose on earth, shall be loosed in heaven. Again I say unto you, That if two of you shall agree on earth as touching any thing that they shall ask, it shall be done for them of my Father which is in heaven. For where two or three are gathered together in my name, there am I in the midst of them.

This represents the church in prayer to inforce discipline in order that its members who have been overtaken by faults, may yield readily to the disciplinary process. In addition, it is the church called together in a concert of prayer in order to repair the waste and friction ensuing upon the cutting off of a church offender. This last direction as to a concert of prayer is that the whole matter may be referred to Almighty God for his approval and ratification.

All this means that the main, the concluding and the all powerful agency in the church is prayer, whether it be, as we have seen in the ninth chapter of Matthew, to thrust out laborers into God's earthly harvest fields, or to exclude from the church a violator of unity, law and order, who will neither listen to his brethren nor repent and confess his fault.

It means that church discipline, now a lost art in the modern church, must go hand in hand with prayer, and that the church which has no disposition to separate wrong-doers from the church, and which has no excommunication spirit for incorrigible offenders against law and order, will have no communication with God. Church purity must precede the church's prayers. The unity of discipline in the church precedes the unity of prayers by the church.

Let it be noted with emphasis that a church which is careless of discipline will be careless in praying. A church which tolerates evildoers in its communion, will cease to pray, will cease to pray with agreement, and will cease to be a church gathered together in prayer in Christ's name.

This matter of church discipline is an important one in the Scriptures. The need of watchfulness over the lives of its members belongs to the church of God. The church is an organization for mutual help, and it is charged with the watch care of all of its members. Disorderly conduct cannot be passed by unnoticed. The course of procedure in such cases is clearly given in the eighteenth chapter of Matthew, which has been heretofore referred to. Furthermore, Paul, in Galatians 6:1, gives explicit directions as to those who fall into sin in the church:

> Brethren, if a man be overtaken in a fault, ye which are spiritual restore such a one in the spirit of meekness, considering thyself lest thou also be tempted.

The work of the church is not alone to members but it is to watch over and guard them after they have entered the church. And if any are overtaken by sin, they must be sought out, and if they cannot be cured of their faults, then excision must take place. This is the doctrine our Lord lays down.

It is somewhat striking that the church at Ephesus, (Rev. 2) though it had left its first love, and had sadly declined in vital godliness and in those things which make up spiritual life, yet it receives credit for this good quality: "Thou canst not bear them that are evil."

While the church at Pergamos was admonished because it had there among its membership those who taught such hurtful doctrines that were a stumbling-block to others. And not so much that such characters were in the church, but that they were tolerated. The impression is that the church leaders were blind to the presence of such hurtful characters, and hence were indisposed to administer discipline. This indisposition was an unfailing sign of prayerlessness in the membership. There was no union of prayer effort looking to cleansing the church and keeping it clean.

This disciplinary idea stands out prominently in the apostle Paul's writings to the churches. The church at Corinth had a notorious case of fornication where a man had married his step-mother, and this church had been careless about this iniquity. Paul rather sharply reproved this church and gave explicit command to this effect: "Therefore put away from among yourselves that wicked person." Here was concert of action on the part of praying people demanded by Paul.

As good a church as that at Thessalonica needed instruction and caution on this matter of looking after disorderly persons. So we hear Paul saying to them:

> Now we command you, brethren, in the name of our Lord Jesus Christ, that ye withdraw yourselves from every brother that walketh disorderly.

Mark you. It is not the mere presence of disorderly persons in a church which merits the displeasure of God. It is when they are tolerated under the mistaken plea of "bearing with them," and no steps are taken either to cure them of their evil practices or exclude them from the fellowship of the church. And this glaring neglect on the part of the church of its wayward members, is but a sad sign of a lack of praying, for a praying church, given to mutual praying, agreement praying, is keen to discern when a brother is over-taken in a fault, and seeks either to restore him, or to cut him off if he be incorrigible.

Much of this dates back to the lack of spiritual vision on the part of church leaders. The Lord by the mouth of the prophet Isaiah once asked the very pertinent, suggestive question, "And who is blind but my servant?" This blindness in leadership in the church is no more patent than in this question of seeing evildoers in the church, in caring for them, and when the effort to restore them fails, to withdraw fellowship from them and let them be "as a heathen man and a publican." The truth is there is such a lust for members in the church in these modern times, that the officials and preachers have entirely lost sight of the members who have violated baptismal covenants, and who are living in open disregard of God's Word. The idea now is *quantity* in membership, *not quality*. The purity of the church is put in the background in the craze to secure numbers, and to pad the church rolls and make large figures in statistical columns. Prayer, much prayer, mutual prayer, would bring the church back to scriptural standards, and would purge the church of many wrongdoers, while it might cure not a few of their evil lives.

Prayer and church discipline are not new revelations of the Christian dispensation. These two things had a high place in the Jewish church. Instances are too numerous to mention all of them. Ezra is a case in point. When he returned from the captivity, he found a sad and distressing condition of things among the Lord's people who were left in the land. They had not separated themselves from the surrounding heathen people, and had intermarried with them, contrary to divine commands. And those high in the church were involved, the priests and the Levites with others. Ezra was greatly moved at the account given him, and rent his garments and wept and prayed. Evildoers in the church did not meet his approval, nor did he shut his eyes to them nor excuse them, neither did he compromise the situation. When he had finished confessing the sins of the people and his praying, the people assembled themselves before him and joined him in a covenant agreement to put away from them their evil doings, and wept and prayed in company with Ezra.

The result was that the people thoroughly repented of their transgressions, and Israel was reformed. Praying and a good man, who was neither blind nor unconcerned, did the deed.

Of Ezra it is written, "For he mourned because of the transgression of them that had been carried away." So it is with every praying man in the church when he has eyes to see the transgression of evildoers in the church, who has a heart to grieve over them, and who has a spirit in him so concerned about the church that he prays about it.

Blessed is that church who has praying leaders, who can see that which is disorderly in the church, who are grieved about it, and who put forth their hands to correct the evils which harm God's cause as a weight to its progress. One point in the indictment against those "Who are at ease in Zion," referred to by Amos, is that "they are not grieved for the affliction of Joseph." And this same indictment could be brought against church leaders of modern time. They are not grieved because the members are engulfed in a craze for worldly, carnal things, nor when there are those in the church walking openly in disorder, whose lives scandalize religion. Of course such leaders do not pray over the matter, for praying would beget a spirit of solicitude in them for these evildoers, and would drive away the spirit of unconcern which possesses them.

It would be well for prayerless church leaders and careless pastors to read the account of the ink horn man in Ezekiel nine, where God instructed the prophet to send through the city certain men who would destroy those in the city because of the great evils found therein. But certain persons were to be spared. These were they who "sigh and cry for all the abominations that be done in the midst of the city." The man with the ink horn was to mark every one of these sighers and mourners so that they would escape the impending destruction. Please note that the instructions were that the slaying of those who did not mourn and sigh should "Begin at my sanctuary."

What a lesson for nonpraying, unconcerned officials of the modern church! How few there are who "sigh and cry" for present abominations in the land, and who are grieved over the desolations of Zion! What need for "two or three to be gathered together" in a concert of prayer over these conditions, and in the secret place weep and pray for the sins in Zion!

This concert of prayer, this agreement in praying, taught by our Lord in the nineteenth chapter of Matthew, finds proof and illustration elsewhere.

This was the kind of prayer which Paul referred to in his request to his Roman brethren, recorded in Romans 15:30:

> Now I beseech you, brethren, for the Lord Jesus Christ's sake, and for the love of the Spirit, that ye strive together with me in your prayers to God for me; that I may be delivered from them that do not believe in Judea.

Here is unity in prayer, prayer by agreement, and prayer which drives directly at deliverance from unbelieving and evil men, the same kind of prayer urged by our Lord, and the end practically the same, deliverance from unbelieving men, that deliverance wrought either by bringing them to repentance or by exclusion from the church.

The same idea is found in 2 Thessalonians 3:1:

> Finally, brethren, pray for us that the word of the Lord may have free course and be glorified, even as it is with you; and that we may be delivered from unreasonable and wicked men.

Here is united prayer requested by an apostle, among other things, for deliverance from wicked men, that same that the church of God needs in this day. By joining their prayers to his, there was the desired end of riddance from men who were hurtful to the church of God and who were a hindrance to the running of the Word of the Lord. Let us ask, are there not in the present-day church those who are a positive hindrance to the on going of the Word of the Lord? What better course is there than to jointly pray over the question, at the same time using the Christ-given course of discipline first to save them, but failing in that course, to excise them from the body?

Does that seem a harsh course? Then our Lord was guilty of harshness himself, for he ends these directions by saying, "But if he neglect to hear the church, let him be unto thee as a heathen man and a publican."

No more is this harshness than is the art of the skillful surgeon, who sees the whole body and its members endangered by a gangrenous limb, and severs the limb from the body for the good of the whole. No more was it harshness in the captain and crew of the vessel on which Jonah was found, when the storm arose threatening destruction to all on board, to cast the fleeing prophet overboard. What seems harshness is obedience to God, is for the welfare of the church, and is wise in the extreme.

12

The Universality of Prayer

PRAYER is far-reaching in its influence and worldwide in its effects. It affects all men, affects them everywhere, and affects them in all things. It touches man's interest in time and eternity. It lays hold upon God and moves him to interfere in the affairs of earth. It moves the angels to minister to men in this life. It restrains and defeats the devil in his schemes to ruin man. Prayer goes everywhere and lays its hand upon everything. There is a universality in prayer. When we talk about prayer and its work we must use universal terms. It is individual in its application and benefits, but it is general and worldwide at the same time in its good influences. It blesses man in every event of life, furnishes him help in every emergency, and gives him comfort in every trouble. There is no experience through which man is called to go but prayer is there as a helper, a comforter and a guide.

When we speak of the universality of prayer, we discover many sides to it. First, it may be marked that all men ought to pray. Prayer is intended for all men, because all men need God and need what God has and what prayer only can secure. As men are called upon to pray everywhere, by consequence all men must pray, for men are everywhere. Universal terms are used when men are commanded to pray, while there is a promise in universal terms to all who call upon God for pardon, for mercy and for help:

> For there is no difference; for the same Lord over all is rich unto all that call upon him. For whosoever shall call upon the name of the Lord shall be saved.

As there is no difference in the state of sin in which men are found, and all men need the saving grace of God which only can bless them, and as this saving grace is obtained only in answer to prayer, therefore all men are called on to pray because of their very needs.

It is a rule of scriptural interpretation that whenever a command issues with no limitation, it is universal in binding force. So the words of the Lord in Isaiah are to the point:

> Seek ye the Lord while he may be found; call ye upon him while he is near. Let the wicked forsake his way, and the unrighteous man his thoughts, and let him return unto the Lord, who will have mercy, and to our God who will abundantly pardon.

138

So that as wickedness is universal, and as pardon is needed by all men, so all men must seek the Lord while he may be found, and must call upon him while he is near. Prayer belongs to all men because all men are redeemed in Christ. It is a privilege for every man to pray, but it is no less a duty for them to call upon God. No sinner is barred from the mercy seat. All are welcomed to approach the throne of grace with all their wants and woes, with all their sins and burdens.

> Come all the world, come, sinner thou,
> All things in Christ are ready now.

Whenever a poor sinner turns his eyes to God, no matter where he is nor what his guilt and sinfulness, the eye of God is upon him and his ear is opened to his prayers.

But men may pray everywhere, since God is accessible in every clime and under all circumstances. "I will therefore that men pray everywhere, lifting up holy hands, without wrath and doubting."

No locality is too distant from God on earth to reach heaven. No place is so remote that God cannot see and hear one who looks toward him and seeks his face. Oliver Holden puts into a hymn these words:

> Then, my soul, in every strait,
> To thy Father come and wait;
> He will answer every prayer;
> God is present everywhere.

There is just this modification of the idea that one can pray everywhere. Some places, because of the evil business carried on there, or because of the environments which belong there, growing out of the place itself, the moral character of those who carry on the business, and of those who support it, are localities where prayer would not be in place. We might list the saloon, the theater, the opera, the card table, the dance, and other like places of worldly amusement. Prayer is so much out of place at such places that no one would ever presume to pray. Prayer would be an intrusion, so regarded by the owners, the patrons and the supporters of such places. Furthermore those who attend such places are not praying people. They belong almost entirely to the prayerless crowd of worldlings.

While we are to pray everywhere, it unquestionably means that we are not to frequent places where we cannot pray. To pray everywhere is to pray in all legitimate places, and to attend especially those places where prayer is welcome, and is given a gracious hospitality. To pray everywhere is to preserve the spirit of prayer in places of business, in our intercourse with men, and in the privacy of the home amid all of its domestic cares.

The model prayer of our Lord, called familiarly "The Lord's Prayer," is the universal prayer, because it is peculiarly adapted to all men everywhere in all circumstances in all times of need. It can be put in the mouths of all people in all nations, and in all times. It is a model of praying which needs no amendment nor alteration for every family, people and nation.

Furthermore, prayer has its universal application in that all men are to be the subjects of prayer. All men everywhere are to be prayed for. Prayer must take in all of Adam's fallen race because all men are fallen in Adam, redeemed in Christ, and are benefited by prayers for them. This is Paul's doctrine in his prayer directory in 1 Timothy 2:1:

> I exhort, therefore, that first of all, supplications, prayers, intercessions and giving of thanks be made for all men.

There is strong scriptural warrant, therefore, for reaching out and embracing all men in our prayers, since not only are we commanded thus to pray for them, but the reason given is that Christ gave himself a ransom for all men, and all men are provisionally beneficiaries of the atoning death of Jesus Christ.

But lastly, and more at length, prayer has a universal side in that all things which concern us are to be prayed about, while all things which are for our good, physical, social, intellectual, spiritual, and eternal, are subjects of prayer. Before, however, we consider this phase of prayer let us stop and again look at the universal prayer for all men. As a special class to be prayed for, we may mention those who have control in state or who bear rule in the church. Prayer has mighty potencies. It makes good rulers, and makes them better rulers. It restrains the lawless and the despotic. Rulers are to be prayed for. They are not out of the reach and the control of prayer, because they are not out of the reach and control of God. Wicked Nero was on the throne of Rome when Paul wrote these words to Timothy urging prayer for those in authority.

Christian lips are to breathe prayers for the cruel and infamous rulers in state as well as for the righteous and the benign governors and princes. Prayer is to be as far-reaching as the race, for all men." Humanity is to burden our hearts as we pray, and all men are to engage our thoughts in approaching a throne of grace. In our praying hours, all men must have a place. The wants and woes of the entire race are to broaden and make tender our sympathies, and inflame our petitions. No little man can pray. No man with narrow views of God, of his plan to save men, and of the universal needs of all men, can pray effectually. It takes a broadminded man, who understands God and his purposes in the atonement, to pray well. No cynic can pray. Prayer is the divinest philanthropy, as well as giant-great-heartedness. Prayer comes from a big heart, filled with thoughts about all men and with sympathies for all men.

Prayer runs parallel with the will of God, "who will have all men to be saved and to come unto the knowledge of the truth."

Prayer reaches up to heaven, and brings heaven down to earth. Prayer has in its hands a double blessing. It rewards him who prays, and blesses him who is prayed for. It brings peace to warring passions and calms warring elements. Tranquility is the happy fruit of true praying. There is an inner calm which comes to him who prays, and an outer calm as well. Prayer creates "quiet and peaceable lives in all godliness and honesty."

Right praying not only makes life beautiful in peace, but redolent in righteousness and weighty in influence. Honesty, gravity, integrity, and weight in character are the natural and essential fruits of prayer.

It is this kind of worldwide, large-hearted, unselfish praying which pleases God well, and which is acceptable in his sight, because it cooperates with his will and runs in gracious streams to all men and to each man. It is this kind of praying which the man Christ Jesus did when on earth, and the same kind which he is now doing at his Father's right hand in heaven, as our mighty intercessor. He is the pattern of prayer. He is between God and man, the one mediator, who gave himself a ransom for all men, and for each man.

So it is that true prayer links itself to the will of God, and runs in streams of solicitude, and compassion, and intercession for all men. As Jesus Christ died for every one involved in the fall, so prayer girdles every one and gives itself for the benefit of every one. Like our one mediator between God and man, he who prays stands midway between God and man, with prayers, supplications, "and strong cryings and tears." Prayer holds in its grasp the movements of the race of man, and embraces the destinies of men for all eternity. The king and the beggar are both affected by it. It touches heaven and moves earth. Prayer holds earth to heaven and brings heaven in close contact with earth.

> Your guides and brethren bear
> Forever on your mind;
> Extend the arms of mighty prayer
> In grasping all mankind.

13

Prayer and Missions

MISSIONS mean the giving of the gospel to those of Adam's fallen race who have never heard of Christ and his atoning death. It means the giving to others the opportunity to hear of salvation through our Lord Jesus Christ, and allowing others to have a chance to receive, and accept the blessings of the gospel, as we have it in christianized lands. It means that those who enjoy the benefits of the gospel give these same religious advantages and gospel privileges to all of mankind. Prayer has a great deal to do with missions. Prayer is the hand-maid of missions. The success of all real missionary effort is dependent on prayer. The life and spirit of missions are the life and spirit of prayer. Both prayer and missions were born in the divine mind. Prayer and missions are bosom companions. Prayer creates and makes missions successful, while missions lean heavily on prayer. In the seventy-second Psalm, one which deals with the Messiah, it is stated that "prayer shall be made for him continually." Prayer would be made for his coming to save man, and prayer would be made for the success of the plan of salvation which he would come to set on foot.

The Spirit of Jesus Christ is the spirit of missions. Our Lord Jesus Christ was himself the first missionary. His promise and advent composed the first missionary movement. The missionary spirit is not simply a phase of the gospel, not a mere feature of the plan of salvation, but is its very spirit and life. The missionary movement is the church of Jesus Christ marching in militant array, with the design of possessing the whole world of mankind for Christ. Whoever is touched by the Spirit of God is fired by the missionary spirit. An anti-missionary Christian is a contradiction in terms. We might say that it would be impossible to be an anti-missionary Christian because of the impossibility for the divine and human forces to put men in such a state as not to align them with the missionary cause. Missionary impulse is the heartbeat of our Lord Jesus Christ, sending the vital forces of himself through the whole body of the church. The spiritual life of God's people rises or falls with the force of those heartbeats. When these life forces cease, then death ensues. So that anti-missionary churches are dead churches, just as anti-missionary Christians are dead Christians.

The craftiest wile of Satan, if he cannot prevent a great movement for God, is to debauch the movement. If he can put the movement first, and the spirit of the movement in the background, he has materialized and thoroughly debauched the movement. Mighty prayer only will save the movement from being materialized, and keep the spirit of the movement strong and controlling.

The key of all missionary success is prayer. That key is in the hands of the home churches. The trophies won by our Lord in heathen lands will be won by praying missionaries, not by professional workers in foreign lands. More especially will this success be won by saintly praying in the churches at home. The home church on her knees fasting and praying, is the great base of spiritual supplies, the sinews of war, and the pledge of victory in this dire and final conflict. Financial resources are not the real sinews of war in this fight. Machinery in itself carries no power to break down heathen walls, open effectual doors and win heathen hearts to Christ. Prayer alone can do the deed.

Aaron and Hur did not more surely give victory to Israel through Moses, than a praying church through Jesus Christ will give victory on every battlefield in heathen lands. It is as true in foreign fields as it is in home lands. The praying church wins the contest. The home church has done but a paltry thing when she has furnished the money to establish missions and support her missionaries. Money is important, but money without prayer is powerless in the face of the darkness, the wretchedness and the sin in unchristianized lands. Prayerless giving breeds barrenness and death. Poor praying at home is the solution of poor results in the foreign field. Prayerless giving is the secret of all crises in the missionary movements of the day, and is the occasion of the accumulation of debts in missionary boards.

It is all right to urge men to give of their means to the missionary cause. But it is much more important to urge them to give their prayers to the movement. Foreign missions need, today, more the power of prayer than the power of money. Prayer can make even poverty in the missionary cause move on amidst difficulties and hindrances. Much money without prayer is helpless and powerless in the face of the utter darkness and sin and wretchedness on the foreign field.

This is peculiarly a missionary age. Protestant Christianity is stirred as it never was before in the line of aggression in pagan lands. The missionary movement has taken on proportions that awaken hope, kindle enthusiasm, and which demand the attention, if not the interest, of the coldest and the most lifeless. Nearly every church has caught the contagion, and the sails of their proposed missionary movements are spread wide to catch the favoring breezes. Herein is the danger just now, that the missionary movement will go ahead of the missionary spirit. This has always been the peril of the church, losing the substance in the shade, losing the spirit in the outward shell, and contenting itself in the mere parade of the movement, putting the force of effort in the movement and not in the spirit.

The magnificence of this movement may not only blind us to the spirit of it, but the spirit which should give life and shape to the movement may be lost in the wealth of the movement as the ship, borne by favoring winds, may be lost when these winds swell to a storm.

Not a few of us have heard many eloquent and earnest speeches stressing the imperative need of money for missions where we have heard only one stressing the imperative need of prayer. All our plans and devices drive to the one end of raising money, not to quicken faith and promote prayer. The common idea among church leaders is that if we get the money, prayer will come as a matter of course. The very reverse is the truth. If we get the church at the business of praying, and thus secure the spirit of missions, money will more than likely come as a matter of course. Spiritual agencies and spiritual forces never come as a matter of course. Spiritual duties and spiritual factors, left to the "matter of course" law, will surely fall out and die. Only the things which are stressed live and rule in the spiritual realm. They who give, will not necessarily pray. Many in our churches are liberal givers who are noted for their prayerlessness. One of the evils of the present-day missionary movement lies just there. Giving is entirely removed from prayer. Prayer receives scant attention, while giving stands out prominently. They who truly pray will be moved to give. Praying creates the giving spirit. The praying ones will give liberally and self-denyingly. He who enters his closet to God, will also open his purse to God. But perfunctory, grudging, assessment-giving kills the very spirit of prayer. Emphasizing the material to the neglect of the spiritual, by an inexorable law retires and discounts the spiritual.

It is truly wonderful how great a part money plays in the modern religious movements, and how little prayer plays in them. In striking contrast with that statement, it is marvelous how little a part money played in primitive Christianity as a factor in spreading the gospel, and how wonderful a part prayer played in it.

The grace of giving is nowhere cultured to a richer growth than in the closet. If all our missionary boards and secretaryships were turned into praying bands, until the agony of real prayer and travail with Christ for a perishing world came on them, real estate, bank stocks, United States bonds would be in the market for the spreading of Christ's gospel among men. If the spirit of prayer prevailed, missionary boards whose individual members are worth millions, would not be staggering under a load of debt and great churches would not have a yearly deficit and a yearly grumbling, grudging, and pressure to pay a beggarly assessment to support a mere handful of missionaries, with the additional humiliation of debating the question of recalling some of them. The ongoing of Christ's kingdom is locked up in the closet of prayer by Christ himself, and not in the contribution box.

The prophet Isaiah, looking down the centuries with the vision of a seer, thus expresses his purpose to continue in prayer and give God no rest till Christ's kingdom be established among men:

For Zion's sake will I not hold my peace, and for Jerusalem's sake I will not rest till the righteousness thereof goeth forth as brightness, and the salvation thereof as a lamp that burneth.

Then, foretelling the final success of the Christian church, he thus speaks:

And the Gentiles shall see thy righteousness, and all kings thy glory, and thou shalt be called by a new name, which the mouth of the Lord shall name.

Then the Lord, himself, by the mouth of this evangelical prophet, declares as follows:

I have set watchmen upon thy walls, O Jerusalem, which shall never hold their peace, day nor night. Ye that make mention of the Lord, keep not silence. And give him no rest till he establish and till he make Jerusalem a praise in the earth.

In the margin of our Bible, it reads, "Ye that are the Lord's remembrances." The idea is, that these praying ones are those who are the Lord's remembrances, those who remind him of what he has promised, and who give him no rest till God's church is established in the earth.

And one of the leading petitions in the Lord's Prayer deals with this same question of the establishing of God's kingdom and the progress of the gospel in the short, pointed petition, "Thy kingdom come," with the added words, "Thy will be done on earth as it is done in heaven."

The missionary movement in the apostolic church was born in an atmosphere of fasting and prayer. The very movement looking to offering the blessings of the Christian church to the Gentiles was on the housetop on the occasion when Peter went up there to pray, and God showed him his divine purpose to extend the privileges of the gospel to the Gentiles, and to break down the middle wall of partition between Jew and Gentile.

But more specifically Paul and Barnabas were definitely called and set apart to the missionary field at Antioch when the church there had fasted and prayed. It was then the Holy Spirit answered from heaven: "Separate me Barnabas and Saul for the work whereunto I have called them."

Please note this was not the call to the ministry of Paul and Barnabas, but more particularly their definite call to the foreign field. Paul had been called to the ministry years before this, even at his conversion. This was a subsequent call to a work born of special and continued prayer in the church at Antioch. God calls men not only to the ministry but to be missionaries. Missionary work is God's work. And it is the God-called men who are to do it. These are the kind of missionaries which have wrought well and successfully in the foreign field in the past, and the same kind will do the work in the future, or it will not be done.

It is praying missionaries who are needed for the work, and it is a praying church who sends them out, which are prophecies of the success which is promised. The sort of religion to be exported by missionaries is of the praying sort. The religion to which the heathen world is to be converted is a religion of prayer, and a religion of prayer to the true God. The heathen world already prays to its idols and false gods. But they are to be taught by praying missionaries, sent out by a praying church, to cast away their idols and to begin to call upon the name of the Lord Jesus Christ. No prayerless church can transport to heathen lands a praying religion. No prayerless missionary can bring heathen idolaters who know not our God to their knees in true prayer until he becomes preeminently a man of prayer. As it takes praying men at home to do God's work, none the less does it take praying missionaries to bring those who sit in darkness to the light.

The most noted and most successful missionaries have been preeminently men of prayer. David Livingstone, William Taylor, Adoniram Judson, Henry Martyn, and Hudson Taylor, with many more, form a band of illustrious praying men whose impress and influence still abide where they labored. No prayerless man is wanted for this job. Above everything else, the primary qualification for every missionary is prayer. Let him be, above everything else, a man of prayer. And when the crowning day comes, and the records are made up and read at the great judgment day, then it will appear how well praying men wrought in the hard fields of heathendom, and how much was due to them in laying the foundations of Christianity in those fields.

The one only condition which is to give worldwide power to this gospel is prayer, and the spread of this gospel will depend on prayer. The energy which was to give it marvelous momentum and conquering power over all its malignant and powerful foes is the energy of prayer.

The fortunes of the kingdom of Jesus Christ are not made by the feebleness of its foes. They are strong and bitter and have ever been strong, and ever will be. But mighty prayer—this is the one great spiritual force which will enable the Lord Jesus Christ to enter into full possession of his kingdom, and secure for him the heathen as his inheritance, and the uttermost part of the earth for his possession.

It is prayer which will enable him to break his foes with a rod of iron, that will make these foes tremble in their pride and power, who are but frail potter's vessels, to be broken in pieces by one stroke of his hand. A person who can pray is the mightiest instrument Christ has in this world. A praying church is stronger than all the gates of hell.

God's decree for the glory of his Son's kingdom is dependent on prayer for its fulfillment: "Ask of me, and I will give thee the heathen for thy inheritance, and the uttermost part of the earth for thy possession." God the Father gives nothing to his Son except through prayer. And the reason why the church has not received more in the missionary work in which it is engaged is the lack of prayer. "Ye have not, because ye ask not."

Every dispensation foreshadowing the coming of Christ when the world has been evangelized, at the end of time, rests upon these constitutional provisions, God's decree, his promises and prayer. However far away that day of victory by distance or time, or remoteness of shadowy type, prayer is the essential condition on which the dispensation becomes strong, typical and representative. From Abraham, the first of the nation of the Israelites, the friend of God, down to this dispensation of the Holy Spirit, this has been true.

> The nations call! from sea to sea
> Extends the thrilling cry,
> Come over, Christians, if there be,
> And help us, ere we die.
>
> Our hearts, O Lord, the summons feel;
> Let hand with heart combine,
> And answer to the world's appeal,
> By giving that is thine.

Our Lord's plan for securing workers in the foreign missionary field is the same plan he set on foot for obtaining preachers. It is by the process of praying. It is the prayer plan as distinguished from all manmade plans. These mission workers are to be "sent men." God must send them. They are God-called, divinely moved to this great work. They are inwardly moved to enter the harvest fields of the world and gather sheaves for the heavenly garners. Men do not choose to be missionaries any more than they choose to be preachers. God sends out laborers in his harvest fields in answer to the prayers of his church. Here is the divine plan as set forth by our Lord:

> But when he saw the multitudes, he was moved with compassion on them, because they fainted, and were as sheep having no shepherd. Then saith he unto his disciples, The harvest truly is plenteous, but the laborers are few. Pray ye, therefore, the Lord of the harvest that he will send forth laborers into his harvest.

It is the business of the home church to do the praying. It is the Lord's business to call and send forth the laborers. The Lord does not do the praying. The church does not do the calling. And just as our Lord's compassions were aroused by the sight of multitudes, weary, hungry, and scattered, exposed to evils, as sheep having no shepherd, so whenever the church has eyes to see the vast multitudes of earth's inhabitants, descendants of Adam, weary in soul, living in darkness, and wretched and sinful, will it be moved to compassion, and begin to pray the Lord of the harvest to send forth laborers into his harvest.

Missionaries, like ministers, are born of praying people. A praying church begets laborers in the harvest field of the world. The scarcity of missionaries argues a non-praying church. It is all right to send trained men to the foreign field, but first of all they must be God-sent. The sending is the fruit of prayer. As praying men are the occasion of sending them, so in turn the workers must be praying men. And the prime mission of these praying missionaries is to convert prayerless heathen men into praying men. Prayer is the proof of their calling, their divine credentials, and their work.

He who is not a praying man at home needs the one fitness to become a mission worker abroad. He who has not the spirit which moves him toward sinners at home, will hardly have a spirit of compassion for sinners abroad. Missionaries are not made of men who are failures at home. He who will be a man of prayer abroad must, before anything else, be a man of prayer in his home church. If he be not engaged in turning sinners away from their prayer- less ways at home, he will hardly succeed in turning away the heathen from their prayerless ways. In other words, it takes the same spiritual qualifications for being a home worker as it does for being a foreign worker.

God in his own way, in answer to the prayers of his church, calls men into his harvest fields. Sad will be the day when Missionary Boards and churches overlook that fundamental fact, and send out their own chosen men indepen- dent of God.

Is the harvest great? Are the laborers few? Then "pray ye the Lord of the harvest to send forth laborers into his harvest." Oh, that a great wave of prayer would sweep over the church asking God to send out a great army of laborers into the needy harvest fields of the earth! No danger of the Lord of the harvest sending out too many laborers and crowding the fields. He who calls will most certainly provide the means for supporting those whom he calls and sends forth.

The one great need in the modern missionary movement is intercessors. They were scarce in the days of Isaiah. This was his complaint:

> And he saw that there was no man, and wondered that there was no intercessor.

So today there is great need of intercessors, first, for the needy harvest fields of earth, born of a Christlike compassion for the thousands without the gospel; and then intercessors for laborers to be sent forth by God into the needy fields of earth.

The Possibilities of Prayer

1

The Ministry of Prayer

THE ministry of prayer has been the peculiar distinction of all of God's saints. This has been the secret of their power. The energy and the soul of their work has been the closet. The need of help outside of man being so great, man's natural inability to always judge kindly, justly, and truly, and to act the Golden Rule, so prayer is enjoined by Christ to enable man to act in all these things according to the divine will. By prayer, the ability is secured to feel the law of love, to speak according to the law of love, and to do everything in harmony with the law of love.

God can help us. God is a father. We need God's good things to help us to "do justly, to love mercy, and to walk humbly before God." We need divine aid to act brotherly, wisely, and nobly, and to judge truly, and charitably. God's help to do all these things in God's way is secured by prayer. "Ask, and ye shall receive; seek, and ye shall find; knock, and it shall be opened unto you."

In the marvelous output of Christian graces and duties, the result of giving ourselves wholly to God, recorded in the twelfth chapter of Romans, we have the words, "Continuing instant in prayer," preceded by "rejoicing in hope, patient in tribulation," followed by, "Distributing to the necessity of the saints, given to hospitality." Paul thus writes as if these rich and rare graces and unselfish duties, so sweet, bright, generous, and unselfish, had for their center and source the ability to pray.

This is the same word which is used of the prayer of the disciples which ushered in Pentecost with all of its rich and glorious blessings of the Holy Spirit. In Colossians, Paul presses the word into the service of prayer again, "Continue in prayer, and watch in the same with thanksgiving." The word in its background and root means strong, the ability to stay, and persevere steadfast, to hold fast and firm, to give constant attention to.

In Acts, chapter six, it is translated, "Give ourselves continually to prayer." There is in it constancy, courage, unfainting perseverance. It means giving such marked attention to, and such deep concern to a thing, as will make it conspicuous and controlling.

This is an advance in demand on "continue." Prayer is to be incessant, without intermission, earnestly, no check in desire, in spirit or in act, the spirit and the life always in the attitude of prayer. The knees may not always be

151

bent, the lips may not always be vocal with words of prayer, but the spirit is always in the act of prayer.

There ought to be no adjustment of life or spirit for closet hours. The closet spirit should sweetly rule and adjust all times and occasions. Our activities and work should be performed in the same spirit which makes our devotion and closet time sacred. "Without intermission, incessantly, earnestly," describes an opulence, and energy, and unabated and ceaseless strength and fullness of effort; like the full and exhaustless and spontaneous flow of an artesian stream. Touch the man of God who thus understands prayer, at any point, at any time, and a full current of prayer is seen flowing from him.

But all these untold benefits, of which the Holy Spirit is made to us the conveyor, go back in their disposition and results to prayer. Not on a little process and a mere performance of prayer is the coming of the Holy Spirit and of his great grace conditioned, but on prayer set on fire, by an unquenchable desire, with such a sense of need as cannot be denied, with a fixed determination which will not let go, and which will never faint till it wins the greatest good and gets the best and last blessing God has in store for us.

The first Christ, Jesus, our great high priest, forever blessed and adored be his name, was a gracious comforter, a faithful guide, a gifted teacher, a fearless advocate, a devoted friend, and an all-powerful intercessor. The other, "another comforter," the Holy Spirit, comes into all these blessed relations of fellowship, authority and aid, with all the tenderness, sweetness, fulness and efficiency of the first Christ.

Was the first Christ, the Christ of prayer? Did he offer prayers and supplications, with strong crying and tears unto God? Did he seek the silence, the solitude and the darkness that he might pray unheard and unwitnessed save by heaven, in his wrestling agony, for man with God? Does he ever live, enthroned above at the Father's right hand, there to pray for us?

Then how truly does the other Christ, the other comforter, the Holy Spirit, represent Jesus Christ as the Christ of prayer! This other Christ, the comforter, plants himself not in the waste of the mountain nor far into the night, but in the chill and the night of the human heart, to rouse it to the struggle, and to teach it the need and form of prayer. How the divine comforter, the spirit of truth, puts into the human heart the burden of earth's almighty need, and makes the human lips give voice to its mute and unutterable groanings!

What a mighty Christ of prayer is the Holy Spirit! How he quenches every flame in the heart but the flame of heavenly desire! How he quiets, like a weaned child, all the self-will, until in will, in brain, and in heart, and by mouth, we pray only as he prays. "Making intercession for the saints, according to the will of God."

2

Prayer and the Promises

WITHOUT the promise prayer is eccentric and baseless. Without prayer, the promise is dim, voiceless, shadowy, and impersonal. The promise makes prayer dauntless and irresistible. The apostle Peter declares that God has given to us "exceeding great and precious promises." "Precious" and "exceeding great" promises they are, and for this very cause we are to "add to our faith," and supply virtue. It is the addition which makes the promises current and beneficial to us. It is prayer which makes the promises weighty, precious and practical. The apostle Paul did not hesitate to declare that God's grace so richly promised was made operative and efficient by prayer. "Ye also helping together by prayer for us."

The promises of God are "exceeding great and precious," words which clearly indicate their great value and their broad reach, as grounds upon which to base our expectations in praying. Howsoever exceeding great and precious they are, their realization, the possibility and condition of that realization, are based on prayer. How glorious are these promises to the believing saints and to the whole church! How the brightness and bloom, the fruitage and cloudless midday glory of the future beam on us through the promises of God! Yet these promises never brought hope to bloom or fruit to a prayerless heart. Neither could these promises, were they a thousandfold increased in number and preciousness, bring millennium glory to a prayerless church. Prayer makes the promise rich, fruitful and a conscious reality.

Prayer as a spiritual energy, and illustrated in its enlarged and mighty working, makes way for and brings into practical realization the promises of God.

God's promises cover all things which pertain to life and godliness, which relate to body and soul, which have to do with time and eternity. These promises bless the present and stretch out in their benefactions to the illimitable and eternal future. Prayer holds these promises in keeping and in fruition. Promises are God's golden fruit to be plucked by the hand of prayer. Promises are God's incorruptible seed, to be sown and tilled by prayer.

Prayer and the promises are interdependent. The promise inspires and energizes prayer, but prayer locates the promise, and gives it realization and location. The promise is like the blessed rain falling in full showers, but prayer, like the pipes which transmit, preserve and direct the rain, localizes and precipitates these promises, until they become local and personal, and bless, refresh and fertilize. Prayer takes hold of the promise and conducts it to its marvelous ends, removes the obstacles, and makes a highway for the promise to its glorious fulfillment.

While God's promises are "exceeding great and precious," they are specific, clear and personal. How pointed and plain God's promise to Abraham:

> And the angel of the Lord called unto Abraham out of heaven the second time, And said, "By myself have I sworn, saith the Lord, for because thou hast done this thing, and hast not withheld thy son, thine only son; That in blessing I will bless thee, and in multiplying I will multiply thy seed as the stars of heaven, and as the sand which is upon the seashore; and thy seed shall possess the gate of his enemies; And in thy seed shall all the nations of the earth be blessed; because thou hast obeyed my voice."

But Rebekah through whom the promise is to flow is childless. Her barren womb forms an invincible obstacle to the fulfillment of God's promise. But in the course of time children are born to her.

Isaac becomes a man of prayer through whom the promise is to be realized, and so we read:

> And Isaac entreated the Lord for his wife, because she was barren, and the Lord was entreated for him, and Rebekah his wife conceived.

Isaac's praying opened the way for the fulfillment of God's promise, and carried it on to its marvelous fulfillment, and made the promise effectual in bringing forth marvelous results.

God spoke to Jacob and made definite promises to him:

> Return unto the land of thy fathers, and to thy kindred, and I will be with thee.

Jacob promptly moves out on the promise, but Esau confronts him with his awakened vengeance and his murderous intention, more dreadful because of the long years, unappeased and waiting. Jacob throws himself directly on God's promise by a night of prayer, first in quietude and calmness, and then when the stillness, the loneliness and the darkness of the night are upon him, he makes the all-night wrestling prayer.

> With thee I mean all night to stay,
> And wrestle till the break of day.

God's being is involved, his promise is at stake, and much is involved in the issue. Esau's temper, his conduct and his character are involved. It is a notable occasion. Much depends upon it. Jacob pursues his case and presses his plea with great struggles and hard wrestling. It is the highest form of importunity. But the victory is gained at last. His name and nature are changed and he becomes a new and different man. Jacob himself is saved first of all. He is blessed in his life and soul. But more still is accomplished. Esau undergoes a radical change of mind. He who came forth with hate and revenge in his heart against his own brother, seeking Jacob's destruction, is strangely and wonderfully affected, and he is changed and his whole attitude toward his brother becomes radically different. And when the two brothers meet, love takes the place of fear and hate, and they vie with each other in showing true brotherly affection.

The promise of God is fulfilled. But it took all that night of importunate praying to do the deed. It took that fearful night of wrestling on Jacob's part to make the promise sure and cause it to bear fruit. Prayer wrought the marvelous deed. So prayer of the same kind will produce like results in this day. It was God's promise and Jacob's praying which crowned and crowded the results so wondrously.

"Go show thyself to Ahab and I will send rain on the earth," was God's command and promise to his servant Elijah after the sore famine had cursed the land. Many glorious results marked that day of heroic faith and dauntless courage on Elijah's part. The sublime issue with Israel had been successful, the fire had fallen, Israel had been reclaimed, the prophets of Baal had been killed, but there was no rain. The one thing, the only thing, which God had promised, had not been given. The day was declining, and the awestruck crowds were faint, and yet held by an invisible hand.

Elijah turns from Israel to God and from Baal to the one source of help for a final issue and a final victory. But seven times is the restless eagerness of the prophet stayed. Not till the seventh repeated time is his vigilance rewarded and the promise pressed to its final fulfillment. Elijah's fiery, relentless praying bore to its triumphant results the promise of God, and rain descended in full showers.

> Thy promise, Lord, is ever sure,
> And they that in thy house would dwell
> That happy station to secure,
> Must still in holiness excel.

Our prayers are too little and feeble to execute the purposes or to claim the promises of God with appropriating power. Marvelous purposes need marvelous praying to execute them. Miracle-making promises need miracle-making praying to realize them. Only divine praying can operate divine promises or carry out divine purposes. How great, how sublime, and how exalted are the promises God makes to his people! How eternal are the purposes of God! Why are we so impoverished in experience and so low in life when God's promises are so "exceeding great and precious"? Why do the eternal purposes of God move so tardily? Why are they so poorly executed? Our failure to appropriate the divine promises and rest our faith on them, and to pray believingly is the solution. "We have not because we ask not." We ask and receive not because we ask amiss.

Prayer is based on the purpose and promise of God. Prayer is submission to God. Prayer has no sigh of disloyalty against God's will. It may cry out against the bitterness and the dread weight of an hour of unutterable anguish: "If it be possible, let this cup pass from me." But it is surcharged with the sweetest and promptest submission. "Yet not my will, but thine be done."

But prayer in its usual uniform and deep current is conscious conformity to God's will, based upon the direct promise of God's Word, and under the illumination and application of the Holy Spirit. Nothing is surer than that the Word of God is the sure foundation of prayer. We pray just as we believe God's Word. Prayer is based directly and specifically upon God's revealed promises in Christ Jesus. It has no other ground upon which to base its plea. All else is shadowy, sandy, fickle. Not our feelings, not our merits, not our works, but God's promise is the basis of faith and the solid ground of prayer.

> Now I have found the ground wherein
> Sure my soul's anchor may remain;
> The wounds of Jesus—for my sin,
> Before the world's foundation slain.

The converse of this proposition is also true. God's promises are dependent and conditioned upon prayer to appropriate them and make them a conscious realization. The promises are inwrought in us, appropriated by us, and held in the arms of faith by prayer. Let it be noted that prayer gives the promises their efficiency, localizes and appropriates them, and utilizes them. Prayer puts the promises to practical and present uses. Prayer puts the promises as the seed in the fructifying soil. Promises, like the rain, are general. Prayer embodies, precipitates, and locates them for personal use. Prayer goes by faith into the great fruit orchard of God's exceeding great and precious promises, and with hand and heart picks the ripest and richest fruit. The promises, like electricity, may sparkle and dazzle and yet be impotent for good till these dynamic, life-giving currents are chained by prayer, and are made the mighty forces which move and bless.

3

Prayer and the Promises
(*Continued*)

THE great promises find their fulfillment along the lines of prayer. They inspire prayer, and through prayer the promises flow out to their full realization and bear their ripest fruit.

The magnificent and sanctifying promise in Ezekiel, thirty-sixth chapter, a promise finding its full, ripe, and richest fruit in the New Testament, is an illustration of how the promise waits on prayer:

> Then will I sprinkle clean water upon you, and ye shall be clean; from all your filthiness, and from all your idols will I cleanse you. A new heart also will I give you, and a new spirit will I put within you; and I will take away the stony heart out of your flesh, and I will give you a heart of flesh. And I will put my Spirit within you, and cause you to walk in my statutes, and ye shall keep my judgments and do them. And ye shall dwell in the land that I gave to your fathers; and ye shall be my people, and I will be your God.

And concerning this promise, and this work, God definitely says:

> I will yet for this be inquired of by the house of Israel, to do it for them.

The more truly men have prayed for these rich things, the more fully have they entered into this exceeding great and precious promise, for in its initial, and final results as well as in all of its processes, realized, it is entirely dependent on prayer.

> Give me a new, a perfect heart,
> From doubt, and fear, and sorrow free;
> The mind which was in Christ impart,
> And let my spirit cleave to thee.
>
> "O take this heart of stone away!
> Thy sway it doth not, cannot own;
> In me no longer let it stay;
> O take away this heart of stone!"

No new heart ever throbbed with its pulsations of divine life in one whose lips have never sought in prayer with contrite spirit, that precious boon of a perfect heart of love and cleanness. God never has put his Spirit into the realm of a human heart which had never invoked by ardent praying the coming and indwelling of the Holy Spirit. A prayerless spirit has no affinity for a clean heart. Prayer and a pure heart go hand in hand. Purity of heart follows praying, while prayer is the natural, spontaneous outflowing of a heart made clean by the blood of Jesus Christ.

In this connection let it be noted that God's promises are always personal and specific. They are not general, indefinite, vague. They do not have to do with multitudes and classes of people in a mass, but are directed to individuals. They deal with persons. Each believer can claim the promise as his own. God deals with each one personally. So that every saint can put the promises to the test. "Prove me now herewith, saith the Lord." No need of generalizing, nor of being lost in vagueness. The praying saint has the right to put his hand upon the promise and claim it as his own, one made especially to him, and one intended to embrace all his needs, present and future.

> Though troubles assail,
> And dangers affright,
> Though friends should all fail,
> And foes all unite,
>
> Yet one thing secures us,
> Whatever betide,
> The promise assures us,
> The Lord will provide.

Jeremiah once said, speaking of the captivity of Israel and of its ending, speaking for Almighty God: "After seventy years be accomplished at Babylon, I will visit you, and will perform my good word toward you, in causing you to return to this place."

But this strong and definite promise of God was accompanied by these words, coupling the promise with prayer: "Then shall ye call upon me, and ye shall go and pray unto me, and I will hearken unto you. And ye shall seek me and find me, when ye shall search for me with all your heart." This seems to indicate very clearly that the promise was dependent for its fulfillment on prayer.

In Daniel we have this record,

> I, Daniel, understood by books the number of the years whereof the word of the Lord came to Jeremiah, the prophet, that he would accomplish seventy years in the desolations of Jerusalem. And I set my face unto the Lord God to seek by prayer and supplications with fastings and sackcloth and ashes.

So Daniel, as the time of the captivity was expiring, set himself in mighty prayer in order that the promise should be fulfilled and the captivity be brought to an end. It was God's promise by Jeremiah and Daniel's praying which broke the chains of Babylonian captivity, set Israel free and brought God's ancient people back to their native land. The promise and prayer went together to carry out God's purpose and to execute his plans.

God had promised through his prophets that the coming Messiah should have a forerunner. How many homes and wombs in Israel had longed for the coming to them of this great honor! Perchance Zachariah and Elizabeth were the only ones who were trying to realize by prayer this great dignity and blessing. At least we do know that the angel said to Zachariah, as he announced to him the coming of this great personage, "Thy prayer is heard." It was then that the word of the Lord as spoken by the prophets and the prayer of the old priest and his wife brought John the Baptist into the withered womb, and into the childless home of Zachariah and Elizabeth.

The promise given to Paul, engraven on his apostolic commission, as related by him after his arrest in Jerusalem, when he was making his defense before King Agrippa, was on this wise: "Delivering thee from the people and from the Gentiles, unto whom I now send thee." How did Paul make this promise efficient? How did he make the promise real? Here is the answer. In trouble by men, Jew and Gentile, pressed by them sorely, he writes to his brethren at Rome, with a pressing request for prayer:

> Now I beseech you, brethren, for the Lord Jesus Christ's sake, and for the love of the Spirit, that ye strive together with me in your prayers to God for me; That I may be delivered from them that do not believe in Judea.

Their prayers, united with his prayer, were to secure his deliverance and secure his safety, and were also to make the apostolic promise vital and cause it to be fully realized.

All is to be sanctified and realized by the Word of God and prayer. God's deep and wide river of promise will turn into a deadly influence or be lost in the abyss, if we do not utilize these promises by prayer, and receive their full and life-giving waters into our hearts.

The promise of the Holy Spirit to the disciples was in a very marked way the "promise of the Father," but it was realized only after many days of continued and importunate praying. The promise was clear and definite that the disciples should be endued with power from on high, but as a condition of receiving that power of the Holy Spirit, they were instructed to "tarry in the city of Jerusalem till ye be endued with power from on high." The fulfillment of the promise depended upon the "tarrying." The promise of this "enduement of power" was made sure by prayer. Prayer sealed it to glorious results. So we find it written, "These continued with one accord, in prayer and supplication, with the women." And it is significant that it was while they were praying, resting their expectations on the surety of the promise, that the Holy Spirit fell upon them and they were all "filled with the Holy Spirit." The promise and the prayer went hand in hand.

After Jesus Christ made this large and definite promise to his disciples, he ascended on high, and was seated at his Father's right hand of exaltation and power. Yet the promise given by him of sending the Holy Spirit was not fulfilled by his enthronement merely, nor by the promise only, nor by the fact that the prophet Joel had foretold with transported raptures of the bright day of the Spirit's coming. Neither was it that the Spirit's coming was the only hope of God's cause in this world. All these all-powerful and all-engaging reasons were not the immediate operative cause of the coming of the Holy Spirit. The solution is found in the attitude of the disciples. The answer is found in the fact that the disciples, with the women, spent several days in that upper room, in earnest, specific, continued prayer. It was prayer that brought to pass the famous day of Pentecost. And as it was then, so it can be now. Prayer can bring a Pentecost in this day if there be the same kind of praying, for the promise has not exhausted its power and vitality. The "promise of the Father" still holds good for the present-day disciples.

Prayer, mighty prayer, united, continued, earnest prayer, for nearly two weeks, brought the Holy Spirit to the church and to the world in pentecostal glory and power. And mighty continued and united prayer will do the same now.

> Lord God, the Holy Ghost,
> In this accepted hour;
> As on the day of Pentecost,
> Descend in all thy power.
>
> We meet with one accord,
> In our appointed place,
> And wait the promise of our Lord,
> The Spirit of all grace.

Nor must it be passed by that the promises of God to sinners of every kind and degree are equally sure and steadfast, and are made real and true by the earnest cries of all true penitents. It is just as true with the divine promises made to the unsaved when they repent and seek God, that they are realized in answer to the prayers of brokenhearted sinners, as it is true that the promises to believers are realized in answer to their prayers. The promise of pardon and peace was the basis of the prayers of Saul of Tarsus during those days of darkness and distress in the house of Judas, when the Lord told Ananias in order to allay his fears, "Behold he prayeth."

The promise of mercy and an abundant pardon is tied up with seeking God and calling upon him by Isaiah:

Seek ye the Lord while he may be found, and call ye upon him while he is near. Let the wicked forsake his way and the unrighteous man his thoughts; and let him return unto the Lord, and he will have mercy, and to our God, for he will abundantly pardon.

The praying sinner receives mercy because his prayer is grounded on the promise of pardon made by him whose right it is to pardon guilty sinners. The penitent seeker after God obtains mercy because there is a definite promise of mercy to all who seek the Lord in repentance and faith. Prayer always brings forgiveness to the seeking soul. The abundant pardon is dependent upon the promise made real by the promise of God to the sinner.

While salvation is promised to him who believes, the believing sinner is always a praying sinner. God has no promise of pardon for a prayerless sinner just as he has no promise for the prayerless professor of religion. "Behold he prayeth" is not only the unfailing sign of sincerity and the evidence that the sinner is proceeding in the right way to find God, but it is also the unfailing prophecy of an abundant pardon. Get the sinner to praying according to the divine promise, and he then is near the kingdom of God. The very best sign of the returning prodigal is that he confesses his sins and begins to ask for the lowliest place in his father's house.

It is the divine promise of mercy, of forgiveness and of adoption which gives the poor sinner hope. This encourages him to pray. This moves him in distress to cry out, "Jesus, thou Son of David, have mercy upon me."

> Thy promise is my only plea,
> With this I venture nigh;
> Thou call'st the burdened soul to thee,
> And such, O Lord, am I.

How large are the promises made to the saint! How great the promises given to poor, hungry-hearted, lost sinners, ruined by the fall! And prayer has arms sufficient to encompass them all, and prove them. How great the encouragement to all souls, these promises of God! How firm the ground on which to rest our faith! How stimulating to prayer! What firm ground on which to base our pleas in praying!

> The Lord hath promised good to me,
> His word my hope secures;
> He will my shield and portion be
> As long as life endures.

4

Prayer—Its Possibilities

How vast are the possibilities of prayer! How wide is its reach! What great things are accomplished by this divinely appointed means of grace! It lays its hand on Almighty God and moves him to do what he would not otherwise do if prayer was not offered. It brings things to pass which would never otherwise occur. The story of prayer is the story of great achievements. Prayer is a wonderful power placed by Almighty God in the hands of his saints, which may be used to accomplish great purposes and to achieve unusual results. Prayer reaches to everything, takes in all things great and small which are promised by God to the children of men. The only limit to prayer are the promises of God and his ability to fulfill those promises. "Open thy mouth wide and I will fill it."

The records of prayer's achievements are encouraging to faith, cheering to the expectations of saints, and is an inspiration to all who would pray and test its value. Prayer is no mere untried theory. It is not some strange unique scheme, concocted in the brains of men, and set on foot by them, an invention which has never been tried nor put to the test. Prayer is a divine arrangement in the moral government of God, designed for the benefit of men and intended as a means for furthering the interests of his cause on earth, and carrying out his gracious purposes in redemption and providence. Prayer proves itself. It is susceptible of proving its virtue by those who pray. Prayer needs no proof other than its accomplishments. If any man will do his will, he shall know of the doctrine." If any man will know the virtue of prayer, if he will know what it will do, let him pray. Let him put prayer to the test.

What a breadth is given to prayer! What heights it reaches! It is the breathing of a soul inflamed for God, and inflamed for man. It goes as far as the gospel goes, and is as wide, compassionate, and prayerful as is that gospel.

How much of prayer do all these unpossessed, alienated provinces of earth demand to enlighten them, to impress them and to move them toward God and his Son, Jesus Christ? Had the professed disciples of Christ only have prayed in the past as they ought to have done, the centuries would not have found these provinces still bound in death, in sin, and in ignorance.

Alas! how the unbelief of men has limited the power of God to work through prayer! What limitations have disciples of Jesus Christ put upon prayer by their prayerlessness! How the church, with her neglect of prayer, has hedged about the gospel and shut up doors of access!

Prayer possibilities open doors for the entrance of the gospel: "Withal praying also for us that God would open to us a door of utterance." Prayer opened for the apostles doors of utterance, created opportunities and made openings to preach the gospel. The appeal by prayer was to God, because God was moved by prayer. God was thereby moved to do his own work in an enlarged way and by new ways. Prayer possibility gives not only great power, and opens doors to the gospel, but it gives facility as well to the gospel. Prayer makes the gospel to go fast and to move with glorious swiftness. A gospel projected by the mighty energies of prayer is neither slow, lazy nor dull. It moves with God's power, with God's radiance and with angelic swiftness.

"Brethren, pray for us that the word of the Lord may have free course and be glorified," is the request of the apostle Paul, whose faith reached to the possibilities of prayer for the preached Word. The gospel moves altogether too slowly, often timidly, idly, and with feeble steps. What will make this gospel go rapidly like a race runner? What will give this gospel divine radiance and glory, and cause it to move worthy of God and of Christ? The answer is at hand. Prayer, more prayer, better prayer will do the deed. This means of grace will give fast going, splendor, and divinity to the gospel.

The possibilities of prayer reach to all things. Whatever concerns man's highest welfare, and whatever has to do with God's plans and purposes concerning men on earth, is a subject for prayer. In "whatsoever ye shall ask," is embraced all that concerns us or the children of men and God. And whatever is left out of "whatsoever" is left out of prayer. Where will we draw the lines which leave out or which will limit the word "whatsoever"? Define it, and search out and publish the things which the word does not include. If "whatsoever" does not include all things, then add to it the word "anything." "If ye shall ask anything in my name, I will do it."

What riches of grace, what blessings, spiritual and temporal, what good for time and eternity, would have been ours had we learned the possibilities of prayer and our faith had taken in the wide range of the divine promises to us to answer prayer! What blessings on our times and what furtherance to God's cause had we but learned how to pray with large expectations! Who will rise up in this generation and teach the church this lesson? It is a child's lesson in simplicity, but who has learned it well enough to put prayer to the test? It is a great lesson in its matchless and universal good. The possibilities of prayer are unspeakable, but the lesson of prayer which realizes and measures up to these possibilities, who has learned?

In his discourse in John fifteen, our Lord seems to connect friendship for him with prayer, and his choosing of his disciples seemed to have been with a design that through prayer they should bear much fruit.

> Ye are my friends if ye do whatsoever I command you. Ye have not chosen me, but I have chosen you, and ordained you, that ye should go and bring forth fruit, and that your fruit should remain; that whatsoever ye shall ask the Father in my name, he may give it to you.

Here we have again the undefined and unlimited word, "whatsoever," as covering the rights and the things for which we are to pray in the possibilities of prayer.

We have still another declaration from Jesus:

> Verily, verily, I say unto you, Whatsoever ye shall ask the Father in my name, he will give it to you. Hitherto ye have asked nothing in my name; ask, and ye shall receive, that your joy may be full.

Here is a very definite exhortation from our Lord to largeness in praying. Here we are definitely urged by him to ask for large things, and announced with the dignity and solemnity indicated by the double amen, "Verily, Verily." Why these marvelous urgencies in this last recorded and vital conversation of our Lord with his disciples? The answer is that our Lord might prepare them for the new dispensation, in which prayer was to have such marvelous results, and in which prayer was to be the chief agency to conserve and make aggressive his gospel.

In our Lord's language to his disciples about choosing them that should bear fruit, he clearly teaches us that this matter of praying and fruit-bearing is not a petty business of our choice, or a secondary matter in relation to other matters, but that he has chosen us for this very business of praying. He had specially in mind our praying, and he has chosen us of his own divine selection, and he expects us to do this one thing of praying and to do it intelligently and well. For he before says that he had made us his friends, and had brought us into bosom confidence with him, and also into free and full conference with him. The main object of choosing us as his disciples and of friendship for him was that we might be the better fitted to bear the fruit of prayer.

Let us not forget that we are noting the possibilities of the true praying ones. "Anything" is the word of area and circumference. How far it reaches we may not know. How wide it spreads, our minds fail to discover. What is there which is not within its reach? Why does Jesus repeat and exhaust these words, all-inclusive and boundless words, if he does not desire to emphasize the unbounded magnificence and illimitable munificence of prayer? Why does he press men to pray, so that our very poverty might be enriched and our limitless inheritance by prayer be secured?

We affirm with absolute certainty that Almighty God answers prayer. The vast possibilities, and the urgent necessity of prayer lie in this stupendous fact that God hears and answers prayer. And God hears and answers all prayer. He hears and answers every prayer, where the true conditions of praying are met.

Either this is so or it is not. If not, then is there nothing in prayer. Then prayer is but the recitation of words, a mere verbal performance, an empty ceremony. Then prayer is an altogether useless exercise. But if what we have said is true, then are there vast possibilities in prayer. Then is it far reaching in its scope, and wide in its range. Then is it true that prayer can lay its hand upon Almighty God and move him to do great and wonderful things.

The benefits, the possibilities and the necessity of prayer are not merely subjective but are peculiarly objective in their character. Prayer aims at a definite object. Prayer has a direct design in view. Prayer always has something specific before the mind's eye. There may be some subjective benefits which accrue from praying, but this is altogether secondary and incidental. Prayer always drives directly at an object and seeks to secure a desired end. Prayer is asking, seeking and knocking at a door for something we have not, which we desire, and which God has promised to us.

Prayer is a direct address to God. "In everything let your requests be made known unto God." Prayer secures blessings, and makes men better because it reaches the ear of God. Prayer is only for the betterment of men when it has affected God and moved him to do something for men. Prayer affects men by affecting God. Prayer moves men because it moves God to move men. Prayer influences men by influencing God to influence them. Prayer moves the hand that moves the world.

> That power is prayer, which soars on high,
> Through Jesus to the throne;
> And moves the hand which moves the world,
> To bring salvation down.

The utmost possibilities of prayer have rarely been realized. The promises of God are so great to those who truly pray, when he puts himself so fully into the hands of the praying ones, that it almost staggers our faith and causes us to hesitate with astonishment. His promise to answer, and to do and to give "all things," "anything," "whatsoever," and "all things whatsoever," is so large, so great, so exceeding broad, that we stand back in amazement and give ourselves to questioning and doubt. We "stagger at the promises through unbelief." Really the answers of God to prayer have been pared down by us to our little faith, and have been brought down to the low level of our narrow notions about God's ability, liberality, and resources. Let us ever keep in mind and never for one moment allow ourselves to doubt the statement that God means what he says in all of his promises. God's promises are his own word. His veracity is at stake in them. To question them is to doubt his veracity. He cannot afford to prove faithless to his word. "In hope of eternal life, which God that cannot lie, promised before the world began." His promises are for plain people, and he means to do for all who pray just what he says he will do. "For he is faithful that hath promised."

Unfortunately we have failed to lay ourselves out in praying. We have limited the Holy One of Israel. The ability to pray can be secured by the grace and power of the Holy Spirit, but it demands so strenuous and high a character that it is a rare thing for a man or woman to be on "praying ground and on pleading terms with God." It is as true today as it was in the days of Elijah, that "the fervent, effectual prayer of a righteous man availeth much." How much such a prayer avails, who can tell?

The possibilities of prayer are the possibilities of faith. Prayer and faith are Siamese twins. One heart animates them both. Faith is always praying. Prayer is always believing. Faith must have a tongue by which it can speak. Prayer is the tongue of faith. Faith must receive. Prayer is the hand of faith stretched out to receive. Prayer must rise and soar. Faith must give prayer the wings to fly and soar. Prayer must have an audience with God. Faith opens the door, and access and audience are given. Prayer asks. Faith lays its hand on the thing asked for.

God's omnipotent power is the basis of omnipotent faith and omnipotent praying. "All things are possible to him that believeth," and "all things whatsoever" are given to him who prays. God's decree and death yield readily to Hezekiah's faith and prayer. When God's promise and man's praying are united by faith, then "nothing shall be impossible." Importunate prayer is so all-powerful and irresistible that it obtains promises, or wins where the prospect and the promise seem to be against it. In fact, the New Testament promise includes all things in heaven and in earth. God, by promise, puts all things he possesses into man's hands. Prayer and faith put man in possession of this boundless inheritance.

Prayer is not an indifferent or a small thing. It is not a sweet little privilege. It is a great prerogative, far-reaching in its effects. Failure to pray entails losses far beyond the person who neglects it. Prayer is not a mere episode of the Christian life. Rather the whole life is a preparation for and the result of prayer. In its condition, prayer is the sum of religion. Faith is but a channel of prayer. Faith gives it wings and swiftness. Prayer is the lungs through which holiness breathes. Prayer is not only the language of spiritual life, but also makes its very essence and forms its real character.

> O for a faith that will not shrink
> Though pressed by every foe;
> That will not tremble on the brink
> Of any earthly woe.
>
> Lord, give us such a faith as this,
> And then, whate'er may come,
> We'll taste e'en here, the hallowed bliss
> Of our eternal home.

5

Prayer—Its Possibilities

(Continued)

AFTER a comprehensive and cursory view of the possibilities of prayer, as mapped out in what has been said, it is important to descend to particulars, to Bible facts and principles in regard to this great subject. What are the possibilities of prayer as disclosed by divine revelation? The necessity of prayer and its being are coexistent with man. Nature, even before a clear and full revelation, cries out in prayer. Man is, therefore prayer is. God is, therefore prayer is. Prayer is born of the instincts, the needs and the cravings and the very being of man.

The prayer of Solomon at the dedication of the temple is the product of inspired wisdom and piety, and gives a lucid and powerful view of prayer in the wideness of its range, the minuteness of its details, and its abounding possibilities and its urgent necessity. How minute and exactly comprehending is this prayer! National and individual blessings are in it, and temporal and spiritual good is embraced by it. Individual sins, national calamities, sins, sickness, exile, famine, war, pestilence, mildew, drought, insects, damage to crops, whatever affects husbandry, enemies—whatsoever sickness, one's own sore, one's own guilt, one's own sin—one and all are in this prayer, and all are for prayer.

For all these evils prayer is the one universal remedy. Pure praying remedies all ills, cures all diseases, relieves all situations, however dire, calamitous, fearful, and despairing. Prayer to God, pure praying, relieves dire situations because God can relieve when no one else can. Nothing is too hard for God. No cause is hopeless which God undertakes. No case is mortal when Almighty God is the physician. No conditions are despairing which can deter or defy God.

Almighty God heard this prayer of Solomon, and committed himself to undertake, to relieve and to remedy if real praying be done, despite all adverse and inexorable conditions. He will always relieve, answer and bless if men will pray from the heart, and if they will give themselves to real, true praying.

This is the record of what God said to him after Solomon had finished his magnificent, illimitable and all-comprehending prayer:

And the Lord appeared to Solomon by night, and said to him, I have heard thy prayer, and have chosen this place to myself for a house of sacrifice. If I shut up heaven that there be no rain, or if I command the locusts that they devour the land, or if I send pestilence among the people; If my people which are called by my name, shall humble themselves and pray, and seek my face, and turn from their wicked ways, then will I hear from heaven, and will forgive their sin, and will heal their land; Now my eyes shall be open, and my ears attentive to the prayer that is made in this place. For now I have chosen and sanctified this house, that my name may be there forever."

God put no limitation to his ability to save through true praying. No hopeless conditions, no accumulation of difficulties, and no desperation in distance or circumstance can hinder the success of real prayer. The possibilities of prayer are linked to the infinite integrity and omnipotent power of God. There is nothing too hard for God to do. God is pledged that if we ask, we shall receive. God can withhold nothing from faith and prayer.

> The thing surpasses all my thought,
> But faithful is my Lord;
> Through unbelief I stagger not,
> For God hath spoke the word.
>
> Faith, mighty faith, the promise sees,
> And looks to that alone;
> Laughs at impossibilities,
> And cries, "It shall be done!"

The many statements of God's Word fully set forth the possibilities and far-reaching nature of prayer. How full of pathos! Call upon me in the day of trouble; I will deliver thee, and thou shalt glorify me." Again, read the cheering words: "He shall call upon me, and I will answer him; I will be with him in trouble; I will deliver him and honor him."

How diversified the range of trouble! How almost infinite its extent! How universal and dire its conditions! How despairing its waves! Yet the range of prayer is as great as trouble, is as universal as sorrow, as infinite as grief. And prayer can relieve all these evils which come to the children of men. There is no tear which prayer cannot wipe away or dry up. There is no depression of spirits which it cannot relieve and elevate. There is no despair which it cannot dispel.

"Call unto me, and I will answer thee, and show thee great things and difficult, which thou knowest not." How broad these words of the Lord, how great the promise, how cheering to faith! They really challenge the faith of the saint. Prayer always brings God to our relief to bless and to aid, and brings marvelous revelations of his power. What impossibilities are there with God? Name them. "Nothing," he says, "is impossible to the Lord." And all the possibilities in God are in prayer.

Samuel, under the judges of Israel, will fully illustrate the possibility and the necessity of prayer. He himself was the beneficiary of the greatness of faith and prayer in a mother who knew what praying meant. Hannah, his mother, was a woman of mark, in character and in piety, who was childless. That privation was a source of worry and weakness and grief. She sought God for relief, and prayed and poured out her soul before the Lord. She continued her praying, in fact she multiplied her praying, to such an extent that to old Eli she seemed to be intoxicated, almost beside herself in the intensity of her supplications. She was specific in her prayers. She wanted a child. For a man child she prayed.

And God was specific in his answer. A man child God gave her, a man indeed he became. He was the creation of prayer, and grew himself to a man of prayer. He was a mighty intercessor, especially in emergencies in the history of God's people. The epitome of his life and character is found in the statement, "Samuel cried unto the Lord for Israel, and the Lord heard him." The victory was complete, and the ebenezer was the memorial of the possibilities and necessity of prayer.

Again, at another time, Samuel called to the Lord, and thunder and rain came out of season in wheat harvest. Here are some statements concerning this mighty intercessor, who knew how to pray, and whom God always regarded when he prayed: "Samuel cried unto the Lord all night."

Says he at another time in speaking to the Lord's people, "Moreover, as for me, God forbid that I should sin against the Lord in ceasing to pray for you."

These great occasions show how this notable ruler of Israel made prayer a habit, and that this was a notable and conspicuous characteristic of his dispensation. Prayer was no strange exercise to Samuel. He was accustomed to it. He was in the habit of praying, knew the way to God, and received answers from God. Through Samuel and his praying God's cause was brought out of its low, depressed condition, and a great national revival began, of which David was one of its fruits.

Samuel was one of the notable men of the old dispensation who stood out prominently as one who had great influence with God in prayer. God could not deny Samuel anything he asked of God. Samuel's praying always affected God, and moved God to do what would not have otherwise been done had Samuel not prayed. Samuel stands out as a striking illustration of the possibilities of prayer. He shows conclusively the achievements of prayer.

Jacob is an illustration for all time of the commanding and conquering forces of prayer. God came to him as an antagonist. He grappled Jacob, and shook him as if he were in the embrace of a deadly foe. Jacob, the deceitful supplanter, the wily, unscrupulous trader, had no eyes to see God. His perverted principles, and his deliberate overreaching and wrongdoing had blinded his vision.

To reach God, to know God, and to conquer God, was the demand of this critical hour. Jacob was alone, and all night witnessed to the intensity of the struggle, its changing issues, and its veering fortunes, as well as the receding and advancing lines in the conflict. Here was the strength of weakness, the power of self-despair, the energy of perseverance, the elevation of humility, and the victory of surrender. Jacob's salvation issued from the forces which he massed in that all-night conflict.

He prayed and wept and importuned until the fiery hate of Esau's heart died and it was softened into love. A greater miracle was wrought on Jacob than on Esau. His name, his character, and his destiny were changed by that all-night praying. Here is the record of the results of that night's praying struggle: "As a prince hast thou power with God and with men, and hast prevailed." "By his strength he had power with God, yea, he had power over the angel and prevailed."

What forces lie in importunate prayer! What mighty results are gained by it in one night's struggle in praying! God is affected and changed in attitude, and two men are transformed in character and destiny.

6

Prayer—Its Possibilities
(Continued)

THE possibilities of prayer are seen in its results in temporal matters. Prayer reaches to everything which concerns man, whether it be his body, his mind, or his soul. Prayer embraces the very smallest things of life. Prayer takes in the wants of the body, food, raiment, business, finances, in fact everything which belongs to this life, as well as those things which have to do with the eternal interests of the soul. Its achievements are seen not only in the large things of earth, but more especially in what might be called the little things of life. It brings to pass not only large things, speaking after the manner of men, but also the small things.

Temporal matters are of a lower order than the spiritual, but they concern us greatly. Our temporal interests make up a great part of our lives. They are the main source of our cares and worries. They have much to do with our religion. We have bodies, with wants, pains, disabilities, and limitations. That which concerns our bodies necessarily engages our minds. These are subjects of prayer, and prayer takes in all of them, and large are the accomplishments of prayer in this realm of our being.

Our temporal matters have much to do with our health and happiness. They form our relations. They are tests of honesty and belong to the sphere of justice and righteousness. Not to pray about temporal matters is to leave God out of the largest sphere of our being. He who cannot pray in everything, as we are charged to do by Paul in Philippians, fourth chapter, has never learned in any true sense the nature and worth of prayer. To leave business and time out of prayer is to leave religion and eternity out of it. He who does not pray about temporal matters cannot pray with confidence about spiritual matters. He who does not put God by prayer in his struggling toil for daily bread will never put him in his struggle for heaven. He who does not cover and supply the wants of the body by prayer will never cover and supply the wants of his soul. Both body and soul are dependent on God, and prayer is but the crying expression of that dependence.

The Syrophoenician woman prayed for the health things. In fact the Old Testament is but the record of God in dealing with his people through the divine appointment of prayer. Abraham prayed that Sodom might be saved from destruction. Abraham's servant prayed and received God's direction in choosing a wife for Isaac. Hannah prayed, and Samuel was given to her. Elijah prayed, and no rain came for three years. And he prayed again, and the clouds gave rain. Hezekiah was saved from a mortal sickness by his praying. Jacob's praying saved him from Esau's revenge. The old Bible is the history of prayer for temporal blessings as well as for spiritual blessings.

In the New Testament we have the same principles illustrated and enforced. Prayer in this section of God's Word covers the whole realm of good, both temporal and spiritual. Our Lord, in his universal prayer, the prayer for humanity, in every clime, in every age and for every condition, puts in it the petition, "Give us this day our daily bread." This embraces all necessary earthly good.

In the Sermon on the Mount, a whole paragraph is taken up by our Lord about food and raiment, where he is cautioning against undue care or anxiety for these things, and at the same time encouraging a faith which takes in and claims all these necessary bodily comforts and necessities. And this teaching stands in close connection with his teachings about prayer. Food and raiment are taught as subjects of prayer. Not for one moment is it even hinted that they are things beneath the notice of a great God, nor too material and earthly for such a spiritual exercise as prayer.

The Syrophoenician woman prayed for the health of her daughter. Peter prayed for Dorcas to be brought back to life. Paul prayed for the father of Publius on his way to Rome, when cast on the island by a shipwreck, and God healed the man who was sick with a fever. He urged the Christians at Rome to strive with him together in prayer that he might be delivered from bad men.

When Peter was put in prison by Herod, the church was instant in prayer that Peter might be delivered from the prison, and God honored the praying of these early Christians. John prayed that Gaius might "prosper and be in health, even as his soul prospered."

The divine directory in James, fifth chapter, says: "Is any among you afflicted, let him pray. Is any sick among you? Let him call for the elders of the church, and let them pray over him."

Paul, in writing to the Philippians, fourth chapter, says: "Be careful for nothing; but in everything, by prayer and supplication, with thanksgiving, let your requests be made known to God." This provides for all kinds of cares—business cares, home cares, body cares, and soul cares. All are to be brought to God by prayer, and at the mercy seat our minds and souls are to be unburdened of all that affects us or causes anxiety or uneasiness. These words of Paul stand in close connection with what he says about temporal matters specially: "But now I rejoiced in the Lord greatly that now at the last your care of me hath flourished—again: wherein ye were also careful, but ye lacked opportunity. Not that I speak in respect to want, for I have learned in whatsoever state I am, therewith to be content."

And Paul closes his epistle to these Christians with the words, which embrace all temporal needs as well as spiritual wants:

But my God shall supply all your need, according to his riches in glory, by Christ Jesus.

Unbelief in the doctrine that prayer covers all things which have to do with the body and business affairs, breeds undue anxiety about earth's affairs, causes unnecessary worry, and creates very unhappy states of mind. How much needless care we would save ourselves if we but believed in prayer as the means of relieving those cares, and would learn the happy art of casting all our cares in prayer upon God, "who careth for us!" Unbelief in God as one who is concerned about even the smallest affairs which affect our happiness and comfort limits the holy one of Israel, and makes our lives altogether devoid of real happiness and sweet contentment.

We have in the instance of the failure of the disciples to cast the devil out of the lunatic son, brought to them by his father, while Jesus was on the Mount of Transfiguration, a suggestive lesson of the union of faith, prayer, and fasting, and the failure to reach the possibilities and obligations of an occasion. The disciples ought to have cast the devil out of the boy. They had been sent out to do this very work, and had been empowered by their Lord and master to do it. And yet they signally failed. Christ reproved them with sharp upbraidings for not doing it. They had been sent out on this very specific mission. This one thing was specified by our Lord when he sent them out. Their failure brought shame and confusion on them, and discounted their Lord and master and his cause. They brought him into disrepute, and reflected very seriously upon the cause which they represented. Their faith to cast out the devil had signally failed, simply because it had not been nurtured by prayer and fasting. Failure to pray broke the ability of faith, and failure came because they had not the energy of a strong authoritative faith.

The promise reads, and we cannot too often refer to it, for it is the very basis of our faith and the ground on which we stand when we pray: "All things whatsoever ye ask in prayer, believing, ye shall receive." What enumeration table can tabulate, itemize, and aggregate "all things whatsoever"? The possibilities of prayer and faith go to the length of the endless chain, and cover the unmeasurable area.

In Hebrews eleven, the sacred penman, wearied with trying to specify the examples of faith, and to recite the wonderful exploits of faith, pauses a moment, and then cries out, giving us almost unheard of achievements of prayer and faith as exemplified by the saints of the olden times. Here is what he says:

And what shall I say more? For the time would fail me to tell of Gideon, of Barak, of Samson, of Jephthah, of David also; and Samuel, and the prophets; Who through faith, subdued kingdoms, wrought righteousness, obtained promises, stopped the mouths of lions; Quenched the violence of fire, escaped the edge of the sword, out of weakness were made strong, waxed valiant in fight, turned to flight the armies of the aliens; Women received their dead raised to life again, and others were tortured, not accepting deliverance; that they might obtain a better resurrection.

What an illustrious record is this! What marvelous accomplishments, wrought not by armies, or by man's superhuman strength, nor by magic, but all accomplished simply by men and women noted alone for their faith and prayer! Hand in hand with these records of faith's illimitable range are the illustrious records of prayer, for they are all one. Faith has never won a victory nor gained a crown where prayer was not the weapon of the victory, and where prayer did not jewel the crown. If "all things are possible to him that believeth," then all things are possible to him that prays.

> Depend on him; thou canst not fail;
> Make all thy wants and wishes known:
> Fear not; his merits must prevail;
> Ask but in faith, it shall be done.

7

Prayer—Its Wide Range

THE possibilities of prayer are gauged by faith in God's ability to do. Faith is the one prime condition by which God works. Faith is the one prime condition by which man prays. Faith draws on God to its full extent. Faith gives character to prayer. A feeble faith has always brought forth feeble praying. Vigorous faith creates vigorous praying. At the close of a parable, "And he spake a parable unto them to this end, that men always ought to pray, and not to faint," in which he stressed the necessity of vigorous praying, Christ asks this pointed question, "When the Son of Man cometh, shall he find faith on the earth?"

In the case of the lunatic child which the father brought first to the disciples, who could not cure him, and then to the Lord Jesus Christ, the father cried out with all the pathos of a declining faith and of a great sorrow, "If thou canst do anything for us, have compassion on us and help us." And Jesus said unto him, "If thou canst believe, all things are possible to him that believeth." The healing turned on the faith in the ability of Christ to heal the boy. The ability to do was in Christ essentially and eternally, but the doing of the thing turned on the ability of the faith. Great faith enables Christ to do great things.

We need a quickening faith in God's power. We have hedged God in till we have little faith in his power. We have conditioned the exercise of his power till we have a little God, and a little faith in a little God.

The only condition which restrains God's power, and which disables him to act, is unfaith. He is not limited in action nor restrained by the conditions which limit men.

The conditions of time, place, nearness, ability, and all others which could possibly be named, upon which the actions of men hinge, have no bearing on God. If men will look to God and cry to him with true prayer, he will hear and can deliver, no matter how dire may be their state, how remediless their conditions may be.

Strange how God has to school his people in his ability to do! He made a promise to Abraham and Sarah that Isaac would be born. Abraham was then nearly one hundred years old, and Sarah was barren by natural defect, and had passed into a barren age. She laughed at the preposterous thought of having a child. God asked, "Why did Sarah laugh? Is anything too hard for the Lord?" And God fulfilled his promise to these old people to the letter.

Moses hesitated to undertake God's purpose to liberate Israel from Egyptian bondage, because of his inability to talk well. God checks him at once by an inquiry:

> And Moses said unto the Lord, O my Lord, I am not eloquent, neither heretofore, nor since thou hast spoken unto thy servant; but I am slow of speech and of a slow tongue. And the Lord said unto him, Who hath made man's mouth? or who maketh the dumb, or deaf, or the seeing, or the blind? Have not I the Lord? Now, therefore, go, and I will be with thy mouth, and teach thee what thou shalt say.

When God said he would feed the children of Israel a whole month with meat, Moses questioned his ability to do it. The Lord said unto Moses, "Is the Lord's hand waxed short? Thou shalt see now whether my word shall come to pass unto thee or not."

Nothing is too hard for the Lord to do. As Paul declared, "He is able to do exceeding abundantly above all that we can ask or think." Prayer has to do with God, with his ability to do. The possibility of prayer is the measure of God's ability to do.

The "all things," the "all things whatsoever," and the "anything," are all covered by the ability of God. The urgent entreaty reads, "Ask whatsoever ye will," because God is able to do anything and all things that my desires may crave, and that he has promised. In God's ability to do, he goes far beyond man's ability to ask. Human thoughts, human words, human imaginations, human desires, and human needs cannot in any way measure God's ability to do.

Prayer in its legitimate possibilities goes out on God himself. Prayer goes out with faith not only in the promise of God, but also faith in God himself, and in God's ability to do. Prayer goes out not on the promise merely, but "obtains promises," and creates promises.

Elijah had the promise that God would send the rain, but no promise that he would send the fire. But by faith and prayer he obtained the fire, as well as the rain, but the fire came first.

Daniel had no specific promise that God would make known to him the dream of the king, but he and his associates joined in united prayer, and God revealed to Daniel the king's dream and the interpretation, and their lives were spared thereby.

Hezekiah had no promise that God would cure him of his desperate sickness which threatened his life. On the contrary, the word of the Lord came to him by the mouth of the prophet, that he should die. However, he prayed against this decree of Almighty God, with faith, and he succeeded in obtaining a reversal of God's word and lived.

God makes it marvelous when he says by the mouth of his prophet: "Thus saith the Lord, the Holy One of Israel and his Maker: Ask me of things to come, concerning my sons, and concerning the work of my hands, command ye me." And in this strong promise in which he commits himself into the hands of his praying people, he appeals in it to his great creative power: "I have created the earth and made man upon it. I, even my hands, have stretched out the heavens, and all their hosts have I commanded."

The majesty and power of God in making man and man's world, and constantly upholding all things, are ever kept before us as the basis of our faith in God, and as an assurance and urgency to prayer. Then God calls us away from what he himself has done, and turns our minds to himself personally. The infinite glory and power of his person are set before our contemplation: "Remember ye not the former things neither consider the things of old?" He declares that he will do a "new thing," that he does not have to repeat himself, that all he has done neither limits his doing nor the manner of his doing, and that if we have prayer and faith, he will so answer our prayers and so work for us, that his former work shall not be remembered nor come into mind. If men would pray as they ought to pray, the marvels of the past would be more than reproduced. The gospel would advance with a facility and power it has never known. Doors would be thrown open to the gospel, and the Word of God would have a conquering force rarely, if ever, known before.

If Christians prayed as Christians ought, with strong commanding faith, with earnestness and sincerity, men, God-called men, God-empowered men everywhere, would be all burning to go and spread the gospel worldwide. The Word of the Lord would run and be glorified as never known heretofore. The God-influenced men, the God-inspired men, the God-commissioned men, would go and kindle the flame of sacred fire for Christ, salvation and heaven, everywhere in all nations, and soon all people would hear the glad tidings of salvation and have an opportunity to receive Jesus Christ as their personal savior. Let us read another one of those large illimitable statements in God's Word, which are a direct challenge to prayer and faith:

He that spared not his own Son, but delivered him up for us all, how shall he not with him freely give us all things?

What a basis have we here for prayer and faith, illimitable, measureless in breadth, in depth, and in height! The promise to give us all things is backed up by the calling to our remembrance of the fact that God freely gave his only begotten Son for our redemption. God giving his Son is the assurance and guarantee that he will freely give all things to him who believes and prays.

What confidence have we in this divine statement for inspired asking! What holy boldness we have here for the largest asking! No commonplace tameness should restrain our largest asking. Large, larger, and largest asking magnifies grace and adds to God's glory. Feeble asking impoverishes the asker, and restrains God's purposes for the greatest good and obscures his glory.

How enthroned, magnificent, and royal the intercession of our Lord Jesus Christ at his Father's right hand in heaven! The benefits of his intercession flow to us through our intercessions. Our intercession ought to catch by contagion, and by necessity the inspiration and largeness of Christ's great work at his Father's right hand. His business and his life are to pray. Our business and our lives ought to be to pray, and to pray without ceasing.

Failure in our intercession affects the fruits of his intercession. Lazy, heartless, feeble, and indifferent praying by us mars and hinders the effects of Christ's praying.

8

Prayer—Facts and History

THE possibilities of prayer are established by the facts and the history of prayer. Facts are stubborn things. Facts are the true things. Theories may be but speculations. Opinions may be wholly at fault. But facts must be deferred to. They cannot be ignored. What are the possibilities of prayer judged by the facts? What is the history of prayer? What does it reveal to us? Prayer has a history, written in God's Word and recorded in the experiences and lives of God's saints. History is truth teaching by example. We may miss the truth by perverting the history, but the truth is in the facts of history.

> He spake with Abraham at the oak,
> He called Elisha from the plough;
> David he from the sheepfolds took,
> Thy day, thine hour of grace, is now.

God reveals the truth by the facts. God reveals himself by the facts of religious history. God teaches us his will by the facts and examples of Bible history. God's facts, God's Word, and God's history are all in perfect harmony, and have much of God in them all. God has ruled the world by prayer; and God still rules the world by the same divinely ordained means.

The possibilities of prayer cover not only individuals but also reach to cities and nations. They take in classes and peoples. The praying of Moses was the one thing which stood between the wrath of God against the Israelites and his declared purpose to destroy them and the execution of that divine purpose, and the Hebrew nation still survived. Notwithstanding Sodom was not spared, because ten righteous men could not be found inside its limits, yet the little city of Zoar was spared because Lot prayed for it as he fled from the storm of fire and brimstone which burned up Sodom. Nineveh was saved because the king and its people repented of their evil ways and gave themselves to prayer and fasting.

Paul in his remarkable prayer in Ephesians, chapter three, honors the illimitable possibilities of prayer and glorifies the ability of God to answer prayer. Closing that memorable prayer, so far-reaching in its petitions, and setting forth the very deepest religious experience, he declares that "God is able to do exceeding abundantly above all that we can ask or think." He makes prayer all-inclusive, comprehending all things, great and small. There is no time nor place which prayer does not cover and sanctify. All things in earth and in heaven, everything for time and for eternity, all are embraced in prayer. Nothing is too great and nothing is too small to be subject of prayer. Prayer reaches down to the least things of life and includes the greatest things which concern us.

> If pain afflict or wrongs oppress,
> If cares distract, or fears dismay;
> If guilt deject, or sin distress,
> In every case still watch and pray.

One of the most important, far-reaching, peace-giving, necessary, and practical prayer possibilities we have in Paul's words in Philippians, chapter four, dealing with prayer as a cure for undue care:

> Be careful for nothing; but in everything, by prayer and supplication, with thanksgiving, let your requests be made known unto God. And the peace of God which passeth all understanding shall keep your hearts and minds through Christ Jesus.

"Cares" are the epidemic evil of mankind. They are universal in their reach. They belong to man in his fallen condition. The predisposition to undue anxiety is the natural result of sin. Care comes in all shapes, at all times, and from all sources. It comes to all of every age and station. There are the cares of the home circle, from which there is no escape save in prayer. There are the cares of business, the cares of poverty, and the cares of riches. Ours is an anxious world, and ours is an anxious race. The caution of Paul is well addressed, "In nothing be anxious." This is the divine injunction, and that we might be able to live above anxiety and freed from undue care, "In everything, by prayer and supplication, let your requests be made known unto God." This is the divinely prescribed remedy for all anxious cares, for all worry, for all inward fretting.

The word careful means to be drawn in different directions, distracted, anxious, disturbed, annoyed in spirit. Jesus had warned against this very thing in the Sermon on the Mount, where he had earnestly urged his disciples, "Take no thought for the morrow," in things concerning the needs of the body. He was endeavoring to show them the true secret of a quiet mind, freed from anxiety and unnecessary care about food and raiment. Tomorrow's evils were not to be considered. He was simply teaching the same lesson found in Psalm 37:3, "Trust in the Lord, and do good; so shalt thou dwell in the land, and verily thou shalt be fed." In cautioning against the fears of tomorrow's prospective evils, and the material wants of the body, our Lord was teaching the great lesson of an implicit and childlike confidence in God. "Commit thy way unto the Lord: trust also in him, and he shall bring it to pass."

> "Day by day," the promise reads,
> Daily strength for daily needs
> Cast foreboding fears away;
> Take the manna of today.

Paul's direction is very specific, "Be careful for nothing." Be careful for not one thing. Be careful for not anything, for any condition, chance, or happening. Be troubled about not anything which creates one disturbing anxiety. Have a mind freed from all anxieties, all cares, all fretting, and all worries. Cares divide, distract, bewilder, and destroy unity, power, and quietness of mind. Cares are fatal to weak piety and are enfeebling to strong piety. What great need to guard against them and learn the one secret of their cure, even prayer!

What boundless possibilities there are in prayer to remedy the situation of mind of which Paul is speaking! Prayer over everything can quiet every distraction, hush every anxiety, and lift every care from care-enslaved lives and from care-bewildered hearts. The prayer specific is the perfect cure for all ills of this character which belong to anxieties, cares, and worries. Only prayer in everything can drive dull care away, relieve unnecessary heart burdens, and save from the besetting sin of worrying over things which we cannot help. Only prayer can bring into the heart and mind the "peace which passeth all understanding," and keep mind and heart at ease, free from burdensome care.

Oh, the needless heart burdens borne by fretting Christians! How few know the real secret of a happy Christian life, filled with perfect peace, hid from the storms and billows of a fretting careworn life! Prayer has a possibility of saving us from carefulness, the bane of human lives. Paul in writing to the Corinthians says, "I would have you without carefulness," and this is the will of God. Prayer has the ability to do this very thing. "Casting all your care on him, for he careth for you," is the way Peter puts it, while the psalmist says, "Fret not thyself in any wise to do evil." Oh, the blessedness of a heart at ease from all inward care, exempt from undue anxiety, in the enjoyment of the peace of God which passeth all understanding!

Paul's injunction which includes both God's promise and his purpose, and which immediately precedes his entreaty to be "careful for nothing," reads on this wise:

> Rejoice in the Lord always, and again I say, Rejoice. Let your moderation be made known to all men. The Lord is at hand.

In a world filled with cares of every kind, where temptation is the rule, where there are so many things to try us, how is it possible to rejoice always?

We look at the naked, dry command, and we accept it and reverence it as the Word of God, but no joy comes. How are we to let our moderation, our mildness, and our gentleness be universally and always known? We resolve to be benign and gentle. We remember the nearness of the Lord, but still we are hasty, quick, hard, and salty. We listen to the divine charge, "Be careful for nothing," yet still we are anxious, care-worn, care-eaten, and care-tossed. How can we fulfill the divine word, so sweet and so large in promise, so beautiful in the eye, and yet so far from being realized? How can we enter upon the rich patrimony of being true, honest, just, pure, and possess lovely things? The recipe is infallible, the remedy is universal, and the cure is unfailing. It is found in the words which we have so often herein referred to of Paul: "Be careful for nothing, but in everything, by prayer and supplication, with thanksgiving, let your requests be made known unto God."

This joyous, care-free, peaceful experience bringing the believer into a joyousness, living simply by faith day by day, is the will of God. Writing to the Thessalonians, Paul tells them: "Rejoice evermore; pray without ceasing, and in everything give thanks, for this is the will of God in Christ Jesus concerning you." So that not only is it God's will that we should find full deliverance from all care and undue anxiety, but he has also ordained prayer as the means by which we can reach that happy state of heart.

The Revised Version makes some changes in the passage of Paul, about which we have been speaking. The reading there is "In nothing be anxious," and "the peace of God shall guard your hearts and your minds." And Paul puts the antecedent in the air of prayer, which is "Rejoice in the Lord always." That is, be always glad in the Lord, and be happy with him. And that you may thus be happy, "Be careful for nothing." This rejoicing is the doorway for prayer, and its pathway, too. The sunshine and buoyancy of joy in the Lord are the strength and boldness of prayer, the means of its victory. "Moderation" makes the rainbow of prayer. The word means mildness, fairness, gentleness, sweet reasonableness. The Revised Version changes it to "forbearance," with the margin reading "gentleness." What rare ingredients and beautiful colorings! These are colorings and ingredients which make a strong and beautiful character and a wide and positive reputation. A rejoicing, gentle spirit, positive in reputation, is well fitted for prayer, rid of the distractions and unrest of care.

9

Prayer—Facts and History
(*Continued*)

It is to the closet Paul directs us to go. The unfailing remedy for all burdensome, distressing care is prayer. The place where the Lord is at hand is the closet of prayer. There he is always found, and there he is at hand to bless, to deliver and to help. The one place where the Lord's presence and power will be more fully realized than any other place is the closet of prayer.

Paul gives the various terms of prayer, supplication and giving of thanks as the complement of true praying. The soul must be in all of these spiritual exercises. There must be no half-hearted praying, no abridging its nature, and no abating its force, if we would be freed from this undue anxiety which causes friction and internal distress, and if we would receive the rich fruit of that peace which passeth all understanding. He who prays must be an earnest soul, abounding in spiritual attributes.

"In everything, let your requests be made known unto God," says Paul. Nothing is too great to be handled in prayer, or to be sought in prayer. Nothing is too small to be weighed in the secret councils of the closet, and nothing is too little for its final judgment. As care comes from every source, so prayer goes to every source. As there are no small things in prayer, so there are no small things with God. He who counts the hairs of our head, and who is not too lofty and high to notice the little sparrow which falls to the ground, is not too great and high to note everything which concerns the happiness, the needs and the safety of his children. Prayer brings God into what men are pleased to term the little affairs of life. The lives of people are made up of these small matters, and yet how often do great consequences come from small beginnings?

> There is no sorrow, Lord, too light.
> To bring in prayer to thee;
> There is no anxious care too slight
> To wake thy sympathy.
>
> There is no secret sigh we breathe,
> But meets thine ear divine,
> And every cross grows light beneath
> The shadow, Lord, of thine.

As everything by prayer is to be brought to the notice of Almighty God, so we are assured that whatever affects us concerns him. How comprehensive is this direction about prayer! "In everything by prayer." There is no distinction here between temporal and spiritual things. Such a distinction is against faith, wisdom and reverence. God rules everything in nature and in grace. Man is affected for time and eternity by things secular as well as by things spiritual. Man's salvation hangs on his business as well as on his prayers. A man's business hangs on his prayers just as it hangs on his diligence.

The chief hindrances to piety, the wiliest and the deadliest temptations of the devil, are in business, and lie alongside the things of time. The heaviest, the most confusing and the most stupefying cares lie beside secular and worldly matters. So in everything which comes to us and which concerns us, in everything which we want to come to us, and in everything which we do not want to come to us, prayer is to be made for all. Prayer blesses all things, brings all things, relieves all things, and prevents all things. Everything as well as every place and every hour is to be ordered by prayer. Prayer has in it the possibility to affect everything which affects us. Here are the vast possibilities of prayer.

How much is the bitter of life sweetened by prayer! How are the feeble made strong by prayer! Sickness flees before the health of prayer. Doubts, misgivings, and trembling fears retire before prayer. Wisdom, knowledge, holiness, and heaven are at the command of prayer. Nothing is outside of prayer. It has the power to gain all things in the provision of our Lord Jesus Christ. Paul covers all departments and sweeps the entire field of human concern, conditions, and happenings by saying, "In everything by prayer."

Supplications and thanksgiving are to be joined with prayer. It is not the dignity of worship, the gorgeousness of ceremonials, the magnificence of its ritual, nor the plainness of its sacraments, which avail. It is not simply the soul's hallowed and lowly abasement before God, neither the speechless awe, which benefits in this prayer service, but the intensity of supplication, the looking and the lifting of the soul in ardent plea to God for the things desired and for which request is made.

The radiance and gratitude and utterance of thanksgiving must be there. This is not simply the poetry of praise, but the deep-toned words and the prose of thanks. There must be hearty thanks, which remembers the past, sees God in it, and voices that recognition in sincere thanksgiving. The hidden depths within must have utterance. The lips must speak the music of the soul. A heart enthused of God, a heart illumined by his presence, a life guided by his right hand, must have something to say for God in gratitude. Such is to recognize God in the events of past life, to exalt God for his goodness, and to honor God who has honored it.

"Make known your requests unto God." The "requests" must be made known unto God. Silence is not prayer. Prayer is asking God for something which we have not, which we desire, and which he has promised to give in answer to prayer. Prayer is really verbal asking. Words are in prayer. Strong words and true words are found in prayer. Desires in prayer are put in words. The praying one is a pleader. He urges his prayer by arguments, promises, and needs.

Sometimes loud words are in prayer. The psalmist said, "Evening, morning and at noon will I pray, and cry aloud." The praying one wants something which he has not got. He wants something which God has in his possession, and which he can get by praying. He is beggared, bewildered, oppressed, and confused. He is before God in supplication, in prayer, and in thanksgiving. These are the attitudes, the incense, the paraphernalia, and the fashion of this hour, the court attendance of his soul before God.

"Requests" mean to ask for one's self. The man is in a strait. He needs something, and he needs it badly. Other help has failed. It means a plea for something to be given which has not been done. The request is for the giver—not alone his gifts but himself. The requests of the praying one are to be made known unto God. The requests are to be brought to the knowledge of God. It is then that cares fly away, anxieties disappear, worries depart, and the soul gets at ease. Then there steals into the heart "the peace of God that passeth all understanding."

> Peace! doubting heart, my God's I am,
> Who formed me man, forbids my fear;
> The Lord hath called me by my name;
> The Lord protects, forever near;
> His blood for me did once atone,
> And still he loves and guards his own.

In James, chapter five, we have another marvelous description of prayer and its possibilities. It has to do with sickness and health, sin and forgiveness, and rain and drought. Here we have James' directory for praying:

> Is any among you afflicted? Let him pray. Is any merry? Let him sing psalms. Is any sick among you? Let him call for the elders of the church, and let them pray over him, anointing him with oil in the name of the Lord. And the prayer of faith shall save the sick; and the Lord shall raise him up; and if he have committed sins, they shall be forgiven him. Confess your faults one to another, and pray one for another, that ye may be healed. The effectual, fervent prayer of a righteous man availeth much. Elijah was a man subject to like passions as we are, and he prayed earnestly that it might not rain, and it rained not on the earth by the space of three years and six months. And he prayed again, and the heaven gave rain, and the earth brought forth her fruit.

Here is prayer for one's own needs and intercessory prayer for others; prayer for physical needs and prayer for spiritual needs; prayer for drought and prayer for rain; prayer for temporal matters and prayer for spiritual things. How vast the reach of prayer! How wonderful under these words its possibilities!

Here is the remedy for affliction and depression of every sort, and here we find the remedy for sickness and for rain in the time of drought. Here is the way to obtain forgiveness of sins. A stroke of prayer paralyzes the energies of nature, stays its clouds, rain and dew, and blasts field and farm like the simoon. Prayer brings clouds, and rain and fertility to the famished and wasted earth.

The general statement, "The effectual, fervent prayer of a righteous man availeth much," is a statement of prayer as an energetic force. Two words are used. One signifies power in exercise, operative power, while the other is power as an endowment. Prayer is power and strength, a power and strength which influences God, and is most salutary, widespread, and marvelous in its gracious benefits to man. Prayer influences God. The ability of God to do for man is the measure of the possibility of prayer.

> Thou art coming to a king,
> Large petitions with thee bring;
> For his grace and power are such
> None can ever ask too much.

10

Answered Prayer

IT is answered prayer which brings praying out of the realm of dry, dead things, and makes praying a thing of life and power. It is the answer to prayer which brings things to pass, changes the natural trend of things, and orders all things according to the will of God. It is the answer to prayer which takes praying out of the regions of fanaticism, and saves it from being Utopian, or from being merely fanciful. It is the answer to prayer which makes praying a power for God and for man, and makes praying real and divine. Unanswered prayers are training schools for unbelief, an imposition and a nuisance, an impertinence to God and to man.

Answers to prayer are the only surety that we have prayed aright. What marvelous power there is in prayer! What untold miracles it works in this world! What untold benefits to men does it secure to those who pray! Why is it that the average prayer by the million goes a begging for an answer?

The millions of unanswered prayers are not to be solved by the mystery of God's will. We are not the sport of his sovereign power. He is not playing at "make-believe" in his marvelous promises to answer prayer. The whole explanation is found in our wrong praying. "We ask and receive not because we ask amiss." If all unanswered prayers were dumped into the ocean, they would come very near filling it. Child of God, can you pray? Are your prayers answered? If not, why not? Answered prayer is the proof of your real praying.

The efficacy of prayer from a Bible standpoint lies solely in the answer to prayer. The benefit of prayer has been well and popularly maximized by the saying, "It moves the arm which moves the universe." To get unquestioned answers to prayer is not only important as to the satisfying of our desires, but is also the evidence of our abiding in Christ. It becomes more important still. The mere act of praying is no test of our relation to God. The act of praying may be a real dead performance. It may be the routine of habit. But to pray and receive clear answers, not once or twice, but daily, this is the sure test, and is the gracious point of our vital connection with Jesus Christ.

Read our Lord's words in this connection:

> If ye abide in me, and my words abide in you, ye shall ask what ye will, and it shall be done unto you.

187

To God and to man, the answer to prayer is the all-important part of our praying. The answer to prayer, direct and unmistakable, is the evidence of God's being. It proves that God lives, that there is a God, an intelligent being, who is interested in his creatures, and who listens to them when they approach him in prayer. There is no proof so clear and demonstrative that God exists than prayer and its answer. This was Elijah's plea: "Hear me, O Lord, hear me, that this people may know that thou art the Lord God."

The answer to prayer is the part of prayer which glorifies God. Unanswered prayers are dumb oracles which leave the praying ones in darkness, doubt, and bewilderment, and which carry no conviction to the unbeliever. It is not the act or the attitude of praying which gives efficacy to prayer. It is not abject prostration of the body before God, the vehement or quiet utterance to God, the exquisite beauty and poetry of the diction of our prayers, which do the deed. It is not the marvelous array of argument and eloquence in praying which makes prayer effectual. Not one or all of these are the things which glorify God. It is the answer which brings glory to his name.

Elijah might have prayed on Carmel's heights till this good day with all the fire and energy of his soul, and if no answer had been given, no glory would have come to God. Peter might have shut himself up with Dorcas' dead body till he himself died on his knees, and if no answer had come, no glory to God nor good to man would have followed, but only doubt, blight, and dismay.

Answer to prayer is the convincing proof of our right relations to God. Jesus said at the grave of Lazarus:

> Father, I thank thee that thou hast heard me. And I knew that thou hearest me always, but because of the people that stand by I said it, that they may believe that thou hast sent me.

The answer of his prayer was the proof of his mission from God, as the answer to Elijah's prayer was made to the woman whose son he raised to life. She said, "Now by this I know that thou art a man of God." He is highest in the favor of God who has the readiest access and the greatest number of answers to prayer from Almighty God.

Prayer ascends to God by an invariable law, even by more than law, by the will, the promise, and the presence of a personal God. The answer comes back to earth by all the promise, the truth, the power, and the love of God.

Not to be concerned about the answer to prayer is not to pray. What a world of waste there is in praying. What myriads of prayers have been offered for which no answer is returned, no answer longed for, and no answer is expected! We have been nurturing a false faith and hiding the shame of our loss and inability to pray, by the false, comforting plea that God does not answer directly or objectively, but indirectly and subjectively. We have persuaded ourselves that by some kind of hocus pocus of which we are wholly unconscious in its process and its results, we have been made better.

Conscious that God has not answered us directly, we have solaced ourselves with the delusive unction that God has in some impalpable way, and with unknown results, given us something better. Or we have comforted and nurtured our spiritual sloth by saying that it is not God's will to give it to us. Faith teaches God's praying ones that it is God's will to answer prayer. God answers all prayers and every prayer of his true children who truly pray.

> Prayer makes the darkened cloud withdraw,
> Prayer climbs the ladder Jacob saw;
> Gives exercise to faith and love,
> Brings every blessing from above.

The emphasis in the Scriptures is always given to the answer to prayer. All things from God are given in answer to prayer. God himself, his presence, his gifts and his grace, one and all, are secured by prayer. The medium by which God communicates with men is prayer. The most real thing in prayer, its very essential end, is the answer it secures. The mere repetition of words in prayer, the counting of beads, the multiplying mere words of prayer, as works of supererogation, as if there was virtue in the number of prayers to avail, is a vain delusion, an empty thing, a useless service. Prayer looks directly to securing an answer. This is its design. It has no other end in view.

Communion with God of course is in prayer. There is sweet fellowship there with our God through his Holy Spirit. Enjoyment of God there is in praying, sweet, rich, and strong. The graces of the Spirit in the inner soul are nurtured by prayer, kept alive and promoted in their growth by this spiritual exercise. But not one nor all of these benefits of prayer have in them the essential end of prayer. The divinely appointed channel through which all good and all grace flows to our souls and bodies is prayer.

> Prayer is appointed to convey
> The blessings God designs to give.

Prayer is divinely ordained as the means by which all temporal and spiritual good are gained to us. Prayer is not an end in itself. It is not something done to be rested in, something we have done, about which we are to congratulate ourselves. It is a means to an end. It is something we do which brings us something in return, without which the praying is valueless. Prayer always aims at securing an answer.

We are rich, strong, good, and holy by answered prayer. It is not the mere performance, the attitude, nor the words of prayer, which bring benefit to us, but it is the answer sent direct from heaven. Conscious, real answers to prayer bring real good to us. This is not praying merely for self, or simply for selfish ends. The selfish character cannot exist when the prayer conditions are fulfilled.

It is by these answered prayers that human nature is enriched. The answered prayer brings us into constant and conscious communion with God, awakens and enlarges gratitude, and excites the melody and lofty inspiration of praise. Answered prayer is the mark of God in our praying. It is the exchange with heaven, and it establishes and realizes a relationship with the unseen. We give our prayers in exchange for the divine blessing. God accepts our prayers through the atoning blood and gives himself, his presence, and his grace in return.

All holy affections are affected by answered prayers. By the answers to prayer all holy principles are matured, and faith, love, and hope have their enrichment by answered prayer. The answer is found in all true praying. The answer is in prayer strongly as an aim, a desire expressed, and its expectation and realization give importunity and realization to prayer. It is the fact of the answer which makes the prayer, and which enters into its very being. To seek no answer to prayer takes the desire, the aim, and the heart out of prayer. It makes praying a dead thing, fit only for dumb idols. It is the answer which brings praying into Bible regions, and makes it a desire realized, a pursuit, an interest, that clothes it with flesh and blood, and makes it a prayer, throbbing with all the true life of prayer, affluent with all the paternal relations of giving and receiving, of asking and answering.

God holds all good in his own hands. That good comes to us through our Lord Jesus Christ because of his all atoning merits, by asking it in his name. The only and the sole command in which all the others of its class belong, is "Ask, seek, knock." And the one and sole promise is its counterpart, its necessary equivalent and results: "It shall be given—ye shall find—it shall be opened unto you."

God is so much involved in prayer and its hearing and answering, that all of his attributes and his whole being are centered in that great fact. It distinguishes him as peculiarly beneficent, wonderfully good, and powerfully attractive in his nature. "O thou that hearest prayer! To thee shall all flesh come."

>Faithful, O Lord, thy mercies are
>A rock that cannot move;
>A thousand promises declare
>Thy constancy of love.

Not only does the Word of God stand surety for the answer to prayer, but all the attributes of God conspire to the same end. God's veracity is at stake in the engagements to answer prayer. His wisdom, his truthfulness and his goodness are involved. God's infinite and inflexible rectitude is pledged to the great end of answering the prayers of those who call upon him in time of need. Justice and mercy blend into oneness to secure the answer to prayer. It is significant that the very justice of God comes into play and stands hard by

God's faithfulness in the strong promise God makes of the pardon of sins and of cleansing from sin's pollutions:

> If we confess our sins, he is faithful and just to forgive us our sins and to cleanse us from all unrighteousness.

God's kingly relation to man, with all of its authority, unites with the fatherly relation and with all of its tenderness to secure the answer to prayer.

Our Lord Jesus Christ is most fully committed to the answer of prayer. "Whatsoever ye shall ask in my name, that will I do, that the Father may be glorified in the Son." How well assured the answer to prayer is, when that answer is to glorify God the Father! And how eager Jesus Christ is to glorify his Father in heaven! So eager is he to answer prayer which always and everywhere brings glory to the Father, that no prayer offered in his name is denied or overlooked by him. Says our Lord Jesus Christ again, giving fresh assurance to our faith, "If ye shall ask anything in my name, I will do it." So says he once more, "Ask what ye will, and it shall be done unto you."

> Come, my soul, thy suit prepare,
> Jesus loves to answer prayer;
> He himself has bid thee pray,
> Therefore will not say thee nay.

11

Answered Prayer
(*Continued*)

God has committed himself to us by his Word in our praying. The Word of God is the basis and the inspiration and the heart of prayer. Jesus Christ stands as the illustration of God's Word, its illimitable good in promise as well as in realization. God takes nothing by halves. He gives nothing by halves. We can have the whole of him when he has the whole of us. His words of promise are so far-reaching, and so all-comprehending, that they seem to have deadened our comprehension and have paralyzed our praying. This appears when we consider those large words, when he almost exhausts human language in promises, as in "whatever," "anything," and in the all-inclusive "whatsoever," and "all things." These oft-repeated promises, so very great, seem to daze us, and instead of allowing them to move us to asking, testing, and receiving, we turn away full of wonder, but empty handed and with empty hearts.

We quote another passage from our Lord's teaching about prayer. By the most solemn verification, he declares as follows:

> And in that day ye shall ask me nothing; Verily, Verily, I say unto you: Whatsoever ye shall ask the Father in my name, he will give it to you. Hitherto ye have asked nothing in my name. Ask, and ye shall receive, that your joy may be full.

Twice in this passage he declares the answer, and pledging his father, "He will give it to you," and declaring with impressive and most suggestive emphasis, "Ask, and ye shall receive." So strong and so often did Jesus declare and repeat the answer as an inducement to pray, and as an inevitable result of prayer, the apostles held it as so fully and invincibly established, that prayer would be answered, they held it to be their main duty to urge and command men to pray. So firmly were they established as to the truth of the law of prayer as laid down by our Lord, that they were led to affirm that the answer to prayer was involved in and necessarily bound up with all right praying. God the Father and Jesus Christ, his Son, are both strongly committed by all the truth of their word and by the fidelity of their character, to answer prayer.

Not only do these and all the promises pledge Almighty God to answer prayer, but they assure us that the answer will be specific, and that the very thing for which we pray will be given.

Our Lord's invariable teaching was that we receive that for which we ask, and obtain that for which we seek, and have that door opened at which we knock. This is according to our heavenly Father's direction to us, and his giving to us for our asking. He will not disappoint us by not answering, neither will he deny us by giving us some other thing for which we have not asked, or by letting us find some other thing for which we have not sought, or by opening to us the wrong door, at which we were not knocking. If we ask bread, he will give us bread. If we ask an egg, he will give us an egg. If we ask a fish, he will give us a fish. Not something like bread, but bread itself will be given unto us. Not something like a fish, but a fish will be given. Not evil will be given us in answer to prayer, but good.

Earthly parents, though evil in nature, give for the asking, and answer to the crying of their children. The encouragement to prayer is transferred from our earthly father to our heavenly Father, from the evil to the good, to the supremely good; from the weak to the omnipotent, our heavenly Father, centering in himself all the highest conceptions of fatherhood, abler, readier, and much more than the best, and much more than the ablest earthly father. "How much more," who can tell? Much more than our earthly father, will he supply all our needs, give us all good things, and enable us to meet every difficult duty and fulfill every law, though hard to flesh and blood, but made easy under the full supply of our heavenly Father's beneficent and exhaustless help.

Here we have in symbol and as initial, more than an intimation of the necessity, not only of perseverance in prayer, but of the progressive stages of intentness and effort in the outlay of increasing spiritual force. Asking, seeking, and knocking. Here is an ascending scale from the mere words of asking, to a settled attitude of seeking, resulting in a determined, clamorous and vigorous direct effort of praying.

Just as God has commanded us to pray always, to pray everywhere, and to pray in everything, so he will answer always, everywhere and in everything.

God has plainly and with directness committed himself to answer prayer. If we fulfill the conditions of prayer, the answer is bound to come. The laws of nature are not so invariable and so inexorable as the promised answer to pray. The ordinances of nature might fail, but the ordinances of grace can never fail. There are no limitations, no adverse conditions, no weakness, no inability, which can or will hinder the answer to prayer. God's doing for us when we pray has no limitations, is not hedged about, by provisos in himself, or in the peculiar circumstances of any particular case. If we really pray, God masters and defies all things and is above all conditions.

God explicitly says, "Call unto me, and I will answer." There are no limitations, no hedges, no hindrances in the way of God fulfilling the promise. His word is at stake. His word is involved. God solemnly engages to answer prayer. Man is to look for the answer, be inspired by the expectation of the answer, and may with humble boldness demand the answer. God, who cannot lie, is bound to answer. He has voluntarily placed himself under obligation to answer the prayer of him who truly prays.

> To God your every want
> In instant prayer display;
> Pray always; pray, and never faint;
> Pray, without ceasing, pray.
>
> In fellowship, alone,
> To God with faith draw near;
> Approach his courts, beseech his throne,
> With all the power of prayer.

The prophets and the men of God of Old Testament times were unshaken in their faith in the absolute certainty of God fulfilling his promises to them. They rested in security on the word of God, and had no doubt whatever either as to the fidelity of God in answering prayer or of his willingness or ability. So much so that their history is marked by repeated asking and receiving at the hands of God.

The same is true of the early church. They received without question the doctrine their Lord and Master had so often affirmed that the answer to prayer was sure. The certainty of the answer to prayer was as fixed as God's Word was true. The Holy Spirit dispensation was ushered in by the disciples carrying this faith into practice. When Jesus told them to "Tarry at Jerusalem till they were endued with power from on high," they received it as a sure promise that if they obeyed the command, they would certainly receive the divine power. So in prayer for ten days they tarried in the upper room, and the promise was fulfilled. The answer came just as Jesus said.

So when Peter and John were arrested for healing the man who sat at the beautiful gate of the temple, after being threatened by the rulers in Jerusalem, they were released. "And being let go, they went to their own company," they went to those with whom they were in affinity, those of like minds, and not to men of the world. Still believing in prayer and its power, they gave themselves to prayer, the prayer itself being recorded in Acts, chapter four. They recited some things to the Lord, and "when they had prayed, the place was shaken where they were assembled together, and they were filled with the Holy Spirit, and they spake the word of God with boldness."

Here they were refilled for this special occasion with the Holy Spirit. The answer to prayer responded to their faith and prayer. The fullness of the Spirit always brings boldness. The cure for fear in the face of threatenings of the enemies of the Lord is being filled with the Spirit. This gives power to speak the word of the Lord with boldness. This gives courage and drives away fear.

12

Answered Prayer
(*Continued*)

WE put it to the front. We unfold it on a banner never to be lowered or folded, that God does hear and answer prayer. God has always heard and answered prayer. God will forever hear and answer prayer. He is the same yesterday, today and forever, ever blessed, ever to be adored. Amen. He changes not. As he has always answered prayer, so will he ever continue to do so.

To answer prayer is God's universal rule. It is his unchangeable and irrepealable law to answer prayer. It is his invariable, specific and inviolate promise to answer prayer. The few denials to prayer in the Scriptures are the exceptions to the general rule, suggestive and startling by their fewness, exception and emphasis.

The possibilities of prayer, then, lie in the great truth, illimitable in its broadness, fathomless in its depths, exhaustless in its fullness, that God answers every prayer from every true soul who truly prays.

God's Word does not say, "Call unto me, and you will thereby be trained into the happy art of knowing how to be denied. Ask, and you will learn sweet patience by getting nothing." Far from it. But it is definite, clear and positive: "Ask, and it shall be given unto you."

We have this case among many in the Old Testament:

> Jabez called on the God of Israel, saying, O that thou wouldst bless me indeed, and enlarge my coast, and that thy hand might be with me, and that thou wouldst keep me from evil, that it may not grieve me.

And God readily granted him the things which he had requested.

Hannah, distressed in soul because she was childless, and desiring a man child, repaired to the house of prayer, and prayed, and this is the record she makes of the direct answer she received: "For this child I prayed, and the Lord hath given me the petition which I asked of him."

God's promises and purposes go direct to the fact of giving for the asking. The answer to our prayers is the motive constantly presented in the Scriptures to encourage us to pray and to quicken us in this spiritual exercise. Take such strong, clear passages as these:

195

Call unto me, and I will answer thee. He shall call unto me, and I will answer. Ask, and it shall be given you. Seek, and ye shall find. Knock, and it shall be opened unto you.

This is Jesus Christ's law of prayer. He does not say, "Ask, and something shall be given you." Nor does he say, "Ask, and you will be trained into piety." But it is that when you ask, the very thing asked for will be given. Jesus does not say, "Knock, and some door will be opened." But the very door at which you are knocking will be opened. To make this doubly sure, Jesus Christ duplicates and reiterates the promise of the answer: "For every one that asketh, receiveth; and he that seeketh, findeth; and to him that knocketh, it shall be opened."

Answered prayer is the spring of love, and is the direct encouragement to pray. "I love the Lord because he hath heard my voice and my supplications. Because he hath inclined his ear unto me, therefore will I call upon him as long as I live."

The certainty of the father's giving is assured by the father's relation, and by the ability and goodness of the father. Earthly parents, frail, infirm, and limited in goodness and ability, give when the child asks and seeks. The parental heart responds most readily to the cry for bread. The hunger of the child touches and wins the father heart. So God, our heavenly Father, is as easily and strongly moved by our prayers as the earthly parent. "If ye being evil, know how to give good gifts unto your children, how much more shall your Father in heaven give good gifts unto them that ask him?" "Much more," just as much more does God's goodness, tenderness and ability exceed that of man's.

Just as the asking is specific, so also is the answer specific. The child does not ask for one thing and get another. He does not cry for bread, and get a stone. He does not ask for an egg, and receive a scorpion. He does not ask for a fish, and get a serpent. Christ demands specific asking. He responds to specific praying by specific giving.

To give the very thing prayed for, and not something else, is fundamental to Christ's law of praying. No prayer for the cure of blind eyes did he ever answer by curing deaf ears. The very thing prayed for is the very thing which he gives. The exceptions to this are confirmatory of this great law of prayer. He who asks for bread gets bread, and not a stone. If he asks for a fish, he receives a fish, and not a serpent. No cry is so pleading and so powerful as the child's cry for bread. The cravings of hunger, the appetite felt, and the need realized, all create and propel the crying of the child. Our prayers must be as earnest, as needy, and as hungry as the hungry child's cry for bread. Simple, artless, direct, and specific must be our praying, according to Christ's law of prayer and his teaching of God's fatherhood.

The illustration and enforcement of the law of prayer are found in the specific answers given to prayer. Gethsemane is the only seeming exception. The prayer of Jesus Christ in that awful hour of darkness and hell was conditioned on these words, "If it be possible, let this cup pass from me." But beyond these utterances of our Lord was the soul and life prayer of the willing, suffering divine victim, "Nevertheless not as I will, but as thou wilt." The prayer was answered, the angel came, strength was imparted, and the meek sufferer in silence drank the bitter cup.

Two cases of unanswered prayer are recorded in the Scriptures in addition to the Gethsemane prayer of our Lord. The first was that of David for the life of his baby child, but for good reasons to Almighty God the request was not granted. The second was that of Paul for the removal of the thorn in the flesh, which was denied. But we are constrained to believe these must have been notable as exceptions to God's rule, as illustrated in the history of prophet, priest, apostle and saint, as recorded in the divine Word. There must have been unrevealed reasons which moved God to veer from his settled and fixed rule to answer prayer by giving the specific thing prayed for.

Our Lord did not hold the Syrophoenician woman in the school of unanswered prayer to test and mature her faith, neither did he answer her prayer by healing or saving her husband. She asks for the healing of her daughter, and Christ healed the daughter. She received the very thing for which she asked the Lord Jesus Christ. It was in the school of answered prayer our Lord disciplined and perfected her faith, and it was by giving her a specific answer to her prayer. Her prayer centered on her daughter. She prayed for the one thing, the healing of her child. And the answer of our Lord centered likewise on the daughter.

We tread altogether too gingerly upon the great and precious promises of God, and too often we ignore them wholly. The promise is the ground on which faith stands in asking of God. This is the one basis of prayer. We limit God's ability. We measure God's ability and willingness to answer prayer by the standard of men. We limit the Holy One of Israel. How full of benefaction and remedy to suffering mankind are the promises as given us by James in his Epistle, fifth chapter! How personal and mediate do they make God in prayer! They are a direct challenge to our faith. They are encouraging to large expectations in all the requests we make of God. Prayer affects God in a direct manner, and has its aim and end in affecting him. Prayer takes hold of God, and induces him to do large things for us, whether personal or relative, temporal or spiritual, earthly or heavenly.

The great gap between Bible promises to prayer and the income from praying is almost unspeakably great, so much so that it is a prolific source of infidelity. It breeds unbelief in prayer as a great moral force, and begets doubt really as to the power of prayer. Christianity needs today, above all things else, men and women who can in prayer put God to the test and who can prove his promises. When this happy day for the world begins, it will be earth's brightest day, and will be heaven's dawning day on earth. These are the sort of men and women needed in this modern day in the church. It is not educated men who are needed for the times. It is not more money that is required. It is not more machinery, more organization, more ecclesiastical laws, but it is men and women who know how to pray, who can in prayer lay hold upon God and bring him down to earth, and move him to take hold of earth's affairs mightily and put life and power into the church and into all of its machinery.

The church and the world greatly need saints who can bridge this wide gap between the praying done and the small number of answers received. Saints are needed whose faith is bold enough and sufficiently far-reaching to put God to the test. The cry comes even now out of heaven to the people of the present-day church, as it sounded forth in the days of Malachi: "Prove me now herewith, saith the Lord of hosts." God is waiting to be put to the test by his people in prayer. He delights in being put to the test on his promises. It is his highest pleasure to answer prayer to prove the reliability of his promises. Nothing worthy of God nor of great value to men will be accomplished till this is done.

Our gospel belongs to the miraculous. It was projected on the miraculous plane. It cannot be maintained but by the supernatural. Take the supernatural out of our holy religion, and its life and power are gone, and it degenerates into a mere mode of morals. The miraculous is divine power. Prayer has in it this same power. Prayer brings this divine power into the ranks of men and puts it to work. Prayer brings into the affairs of earth a supernatural element. Our gospel when truly presented is the power of God. Never was the church more in need of those who can and will test Almighty God. Never did the church need more than now those who can raise up everywhere memorials of God's supernatural power, memorials of answers to prayer, memorials of promises fulfilled. These would do more to silence the enemy of souls, the foe of God and the adversary of the church than any modern scheme or present-day plan for the success of the gospel. Such memorials reared by praying people would dumbfound God's foes, strengthen weak saints, and would fill strong saints with triumphant rapture.

The most prolific source of infidelity, and that which maligns and hinders praying, and that which obscures the being and glory of God most effectually, is unanswered prayer. Better not to pray at all than to go through a dead form, which secures no answer, brings no glory to God, and supplies no good to man. Nothing so hardens the heart and nothing so blinds us to the unseen and the eternal, as this kind of prayerless praying.

13

Prayer Miracles

THE earthly career of our Lord Jesus Christ was no mere episode, a sort of interlude, in his eternal life. What he was and what he did on earth was neither abnormal nor divergent, but characteristic. What he was and what he did on earth is but the figure and the illustration of what he is and what he is doing in heaven. He is "the same yesterday and today, and forever." This statement is the divine summary of the eternal unity and changelessness of his character. His earthly life was made up largely of hearing and answering prayer. His heavenly life is devoted to the same divine business. Really the Old Testament is the record of God hearing and answering prayer. The whole Bible deals largely with this all important subject.

Christ's miracles are object lessons. They are living pictures. They talk to us. They have hands which take hold of us. Many valuable lessons do these miracles teach us. In their diversity, they refresh us. They show us the matchless power of Jesus Christ, and at the same time discover to us his marvelous compassion for suffering humanity. These miracles disclose to us his ability to endlessly diversify his operations. God's method in working with man is not the same in all cases. He does not administer his grace in rigid ruts. There is endless variety in his movements. There is marvelous diversity in his operations. He does not fashion his creations in the same mold. Just so our Lord is not circumscribed in his working nor trammeled by models. He works independently. He is his own architect. He furnishes his own patterns which have unlimited variety.

When we consider our Lord's miracles, we discover that quite a number were performed unconditionally. At least there were no conditions accompanying them so far as the divine record shows. At his own instance, without being solicited to do so, to glorify God and to manifest his own glory and power, this class of miracles was wrought. Many of his mighty works were performed at the moving of his compassion and at the call of suffering and need, as well as at the call of his power. But a number of them were performed by him in answer to prayer. Some were wrought in answer to the personal prayers of those who were afflicted. Others were performed in answer to the prayers of the friends of those who were afflicted. Those miracles wrought in answer to prayer are very instructive in the uses of prayer. In these conditional miracles, faith holds the primacy and prayer is faith's deputy. We have an illustration of the importance of faith as the condition on which the exercise of Christ's power was based, or the channel through which it flowed, in the incident of a visit he made to Nazareth with its results, or rather its lack of results. Here is the record of the case:

> And he could there do no mighty work, save that he laid his hands upon a few sick folk, and healed them. And he marvelled because of their unbelief.

Those people at Nazareth may have prayed our Lord to raise their dead, or open the eyes of the blind, or heal the lepers, but it was all in vain. The absence of faith, however much of performance may be seen, restrains the exercise of God's power, paralyzes the arm of Christ, and turns to death all signs of life. Unbelief is the one thing which seriously hinders Almighty God in doing mighty works. Matthew's record of this visit to Nazareth says, "And he did not any mighty works there because of their unbelief." Lack of faith ties the hands of Almighty God in his working among the children of men. Prayer to Christ must always be based, backed, and impregnated with faith.

The miracle of miracles in the earthly career of our Lord, the raising of Lazarus from the dead, was remarkable for its prayer accompaniment. It was really a prayer issue, something after the issue between the prophets of Baal and Elijah. It was not a prayer for help. It was one of thanksgiving and assured confidence. Let us read it:

> And Jesus lifted up his eyes and said, Father, I thank thee that thou hast heard me. And I know that thou hearest me always. But because of the people that stand by, I said it, that they may believe that thou hast sent me.

It was a prayer mainly for the benefit of those who were present, that they might know that God was with him because he had answered his prayers, and that faith in God might be radiated in their hearts.

Answered prayers are sometimes the most convincing and faith-creating forces. Unanswered prayers chill the atmosphere and freeze the soil of faith. If Christians knew how to pray so as to have answers to their prayers, evident, immediate, and demonstrative answers from God, faith would be more widely diffused, would become more general, would be more profound, and would be a much more mighty force in the world.

What a valuable lesson of faith and intercessory prayer does the miracle of the healing of the centurion's servant bring to us! The simplicity and strength of the faith of this Roman officer are remarkable, for he believed that it was not needful for our Lord to go directly to his house to have his request granted, "But speak the word only, and my servant shall be healed." And our Lord puts his mark upon this man's faith by saying, "Verily I say unto you, I have not found so great faith, no, not in Israel." This man's prayer was the expression of his strong faith, and such faith brought the answer promptly.

The same invaluable lesson we get from the prayer miracle of the case of the Syrophoenician woman who went to our Lord in behalf of her stricken daughter, making her daughter's case her own, by pleading, "Lord, help me." Here was importunity, holding on, pressing her case, refusing to let go or to be denied. A strong case it was of intercessory prayer and its benefits. Our Lord seemingly held her off for a while but at last yielded, and put his seal upon her strong faith: "O woman, great is thy faith! Be it unto thee even as thou wilt." What a lesson on praying for others and its large benefits!

Individual cases could be named, where the afflicted persons interceded for themselves, illustrations of wonderful things wrought by our Lord in answer to the cries of those who were afflicted. As we read the evangelists' record, the pages fairly glisten with records of our Lord's miracles wrought in answer to prayer, showing the wonderful things accomplished by the use of this divinely appointed means of grace.

If we turn back to Old Testament times, we have no lack of instances of prayer miracles. The saints of those days were well acquainted with the power of prayer to move God to do great things. Natural laws did not stand in the way of Almighty God when he was appealed to by his praying ones. What a marvelous record is that of Moses as those successive plagues were visited upon Egypt in the effort to make Pharaoh let the children of Israel go that they might serve God! As one after another of these plagues came, Pharaoh would beseech Moses, "Entreat the Lord your God that he may take away this death." And as the plagues themselves were miracles, prayer removed them as quickly as they were sent by Almighty God. The same hand which sent these destructive agencies upon Egypt was moved by the prayers of his servant Moses to remove these same plagues. And the removal of the plagues in answer to prayer was as remarkable a display of divine power as was the sending of the plagues in the first instance. The removal in answer to prayer would do as much to show God's being and his power as would the plagues themselves. They were miracles of prayer.

All down the line in Old Testament days we see these prayer miracles. God's praying servants had not the least doubt that prayer would work marvelous results and bring the supernatural into the affairs of earth. Miracles and prayer went hand in hand. They were companions. The one was the cause, the other was the effect. The one brought the other into existence. The miracle was the proof that God heard and answered prayer. The miracle was the divine demonstration that God, who was in heaven, interfered in earth's affairs, intervened to help men, and worked supernaturally if need be to accomplish his purposes in answer to prayer.

Passing to the days of the early church, we find the same divine record of prayer miracles. The sad news came to Peter that Dorcas was dead and he was wanted at Joppa. Promptly he made his way to that place. Peter put everybody out of the room, and then he kneeled down and prayed, and with faith said, "Tabitha, arise," and she opened her eyes and sat up. Knee work on the part of Peter did the work. Prayer brought things to pass and saved Dorcas for further work on earth.

Paul was on that noted journey to Rome under guard, and had been shipwrecked on an island. The chief man of the island was Publius, and his old father was critically ill of a bloody flux. Paul laid his hands on the old man, and prayed for him, and God came to the rescue and healed the sick man. Prayer brought the thing desired to pass. God interfered with the laws of nature, either suspending or setting them aside for a season, and answered the prayer of this praying servant of his. And the answer to prayer among those heathen people convinced them that a supernatural power was at work among them. In fact so true was this that they seemed to think a supernatural being had come among them.

After Herod killed James with the sword, Herod had Peter put in prison. The young church was greatly concerned, but they neither lost heart nor gave themselves over to needless fretting and worrying. They had learned before this from whence their help came. They had been schooled in the lesson of prayer. God had intervened before in the behalf of his servants and interfered when his cause was at stake. "Prayer was made without ceasing of the church unto God for him." An angel on swift wings comes to the rescue, and in a marvelous and supernatural way releases Peter and leaves the prison doors locked. Locks and prison doors and an unfriendly king cannot stand in the way of Almighty God when his people cry in prayer unto him. Miracles if need be will be wrought in their behalf to fulfill his promises and to carry forward his plans. After this order does the Word of God illustrate and enlarge and confirm the possibilities of prayer by what may be termed "Prayer miracles."

How quickly to our straits follow our enlargements! God wrought a wonderful work through Samson in enabling him with a crude instrument, the jawbone of an ass, to slay a thousand men, giving him a great deliverance. Shortly afterward Samson was abnormally thirsty, and he was unable to obtain any water. It seemed as if he would perish with thirst. God had saved him from the hands of the Philistines. Could he not as well save him from thirst? "So Samson cried unto the Lord, and God clave a hollow place that was in the jaw, and there came water thereout, and when he had drunk, his spirit came again and he revived." God could bring water out of the jawbone just as well as he could give victory by it to Samson. God could change that which had been death-dealing to his enemies and make it life-giving to his servant. God can and will work a miracle in answer to prayer to deliver his friends, sooner than he will work one to destroy his enemies. He does both, however, in answer to prayer.

All natural forces are under God's control. He did not create the world and put it under law, and then retire from it, to work out its own destiny, irrespective of the welfare of his intelligent creatures. Natural laws are simply God's laws, by which he governs and regulates all things in nature. Nature is nothing but God's servant. God is above nature, God is not the slave of nature. This being true, God can and will suspend the working of nature's laws, can hold them in abeyance by his almighty hand, can for the time being set them aside, to fulfill his higher purposes in redemption. It is no violation of nature's laws when, in answer to prayer, he who is above nature makes nature his servant, and causes nature to carry out his plans and purposes.

This is the explanation of that wonderful prayer miracle of Old Testament times, when Joshua, in the strength and power of the Lord God, commanded the sun and moon to stand still to give time to complete the victory over the enemies of Israel. Why should it be thought a thing incredible that the God of nature and of grace should interfere with his own natural laws for a short season in answer to prayer, and for the good of his cause? Is God tied hand and foot? Has he so circumscribed himself that he cannot operate the law of prayer? Is the law of nature superior to the law of prayer? Not by any means. He is the God of prayer as well as the God of nature. Both prayer and nature have God as their maker, their ruler and their executor. And prayer is God's servant, just as nature is his servant.

The prayer force in God's government is as strong as any other force, and all natural and other forces must give way before the force of prayer. Sun, moon and stars are under God's control in answer to prayer. Rain, sunshine and drought obey his will. "Fire and hail, snow and vapor, stormy wind fulfilling his word." Disease and health are governed by him. All, all things in heaven and earth, are absolutely under the control of him who made heaven and earth, and who governs all things according to his own will.

Prayer still works miracles among men and brings to pass great things. It is as true now as when James wrote his epistle, "The effectual fervent, prayer of a righteous man availeth much." And when the records of eternity are read out to an assembled world, then will it appear how much prayer has wrought in this world. Little is now seen of the fruits of prayer compared to all that it has accomplished and is accomplishing. At the judgment day, then will God disclose the things which were brought to pass in this world through the prayers of the saints. Many occurrences which are now taken as a matter of course will then be seen to have happened because of the Lord's praying ones.

The work of George Muller in Bristol, England, was a miracle of the nineteenth century. It will take the opening of the books at the great judgment day to disclose all he wrought through prayer. This godly man never asked anyone for money for running expenses at his orphanage where hundreds of fatherless and motherless children were cared for. His practice was always to ask God for just what was needed, and the answers which came to him read like a record of apostolic times. He prayed for everything and trusted implicitly to God to supply all his needs. And it is a matter of record that never did he and the orphans ever lack for any good thing.

Of a holy man who has done so much for Christ and suffering humanity, it was said at the grave about him:

He prayed up the walls of an hospital, and the hearts of the nurses. He prayed mission stations into being, and missionaries into faith. He prayed open the hearts of the rich, and gold from the most distant lands.

Luther is quoted as once saying: "The Christian's trade is praying." Certainly, for a great reason, the preacher's trade should be praying. We fear greatly that many preachers know nothing of this trade of praying, and hence they never succeed at this trade. A severe apprenticeship in the trade of praying must be served in order to become a journeyman in it. Not only is it true that there are few journeymen at work at this praying trade, but many have never even been apprentices at praying. No wonder so little is accomplished by them. God and the supernatural are left out of their programs.

Many do not understand this trade of praying because they have never learned it, and hence do not work at it. Many miracles ought to be worked by our praying. Why not? Is the arm of the Lord shortened that he cannot save? Is his ear heavy that he cannot hear? Has prayer lost its power because iniquity abounds and the love of many has grown cold? Has God changed from what he once was? To all these queries we enter an emphatic negative. God can as easily today work miracles by praying as he did in the days of old. "I am the Lord; I change not." "Is anything too hard for the Lord?"

He who works miracles by praying will first of all work the chief miracle on himself. Oh, that we might fully understand well the Christian's trade of praying, and follow the trade day by day and thus make for ourselves great spiritual wealth!

14

Wonders of God Through Prayer

IN the fearful contest in this world between God and the devil, between good and evil, and between heaven and hell, prayer is the mighty force for overcoming Satan, giving dominion over sin, and defeating hell. Only praying leaders are to be counted on in this dreadful conflict. Praying men alone are to be put to the front. These are the only sort who are able to successfully contend with all the evil forces.

The prayers of all saints are a perpetual force against all the powers of darkness. These prayers are a mighty energy in overcoming the world, the flesh and the devil, and in shaping the destiny of God's movements, to overcome evil and get the victory over the devil and all his works. The character and energy of God's movements lie in prayer. Victory is to come at the end of praying.

The wonders of God's power are to be kept alive, made real and present, and repeated only by prayer. God is not now so evident in the world, so almighty in manifestation as of old, not because miracles have passed away, nor because God has ceased to work, but because prayer has been shorn of its simplicity, its majesty, and its power. God still lives, and miracles still live while God lives and acts, for miracles are God's ways of acting. Prayer is dwarfed, withered, and petrified when faith in God is staggered by doubts of his ability, or through the shrinking caused by fear. When faith has a telescopic, far-off vision of God, prayer works no miracles, and brings no marvels of deliverance. But when God is seen by faith's closest, fullest eye, prayer makes a history of wonders.

Think about God. Make much of him, till he broadens and fills the horizon of faith. Then prayer will come into its marvelous inheritance of wonders. The marvels of prayer are seen when we remember that God's purposes are changed by prayer, God's vengeance is stayed by prayer, and God's penalty is remitted by prayer. The whole range of God's dealing with man is affected by prayer. Here is a force which must be increasingly used, that of prayer, a force to which all the events of life ought to be subjected.

To "pray without ceasing," to pray in everything, and to pray everywhere—these commands of continuity are expressive of the sleepless energy of prayer, of the exhaustless possibilities of prayer, and of its exacting necessity. Prayer can do all things. Prayer must do all things.

> Prayer is the simplest form of speech
> That infant lips can try;
> Prayer the sublimest strains that reach
> The majesty on high.

Prayer is asking God for something, and for something which he has promised. Prayer is using the divinely appointed means for obtaining what we need and for accomplishing what God proposes to do on earth.

> Prayer is appointed to convey
> The blessings God designs to give;
> Long as they live should Christians pray,
> They learn to pray when first they live.

And prayer brings to us blessings which we need, and which only God can give, and which prayer can alone convey to us.

In their broadest fullness, the possibilities of prayer are to be found in the very nature of prayer. This service of prayer is not a mere rite, a ceremony through which we go, a sort of performance. Prayer is going to God for something needed and desired. Prayer is simply asking God to do for us what he has promised us he will do if we ask him. The answer is a part of prayer, and is God's part of it. God's doing the thing asked for is as much a part of the prayer as the asking of the thing is prayer. Asking is man's part. Giving is God's part. The praying belongs to us. The answer belongs to God.

Man makes the plea and God makes the answer. The plea and the answer compose the prayer. God is more ready, more willing and more anxious to give the answer than man is to give the asking. The possibilities of prayer lie in the ability of man to ask large things and in the ability of God to give large things.

God's only condition and limitation of prayer is found in the character of the one who prays. The measure of our faith and praying is the measure of his giving. As our Lord said to the blind man, "according to your faith be it unto you," so it is the same in praying, "According to the measure of your asking, be it unto you." God measures the answer according to the prayer. He is limited by the law of prayer in the measure of the answers he gives to prayer. As is the measure of prayer, so will be the answer.

If the person praying has the characteristics which warrant praying, then the possibilities are unlimited. They are declared to be "all things whatsoever." Here is no limitation in character or kind, in circumference or condition. The man who prays can pray for anything and for everything, and God will give everything and anything. If we limit God in the asking, he will be limited in the giving.

Looking ahead, God declares in his Word that the wonder of wonders will be so great in the last days that everything animate and inanimate will be excited by his power:

> For behold, I create new heavens and a new earth; and the former shall not be remembered nor come to mind. But be ye glad and rejoice, forever, in that which I create; for behold I create Jerusalem a rejoicing, and her people a joy.

But these days of God's mighty working, the days of his magnificent and wonder-creating power, will be days of magnificent praying.

> And it shall come to pass that before they call, I will answer, and while they are yet speaking, I will hear.

It has ever been so. God's marvelous, miracle-working times have been times of marvelous, miracle-working praying. The greatest thing in God's worship by his own estimate is praying. Its chief service and its distinguishing feature is prayer:

> Even them will I bring to my holy mountain, and make them joyful in my house of prayer; their burnt offering and their sacrifices shall be accepted upon my altar, for my house shall be called a house of prayer for all people.

This was true under all the gorgeous rites and parade of ceremonies under the Jewish worship. Sacrifice, offering, and the atoning blood were all to be impregnated with prayer. The smoke of burnt offering and perfumed incense which filled God's house was to be but the flame of prayer, and all of God's people were to be anointed priests to minister at his altar of prayer. So all things were to be done with mighty prayer, because mighty prayer was the fruitage and inspiration of mighty faith. But much more is it now true every way under the more simple service of the gospel.

The course of nature, the movements of the planets, and the clouds, have yielded to the influence of prayer, and God has changed and checked the order of the sun and the seasons under the mighty energies of prayer. It is only necessary to note the remarkable incident when Joshua, through this divine means of prayer, caused the sun and the moon to stand still so that a more complete victory could be given to the armies of Israel in the contest with the armies of the Amorites.

If we believe God's Word, we are bound to believe that prayer affects God, and affects him mightily; that prayer avails, and that prayer avails mightily. There are wonders in prayer because there are wonders in God. Prayer has no talismanic influence. It is no mere fetish. It has no so-called powers of magic. It is simply making known our requests to God for things agreeable to his will in the name of Christ. It is just yielding our requests to a father, who knows all things, who has control of all things, and who is able to do all things.

Prayer is infinite ignorance trusting to the wisdom of God. Prayer is the voice of need crying out to him who is inexhaustible in resources. Prayer is helplessness reposing with childlike confidence on the word of its Father in heaven. Prayer is but the verbal expression of the heart of perfect confidence in the infinite wisdom, the power and the riches of Almighty God, who has placed at our command in prayer everything we need.

How all the gracious results of such gracious times are to come to the world through prayer, we are taught in God's Word. God's heart seems to overflow with delight at the prospect of thus blessing his people. By the mouth of the prophet Joel, God thus speaks:

> Fear not, O land; be glad and rejoice; for the Lord will do great things." Be not afraid, ye beasts of the field; for the pastures of the wilderness do spring, for the tree beareth her fruit, the fig-tree and the vine do yield their strength. Be glad then, ye children of Zion, and rejoice in the Lord your God; for he hath given you the former rain moderately, and he will cause to come down for you the rain, the former rain, and the latter rain in the first month. And the floors shall be full of wheat, and the vats shall overflow with wine and oil. And I will restore to you the years that the locust hath eaten, the canker worm and the caterpillar, and the palmer worm, my great army which I sent among you. And ye shall eat in plenty, and be satisfied, and praise the name of the Lord your God, that hath dealt wondrously with you; and my people shall never be ashamed. And ye shall know that I am in the midst of Israel, and that I am the Lord your God, and none else; and my people shall never be ashamed.

What wonderful material things are these which God proposes to bestow upon his people! They are marvelous temporal blessings he promises to bestow on them. They almost astonish the mind when they are studied. But God does not restrict his large blessings to temporal things. Looking down the ages, he foresees Pentecost, and makes these exceeding great and precious promises concerning the outpouring of the Holy Spirit, these very words being quoted by Peter on that glad day of Pentecost:

> And it shall come to pass afterward, that I will pour out my Spirit upon all flesh; and your sons shall prophesy, your old men shall dream dreams, your young men shall see visions; And also upon the servants and upon the hand maidens in those days will I pour out my Spirit. And I will show wonders in the heavens and in the earth, blood, and fire, and pillars of smoke; The sun shall be turned into darkness, and the moon into blood, before the great and the terrible day of the Lord shall come. And it shall come to pass that whosoever shall call on the name of the Lord shall be delivered; for in Mount Zion and in Jerusalem shall be deliverance, as the Lord hath said, and in the remnant whom the Lord shall call.

But these marvelous blessings will not be bestowed upon the people by sovereign power, nor be given unconditionally. God's people must do something precedent to such glorious results. Fasting and prayer must play an important part as conditions of receiving such large blessings. By the mouth of the same prophet, God thus speaks:

> Therefore also now, saith the Lord, turn ye to me with all your heart, and with fasting, and with weeping, and with mourning; And rend your heart, and not your garments; and turn unto the Lord your God; for he is gracious and merciful, slow to anger, and of great kindness, and repenteth him of the evil. Who knoweth if he will turn and repent, and leave a blessing behind him, even a meat offering, and a drink offering, unto the Lord your God? Blow the trumpet in Zion; sanctify a fast, call a solemn assembly. Gather the people; sanctify the congregation; assemble the elders; gather the children; and those that suck the breasts; let the bridegroom go forth of his chamber, and the bride out of her closet. Let the priests, the ministers of the Lord, weep between the porch and the altar, and let them say, Spare thy people, O Lord, and give not thine heritage to reproach, that the heathen should rule over them; Wherefore should they say among the people, Where is their God? Then will the Lord be jealous for his land, and pity his people. Yea, the Lord will answer and say unto his people, Behold I will send you corn, and wine, and oil, and ye shall be satisfied therewith; and I will no more make you a reproach among the heathen."

Prayer reaches even as far as the presence of God goes. It reaches everywhere because God is everywhere. Let us read from Psalm 139:1:

> If I ascend up into heaven, thou art there; if I make my bed in hell, behold thou art there. If I take the wings of the morning and dwell in the uttermost part of the sea; Even there shall thy hand lead me, and thy right hand shall hold me."

This may be said as truly of prayer as it is said of the God of prayer. The mysteries of death have been fathomed by prayer, and its victims have been brought back to life by the power of prayer, because God holds dominion over death, and prayer reaches where God reigns. Elisha and Elijah both invaded the realms of death by their prayers, and asserted and established the power of God as the power of prayer. Peter by prayer brings back to life the saintly Dorcas to the early church. Paul doubtless exercised the power of prayer as he fell upon and embraced Eutychus who fell out of the window when Paul preached at night.

Our Lord several times explicitly declared the far-reaching possibilities and the unlimited nature of prayer as covering "all things whatsoever." The conditions of prayer are exalted into a personal union with himself. That successful praying glorified God was the condition upon which laborers of first quality and sufficient in numbers were to be secured to press forward God's work in the world. The giving of all good things is conditioned upon asking for them. The giving of the Holy Spirit to God's children is based upon the asking of the children of God. God's will on earth can be secured only by prayer. Daily bread is obtained and sanctified by prayer. Reverence, forgiveness of sins, and deliverance from the evil one, and salvation from temptation, are in the hands of prayer.

The first jeweled foundation Christ lays as the basic principle of his religion in the Sermon on the Mount reads on this wise: "Blessed are the poor in spirit, for theirs is the kingdom of heaven." As prayer follows from the inner sense of need, and prayer is the utterance of a deep poverty-stricken spirit, so it is evident he who is "poor in spirit" is where he can pray and where he does pray.

Prayer is a tremendous force in the world. Take this picture of prayer and its wonderful possibilities. God's cause is quiet and motionless on the earth. An angel, strong and impatient to be of service, waits round about the throne of God in heaven, and to move things on earth and give impetus to the movements of God's cause in this world, he gathers all the prayers of all God's saints in all ages, and puts them before God just like Aaron used to cloud, flavor, and sweeten himself with the delicious incense when he entered the holy sanctuary, made aweful by the immediate presence of God. The angel impregnates all the air with that holy offering of prayers, and then takes its fiery body and casts it on the earth.

Note the remarkable result. "There were voices and thunderings and lightnings and an earthquake." What tremendous force is this which has thus convulsed the earth? The answer is that it is the "prayers of the saints," turned loose by the angel round about the throne, who has charge of those prayers. This mighty force is prayer, like the power of earth's mightiest dynamite.

Take another fact showing the wonders of prayer wrought by Almighty God in answer to the praying of his true prophet. The nation of God's people was fearfully apostate in head and heart and life. A man of God went to the apostate king with the fearful message which meant so much to the land, "There shall not be rain nor dew these years but according to my word." Whence this mighty force which can stay the clouds, seal up the rain, and hold back the dew? Who is this who speaks with such authority? Is there any force which can do this on earth? Only one, and that force is prayer, wielded in the hands of a praying prophet of God. It is he who has influence with God and over God in prayer, who thus dares to assume such authority over the forces of nature. This man Elijah is skilled in the use of that tremendous force. "And Elijah prayed earnestly, and it rained not on the earth for three years and six months."

But this is not all the story. He who could by prayer lock up the clouds and seal up the rain, could also unlock the clouds and unseal the rain by the same mighty power of prayer. "And he prayed again, and the heaven gave rain, and the earth gave forth her fruit."

Mighty is the power of prayer. Wonderful are its fruits. Remarkable things are brought to pass by men of prayer. Many are the wonders of prayer wrought by an almighty hand. The evidences of prayer's accomplishments almost stagger us. They challenge our faith. They encourage our expectations when we pray.

From a cursory summary like this, we get a bird's-eye view of the large possibilities of prayer and the urgent necessity of prayer. We see how God commits himself into the hands of those who truly pray. Great are the wonders of prayer because great is the God who hears and answers prayer. Great are these wonders because great are the rich promises made by a great God to those who pray.

We have seen prayer's far-reaching possibilities and its absolute, unquestioned necessity, and we have also seen that the foregoing particulars and elaboration were requisite in order to bring the subject more clearly, truly and strongly before our minds. The church more than ever needs profound convictions of the vast importance of prayer in prosecuting the work committed to it. More praying must be done and better praying if the church shall be able to perform the difficult, delicate, and responsible task given to it by her Lord and master. Defeat awaits a nonpraying church. Success is sure to follow a church given to much prayer. The supernatural element in the church, without which it must fail, comes only through praying. More time, in this busy bustling age, must be given to prayer by a God-called church. More thought must be given to prayer in this thoughtless, silly age of superficial religion. More heart and soul must be in the praying that is done if the church would go forth in the strength of her Lord and perform the wonders which is her heritage by divine promise.

> O Spirit of the living God,
> In all thy plenitude of grace,
> Where'er the foot of man hath trod,
> Descend on our apostate race.
>
> Give tongues of fire and hearts of love,
> To preach the reconciling word,
> Give power and unction from above,
> Where'er the joyful sound is heard.

It might be in order to give an instance or two in the life of Rev. John Wesley, showing some remarkable displays of spiritual power. Many times it is stated this noted man gathered his company together, and prayed all night, or till the mighty power of God came upon them. It was at a watch night service, at Fetter Lane, December 31, 1738, when Charles and John Wesley, with Whitfield, sat up till after midnight singing and praying. This is the account:

> About three o'clock in the morning, as we were continuing instant in prayer, the power of God came mightily upon us, so that many cried out for exceeding joy, and many fell to the ground. As soon as we had recovered a little from that awe and amazement at the presence of his majesty, we broke out with one voice,

"We praise thee, O God! We acknowledge thee to be the Lord!"

On another occasion, Mr. Wesley gives us this account:

> After midnight, about a hundred of us walked home together, singing, rejoicing and praising God.

Often does this godly man make the record to this effect, "We continued in ministering the Word and in prayer and praise till morning."

One of his all-night wrestlings in prayer alone with God is said to have greatly affected a Catholic priest, who was really awakened by the occurrence to a realization of his spiritual condition.

As often as God manifested his power in scriptural times in working wonders through prayer, he has not left himself without witness in modern times. Prayer brings the Holy Spirit upon men today in answer to importunate, continued prayer just as it did before Pentecost. The wonders of prayer have not ceased.

15

Prayer and Divine Providence

PRAYER and the divine providence are closely related. They stand in close companionship. They cannot possibly be separated. So closely connected are they that to deny one is to abolish the other. Prayer supposes a providence, while providence is the result of and belongs to prayer. All answers to prayer are but the intervention of the providence of God in the affairs of men. Providence has to do specially with praying people. Prayer, providence, and the Holy Spirit are a trinity, which cooperate with each other and are in perfect harmony with one another. Prayer is but the request of man for God through the Holy Spirit to interfere in behalf of him who prays.

What is termed providence is the divine superintendence over earth and its affairs. It implies gracious provisions which Almighty God makes for all his creatures, animate and inanimate, intelligent or otherwise. Once we admit that God is the creator and preserver of all men, and concede that he is wise and intelligent, we are logically driven to the conclusion that Almighty God has a direct superintendence of those whom he has created and whom he preserves in being. In fact, creation and preservation suppose a superintending providence. What is called divine providence is simply Almighty God governing the world for its best interests, and overseeing everything for the good of mankind.

Men talk about a "general providence" as separate from a "special providence." There is no general providence but what is made up of special providences. A general supervision on the part of God supposes a special and individual supervision of each person, yes, even every creature, animal and all alike.

God is everywhere, watching, superintending, overseeing, governing everything in the highest interest of man, and carrying forward his plans and executing his purposes in creation and redemption. He is not an absentee God. He did not make the world with all that is in it, and turn it over to so-called natural laws, and then retire into the secret places of the universe having no regard for it or for the working of his laws. His hand is on the throttle. The work is not beyond his control. Earth's inhabitants and its affairs are not running independently of Almighty God.

Any and all providences are special providences, and prayer and this sort of providences work hand in hand. God's hand is in everything. None are beyond him nor beneath his notice. Not that God orders everything which comes to pass. Man is still a free agent, but the wisdom of Almighty God comes out when we remember that while man is free, and the devil is abroad in the land, God can superintend and overrule earth's affairs for the good of man and for his glory, and cause even the wrath of man to praise him.

Nothing occurs by accident under the superintendence of an all-wise and perfectly just God. Nothing happens by chance in God's moral or natural government. God is a God of order, a God of law, but nonetheless a superintendent in the interest of his intelligent and redeemed creatures. Nothing can take place without the knowledge of God.

> His all surrounding sight surveys
> Our rising and our rest;
> Our public walks, our private ways,
> The secrets of our breasts.

Jesus Christ sets this matter at rest when he says, "Are not two sparrows sold for a farthing? and one of them shall not fall on the ground without your Father. But the very hairs of your head are all numbered. Fear ye not, therefore, ye are of more value than many sparrows."

God cannot be ruled out of the world. The doctrine of prayer brings him directly into the world, and moves him to a direct interference with all of this world's affairs.

To rule Almighty God out of the providences of life is to strike a direct blow at prayer and its power. Nothing takes place in the world without God's consent, yet not in a sense that he either approves everything or is responsible for all things which happen. God is not the author of sin.

The question is sometimes asked, "Is God in everything?" as if there are some things which are outside of the government of God, beyond his attention, with which he is not concerned. If God is not in everything, what is the Christian doing praying according to Paul's directions to the Philippians?

> Be careful for nothing, but in everything, by prayer and supplication, with thanksgiving, let your requests be made known unto God.

Are we to pray for some things and about things with which God has nothing to do? According to the doctrine that God is not in everything, then we are outside the realm of God when "in everything we make our requests unto God."

Then what will we do with that large promise so comforting to all of God's saints in all ages and in all climes, a promise which belongs to prayer and which is embraced in a special providence: "And we know that all things work together for good to them that love God"?

If God is not in everything, then what are the things we are to expect from the "all things" which "work together for good to them that love God"? And if God is not in everything, in his providence what are the things which are to be left out of our praying? We can lay it down as a proposition, borne out by Scripture, which has a sure foundation, that nothing ever comes into the life of God's saints without his consent. God is always there when it occurs. He is not far away. He whose eye is on the sparrow is also upon his saints. His presence which fills immensity is always where his saints are. "Certainly I will be with thee," is the word of God to every child of his.

"The angel of the Lord encampeth round about them that fear him and delivereth them." And without God's permission, nothing can touch those who fear God. Nothing can break through the encampment without the permission of the captain of the Lord's hosts. Sorrows, afflictions, want, trouble, or even death, cannot enter this divine encampment without the consent of Almighty God, and even then it is to be used by God in his plans for the good of his saints and for carrying out his plans and purposes:

> For I am persuaded that neither death, nor life, nor angels, nor principalities, nor powers, nor things present, nor things to come, Nor height, nor depth, nor any other creature, shall be able to separate us from the love of God which is in Christ Jesus our Lord.

These evil things, unpleasant and afflictive, may come with divine permission, but God is on the spot, his hand is in all of them, and he sees to it that they are woven into his plans. He causes them to be overruled for the good of his people, and eternal good is brought out of them. These things, with hundreds of others, belong to the disciplinary processes of Almighty God in administering his government for the children of men.

The providence of God reaches as far as the realm of prayer. It has to do with everything for which we pray. Nothing is too small for the eye of God, nothing too insignificant for his notice and his care. God's providence has to do with even the stumbling of the feet of his saints:

> For he shall give his angels charge concerning thee, to keep thee in all thy ways. They shall bear thee up in their hands, lest thou dash thy foot against a stone.

Read again our Lord's words about the sparrow, for he says, "Five sparrows are sold for two farthings, and not one of them is forgotten before God." Paul asks the pointed question, "Doth God care for oxen?" His care reaches to the smallest things and has to do with the most insignificant matters which concern men. He who believes in the God of providence is prepared to see his hand in all things which come to him, and can pray over everything.

Not that the saint who trusts the God of providence, and who takes all things to God in prayer, can explain the mysteries of divine providence, but the praying ones recognize God in everything, see him in all that comes to them, and are ready to say as John said to Peter at the Sea of Galilee, "It is the Lord."

Praying saints do not presume to interpret God's dealings with them nor undertake to explain God's providences, but they have learned to trust God in the dark as well as in the light, to have faith in God even when "cares like a wild deluge come, and storms of sorrow fall."

"Though he slay me, yet will I trust him." Praying saints rest themselves on the words of Jesus to Peter, "What I do thou knowest not now but thou shalt know hereafter." None but the praying ones can see God's hands in the providences of life. "Blessed are the pure in heart, for they shall see God," shall see God here in his providences, in his Word, in his church. These are they who do not rule God out of earth's affairs, and who believe God interferes with matters of earth for them.

While God's providence is over all men, yet his supervision and administration of his government are peculiarly in the interest of his people.

Prayer brings God's providence into action. Prayer puts God to work in overseeing and directing earth's affairs for the good of men. Prayer opens the way when it is shut up or straitened.

Providence deals more especially with temporalities. It is in this realm that the providence of God shines brightest and is most apparent. It has to do with food and raiment, with business difficulties, with strangely interposing and saving from danger, and with helping in emergencies at very opportune and critical times.

The feeding of the Israelites during the wilderness journey is a striking illustration of the providence of God in taking care of the temporal wants of his people. His dealings with those people show how he provided for them in that long pilgrimage.

> Day by day the manna fell,
> O to learn this lesson well!
> Still by constant mercy fed,
> Give me, Lord, my daily bread.
>
> Day by day the promise reads,
> Daily strength for daily needs;
> Cast foreboding fears away,
> Take the manna of today.

Our Lord teaches this same lesson of a providence which clothes and feeds his people in the Sermon on the Mount when he says, "Take no thought what ye shall eat, or what ye shall drink, nor yet for your body, what ye shall put on." Then he directs attention to the fact that it is God's providence which feeds the fowls of the air, clothes the lilies of the field, and asks if God does all this for birds and flowers, will he not care for them?

All of this teaching leads up to the need of a childlike, implicit trust in an overruling providence, which looks after the temporal wants of the children of men. And let it be noted specially that all this teaching stands closely connected in the utterances of our Lord with what he says about prayer, thus closely connecting a divine oversight with prayer and its promises.

We have an impressive lesson on divine providence in the case of Elijah when he was sent to the brook Cherith, where God actually employed the ravens to feed his prophet. Here was an interposition so plain that God cannot be ruled out of life's temporalities. Before God will allow his servant to want bread, he moves the birds of the air to do his bidding and take care of his prophet.

Nor was this all. When the brook ran dry, God sent him to a poor widow, who had just enough meal and oil for the urgent needs of the good woman and her son. Yet she divided with him her last morsel of bread. What was the result? The providence of God interposed, and as long as the drought lasted, the cruse of oil never failed nor did the meal in the barrel give out.

The Old Testament sparkles with illustrations of the provisions of Almighty God for his people, and shows clearly God's overruling providence. In fact the Old Testament is largely the account of a providence which dealt with a peculiar people, anticipating their every temporal want, which ministered to them in emergencies, and which sanctified to them their troubles.

It is worth while to read that old hymn of Newton's, which has in it so much of the providence of God:

> Though troubles assail, and dangers affright,
> Though friends should all fail, and foes all unite,
> Yet one thing secures me, whatever betide,
> The promise assures us, the Lord will provide.
>
> The birds without barns, or storehouse are fed,
> From them let us learn, to trust for our bread;
> His saints what is fitting, shall ne'er be denied,
> So long as it's written, the Lord will provide.

In fact, many of our old hymns are filled with sentiments in song about a divine providence, which are worthwhile to be read and sung even in this day.

God is in the most afflictive and sorrowing events of life. All such events are subjects of prayer, and this is so for the reason that everything which comes into the life of the praying one is in the providence of God, and takes place under his superintending hand. Some would rule God out of the sad and hard things of life. They tell us that God has nothing to do with certain events which bring such grief to us. They say that God is not in the death of children, that they die from natural causes, and that it is but the working of natural laws.

Let us ask what are nature's laws but the laws of God, the laws by which God rules the world? And what is nature anyway? And who made nature?

How great is the need to know that God is above nature, is in control of nature, and is in nature! We need to know that nature or natural laws are but the servants of Almighty God who made these laws, and that he is directly in them, and they are but the divine servants to carry out God's gracious designs, and are made to execute his gracious purposes. The God of providence, the God to whom the Christians pray, and the God who interposes in behalf of the children of men for their good, is above nature, in perfect and absolute control of all that belongs to nature. And no law of nature can crush the life out of even a child without God giving his consent, without such a sad event occurring directly under his all-seeing eye, and without his being immediately present.

David believed this doctrine when he fasted and prayed for the life of his child, for why pray and fast for a baby to be spared, if God has nothing to do with its death should it die?

Moreover, "does God care for oxen," and have a direct oversight of the sparrows which fall to the ground, and yet have nothing to do with the going out of this world of an immortal child? Still further, the death of a child, no matter if it should come alone as some people claim by the operation of the laws of nature, let it be kept in mind that it is a great affliction to the parents of the child. Where do these parents come in under any such doctrine? It becomes a great sorrow to mother and father. Are they not to recognize the hand of God in the death of the child? And to them is there no providence or divine oversight in the taking away of their child? David recognized the facts clearly that God had to do with keeping his child in life; that prayer might avail in saving his child from death, and that when the child died it was because God had ordered it. Prayer and providence in all this affair worked in harmonious cooperation, and David thoroughly understood it. No child ever dies without the direct permission of Almighty God, and such an event takes place in his providence for wise and beneficent ends. God works it into his plans concerning the child himself and the parents and all concerned. Moreover, it is a subject of prayer whether the child lives or dies.

> In each event of life how clear,
> Thy ruling hand I see;
> Each blessing to my soul most dear,
> Because conferred by thee.

16

Prayer and Divine Providence
(Continued)

Two kinds of providences are seen in God's dealings with men, direct providences and permissive providences. God orders some things, others he permits. But when he permits an afflictive dispensation to come into the life of his saint, even though it originates in a wicked mind, and it is the act of a sinner, yet before it strikes his saint and touches him, it becomes God's providence to the saint. In other words, God consents to some things in this world, many of them very painful and afflictive, without in the least being responsible for them, or in the least excusing him who originates them, but such events or things always become to the saint of God the providence of God to him. So the saint can say in each and all of these sad and distressing experiences, "It is the Lord; let him do what seemeth him good." Or with the psalmist, he may say, "I was dumb; I opened not my mouth, because thou didst it."

This was the explanation of all of Job's severe afflictions. They came to him in the providence of God, even though they had their origin in the mind of Satan, who devised them and put them into execution. God gave Satan permission to afflict Job, to take away his property, and to rob him of his children. But Job did not attribute these things to blind chance, nor to accident, neither did he charge them to satanic agency, but said, "The Lord hath given, and the Lord hath taken away; blessed be the name of the Lord." He took these things as coming from his God, whom he feared and served and trusted.

And to the same effect are Job's words to his wife when she left God out of the question, and wickedly told her husband, "Curse God and die." Job replied, "Thou speakest as one of the foolish women speaketh. What! Shall we receive good at the hand of God, and shall we not receive evil?"

It is no surprise under such a view of God's dealings with Job that it should be recorded of this man of faith, "In all this did not Job sin with his lips," and in another place was it said, "In all this Job sinned not, nor charged God foolishly." In nothing concerning God and the events of life do men talk more foolishly and even wickedly than in ignorantly making up their judgments on the providences of God in this world. O that we had men after the type of Job, who though afflictions and privations are severe in the extreme, yet they see the hand of God in providence and openly recognize God in it.

The sequel to all these painful experiences are but illustrations of that familiar text of Paul, "And we know that all things work together for good to them that love God." Job received back more in the end than was ever taken away from him. He emerged from under these tremendous troubles with victory, and became till this day the exponent and example of great patience and strong faith in God's providences. "Ye have heard of the patience of Job," rings down the line of divine revelation. God took hold of the evil acts of Satan, and worked them into his plans and brought great good out of them. He made evil work out for good without in the least endorsing the evil or conniving at it.

We have the same gracious truth of divine providence evidenced in the story of Joseph and his brethren, who sold him wickedly into Egypt and forsook him and deceived their old father. All this had its origin in their evil minds. And yet when it reached God's plans and purposes, it became God's providence both to Joseph and to the future of Jacob's descendants. Hear Joseph as he spoke to his brethren after he had revealed himself to them down in Egypt, as he traced all the painful events back to the mind of God and made them have to do with fulfilling God's purposes concerning Jacob and his posterity:

> Now therefore be not grieved nor angry with yourselves that ye sold me hither; for God did send me before you to preserve life. And God sent me before you to preserve you a posterity on the earth, and to save your lives by a great deliverance. So that it was not you that sent me hither, but God.

Cowper's well-known hymn might well be read in this connection, one verse of which is sufficient just now:

> God moves in a mysterious way, his wonders to perform;
> He plants his footsteps in the sea, and rides upon the storm.

The very same line of argument appears in the betrayal of our Lord by Judas. Of course it was the wicked act of an evil man, but it never touched our Lord till the Father gave his consent, and God took the evil design of Judas and worked it into his own plans for the redemption of the world. It did not excuse Judas in the least that good came out of his wicked act, but it does magnify the wisdom and greatness of God in so overruling it that man's redemption was secured. It is so always in God's dealings with man. Things which come to us from second causes are no surprise to God, nor are they beyond his control. His hand can take hold of them in answer to prayer and he can make afflictions, from whatever quarter they may come, "work for us a far more exceeding and eternal weight of glory."

The providence of God goes before his saints, opens the way, removes difficulties, solves problems and brings deliverances when escape seems hopeless. God brought Israel out of Egypt by the hand of Moses, his chosen leader of that people. They came to the Red Sea. But there were the waters in front, with no crossing nor bridges. On one side were high mountains, and behind came the hosts of Pharaoh. Every avenue of escape was closed. There seemed no hope. Despair almost reigned. But there was one way open which men overlooked, and that was the upward way. A man of prayer, Moses, the man of faith in God, was on the ground. This man of prayer, who recognized God in providence, with commanding force, spoke to the people on this wise:

> Fear ye not; stand still and see the salvation of the Lord.

With this he lifted up his rod, and according to divine command, he stretched his hand over the sea. The waters divided, and the command issued forth, "Speak unto the children of Israel that they go forward." And Israel went over the sea dry shod. God had opened a way, and what seemed an impossible emergency was remarkably turned into a wonderful deliverance. Nor is this the only time that God has interposed in behalf of his people when their way was shut up.

The whole history of the Jews is the story of God's providence. The Old Testament cannot be accepted as true without receiving the doctrine of a divine, overruling providence. The Bible is preeminently a divine revelation. It reveals things. It discovers, uncovers, brings to light things concerning God, his character, and his manner of governing this world, and its inhabitants, not discoverable by human reason, by science or by philosophy. The Bible is a book in which God reveals himself to men. And this is particularly true when we consider God's care of his creatures and his oversight of the world, his superintendent of its affairs. And to dispute the doctrine of providence is to discredit the entire revelation of God's Word. Everywhere this Word discovers God's hand in man's affairs.

The Old Testament especially, but also the New Testament, is the story of prayer and providence. It is the tale of God's dealings with men of prayer, men of faith in his direct interference in earth's affairs, and with God's manner of superintending the world in the interest of his people and in carrying forward his work in his plans and purposes in creation and redemption.

Praying men and God's providence go together. This was thoroughly understood by the praying ones of the Scripture. They prayed over everything because God had to do with everything. They took all things to God in prayer because they believed in a divine providence which had to do with all things. They believed in an everpresent God, who had not retired into the secret recesses of space, leaving his saints and his creatures to the mercy of a tyrant, called nature, and its laws, blind, unyielding, with no regard for anyone who stood in its way. If that be the correct conception of God, why pray to him? He is too far away to hear them when they pray, and too unconcerned to trouble himself about those on earth.

These men of prayer had an implicit faith in a God of special providence, who would gladly, promptly, and readily respond to their cries for help in times of need and in seasons of distress.

The so-called "laws of nature" did not trouble them in the least. God was above nature, in control of nature, while nature was but the servant of Almighty God. Nature's laws were but his own laws, since nature was but the offspring of the divine hand. Laws of nature might be suspended and no evil would result. Every intelligent person is conversant every day when he sees man overruling and overcoming the law of gravitation, and no one is surprised or raises his hand or voice in horror at the thought of nature's laws being violated. God is a God of law and order, and all his laws in nature, in providence and in grace work together in perfect accord, with no clash or disharmony.

God suspends or overcomes the laws of disease and rain often without or independent of prayer. But quite often he does this in answer to prayer. Prayer for rain or for dry weather is not outside the moral government of God, nor is it asking God to violate any law which he has made, but only asking him to give rain in his own way, according to his own laws. So also the prayer for the rebuking of disease is not a request at war with law either natural or otherwise, but is a prayer in accordance with law, even the law of prayer, a law set in operation by Almighty God as the so-called natural law which governs rain or which controls disease.

The believer in the law of prayer has strong ground on which to base his plea. And the believer in a divine providence, the companion of prayer, stands equally on strong granite foundations, from which he need not be shaken. These twin doctrines stand fast and will abide forever.

> In every condition, in sickness, in health,
> In poverty's vale or abounding in wealth;
> At home or abroad, on the land or the sea,
> As thy days may demand shall thy strength ever be.

BOOK

◆4◆

The Reality of Prayer

1

Prayer—A Privilege, Princely, Sacred

THE word *prayer* expresses the largest and most comprehensive approach to God. It gives prominence to the element of devotion. It is communion and fellowship with God. It is enjoyment of God. It is access to God. *Supplication* is a more restricted and more intense form of prayer, accompanied by a sense of personal need, limited to the seeking in an urgent manner of a supply for pressing need. Supplication is the very soul of prayer in the way of pleading for some one thing, greatly needed, and the need intensely felt.

Intercession is an enlargement in prayer, a going out in broadness and fullness from self to others. Primarily, it does not center in praying for others, but refers to the freeness, boldness and childlike confidence of the praying. It is the fullness of confiding influence in the soul's approach to God, unlimited and unhesitating in its access and its demands. This influence and confident trust is to be used for others.

Prayer always, and everywhere is an immediate and confiding approach to, and a request of, God the Father. In the prayer universal and perfect, as the pattern of all praying, it is "Our Father, who art in heaven." At the grave of Lazarus, Jesus lifted up his eyes and said, "Father." In his high-priestly prayer, Jesus lifted up his eyes to heaven, and said, "Father." Personal, familiar, and filial was all his praying. Strong, too, and touching and tearful, was his praying. Read these words of Paul:

> Who in the days of his flesh, when he had offered up prayers and supplications, with strong crying and tears, unto him that was able to save him from death, and was heard in that he feared (Heb. 5: 7).

So elsewhere (James 1:5) we have "asking" set forth as prayer: "If any of you lack wisdom, let him ask of God, who giveth to all men liberally, and upbraideth not, and it shall be given him."

Asking of God and receiving from the Lord—direct application to God, immediate connection with God—that is prayer.

In John 5:13 we have this statement about prayer:

And this is the confidence that we have in him, that if we ask anything according to his will, he heareth us. And if we know that he heareth us, whatsoever we ask, we know that we have the petitions that we desired of him.

In Philippians 4: 6 we have these words about prayer:

"Be careful for nothing, but in everything, by prayer and supplication, with thanksgiving, let your requests be made known unto God."

What is God's will about prayer? First of all, it is God's will that we pray. "Jesus Christ spake a parable unto them to this end, that men ought always to pray, and not to faint."

Paul writes to young Timothy about the first things which God's people are to do, and first among the first he puts prayer: "I exhort, therefore, that first of all, supplications, prayers, intercessions, and giving of thanks, be made for all men" (1 Tim. 2:1).

In connection with these words Paul declares that the will of God and the redemption and mediation of Jesus Christ for the salvation for all men are all vitally concerned in this matter of prayer. In this his apostolical authority and solicitude of soul conspire with God's will and Christ's intercession to will that "the men pray everywhere."

Note how frequently prayer is brought forward in the New Testament: "Continuing instant in prayer"; "Pray without ceasing"; "Continue in prayer, and watch in the same with thanksgiving"; "Be ye sober and watch unto prayer"; Christ's clarion call was "watch and pray." What are all these and others, if it is not the will of God that men should pray?

Prayer is complementary, made efficient and cooperative with God's will, whose sovereign sway is to run parallel in extent and power with the atonement of Jesus Christ. He, through the eternal Spirit, by the grace of God, "tasted death for every man." We, through the eternal Spirit, by the grace of God, *pray* for every man.

But how do I know that I am praying by the will of God? Every true attempt to pray is in response to the will of God. Bungling it may be and untutored by human teachers, but it is acceptable to God, because it is in obedience to his will. If I will give myself up to the inspiration of the Spirit of God, who commands me to pray, the details and the petitions of that praying will all fall into harmony with the will of him who wills that I should pray.

Prayer is no little thing, no selfish and small matter. It does not concern the petty interests of one person. The littlest prayer broadens out by the will of God till it touches all words, conserves all interests, and enhances man's greatest wealth, and God's greatest good. God is so concerned that men pray that he has promised to answer prayer. He has not promised to do something general if we pray, but he has promised to do the very thing for which we pray.

Prayer, as taught by Jesus in its essential features, enters into all the relations of life. It sanctifies brotherliness. To the Jew, the altar was the symbol and place of prayer. The Jew devoted the altar to the worship of God. Jesus Christ takes the altar of prayer and devotes it to the worship of the brotherhood. How Christ purifies the altar and enlarges it! How he takes it out of the sphere of a mere performance, and makes its virtue to consist, not in the mere act of praying, but in the spirit which actuates us toward men. Our spirit toward folks is of the life of prayer. We must be at peace with men, and, if possible, have them at peace with us, before we can be at peace with God. Reconciliation with men is the forerunner of reconciliation with God. Our spirit and words must embrace men before they can embrace God. Unity with the brotherhood goes before unity with God. "Therefore, if thou bring thy gift to the altar, and there rememberest that thy brother hath aught against thee; leave there thy gift before the altar, and go thy way. First, be reconciled to thy brother, and then come and offer thy gift (Matt. 5:23).

Nonpraying is lawlessness, discord, anarchy. Prayer, in the moral government of God, is as strong and far-reaching as the law of gravitation in the material world, and it is as necessary as gravitation to hold things in their proper sphere and in life.

The space occupied by prayer in the Sermon on the Mount reveals its esteem by Christ and the importance it holds in his system. Many important principles are discussed in a verse or two. The Sermon consists of one hundred and eleven verses, and eighteen are about prayer directly, and others indirectly.

Prayer was one of the cardinal principles of piety in every dispensation and to every child of God. It did not pertain to the business of Christ to originate duties, but to recover, to recast, to spiritualize, and to reinforce those duties which are cardinal and original.

With Moses the great features of prayer are prominent. He never beats the air nor fights a sham battle. The most serious and strenuous business of his serious and strenuous life was prayer. He is much at it with the intensest earnestness of his soul. Intimate as he was with God, his intimacy did not abate the necessity of prayer. This intimacy only brought clearer insight into the nature and necessity of prayer, and led him to see the greater obligations to pray, and to discover the larger results of praying. In reviewing one of the crises through which Israel passed, when the very existence of the nation was imperilled, he writes: "I fell down before the Lord forty days and forty nights." Wonderful praying and wonderful results! Moses knew how to do wonderful praying, and God knew how to give wonderful results.

The whole force of Bible statement is to increase our faith in the doctrine that prayer affects God, secures favors from God, which can be secured in no other way, and which will not be bestowed by God if we do not pray. The whole canon of Bible teaching is to illustrate the great truth that God hears and answers prayer. One of the great purposes of God in his book is to impress on us indelibly the great importance, the priceless value, and the absolute necessity of asking God for the things which we need for time and eternity. He urges us by every consideration, and presses and warns us by every interest. He points us to his own Son, turned over to us for our good, as his pledge that prayer will be answered, teaching us that God is our Father, able to do all things for us and to give all things to us, much more than earthly parents are able or willing to do for their children.

Let us thoroughly understand ourselves and understand, also, this great business of prayer. Our one great business is prayer, and we will never do it well unless we fasten it by all binding force. We will never do it well without arranging the best conditions of doing it well. Satan has suffered so much by good praying that all his wily, shrewd, and ensnaring devices will be used to cripple its performances.

We must, by all the fastenings we can find, cable ourselves to prayer. To be loose in time and place is to open the door to Satan. To be exact, prompt, unswerving, and careful in even the little things, is to buttress ourselves against the evil one.

Prayer, by God's very oath, is put in the very stones of God's foundations, as eternal as its companion, "And men shall pray for him continually." This is the eternal condition which advances his cause, and makes it powerfully aggressive. Men are to always pray for it. Its strength, beauty, and aggression lie in their prayers. Its power lies simply in its power to pray. No power is found elsewhere but in its ability to pray. "For my house shall be called the house of prayer for all people." It is based on prayer, and carried on by the same means.

Prayer is a privilege, a sacred, princely privilege. Prayer is a duty, an obligation most binding, and most imperative, which should hold us to it. But prayer is more than a privilege, more than a duty. It is a means, an instrument, a condition. Not to pray is to lose much more than to fail in the exercise and enjoyment of a high, or sweet privilege. Not to pray is to fail along lines far more important than even the violation of an obligation.

Prayer is the appointed condition of getting God's aid. This aid is as manifold and illimitable as God's ability, and as varied and exhaustless is this aid as man's need. Prayer is the avenue through which God supplies man's wants. Prayer is the channel through which all good flows from God to man, and all good from men to men. God is the Christian's father. Asking and giving are in that relation.

Man is the one more immediately concerned in this great work of praying. It ennobles man's reason to employ it in prayer. The office and work of prayer is the divinest engagement of man's reason. Prayer makes man's reason to shine. Intelligence of the highest order approves prayer. He is the wisest man who prays the most and the best. Prayer is the school of wisdom as well as of piety.

Prayer is not a picture to handle, to admire, to look at. It is not beauty, coloring, shape, attitude, imagination, or genius. These things do not pertain to its character or conduct. It is not poetry nor music. Its inspiration and melody come from heaven. Prayer belongs to the spirit, and at times it possesses the spirit and stirs the spirit with high and holy purposes and resolves.

2

Prayer—Fills Man's Poverty with God's Riches

WE have much fine writing and learned talk about the subjective benefits of prayer; how prayer secures its full measure of results, not by affecting God, but by affecting us, by becoming a training school for those who pray. We are taught by such teachers that the province of prayer is not to get, but to train. Prayer thus becomes a mere performance, a drill-sergeant, a school, in which patience, tranquility, and dependence are taught. In this school, denial of prayer is the most valuable teacher. How well all this may look, and how reasonable soever it may seem, there is nothing of it in the Bible. The clear and oft repeated language of the Bible is that prayer is to be answered by God; that God occupies the relation of a father to us, and that as Father he gives to us when we ask the things for which we ask. The best praying, therefore, is the praying that gets an answer.

The possibilities and necessity of prayer are graven in the eternal foundations of the gospel. The relation that is established between the Father and the Son and the decreed covenant between the two, has prayer as the base of its existence, and the conditions of the advance and success of the gospel. Prayer is the condition by which all foes are to be overcome and all the inheritance is to be possessed.

These are axiomatic truths, though they may be very homely ones. But these are the times when Bible axioms need to be stressed, pressed, repeated and reiterated. The very air is rife with influences, practices and theories which sap foundations, and the most veritable truths and the most self-evident axioms go down by insidious and invisible attacks.

More than this: the tendency of these times is to an ostentatious parade of doing, which enfeebles the life and dissipates the spirit of praying. There may be kneeling, and there may be standing in prayerful attitude. There may be much bowing of the head, and yet there may be no serious, real praying. Prayer is real work. Praying is vital work. Prayer has in its keeping the very heart of worship. There may be the exhibit, the circumstance, and the pomp of praying, and yet no real praying. There may be much attitude, gesture, and verbiage, but no praying.

230

Who can approach into God's presence in prayer? Who can come before the great God, maker of all worlds, the God and Father of our Lord Jesus Christ, who holds in his hands all good, and who is all powerful and able to do all things? Man's approach to this great God—what lowliness, what truth, what cleanness of hands, and purity of heart is needed and demanded!

Everywhere in Scripture we are impressed that it is most important and urgent that men pray, that they be skilled in the homiletic didactics of prayer. That is a thing of the heart, not of the schools. It is more of feeling than of words. Praying is the best school in which to learn to pray, prayer the best dictionary to define the art and nature of praying.

We repeat and reiterate. Prayer is not a mere habit, riveted by custom and memory, something which must be gone through with, its value depending upon the decency and perfection of the performance. Prayer is not a duty which must be performed, to ease obligation and to quiet conscience. Prayer is not mere privilege, a sacred indulgence to be taken advantage of, at leisure, at pleasure, at will, and no serious loss attending its omission.

Prayer is a solemn service due to God, an adoration, a worship, an approach to God for some request, the presenting of some desire, the expression of some need to him, who supplies all need, and who satisfies all desires; who, as a Father, finds his greatest pleasure in relieving the wants and granting the desires of his children. Prayer is the child's request, not to the winds nor to the world, but to the Father. Prayer is the outstretched arms of the child for the Father's help. Prayer is the child's cry calling to the Father's ear, the Father's heart, and to the Father's ability, which the Father is to hear, the Father is to feel, and which the Father is to relieve. Prayer is the seeking of God's great and greatest good, which will not come if we do not pray.

Prayer is an ardent and believing cry to God for some specific thing. God's rule is to answer by giving the specific thing asked for. With it may come much of other gifts and graces. Strength, serenity, sweetness, and faith may come as the bearers of the gifts. But even they come because God hears and answers prayer.

We do but follow the plain letter and spirit of the Bible when we affirm that God answers prayer, and answers by giving us the very things we desire, and that the withholding of that which we desire and the giving of something else is not the rule, but rare and exceptional. When his children cry for bread he gives them bread.

Revelation does not deal in philosophical subtleties, nor verbal niceties and hair-splitting distinctions. It unfolds relationships, declares principles, and enforces duties. The heart must define, the experience must realize. Paul came on the stage too late to define prayer. That which had been so well done by patriarchs and prophets needed no return to dictionaries. Christ is himself the illustration and definition of prayer. He prayed as man had never prayed. He put prayer on a higher basis, with grander results and simpler being than it had ever known. He taught Paul how to pray by the revelation of himself, which is the first call to prayer, and the first lesson in praying. Prayer, like love, is too ethereal and too heavenly to be held in the gross arms of chilly definitions. It belongs to heaven, and to the heart, and not to words and ideas only.

Prayer is no petty invention of man, a fancied relief for fancied ills. Prayer is no dreary performance, dead and death-dealing, but is God's enabling act for man, living and life-giving, joy and joy-giving. Prayer is the contact of a living soul with God. In prayer, God stoops to kiss man, to bless man, and to aid man in everything that God can devise or man can need. Prayer fills man's emptiness with God's fullness. It fills man's poverty with God's riches. It puts away man's weakness with God's strength. It banishes man's littleness with God's greatness. Prayer is God's plan to supply man's great and continuous need with God's great and continuous abundance.

What is this prayer to which men are called? It is not a mere form, a child's play. It is serious, difficult work, the manliest, the mightiest work, the divinest work which man can do. Prayer lifts men out of the earthliness and links them with the heavenly. Men are never nearer heaven, nearer God, never more Godlike, never in deeper sympathy and truer partnership with Jesus Christ, than when praying. Love, philanthropy, holy affiances,—all of them helpful and tender for men—are born and perfected by prayer.

Prayer is not merely a question of duty, but of salvation. Are men saved who are not men of prayer? Is not the gift, the inclination, the habit of prayer, one of the elements or characteristics of salvation? Can it be possible to be in affinity with Jesus Christ and not be prayerful? Is it possible to have the Holy Spirit and not have the spirit of prayer? Can one have the new birth and not be born to prayer? Is not the life of the Spirit and the life of prayer coordinate and consistent? Can brotherly love be in the heart which is unschooled in prayer?

We have two kinds of prayer named in the New Testament—prayer and supplication. Prayer denotes prayer in general. Supplication is a more intense and more special form of prayer. These two, supplication and prayer, ought to be combined. Then we would have devotion in its widest and sweetest form, and supplication with its most earnest and personal sense of need.

In Paul's prayer directory, found in the sixth chapter of Ephesians, we are taught to be always in prayer, as we are always in the battle. The Holy Spirit is to be sought by intense supplication, and our supplications are to be charged by his vitalizing, illuminating, and ennobling energy. Watchfulness is to fit us for this intense praying and intense fighting. Perseverance is an essential element in successful praying, as in every other realm of conflict. The saints universal are to be helped on to victory by the aid of our prayers. Apostolic courage, ability, and success are to be gained by the prayers of the soldier saints everywhere.

It is only those of deep and true vision who can administer prayer. These "living creatures," in Revelation 4:6, are described as "full of eyes before and behind," "full of eyes within." Eyes are for seeing. Clearness, intensity, and perfection of sight are in it. Vigilance and profound insight are in it, the faculty of knowing. It is by prayer that the eyes of our hearts are opened. Clear, profound knowledge of the mysteries of grace is secured by prayer. These "living creatures" had eyes "within and without." They were "full of eyes." The highest form of life is intelligent. Ignorance is degrading and low, in the spiritual realm as it is in other realms. Prayer gives us eyes to see God. Prayer is seeing God. The prayer life is knowledge without and within. All vigilance without, all vigilance within. There can be no intelligent prayer without knowledge within. Our inner condition and our inner needs must be felt and known.

It takes prayer to minister. It takes life, the highest form of life, to minister. Prayer is the highest intelligence, the profoundest wisdom, the most vital, the most joyous, the most efficacious, the most powerful of all vocations. It is life, radiant, transporting, eternal life. Away with dry forms, with dead, cold habits of prayer! Away with sterile routine, with senseless performances, and petty playthings in prayer! Let us get at the serious work, the chief business of men, that of prayer. Let us work at it skillfully. Let us seek to be adepts in this great work of praying. Let us be master-workmen, in this high art of praying. Let us be so in the habit of prayer, so devoted to prayer, so filled with its rich spices, so ardent by its holy flame, that all heaven and earth will be perfumed by its aroma, and nations yet in the womb will be blest by our prayers. Heaven will be fuller and brighter in glorious inhabitants, earth will be better prepared for its bridal day, and hell robbed of many of its victims, because we have lived to pray.

There is not only a sad and ruinous neglect of any attempt to pray, but there is an immense waste in the seeming praying which is done, as official praying, state praying, mere habit praying. Men cleave to the form and semblance of a thing after the heart and reality have gone out of it. This finds illustrations in many who seem to pray. Formal praying has a strong hold and a strong following.

Hannah's statement to Eli and her defense against his charge of hypocrisy was: "I have poured out my soul before the Lord." God's serious promise to the Jews was,

> Then shall ye call upon me, and ye shall go and pray unto me, and I will hearken unto you. And ye shall seek me and find me when ye shall search for me with all your heart.

Let all the present day praying be measured by these standards, "Pouring out the soul before God," and "Seeking with all the heart," and how much of it will be found to be mere form, waste, worthless. James says of Elijah that he "prayed with prayer." In Paul's directions to Timothy about prayer, (1 Tim. 1:8) we have a comprehensive verbal description of prayer in its different departments, or varied manifestations. They are all in the plural form, supplications, prayers, and intercessions. They declare the many-sidedness, the endless diversity, and the necessity of going beyond the formal simplicity of a single prayer, and press and add prayer upon prayer, supplication to supplication, intercession over and over again, until the combined force of prayers in their most superlative modes, unite their aggregation and pressure with cumulative power to our praying. The unlimited superlative and the unlimited plural are the only measures of prayer. The one term of "prayer" is the common and comprehensive one for the act, the duty, the spirit, and the service we call prayer. It is the condensed statement of worship. The heavenly worship does not have the element of prayer so conspicuous. Prayer is the conspicuous, all-important essence and the all-coloring ingredient of earthly worship, while praise is the preeminent, comprehensive, all-coloring, all-inspiring element of the heavenly worship.

3

Prayer—
The All-Important Essence
of Earthly Worship

THE Jewish law and the prophets know something of God as a Father. Occasional and imperfect, yet comforting glimpses they had of the great truth of God's Fatherhood, and of our sonship. Christ lays the foundation of prayer deep and strong with this basic principle. The law of prayer, the right to pray, rests on sonship. "Our Father" brings us into the closest relationship to God. Prayer is the child's approach, the child's plea, the child's right. It is the law of prayer that looks up, that lifts up the eye to "Our Father, who art in heaven." Our Father's house is our home in heaven. Heavenly citizenship and heavenly homesickness are in prayer. Prayer is an appeal from the lowness, from the emptiness, from the need of earth, to the highness, the fullness and to the all-sufficiency of heaven. Prayer turns the eye and the heart heavenward with a child's longings, a child's trust and a child's expectancy. To hallow God's name, to speak it with bated breath, to hold it sacredly, this also belongs to prayer.

In this connection it might be said that it is requisite to dictate to children the necessity of prayer for their salvation. But alas! Unhappily it is thought sufficient to tell them there is a heaven and a hell; that they must avoid the latter place and seek to reach the former. Yet they are not taught the easiest way to arrive at salvation. The only way to heaven is by the route of prayer, such prayer of the heart which every one is capable of. It is prayer, not of reasonings which are the fruits of study, or of the exercise of the imagination, which fills the mind with wondering objects, but which fails to settle salvation, but the simple, confidential prayer of the child to his Father in heaven.

Poverty of spirit enters into true praying. "Blessed are the poor in spirit, for theirs is the kingdom of heaven." "The poor" means paupers, beggars, those who live on the bounties of others, who live by begging. Christ's people live by asking. "Prayer is the Christian's vital breath." It is his affluent inheritance, his daily annuity.

In his own example, Christ illustrates the nature and necessity of prayer. Everywhere he declares that he who is on God's mission in this world will pray. He is an illustrious example of the principle that the more devoted the

235

man is to God, the more prayerful will he be. The diviner the man, the more of the Spirit of the Father and of the Son he has, the more prayerful will he be. And, conversely, it is true that the more prayerful he is, the more of the Spirit of the Father and of the Son will he receive.

At the great events and crowning periods of the life of Jesus we find him in prayer—at the beginning of his ministry, at the fords of the Jordan, when the Holy Spirit descended upon him; just prior to the transfiguration, and in the garden of Gethsemane. Well do the words of Peter come in here: "Leaving us an example that ye should follow his steps."

There is an important principle of prayer found in some of the miracles of Christ. It is the progressive nature of the answer to prayer. Not at once does God always give the full answer to prayer, but rather progressively, step by step. Mark (8: 22) describes a case which illustrates this important truth, too often overlooked:

> And he cometh to Bethsaida; and they bring a blind man unto him, and besought him to touch him. And he took the blind man by the hand, and led him out of the town; and when he had spit on his eyes, and put his hands upon him, he asked him if he saw aught. "And he looked up; and said, 'I see men as trees, walking.'" After that he put his hands again upon his eyes, and made him look up; and he was restored, and saw every man clearly.

Alone he has to take us at times, aside from the world, where he can have us all to himself, and there speak to and deal with us.

We have three cures for blindness in the life of our Lord, which illustrate the nature of God's working in answering prayer, and show the exhaustless variety and the omnipotence of his working.

In the first case Christ came incidentally on a blind man at Jerusalem, made clay, softened it by spittle, and smeared it on the eyes and then commanded the man to go and wash in the pool of Siloam. The gracious results lay at the end of his action—washing. The failure to go and wash would have been fatal to the cure. No one, not even the blind man, in this instance, requested the cure.

In the second case the parties who bring the blind man, back their bringing with earnest prayer for cure; they beseech Christ to simply touch him, as though their faith would relieve the burden of a heavy operation. But he took the man by the hand and led him out of the town and apart from the people. Alone, and in secret, this work was to be done. He spat on his eyes and put his hands on them. The response was not complete, rather it was a dawning of light, a partial recovery. The first gracious communication but gave him a disordered vision, the second stroke perfected the cure. The man's submissive faith in giving himself up to Christ to be led away into privacy and alone, were prominent features of the cure, as also the gradual reception of sight, and the necessity of a second stroke to finish the perfect work.

The third was the case of blind Bartimaeus. It was the urgency of faith declaring itself in clamorous utterances, rebuked by those who were following Christ, but intensified and emboldened by opposition.

The first case comes on Christ unawares; the second was brought with specific intent to him; the last goes after Christ with irresistible urgency, met by the resistance of the multitude and the seeming indifference of Christ. The cure, though, was without the interposition of any agent, no taking by the hand, no gentle or severe touch, no spittle, nor clay, nor washing—a word only and his sight, full-orbed, came instantly. Each one had experienced the same divine power, the same blessed results, but with marked diversity in the expression of their faith and the mode of their cure. Suppose, at their meeting, the first had set up the particulars and process of his cure, the spittle, the clay, the washing in Siloam as the only divine process, as the only genuine credentials of a divine work, how far from the truth, how narrow and misleading such a standard of decision! Not methods, but results, are the tests of the divine work.

Each one could say: "This one thing I know, whereas I was blind I now see." The results were conscious results; that Christ did the work they knew; faith was the instrument, but its exercise different; the method of Christ's working different; the various steps that brought them to the gracious end on their part and on his part at many points strikingly dissimilar.

What are the limitations of prayer? How far do its benefits and possibilities reach? What part of God's dealing with man, and with man's world, is unaffected by prayer? Do the possibilities of prayer cover all temporal and spiritual good? The answers to these questions are of transcendental importance. The answer will gauge the effort and results of our praying. The answer will greatly enhance the value of prayer, or will greatly depress prayer. The answer to these important questions are fully covered by Paul's words on prayer: "Be careful for nothing, but in everything, by prayer and supplication, with thanksgiving, let your requests be made known unto God" (Phil. 4:6).

4

God Has Everything
to Do with Prayer

PRAYER is God's business to which men can attend. Prayer is God's necessary business, which men only can do, and that men must do. Men who belong to God are obliged to pray. They are not obliged to grow rich, nor to make money. They are not obliged to have large success in business. These are incidental, occasional, merely nominal, as far as integrity to heaven and loyalty to God are concerned. Material successes are immaterial to God. Men are neither better nor worse with those things or without them. They are not sources of reputation nor elements of character in the heavenly estimates. But to pray, to really pray, is the source of revenue, the basis of reputation, and the element of character in the estimation of God. Men are obliged to pray as they are obliged to be religious. Prayer is loyalty to God. Non-praying is to reject Christ and to abandon heaven. A life of prayer is the only life which heaven counts.

God is vitally concerned that men should pray. Men are bettered by prayer, and the world is bettered by praying. God does his best work for the world through prayer. God's greatest glory and man's highest good are secured by prayer. Prayer forms the godliest men and makes the godliest world.

God's promises lie like giant corpses without life, only for decay and dust unless men appropriate and vitalize these promises by earnest and prevailing prayer.

Promise is like the unsown seed, the germ of life in it, but the soil and culture of prayer are necessary to germinate and culture the seed. Prayer is God's life-giving breath. God's purposes move along the pathway made by prayer to their glorious designs. God's purposes are always moving to their high and beneficial ends, but the movement is along the way marked by unceasing prayer. The breath of prayer in man is from God.

God has everything to do with prayer, as well as everything to do with the one who prays. To him who prays, and as he prays, the hour is sacred because it is God's hour. The occasion is sacred because it is the occasion of the soul's approach to God, and of dealing with God. No hour is more hallowed because it is the occasion of the soul's mightiest approach to God, and of the

238

fullest revelation from God. Men are Godlike and men are blessed, just as the hour of prayer has the most of God in it. Prayer makes and measures the approach of God. He knows not God who knows not how to pray. He has never seen God whose eye has not been couched for God in the closet. God's vision place is the closet. His dwelling place is in secret. "He that dwelleth in the secret place of the most high shall abide under the shadow of the Almighty."

He has never studied God who has not had his intellect broadened, strengthened, clarified and uplifted by prayer. Almighty God commands prayer, God waits on prayer to order his ways, and God delights in prayer. To God, prayer is what the incense was to the Jewish temple. It impregnates everything, perfumes everything and sweetens everything.

The possibilities of prayer cover the whole purposes of God through Christ. God conditions all gifts in all dispensations to his Son on prayer: "Ask of me," saith God the Father to the Son, as that Son was moving earthward on the stupendous enterprise for a world's salvation, "and I will give thee the heathen for thy inheritance, and the uttermost parts of the earth for thy possession." Hinging on prayer were all the means and results and successes of that wonderful and divine movement for man's salvation. Broad and profound, mysterious and wonderful was the scheme.

The answer to prayer is assured not only by the promises of God, but by God's relation to us as a Father.

> But thou, when thou prayest, enter into thy closet, and when thou has shut thy door, pray to thy Father, which is in secret; and thy Father, which seeth in secret, shall reward thee openly.

Again, we have these words:

> If ye, being evil, know how to give good gifts unto your children, how much more shall your Father, which is in heaven, give good things to them that ask him?

God encourages us to pray, not only by the certainty of the answer, but by the munificence of the promise, and the bounty of the giver. How princely the promise! "All things whatsoever." And when we add to that "whatsoever" the promise which covers all things and everything, without qualification, exception or limitation, "anything," this is to expand and make minute and specific the promise. The challenge of God to us is "Call unto me, and I will answer thee, and show thee great and mighty things which thou knowest not." This includes, like the answer to Solomon's prayer, that which was specifically prayed for, but embraces vastly more of great value and of great necessity.

Almighty God seems to fear we will hesitate to ask largely, apprehensive that we will strain his ability. He declares that he is "able to do exceeding abundantly above all that we can ask or think." He almost paralyses us by giving us a *carte blanche,* "Ask of me things to come concerning my sons, and concerning the work of my hands, command ye me." How he charges, commands and urges us to pray! He goes beyond promise and says: "Behold my Son! I have given him to you." "He that spared not his own Son, but delivered him up for us all, how shall he not with him freely give us all things?"

God gave us all things in prayer by promise because he had given us all things in his Son. Amazing gift—his Son! Prayer is as illimitable as his own blessed Son. There is nothing on earth nor in heaven, for time or eternity, that God's Son did not secure for us. By prayer God gives us the vast and matchless inheritance which is ours by virtue of his Son. God charges us to "come boldly to the throne of grace." God is glorified and Christ is honored by large asking.

That which is true of the promises of God is equally true of the purposes of God. We might say that God does nothing without prayer. His most gracious purposes are conditioned on prayer. His marvelous promises in the thirty-sixth chapter of Ezekiel are subject to this qualification and condition: "Thus saith the Lord God: I will yet for this be inquired of by the house of Israel to do it for them."

In the second psalm the purposes of God to his enthroned Christ are decreed on prayer, as has been previously quoted. That decree which promises to him the heathen for his inheritance relies on prayer for its fulfillment: "Ask of me." We see how sadly the decree has failed in its operation, not because of the weakness of God's purpose, but by the weakness of man's praying. It takes God's mighty decree and man's mighty praying to bring to pass these glorious results.

In the seventy-second psalm we have an insight into the mighty potencies of prayer as the force which God moves on the conquest of Christ: "Prayer shall be made for him continually." In this statement Christ's movements are put into the hands of prayer.

When Christ, with a sad and sympathizing heart, looked upon the ripened fields of humanity, and saw the great need of laborers, his purposes were for more laborers, and so He charged them, "Pray ye therefore the Lord of the harvest that he will send forth laborers into his harvest."

In Ephesians, chapter three, Paul reminds those believers of the eternal purposes of God, and how he was bowing his knees to God so that eternal purpose might be accomplished, and also that they "might be filled with all the fullness of God."

We see in Job how God conditioned his purposes for Job's three friends on Job's praying, and God's purposes in regard to Job were brought about by the same means.

In the first part of Revelation, (chapter eight) the relation and necessity of saintly prayers to God's plans and operations in executing the salvation of men is set forth in rich, expressive symbol, wherein the angels have to do with the prayers of the saints.

Prayer gives efficiency and utility to the promises. The mighty ongoing of

God's purposes rests on prayer. The representatives of the church in heaven and of all creation before the throne of God "have every one of them golden vials of odors which are the prayers of the saints."

We have said before, and repeat it, that prayer is based not simply on a promise, but on a relationship. The returning penitent sinner prays on a promise. The child of God prays on the relation of a child. What the father has belongs to the child for present and prospective uses. The child asks, the father gives. The relationship is one of asking and answering, of giving and receiving. The child is dependent upon the father, must look to the father, must ask of the father, and must receive of the father.

We know how with earthly parents asking and giving belong to this relation, and how in the very act of asking and giving, the relationship of parent and child is cemented, sweetened, and enriched. The parent finds his wealth of pleasure and satisfaction in giving to an obedient child, and the child finds his wealth in the father's loving and continuous giving.

Prayer affects God more powerfully than his own purposes. God's will, words, and purposes are all subject to review when the mighty potencies of prayer come in. How mighty prayer is with God may be seen as he readily sets aside his own fixed and declared purposes in answer to prayer. The whole plan of salvation had been blocked had Jesus Christ prayed for the twelve legions of angels to carry dismay and ruin to his enemies.

The fasting and prayers of the Ninevites changed God's purposes to destroy that wicked city, after Jonah had gone there and cried unto the people, "Yet forty days and Nineveh shall be destroyed."

Almighty God is concerned in our praying. He wills it, he commands it, he inspires it. Jesus Christ in heaven is ever praying. Prayer is his law and his life. The Holy Spirit teaches us how to pray. He prays for us with "groanings which cannot be uttered." All these show the deep concern of God in prayer. It discloses very clearly how vital it is to his work in this world, and how far-reaching are its possibilities. Prayer forms the very center of the heart and will of God concerning men. "Rejoice evermore, pray without ceasing, and in everything give thanks. For this is the will of God in Christ Jesus concerning you." Prayer is the pole star around which rejoicing and thanksgiving revolve. Prayer is the heart sending its full and happy pulsations up to God through the glad currents of joy and thanksgiving.

By prayer God's name is hallowed. By prayer God's kingdom comes. By prayer is his kingdom established in power and made to move with conquering force swifter than the light. By prayer God's will is done till earth rivals heaven in harmony and beauty. By prayer daily toil is sanctified and enriched, and pardon is secured, and Satan is defeated. Prayer concerns God, and concerns man in every way.

God has nothing too good to give in answer to prayer. There is no vengeance pronounced by God so dire which does not yield to prayer. There is no justice so flaming that is not quenched by prayer.

Take the record and attitude of heaven against Saul of Tarsus. That attitude is changed and that record is erased when the astonishing condition is announced, "Behold he prayeth." The deserter Jonah is alive, and on dry ground, with scarce the taste of the sea or the smell of its weeds about him, as he prays.

> Out of the belly of hell cried I, and thou heardst my voice. The waters compassed me about, even to the soul; the depth closed me round about, the weeds were wrapped about my head. I went down to the bottoms of the mountains; the earth with her bars was about me for ever; yet hast thou brought up my life from corruption, O Lord my God. When my soul fainted within me I remembered the Lord: and my prayer came in unto thee, into thine holy temple. And the Lord spake unto the fish, and it vomited out Jonah upon the dry land.

Prayer has all the force of God in it. Prayer can get anything which God has. Thus prayer has all of its plea and its claim in the name of Jesus Christ, and there is nothing to good or great for God to give that name.

It must be borne in mind that there is no test surer than this thing of prayer of our being in the family of God. God's children pray. They repose in him for all things. They ask him for all things—for everything. The faith of the child in the father is evinced by the child's asking. It is the answer to prayer which convinces men not only that there is a God, but that he is a God who concerns himself about men, and about the affairs of this world. Answered prayer brings God nigh, and assures men of his being. Answered prayer is the credential of our relation to and our representative of him. Men who do not get answers to prayer from God cannot represent him.

The possibilities of prayer are found in the illimitable promise, the willingness and the power of God to answer prayer, to answer all prayer, to answer every prayer, and to supply fully the illimitable need of man. None are so needy as man, none are so able and anxious to supply every need and any need as God.

Preaching should no more fully declare and fulfill the will of God for the salvation of all men, than should the prayers of God's saints declare the same great truth, as they wrestle in their closet for this sublime end. God's heart is set on the salvation of all men. This concerns God. He has declared this in the death of his Son by an unspeakable voice, and every movement on earth for this end pleases God. And so he declares that our prayers for the salvation of all men are well pleasing in his sight. The sublime and holy inspiration of pleasing God should ever move us to prayer for all men. God eyes the closet, and nothing we can do pleases him better than our large-hearted, ardent praying for all men. It is the embodiment and test of our devotion to God's will and of our sympathetic loyalty to God.

In 1 Timothy 2:13 the apostle Paul does not descend to a low plane, but presses the necessity of prayer by the most forceful facts. Jesus Christ, a man, the God-man, the highest illustration of manhood, is the mediator between God and man. Jesus Christ, this divine man, died for all men. His life is but an intercession for all men. His death is but a prayer for all men. On earth, Jesus Christ knew no higher law, no holier business, no diviner life, than to plead for men. In heaven he knows no more royal estate, no higher theme, than to intercede for men. On earth he lived and prayed and died for men. His life, his death and his exaltation in heaven all plead for men.

Is there any work, higher work for the disciple to do than his Lord did? Is there any loftier employment, more honorable, more divine, than to pray for men? To take their woes, their sins, and their perils before God; to be one with Christ? To break the slavery which binds them, the hell which holds them and lift them to immortality and eternal life?

5

Jesus Christ,
the Divine Teacher of Prayer

JESUS Christ was the divine teacher of prayer. Its power and nature had been illustrated by many a saint and prophet in olden times, but modern sainthood and modern teachers of prayer had lost their inspiration and life. Religiously dead, teachers and superficial ecclesiastics had forgotten what it was to pray. They did much of saying prayers, on state occasions, in public, with much ostentation and parade, but pray they did not. To them it was almost a lost practice. In the multiplicity of saying prayers they had lost the art of praying.

The history of the disciples during the earthly life of our Lord was not marked with much devotion. They were much enamored by their personal association with Christ. They were charmed by his words, excited by his miracles, and were entertained and concerned by the hopes which a selfish interest aroused in his person and mission. Taken up with the superficial and worldly views of his character, they neglected and overlooked the deeper and weightier things which belonged to him and his mission. The neglect of the most obliging and ordinary duties by them was a noticeable feature in their conduct. So evident and singular was their conduct in this regard, that it became a matter of grave inquiry on one occasion and severe chiding on another.

> And they said unto him, Why do the disciples of John fast often, and make prayers, and likewise the disciples of the Pharisees; but thine eat and drink? And he said unto them, Can ye make the children of the bridechamber fast, while the bridegroom is with them? But the days will come, when the bridegroom shall be taken away from them, and then shall they fast in those days.

In the example and the teaching of Jesus Christ, prayer assumes its normal relation to God's person, God's movements, and God's Son. Jesus Christ was essentially the teacher of prayer by precept and example. We have glimpses of his praying which, like indices, tell how full of prayer the pages, chapters, and volumes of his life were. The epitome which covers not one segment only, but the whole circle of his life, and character, is preeminently that of prayer!

244

"In the days of his flesh," the divine record reads, "when he had offered up prayers and supplications, with strong crying and tears." The suppliant of all suppliants he was, the intercessor of all intercessors. In lowliest form he approached God, and with strongest pleas he prayed and supplicated.

Jesus Christ teaches the importance of prayer by his urgency to his disciples to pray. But he shows us more than that. He shows how far prayer enters into the purposes of God. We must ever keep in mind that the relation of Jesus Christ to God is the relation of asking and giving, the Son ever asking, the Father ever giving. We must never forget that God has put the conquering, inheriting and expanding forces of Christ's cause in prayer.

> Ask of me, and I will give thee the heathen for thy inheritance, and the uttermost part of the earth for thy possession.

This was the clause embodying the royal proclamation and the universal condition when the Son was enthroned as the world's mediator, and when he was sent on his mission of receiving grace and power. We very naturally learn from this how Jesus would stress praying as the one sole condition of his receiving his possession and inheritance.

Necessarily in this study on prayer, lines of thought will cross each other, and the same Scripture passage or incident will be mentioned more than once, simply because a passage may teach one or more truths. This is the case when we speak of the vast comprehensiveness of prayer. How all-inclusive Jesus Christ makes prayer! It has no limitations in extent or things! The promises to prayer are Godlike in their magnificence, wideness, and universality. In their nature these promises have to do with God—with him in their inspiration, creation, and results. Who but God could say, "All things whatsoever ye ask in prayer, believing, ye shall receive?" Who can command and direct "All things whatsoever" but God? Neither man nor chance nor the law of results are so far lifted above change, limitations, or condition, nor have in them mighty forces which can direct and result all things, as to promise the bestowment and direction of all things.

Whole sections, parables, and incidents were used by Christ to inforce the necessity and importance of prayer. His miracles are but parables of prayer. In nearly all of them prayer figures distinctly, and some features of it are illustrated. The Syrophoenician woman is a preeminent illustration of the ability and the success of importunity in prayer. The case of blind Bartimaeus has points of suggestion along the same line. Jairus and the centurion illustrate and impress phases of prayer. The parable of the Pharisee and the publican inforces humility in prayer, declares the wondrous results of praying, and shows the vanity and worthlessness of wrong praying. The failure to inforce church discipline and the readiness of violating the brotherhood, are all used to make an exhibit of far-reaching results of agreed praying, a record of which we have in Matthew 18:19.

It is of prayer in concert that Christ is speaking: two agreed ones, two whose hearts have been keyed into perfect symphony by the Holy Spirit. Anything that they shall ask, it shall be done. Christ had been speaking of discipline in the church, how things were to be kept in unity, and how the fellowship of the brethren was to be maintained, by the restoration of the offender or by his exclusion. Members who had been true to the brotherhood of Christ, and who were laboring to preserve that brotherhood unbroken, would be the agreed ones to make appeals to God in united prayer.

In the Sermon on the Mount, Christ lays down constitutional principles. Types and shadows are retired, and the law of spiritual life is declared. In this foundation law of the Christian system prayer assumes a conspicuous, if not a paramount, position. It is not only wide, all-commanding, and comprehensive in its own sphere of action and relief, but it is ancillary to all duties. Even the one demanding kindly and discriminating judgment toward others, and also the royal injunction, the golden rule of action, these owe their being to prayer.

Christ puts prayer among the statutory promises. He does not leave it to natural law. The law of need, demand, and supply, of helplessness, of natural instincts, or the law of sweet, high, attractive privilege—these howsoever strong as motives of action, are not the basis of praying. Christ puts it as spiritual law. Men must pray. Not to pray is not simply a privation, an omission, but a positive violation of law, of spiritual life, a crime, bringing disorder and ruin. Prayer is law worldwide and eternity-reaching.

In the Sermon on the Mount many important utterances are dismissed with a line or a verse, while the subject of prayer occupies a large space. To it Christ returns again and again. He bases the possibilities and necessities of prayer on the relation of father and child, the child crying for bread, and the father giving that for which the child asks. Prayer and its answer are in the relation of a father to his child. The teaching of Jesus Christ on the nature and necessity of prayer as recorded in his life, is remarkable. He sends men to their closets. Prayer must be a holy exercise, untainted by vanity or pride. It must be in secret. The disciple must live in secret. God lives there, is sought there and is found there. The command of Christ as to prayer is that pride and publicity should be shunned. Prayer is to be in private.

> But thou when thou prayest, enter into thy closet, and shut thy door, and pray to thy Father in secret. And thy Father, which seeth in secret, shall reward thee openly.

The Beatitudes are not only to enrich and adorn, but they are the material out of which spiritual character is built. The very first one of these fixes prayer in the very foundation of spiritual character, not simply to adorn, but to compose. "Blessed are the poor in spirit." The word *poor* means a pauper, one who lives by begging. The real Christian lives on the bounties of another, whose bounties he gets by asking. Prayer then becomes the basis of Christian character, the Christian's business, his life and his living. This is Christ's law of prayer, putting it into the very being of the Christian. It is his first step, and his first breath, which is to color and to form all his afterlife. Blessed are the poor ones, for they only can pray.

> Prayer is the Christian's vital breath,
> The Christian's native air;
> His watchword at the gates of death;
> He enters heaven with prayer.

From praying Christ eliminates all self-sufficiency, all pride, and all spiritual values. The poor in spirit are the praying ones. Beggars are God's princes. They are God's heirs. Christ removes the rubbish of Jewish traditions and glosses from the regulations of the prayer altar.

> Ye have heard that it was said by them of old time, Thou shalt not kill: and whosoever shall kill shall be in danger of the judgment: But I say unto you, that whosoever is angry with his brother shall be in danger of the judgment: and whosoever shall say to his brother, Raca, shall be in danger of the council: but whosoever shall say, thou fool shall be in danger of hell fire. Therefore if thou bring thy gift to the altar and there rememberest that thy brother has aught against thee: Leave there thy gift before the altar, and go thy way; first, be reconciled to thy brother, and then come and offer thy gift.

He who essays to pray to God with an angry spirit, with loose and irreverent lips, with an irreconciled heart, and with unsettled neighborly scores, spends his labor for that which is worse than naught, violates the law of prayer, and adds to his sin.

How rigidly exacting is Christ's law of prayer! It goes to the heart, and demands that love be enthroned there, love to the brotherhood. The sacrifice of prayer must be seasoned and perfumed with love, by love in the inward parts. The law of prayer, its creator and inspirer, is love.

Praying must be done. God wants it done. He commands it. Man needs it and man must do it. Something must surely come of praying, for God engages that something shall come out of it, if men are in earnest and are persevering in prayer.

After Jesus teaches "Ask and it shall be given you," etc., he encourages real praying, and more praying. He repeats and avers with redoubled assurance, "For every one that asketh receiveth." No exception. "Every one." "He that seeketh, findeth." Here it is again, sealed and stamped with infinite veracity. Then closed and signed, as well as sealed, with divine attestation, "To him that knocketh it shall be opened." Note how we are encouraged to pray by our relation to God!

If ye then, being evil, know how to give good gifts unto your children, how much more shall your Father which is in heaven give good things. to them that ask him?

The relation of prayer to God's work and God's rule in this world is most fully illustrated by Jesus Christ in both his teaching and his practice. He is first in every way and in everything. Among the rulers of the church he is primary in a preeminent way. He has the throne. The golden crown is his in eminent preciousness. The white garments enrobe him in preeminent whiteness and beauty. In the ministry of prayer he is a divine example as well as the divine teacher. His example is affluent, and his prayer teaching abounds. How imperative the teaching of our Lord when he affirms that "men ought always to pray and not to faint!" and then presents a striking parable of an unjust judge and a poor widow to illustrate and enforce his teaching. It is a necessity to pray. It is exacting and binding for men always to be in prayer. Courage, endurance, and perseverance are demanded that men may never faint in prayer. "And shall not God avenge his own elect that cry day and night unto him?"

This is his strong and indignant questioning and affirmation. Men must pray according to Christ's teaching. They must not get tired nor grow weary in praying. God's character is the assured surety that much will come of the persistent praying of true men.

Doubtless the praying of our Lord had much to do with the revelation made to Peter and the confession he made to Christ, "Thou art the Christ, the Son of the living God." Prayer mightily affects and molds the circle of our associates. Christ made disciples and kept them disciples by praying. His twelve disciples were much impressed by his praying. Never man prayed like this man. How different his praying from the cold, proud, self-righteous praying which they heard and saw on the streets, in the synagogue, and in the temple.

6

Jesus Christ,
the Divine Teacher of Prayer
(Continued)

LET it not be forgotten that prayer was one of the great truths which he came into the world to teach and illustrate. It was worth a trip from heaven to earth to teach men this great lesson of prayer. A great lesson it was, a very difficult lesson for men to learn. Men are naturally averse to learning this lesson of prayer. The lesson is a very lowly one. None but God can teach it. It is a despised beggary, a sublime, and heavenly vocation. The disciples were very stupid scholars, but were quickened to prayer by hearing him pray and talk about prayer.

The dispensation of Christ's personality, was not and could not be the dispensation in its fullest and highest sense of need and dependence, yet Christ did try to impress on his disciples not alone a deep necessity of the necessity of prayer in general, but also the importance of prayer to them in their personal and spiritual needs. And there came moments to them when they felt the need of a deeper and more thorough schooling in prayer and of their grave neglect in this regard. One of these hours of deep conviction on their part and of eager inquiry was when he was praying at a certain place and time, and they saw him, and they said to him, "Lord, teach us to pray, as John also taught his disciples."

As they listened to him praying, they felt very keenly their ignorance and deficiency in praying. Who has not felt the same deficiency and ignorance? Who has not longed for a teacher in the divine art of praying?

The conviction which these twelve men had of their defect in prayer arose from hearing their Lord and master pray, but likewise from a sense of serious defect even when compared with John the Baptist's training of his disciples in prayer. As they listened to their Lord pray (for unquestionably he must have been seen and heard by them as he prayed, who prayed with marvelous simplicity, and power, so human and so divine) such praying had a stimulating charm for them. In the presence and hearing of his praying, very keenly they felt their ignorance and deficiency in prayer. Who has not felt the same ignorance and deficiency?

We do not regret the schooling our Lord gave these twelve men, for in schooling them he schools us. The lesson is one already learned in the law of Christ. But so dull were they, that many a patient emphasis and reiteration was required to instruct them in this divine art of prayer. And likewise so dull are we and inept that many a wearying patient repetition must be given us before we will learn any important lesson in the all-important school of prayer.

This divine teacher of prayer lays himself out to make it clear and strong that God answers prayer, assuredly, certainly, inevitably; that it is the duty of the child to ask, and to press, and that the Father is obliged to answer, and to give for the asking. In Christ's teaching, prayer is no sterile, vain performance, not a mere rite, a form, but a request for an answer, a plea to gain, the seeking of a great good from God. It is a lesson of getting that for which we ask, of finding that for which we seek, and of entering the door at which we knock.

A notable occasion we have as Jesus comes down from the Mount of Transfiguration. He finds his disciples defeated, humiliated, and confused in the presence of their enemies. A father has brought his child possessed with a demon to have the demon cast out. They tried to do it but failed. They had been commissioned by Jesus and sent to do that very work, but had signally failed.

> And when he was come into the house, his disciples asked him privately, saying, Why could not we cast him out? And he said unto them, This kind can come forth by nothing but by prayer and fasting.

Their faith had not been cultured by prayer. They failed in prayer before they failed in ability to do their work. They failed in faith because they had failed in prayer. That one thing which was necessary to do God's work was prayer. The work which God sends us to do cannot be done without prayer.

In Christ's teaching on prayer we have another pertinent statement. It was in connection with the cursing of the barren fig tree:

> Jesus answered and said unto them, Verily I say unto you, if ye have faith, and doubt not, ye shall not only do this which is done to the fig tree, but also if ye shall say unto this mountain, Be thou removed and be thou cast into the sea; it shall be done. And all things whatsoever ye shall ask in prayer, believing, ye shall receive.

In this passage we have faith and prayer, their possibilities, and powers joined. A fig tree had been blasted to the roots by the word of the Lord Jesus. The power and quickness of the result surprised the disciples. Jesus says to them that it need be no surprise to them or such a difficult work to be done. "If ye have faith" its possibilities to affect will not be confined to the little fig tree, but the gigantic, rock-ribbed, rock-founded mountains can be uprooted and moved into the sea. Prayer is leverage of this great power of faith.

It is well to refer again to the occasion when the heart of our Lord was so deeply moved with compassion as he beheld the multitudes because they fainted and were scattered as having no shepherd. Then it was he urged on his disciples the injunction, "Pray ye the Lord of the harvest that he would send forth laborers into his harvest," clearly teaching them that it belonged to God to call into the ministry men whom he will, and that in answer to prayer the Holy Spirit does this very work.

Prayer is as necessary now as it was then to secure the needed laborers to reap earthly harvests for the heavenly garners. Has the church of God ever learned this lesson of so vital and exacting import? God alone can choose the laborers and thrust them out, and this choosing he does not delegate to man, or church, convocation, synod, association, or conference. And God is moved to this great work of calling men into the ministry by prayer. Earthly fields are rotting. They are untilled because prayer is silent. The laborers are few. Fields are unworked because prayer has not worked with God.

We have the prayer promise and the prayer ability put in a distinct form in the higher teachings of prayer by our Lord: "If ye abide in me, and my words abide in you, ye shall ask what ye will, and it shall be done unto you."

Here we have a fixed attitude of life as the condition of prayer. Not simply a fixed attitude of life toward some great principles or purposes, but the fixed attitude and unity of life with Jesus Christ. To live in him, to dwell there, to be one with him, to draw all life from him, to let all life from him flow through us—this is the attitude of prayer and the ability to pray. No abiding in him can be separated from his Word abiding in us. It must live in us to give birth to and food for prayer. The attitude of the person of Christ is the condition of prayer.

The Old Testament saints had been taught that "God had magnified his word above all his name." New Testament saints must learn fully how to exalt by perfect obedience that Word issuing from the lips of him who is the Word. Praying ones under Christ must learn what praying ones under Moses had already learned, that "man shall not live by bread alone, but by every word that proceedeth out of the mouth of God." The life of Christ flowing through us and the words of Christ living in us, these give potency to prayer. They breathe the spirit of prayer, and make the body, blood, and bones of prayer. Then it is Christ praying in me and through me, and "all things which I will" are the will of God. My will becomes the law and the answer, for it is written "Ye shall ask what ye will, and it shall be done unto you."

Our Lord puts fruit bearing to the front in our praying:

> Ye have not chosen me, but I have chosen you, and ordained you, that ye shall go and bring forth fruit and that your fruit shall remain, that whatsoever ye shall ask of the Father in my name, he may give it you.

Barrenness cannot pray. Fruit-bearing capacity and reality only can pray. It is not past fruitfulness, but present: "That your fruit should remain." Fruit, the product of life, is the condition of praying. A life vigorous enough to bear fruit, much fruit, is the condition and the source of prayer.

> And in that day ye shall ask me nothing. Verily, verily, I say unto you, Whatsoever ye shall ask the Father in my name, he will give it you. Hitherto have ye asked nothing in my name: ask and ye shall receive, that your joy may be full. In that day ye shall ask me nothing.

It is not solving riddles, not revealing mysteries, not curious questionings. This is not our attitude, not our business under the dispensation of the Spirit, but to pray, and to pray largely. Much true praying increases man's joy and God's glory.

"Whatsoever ye shall ask in my name, I will give," says Christ, and the Father will give. Both Father and Son are pledged to give the very things for which we ask. But the condition is in his name. This does not mean that his name is talismanic, to give value by magic. It does not mean that his name in beautiful settings of pearl will give value to prayer. It is not that his name perfumed with sentiment and larded in and closing up our prayers and doings will do the deed. How fearful the statement:

> Many will say unto me in that day, Lord, Lord, have we not prophesied in thy name? and in thy name cast out devils? and in thy name done many wonderful works? And then will I profess unto them, I never knew you. Depart from me, ye that work iniquity.

How blasting the doom of these great workers and doers who claim to work in his name!

It means far more than sentiment, verbiage, and nomenclature. It means to stand in his stead, to bear his nature, to stand for all for which he stood, for righteousness, truth, holiness and zeal. It means to be one with God as he was, one in spirit, in will and in purpose. It means that our praying is singly and solely for God's glory through his Son. It means that we abide in him, that Christ prays through us, lives in us and shines out of us; that we pray by the Holy Spirit according to the will of God.

Even amid the darkness of Gethsemane, with the stupor which had settled upon the disciples, we have the sharp warning from Christ to his sluggish disciples, "Watch and pray lest ye enter into temptation. The spirit truly is willing, but the flesh is weak." How needful to hear such a warning, to awaken all our powers, not simply for the great crises of our lives, but as the inseparable and constant attendants of a career marked with perils and dangers on every hand.

As Christ nears the close of his earthly mission, nearer to the greater and more powerful dispensation of the Spirit, his teaching about prayer takes on a more absorbing and higher form. It has now become a graduating school. His connection with prayer becomes more intimate and more absolute. He becomes in prayer what he is in all else pertaining to our salvation, the beginning and the end, the first and the last. His name becomes all potent. Mighty works are to be done by the faith which can pray in his name. Like his nature, his name covers all needs, embraces all worlds, and gets all good.

> Believest thou not that I am in the Father and the Father in me? The words that I speak unto you I speak not of myself: but the Father that dwelleth in me, he doeth the works. Believe me that I am in the Father and the Father in me: or else believe me for the very works' sake. Verily, verily, I say unto you, He that believeth on me, the works that I do shall he do also; and greater works than these shall he do; because I go unto my Father. And whatsoever ye shall ask in my name, than will I do, that the Father may be glorified in the Son. If ye shall ask anything in my name I will do it.

The Father, the Son and the praying one are all bound up together. All things are in Christ, and all things are in prayer in his name. "If ye shall ask anything in my name." The key which unlocks the vast storehouse of God is prayer. The power to do greater works than Christ did lies in the faith which can grasp his name truly and in true praying.

In the last of his life, note how he urges prayer as a preventive of the many evils to which they were exposed. In view of the temporal and fearful terrors of the destruction of Jerusalem, he charges them to this effect: "Pray ye that your flight be not in winter."

How many evils in this life which can be escaped by prayer! How many fearful temporal calamities can be mitigated, if not wholly relieved, by prayer! Notice how, amid the excesses and stupefying influences to which we are exposed in this world, Christ charges us to pray:

> And take heed to yourselves, lest at any time your hearts be overcharged with surfeiting, and drunkenness, and cares of this life, and so that day come upon you unawares. For as a snare shall it come on all them that dwell on the face of the whole earth. Watch ye therefore and pray always, that ye may be accounted worthy to escape all these things that shall come to pass, and to stand before the Son of man.

In view of the uncertainty of Christ's coming to judgment, and the uncertainty of our going out of this world, he says:

> But of that day and that hour knoweth no man, no, not the angels which are in heaven, neither the Son, but the Father. Take ye heed, watch and pray, for ye know not when the time is.

We have the words of Jesus as given in his last interview with his twelve disciples, found in the Gospel of John, chapters fourteen to seventeen, inclusive. These are true, solemn parting words. The disciples were to move out into the regions of toil, and peril, bereft of the personal presence of their Lord and master. They were to be impressed that prayer would serve them in everything, and its use, and unlimited possibilities would in some measure supply their loss, and by it they would be able to command all the possibilities of Jesus Christ and God the Father.

It was the occasion of momentous interest to Jesus Christ. His work was to receive its climax and crown in his death and his resurrection. His glory and the success of his work and of its execution, under the mastery and direction of the Holy Spirit, was to be committed to his apostles. To them it was an hour of strange wonderment and of peculiar, mysterious sorrow, only too well assured of the fact that Jesus was to leave them. Dark and impalpable was all else.

He was to give them his parting words and pray his parting prayer. Solemn, vital truths were to be the weight and counsel of that hour. He speaks to them of heaven. Young men, strong though they were, yet they could not meet the duties of their preaching life and their apostolic life, without the fact, the thought, the hope, and the relish of heaven. These things were to be present constantly in all sweetness, in all their vigor, in all freshness, in all brightness. He spoke to them about their spiritual and conscious connection with himself, an abiding indwelling, so close and continuous that his own life would flow into them, as the life of the vine flows into the branches. Their lives and their fruitfulness were dependent on this. Then praying was urged on them as one of the vital, essential forces. This was the one thing upon which all the divine force depended, and this was the avenue and agency through which the divine life and power were to be secured and continued in their ministry.

He spoke to them about prayer. He had taught them many lessons upon this all-important subject as they had been together. This solemn hour he seizes to perfect his teaching. They must be made to realize that they have an illimitable and exhaustless storehouse of good in God and that they can draw on him at all times and for all things without stint, as Paul said in after years to the Philippians, "My God shall supply all your need according to his riches in glory by Christ Jesus."

7

Jesus Christ,
an Example of Prayer

THE Bible record of the life of Jesus Christ gives but a glance of his busy doing, a small selection of his many words, and only a brief record of his great works. But even in this record we see him as being much in prayer. Even though busy and exhausted by the severe strain and toils of his life, "in the morning a great while before day, he rose up and went out and departed into a desert place, and there prayed." Alone in the desert and in the darkness with God! Prayer filled the life of our Lord while on earth. His life was a constant stream of incense sweet and perfumed by prayer. When we see how the life of Jesus was but one of prayer, then we must conclude that to be like Jesus is to pray like Jesus and is to live like Jesus. A serious life it is to pray as Jesus prayed.

We cannot follow any chronological order in the praying of Jesus Christ. What were his steps of advance and skill in the divine art of praying we know not. He is in the act of prayer when we find him at the fords of the Jordan, when the waters of baptism, at the hands of John the Baptist, are on him. So passing over the three years of his ministry, when closing the drama of his life in that terrible baptism of fear, pain, suffering, and shame, we find him in the spirit, and also in the very act of praying. The baptism of the cross, as well as the baptism of the Jordan, are sanctified by prayer. With the breath of prayer in his last sigh, he commits his spirit to God. In his first recorded utterances, as well as his first acts, we find him teaching his disciples how to pray as his first lesson, and as their first duty. Under the shadow of the cross, in the urgency and importance of his last interview with his chosen disciples, he is at the same all-important business, teaching the world's teachers how to pray, trying to make prayerful those lips and hearts out of which were to flow the divine deposits of truth.

The great eras of his life were created and crowned with prayer. What were his habits of prayer during his stay at home and his toil as a carpenter in Nazareth, we have no means of knowing. God has veiled it, and guess and speculation are not only vain and misleading, but proud and prurient. It would be presumptuous searching into that which God has hidden, which

255

would make us seek to be wise above that which was written, trying to lift up the veil with which God has covered his own revelation.

We find Christ in the presence of the famed, the prophet and the preacher. He has left his Nazareth home and his carpenter shop by God's call. He is now at a transitional point. He has moved out to his great work. John's baptism and the baptism of the Holy Spirit are prefatory and are to qualify him for that work. This epochal and transitional period is marked by prayer.

> Now when all the people were baptized, it came to pass that Jesus, being also baptized, and praying, the heaven was opened.
> And the Holy Spirit descended in a bodily shape like a dove upon him, and a voice came from heaven, which said, thou art my beloved Son; in thee I am well pleased.

It is a supreme hour in his history, different and in striking contrast with, but not in opposition to, the past. The descent and abiding of the Holy Spirit in all his fullness, the opening heavens, and the attesting voice which involved God's recognition of his only Son—all these are the result, if not the direct creation and response to his praying on that occasion.

"As he was praying," so we are to be praying. If we would pray as Christ prayed, we must be as Christ was, and must live as Christ lived. The Christ character, the Christ life, and the Christ spirit, must be ours if we would do the Christ praying, and would have our prayers answered as he had his prayers answered. The business of Christ even now in heaven at his Father's right hand is to pray. Certainly if we are his, if we love him, if we live for him, and if we live close to him, we will catch the contagion of his praying life, both on earth and in heaven. We will learn his trade and carry on his business on earth.

Jesus Christ loved all men, he tasted death for all men, he intercedes for all men. Let us ask then, are we the imitators, the representatives, and the executors of Jesus Christ? Then must we in our prayers run parallel with his atonement in its extent. The atoning blood of Jesus Christ gives sanctity and efficiency to our prayers. As worldwide, as broad, and as human as the man Christ Jesus was, so must be our prayers. The intercessions of Christ's people must give currency and expedition to the work of Christ, carry the atoning blood to its beneficial ends, and help to strike off the chains of sin from every ransomed soul. We must be as praying, as tearful, and as compassionate as was Christ.

Prayer affects all things. God blesses the person who prays. He who prays goes out on a long voyage for God and is enriched himself while enriching others, and is blessed himself while the world is blessed by his praying. "To live a quiet and peaceable life in all godliness and honesty" is the wealthiest wealth.

The praying of Christ was real. No man prayed as he prayed. Prayer pressed upon him as a solemn, all-imperative, all-commanding duty, as well as a royal privilege in which all sweetness was condensed, alluring, and absorbing. Prayer was the secret of his power, the law of his life, the inspiration of his toil and the source of his wealth, his joy, his communion, and his strength.

To Christ Jesus prayer occupied no secondary place, but was exacting and paramount, a necessity, a life, the satisfying of a restless yearning and a preparation for heavy responsibilities.

Closeting with his Father in counsel and fellowship, with vigor and in deep joy, all this was his praying. Present trials, future glory, the history of his church, and the struggles and perils of his disciples in all times and to the very end of time all these things were born and shaped by his praying.

Nothing is more conspicuous in the life of our Lord than prayer. His campaigns were arranged and his victories were gained in the struggles and communion of his all-night praying. By prayer he rent the heavens. Moses and Elijah and the transfiguration glory wait on his praying. His miracles and teaching had their power from the same source. Gethsemane's praying crimsoned Calvary with serenity and glory. His high-priestly prayer makes the history and hastens the triumph of his church on earth. What an inspiration and command to pray is the prayer life of Jesus Christ while in this world! What a comment it is on the value, the nature and the necessity of prayer!

The dispensation of the person of Jesus Christ was a dispensation of prayer. A synopsis of his teaching and practice of prayer was that "Men ought always to pray and not to faint."

As the Jews prayed in the name of their patriarchs and invoked the privileges granted to them by covenant with God; as we have a new name and a new covenant, more privileged and more powerful and more all-comprehensive, more authoritative and more divine; and as far as the Son of God is lifted above the patriarchs in divinity, glory, and power, by so much should our praying exceed theirs in range of largeness, glory, and power of results.

Jesus Christ prayed to God as Father. Simply and directly did he approach God in the charmed and revered circle of the Father. The awful, repelling fear was entirely absent, lost in the supreme confidence of a child.

Jesus Christ crowns his life, his works, and his teaching with prayer. How his Father attests his relationship and puts on him the glory of answered prayer at his baptism and transfiguration when all other glories are growing dim in the night which settles on him! What almighty potencies are in prayer when we are charged and surcharged with but one inspiration and aim! "Father, glorify thy name." This sweetens all, brightens all, conquers all and gets all. Father, glorify thy name." That guiding star will illumine the darkest night and calm the wildest storm and will make us brave and true. An imperial principle it is. It will make an imperial Christian.

The range and potencies of prayer, so clearly shown by Jesus in life and teaching, but reveal the great purposes of God. They not only reveal the Son in the reality and fullness of his humanity, but also reveal the Father.

Christ prayed as a child. The spirit of a child was found in him. At the grave of Lazarus "Jesus lifted up his eyes and said, 'Father.'" Again we hear him begin his prayer after this fashion: "In that hour Jesus rejoiced in spirit, and said, 'I thank thee, O Father.'" So also on other occasions we find him in praying addressing God as his Father, assuming the attitude of the child asking something of the Father. What confidence, simplicity, and artlessness! What readiness, freeness, and fullness of approach are all involved in the spirit of a child! What confiding trust, what assurance, what tender interest! What profound solicitudes, and tender sympathy on the Father's part! What respect deepening into reverence! What loving obedience and grateful emotions glow in the child's heart! What divine fellowship and royal intimacy! What sacred and sweet emotions! All these meet in the hour of prayer when the child of God meets his Father in heaven, and when the Father meets his child! We must live as children if we would ask as children. We must act as children if we would pray as children. The spirit of prayer is born of the child spirit.

The profound reverence in this relation of paternity must forever exclude all lightness, frivolity, and pertness, as well as all undue familiarity. Solemnity and gravity become the hour of prayer. It has been well said: The worshiper who invokes God under the name of Father and realizes the gracious and beneficent love of God must at the same time remember and recognize God's glorious majesty, which is neither annulled nor impaired, but rather supremely intensified through his fatherly love. An appeal to God as Father, if not associated with reverence and homage before the divine majesty, would betray a want of understanding of the character of God." And, we might add, would show a lack of the attributes of a child.

Patriarchs and prophets knew something of the doctrine of the fatherhood of God to God's family. They "saw it afar off, were persuaded of it, and embraced it," but understood it not, in all its fullness, "God having provided some better thing for us, that they without us should not be made perfect."

"Behold he prayeth!" was God's response, to the wonderment and surprise of the timid Ananias, in regard to Saul of Tarsus. "Behold he prayeth!" applied to Christ has in it far more of wonderment and mystery and surprise. He, the maker of all worlds, the Lord of angels and of men, co-equal and co-eternal with the everlasting God; the "brightness of the Father's glory and the express image of his person"; "fresh from his Father's glory and from his Father's throne."—"Behold he prayeth!" To find him in lowly, dependent attitude of prayer, the suppliant of all suppliants, his richest legacy and his royal privilege to pray—this is the mystery of all mysteries, the wonder of all wonders.

Hebrews 5:7 gives in brief and comprehensive statement the habit of our Lord in prayer—"Who, in the days of his flesh, when he had offered up prayers and supplications, with strong crying and tears, unto him that was able to save him from death, and was heard in that he feared." We have in this description of our Lord's praying the outgoing of great spiritual forces. He prayed with "prayers and supplications." It was no formal, tentative effort. He was intense, personal, and real. He was a pleader for God's good. He was in great need and he must cry with "strong cryings," made stronger still by his tears. In an agony the Son of God wrestled. His praying was no playing a mere part. His soul was engaged, and all his powers were taxed to a strain. Let us pause and look at him and learn how to pray in earnest. Let us learn how to win in an agony of prayer that which seems to be withheld from us. A beautiful word is that, "feared," which occurs only twice in the New Testament, the fear of God.

Jesus Christ was always a busy man with his work, but never too busy to pray. The divinest of business filled his heart and filled his hands, consumed his time, exhausted his nerves. But with him even God's work must not crowd out God's praying. Saving people from sin or suffering must not, even with Christ, be substituted for praying, nor abate in the least the time or the intensity of these holiest of seasons. He filled the day with working for God; He employed the night with praying to God. The day-working made the night-praying a necessity. The night-praying sanctified and made successful the day-working. Too busy to pray gives religion Christian burial, it is true, but kills it nevertheless.

In many cases only the bare fact, yet important and suggestive fact, is stated that he prayed. In other cases the very words which came out of his heart and fell from his lips are recorded. The man of prayer by preeminence was Jesus Christ. The epochs of his life were created by prayer, and all the minor details, outlines, and forms of his life were inspired, colored, and impregnated by prayer. The prayer words of Jesus were sacred words.

By them God speaks to God, and by them God is revealed and prayer is illustrated and enforced. Here is prayer in its purest form and in its mightiest potencies. It would seem that earth and heaven would uncover head and open ears most wide to catch the words of his praying who was truest God and truest man, and divinest of suppliants, who prayed as never man prayed. His prayers are our inspiration and pattern to pray.

8

Prayer Incidents
in the Life of Our Lord

ONE of Christ's most impassioned and sublime paeans of prayer and praise is recorded by both Matthew and Luke, with small verbal contrasts and with some diversity of detail and environments. He is reviewing the poor results of his ministry and remarking upon the feeble responses of man to God's vast outlay of love and mercy. He is arraigning the ingratitude of men to God, and is showing the fearfully destructive results of their indifference with their increased opportunities, favors and responsibilities

In the midst of these arraignments, denunciations, and woes, the seventy disciples return to report the results of their mission. They were full of exhilaration at their success, and evinced it with no little self-gratulation. The spirit of Jesus was diverted, relieved, and refreshed by their animation, catching somewhat the contagion of their joy, and sharing in their triumph. He rejoiced, gave thanks, and prayed a prayer wonderful for its brevity, its inspiration and its revelation:

> In that hour Jesus rejoiced in spirit, and said, I thank thee, O Father, Lord of heaven and earth, that thou hast hid these things from the wise and prudent, and hast revealed them unto babes: even so, Father; for so it seemed good in thy sight.
>
> All things are delivered to me of my Father; and no man knoweth who the Son is, but the Father; and who the Father is, but the Son, and he to whom the Son will reveal him.

The Christ life was in the image of his Father. He was the "express image of his person." And so the spirit of prayer with Christ was to do God's will. His constant assertion was that he "came to do his Father's will," and not his own will. When the fearful crisis came in his life in Gethsemane, and all its darkness, direness and dread, with the crushing weight of man's sins and sorrows which were pressing down upon him, his spirit and frame crushed, and almost expiring, then he cried out for relief, yet it was not his will which was to be followed. It was only an appeal out of weakness and death for God's relief in God's way. God's will was to be the law and the rule of his relief, if relief came.

260

So he who follows Christ in prayer must have God's will as his law, his rule, and his inspiration. In all praying, it is the man who prays. The life and the character flow into the closet. There is a mutual action and reaction. The closet has much to do with making the character, while the character has much to do with making the closet. It is "the effectual fervent prayer of the righteous man which availeth much." It is with them who "call upon the Lord out of a pure heart" we are to consort. Christ was the greatest of pray-ers because he was the holiest of men. His character is the praying character. His spirit is the life and power of prayer. He is not the best pray-er who has the greatest fluency, the most brilliant imagination, the richest gifts, and the most fiery ardor, but he who has imbibed most of the spirit of Christ.

It is he whose character is the nearest to a facsimile of Christ upon whom God's power is bestowed and to whom God's person and will are revealed. "Hid these things from the wise and prudent," those, for instance, who are wise in their own eyes, skilled in letters, cultured, learned, philosophers, scribes, doctors, rabbis. "Prudent"—one who can put things together, having insight, comprehension, expression. God's revelation of himself and his will cannot be sought out and understood by reason, intelligence, or great learning. Great men and great minds are neither the channels nor depositories of God's revelation by virtue of their culture, braininess, nor wisdom. God's system in redemption and providence is not to be thought out, open only to the learned and wise. The learned and the wise, following their learning and their wisdom, have always sadly and darkly missed God's thoughts and God's ways.

The condition of receiving God's revelation and of holding God's truth is one of the heart, not one of the head. The ability to receive and search out is like that of the child, the babe, the synonym of docility, innocence and simplicity. These are the conditions on which God reveals himself to men. The world by wisdom cannot know God. The world by wisdom can never receive nor understand God, because God reveals himself to men's hearts, not to their heads. Only hearts can ever know God, can feel God, can see God, and can read God in his book of books. God is not grasped by thought but by feeling. The world gets God by revelation, not by philosophy. It is not apprehension, the mental ability to grasp God, but plasticity, ability to be impressed, that men need. It is not by hard, strong, stern, great reasoning that the world gets God or gets hold of God, but by big, soft, pure hearts. Not so much do men need light to see God as they need hearts to feel God.

Human wisdom, great natural talents, and the culture of the schools, howsoever good they may be, can neither be the repositories nor conservers of God's revealed truth. The tree of knowledge has been the bane of faith, ever essaying to reduce revelation to a philosophy and to measure God by man. In its pride, it puts God out and puts man into God's truth. To become babes again, on our mother's bosom, quieted, weaned, without clamor or protest, is the only position in which to know God. A calmness on the surface, and in the depths of the soul, in which God can mirror his will, his Word and himself—this is the attitude toward him through which he can reveal himself, and this attitude is the right attitude of prayer.

Our Lord taught us the lesson of prayer by putting into practice in his life what he taught by his lips. Here is a simple but important statement, full of meaning: "And when he had sent the multitudes away, he went up into a mountain apart to pray: and when the evening was come he was there alone."

The multitudes had been fed and were dismissed by our Lord.

The divine work of healing and teaching must be stayed awhile in order that time, place and opportunity for prayer might be secured,—prayer, the divinest of all labor, the most important of all ministries. Away from the eager, anxious, seeking multitudes, he has gone while the day is yet bright, to be alone with God. The multitudes tax and exhaust him. The disciples are tossed on the sea, but calmness reigns on the mountain top where our Lord is kneeling in secret prayer—where prayer rules. "When Jesus therefore perceived that they would come and take him by force, to make him a king, he departed again into a mountain alone."

He must be alone in that moment with God. Temptation was in that hour. The multitude had feasted on the five loaves and the two fishes. Filled with food and excited beyond measure, they would fain make him king. He flees from the temptation to secret prayer, for here is the source of his strength to resist evil. What a refuge was secret prayer even to him! What a refuge to us from the world's dazzling and delusive crowns! What safety there is to be alone with God when the world tempts us, allures us, attracts us!

The prayers of our Lord are prophetic and illustrative of the great truth that the greatest measure of the Holy Spirit, the attesting voice and opening heavens are only secured by prayer. This is suggested by his baptism by John the Baptist, when he prayed as he was baptized, and immediately the Holy Spirit descended upon him like a dove. More than prophetic and illustrative is this hour to him. This critical hour is real and personal, consecrating and qualifying him for God's highest purposes. Prayer to him, just as it is to us, was a necessity, an absolute, invariable condition of securing God's fullest, consecrating and qualifying power. The Holy Spirit came upon him in fullness of measure and power in the very act of prayer.

And so the Holy Spirit comes upon us in fullness of measure and power only in answer to ardent and intense praying. The heavens were opened to Christ, and access and communion established and enlarged by prayer. Freedom and fullness of access and closeness of communion are secured to us as the heritage of prayer. The voice attesting his sonship came to Christ in prayer. The witness of our sonship, clear and indubitable, is secured only by praying. The constant witness of our sonship can only be retained by those who pray without ceasing. When the stream of prayer is shallow and arrested, the evidence of our sonship becomes faint and inaudible.

9

Prayer Incidents
in the Life of Our Lord
(Continued)

WE note that from the revelation and inspiration of a transporting prayer-hour of Christ, as its natural sequence, there sounds out that gracious encouraging proclamation for heavy-hearted, restless, weary souls of earth, which has so impressed, arrested and drawn humanity as it has fallen on the ears of heavy-laden souls, which has so sweetened and relieved men of their toils and burdens:

> Come unto me, all ye that labor and are heavy laden, and I will give you rest. Take my yoke upon you, and learn of me; for I am meek and lowly in heart: and ye shall find rest unto your souls. For my yoke is easy, and my burden is light.

At the grave of Lazarus and as preparatory to and as a condition of calling him back to life, we have our Lord calling upon his Father in heaven. "Father I thank thee that thou hast heard me, and I know that thou hearest me always." The lifting to heaven of Christ's eyes—how much was there in it! How much of confidence and plea was in that look to heaven! His very look, the lifting up of his eyes, carried his whole being heavenward, and caused a pause in that world, and drew attention and help. All heaven was engaged, pledged and moved when the Son of God looked up at this grave. O for a people with the Christlike eye, heaven lifted and heaven arresting! As it was with Christ, so ought we to be so perfected in faith, so skilled in praying, that we could lift our eyes to heaven and say with him, with deepest humility, and with commanding confidence, "Father, I thank thee that thou hast heard me."

Once more we have a very touching and beautiful and instructive incident in Christ's praying, this time having to do with infants in their mothers' arms, parabolic as well as historical:

> Then were there brought unto him little children, that he should put his hands on them, and pray: and the disciples rebuked them. But when Jesus saw it he was much displeased, and said unto them, Suffer the little children to come unto me, and forbid them not; for of such is the kingdom of God. Verily I

263

say unto you, whosoever shall not receive the kingdom of God as a little child, he shall not enter therein. And he took them up in his arms, put his hands upon them and blessed them.

This was one of the few times when stupid ignorance and unspiritual views aroused his indignation and displeasure. Vital principles were involved. The foundations were being destroyed, and worldly views actuated the disciples. Their temper and their words in rebuking those who brought their infants to Christ were exceedingly wrong. The very principles which he came to illustrate and propagate were being violated. Christ received the little ones. The big ones must become little ones. The old ones must become young ones ere Christ will receive them. Prayer helps the little ones. The cradle must be invested with prayer. We are to pray for our little ones. The children are now to be brought to Jesus Christ by prayer, as he is in heaven and not on earth. They are to be brought to him early for his blessing, even when they are infants. His blessing descends upon these little ones in answer to the prayers of those who bring them. With untiring importunity are they to be brought to Christ in earnest, persevering prayer by their fathers and mothers. Before they know anything about coming of their own accord, parents are to present them to God in prayer, seeking his blessing upon their offspring and at the same time asking for wisdom, for grace and divine help to rear them that they may come to Christ when they arrive at the years of accountability of their own accord.

Holy hands and holy praying have much to do with guarding and training young lives and to form young characters for righteousness and heaven. What graciousness, simplicity, kindness, unworldliness, condescension and meekness, linked with prayerfulness, are in this act of this divine teacher!

It was as Jesus was praying that Peter made that wonderful confession of his faith that Jesus was the Son of God:

> And it came to pass, as he was alone praying, his disciples were with him; and he asked them, saying, "Whom say the people that I am?" And they said, "Some say that thou art John the Baptist; some, Elijah; and others, Jeremiah or one of the prophets." He saith unto them, "But whom say ye that I am?" And Simon Peter answered and said, "Thou art the Christ, the Son of the living God." And Jesus answered and said unto him, "Blessed art thou, Simon Bar-jonah; for flesh and blood hath not revealed it unto thee, but my Father which is in heaven. And I say also unto thee, that thou art Peter, and upon this rock I will build my church: and the gates of hell shall not prevail against it. And I will give unto thee the keys of the kingdom of heaven; and whatsoever thou shalt bind on earth shall be bound in heaven; and whatsoever thou shalt loose on earth shall be loosed in heaven."

It was after our Lord had made large promises to his disciples that he had appointed unto each of them a kingdom, and that they should sit at his table in his kingdom and sit on thrones judging the twelve tribes of Israel, that he gave those words of warning to Simon Peter, telling him that he had prayed for Peter.

> And the Lord said, Simon, Simon, behold Satan hath desired to have you, so that he may sift you as wheat. But I have prayed for thee that thy faith fail not. And when thou art converted, strengthen thy brethren.

Happy Peter, to have such a one as the Son of God to pray for him! Unhappy Peter, to be so in the toils of Satan as to demand so much of Christ's solicitude! How intense are the demands upon our prayers for some specific cases! Prayer must be personal to be to the fullest extent beneficial. Peter drew on Christ's praying more than any other disciple because of his exposure to greater perils. Pray for the most impulsive, the most imperiled ones by name. Our love and their danger give frequency, inspiration, intensity, and personality to praying.

We have seen how Christ had to flee from the multitude after the magnificent miracle of feeding the five thousand as they sought to make him king. Then prayer was his escape and his refuge from this strong worldly temptation. He returns from that night of prayer with strength and calmness, and with a power to perform that other remarkable miracle of great wonder of walking on the sea.

Even the loaves and fishes were sanctified by prayer before he served them to the multitude. "He looked up to heaven and gave thanks." Prayer should sanctify our daily bread and multiply our seed sown.

He looked up to heaven and heaved a sigh when he touched the tongue of the deaf man who had an impediment in his speech. Much akin was this sigh to that groaning in spirit which he evinced at the grave of Lazarus. "Jesus therefore again groaning in himself, cometh to the grave." Here was the sigh and groan of the Son of God over a human wreck, groaning that sin and hell had such a mastery over man; troubled that such a desolation and ruin were man's sad inheritance. This is a lesson to be ever learned by us. Here is a fact ever to be kept in mind and heart and which must ever, in some measure, weigh upon the inner spirits of God's children. We who have received the first fruit of the Spirit groan within ourselves at sin's waste, and death, and are filled with longings for the coming of a better day.

Present in all great praying, making and marking it, is the man. It is impossible to separate the praying from the man. The constituent elements of the man are the constituents of his praying. The man flows through his praying. Only the fiery Elijah could do Elijah's fiery praying. We can get holy praying only from a holy man. Holy being can never exist without holy doing. Being is first, doing comes afterward. What we are gives being, force, and inspiration to what we do. Character, that which is graven deep, ineradicably, imperishably within us, colors all we do.

The praying of Christ, then, is not to be separated from the character of Christ. If he prayed more unweariedly, more self-denyingly, more holily, more simply and directly than other men, it was because these elements entered more largely into his character than into that of others.

The transfiguration marks another epoch in his life, and that was preeminently a prayer epoch. Luke gives an account with the purpose and aim of the event:

> And it came to pass about an eight days after these sayings, he took Peter and John and James, and went up into a mountain to pray. And as he prayed, the fashion of his countenance was altered, and his raiment was white and glistering. And, behold, there talked with him two men, which were Moses and Elijah: Who appeared in glory, and spake of his decease which he should accomplish at Jerusalem.

The selection was made of three of his disciples for an inner circle of associates, in prayer. Few there be who have the spiritual tastes or aptitude for this inner circle. Even these three favored ones could scarcely stand the strain of that long night of praying. We know that he went up on that mountain to pray, not to be transfigured. But it was as he prayed, the fashion of his countenance was altered and his raiment became white and glistering. There is nothing like prayer to change character and whiten conduct. There is nothing like prayer to bring heavenly visitants and to gild with heavenly glory earth's mountain to us, dull and drear. Peter calls it the holy mount, made so by prayer.

Three times did the voice of God bear witness to the presence and person of his Son, Jesus Christ—at his baptism by John the Baptist, and then at his transfiguration the approving, consoling, and witnessing voice of his Father was heard. He was found in prayer both of these times. The third time the attesting voice came, it was not on the heights of his transfigured glory, nor was it as he was girding himself to begin his conflict and to enter upon his ministry, but it was when he was hastening to the awful end. He was entering the dark mystery of his last agony, and looking forward to it. The shadows were deepening, a dire calamity was approaching and an unknown and untried dread was before him. Ruminating on his approaching death, prophesying about it, and forecasting the glory which would follow, in the midst of his high and mysterious discourse, the shadows come like a dread eclipse and he bursts out in an agony of prayer:

> Now is my soul troubled; and what shall I say? Father, save me from this hour: but for this cause came I unto this hour. Father, glorify thy name. Then came there a voice from heaven, saying, I have both glorified it and will glorify it again. The people therefore that stood by, and heard it, said that it thundered: others said, An angel spake to him. Jesus answered and said, This voice came not because of me, but for your sakes.

But let it be noted that Christ is meeting and illuminating this fateful and distressing hour with prayer. How even thus early the flesh reluctantly shrank from the contemplated end!

How fully does his prayer on the cross for his enemies synchronize with all he taught about love to our enemies, and with mercy and forgiveness to those who have trespassed against us! "Then said Jesus, Father, forgive them; for they know not what they do." Apologizing for his murderers and praying for them, while they were jeering and mocking him at his death pains and their hands were reeking with his blood! What amazing generosity, pity, and love!

Again, take another one of the prayers on the cross. How touching the prayer and how bitter the cup! How dark and desolate the hour as he exclaims, "My God, my God, why hast thou forsaken me?" This is the last stroke that rends in twain his heart, more exquisite in its bitterness and its anguish and more heart-piercing than the kiss of Judas. All else was looked for, all else was put in his book of sorrows. But to have his Father's face withdrawn, God-forsaken, the hour when these distressing words escaped the lips of the dying Son of God! And yet how truthful he is! How childlike we find him! And so when the end really comes, we hear him again speaking to his Father: "Father, into thy hands I commit my spirit. And having said this, he gave up the ghost."

10

Our Lord's Model Prayer

JESUS gives us the pattern prayer in what is commonly known as "The Lord's Prayer." In this model, perfect prayer he gives us a law form to be followed, and yet one to be filled in and enlarged as we may decide when we pray. The outlines and form are complete, yet it is but an outline, with many a blank, which our needs and convictions are to fill in.

Christ puts words on our lips, words which are to be uttered by holy lives. Words belong to the life of prayer. Wordless prayers are like human spirits; pure and high they may be, but too ethereal and impalpable for earthly conflicts and earthly needs and uses. We must have spirits clothed in flesh and blood, and our prayers must be likewise clothed in words to give them point and power, a local habitation, and a name.

This lesson of The Lord's Prayer, drawn forth by the request of the disciples, "Lord, teach us to pray," has something in form and verbiage like the prayer sections of the Sermon on the Mount. It is the same great lesson of praying to "Our Father which art in heaven," and is one of insistent importunity. No prayer lesson would be complete without it. It belongs to the first and last lessons in prayer. God's fatherhood gives shape, value and confidence to all our praying.

He teaches us that to hallow God's name is the first and the greatest of prayers. A desire for the glorious coming and the glorious establishment of God's glorious kingdom follows in value and in sequence the hallowing of God's name. He who really hallows God's name will hail the coming of the kingdom of God, and will labor and pray to bring that kingdom to pass and to establish it. Christ's pupils in the school of prayer are to be taught diligently to hallow God's name, to work for God's kingdom, and to do God's will perfectly, completely and gladly, as it is done in heaven.

Prayer engages the highest interest and secures the highest glory of God. God's name, God's kingdom, and God's will are all in it. Without prayer his name is profaned, his kingdom fails, and his will is decried and opposed. God's will can be done on earth as it is done in heaven. God's will done on earth makes earth like heaven. Importunate praying is the mighty energy which establishes God's will on earth as it is established in heaven.

He is still teaching us that prayer sanctifies and makes hopeful and sweet our daily toil for daily bread. Forgiveness of sins is to be sought by prayer, and the great prayer plea we are to make for forgiveness is that we have forgiven all those who have sinned against us. It involves love for our enemies so far as to pray for them, to bless them and not curse them, and to pardon their offenses against us whatever those offenses may be.

We are to pray, "Lead us not into temptation," that is, that while we thus pray, the tempter and the temptation are to be watched against, resisted and prayed against.

All these things he had laid down in this law of prayer, but many a simple lesson of comment, expansion, and expression he adds to his statute law.

In this prayer he teaches his disciples, so familiar to thousands in this day who learned it at their mother's knees in childhood, the words are so childlike that children find their instruction, edification and comfort in them as they kneel and pray. The most glowing mystic and the most careful thinker finds his own language in these simple words of prayer. Beautiful and revered as these words are, they are our words for solace, help and learning.

He led the way in prayer that we might follow his footsteps. Matchless leader in matchless praying! Lord, teach us to pray as thou didst thyself pray!

How marked the contrast between the high-priestly prayer and this "Lord's Prayer," this copy for praying he gave to his disciples as the first elements of prayer. How simple and childlike! No one has ever approached in composition a prayer so simple in its petitions and yet so comprehensive in all of its requests.

How these simple elements of prayer as given by our Lord commend themselves to us! This prayer is for us as well as for those to whom it was first given. It is for the child in the A B C of prayer, and it is for the graduate of the highest institutions of learning. It is a personal prayer, reaching to all our needs and covering all our sins. It is the highest form of prayer for others. As the scholar can never in all his after studies or learning dispense with his A B C, and as the alphabet gives form, color, and expression to all after learning, impregnating all, and grounding all, so the learner in Christ can never dispense with the Lord's Prayer. But he may make it form the basis of his higher praying, this intercession for others in the high-priestly prayer.

The Lord's Prayer is ours by our mother's knee and fits us in all the stages of a joyous Christian life. The high-priestly prayer is ours also in the stages and office of our royal priesthood as intercessors before God. Here we have oneness with God, deep spiritual unity, and unswerving loyalty to God, living and praying to glorify God.

11

Our Lord's High-Priestly Prayer

WE come now to consider our Lord's high-priestly prayer, as found recorded in the seventeenth chapter of John's Gospel.

Obedience to the Father and abiding in the Father, these belong to the Son, and these belong to us, as partners with Christ in his divine work of intercession. How tenderly and with what pathos and how absorbingly he prays for his disciples! "I pray for them; I pray not for the world." What a pattern of prayerfulness for God's people! For God's people are God's cause, God's church, and God's kingdom. Pray for God's people, for their unity, their sanctification, and their glorification. How the subject of their unity pressed upon him! These walls of separation, these alienations, these riven circles of God's family, and these warring tribes of ecclesiastics—how he is torn and bleeds and suffers afresh at the sight of these divisions! Unity—that is the great burden of that remarkable high-priestly prayer. "That they may be one, even as we are one." The spiritual oneness of God's people—that is the heritage of God's glory to them, transmitted by Christ to his church.

First of all, in this prayer, Jesus prays for himself, not now the suppliant as in Gethsemane, not weakness, but strength now. There is not now the pressure of darkness and of hell, but passing for the time over the fearful interim, he asks that he may be glorified, and that his exalted glory may secure glory to his Father. His sublime loyalty and fidelity to God are declared, that fidelity to God which is of the very essence of interceding prayer. Our devoted lives pray. Our unswerving loyalty to God are eloquent pleas to him, and give access and confidence in our advocacy. This prayer is gemmed, but its walls are adamant. What profound and granite truths! What fathomless mysteries! What deep and rich experiences do such statements as these involve:

> And this is life eternal, that they might know thee, the only true God, and Jesus Christ whom thou hast sent. And all mine are thine, and thine are mine, and I am glorified in them. And I have declared unto them thy name, and will declare it, that the love wherewith thou hast loved me may be in them, and I in them. And now, O Father, glorify thou me with thine own self with the glory which I had with thee before the world was.

Let us stop and ask, have we eternal life? Do we know God experimentally, consciously, and do we know him really and personally? Do we know Jesus Christ as a person, and as a personal Savior? Do we know him by a heart acquaintance, and know him well? This, this only, is eternal life. And is Jesus glorified in us? Let us continue this personal inquiry. Do our lives prove his divinity? And does Jesus shine brighter because of us? Are we opaque or transparent bodies, and do we darken or reflect his pure light? Once more let us ask: Do we seek God's glory? Do we seek glory where Christ sought it? "Glorify thou me with thy own self." Do we esteem the presence and the possession of God our most excellent glory and our supreme good?

How closely does he bind himself and his Father to his people! His heart centers upon them in this high hour of holy communion with his Father.

> I have manifested thy name unto the men which thou gavest me out of the world; thine they were, and thou gavest them me; and they have kept thy word. Now they have known that all things whatsoever thou hast given me are of thee. For I have given unto them the words which thou gavest me; and they have received them, and have known surely that I came out from thee, and they have believed that thou didst send me. I pray for them; I pray not for the world; but for them which thou hast given me; for they are thine. And all mine are thine, and thine are mine; and I am glorified in them.

He prays also for keeping for these disciples. Not only were they to be chosen, elected and possessed, but were to be kept by the Father's watchful eyes and by the Father's omnipotent hand.

> And now I am no more in the world, but these are in the world, and I come to thee. Holy Father, keep through thine own name those whom thou hast given me, that they may be one, as we are.

He prays that they might be kept by the holy Father, in all holiness by the power of his name. He asks that his people may be kept from sin, from all sin, from sin in the concrete and sin in the abstract, from sin in all its shapes of evil, from all sin in this world. He prays that they might not only be fit and ready for heaven, but ready and fit for earth, for its sweetest privileges, its sternest duties, its deepest sorrows, and its richest joys; ready for all of its trials, consolations, and triumphs. "I pray not that thou shouldest take them out of the world, but that thou shouldest keep them from the evil."

He prays that they may be kept from the world's greatest evil, which is sin. He desires that they may be kept from the guilt, the power, the pollution, and the punishment of sin. The Revised Version makes it read, "That thou shouldest keep them from the evil one." Kept from the devil, so that he might not touch them, nor find them, nor have a place in them; that they might be all owned, possessed, filled and guarded by God. "Kept by the power of God through faith unto salvation."

He places us in the arms of his Father, on the bosom of his Father, and in the heart of his Father. He calls God into service, puts him to the front, and places us under his Father's closer keeping, under his Father's shadow, and under the covert of his Father's wing. The Father's rod and staff are for our security, for our comfort, for our refuge, for our strength and guidance.

These disciples were not to be taken out of the world, but kept from its evil, its monster evil, which is itself. "This present evil world." How the world seduces, dazzles, and deludes the children of men! His disciples are chosen out of the world, out of the world's bustle and earthliness, out of its all-devouring greed of gain, out of its money-desire, money-love, and money-toil. Earth draws and holds as if it was made out of gold and not out of dirt; as though it was covered with diamonds and not with graves.

"They are not of the world, even as I am not of the world." Not only from sin and Satan were they to be kept, but also from the soil, stain, and the taint of worldliness, as Christ was free from it. Their relation to Christ was not only to free them from the world's defiling taint, its unhallowed love, and its criminal friendships, but the world's hatred would inevitably follow their Christlikeness. No result so necessarily and universally follows its cause as this. "The world hath hated them because they are not of the world, even as I am not of the world."

How solemn and almost awful the repetition of the declaration, "They are not of the world, even as I am not of the world." How pronounced, radical, and eternal was our Lord Christ's divorce from the world! How pronounced, radical, and eternal is that of our Lord's true followers from the world! The world hates the disciple as it hated his Lord, and will crucify the disciple just as it crucified his Lord. How pertinent the question, Have we Christ's unworldliness? Does the world hate us as it hated our Lord? Are his words fulfilled in us?

> If the world hate you, ye know that it hated me before it hated you. If ye were of the world, the world would love his own; but because ye are not of the world, but I have chosen you out of the world, therefore the world hateth you.

He puts himself before us clear cut as the full portraiture of an unworldly Christian. Here is our changeless pattern. "They are not of the world even as I am not of the world." We must be cut after this pattern.

The subject of their unity pressed on him. Note how he called his Father's attention to it, and see how he pleaded for this unity of his followers:

> And now I am no more in the world, but these are in the world and I come to thee. Holy Father, keep through thine own name those whom thou hast given me, that they may be one, as we are.

Again he returns to it as he sees the great crowds flocking to his standard as the ages pass on:

> That they all may be one; as thou, Father, art in me, and I in thee, that they
> also may be one in us; that the world may believe that thou hast sent me. And
> the glory which thou gavest me I have given them; that they may be one, even
> as we are one. I in them and thou in me that they may be made perfect in one;
> and that the world may know that thou hast sent me, and hast loved them, as
> thou hast loved me."

Notice how intently his heart was set on this unity. What shameful history, and what bloody annals has this lack of unity written for God's church! These walls of separations, these alienations, these riven circles of God's family, these warring tribes of men, and these internecine, fratricidal wars! He looks ahead and sees how Christ is torn, how he bleeds and suffers afresh in all these sad things of the future. The unity of God's people was to be the heritage of God's glory promised to them. Division and strife are the devil's bequest to the church, a heritage of failure, weakness, shame, and woe.

The oneness of God's people was to be the one credential to the world of the divinity of Christ's mission on earth. Let us ask in all candor, are we praying for this unity as Christ prayed for it? Are we seeking the peace, the welfare, the glory, the might, and the divinity of God's cause as it is found in the unity of God's people?

Going back again, note, please, how he puts himself as the exponent and the pattern of this unworldliness which he prays may possess his disciples. He sends them into the world just as his Father sent him into the world. He expects them to be and do, just as he was and as he did for his Father. He sought the sanctification of his disciples that they might be wholly devoted to God and purified from all sin. He desired in them a holy life and a holy work for God. He devoted himself to death in order that they might be devoted in life to God. For a true sanctification he prayed, a real, whole, and thorough sanctification, embracing soul, body, and mind, for time and eternity. With him the word itself had much to do with their true sanctification.

> Sanctify them through thy truth; thy word is truth. And for their sakes I
> sanctify myself, that they also might be sanctified by the truth.

Entire devotedness was to be the type of their sanctification. His prayer for their sanctification marks the pathway to full sanctification. Prayer is that pathway. All the ascending steps to that lofty position of entire sanctification are steps of prayer, increasing prayerfulness in spirit and increasing prayerfulness in fact. "Pray without ceasing is the imperative prelude to "the very God of peace sanctify you wholly." And prayer is but the continued interlude and doxology of this rich grace in the heart:

> I pray God your whole spirit and soul and body be preserved blameless unto
> the coming of our Lord Jesus Christ. Faithful is he that calleth you, who also
> will do it.

We can only meet our full responsibilities and fulfill our high mission when we go forth sanctified as Christ our Lord was sanctified. He sends us into the world just as his Father sent him into the world. He expects us to be as he was, to do as he did, and to glorify the Father just as he glorified the Father.

What longings he had to have us with him in heaven: "Father, I will that they also whom thou hast given me, be with me where I am; that they may behold my glory, which thou hast given me." What response do our truant hearts make to this earnest, loving, Christly longing? Are we as eager for heaven as he is to have us there? How calm, how majestic and how authoritative is his "I will"!

He closes his life with inimitable calmness, confidence and sublimity. "I have glorified thee on the earth; I have finished the work which thou gavest me to do."

The annals of earth have nothing comparable to it in real serenity and sublimity. May we come to our end thus in supreme loyalty to Christ.

12

The Gethsemane Prayer

WE come to Gethsemane. What a contrast! The high-priestly prayer had been one of intense feelings of universal grasp, and of worldwide and illimitable sympathy and solicitude for his church. Perfect calmness and perfect poise reigned. Majestic he was and simple and free from passion or disquiet. The royal intercessor and advocate for others, his petitions are like princely edicts, judicial and authoritative. How changed now! In Gethsemane he seems to have entered another region, and becomes another man. His high-priestly prayer, so exquisite in its tranquil flow, so unruffled in its strong, deep current, is like the sun, moving in meridian, unsullied glory, brightening, vitalizing, ennobling, and blessing everything. The Gethsemane prayer is that same sun declining in the west, plunged into an ocean of storm and cloud, storm-covered, storm-eclipsed with gloom, darkness and terror on every side.

The prayer in Gethsemane is exceptional in every way. The super-incumbent load of the world's sin is upon him. The lowest point of his depression has been reached. The bitterest cup of all, his bitter cup, is being pressed to his lips. The weakness of all his weaknesses, the sorrow of all his sorrows, the agony of all his agonies are now upon him. The flesh is giving out with its fainting and trembling pulsations, like the trickling of his heart's blood. His enemies have thus far triumphed. Hell is in a jubilee and bad men are joining in the hellish carnival.

Gethsemane was Satan's hour, Satan's power, and Satan's darkness. It was the hour of massing all of Satan's forces for a final, last conflict. Jesus had said, "The prince of this world cometh and findeth nothing in me." The conflict for earth's mastery is before him. The spirit led and drove him into the stern conflict and severe temptation of the wilderness. But his comforter, his leader and his inspiration through his matchless history, seems to have left him now. "He began to be sorrowful and very heavy," and we hear him under this great pressure exclaiming, "My soul is exceeding sorrowful, even unto death." The depression, conflict, and agony had gone to the very core of his spirit, and had sunk him to the very verge of death. "Sore amazed" he was.

Surprise and awe depress his soul. "Very heavy" was the hour of hell's midnight which fell upon his spirit. Very heavy was this hour when all the sins of all the world, of every man, of all men, fell upon his immaculate soul, with all their stain and all their guilt.

He cannot abide the presence of his chosen friends. They cannot enter into the depths and demands of this fearful hour. His trusted and set watchers were asleep. His Father's face is hid. His Father's approving voice is silent. The Holy Spirit, who had been with him in all the trying hours of his life, seems to have withdrawn from the scene. Alone he must drink the cup, alone he must tread the winepress of God's fierce wrath and of Satan's power and darkness, and of man's envy, cruelty, and vindictiveness. The scene is well described by Luke:

> And he came out and went, as he was wont, to the Mount of Olives: and his disciples also followed him. And when he was at the place, he said unto them, Pray that ye enter not into temptation. And he was withdrawn from them about a stone's cast, and kneeled down and prayed.
> Saying, Father, if thou be willing remove this cup from me; nevertheless, not my will, but thine, be done. And there appeared an angel unto him from heaven, strengthening him. And being in an agony he prayed more earnestly; and his sweat was as it were great drops of blood falling down to the ground. And when he rose up from prayer, and was come to his disciples, he found them sleeping for sorrow. And said unto them, Why sleep ye? Rise and pray, lest ye enter into temptation.

The prayer agony of Gethsemane crowns Calvary with glory and while the prayers offered by Christ on the cross are the union of weakness and strength, of deepest agony and desolation, accompanied with sweetest calm, divinest submission, and implicit confidence.

Nowhere in prophet or priest, king or ruler, of synagogue or church, does the ministry of prayer assume such marvels of variety, power and fragrance as in the life of Jesus Christ. It is the aroma of God's sweetest spices, aflame with God's glory, and consumed by God's will.

We find in this Gethsemane prayer that which we find nowhere else in the praying of Christ. "O my Father, if it be possible, let this cup pass from me; nevertheless, not as I will, but as thou wilt." This is different from the whole tenor and trend of his praying and doing. How different from his high-priestly prayer! "Father, I will," is the law and life of that prayer. In his last directions for prayer, he makes our will the measure and condition of prayer. If ye abide in me, and my words abide in you, ye shall ask what ye will, and it shall be done unto you." He said to the Syrophoenician woman, "Great is thy faith! Be it unto thee as thou wilt."

But in Gethsemane his praying was against the declared will of God. The pressure was so heavy upon him, the cup was so bitter, the burden was so strange and intolerable, that the flesh cried out for relief. Prostrate, sinking, sorrowful unto death, he sought to be relieved from that which seemed too heavy to bear. He prayed, however, not in revolt against God's will, but in submission to that will, and yet to change God's plan and to alter God's purposes he prayed. Pressed by the weakness of the flesh, and by the powers of hell in all their dire, hellish malignity, and might, Jesus was on this only one occasion constrained to pray against the will of God. He did it, though, with great wariness and pious caution. He did it with declared and inviolable submission to God's will. But this was exceptional.

Simple submission to God's will is not the highest attitude of the soul to God. Submission may be seeming, induced by conditions, nothing but an inforced surrender, not cheerful but grudging, only a temporary expedient, a fitful resolve. When the occasion or calamity which called it forth is removed, the will returns to its old ways and to its old self.

Jesus Christ prayed always with this one exception in conformity with the will of God. He was one with God's plan, and one with God's will. To pray in conformity with God's will was the life and law of Christ. The same was law of his praying. Conformity, to live one with God, is a far higher and diviner life than to live simply in submission to God. To pray in conformity—together with God—is a far higher and diviner way to pray than mere submission. At its best state, submission is non-rebellion, an acquiescence, which is good, but not the highest. The most powerful form of praying is positive, aggressive, mightily outgoing, and creative. It molds things, changes things, and brings things to pass.

Conformity means to "stand perfect and complete in all the will of God." It means to delight to do God's will, to run with eagerness and ardor to carry out his plans. Conformity to God's will involves submission, patient, loving, sweet submission. But submission in itself falls short of and does not include conformity. We may be submissive but not conformed. We may accept results against which we have warred, and even be resigned to them.

Conformity means to be one with God, both in result and in processes. Submission may be one with God in the end. Conformity is one with God in the beginning, and the end. Jesus had conformity, absolute and perfect, to God's will, and by that he prayed. This was the single point where there was a drawing back from God's processes, extorted by insupportable pain, fear, and weariness. His submission was abject, loyal, and confiding, as his conformity had been constant and perfect. Conformity is the only true submission, the most loyal, the sweetest, and the fullest.

Gethsemane has its lessons of humble supplications as Jesus knelt alone in the garden. Of burdened prostration, as he fell on his face, of intense agony, of distressing dread, of hesitancy and shrinking back, of crying out for relief—yet amid it all of cordial submission to God, accompanied with a singleness of purpose for his glory.

Satan will have for each of us his hour and power of darkness and for each of us the bitter cup and the fearful spirit of gloom.

We can pray against God's will, as Moses did, to enter the promised land; as Paul did about the thorn in the flesh; as David did for his doomed child; as

Hezekiah did to live. We must pray against God's will when the stroke is the heaviest, the sorrow is the keenest, and the grief is the deepest. We may lie prostrate all night, as David did, through the hours of darkness. We may pray for hours, as Jesus did, and in the darkness of many nights, not measuring the hours by the clock, nor the nights by the calendar. It must all be, however, the prayer of submission.

When sorrow and the night and desolation of Gethsemane fall in heaviest gloom on us, we ought to submit patiently and tearfully, if need be, but sweetly and resignedly, without tremor, or doubt, to the cup pressed by a Father's hand to our lips. "Not my will, but thine, be done," our broken hearts shall say. In God's own way, mysterious to us, that cup has in its bitterest dregs, as it had for the Son of God, the gem and gold of perfection. We are to be put into the crucible to be refined. Christ was made perfect in Gethsemane, not by the prayer, but by the suffering. "For it became him to make the captain of their salvation perfect through suffering." The cup could not pass because the suffering must go on and yield its fruit of perfection. Through many an hour of darkness and of hell's power, through many a sore conflict with the prince of this world, by drinking many a bitter cup, we are to be made perfect. To cry out against the terrific and searching flame of the crucible of a Father's painful processes is natural and is no sin, if there be perfect acquiescence in the answer to our prayer, perfect submission to God's will, and perfect devotion to his glory.

If our hearts are true to God, we may plead with him about his way, and seek relief from his painful processes. But the fierce fire of the crucible and the agonizing victim with his agonizing and submissive prayer, is not the normal and highest form of majestic and all-commanding prayer. We can cry out in the crucible, and can cry out against the flame which purifies and perfects us. God allows this, hears this, and answers this, not by taking us out of the crucible, nor by mitigating the fierceness of the flame, but by sending more than an angel to strengthen us. And yet crying out thus, with full submission, does not answer the real high, worldwide, royal and eternity-reaching behests of prayer.

The prayer of submission must not be so used as to vitiate or substitute the higher and mightier prayer of faith. Nor must it be so stressed as to break down importunate and prevailing prayer, which would be to disarm prayer of its efficiency and discrown its glorious results and would be to encourage listless, sentimental, and feeble praying.

We are ever ready to excuse our lack of earnest and toilsome praying by a fancied and delusive view of submission. We often end praying just where we ought to begin. We quit praying when God waits and is waiting for us to really pray. We are deterred by obstacles from praying, or we succumb to difficulties, and call it submission to God's will. A world of beggarly faith, of spiritual laziness, and of halfheartedness in prayer, is covered under the high and pious name of submission. To have no plan but to seek God's plan and carry it out, is of the essence and inspiration of Christlike praying. This is far more than putting in a clause of submission. Jesus did this once in seeking to change the purpose of God, but all his other praying was the output of being perfectly at one with the plans and purposes of God. It is after this order we pray when we abide in him and when his word abides in us. Then we ask what we will and it is done. It is then our prayers fashion and create things. Our wills then become God's will and his will becomes ours. The two become one, and there is not a note of discord.

"And this is the confidence that we have in him, that, if we ask anything according to his will, he heareth us." And if we know that he hears us, whatsoever we ask, we know that we have the petitions that we desired of him. And then it proves true: "And whatsoever we ask, we receive of him, because we keep his commandments, and do those things that are pleasing in his sight."

What restraint, forbearance, self-denial, and loyalty to duty to God, and what deference to the Old Testament Scriptures are in that statement of our Lord:

> Thinkest thou that I cannot now pray to my Father, and he shall presently give me more than twelve legions of angels? But how then shall the scriptures be fulfilled, that thus it must be?

13

The Holy Spirit and Prayer

THE gospel without the Holy Spirit would be vain and negatory. The gift of the Holy Spirit was vital to the work of Jesus Christ in the atonement. As Jesus did not begin his work on earth till he was anointed by the Holy Spirit, so the same Holy Spirit is necessary to carry forward and make effective the atoning work of the Son of God. As his anointing by the Holy Spirit at his baptism was an era in his life, so also is the coming of the Holy Spirit at Pentecost a great era in the work of redemption in making effective the work of Christ's church.

The Holy Spirit is not only the bright lamp of the Christian dispensation, its teacher and guide, but is the divine helper.

He is the enabling agent in God's new dispensation of doing. As the pilot takes his stand at the wheel to guide the vessel, so the Holy Spirit takes up his abode in the heart to guide and empower all its efforts. The Holy Spirit executes the whole gospel through the man by his presence and control of the spirit of the man.

In the execution of the atoning work of Jesus Christ, in its general and more comprehensive operation, or in its minute and personal application, the Holy Spirit is the one efficient agent, absolute and indispensable.

The gospel cannot be executed but by the Holy Spirit. He only has the regal authority to do this royal work. Intellect cannot execute it, neither can learning, nor eloquence, nor truth, not even the revealed truth can execute the gospel. The marvelous facts of Christ's life told by hearts unanointed by the Holy Spirit will be dry and sterile, or "like a story told by an idiot, full of sound and fury, signifying nothing." Not even the precious blood can execute the gospel. Not any, nor all of these, though spoken with angelic wisdom, angelic eloquence, can execute the gospel with saving power. Only tongues set on fire by the Holy Spirit can witness the saving power of Christ with power to save others.

No one dared move from Jerusalem to proclaim or utter the message along its streets to the dying multitudes till the Holy Spirit came in baptismal power. John could not utter a word, though he had pillowed his head on Christ's bosom and caught the pulsations of Christ's heart, and though his brain was full of the wondrous facts of that life and of the wondrous words which fell from his lips. John must wait till a fuller and richer endowment than all of these came on him. Mary could not live over that Christ-life in the home of John, though she had nurtured the Christ and stored heart and mind full of holy and motherly memories, till she was empowered by the Holy Spirit.

The coming of the Holy Spirit is dependent upon prayer, for prayer only can compass with its authority and demands the realm where this person of the Godhead has his abode. Even Christ was subject to this law of prayer. With him, it is, it ever has been, and ever will be, "Ask, and it shall be given you; seek and ye shall find; knock, and it shall be opened unto you." To his disconsolate disciples, he said, "I will pray the Father, and he will give you another comforter." This law of prayer for the Holy Spirit presses on the master and on the disciples as well. Of so many of God's children it may truly be said, "Ye have him not because ye ask not." And of many others it might be said, "Ye have him in faint measure because ye pray for him in faint measure."

The Holy Spirit is the spirit of all grace and of each grace as well. Purity, power, holiness, faith, love, joy, and all grace are brought into being and perfected by him. Would we grow in grace in particular? Would we be perfect in all graces? We must seek the Holy Spirit by prayer.

We urge the seeking of the Holy Spirit. We need him, and we need to stir ourselves up to seek him. The measure we receive of him will be gauged by the fervor of faith and prayer with which we seek him. Our ability to work for God, and to pray to God, and live for God, and affect others for God will be dependent on the measure of the Holy Spirit received by us, dwelling in us, and working through us.

Christ lays down the clear and explicit law of prayer in this regard for all of God's children. The world needs the Holy Spirit to convict it of sin and of righteousness and judgment to come and to make it feel its guiltiness in God's sight. And this spirit of conviction on sinners comes in answer to the prayers of God's people. God's children need him more and more, need his life, his more abundant life, his super-abundant life. But that life begins and ever increases as the child of God prays for the Holy Spirit. "If ye, then, being evil, know how to give good gifts unto your children, how much more shall your heavenly Father give the Holy Spirit to them that ask him?" This is the law, a condition brightened by a promise and sweetened by a relationship.

The gift of the Holy Spirit is one of the benefits flowing to us from the glorious presence of Christ at the right hand of God, and this gift of the Holy Spirit, together with all the other gifts of the enthroned Christ, are secured to us by prayer as the condition. The Bible by express statement, as well as by its general principles and clear and constant intimations, teaches us that the gift of the Holy Spirit is connected with and conditioned in prayer. That the Holy Spirit is in the world as God is in the world, is true. That the Holy Spirit is in the world as Christ is in the world is also true. And it is also true that there is nothing predicated of him being in us and in the world that is not predicated of God and Christ being in us, and in the world. The Holy Spirit was in the world in measure before Pentecost, and in the measure of his operation then he was prayed for and sought for, and the principles are unchanged. The truth is, if we cannot pray for the Holy Spirit we cannot pray for any good thing from God, for he is the sum of all good to us. The truth is we seek after the Holy Spirit just as we seek after God, just as we seek after Christ, with strong cryings and tears, and we are to seek always for more and more of his gifts, and power, and grace. The truth is, that the presence and power of the Holy Spirit at any given meeting is conditioned on praying faith.

Christ lays down the doctrine that the reception of the Holy Spirit is conditioned on prayer, and he himself illustrated this universal law, for when the Holy Spirit came upon him at his baptism, he was praying. The apostolic church in action illustrates the same great truth.

A few days after Pentecost the disciples were in an agony of prayer, "and when they had prayed, the place was shaken where they were assembled together; and they were all filled with the Holy Spirit." This incident destroys every theory which denies prayer as the condition of the coming and re-coming of the Holy Spirit after Pentecost, and confirms the view that Pentecost as the result of a long struggle of prayer is illustrative and confirmatory that God's great and most precious gifts are conditioned on asking, seeking, knocking, prayer, ardent, importunate prayer.

The same truth comes to the front very prominently in Philip's revival at Samaria. Though filled with joy by believing in Christ, and though received into the church by water baptism, they did not receive the Holy Spirit till Peter and John went down there and prayed with and for them.

Paul's praying was God's proof to Ananias that Paul was in a state which conditioned him to receive the Holy Spirit.

The Holy Spirit is not only our teacher, our inspirer and our revealer, in prayer, but the power of our praying in measure and force is measured by the Spirit's power working in us, as the will and work of God, according to God's good pleasure. In the third chapter of Ephesians, after the marvelous prayer of Paul for the church, he seemed to be apprehensive that they would think he had gone beyond the ability of God in his large asking. And so he closes his appeal for them with the words, that God was "able to do exceeding abundantly above all that we ask or think." The power of God to do for us was measured by the power of God in us. "According to," says the apostle, that is, after the measure of, "the power that worketh in us." The projecting power of praying outwardly was the projecting power of God in us. The feeble operation of God in us brings feeble praying. The mightiest operation of God in us brings the mightiest praying. The secret of prayerlessness is the absence of the work of the Holy Spirit in us. The secret of feeble praying everywhere is the lack of God's Spirit in his mightiness.

The ability of God to answer and work through our prayers is measured by the divine energy that God has been enabled to put in us by the Holy Spirit.

The projecting power of praying is the measure of the Holy Spirit in us. So the statement of James in the fifth chapter of his epistle is to this effect: "The fervent effectual prayer of a righteous man availeth much." The prayer wrought in the heart by the almighty energy of the Holy Spirit works mightily in its results just as Elijah's prayer did.

Would we pray efficiently and mightily? Then the Holy Spirit must work in us efficiently and mightily. Paul makes the principle of universal application. "Whereunto I also labor, striving according to his working, which worketh in me mightily." All labor for Christ which does not spring from the Holy Spirit working in us, is inconsequential and vain. Our prayers and activities are so feeble and resultless, because he has not worked in us and cannot work in us his glorious work. Would you pray with mighty results? Seek the mighty workings of the Holy Spirit in your own spirit.

Here we have the initial lesson in prayer for the Holy Spirit which was to enlarge to its full fruitage in Pentecost. It is to be noted that in John 14:16, where Jesus engages to pray the Father to send another comforter, who would dwell with his disciples and be in them, that this is not a prayer that the Holy Spirit might do his work in making us children of God by regeneration, but it was for that fuller grace and power and person of the Holy Spirit which we can claim by virtue of our relation as children of God. His work in us to make us the children of God and his person abiding with us and in us, as children of God, are entirely different stages of the same Spirit in his relation to us. In this latter work, his gifts and works are greater, and his presence, even himself, is greater than his works or gifts. His work in us prepares us for himself. His gifts are the dispensations of his presence. He puts and makes us members of the body of Christ by his work. He keeps us in that body by his presence and person. He enables us to discharge the functions as members of that body by his gifts.

The whole lesson culminates in asking for the Holy Spirit as the great objective point of all praying. In the direction in the Sermon on the Mount, we have the very plain and definite promise, "If ye, being evil, know how to give good gifts unto your children, how much more shall your Father in heaven give good things to them that ask him?" In Luke we have "good things" substituted by "the Holy Spirit." All good is comprehended in the Holy Spirit and he is the sum and climax of all good things.

How complex, confusing, and involved is many a human direction about obtaining the gift of the Holy Spirit as the abiding comforter, our sanctifier and the one who empowers us. How simple and direct is our Lord's direction—ASK! This is plain and direct. Ask with urgency, ask without fainting. Ask, seek, knock, till he comes. Your heavenly Father will surely send him if you ask for him. Wait in the Lord for the Holy Spirit. It is the child waiting, asking, urging, and praying perseveringly for the Father's greatest gift and for the child's greatest need, the Holy Spirit.

How are we to obtain the Holy Spirit so freely promised to those who seek

284 The Reality of Prayer

him believingly? Wait, press, and persevere with all the calmness and with all the ardor of a faith which knows no fear, which allows no doubt, a faith which staggers not at the promise through unbelief, a faith which in its darkest and most depressed hours against hope believes in hope, which is brightened by hope and strengthened by hope, and which is saved by hope.

Wait and pray—here is the key which unlocks every castle of despair, and which opens every treasure store of God. It is the simplicity of the child's asking of the Father, who gives with a largeness, liberality, and cheerfulness, infinitely above everything ever known to earthly parents. Ask for the Holy Spirit—seek for the Holy Spirit—knock for the Holy Spirit. He is the Father's greatest gift for the child's greatest need.

In these three words, *ask, seek* and *knock*, given us by Christ, we have the repetition of the advancing steps of insistency and effort. He is laying himself out in command and promise in the strongest way, showing us that if we will lay ourselves out in prayer and will persevere, rising to higher and stronger attitudes and sinking to deeper depths of intensity and effort, that the answer must inevitably come. So that it is true the stars would fail to shine before the asking, the seeking and the knocking would fail to obtain what is needed and desired.

There is no elect company here, only the election of undismayed, importunate, never-fainting effort in prayer: "For to him that knocketh, it shall be opened." Nothing can be stronger than this declaration assuring us of the answer unless it be the promise upon which it is based, "And I say unto you, ask and it shall be given you."

14

The Holy Spirit,
Our Helper in Prayer

ONE of the revelations of the New Testament concerning the Holy Spirit is that he is our helper in prayer. So we have in the following incident in our Lord's life the close connection between the Holy Spirit's work and prayer :

> At that time Jesus rejoiced in spirit and said, I thank thee, O Father, Lord of heaven and earth, that thou hast hid these things from the wise and prudent, and hast revealed them unto babes; even so, Father, for it seemed good in thy sight—Luke 10:21.

Here we have revelations of what God is to us. Only the child's heart can know the Father, and only the child's heart can reveal the Father. It is by prayer only that all things are delivered to us by the Father through the Son. It is only by prayer that all things are revealed to us by the Father and by the Son. It is only in prayer that the Father gives himself to us, which is much more every way than all other things whatsoever.

The Revised Version reads: "At that same hour Jesus rejoiced in the Holy Spirit." This sets forth that great truth not generally known, or if known, ignored, that Jesus Christ was generally led by the Holy Spirit, and that his joy and his praying, as well as his working, and his life, were under the inspiration, law and guidance of the Holy Spirit.

Turn to and read Romans 8:2:

> Likewise the spirit also helpeth our infirmities; for we know not what we should pray for as we ought.

This text is most pregnant and vital, and needs to be quoted. Patience, hope, and waiting help us in prayer. But the greatest and the divinest of all helpers is the Holy Spirit. He takes hold of things for us. We are dark and confused, ignorant and weak in many things, in fact in everything pertaining to the heavenly life, especially in the simple service of prayer. There is an "ought" on us, an obligation, a necessity to pray, a spiritual necessity upon us of the most absolute and imperative kind. But we do not feel the obligation and have no ability to meet it. The Holy Spirit helps us in our weaknesses, gives wisdom to our ignorance, turns ignorance into wisdom, and changes our weakness into strength. The Spirit himself does this. He helps and takes hold with us as we tug and toil. He adds his wisdom to our ignorance, gives his strength to our weakness. He pleads for us and in us. He quickens, illumines, and inspires our prayers. He proclaims and elevates the matter of our prayers, and inspires the words and feelings of our prayers. He works mightily in us so that we can pray mightily. He enables us to pray always and ever according to the will of God.

In 1 John 5: 14 we have these words:

> And this is the confidence that we have in him, that, if we ask anything according to his will, he heareth us: And if we know that he hear us, whatsoever we ask, we know that we have the petitions that we desired of him.

That which gives us boldness and so much freedom and fullness of approach toward God, the fact and basis of that boldness and liberty of approach, is that we are asking "according to the will of God." This does not mean submission, but conformity. "According to" means after the standard, conformity, agreement. We have boldness and all freedom of access to God because we are praying in conformity to his will. God records his general will in his Word, but he has this special work in praying for us to do. His "things are prepared for us," as the prophet says, who "wait upon him." How can we know the will of God in our praying? What are the things which God designs specially for us to do and pray? The Holy Spirit reveals them to us perpetually.

> The Spirit itself maketh intercession for us with groanings which cannot be uttered. And he that searcheth the hearts knoweth what is the mind of the Spirit because he maketh intercession for the saints according to the will of God.

Combine this text with those words of Paul in 1 Corinthians 2:8–16:

> But as it is written, eye hath not seen, nor ear heard, neither have entered into the heart of man, the things which God hath prepared for them that love him. But God hath revealed them unto us by his spirit; for the spirit searcheth all things, yea, the deep things of God. For what man knoweth the things of a man, save the spirit of man which is in him? Even so the things of God knoweth no man, but the spirit of God. Now we have received, not the spirit of the world, but the spirit which is of God; that we might know the things that are freely given to us of God. Which things also we speak, not in the words which man's wisdom teacheth, but which the Holy Spirit teacheth, comparing spiritual things with spiritual. But the natural man receiveth not the things of the Spirit of God; for they are foolishness unto him; neither can he know them,

because they are spiritually discerned. But he that is spiritual judgeth all things, yet he himself is judged of no man. For who hath known the mind of the Lord, that he may instruct him? But we have the mind of Christ.

"Revealed to us by the Spirit." Note those words. God searches the heart where the Spirit dwells and knows the mind of the Spirit. The Spirit who dwells in our hearts searches the deep purposes and the will of God, and reveals those purposes and will of God to us, that we might know the things which are freely given to us of God. Our spirits are so fully indwelt by the Spirit of God, so responsive and obedient to his illumination and to his will, that we ask with holy boldness and freedom the things which the Spirit of God has shown us as the will of God, and faith is assured. Then we know that "we have the petitions that we have asked."

The natural man prays, but prays according to his own will, fancy, and desire. If he has ardent desires and groanings, they are the fire and agony of nature simply, and not that of the Spirit. What a world of natural praying there is, which is selfish, self-centered, self-inspired! The Spirit, when he prays through us, or helps us to meet the mighty "oughtness" of right praying, trims our praying down to the will of God, and then we give heart and expression to his unutterable groanings. Then we have the mind of Christ, and pray as he would pray. His thoughts, purposes, and desires are our desires, purposes, and thoughts.

This is not a new and different Bible from that which we already have, but it is the Bible we have, applied personally by the Spirit of God. It is not new texts, but rather the Spirit's embellishing of certain texts for us at the time.

It is the unfolding of the word by the Spirit's light, guidance, teaching, enabling us to perform the great office of intercessors on earth, in harmony with the great intercessions of Jesus Christ at the Father's right hand in heaven.

We have in the Holy Spirit an illustration and an enabler of what this intercession is and ought to be. We are charged to supplicate in the Spirit and to pray in the Holy Spirit. We are reminded that the Holy Spirit "helpeth our infirmities," and that while intercession is an art of so divine and so high a nature that though we know not what to pray for as we ought, yet the Spirit teaches us this heavenly science, by making intercession in us "with groanings which cannot be uttered." How burdened these intercessions of the Holy Spirit! How profoundly he feels the world's sin, the world's woe, and the world's loss, and how deeply he sympathizes with the dire conditions, are seen in his groanings which are too deep for utterance and too sacred to be voiced by him. He inspires us to this most divine work of intercession, and his strength enables us to sigh unto God for the oppressed, the burdened and the distressed creation. The Holy Spirit helps us in many ways.

How intense will be the intercessions of the saints who supplicate in the spirit! How vain and delusive and how utterly fruitless and inefficient are prayers without the Spirit! Official prayers they may be, fitted for state occasions, beautiful and courtly, but worth less than nothing as God values prayer.

It is our unfainting praying which will help the Holy Spirit to his mightiest work in us, and at the same time he helps us to these strenuous and exalted efforts in prayer.

We can and do pray by many inspirations and in many ways which are not of God. Many prayers are stereotyped in manner and in matter, in part, if not as a whole. Many prayers are hearty and vehement, but it is natural heartiness and a fleshly vehemence. Much praying is done by dint of habit and through form. Habit is a second nature and holds to the good, when so directed, as well as to the bad. The habit of praying is a good habit, and should be early and strongly formed; but to pray by habit merely is to destroy the life of prayer and allow it to degenerate into a hollow and sham-producing form. Habit may form the bank for the river of prayer, but there must be a strong, deep, pure current, crystal and life-giving, flowing between these two banks. Hannah multiplied her praying, "but she poured out her soul before the Lord." We cannot make our prayer habits too marked and controlling if the life-waters be full and overflow the banks.

Our divine example in praying is the Son of God. Our divine helper in praying is the Holy Spirit. He quickens us to pray and helps us in praying. Acceptable prayer must be begun and carried on by his presence and inspiration. We are enjoined in the Holy Scriptures to "pray in the Holy Spirit." We are charged to "pray always with all prayer and supplication in the Spirit." We are reminded for our encouragement, that "Likewise the Spirit also helpeth our infirmities; for we know not what we should pray for as we ought; but the Spirit itself maketh intercession for us with groanings which cannot be uttered." "And he that searcheth the hearts knoweth what is the mind of the Spirit, because he maketh intercession for the saints according to the will of God."

So ignorant are we in this matter of prayer; so impotent are all other teachers to impart its lessons to our understanding and heart, that the Holy Spirit comes as the infallible and all-wise teacher to instruct us in this divine art. To pray with all your heart and all your strength, with the reason and the will, this is the greatest achievement of the Christian warfare on earth. This is what we are taught to do and enabled to do by the Holy Spirit. If no man can say that Jesus is the Christ but by the Spirit's help; for the much greater reason can no man pray save by the aid of God's Spirit. My mother's lips, now sealed by death, taught me many sweet lessons of prayer; prayers which have bound and held our hearts like golden threads; but these prayers, flowing through the natural channel of a mother's love, cannot serve the purposes of my manhood's warring, stormy life. These maternal lessons are but the A B C of praying. For the higher and graduating lessons in prayer we must have the Holy Spirit. He only can unfold to us the mysteries of the prayer life, its duty and its service.

To pray by the Holy Spirit we must have him always. He does not, like earthly teachers, teach us the lesson and then withdraw. He stays to help us practice the lesson he has taught. We pray, not by the precepts and lessons he has taught, but we pray by him. He is both teacher and lesson. We can only know the lesson because he is ever with us to inspire, to illumine, to explain, to help us to do. We pray not by the truth the Holy Spirit reveals to us, but we pray by the actual presence of the Holy Spirit. He puts the desire in our hearts; kindles that desire by his own flame. We simply give lip and voice and heart to his unutterable groanings. Our prayers are taken up by him and energized and sanctified by his intercession. He prays for us, through us and in us. We pray by him, through him and in him. He puts the prayer in us and we give it utterance and heart.

We always pray according to the will of God when the Holy Spirit helps our praying. He prays through us only "according to the will of God." If our prayers are not according to the will of God they die in the presence of the Holy Spirit. He gives such prayers no countenance, no help. Discountenanced and unhelped by him, prayers, not according to God's will, soon die out of every heart where the Holy Spirit dwells.

We must, as Jude says, "Pray in the Holy Spirit." As Paul says, "with all prayer and supplication in the Spirit." Never forgetting that "the Spirit also helpeth our infirmities; for we know not what we should pray for as we ought: but the Spirit itself maketh intercession for us with groanings which cannot be uttered." Above all, over all, and through all our praying there must be the name of Christ, which includes the power of his blood, the energy of his intercession, the fullness of the enthroned Christ. "Whatsoever ye ask in my name that will I do."

15

The Two Comforters
and Two Advocates

THE fact that man has two divine comforters, advocates, helpers, is declarative of the affluence of God's provisions in the gospel, and also declarative of the settled purpose of God to execute his work of salvation with efficacy and final success. Many-sided are the infirmities and needs of man in his pilgrimage and warfare for heaven. These two Christs can meet with manifold wisdom.

The affluence of God's provision of two intercessors in executing the plan of salvation finds its counterpart in the prayer promise in its unlimited nature, comprehending all things, great and small.

"All things whatsoever ye ask in prayer, believing, ye shall receive." All things we have in Christ, all things we have in the Holy Spirit, and all things we have in prayer.

How much is ours in God's plan and purposes we have in these two Christs, the one ascended to heaven and enthroned, there to intercede for our benefit, the other Christ, his representative, and better substitute, on earth, to work in us and make intercessions for us!

The first Christ was a person. The other Christ, a person, but not clothed in physical form nor subject to human limitations as the first Christ necessarily was. Transient and local was the first Christ. The other Christ not limited to locality, not transient, but abiding; not dealing with the sensible, the material, the fleshly, but entering personally into the mysterious and imperial domain of the spirit, to emancipate and transform into more than Eden beauty that waste and dark realm. The first Christ left his novitiates that they might enter into higher regions of spiritual knowledge. The man Christ withdrew that the spirit Christ might train and school into the deeper mysteries of God; that all the historical and physical might be transmuted into the pure gold of the spiritual. The first Christ brought to us a picture of what we must be. The other Christ mirrored this perfect and fadeless image on our hearts. The first Christ, like David, gathered and furnished the material for the temple. The other Christ out of this material forms God's glorious temple.

The possibilities of prayer, then, are the possibilities of these two divine intercessors. Where are the limitations to results when the Holy Spirit inter-cedes for us with groanings which cannot be uttered, when he so helps us that our prayers run parallel to the will of God, and we pray for the very things and in the very manner in which we ought to pray, schooled in and pressed to these prayers by the urgency of the Holy Spirit! How measureless are the possibilities of prayer when we are filled with all the fullness of God; when we stand perfect and complete in all the will of God?

If the intercession of Moses so wondrously preserved the being and safety of Israel throughout its marvelous history and destiny, what may we not secure through our intercessor, who is so much greater than Moses? All that God has lies open to Christ through prayer. All that Christ has lies open to us through prayer.

If we have the two Christs covering the whole realm of goodness, power, purity, and glory, in heaven and on earth—if we have the better Christ with us here in this world—why is it that we sigh to know the Christ after the flesh as the disciples knew him? Why is it that the mighty work of these two almighty intercessors finds us so barren of heavenly fruit, so feeble in all Christlike principles, so low in the Christlike life, and so marred in the Christlike image? Is it not because our prayers for the Holy Spirit have been so faint and few? The heavenly Christ can come to us in full beauty and power only when we have received the fullness of the present earthly Christ, even the Holy Spirit.

Living always the life of prayer, breathing always the spirit of prayer, being always in the fact of prayer, praying always in the Holy Spirit, the heavenly Christ would become ours by a clearer vision, a deeper love, and a more intimate fellowship than he was to his disciples in the days of his flesh.

We would not disguise nor abate the fact that there is a loss to us by our absent Christ as we will see and know him in heaven. But in our earthly work to be done by us, and above all to be done in us, we will know Christ and the Father better, and can better utilize them by the ministry of the Holy Spirit than would have been possible under the personal, human presence of the Son. So to the loving and obedient ones who are filled with the Spirit, both the Father and the Son "will come unto us and make their abode with us." In the day of the fullness of the indwelling Spirit, "Ye shall know that I am in my Father and ye in me and I in you." Amazing oneness and harmony, wrought by the almighty power of the other Christ!

There is not a note in the archangel's song to which the Holy Spirit does not attune man into sympathy, not a pulsation in the heart of God to which the Holy Spirit-filled heart does not respond with loud amens and joyful hal-lelujahs. Even more than this, by the other Christ, the Holy Spirit, "we know the love of Christ which passeth knowledge." More than this, by the Holy Spirit we are "filled with all the fullness of God." More than this, God is able to do exceeding abundantly above all that we ask or think according to the power of the Holy Spirit which worketh in us.

The presence and power of the other Christ would more than compensate the disciples for the loss of the first Christ. His going away had filled their hearts with a strange sorrow. A loneliness and desolation like an orphan's woe had swept over their hearts and stunned and bewildered them; but he comforted them by telling them that the Holy Spirit would be like the pains of a travailing mother, all forgotten in the untold joy that a man-child was born into the world.

16

Prayer and
the Holy Spirit Dispensation

THE dispensation of the Holy Spirit was ushered in by prayer. Read these words from Acts 1:13—"And when they were come in, they went up into an upper room where abode both Peter and James and John and Andrew, Philip and Thomas, Bartholomew and Matthew, James, the son of Alpheus, and Simon Zelotes, and Judas, the brother of James. These all continued with one accord in prayer and supplication, with the women, and Mary, the mother of Jesus, and with his brethren."

This was the attitude which the disciples assumed after Jesus had ascended to heaven. That meeting for prayer ushered in the dispensation of the Holy Spirit, to which prophets had looked forward with entranced vision. And to prayer in a marked way has this dispensation, which holds in its keeping the fortune of the gospel, been committed.

Apostolic men knew well the worth of prayer and were jealous of the most sacred offices which infringed on their time and strength and hindered them from "giving themselves continually to prayer and to the ministry of the Word." They put prayer first. The Word depends on prayer that it "may have free course and be glorified." Praying apostles make preaching apostles. Prayer gives edge, entrance, and weight to the Word. Sermons conceived by prayer and saturated with prayer are weighty sermons. Sermons may be ponderous with thought, sparkle with the gems of genius and of taste, pleasing and popular, but unless they have their birth and life in prayer, for God's uses, they are trifles, dull and dead.

The Lord of the harvest sends out laborers, full in number and perfect in kind, in answer to prayer. It needs no prophetic ken to declare that if the church had used prayer force to its utmost the light of the gospel would have long since girdled the world.

God's gospel has always waited more on prayer than on anything else for its successes. A praying church is strong though poor in all besides. A prayerless church is weak though rich in all besides. Only praying hearts will build God's kingdom. Only praying hands will put the crown on the Savior's head.

The Holy Spirit is the divinely appointed substitute for and representative of the personal and humanized Christ. How much is he to us! And how we are to be filled by him, live in him, walk in him, and be led by him! How we are to conserve and kindle to a brighter and more consuming glow the holy flame! How careful should we be never to quench that pure flame! How watchful, tender, loving ought we to be so as not to grieve his sensitive, loving nature! How attentive, meek and obedient, never to resist his divine impulses, always to hear his voice, and always to do his divine will. How can all this be done without much and continuous prayer?

The importunate widow had a great case to win against helpless, hopeless despair, but she did it by importunate prayer. We have this great treasure to preserve and enhance, but we have a divine person to entertain and help. We can be enabled to meet our duties only by much prayer.

Prayer is the only element in which the Holy Spirit can live and work. Prayer is the golden chain which happily enslaves him to his happy work in us.

Everything depends upon our having this second Christ, and retaining him in the fullness of his power. With the disciples, Pentecost was made by prayer. With them, Pentecost was continued by giving themselves to continued prayer. Persistent and unwearied prayer is the price we will have to pay for our Pentecost, by instant and continued prayer. Abiding in the fact and in the spirit of prayer is the only surety of our abiding in pentecostal power and purity.

Not only should the many-sided operation of the Holy Spirit in us and for us teach us the necessity of prayer for him, but also his condition with our praying assumes another attitude, the attitude of mutual dependence, that of action and reaction. The more we pray the more he helps us to pray, and the larger the measure of himself he gives to us. We are not only to pray and press and wait for his coming to us, but after we have received him in his fullness, we are to pray for a fuller and still larger bestowment of himself to us. We are to pray for the largest and ever-increasing and constant fullness of capacity. "That ye might be strengthened with might by his Spirit in the inner man," as Paul prayed for the Spirit-baptized Ephesian church. It will be remembered that he also prayed that

> Christ might dwell in your hearts by faith, rooted and grounded in love, measuring up to the breadth, length, depth and height of the most perfect sainthood, and up to the immeasurable love of Christ, being filled with all the fullness of God.

In that wonderful prayer for those Christians, Paul laid himself out to pray to God, and by prayer he sought to fathom the fathomless depths and to measure the illimitable purposes and benefits of God's plan of salvation for immortal souls by the presence and work of the Holy Spirit. Only importunate and invincible prayer can bring the Holy Spirit to us, and secure for us these ineffably gracious results. "Epaphras always laboring fervently in prayers, that ye may stand perfect and complete in all the will of God."

The Word of God provides for a mighty, consciously realized religion in his saints, into whose happy, shining spirits God has been brought as a dweller, and whose heaven-toned lives have been attuned to melody by God's own hand.

Then will it prove true: "He that believeth on me, out of his belly shall flow rivers of living water." Here is a promise concerning the indwelling and outflowing of the Holy Spirit in us, life-giving, fruitful, irresistible, a ceaseless outflow of the river of God in us.

How God needs, how the world needs, how the church needs the flow of this mighty river, more blessed than the Nile, deeper, broader, more overflowing than the Amazon's broad and mighty current! And yet what mere rills we are and have!

O that the church, by the infilling and outflowing of the Holy Spirit, might he able to raise up everywhere memorials of the Holy Spirit's power, which might fix the eye as well as engage the heart! We need, the age needs, the church needs, memorials of God's mighty power, which will silence the enemy and the avenger, dumbfound God's foes, strengthen weak saints, and fill strong ones with triumphant raptures.

A glance at some more of the divine promises concerning this vital question would show us how they need to be projected into the experimental and the actual. "If any man will do his will, he shall know of the doctrine, whether it be of God or whether I speak of myself." How we do need a conscious religion, personal and vital, unspeakable in its joy, and full of glory! The need is for a conscious religion, made so by the Spirit bearing witness that we are the children of God. A religion of "I know" is the only powerful, vital and aggressive religion. "One thing I know, whereas I once was blind, but now I see." We need men and women in these loose days who can verify the above mentioned promise of Christ in their inner consciousness. And yet how many untold thousands of people in all of our churches, who have only a dim, impalpable, hope so, maybe so, I trust so, kind of religion, all dubious, intangible and unstable.

There is certainly a great need in these days in the modern church, first, for Christians to see and seek and obtain the high privilege in the gospel of a heaven-born, clear cut, and happy religious experience, born of the presence of the Holy Spirit, giving an undoubted assurance of sins forgiven, and of adoption into the family of God.

And secondly, there is a need, subsequent to this conscious realization of divine favor in the forgiveness of sins, and added to it, of the reception of the Holy Spirit in his fullness, purifying their hearts by faith, perfecting them in love, overcoming the world, and bestowing a divine, inward power over all sin, both inward and outward, and giving boldness to bear witness and qualifying for real religious service in the church and in the world.

There is a fearfully prevailing agnosticism in the church at this time. We greatly fear that a vast majority of our church members are now in this school of spiritual agnosticism, and really deem it to be a virtue to be there. God's Word gives no encouragement whatever to a shadowy religion and a vague religious experience. It calls us definitely into the realm of knowledge. It crowns religion with the crown of "I know." It passes us from the darkness of sin, doubt, and inward misgiving into the marvelous light, where we see clearly and know fully our personal relations to God.

> "The things unknown to feeble sense,
> Unseen by reason's glimmering ray,
> With strong, commanding confidence,
> Their heavenly origin display."

Two things may be said just here in concluding this part of our study on this subject: First, this sort of biblical religion, heretofore described, comes directly through the office of the Holy Spirit dealing personally with each soul; and secondly, the Holy Spirit in all of his offices pertaining to spiritual life and religious experience is secured by earnest, definite, prevailing prayer.

BOOK

◆5◆

Purpose in Prayer

1

Prayer Is a Keynote

THE more praying there is in the world the better the world will be, the mightier the forces against evil everywhere. Prayer, in one phase of its operation, is a disinfectant and a preventive. It purifies the air; it destroys the contagion of evil. Prayer is no fitful, shortlived thing. It is no voice crying unheard and unheeded in the silence. It is a voice which goes into God's ear, and it lives as long as God's ear is open to holy pleas, as long as God's heart is alive to holy things.

God shapes the world by prayer. Prayers are deathless. The lips that uttered them may be closed in death, the heart that felt them may have ceased to beat, but the prayers live before God, and God's heart is set on them and prayers outlive the lives of those who uttered them; outlive a generation, outlive an age, outlive a world.

That man is the most immortal who has done the most and the best praying. They are God's heroes, God's saints, God's servants, God's deputies. A man can pray better because of the prayers of the past; a man can live holier because of the prayers of the past, the man of many and acceptable prayers has done the truest and greatest service to the incoming generation. The prayers of God's saints strengthen the unborn generation against the desolating waves of sin and evil. Woe to the generation of sons who find their censers empty of the rich incense of prayer; whose fathers have been too busy or too unbelieving to pray, and perils inexpressible and consequences untold are their unhappy heritage. Fortunate are they whose fathers and mothers have left them a wealthy patrimony of prayer.

The prayers of God's saints are the capital stock in heaven by which Christ carries on his great work upon earth. The great throes and mighty convulsions on earth are the results of these prayers. Earth is changed, revolutionized, angels move on more powerful, more rapid wing, and God's policy is shaped as the prayers are more numerous, more efficient.

It is true that the mightiest successes that come to God's cause are created and carried on by prayer. God's day of power; the angelic days of activity and power are when God's church comes into its mightiest inheritance of mightiest faith and mightiest prayer. God's conquering days are when the saints have given themselves to mightiest prayer. When God's house on earth is a house of prayer, then God's house in heaven is busy and all potent in its plans and movements, then his earthly armies are clothed with the triumphs and spoils of victory and his enemies defeated on every hand.

God conditions the very life and prosperity of his cause on prayer. The condition was put in the very existence of God's cause in the world. *Ask of me* is the one condition God puts in the very advance and triumph of his cause.

Men are to pray—to pray for the advance of God's cause. Prayer puts God in full force in the world. To a prayerful man God is present in realized force; to a prayerful church God is present in glorious power, and the second psalm is the divine description of the establishment of God's cause through Jesus Christ. All inferior dispensations have merged in the enthronement of Jesus Christ. God declares the enthronement of his son. The nations are incensed with bitter hatred against his cause. God is described as laughing at their enfeebled hate. The Lord will laugh; The Lord will have them in derision. "Yet have I set my king upon my holy hill of Zion." The decree has passed immutable and eternal:

> I will tell of the decree:
> The Lord said unto me, thou art my Son;
> This day have I begotten thee.
> *Ask of me,* and I will give thee the nations for thine inheritance,
> And the uttermost parts of the earth for thy possession.
> Thou shalt break them with a rod of iron;
> Thou shalt dash them in pieces like a potter's vessel.

Ask of me is the condition—a praying people willing and obedient. "And men shall pray for him continually." Under this universal and simple promise men and women of old laid themselves out for God. They prayed and God answered their prayers, and the cause of God was kept alive in the world by the flame of their praying.

Prayer became a settled and only condition to move his son's kingdom. "Ask, and ye shall receive; seek, and ye shall find; knock, and it shall be opened." The strongest one in Christ's kingdom is he who is the best knocker. The secret of success in Christ's kingdom is the ability to pray. The one who can wield the power of prayer is the strong one, the holy one in Christ's kingdom. The most important lesson we can learn is how to pray.

Prayer is the keynote of the most sanctified life, of the holiest ministry. He does the most for God who is the highest skilled in prayer. Jesus Christ exercised his ministry after this order.

That we ought to give ourselves to God with regard to things both temporal and spiritual, and seek our satisfaction only in fulfilling his will, whether he lead us by suffering, or by consolation, for all would be equal to a soul truly resigned. Prayer is nothing else but a sense of God's presence.—BROTHER LAWRENCE

Be sure you look to your secret duty; keep that up whatever you do. The soul cannot prosper in the neglect of it. Apostasy generally begins at the closet door. Be much in secret fellowship with God. It is secret trading that enriches the Christian.

Pray alone. Let prayer be the key of the morning and the bolt at night. The best way to fight against sin is to fight it on our knees.—PHILIP HENRY

The prayer of faith is the only power in the universe to which the great Jehovah yields. Prayer is the sovereign remedy.—ROBERT HALL

An hour of solitude passed in sincere and earnest prayer, or the conflict with and conquest over a single passion or subtle bosom sin will teach us more of thought, will more effectually awaken the faculty and form the habit of reflection than a year's study in the schools without them.—COLERIDGE

A man may pray night and day and deceive himself, but no man can be assured of his sincerity who does not pray. Prayer is faith passing into act. A union of the will and intellect realizing in an intellectual act. It is the whole man that prays. Less than this is wishing or lip work, a sham or a mummery.

If God should restore me again to health I have determined to study nothing but the Bible. Literature is inimical to spirituality if it be not kept under with a firm hand.—RICHARD CECIL

2

Prayer Can Change God's Purpose

THE possibilities and necessity of prayer, its power and results are manifested in arresting and changing the purposes of God and in relieving the stroke of his power. Abimelech was smitten by God:

> So Abraham prayed unto God: and God healed Abimelech, and his wife, and his maidservants; and they bare children.
> For the Lord had fast closed up all the wombs of the house of Abimelech, because of Sarah, Abraham's wife.

Job's miserable, mistaken, comforters had so deported themselves in their controversy with Job that God's wrath was kindled against them. "My servant Job shall pray for you," said God, "for him will I accept."

And the Lord turned the captivity of Job when he prayed for his friends.

Jonah was in dire condition when "the Lord sent out a great wind into the sea, and there was a mighty tempest." When lots were cast, "the lot fell upon Jonah." He was cast overboard into the sea, but "the Lord had prepared a great fish to swallow up Jonah. . . . Then Jonah prayed unto the Lord his God out of the fish's belly . . . and the Lord spake unto the fish, and it vomited out Jonah upon the dry land."

When the disobedient prophet lifted up his voice in prayer, God heard and sent deliverance.

Pharaoh was a firm believer in the possibilities of prayer, and its ability to relieve. When staggering under the woeful curses of God, he pleaded with Moses to intercede for him. "Intreat the Lord for me," was his pathetic appeal four times repeated when the plagues were scourging Egypt. Four times were these urgent appeals made to Moses, and four times did prayer lift the dread curse from the hard king and his doomed land.

The blasphemy and idolatry of Israel in making the golden calf and declaring their devotions to it were a fearful crime. The anger of God waxed hot, and he declared that he would destroy the offending people. The Lord was very wroth with Aaron also, and to Moses he said, "Let me alone that I may destroy them." But Moses prayed, and kept on praying; day and night he

prayed forty days. He makes the record of his prayer struggle. "I fell down,"
he says,

> before the Lord at the first forty days and nights; I did neither eat bread nor
> drink water because of your sins which ye sinned in doing wickedly in the sight
> of the Lord to provoke him to anger. For I was afraid of the anger and hot dis-
> pleasure wherewith the Lord was hot against you to destroy you. But the Lord
> hearkened to me at this time also. And the Lord was very angry with Aaron to
> have destroyed him. And I prayed for him also at the same time.

"Yet forty days, and Nineveh shall be overthrown." It was the purpose of
God to destroy that great and wicked city. But Nineveh prayed, covered with
sackcloth; sitting in ashes she cried "mightily to God," and "God repented of
the evil that he had said he would do unto them; and he did it not."

The message of God to Hezekiah was: "Set thine house in order; for thou
shalt die and not live." Hezekiah turned his face toward the wall, and prayed
unto the Lord, and said:

> "Remember now, O Lord, I beseech thee, how I have walked before thee in
> truth, and with a perfect heart, and have done that which is good in thy sight."
> And Hezekiah wept sore. God said to Isaiah, "Go, say to Hezekiah, I have heard
> thy prayer, I have seen thy tears; behold, I will add unto thy days fifteen years."

These men knew how to pray and how to prevail in prayer. Their faith in
prayer was no passing attitude that changed with the wind or with their own
feelings and circumstances; it was a fact that God heard and answered, that
his ear was ever open to the cry of his children, and that the power to do
what was asked of him was commensurate with his willingness. And thus
these men, strong in faith and in prayer,

> subdued kingdoms, wrought righteousness, obtained promises, stopped the
> mouths of lions, quenched the power of fire, escaped the edge of the sword,
> from weakness were made strong, waxed mighty in war, turned to fight the
> armies of the aliens.

Everything then, as now, was possible to the men and women who knew
how to pray. Prayer, indeed, opened a limitless storehouse, and God's hand
withheld nothing. Prayer introduced those who practiced it into a world of
privilege, and brought the strength and wealth of heaven down to the aid of
finite man. What rich and wonderful power was theirs who had learned the
secret of victorious approach to God! With Moses it saved a nation; with Ezra
it saved a church.

And yet, strange as it seems when we contemplate the wonders of which
God's people had been witness, there came a slackness in prayer. The mighty
hold upon God, that had so often struck awe and terror into the hearts of

their enemies, lost its grip. The people, backslidden and apostate, had gone off from their praying—if the bulk of them had ever truly prayed. The Pharisee's cold and lifeless praying was substituted for any genuine approach to God, and because of that formal method of praying the whole worship became a parody of its real purpose. A glorious dispensation, and gloriously executed, was it by Moses, by Ezra, by Daniel and Elijah, by Hannah and Samuel; but the circle seems limited and shortlived; the praying ones were few and far between. They had no survivors, none to imitate their devotion to God, none to preserve the roll of the elect.

In vain had the decree established the divine order, the divine call. *Ask of me*. From the earnest and fruitful crying to God they turned their faces to pagan gods, and cried in vain for the answers that could never come. And so they sank into that godless and pitiful state that has lost its object in life when the link with the eternal has been broken. Their favored dispensation of prayer was forgotten; they knew not how to pray.

What a contrast to the achievements that brighten up other pages of holy writ. The power working through Elijah and Elisha in answer to prayer reached down even to the very grave. In each case a child was raised from the dead, and the powers of famine were broken. "The supplications of a righteous man avail much." Elijah was a man of like passions with us. He prayed fervently that it might not rain, and it rained not on the earth for three years and six months. And he prayed again, and the heaven gave rain, and the earth brought forth her fruit. Jonah prayed while imprisoned in the great fish, and he came to dry land, saved from storm and sea and monsters of the deep by the mighty energy of his praying.

How wide the gracious provision of the grace of praying as administered in that marvelous dispensation. They prayed wondrously. Why could not their praying save the dispensation from decay and death? Was it not because they lost the fire without which all praying degenerates into a lifeless form? It takes effort and toil and care to prepare the incense. Prayer is no laggard's work. When all the rich, spiced graces from the body of prayer have by labor and beating been blended and refined and intermixed, the fire is needed to unloose the incense and make its fragrance rise to the throne of God. The fire that consumes creates the spirit and life of the incense. Without fire prayer has no spirit; it is, like dead spices, for corruption and worms.

The casual, intermittent prayer is never bathed in this divine fire. For the man who thus prays is lacking in the earnestness that lays hold of God, determined not to let him go until the blessing comes. "Pray without ceasing," counseled the great apostle. That is the habit that drives prayer right into the mortar that holds the building stones together. "You can do more than pray after you have prayed," said the godly Dr. A. J. Gordon, "but you cannot do more than pray until you have prayed." The story of every great Christian achievement is the history of answered prayer.

"The greatest and the best talent that God gives to any man or woman in this world is the talent of prayer," writes Alexander Whyte. "And the best usury that any man or woman brings back to God when he comes to reckon with them at the end of this world is a life of prayer. And those servants best put their Lord's money 'to the exchangers' who rise early and sit late, as long as they are in this world, ever finding out and ever following after better and better methods of prayer, and ever forming more secret, more steadfast, and more spiritually fruitful habits of prayer, till they literally 'pray without ceasing,' and till they continually strike out into new enterprises in prayer, and new achievements, and new enrichments."

Martin Luther, when once asked what his plans for the following day were, answered: "Work, work, from early until late. In fact, I have so much to do that I shall spend the first three hours in prayer." Cromwell, too, believed in being much upon his knees. Looking on one occasion at the statues of famous men, he turned to a friend and said: "Make mine kneeling, for thus I came to glory."

It is only when the whole heart is gripped with the passion of prayer that the life-giving fire descends, for none but the earnest man gets access to the ear of God.

3

Prayer Has Conditions

MORE praying and better is the secret of the whole matter. More time for prayer, more relish and preparation to meet God, to commune with God through Christ—this has in it the whole of the matter. Our manner and matter of praying ill become us. The attitude and relationship of God and the Son are the eternal relationship of Father and Son, of asking and giving—the Son always asking, the Father always giving:

> *Ask of me,* and I will give *thee* the nations for thine inheritance,
> And the uttermost parts of the earth for thy possession.
> Thou shalt break them with a rod of iron;
> Thou shalt dash them in pieces like a potter's vessel.

Jesus is to be always praying through his people. "And men shall pray for him continually." "For my house shall be called a house of prayer for my peoples." We must prepare ourselves to pray; to be like Christ, to pray like Christ.

Man's access in prayer to God opens everything, and makes his impoverishment his wealth. All things are his through prayer. The wealth and the glory—all things are Christ's. As the light grows brighter and prophets take in the nature of the restoration, the divine record seems to be enlarged. "Thus saith the Lord, the holy one of Israel and his maker, ask me of the things that are to come, concerning my sons, and concerning the work of my hands command ye me. I have made the earth, and created man upon it: I, even my hands, have stretched out the heavens and all their host have I commanded."

To man is given to command God with all this authority and power in the demands of God's earthly kingdom. Heaven, with all it has, is under tribute to carry out the ultimate, final and glorious purposes of God. Why then is the time so long in carrying out these wise benedictions for man? Why then does sin so long reign? Why are the oath-bound covenant promises so long in coming to their gracious end? Sin reigns, Satan reigns, sighing marks the lives of many; all tears are fresh and full.

Why is all this so? We have not prayed to bring the evil to an end; we have not prayed as we must pray. We have not met the conditions of prayer.

Ask of me. Ask of God. We have not rested on prayer. We have not made prayer the sole condition. There has been violation of the primary condition of prayer. We have not prayed aright. We have not prayed at all. God is willing to give, but we are slow to ask. The son, through his saints, is ever praying and God the father is ever answering.

Ask of me. In the invitation is conveyed the assurance of answer; the shout of victory is there and may be heard by the listening ear. The father holds the authority and power in his hands. How easy is the condition, and yet how long are we in fulfilling the conditions! Nations are in bondage; the uttermost parts of the earth are still unpossessed. The earth groans; the world is still in bondage; Satan and evil hold sway.

The father holds himself in the attitude of giver, *Ask of me,* and that petition to God the father empowers all agencies, inspires all movements. The gospel is divinely inspired. Back of all its inspirations is prayer. *Ask of me* lies back of all movements. Standing as the endowment of the enthroned Christ is the oath-bound covenant of the Father, "*Ask of me,* and I will give thee the nations for thine inheritance, and the uttermost parts of the earth for thy possession." "And men shall pray to him continually."

Ever are the prayers of holy men streaming up to God as fragrant as the richest incense. And God in many ways is speaking to us, declaring his wealth and our impoverishment. "I am the maker of all things; the wealth and glory are mine. *Command ye me.*"

We can do all things by God's aid, and can have the whole of his aid by asking. The gospel, in its success and power, depends on our ability to pray. The dispensations of God depend on man's ability to pray. We can have all that God has. *Command ye me.* This is no figment of the imagination, no idle dream, no vain fancy. The life of the church is the highest life. Its office is to pray. Its prayer life is the highest life, the most odorous, the most conspicuous.

The book of Revelation says nothing about prayer as a great duty, a hallowed service, but much about prayer in its aggregated force and energies. It is the prayer force ever living and ever praying; it is all saints' prayers going out as a mighty, living energy while the lips that uttered the words are stilled and sealed in death, while the living church has an energy of faith to inherit the forces of all the past praying and make it deathless.

The statement by the Baptist philosopher, John Foster, contains the purest philosophy and the simple truth of God, for God has no force and demands no conditions but prayer. "More and better praying will bring the surest and readiest triumph to God's cause; feeble, formal, listless praying brings decay and death. The church has its sheet-anchor in the closet; its magazine stores are there."

"I am convinced," Foster continues,

that every man who amidst his serious projects is apprized of his dependence upon God as completely as that dependence is a fact, will be impelled to pray and anxious to induce his serious friends to pray almost every hour. He will not without it promise himself any noble success any more than a mariner would expect to reach a distant coast by having his sails spread in a stagnation of air.

I have intimated my fear that it is visionary to expect an unusual success in the human administration of religion unless there are unusual omens: now a most emphatic spirit of prayer would be such an omen; and the individual who should determine to try its last possible efficacy might probably find himself becoming a much more prevailing agent in his little sphere. And if the whole, or the greater number of the disciples of Christianity were with an earnest and unalterable resolution of each to combine that heaven should not withhold one single influence which the very utmost effort of conspiring and persevering supplication would obtain, it would be a sign that a revolution of the world was at hand.

Edward Payson, one of God's own, says of this statement of Foster, "Very few missionaries since the apostles, probably have tried the experiment. He who shall make the first trial will, I believe, effect wonders. Nothing that I could write, nothing that an angel could write, would be necessary to him who should make this trial.

One of the principal results of the little experience which I have had as a Christian minister is a conviction that religion consists very much in giving God that place in our views and feelings which he actually fills in the universe. We know that in the universe he is all in all. So far as he is constantly all in all to us, so far as we comply with the psalmist's charge to his soul, "My soul, wait thou *only* upon God;" so far, I apprehend, have we advanced toward perfection. It is comparatively easy to wait upon God; but to wait upon him *only*—to feel, so far as our strength, happiness, and usefulness are concerned, as if all creatures and second causes were annihilated, and we were alone in the universe with God, is, I suspect, a difficult and rare attainment. At least, I am sure it is one which I am very far from having made. In proportion as we make this attainment we shall find everything easy; for we shall become, emphatically, men of prayer; and we may say of prayer as Solomon says of money, that it answereth all things.

This same John Foster said, when approaching death: "I never prayed more earnestly nor probably with such faithful frequency. 'Pray without ceasing' has been the sentence repeating itself in the silent thought, and I am sure it must be my practice till the last conscious hour of life. Oh, why not throughout that long, indolent, inanimate half-century past?"

And yet this is the way in which we all act about prayer. Conscious as we are of its importance, of its vital importance, we yet let the hours pass away as a blank and can only lament in death the irremediable loss.

When we calmly reflect upon the fact that the progress of our Lord's kingdom is dependent upon prayer, it is sad to think that we give so little time to the holy exercise. Everything depends upon prayer, and yet we neglect it not only to our own spiritual hurt but also to the delay and injury of our Lord's cause upon earth. The forces of good and evil are contending for the world. If we would, we could add to the conquering power of the army of righteousness, and yet our lips are sealed, our hands hang listlessly by our side, and we jeopardize the very cause in which we profess to be deeply interested by holding back from the prayer chamber.

Prayer is the one prime, eternal condition by which the Father is pledged to put the Son in possession of the world. Christ prays through his people. Had there been importunate, universal, and continuous prayer by God's people, long ere this the earth had been possessed for Christ. The delay is not to be accounted for by the inveterate obstacles, but by the lack of the right asking. We do more of everything else than of praying. As poor as our giving is, our contributions of money exceed our offerings of prayer. Perhaps in the average congregation fifty aid in paying, where one saintly, ardent soul shuts itself up with God and wrestles for the deliverance of the heathen world. Official praying on set or state occasions counts for nothing in this estimate. We emphasize other things more than we do the necessity of prayer.

We are saying prayers after an orderly way, but we have not the world in the grasp of our faith. We are not praying after the order that moves God and brings all divine influences to help us. The world needs more true praying to save it from the reign and ruin of Satan.

We do not pray as Elijah prayed. John Foster puts the whole matter to a practical point. "When the church of God," he says, "is aroused to its obligation and duties and right faith to claim what Christ has promised—'all things whatsoever'—a revolution will take place."

But not all praying is praying. The driving power, the conquering force in God's cause is God himself. "Call upon me and I will answer thee and show thee great and mighty things which thou knowest not," is God's challenge to prayer. Prayer puts God in full force into God's work. "Ask of me things to come, concerning my sons, and concerning the work of my hands command ye me"—God's *carte blanche* to prayer. Faith is only omnipotent when on its knees, and its outstretched hands take hold of God, then it draws to the utmost of God's capacity; for only a praying faith can get God's "all things whatsoever." Wonderful lessons are the Syrophenician woman, the importunate widow, and the friend at midnight, of what dauntless prayer can do in mastering or defying conditions, in changing defeat into victory and triumphing in the regions of despair. Oneness with Christ, the acme of spiritual attainment, is glorious in all things; most glorious in that we can then "ask what we will and it shall be done unto us." Prayer in Jesus' name puts the crowning crown on God, because it glorifies him through the son and pledges the son to give to men "whatsoever and anything" they shall ask.

In the New Testament the marvelous prayer of the Old Testament is put to the front that it may provoke and stimulate our praying, and it is preceded with a declaration, the dynamic energy of which we can scarcely translate. "The supplication of a righteous man availeth much. Elijah was a man of like passions with us, and he prayed earnestly that it might not rain, and it rained not on the earth by the space of three years and six months. And he prayed again, and the heaven gave rain, and the earth brought forth her fruit."

Our paucity in results, the cause of all leanness, is solved by the apostle James—"Ye have not, because ye ask not. Ye ask and receive not, because ye ask amiss, that ye may spend it on your pleasures."

That is the whole truth in a nutshell.

4

Attitudes Regarding Prayer

IT was said of the late C. H. Spurgeon, that he glided from laughter to prayer with the naturalness of one who lived in both elements. With him the habit of prayer was free and unfettered. His life was not divided into compartments, the one shut off from the other with a rigid exclusiveness that barred all intercommunication. He lived in constant fellowship with his Father in heaven. He was ever in touch with God, and thus it was as natural for him to pray as it was for him to breathe.

"What a fine time we have had; let us thank God for it," he said to a friend on one occasion, when, out under the blue sky and wrapped in glorious sunshine, they had enjoyed a holiday with the unfettered enthusiasm of schoolboys. Prayer sprang as spontaneously to his lips as did ordinary speech, and never was there the slightest incongruity in his approach to the divine throne straight from any scene in which he might be taking part.

That is the attitude with regard to prayer that ought to mark every child of God. There are, and there ought to be, stated seasons of communion with God when, everything else shut out, we come into his presence to talk to him and to let him speak to us; and out of such seasons springs that beautiful habit of prayer that weaves a golden bond between earth and heaven. Without such stated seasons the habit of prayer can never be formed; without them there is no nourishment for the spiritual life. By means of them the soul is lifted into a new atmosphere–the atmosphere of the heavenly city, in which it is easy to open the heart to God and to speak with him as friend speaks with friend.

Thus, in every circumstance of life, prayer is the most natural outpouring of the soul, the unhindered turning to God for communion and direction. Whether in sorrow or in joy, in defeat or in victory, in health or in weakness, in calamity or in success, the heart leaps to meet with God just as a child runs to his mother's arms, ever sure that with her is the sympathy that meets every need.

Dr. Adam Clarke, in his autobiography, records that when Mr. Wesley was returning to England by ship, considerable delay was caused by contrary winds. Wesley was reading, when he became aware of some confusion on board, and asking what was the matter, he was informed that the wind was contrary. "Then," was his reply, "let us go to prayer."

After Dr. Clarke had prayed, Wesley broke out into fervent supplication which seemed to be more the offering of faith than of mere desire. "Almighty and everlasting God," he prayed, "thou hast sway everywhere, and all things serve the purpose of thy will, thou holdest the winds in thy fists and sittest upon the water floods, and reignest a king for ever. Command these winds and these waves that they obey thee, and take us speedily and safely to the haven whither we would go."

The power of this petition was felt by all. Wesley rose from his knees, made no remark, but took up his book and continued reading. Dr. Clarke went on deck, and to his surprise found the vessel under sail, standing on her right course. Nor did she change till she was safely at anchor. On the sudden and favorable change of wind, Wesley made no remark; so fully did he *expect to be heard* that he took it for granted that he *was heard*.

That was prayer with a purpose—the definite and direct utterance of one who knew that he had the ear of God, and that God had the willingness as well as the power to grant the petition which he asked of him.

Major D. W. Whittle, in an introduction to the wonders of prayer, says of George Muller, of Bristol:

I met Mr. Muller in the express, the morning of our sailing from Quebec to Liverpool. About half-an-hour before the tender was to take the passengers to the ship, he asked of the agent if a deck chair had arrived for him from New York. He was answered, "No," and told that it could not possibly come in time for the steamer. I had with me a chair I had just purchased, and told Mr. Muller of the place near by, and suggested, as but a few moments remained, that he had better buy one at once. His reply was, "No, my brother. Our heavenly father will send the chair from New York. It is one used by Mrs. Muller. I wrote ten days ago to a brother, who promised to see it forwarded here last week. He has not been prompt, as I would have desired, but I am sure our heavenly father will send the chair. Mrs. Muller is very sick on the sea, and has particularly desired to have this same chair, and not finding it here yesterday, we have made special prayer that our heavenly father would be pleased to provide it for us, and we will trust him to do so." As this dear man of God went peacefully on board, running the risk of Mrs. Muller making the trip without a chair, when, for a couple of dollars, she could have been provided for, I confess I feared Mr. Muller was carrying his faith principles too far and not acting wisely. I was kept at the express office ten minutes after Mr. Muller left. Just as I started to hurry to the wharf, a team drove up the street, and on top of a load just arrived from New York was *Mr. Muller's chair.* It was sent at once to the tender and placed in *my hands* to take to Mr. Muller, just as the boat was leaving the dock (the Lord having a lesson for me). Mr. Muller took it with the happy, pleased expression of a child who has just received a kindness deeply appreciated, and reverently removing his hat and folding his hands over it, he thanked the heavenly father for sending the chair.

One of Melancthon's correspondents writes of Luther's praying:

> I cannot enough admire the extraordinary cheerfulness, constancy, faith, and hope of the man in these trying and vexatious times. He constantly feeds these gracious affections by a very diligent study of the Word of God. *Then not a day passes in which he does not employ in prayer at least three of his very best hours.* Once I happened to hear him at prayer. Gracious God! What spirit and what faith is there in his expressions! He petitions God with as much reverence as if he was in the divine presence, and yet with as firm a hope and confidence as he would address a father or a friend. "I know," said he, "Thou art our father and our God; and therefore I am sure thou wilt bring to naught the persecutors of thy children. For shouldest thou fail to do this thine own cause, being connected with ours, would be endangered. It is entirely thine own concern. We, by thy providence, have been compelled to take a part. Thou therefore wilt be our defense." Whilst I was listening to Luther praying in this manner, at a distance, my soul seemed on fire within me, to hear the man address God so like a friend, yet with so much gravity and reverence; and also to hear him, in the course of his prayer, insisting on the promises contained in the psalms, as if he were sure his petitions would be granted."

Of William Bramwell, a noted Methodist preacher in England, wonderful for his zeal and prayer, the following is related by a sergeant major:

> In July, 1811, our regiment was ordered for Spain, then the seat of a protracted and sanguinary war. My mind was painfully exercised with the thoughts of leaving my dear wife and four helpless children in a strange country, unprotected and unprovided for. Mr. Bramwell felt a lively interest in our situation, and his sympathizing spirit seemed to drink in all the agonized feelings of my tender wife. He supplicated the throne of grace day and night in our behalf. My wife and I spent the evening previous to our march at a friend's house, in company with Mr. Bramwell, who sat in a very pensive mood, and appeared to be in a spiritual struggle all the time. After supper, he suddenly pulled his hand out of his bosom, laid it on my knee, and said: "Brother Riley, mark what I am about to say! You are not to go to Spain. Remember, I tell you, you are not; for I have been wrestling with God on your behalf, and when my heavenly father condescends in mercy to bless me with power to lay hold on himself, I do not easily let him go; no, not until I am favored with an answer. Therefore you may depend upon it that the next time I hear from you, you will be settled in quarters." This came to pass exactly as he said. The next day the order for going to Spain was countermanded.

These men prayed with a purpose. To them God was not far away, in some inaccessible region, but near at hand, ever ready to listen to the call of his children. There was no barrier between. They were on terms of perfect intimacy, if one may use such a phrase in relation to man and his maker. No cloud obscured the face of the father from his trusting child, who could look up into the divine countenance and pour out the longings of his heart. And that is the type of prayer which God never fails to hear. He knows that it comes from a heart at one with his own; from one who is entirely yielded to the heavenly plan, and so he bends his ear and gives to the pleading child the assurance that his petition has been heard and answered.

Have we not all had some such experience when with set and undeviating purpose we have approached the face of our father? In an agony of soul we have sought refuge from the oppression of the world in the anteroom of heaven; the waves of despair seemed to threaten destruction, and as no way of escape was visible anywhere, we fell back, like the disciples of old, upon the power of our Lord, crying to him to save us lest we perish. And then, in the twinkling of an eye, the thing was done. The billows sank into a calm; the howling wind died down at the divine command; the agony of the soul passed into a restful peace as over the whole being there crept the consciousness of the divine presence, bringing with it the assurance of answered prayer and sweet deliverance.

"I tell the Lord my troubles and difficulties, and wait for him to give me the answers to them," says one man of God. "And it is wonderful how a matter that looked very dark will in prayer become clear as crystal by the help of God's Spirit. I think Christians fail so often to get answers to their prayers because they do not wait long enough on God. They just drop down and say a few words, and then jump up and forget it and expect God to answer them. Such praying always reminds me of the small boy ringing his neighbor's doorbell, and then running away as far as he can go."

When we acquire the habit of prayer we enter into a new atmosphere. "Do you expect to go to heaven?" asked someone of a devout Scotsman. "Why, man, I live there," was the quaint and unexpected reply. It was a pithy statement of a great truth, for all the way to heaven is heaven begun to the Christian who walks near enough to God to hear the secrets he has to impart.

This attitude is beautifully illustrated in a story of Horace Bushnell, told by Dr. Parkes Cadman. Bushnell was found to be suffering from an incurable disease. One evening the Rev. Joseph Twichell visited him, and, as they sat together under the starry sky, Bushnell said: "One of us ought to pray." Twichell asked Bushnell to do so, and Bushnell began his prayer; burying his face in the earth, he poured out his heart until, said Twichell, in recalling the incident, "I was afraid to stretch out my hand in the darkness lest I should touch God."

To have God thus near is to enter the holy of holies—to breathe the fragrance of the heavenly air, to walk in Eden's delightful gardens. Nothing but prayer can bring God and man into this happy communion. That was the experience of Samuel Rutherford, just as it is the experience of every one who passes through the same gateway. When this saint of God was confined in jail at one time for conscience's sake, he enjoyed in a rare degree the divine companionship, recording in his diary that Jesus entered his cell, and that at his coming "every stone flashed like a ruby."

Many others have borne witness to the same sweet fellowship, when prayer had become the one habit of life that meant more than anything else to them. David Livingstone lived in the realm of prayer and knew its gracious influence. It was his habit every birthday to write a prayer, and on the next to the last birthday of all, this was his prayer: "O divine one, I have not loved thee earnestly, deeply, sincerely enough. Grant, I pray thee, that before this year is ended I may have finished my task." It was just on the threshold of the year that followed that his faithful men, as they looked into the hut of Ilala, while the rain dripped from the eaves, saw their master on his knees beside his bed in an attitude of prayer. He had died on his knees in prayer.

Stonewall Jackson was a man of prayer. Said he:

> I have so fixed the habit in my mind that I never raise a glass of water to my lips without asking God's blessing, never seal a letter without putting a word of prayer under the seal, never take a letter from the post without a brief sending of my thoughts heavenward, never change my classes in the lecture room without a minute's petition for the cadets who go out and for those who come in.

James Gilmour, the pioneer missionary to Mongolia, was a man of prayer. He had a habit in his writing of never using a blotter. He made a rule when he got to the bottom of any page to wait until the ink dried and spend the time in prayer.

In this way their whole being was saturated with the divine, and they became the reflectors of the heavenly fragrance and glory. Walking with God down the avenues of prayer we acquire something of his likeness, and unconsciously we become witnesses to others of his beauty and his grace. Professor James, in his famous work, *Varieties of Religious Experience*, tells of a man of forty-nine who said:

> God is more real to me than any thought or thing or person. I feel his presence positively, and the more as I live in closer harmony with his laws as written in my body and mind. I feel him in the sunshine or rain; and all mingled with a delicious restfulness most nearly describes my feelings. I talk to him as to a companion in prayer and praise, and our communion is delightful. He answers me again and again, often in words so clearly spoken that it seems my outer ear must have carried the tone, but generally in strong mental impressions. Usually a text of Scripture, unfolding some new view of him and his love for me, and care for my safety . . . That he is mine and I am his never leaves me; it is an abiding joy. Without it life would be a blank, a desert, a shoreless, trackless waste.

Equally notable is the testimony of Sir Thomas Browne, the beloved physician who lived at Norwich in 1605, and was the author of a very remarkable book of wide circulation, *Religio Medici*. In spite of the fact that England was passing through a period of national convulsion and political excitement, he found comfort and strength in prayer. "I have resolved," he wrote in a journal found among his private papers after his death, to pray more and pray always, to pray in all places where quietness inviteth, in the house, on the highway and on the street; and to know no street or passage in this city that may not witness that I have not forgotten God.

And he adds:

I purpose to take occasion of praying upon the sight of any church which I may pass, that God may be worshiped there in spirit, and that souls may be saved there; to pray daily for my sick patients and for the patients of other physicians; at my entrance into any home to say, "May the peace of God abide here;" after hearing a sermon, to pray for a blessing on God's truth, and upon the messenger; upon the sight of a beautiful person to bless God for his creatures, to pray for the beauty of such an one's soul, that God may enrich her with inward graces, and that the outward and inward may correspond; upon the sight of a deformed person, to pray God to give them wholeness of soul, and by and by to give them the beauty of the resurrection.

What an illustration of the praying spirit! Such an attitude represents prayer without ceasing, reveals the habit of prayer in its unceasing supplication, in its uninterrupted communion, in its constant intercession. What an illustration, too, of purpose in prayer! Of how many of us can it be said that as we pass people in the street we pray for them, or that as we enter a home or a church we remember the inmates or the congregation in prayer to God?

The explanation of our thoughtlessness or forgetfulness lies in the fact that prayer with so many of us is simply a form of selfishness; it means asking for something for ourselves—that and nothing more.

And from such an attitude we need to pray to be delivered.

The prayer of faith is the only power in the universe to which the great Jehovah yields. Prayer is the sovereign remedy.—ROBERT HALL

5

Prayer Has No Substitutes

ARE we praying as Christ did? Do we abide in him? Are our pleas and spirit the overflow of his spirit and pleas? Does love rule the spirit—perfect love?

These questions must be considered as proper and relevant at a time like the present. We do fear that we are doing more of other things than prayer. This is not a praying age; it is an age of great activity, of great movements, but one in which the tendency is very strong to stress the seen and the material and to neglect and discount the unseen and the spiritual. Prayer is the greatest of all forces, because it honors God and brings him into active aid.

There can be no substitute, no rival for prayer; it stands alone as the great spiritual force, and this force must be imminent and acting. It cannot be dispensed with during one generation, nor held in abeyance for the advance of any great movement—it must be continuous and particular, always, everywhere, and in everything. We cannot run our spiritual operations on the prayers of the past generation. Many persons believe in the efficacy of prayer, but not many pray. Prayer is the easiest and hardest of all things; the simplest and the sublimest; the weakest and the most powerful; its results lie outside the range of human possibilities—they are limited only by the omnipotence of God.

Few Christians have anything but a vague idea of the power of prayer; fewer still have any experience of that power. The church seems almost wholly unaware of the power God puts into her hand; this spiritual carte blanche on the infinite resources of God's wisdom and power is rarely, if ever, used—never used to the full measure of honoring God. It is astounding how poor the use, how little the benefits. Prayer is our most formidable weapon, but the one in which we are the least skilled, the most averse to its use. We do everything else for the heathen save the thing God wants us to do; the only thing which does any good—makes all else we do efficient.

To graduate in the school of prayer is to master the whole course of a religious life. The first and last stages of holy living are crowned with praying. It is a life trade. The hindrances of prayer are the hindrances in a holy life. The conditions of praying are the conditions of righteousness, holiness, and salvation. A cobbler in the trade of praying is a bungler in the trade of salvation.

Prayer is a trade to be learned. We must be apprentices and serve our time at it. Painstaking care, much thought, practice, and labor are required to be a skillful tradesman in praying. Practice in this, as well as in all other trades, makes perfect. Only toiling hands and hearts make proficients in this heavenly trade.

In spite of the benefits and blessings which flow from communion with God, the sad confession must be made that we are not praying much. A very small number comparatively lead in prayer at the meetings. Fewer still pray in their families. Fewer still are in the habit of praying regularly in their closets. Meetings specially for prayer are as rare as frost in June. In many churches there is neither the name nor the semblance of a prayer meeting. In the town and city churches the prayer meeting in name is not a prayer meeting in fact. A sermon or a lecture is the main feature. Prayer is the nominal attachment.

Our people are not essentially a praying people. That is evident by their lives.

Prayer and a holy life are one. They mutually act and react. Neither can survive alone. The absence of the one is the absence of the other. The monk depraved prayer, substituted superstition for praying, mummeries and routine for a holy life. We are in danger of substituting churchly work and a ceaseless round of showy activities for prayer and holy living. A holy life does not live in the closet, but it cannot live without the closet. If, by any chance, a prayer chamber should be established without a holy life, it would be a chamber without the presence of God in it.

Put the saints everywhere to praying, is the burden of the apostolic effort and the keynote of apostolic success. Jesus Christ had striven to do this in the days of his personal ministry. He was moved by infinite compassion at the ripened fields of earth perishing for lack of laborers, and pausing in his own praying, he tries to awaken the sleeping sensibilities of his disciples to the duty of prayer, as he charges them: "Pray ye the Lord of the harvest that he will send forth laborers into his harvest." And he spake a parable to them to this end, that *men ought* always to pray.

Only glimpses of this great importance of prayer could the apostles get before Pentecost. But the Spirit coming and filling on Pentecost elevated prayer to its vital and all-commanding position in the gospel of Christ. The call to every saint of prayer is the Spirit's loudest and most exacting call. Sainthood's piety is made, refined, perfected, by prayer. The gospel moves with slow and timid pace when the saints are not at their prayers early and late and long.

Where are the Christlike leaders who can teach the modern saints how to pray and put them at it? Do our leaders know we are raising up a prayerless set of saints? Where are the apostolic leaders who can put God's people to praying? Let them come to the front and do the work, and it will be the greatest work that can be done. An increase of educational facilities and a great increase of money force will be the direst curse to religion if they are not sanctified by more and better praying than we are doing.

More praying will not come as a matter of course. The campaign for the twentieth or thirtieth century will not help, but hinder our praying, if we are not careful. Nothing but a specific effort from a praying leadership will avail. None but praying leaders can have praying followers. Praying apostles will beget praying saints. A praying pulpit will beget praying pews. We do greatly need somebody who can set the saints to this business of praying. We are a generation of nonpraying saints. Nonpraying saints are a beggarly gang of saints, who have neither the ardor nor the beauty, nor the power of saints. Who will restore this branch? The greatest will he be of reformers and apostles, who can set the church to praying.

Holy men have, in the past, changed the whole force of affairs, revolutionized character and country by prayer. And such achievements are still possible to us. The power is only wanting to be used. Prayer is but the expression of faith.

Time would fail to tell of the mighty things wrought by prayer, for by it holy ones have

> subdued kingdoms, wrought righteousness, obtained promises, stopped the mouths of lions, quenched the violence of fire, escaped the edge of the sword, out of weakness were made strong, waxed valiant in fight, turned to flight the armies of the aliens, women received their dead raised to life again.

Prayer honors God; it dishonors self. It is man's plea of weakness, ignorance, want; a plea which heaven cannot disregard. God delights to have us pray.

Prayer is not the foe to work, it does not paralyze activity. It works mightily; prayer itself is the greatest work. It springs activity, stimulates desire and effort. Prayer is not an opiate but a tonic, it does not lull to sleep but arouses anew for action. The lazy man does not, will not, cannot pray, for prayer demands energy. Paul calls it a striving, an agony. With Jacob it was a wrestling; with the Syrophenician woman it was a struggle which called into play all the higher qualities of the soul, and which demanded great force to meet.

The closet is not an asylum for the indolent and worthless Christian. It is not a nursery where none but babes belong. It is the battlefield of the church; its citadel; the scene of heroic and unearthly conflicts. The closet is the base of supplies for the Christian and the church. Cut off from it there is nothing left but retreat and disaster. The energy for work, the mastery over self, the deliverance from fear, all spiritual results and graces, are much advanced by prayer. The difference between the strength, the experience, the holiness of Christians is found in the contrast in their praying.

Few, short, feeble prayers, always betoken a low spiritual condition. Men ought to pray much and apply themselves to it with energy and perseverance. Eminent Christians have been eminent in prayer. The deep things of God are learned nowhere else. Great things for God are done by great prayers. He who prays much, studies much, loves much, works much, does much for God and humanity. The execution of the gospel, the vigor of faith, the maturity and excellence of spiritual graces wait on prayer.

6

Characteristics of True Prayer

CHRIST puts importunity as a distinguishing characteristic of true praying. We must not only pray, but we must also pray with great urgency, with intentness and with repetition. We must not only pray, but we must pray again and again. We must not get tired of praying. We must be thoroughly in earnest, deeply concerned about the things for which we ask, for Jesus Christ made it very plain that the secret of prayer and its success lie in its urgency. We must press our prayers upon God.

In a parable of exquisite pathos and simplicity, our Lord taught not simply that men ought to pray, but that men ought to pray with full heartiness, and press the matter with vigorous energy and brave hearts.

> And he spake a parable unto them to the end that they ought always to pray, and not to faint; saying, There was in a city, a judge, which feared not God, and regarded not man: and there was a widow in that city; and she came oft unto him, saying, Avenge me of mine adversary. And he would not for a while: but afterwards he said within himself, Though I fear not God, nor regard man; yet because this widow troubleth me, I will avenge her, lest she wear me out by her continual coming. And the Lord said, "Hear what the unrighteous judge saith. And shall not God avenge his elect, which cry to him day and night, and he is longsuffering over them? I say unto you, that he will avenge them speedily. Howbeit when the Son of man cometh, shall he find faith on the earth?"

The poor woman's case was a most hopeless one, but importunity brings hope from the realms of despair and creates success where neither success nor its conditions existed. There could be no stronger case, to show how unwearied and dauntless importunity gains its ends where everything else fails. The preface to this parable says: "He spake a parable to this end, that men ought always to pray and not to faint." He knew that men would soon get fainthearted in praying, so to hearten us he gives this picture of the marvelous power of importunity.

The widow, weak and helpless, is helplessness personified; bereft of every hope and influence which could move an unjust judge, she yet wins her case solely by her tireless and offensive importunity. Could the necessity of importunity, its power and tremendous importance in prayer, be pictured in deeper or more impressive coloring? It surmounts or removes all obstacles, overcomes every resisting force and gains its ends in the face of invincible hindrances. We can do nothing without prayer. All things can be done by importunate prayer. That is the teaching of Jesus Christ.

Another parable spoken by Jesus emphasizes the same great truth. A man at midnight goes to his friend for a loan of bread. His pleas are strong, based on friendship and the embarrassing and exacting demands of necessity, but these all fail. He gets no bread, but he stays and presses, and waits and gains. Sheer importunity succeeds where all other pleas and influences had failed.

The case of the Syrophoenician woman is a parable in action. She is arrested in her approaches to Christ by the information that he will not see anyone. She is denied his presence, and then in his presence is treated with seeming indifference, with the chill of silence and unconcern: she presses and approaches, the pressure and approach are repulsed by the stern and crushing statement that he is not sent to her kith or kind, that she is reprobated from his mission and power. She is humiliated by being called a dog. Yet she accepts all, overcomes all, wins all by her humble, dauntless, invincible importunity. The Son of God, pleased, surprised, overpowered by her unconquerable importunity, says to her: "O, woman, great is thy faith; be it unto thee even as thou wilt." Jesus Christ surrenders himself to the importunity of a great faith. "And shall not God avenge his own elect which cry day and night unto him, though he bear long with them?"

Jesus Christ puts ability to importune as one of the elements of prayer, one of the main conditions of prayer. The prayer of the Syrophenician woman is an exhibition of the matchless power of importunity, of a conflict more real and involving more of vital energy, endurance, and all the higher elements than was ever illustrated in the conflicts of Isthmia or Olympia.

The first lessons of importunity are taught in the Sermon on the Mount—"Ask, and it shall be given; seek, and ye shall find; knock, and it shall be opened." These are steps of advance—"For every one that asketh, receiveth; and he that seeketh, findeth; and to him that knocketh, it shall be opened."

Without continuance the prayer may go unanswered. Importunity is made up of the ability to hold on, to press on, to wait with unrelaxed and unrelaxable grasp, restless desire and restful patience. Importunate prayer is not an incident, but the main thing, not a performance but a passion, not a need but a necessity.

Prayer in its highest form and grandest success assumes the attitude of a wrestler with God. It is the contest, trial and victory of faith; a victory not secured from an enemy, but from him who tries our faith that he may enlarge it: that tests our strength to make us stronger. Few things give such quickened and permanent vigor to the soul as a long exhaustive season of importunate prayer. It makes an experience, an epoch, a new calendar for the spirit, a new life to religion, a soldierly training. The Bible never wearies in its pressure and illustration of the fact that the highest spiritual good is secured as the return of the outgoing of the highest form of spiritual effort. There is neither encouragement nor room in Bible religion for feeble desires, listless efforts, lazy attitudes; all must be strenuous, urgent, ardent. Inflamed desires, impassioned, unwearied insistence delight heaven. God would have his children incorrigibly earnest and persistently bold in their efforts. Heaven is too busy to listen or respond to half-hearted prayers.

Our whole being must be in our praying; like John Knox, we must say and feel, "Give me Scotland, or I die." Our experience and revelations of God are born of our costly sacrifice, our costly conflicts, our costly praying. The wrestling and all-night praying of Jacob made an era never to be forgotten in Jacob's life, brought God to the rescue, changed Esau's attitude and conduct, changed Jacob's character, saved and affected his life and entered into the habits of a nation.

Our seasons of importunate prayer cut themselves, like the print of a diamond, into our hardest places, and mark with ineffaceable traces our characters. They are the salient periods of our lives! The memorial stones which endure and to which we turn.

Importunity, it may be repeated, is a condition of prayer. We are to press the matter, not with vain repetitions, but with urgent repetitions. We repeat, not to count the times, but to gain the prayer. We cannot quit praying because heart and soul are in it. We pray "with all perseverance." We hang to our prayers because by them we live. We press our pleas because we must have them or die. Christ gives us two most expressive parables to emphasize the necessity of importunity in praying. Perhaps Abraham lost Sodom by failing to press to the utmost his privilege of praying. Joash, we know, lost because he stayed his smiting.

Perseverance counts much with God as well as with man. If Elijah had ceased at his first petition the heavens would have scarcely yielded their rain to his feeble praying. If Jacob had quit praying at decent bedtime he would scarcely have survived the next day's meeting with Esau. If the Syrophenician woman had allowed her faith to faint by silence, humiliation, repulse, or stop midway its struggles, her grief-stricken home would never have been brightened by the healing of her daughter.

Pray and never faint, is the motto Christ gives us for praying. It is the test of our faith, and the severer the trial and the longer the waiting, the more glorious the results.

The benefits and necessity of importunity are taught by Old Testament saints. Praying men must be strong in hope, and faith, and prayer. They must know how to wait and to press, to wait on God and be in earnest in our approaches to him.

Abraham has left us an example of importunate intercession in his passionate pleading with God on behalf of Sodom and Gomorrah, and if, as already indicated, he had not ceased in his asking, perhaps God would not have ceased in his giving. "Abraham left off asking before God left off granting." Moses taught the power of importunity when he interceded for Israel forty days and forty nights, by fasting and prayer. And he succeeded in his importunity.

Jesus, in his teaching and example, illustrated and perfected this principle of Old Testament pleading and waiting. How strange that the only Son of God, who came on a mission direct from his father, whose only heaven on earth, whose only life and law were to do his father's will in that mission—what a mystery that he should be under the law of prayer, that the blessings which came to him were impregnated and purchased by prayer; stranger still that importunity in prayer was the process by which his wealthiest supplies from God were gained. Had he not prayed with importunity, no transfiguration would have been in his history, no mighty works had rendered divine his career. His all-night praying was that which filled with compassion and power his all-day work. The importunate praying of his life crowned his death with its triumph. He learned the high lesson of submission to God's will in the struggles of importunate prayer before he illustrated that submission so sublimely on the cross.

"Whether we like it or not," said Mr. Spurgeon,

> *asking is the rule of the kingdom.* "Ask, and ye shall receive." It is a rule that never will be altered in anybody's case. Our Lord Jesus Christ is the elder brother of the family, but God has not relaxed the rule for him. Remember this text: Jehovah says to his own Son, "Ask of me, and I will give thee the heathen for thine inheritance, and the uttermost parts of the earth for thy possession." If the royal and divine Son of God cannot be exempted from the rule of asking that he may have, you and I cannot expect the rule to be relaxed in our favor. Why should it be? What reason can be pleaded why we should be exempted from prayer? What argument can there be why we should be deprived of the privilege and delivered from the necessity of supplication? I can see none: can you? God will bless Elijah and send rain on Israel, but Elijah must pray for it. If the chosen nation is to prosper, Samuel must plead for it. If the Jews are to be delivered, Daniel must intercede. God will bless Paul, and the nations shall be converted through him, but Paul must pray. Pray he did without ceasing; his epistles show that he expected nothing except by asking for it. If you may have everything by asking, and nothing without asking, I beg you to see how absolutely vital prayer is, and I beseech you to abound in it."

There is not the least doubt that much of our praying fails for lack of persistency. It is without the fire and strength of perseverance. Persistence is of the essence of true praying. It may not be always called into exercise, but it must be there as the reserve force. Jesus taught that perseverance is the essential element of prayer. Men must be in earnest when they kneel at God's footstool.

Too often we get faint-hearted and quit praying at the point where we ought to begin. We let go at the very point where we should hold on strongest. Our prayers are weak because they are not impassioned by an unfailing and irresistible will.

God loves the importunate pleader, and sends him answers that would never have been granted but for the persistency that refuses to let go until the petition craved for is granted.

7

Pray Always

"MEN ought *always* to pray, and not to faint." The words are the words of our Lord, who not only ever sought to impress upon his followers the urgency and the importance of prayer, but set them an example which they alas! have been far too slow to copy.

The *always* speaks for itself. Prayer is not a meaningless function or duty to be crowded into the busy or the weary ends of the day, and we are not obeying our Lord's command when we content ourselves with a few minutes on our knees in the morning rush or late at night when the faculties, tired with the tasks of the day, call out for rest. God is always within call, it is true; his ear is ever attentive to the cry of his child, but we can never get to know him if we use the vehicle of prayer as we use the telephone—or a few words of hurried conversation. Intimacy requires development. We can never know God as it is our privilege to know him, by brief and fragmentary and unconsidered repetitions of intercessions that are requests for personal favors and nothing more. That is not the way in which we can come into communication with heaven's king. "The goal of prayer is the ear of God," a goal that can only be reached by patient and continued and continuous waiting upon him, pouring out our hearts to him and permitting him to speak to us. Only by so doing can we expect to know him, and as we come to know him better we shall spend more time in his presence and find that presence a constant and ever-increasing delight.

Always does not mean that we are to neglect the ordinary duties of life; what it means is that the soul which has come into intimate contact with God in the silence of the prayer-chamber is never out of conscious touch with the Father, that the heart is always going out to him in loving communion, and that the moment the mind is released from the task on which it is engaged, it returns as naturally to God as the bird does to its nest. What a beautiful conception of prayer we get if we regard it in this light, if we view it as a constant fellowship, an unbroken audience with the king. Prayer then loses every vestige of dread which it may once have possessed; we regard it no longer as a duty which must be performed, but rather as a privilege which is to be enjoyed, a rare delight that is always revealing some new beauty.

Thus, when we open our eyes in the morning, our thought instantly mounts heavenward. To many Christians the morning hours are the most precious portion of the day, because they provide the opportunity for the hallowed fellowship that gives the keynote to the day's program. And what better introduction can there be to the never-ceasing glory and wonder of a new day than to spend it alone with God? It is said that Mr. Moody, at a time when no other place was available, kept his morning watch in the coal-shed, pouring out his heart to God, and finding in his precious Bible a true "feast of fat things."

George Muller also combined Bible study with prayer in the quiet morning hours. At one time his practice was to give himself to prayer, after having dressed, in the morning. Then his plan underwent a change. As he himself put it:

> I saw the most important thing I had to do was to give myself to the reading of the Word of God, and to meditation on it, that thus my heart might be comforted, encouraged, warned, reproved, instructed; and that thus, by means of the Word of God, whilst meditating on it, my heart might be brought into experimental communion with the Lord. I began, therefore, to meditate on the New Testament early in the morning. The first thing I did, after having asked in a few words for the Lord's blessing upon his precious Word, was to begin to meditate on the Word of God, searching, as it were, into every verse to get blessing out of it; not for the sake of the public ministry of the Word, not for the sake of preaching on what I had meditated on, but for the sake of obtaining food for my own soul. The result I have found to be almost invariably thus, that after a very few minutes my soul has been led to confession, or to thanksgiving, or to intercession, or to supplication; so that, though I did not, as it were, give myself to prayer, but to meditation, yet it turned almost immediately more or less into prayer.

The study of the Word and prayer go together, and where we find the one truly practiced, the other is sure to be seen in close alliance.

But we do not pray *always*. That is the trouble with so many of us. We need to pray much more than we do and much longer than we do.

Robert Murray McCheyne, gifted and saintly, of whom it was said, that "Whether viewed as a son, a brother, a friend, or a pastor, he was the most faultless and attractive exhibition of the true Christian they had ever seen embodied in a living form," knew what it was to spend much time upon his knees, and he never wearied in urging upon others the joy and the value of holy intercession. "God's children should pray," he said. "They should cry day and night unto him. God hears every one of your cries in the busy hour of the daytime and in the lonely watches of the night." In every way, by preaching, by exhortation when present and by letters when absent, McCheyne emphasized the vital duty of prayer, importunate and unceasing prayer.

In his diary we find this:

> In the morning was engaged in preparing the head, then the heart. This has been frequently my error, and I have always felt the evil of it, especially in prayer. Reform it then, O Lord.

While on his trip to the Holy Land he wrote:

"For much of our safety I feel indebted to the prayers of my people. If the veil of the world's machinery were lifted off how much we would find done in answer to the prayers of God's children.

In an ordination sermon he said to the preacher:

"Give yourself to prayers and the ministry of the Word. If you do not pray, God will probably lay you aside from your ministry, as he did me, to teach you to pray. Remember Luther's maxim, "To have prayed well is to have studied well." Get your texts from God, your thoughts, your words. Carry the names of the little flock upon your breast like the High Priest. Wrestle for the unconverted. Luther spent his last three hours in prayer; John Welch prayed seven or eight hours a day.

He used to keep a plaid blanket on his bed that he might wrap himself in when he rose during the night. Sometimes his wife found him on the ground lying weeping. When she complained, he would say, "O woman, I have the souls of three thousand to answer for, and I know not how it is with many of them." The people he exhorted and charged: "Pray for your pastor. Pray for his body, that he may be kept strong and spared many years. Pray for his soul, that he may be kept humble and holy, a burning and shining light. Pray for his ministry, that it may be abundantly blessed, that he may be anointed to preach good tidings. Let there be no secret prayer without naming him before your God, no family prayer without carrying your pastor in your hearts to God."

"Two things," says his biographer, "he seems never to have ceased from—the cultivation of personal holiness and the most anxious efforts to win souls." The two are the inseparable attendants on the ministry of prayer. Prayer fails when the desire and effort for personal holiness fail. No person is a soulwinner who is not adept in the ministry of prayer. "It is the duty of ministers," says this holy man, "to begin the reformation of religion and manner with themselves, families, etc., with confession of past sin, earnest prayer for direction, grace and full purpose of heart." He begins with himself under the head of "Reformation in Secret Prayer," and he resolves:

I ought not to omit any of the parts of prayer—confession, adoration, thanksgiving, petition and intercession. There is a fearful tendency to omit *confession* proceeding from low views of God and his law, slight views of my heart, and the sin of my past life. This must be resisted. There is a constant tendency to omit *adoration* when I forget to whom I am speaking, when I rush heedlessly into the presence of Jehovah without thought of his awful name and character. When I have little eyesight for his glory, and little admiration of his wonders, I have the native tendency of the heart to omit giving *thanks,* and yet it is specially commanded. Often when the heart is dead to the salvation of others I omit *intercession,* and yet it especially is the spirit of the great advocate who has the name of Israel on his heart. I ought to pray before seeing anyone. Often when I sleep long, or meet with others early, and then have family prayer and breakfast and forenoon callers, it is eleven or twelve o'clock before I begin secret prayer. This is a wretched system; it is unscriptural. Christ rose before day and went into a solitary place. David says, "Early will I seek thee; thou shalt early hear my voice." Mary Magdalene came to the sepulcher while it was yet dark. Family prayer loses much of its power and sweetness; and I can do no good to those who come to seek from me. The conscience feels guilty, the soul unfed, the lamp not trimmed. I feel it is far better to begin with God, to see his face first, to get my soul near him before it is near another. "When I awake I am still with Thee." If I have slept too long, or I am going on an early journey, or my time is in any way shortened, it is best to dress hurriedly and have a few minutes alone with God than to give up all for lost. But in general it is best to have at least one hour alone with God before engaging in anything else. I ought to spend the best hours of the day in communion with God. When I awake in the night I ought to rise and pray as David and John Welch.

McCheyne believed in being *always* in prayer, and his fruitful life, short though that life was, affords an illustration of the power that comes from long and frequent visits to the secret place where we keep tryst with our Lord.

Men of McCheyne's stamp are needed today—praying men, who know how to give themselves to the greatest task demanding their time and their attention; men who can give their whole heart to the holy task of intercession, men who can pray through. God's cause is committed to men; God commits himself to men. Praying men are the deputies of God; they do his work and carry out his plans.

We are obliged to pray if we be citizens of God's kingdom. Prayerlessness is expatriation, or worse, from God's kingdom. It is outlawry, a high crime, a constitutional breach. The Christian who relegates prayer to a subordinate place in his life soon loses whatever spiritual zeal he may have once possessed, and the church that makes little of prayer cannot maintain vital piety, and is powerless to advance the Gospel. The gospel cannot live, fight, conquer without prayer—prayer unceasing, instant, and ardent.

Little prayer is the characteristic of a backslidden age and of a backslidden church. Whenever there is little praying in the pulpit or in the pew, spiritual bankruptcy is imminent and inevitable.

The cause of God has no commercial age, no cultured age, no age of education, no age of money. But it has one golden age, and that is the age of prayer. When its leaders are men of prayer, when prayer is the prevailing element of worship, like the incense giving continual fragrance to its service, then the cause of God will be triumphant.

Better praying and more of it, that is what we need. We need holier men, and more of them, holier women, and more of them, to pray—women like Hannah, who, out of their greatest griefs and temptations brewed their greatest prayers. Through prayer Hannah found her relief. Everywhere the church was backslidden and apostate, her foes were victorious. Hannah gave herself to prayer, and in sorrow she multiplied her praying. She saw a great revival born of her praying. When the whole nation was oppressed, prophet and priest, Samuel was born to establish a new line of priesthood, and her praying warmed into life a new life for God. Everywhere religion revived and flourished. God, true to his promise, "*Ask of me,*" heard and answered, sending a new day of holy gladness to revive his people.

So once more, let us apply the emphasis and repeat that the great need of the church in this and all ages is men of such commanding faith, of such unsullied holiness, of such marked spiritual vigor and consuming zeal, that they will work spiritual revolutions through their mighty praying.

> Natural ability and educational advantages do not figure as factors in this matter; but a capacity for faith, the ability to pray, the power of a thorough consecration, the ability of self-denegration, an absolute losing of one's self in God's glory and an ever present and insatiable yearning and seeking after all the fulness of God. Such pray-ers can set the church ablaze for God, not in a noisy, showy way, but with an intense and quiet heat that melts and moves everything for God.

And, to return to the vital point, secret praying is the test, the gauge, the conserver of man's relation to God. The prayer chamber, while it is the test of the sincerity of our devotion to God, becomes also the measure of the devotion. The self-denial, the sacrifices which we make for our prayer-chambers, the frequency of our visits to that hallowed place of meeting with the Lord, the lingering to stay, the loathness to leave, are values which we put on communion alone with God, the price we pay for the Spirit's trysting hours of heavenly love.

The prayer chamber conserves our relation to God. It hems every raw edge; it tucks up every flowing and entangling garment; girds up every fainting loin. The sheet-anchor holds not the ship more surely and safely than the prayer chamber holds to God. Satan has to break our hold on, and close up our way to the prayer chambers, ere he can break our hold on God or close up our way to heaven.

> Be not afraid to pray; to pray is right;
> Pray if thou canst with hope, but ever pray,
> Though hope be weak or sick with long delay;
> Pray in the darkness if there be no light;
> And if for any wish thou dare not pray
> Then pray to God to cast that wish away.

8

Men Are Called to Pray

THAT the men had quit praying in Paul's time we cannot certainly affirm. They have, in the main, quit praying now. They are too busy to pray. Time and strength and every faculty are laid under tribute to money, to business, to the affairs of the world. Few men lay themselves out in great praying. The great business of praying is a hurried, petty, starved, beggarly business with most men.

St. Paul calls a halt, and lays a levy on men for prayer. Put the men to praying is Paul's unfailing remedy for great evils in church, in state, in politics, in business, in home. Put the men to praying, then politics will be cleansed, business will be thriftier, the church will be holier, the home will be sweeter.

"I exhort, therefore, first of all, that supplications, prayers, intercessions, thanksgivings, be made for all men; for kings and all that are in high place; that we may lead a tranquil and quiet life in all godliness and gravity. This is good and acceptable in the sight of God our savior. . . . I desire, therefore, that the men pray in every place, lifting up holy hands, without wrath and disputing (1 Tim. 2:1–3, 8).

Praying women and children are invaluable to God, but if their praying is not supplemented by praying men, there will be a great loss in the power of prayer—a great breach and depreciation in the value of prayer, great paralysis in the energy of the gospel. Jesus Christ spake a parable unto the people, telling them that men ought always to pray and not faint. Men who are strong in everything else ought to be strong in prayer, and never yield to discouragement, weakness or depression. Men who are brave, persistent, illustrious in other pursuits ought to be full of courage, unfainting, strong-hearted in prayer.

Men are to pray; *all men* are to pray. Men, as distinguished from women, men in their strength in their wisdom. There is an absolute, specific command that the men pray; there is an absolute imperative necessity that men pray. The first of beings, man, should also be first in prayer.

The men are to pray for men. The direction is specific and classified. Just underneath we have a specific direction with regard to women. About prayer, its importance, wideness, and practice the Bible here deals with the men in contrast to, and distinct from, the women. The men are definitely command-

330

ed, seriously charged, and warmly exhorted to pray. Perhaps it was that men were averse to prayer, or indifferent to it; it may be that they deemed it a small thing, and gave to it neither time nor value nor significance. But God would have all men pray, and so the great apostle lifts the subject into prominence and emphasizes its importance.

For prayer is of transcendent importance. Prayer is the mightiest agent to advance God's work. Praying hearts and hands only can do God's work. Prayer succeeds when all else fails. Prayer has won great victories, and rescued, with notable triumph, God's saints when every other hope was gone. Men who know how to pray are the greatest boon God can give to earth—they are the richest gift earth can offer heaven. Men who know how to use this weapon of prayer are God's best soldiers, his mightiest leaders.

Praying men are God's chosen leaders. The distinction between the leaders who God brings to the front to lead and bless his people, and those leaders who owe their position of leadership to a worldly, selfish, unsanctified selection, is this, God's leaders are pre-eminently men of prayer. This distinguishes them as the simple, divine attestation of their call, the seal of their separation by God. Whatever of other graces or gifts they may have, the gift and grace of prayer towers above them all. In whatever else they may share or differ, in the gift of prayer they are one.

What would God's leaders be without prayer? Strip Moses of his power in prayer, a gift that made him eminent in pagan estimate, and the crown is taken from his head, the food and fire of his faith are gone. Elijah, without his praying, would have neither record nor place in the divine legation, his life insipid, cowardly, its energy, defiance, and fire gone. Without Elijah's praying the Jordan would never have yielded to the stroke of his mantle, nor would the stern angel of death have honored him with the chariot and horses of fire. The argument that God used to quiet the fears and convince Ananias of Paul's condition and sincerity is the epitome of his history, the solution of his life and work—"Behold he prayeth."

Paul, Luther, Wesley—what would these chosen ones of God be without the distinguishing and controlling element of prayer? They were leaders for God because mighty in prayer. They were not leaders because of brilliancy in thought, unlimited resources, magnificent culture, or native endowment, but because by the power of prayer they could command the power of God. Praying men means much more than men who say prayers; much more than men who pray by habit. It means men with whom prayer is a mighty force, an energy that moves heaven, and pours untold treasures of good on earth.

Praying men are the safety of the church from the materialism that is affecting all its plans and polity, and which is hardening its lifeblood. The insinuation circulates as a secret, deadly poison that the church is not so dependent on purely spiritual forces as it used to be—that changed times and changed conditions have brought it out of its spiritual straits and dependencies and put it where other forces can bear it to its climax. A fatal snare of this kind has allured the church into worldly embraces, dazzled her leaders, weakened her foundations, and shorn her of much of her beauty and strength. Praying men are the saviors of the church from this material tendency. They pour into it the original spiritual forces, lift it off the sandbars of materialism, and press it out into the ocean depths of spiritual power. Praying men keep God in the church in full force; keep his hand on the helm, and train the church in its lessons of strength and trust.

The number and efficiency of the laborers in God's vineyard in all lands is dependent on the men of prayer. The mightiness of these men of prayer increases, by the divinely arranged process, the number and success of the consecrated labors. Prayer opens wide their doors of access, gives holy aptness to enter, and holy boldness, firmness, and fruitage. Praying men are needed in all fields of spiritual labor. There is no position in the church of God, high or low, which can be well filled without instant prayer. No position where Christians are found does not demand the full play of a faith that always prays and never faints. Praying men are needed in the house of business, as well as in the house of God, that they may order and direct trade, not according to the maxims of this world, but according to Bible precepts and the maxims of the heavenly life.

Men of prayer are needed especially in the positions of church influence, honor, and power. These leaders of church thought, of church work, and of church life should be men of signal power in prayer. It is the praying heart that sanctifies the toil and skill of the hands, and the toil and wisdom of the head. Prayer keeps work in the line of God's will, and keeps thought in the line of God's Word. The solemn responsibilities of leadership, in a large or limited sphere, in God's church should be so hedged about with prayer that between it and the world there should be an impassable gulf, so elevated and purified by prayer that neither cloud nor night should stain the radiance nor dim the sight of a constant meridian view of God. Many church leaders seem to think if they can be prominent as men of business, of money, influence, of thought, of plans, of scholarly attainments, of eloquent gifts, of taking, conspicuous activities, that these are enough, and will atone for the absence of the higher spiritual power which only much praying can give. But how vain and paltry are these in the serious work of bringing glory to God, controlling the church for him, and bringing it into full accord with its divine mission.

Praying men are the men that have done so much for God in the past. They are the ones who have won the victories for God, and spoiled his foes. They are the ones who have set up his kingdom in the very camps of his enemies. There are no other conditions of success in this day. The twentieth century has no relief statute to suspend the necessity or force of prayer—no substitute by which its gracious ends can be secured. We are shut up to this, only praying hands can build for God. They are God's mighty ones on earth, his master builders. They may be destitute of all else, but with the wrestlings and prevailings of a simple-hearted faith they are mighty, the mightiest for God.

Church leaders may be gifted in all else, but without this greatest of gifts they are as Samson shorn of his locks, or as the temple without the divine presence or the divine glory, and on whose altars the heavenly flame has died.

The only protection and rescue from worldliness lie in our intense and radical spirituality; and our only hope for the existence and maintenance of this high, saving spirituality, under God, is in the purest and most aggressive leadership—a leadership that knows the secret power of prayer, the sign by which the church has conquered, and that has conscience, conviction, and courage to hold her true to her symbols, traditions, and power. We need this prayerful leadership; we must have it, that by the perfection and beauty of its holiness, by the strength and elevation of its faith, by the potency and pressure of its prayers, by the authority and spotlessness of its example, by the fire and contagion of its zeal, by the singularity, sublimity, and unworldliness of its piety, it may influence God, and hold and mold the church to its heavenly pattern.

Such leaders, how mightily they are felt. How their flame arouses the church! How they stir it by the force of their pentecostal presence! How they embattle and give victory by the conflicts and triumphs of their own faith! How they fashion it by the impress and importunity of their prayers! How they inoculate it by the contagion and fire of their holiness! How they lead the march in great spiritual revolutions! How the church is raised from the dead by the resurrection call of their sermons! Holiness springs up in their wake as flowers at the voice of spring, and where they tread the desert blooms as the garden of the Lord. God's cause demands such leaders along the whole line of official position from subaltern to superior. How feeble, aimless, or worldly are our efforts, how demoralized and vain for God's work without them!

The gift of these leaders is not in the range of ecclesiastical power. They are God's gifts. Their being, their presence, their number, and their ability are the tokens of his favor; their lack the sure sign of his disfavor, the presage of his withdrawal. Let the church of God be on her knees before the Lord of hosts, that he may more mightily endow the leaders we already have, and put others in rank, and lead all along the line of our embattled front.

The world is coming into the church at many points and in many ways. It oozes in; it pours in; it comes in with brazen front or soft, insinuating disguise; it comes in at the top and comes in at the bottom; and percolates through many a hidden way.

For praying men and holy men we are looking—men whose presence in the church will make it like a censer of holiest incense flaming up to God. With God the man counts for everything. Rites, forms, organizations are of small moment; unless they are backed by the holiness of the man they are offensive in his sight. "Incense is an abomination unto me; the new moons and sabbaths, the calling of assemblies I cannot away with; it is iniquity, even the solemn meeting."

Why does God speak so strongly against his own ordinances? Personal purity had failed. The impure man tainted all the sacred institutions of God and defiled them. God regards the man in so important a way as to put a kind of discount on all else. Men have built him glorious temples and have striven and exhausted themselves to please God by all manner of gifts; but in lofty strains he has rebuked these proud worshipers and rejected their princely gifts.

> Heaven is my throne and the earth is my footstool: where is the house that ye build unto me? and where is the place of my rest? For all those things hath mine hand made, and all those things hath been, saith the Lord. He that killeth an ox is as if he slew a man; he that sacrificeth a lamb, as if he cut off a dog's neck; he that offereth an oblation, as if he offered swine's blood; he that burneth incense, as if he blessed an idol."

Turning away in disgust from these costly and profane offerings, he declares: "But to this man will I look, even to him that is poor and of a contrite spirit, and trembleth at my word.

This truth that God regards the personal purity of the man is fundamental. This truth suffers when ordinances are made much of and forms of worship multiply. The man and his spiritual character depreciate as church ceremonials increase. The simplicity of worship is lost in religious esthetics, or in the gaudiness of religious forms.

This truth that the personal purity of the individual is the only thing God cares for is lost sight of when the church begins to estimate men for what they have. When the church eyes a man's money, social standing, his belongings in any way, then spiritual values are at a fearful discount, and the tear of penitence, the heaviness of guilt are never seen at her portals. Worldly bribes have opened and stained its pearly gates by the entrance of the impure.

This truth that God is looking after personal purity is swallowed up when the church has a greed for numbers. "Not numbers, but personal purity is our aim," said the fathers of Methodism. The parading of church statistics is mightily against the grain of spiritual religion. Eyeing numbers greatly hinders the looking after personal purity. The increase of quantity is generally at a loss of quality. Bulk abates preciousness.

The age of church organization and church machinery is not an age noted for elevated and strong personal piety. Machinery looks for engineers and organizations for generals, and not for saints, to run them. The simplest organization may aid purity as well as strength; but beyond that narrow limit, organization swallows up the individual, and is careless of personal purity; push, activity, enthusiasm, zeal for an organization, come in as the vicious substitutes for spiritual character. Holiness and all the spiritual graces of hardy culture and slow growth are discarded as too slow and too costly for the progress and rush of the age. By dint of machinery, new organizations, and spiritual weakness, results are vainly expected to be secured which can be secured only by faith, prayer, and waiting on God.

The man and his spiritual character is what God is looking after. If men, holy men, can be turned out by the easy processes of church machinery readier and better than by the old-time processes, we would gladly invest in every new and improved patent; but we do not believe it. We adhere to the old way—the way the holy prophets went, the king's highway of holiness.

An example of this is afforded by the case of William Wilberforce. High in social position, a member of Parliament, the friend of Pitt the famous statesman, he was not called of God to forsake his high social position nor to quit Parliament, but he was called to order his life according to the pattern set by Jesus Christ and to give himself to prayer. To read the story of his life is to be impressed with its holiness and its devotion to the claims of the quiet hours alone with God. His conversion was announced to his friends—to Pitt and others—by letter.

In the beginning of his religious career he records:

> My chief reasons for a day of secret prayer are, (1) That the state of public affairs is very critical and calls for earnest deprecation of the divine displeasure. (2) My station in life is a very difficult one, wherein I am at a loss to know how to act. Direction, therefore, should be specially sought from time to time. (3) I have been graciously supported in difficult situations of a public nature. I have gone out and returned home in safety, and found a kind reception has attended me. I would humbly hope, too, that what I am now doing is a proof that God has not withdrawn his Holy Spirit from me. I am covered with mercies.

The recurrence of his birthday led him again to review his situation and employment. "I find," he wrote,

> that books alienate my heart from God as much as anything. I have been framing a plan of study for myself, but let me remember but one thing is needful, that if my heart cannot be kept in a spiritual state without so much prayer, meditation, Scripture reading, etc., as are incompatible with study, I must *seek first* the righteousness of God.

All were to be surrendered for spiritual advance. "I fear," we find him saying,

> that I have not studied the Scriptures enough. Surely in the summer recess I ought to read the Scriptures an hour or two every day, besides prayer, devotional reading, and meditation. God will prosper me better if I wait on him. The experience of all good men shows that without constant prayer and watchfulness the life of God in the soul stagnates. Doddridge's morning and evening devotions were serious matters. Colonel Gardiner always spent hours in prayer in the morning before he went forth. Bonnell practiced private devotions largely morning and evening, and repeated psalms dressing and undressing to raise his mind to heavenly things. I would look up to God to make the means effectual. I fear that my devotions are too much hurried, that I do not read Scripture enough. I must grow in grace; I must love God more; I must feel the power of divine

things more. Whether I am more or less learned signifies not. Whether even I execute the work which I deem useful is comparatively unimportant. But beware my soul of lukewarmness.

The New Year began with the Holy Communion and new vows. "I will press forward," he wrote,

and labor to know God better and love him more. Assuredly I may, because God will give his Holy Spirit to them that ask him, and the Holy Spirit will shed abroad the love of God in the heart. O, then, pray, pray; be earnest, press forward and follow on to know the Lord. Without watchfulness, humiliation and prayer, the sense of divine things must languish.

To prepare for the future he said he found nothing more effectual than private prayer and the serious perusal of the New Testament.

And again:

I must put down that I have lately too little time for private devotions. I can sadly confirm Doddridge's remark that when we go on ill in the closet we commonly do so everywhere else. I must mend here. I am afraid of getting into what Owen calls the trade of sinning and repenting . . . Lord help me, the shortening of private devotions starves the soul; it grows lean and faint. This must not be. I must redeem more time. I see how lean in spirit I become without full allowance of time for private devotions; I must be careful to be watching unto prayer.

At another time he puts on record:

I must try what I long ago heard was the rule of E—— the great upholsterer, who, when he came from Bond Street to his little villa, always first retired to his closet. I have been keeping too late hours, and hence have had but a hurried half hour to myself. Surely the experience of all good men confirms the proposition that without due measure of private devotions, the soul will grow lean.

To his son he wrote:

Let me conjure you not to be seduced into neglecting, curtailing, or hurrying over your morning prayers. Of all things, guard against neglecting God in the closet. There is nothing more fatal to the life and power of religion. More solitude and earlier hours—prayer three times a day at least. How much better might I serve if I cultivated a closer communion with God.

Wilberforce knew the secret of a holy life. Is that not where most of us fail? We are so busy with other things, so immersed even in doing good and in carrying on the Lord's work, that we neglect the quiet seasons of prayer with God, and before we are aware of it our soul is lean and impoverished.

"One night alone in prayer," says Spurgeon,

might make us new men, changed from poverty of soul to spiritual wealth, from trembling to triumphing. We have an example of it in the life of Jacob. Aforetime the crafty shuffler, always bargaining and calculating, unlovely in almost every respect, yet one night in prayer turned the supplanter into a prevailing prince, and robed him with celestial grandeur. From that night he lives on the sacred page as one of the nobility of heaven. Could not we, at least now and then, in these weary earthbound years, hedge about a single night for such enriching traffic with the skies? What, have we no sacred ambition? Are we deaf to the yearnings of divine love? Yet, my brethren, for wealth and for science men will cheerfully quit their warm couches, and cannot we do it now and again for the love of God and the good of souls? Where is our zeal, our gratitude, our sincerity? I am ashamed while I thus upbraid both myself and you. May we often tarry at Jabbok, and cry with Jacob, as he grasped the angel—

> With thee all night I mean to stay,
> And wrestle till the break of day.

Surely, brethren, if we have given whole days to folly, we can afford a space for heavenly wisdom. Time was when we gave whole nights to chambering and wantonness, to dancing and the world's revelry; we did not tire then; we were chiding the sun that he rose so soon, and wishing the hours would lag awhile that we might delight in wilder merriment and perhaps deeper sin. Oh, wherefore, should we weary in heavenly employments? Why grow we weary when asked to watch with our Lord? Up, sluggish heart, Jesus calls thee! Rise and go forth to meet the heavenly friend in the place where he manifests himself.

We can never expect to grow in the likeness of our Lord unless we follow his example and give more time to communion with the Father. A revival of real praying would produce a spiritual revolution.

9

The Possibilities of True Prayer

It may be said with emphasis that no lazy saint prays. Can there be a lazy saint? Can there be a prayerless saint? Does not slack praying cut short saint-hood's crown and kingdom? Can there be a cowardly soldier? Can there be a saintly hypocrite? Can there be virtuous vice? It is only when these impossibilities are brought into being that we then can find a prayerless saint.

To go through the motion of praying is a dull business, though not a hard one. To say prayers in a decent, delicate way is not heavy work. But to pray really, to pray till hell feels the ponderous stroke, to pray till the iron gates of difficulty are opened, till the mountains of obstacles are removed, till the mists are exhaled and the clouds are lifted, and the sunshine of a cloudless day brightens—this is hard work, but it is God's work and man's best labor. Never was the toil of hand, head and heart less spent in vain than when praying. It is hard to wait and press and pray, and hear no voice, but stay till God answers. The joy of answered prayer is the joy of a travailing mother when a man child is born into the world, the joy of a slave whose chains have been burst asunder and to whom new life and liberty have just come.

A bird's-eye view of what has been accomplished by prayer shows what we lost when the dispensation of real prayer was substituted by Pharisaical pretense and sham; it shows, too, how imperative is the need for holy men and women who will give themselves to earnest, Christlike praying.

It is not an easy thing to pray. Back of the praying there must lie all the conditions of prayer. These conditions are possible, but they are not to be seized on in a moment by the prayerless. Present they always may be to the faithful and holy, but cannot exist in nor be met by a frivolous, negligent, laggard spirit. Prayer does not stand alone. It is not an isolated performance. Prayer stands in closest connection with all the duties of an ardent piety. It is the issuance of a character which is made up of the elements of a vigorous and commanding faith. Prayer honors God, acknowledges his being, exalts his power, adores his providence, secures his aid. A sneering half-rationalism cries out against devotion, that it does nothing but pray. But to pray well is to do all things well. If it be true that devotion does nothing but pray, then it does nothing at all. To do nothing but pray fails to do the praying, for the antecedent, coincident, and subsequent conditions of prayer are but the sum of all the energized forces of a practical, working piety.

The possibilities of prayer run parallel with the promises of God. Prayer opens an outlet for the promises, removes the hindrances in the way of their execution, puts them into working order, and secures their gracious ends. More than this, prayer like faith, obtains promises, enlarges their operation, and adds to the measure of their results. God's promises were to Abraham and to his seed, but many a barren womb, and many a minor obstacle stood in the way of the fulfilment of these promises; but prayer removed them all, made a highway for the promises, added to the facility and speediness of their realization, and by prayer the promise shone bright and perfect in its execution.

The possibilities of prayer are found in its allying itself with the purposes of God, for God's purposes and man's praying are the combination of all potent and omnipotent forces. More than this, the possibilities of prayer are seen in the fact that it changes the purposes of God. It is in the very nature of prayer to plead and give directions. Prayer is not a negation. It is a positive force. It never rebels against the will of God, never comes into conflict with that will, but that it does seek to change God's purpose is evident. Christ said, "The cup which my Father hath given me shall I not drink it?" and yet he had prayed that very night, "If it be possible let this cup pass from me." Paul sought to change the purposes of God about the thorn in the flesh. God's purposes were fixed to destroy Israel, and the prayer of Moses changed the purposes of God and saved Israel. In the time of the judges Israelites were apostate and greatly oppressed. They repented and cried unto God and he said: "Ye have forsaken me and served other gods, wherefore I will deliver you no more": but they humbled themselves, put away their strange gods, and God's "soul was grieved for the misery of Israel," and he sent them deliverance by Jephthah.

God sent Isaiah to say to Hezekiah, "Set thine house in order: for thou shalt die, and not live"; and Hezekiah prayed, and God sent Isaiah back to say, "I have heard thy prayer, I have seen thy tears; behold I will add unto thy days fifteen years." "Yet forty days and Nineveh shall be overthrown," was God's message by Jonah. But Nineveh cried mightily to God, and "God repented of the evil that he had said he would do unto them; and he did it not."

The possibilities of prayer are seen from the diverse conditions it reaches and the diverse ends it secures. Elijah prayed over a dead child, and it came to life; Elisha did the same thing; Christ prayed at Lazarus's grave, and Lazarus came forth. Peter kneeled down and prayed beside dead Dorcas, and she opened her eyes and sat up, and Peter presented her alive to the distressed company. Paul prayed for Publius, and healed him. Jacob's praying changed Esau's murderous hate into the kisses of the tenderest brotherly embrace. God gave to Rebecca Jacob and Esau because Isaac prayed for her. Joseph was the child of Rachel's prayers. Hannah's praying gave Samuel to Israel. John the Baptist was given to Elizabeth, barren and past age as she was, in answer to the prayer of Zacharias. Elisha's praying brought famine or harvest to Israel;

as he prayed so it was. Ezra's praying carried the Spirit of God in heart-breaking conviction to the entire city of Jerusalem, and brought them in tears of repentance back to God. Isaiah's praying carried the shadow of the sun back ten degrees on the dial of Ahaz.

In answer to Hezekiah's praying an angel slew one hundred and eighty-five thousand of Sennacherib's army in one night. Daniel's praying opened to him the vision of prophecy, helped him to administer the affairs of a mighty kingdom, and sent an angel to shut the lions' mouths. The angel was sent to Cornelius, and the gospel opened through him to the Gentile world, because his "prayers and alms had come up as a memorial before God."

> And what shall I more say? for the time would fail me to tell of Gideon, and of Barak, and of Samson, and of Jephthah; of David also, and Samuel, and of the prophets"; of Paul and Peter, and John and the Apostles, and the holy company of saints, reformers, and martyrs, who, through praying, "subdued kingdoms, wrought righteousness, obtained promises, stopped the mouths of lions, quenched the violence of fire, escaped the edge of the sword, out of weakness were made strong, waxed valiant in fight, turned to flight the armies of the aliens.

Prayer puts God in the matter with commanding force: "Ask of me things to come concerning my sons," says God, "and concerning the work of my hands command ye me." We are charged in God's Word "always to pray," "in everything by prayer," "continuing instant in prayer," to "pray everywhere," "praying always." The promise is as illimitable as the command is comprehensive. "All things whatsoever ye shall ask in prayer, believing, ye shall receive," "whatever ye shall ask," "if ye shall ask anything." "Ye shall ask what ye will and it shall be done unto you." "Whatsoever ye ask the Father he will give it to you." If there is anything not involved in "All things whatsoever," or not found in the phrase "Ask anything," then these things may be left out of prayer. Language could not cover a wider range, nor involve more fully all *minutia*. These statements are but samples of the all-comprehending possibilities of prayer under the promises of God to those who meet the conditions of right praying.

These passages, though, give but a general outline of the immense regions over which prayer extends its sway. Beyond these the effect of prayer reaches and secures good from regions which cannot be traversed by language or thought. Paul exhausted language and thought in praying, but conscious of necessities not covered and realms of good not reached he covers these impenetrable and undiscovered regions by this general plea, "unto him that is able to do exceeding abundantly above all that we ask or think, according to the power that worketh in us." The promise is, "Call upon me, and I will answer thee, and show thee great and mighty things, which thou knowest not."

James declares that "the effectual, fervent prayer of a righteous man availeth much." How much he could not tell, but illustrates it by the power of Old Testament praying to stir up New Testament saints to imitate by the fervor and influence of their praying the holy men of old, and duplicate and surpass the power of their praying. Elijah, he says, was a man subject to like passions as we are, and he prayed earnestly that it might not rain: and it rained not on the earth by the space of three years and six months. And he prayed again, and the heaven gave rain, and the earth brought forth her fruit.

In the Revelation of John the whole lower order of God's creation, and his providential government, the church and the angelic world, are in the attitude of waiting on the efficiency of the prayers of the saintly ones on earth to carry on the various interests of earth and heaven. The angel takes the fire kindled by prayer and casts it earthward, "and there were voices, and thunderings, and lightnings, and an earthquake." Prayer is the force which creates all these alarms, stirs, and throes. "Ask of me," says God to his son, and to the church of his son, "and I shall give thee the heathen for thine inheritance and the uttermost parts of the earth for thy possessions."

The men who have done mighty things for God have always been mighty in prayer, have well understood the possibilities of prayer, and made most of these possibilities. The Son of God, the first of all and the mightiest of all, has shown us the all-potent and far-reaching possibilities of prayer. Paul was mighty for God because he knew how to use, and how to get others to use, the mighty spiritual forces of prayer.

The seraphim, burning, sleepless, adoring, is the figure of prayer. It is resistless in its ardor, devoted and tireless. There are hindrances to prayer that nothing but pure, intense flame can surmount. There are toils and outlays and endurance which nothing but the strongest, most ardent flame can abide. Prayer may be low-tongued, but it cannot be cold-tongued. Its words may be few, but they must be on fire. Its feelings may not be impetuous, but they must be white with heat. It is the effectual, fervent prayer that influences God.

God's house is the house of prayer; God's work is the work of prayer. It is the zeal for God's house and the zeal for God's work that makes God's house glorious and his work abide.

When the prayer-chambers of saints are closed or are entered casually or coldly, then church rulers are secular, fleshly, materialized; spiritual character sinks to a low level, and the ministry becomes restrained and enfeebled.

When prayer fails, the world prevails. When prayer fails the church loses its divine characteristics, its divine power; the church is swallowed up by a proud ecclesiasticism, and the world scoffs at its obvious impotence.

10

Hindrances to Prayer

WHY do we not pray? What are the hindrances to prayer? This is not a curious nor trivial question. It goes not only to the whole matter of our praying, but to the whole matter of our religion. Religion is bound to decline when praying is hindered. That which hinders praying, hinders religion. He who is too busy to pray will be too busy to live a holy life.

Other duties become pressing and absorbing and crowd out prayer. Choked to death, would be the coroner's verdict in many cases of dead praying, if an inquest could be secured on this dire, spiritual calamity. This way of hindering prayer becomes so natural, so easy, so innocent that it comes on us all unawares. If we will allow our praying to be crowded out, it will always be done. Satan had rather we let the grass grow on the path to our prayer-chamber than anything else. A closed chamber of prayer means gone out of business religiously, or what is worse, made an assignment and carrying on our religion in some other name than God's and to somebody else's glory. God's glory is only secured in the business of religion by carrying that religion on with a large capital of prayer. The apostles understood this when they declared that their time must not be employed in even the sacred duties of almsgiving; they must give themselves, they said, "continually to prayer and to the ministry of the Word," prayer being put first with them and the ministry of the Word having its efficiency and life from prayer.

The process of hindering prayer by crowding out is simple and goes by advancing stages. First, prayer is hurried through. Unrest and agitation, fatal to all devout exercises, come in. Then the time is shortened, relish for the exercise palls. Then it is crowded into a corner and depends on the fragments of time for its exercise. Its value depreciates. The duty has lost its importance. It no longer commands respect nor brings benefit. It has fallen out of estimate, out of the heart, out of the habits, out of the life. We cease to pray and cease to live spiritually.

There is no stay to the desolating floods of worldliness and business and cares, but prayer. Christ meant this when he charged us to watch and pray. There is no pioneering corps for the gospel but prayer. Paul knew that when he declared that "night and day he prayed exceedingly that we might see your face and might perfect that which is lacking in your faith." There is no arriving at a high state of grace without much praying and no staying in those high altitudes without great praying. Epaphras knew this when he "labored fervently in prayers" for the Colossian church, "that they might stand perfect and complete in all the will of God."

The only way to preserve our praying from being hindered is to estimate prayer at its true and great value. Estimate it as Daniel did, who, when he "knew that the writing was signed he went into his house, and his windows being opened to Jerusalem, he kneeled upon his knees three times a day and prayed and gave thanks before his God as he did aforetime." Put praying into the high values as Daniel did, above place, honor, ease, wealth, life. Put praying into the habits as Daniel did. "As he did aforetime" has much in it to give firmness and fidelity in the hour of trial; much in it to remove hindrances and master opposing circumstances.

One of Satan's wiliest tricks is to destroy the best by the good. Business and other duties are good, but we are so filled with these that they crowd out and destroy the best. Prayer holds the citadel for God, and if Satan can by any means weaken prayer he is a gainer so far, and when prayer is dead the citadel is taken. We must keep prayer as the faithful sentinel keeps guard, with sleepless vigilance. We must not keep it half-starved and feeble as a baby, but we must keep it in giant strength. Our prayer-chamber should have our freshest strength, our calmest time, its hours unfettered, without obtrusion, without haste. Private place and plenty of time are the life of prayer. "To kneel upon our knees three times a day and pray and give thanks before God as we did aforetime," is the very heart and soul of religion, and makes men, like Daniel, of "an excellent spirit," "greatly beloved in heaven."

The greatness of prayer, involving as it does the whole man, in the intensest form, is not realized without spiritual discipline. This makes it hard work, and before this exacting and consuming effort our spiritual sloth or feebleness stands abashed.

The simplicity of prayer, its childlike elements form a great obstacle to true praying. Intellect gets in the way of the heart. The child spirit only is the spirit of prayer. It is no holiday occupation to make the man a child again. In song, in poetry, in memory he may wish himself a child again, but in prayer he must be a child again in reality. At his mother's knee, artless, sweet, intense, direct, trustful. With no shade of doubt, no temper to be denied. A desire which burns and consumes which can only be voiced by a cry. It is no easy work to have this childlike spirit of prayer.

If praying were but an hour in the closet, difficulties would face and hinder even that hour, but praying is the whole life preparing for the closet. How difficult it is to cover home and business, all the sweets and all the bitters of life, with the holy atmosphere of the closet! A holy life is the only preparation for prayer. It is just as difficult to pray, as it is to live a holy life. In this we find a wall of exclusion built around our closets; men do not love holy praying, because they do not love and will not do holy living. Montgomery sets forth the difficulties of true praying when he declares the sublimity and simplicity of prayer.

> Prayer is the simplest form of speech
> That infant lips can try.
> Prayer is the sublimest strains that reach
> The Majesty on high.

This is not only good poetry, but also a profound truth as to the loftiness and simplicity of prayer. There are great difficulties in reaching the exalted, angelic strains of prayer. The difficulty of coming down to the simplicity of infant lips is not much less.

Prayer in the Old Testament is called wrestling. Conflict and skill, strenuous, exhaustive effort are involved. In the New Testament we have the terms striving, laboring fervently, fervent, effectual, agony, all indicating intense effort put forth, difficulties overcome. We, in our praises sing out—

> What various hindrances we meet
> In coming to a mercyseat.

We also have learned that the gracious results secured by prayer are generally proportioned to the outlay in removing the hindrances which obstruct our soul's high communion with God.

Christ spake a parable to this end, that men ought always to pray and not to faint. The parable of the importunate widow teaches the difficulties in praying, how they are to be surmounted, and the happy results which follow from valorous praying. Difficulties will always obstruct the way to the closet as long as it remains true,

> That Satan trembles when he sees
> The weakest saint upon his knees.

Courageous faith is made stronger and purer by mastering difficulties. These difficulties but dim the eye of faith to the glorious prize which is to be won by the successful wrestler in prayer. Men must not faint in the contest of prayer, but to this high and holy work they must give themselves, defying the difficulties in the way, and experience more than an angel's happiness in the results. Luther said: "To have prayed well is to have studied well." More than that, to have prayed well is to have fought well. To have prayed well is to have lived well. To pray well is to die well.

Prayer is a rare gift, not a popular, ready gift. Prayer is not the fruit of natural talents; it is the product of faith, of holiness, of deeply spiritual character. Men learn to pray as they learn to love. Perfection in simplicity, in humility in faith—these form its chief ingredients. Novices in these graces are not adept in prayer. It cannot be seized upon by untrained hands; graduates in heaven's highest school of art can alone touch its finest keys, raise its sweetest, highest notes. Fine material, fine finish are requisite. Master workmen are required, for mere journeymen cannot execute the work of prayer.

The spirit of prayer should rule our spirits and our conduct. The spirit of the prayer-chamber must control our lives or the closet hour will be dull and sapless. Always praying in spirit; always acting in the spirit of praying; these make our praying strong. The spirit of every moment is that which imparts strength to the closet communion. It is what we are out of the closet which gives victory or brings defeat to the closet. If the spirit of the world prevails in our non-closet hours, the spirit of the world will prevail in our closet hours, and that will be a vain and idle farce.

We must live for God out of the closet if we would meet God in the closet. We must bless God by praying lives if we would have God's blessing in the closet. We must do God's will in our lives if we would have God's ear in the closet. We must listen to God's voice in public if we would have God listen to our voice in private. God must have our hearts out of the closet, if we would have God's presence in the closet. If we would have God in the closet, God must have us out of the closet. There is no way of praying to God, but by living to God. The closet is not a confessional, simply, but the hour of holy communion and high and sweet communicating and of intense intercession.

Men would pray better if they lived better. They would get more from God if they lived more obediently and well pleasing to God. We would have more strength and time for the divine work of intercession if we did not have to expend so much strength and time settling up old scores and paying our delinquent taxes. Our spiritual liabilities are so greatly in excess of our spiritual assets that our closet time is spent in taking out a decree of bankruptcy instead of being the time of great spiritual wealth for us and for others. Our closets are too much like the sign, "Closed for Repairs."

John said of primitive Christian praying, "Whatsoever we ask we receive of him, because we keep his commandments and do those things which are pleasing in his sight." We should note what illimitable grounds were covered, what illimitable gifts were received by their strong praying: "Whatsoever"—how comprehensive the range and reception of mighty praying; how suggestive the reasons for the ability to pray and to have prayers answered. Obedience, but more than mere obedience, doing the things which please God well. They went to their closets made strong by their strict obedience and loving fidelity to God in their conduct. Their lives were not only true and obedient, but they were thinking about things above obedience, searching for and doing things to make God glad. These can come with eager step and radiant countenance to meet their Father in the closet, not simply to be forgiven, but to be approved and to receive.

It makes much difference whether we come to God as a criminal or a child; to be pardoned or to be approved; to settle scores or to be embraced; for punishment or for favor. Our praying to be strong must be buttressed by holy living. The name of Christ must be honored by our lives before it will honor our intercessions. The life of faith perfects the prayer of faith.

Our lives not only give color to our praying, but they give body to it as well. Bad living makes bad praying. We pray feebly because we live feebly. The stream of praying cannot rise higher than the fountain of living. The closet force is made up of the energy which flows from the confluent streams of living. The feebleness of living throws its faintness into closet homes. We cannot talk to God strongly when we have not lived for God strongly. The closet cannot be made holy to God when the life has not been holy to God. The Word of God emphasizes our conduct as giving value to our praying. "Then shalt thou call and the Lord shalt answer, thou shalt cry and he shall say, 'Here I am.' If thou take away from the midst of thee the yoke, the putting forth the finger, and speaking vanity."

Men are to pray "lifting up holy hands without wrath and doubting." We are to pass the time of our sojourning here in fear if we would call on the father. We cannot divorce praying from conduct. "Whatsoever we ask we receive of him because we keep his commandments and do those things that are pleasing in his sight." "Ye ask and receive not because ye ask amiss that ye may consume it upon your lusts." The injunction of Christ, "Watch and pray," is to cover and guard conduct that we may come to our closets with all the force secured by a vigilant guard over our lives.

Our religion breaks down oftenest and most sadly in our conduct. Beautiful theories are marred by ugly lives. The most difficult as well as the most impressive point in piety is to live it. Our praying suffers as much as our religion from bad living. Preachers were charged in primitive times to preach by their lives or preach not at all. So Christians everywhere ought to be charged to pray by their lives or pray not at all. Of course, the prayer of repentance is acceptable. But repentance means to quit doing wrong and learn to do well. A repentance which does not produce a change in conduct is a sham. Praying which does not result in pure conduct is a delusion. We have missed the whole office and virtue of praying if it does not rectify conduct. It is in the very nature of things that we must quit praying or quit bad conduct. Cold, dead praying may exist with bad conduct, but cold, dead praying is no praying in God's esteem. Our praying advances in power as it rectifies the life. A life growing in its purity and devotion will be a more prayerful life.

The pity is that so much of our praying is without object or aim. It is without purpose. How much praying there is by men and women who never abide in Christ—hasty praying, sweet praying full of sentiment, pleasing praying, but not backed by a life wedded to Christ. Popular praying! How much of this praying is from unsanctified hearts and unhallowed lips! Prayers spring into life under the influence of some great excitement, by some pressing emergency, through some popular clamor, some great peril. But the conditions of prayer are not there. We rush into God's presence and try to link him to our cause, inflame him with our passions, move him by our peril. All things are to be prayed for—but with clean hands, with absolute deference to God's will and abiding in Christ. Prayerless praying by lips and hearts untrained to prayer, by lives out of harmony with Jesus Christ; prayerless praying, which has the form and motion of prayer but is without the true heart of prayer, never moves God to an answer. It is of such praying that James says: "Ye have not because ye ask not; ye ask and receive not, because ye ask amiss."

The two great evils—not asking, and asking in a wrong way. Perhaps the greater evil is wrong asking, for it has in it the show of duty done, of praying when there has been no praying—a deceit, a fraud, a sham. The times of the most praying are not really the times of the best praying. The Pharisees prayed much, but they were actuated by vanity; their praying was the symbol of their hypocrisy by which they made God's house of prayer a den of robbers. Theirs was praying on state occasions—mechanical, perfunctory, professional, beautiful in words, fragrant in sentiment, well ordered, well received by the ears that heard, but utterly devoid of every element of real prayer.

The conditions of prayer are well ordered and clear—abiding in Christ; in his name. One of the first necessities, if we are to grasp the infinite possibilities of prayer, is to get rid of prayerless praying. It is often beautiful in words and in execution; it has the drapery of prayer in rich and costly form, but it lacks the soul of praying. We fall so easily into the habit of prayerless service, of merely filling a program.

If men only prayed on all occasions and in every place where they go through the motion! If there were only holy inflamed hearts back of all these beautiful words and gracious forms! If there were always uplifted hearts in these erect men who are uttering flawless but vain words before God! If there were always reverent bended hearts when bended knees are uttering words before God to please men's ears!

There is nothing that will preserve the life of prayer; its vigor, sweetness, obligations, seriousness and value, so much as a deep conviction that prayer is an approach to God, a pleading with God, an asking of God. Reality will then be in it; reverence will then be in the attitude, in the place, and in the air. Faith will draw, kindle and open. Formality and deadness cannot live in this high and all-serious home of the soul.

Prayerless praying lacks the essential element of true praying; it is not based on desire, and is devoid of earnestness and faith. Desire burdens the chariot of prayer, and faith drives its wheels. Prayerless praying has no burden, because no sense of need; no ardency, because no vision, strength, or glow of faith. No mighty pressure to prayer, no holding on to God with the deathless, despairing grasp, "I will not let thee go except thou bless me." No utter self-abandon, lost in the throes of a desperate, pertinacious, and consuming plea: "Yet now if thou wilt forgive their sin—if not, blot me, I pray thee, out of thy book"; or, "Give me Scotland, or I die." Prayerless praying stakes nothing on the issue, for it has nothing to stake. It comes with empty hands, indeed, but they are listless hands as well as empty. They have never learned the lesson of empty hands clinging to the cross; this lesson to them has no form nor comeliness.

Prayerless praying has not heart in its praying. The lack of heart deprives praying of its reality, and makes it an empty and unfit vessel. Heart, soul, life must be in our praying; the heavens must feel the force of our crying, and must be brought into oppressed sympathy for our bitter and needy state. A need that oppresses us, and has no relief but in our crying to God, must voice our praying.

Prayerless praying is insincere. It has no honesty at heart. We name in words what we do not want in heart. Our prayers give formal utterance to the things for which our hearts are not only not hungry, but for which they really have no taste. We once heard an eminent and saintly preacher, now in heaven, come abruptly and sharply on a congregation that had just risen from prayer, with the question and statement, "What did you pray for? If God should take hold of you and shake you, and demand what you prayed for, you could not tell him to save your life what the prayer was that has just died from your lips." So it always is, prayerless praying has neither memory nor heart. A mere form, a heterogeneous mass, an insipid compound, a mixture thrown together for sound and to fill up, but with neither heart nor aim, is prayerless praying. A dry routine, a dreary drudge, a dull and heavy task is this prayerless praying.

But prayerless praying is much worse than either task or drudge, it divorces praying from living; it utters its words against the world, but with heart and life runs into the world; it prays for humility, but nurtures pride; prays for self-denial, while indulging the flesh. Nothing exceeds in gracious results true praying, but better not to pray at all than to pray prayerless prayers, for they are but sinning, and the worst of sinning is to sin on our knees.

The prayer habit is a good habit, but praying by dint of habit only is a very bad habit. This kind of praying is not conditioned after God's order, nor generated by God's power. It is not only a waste, a perversion, and a delusion, but it is a prolific source of unbelief. Prayerless praying gets no results. God is not reached, self is not helped. It is better not to pray at all than to secure no results from praying. Better for the one who prays, better for others. Men hear of the prodigious results which are to be secured by prayer: the matchless good promised in God's Word to prayer. These keen-eyed worldlings or timid little-faith ones mark the great discrepancy between the results promised and results realized, and are led necessarily to doubt the truth and worth of that which is so big in promise and so beggarly in results. Religion and God are dishonored, doubt and unbelief are strengthened by much asking and no getting.

In contrast with this, what a mighty force prayerful praying is. Real prayer helps God and man. God's kingdom is advanced by it. The greatest good comes to man by it. Prayer can do anything that God can do. The pity is that we do not believe this as we ought, and we do not put it to the test.

The deepest need of the church today is not for any material or external thing, but the deepest need is spiritual. Prayerless work will never bring in the kingdom. We neglect to pray in the prescribed way. We seldom enter the closet and shut the door for a season of prayer. Kingdom interests are pressing on us thick and fast and we must pray. Prayerless giving will never evangelize the world.—A. J. GORDON

11

Prayer Opens Up Divine Resources

THE preceding chapter closed with the statement that prayer can do anything that God can do. It is a tremendous statement to make, but it is a statement borne out by history and experience. If we are abiding in Christ—and if we abide in him we are living in obedience to his holy will—and approach God in his name, then there lie open before us the infinite resources of the divine treasure-house.

The man who truly prays gets from God many things denied to the prayerless man. The aim of all real praying is to get the thing prayed for, as the child's cry for bread has for its end the getting of bread. This view removes prayer clean out of the sphere of religious performances. Prayer is not acting a part or going through religious motions. Prayer is neither official nor formal nor ceremonial, but direct, hearty, intense. Prayer is not religious work which must be gone through, and avails because well done. Prayer is the helpless and needy child crying to the compassion of the father's heart and the bounty and power of a father's hand. The answer is as sure to come as the father's heart can be touched and the father's hand moved.

The object of asking is to receive. The aim of seeking is to find. The purpose of knocking is to arouse attention and get in, and this is Christ's repeated assertion that the prayer without doubt will be answered, its end without doubt secured. Not by some roundabout way, but by getting the very thing asked for.

The value of prayer does not lie in the number of prayers, or the length of prayers, but its value is found in the great truth that we are privileged by our relations to God to unburden our desires and make our requests known to God, and he will relieve by granting our petitions. The child asks because the parent is in the habit of granting the child's requests. As the children of God we need something and we need it badly, and we go to God for it. Neither the Bible nor the child of God knows anything of that half-infidel declaration that we are to answer our own prayers. God answers prayer. The true Christian does not pray to stir himself up, but his prayer is the stirring up of himself to take hold of God. The heart of faith knows nothing of that specious skepticism which stays the steps of prayer and chills its ardor by whispering that prayer does not affect God.

D. L. Moody used to tell a story of a little child whose father and mother had died, and who was taken into another family. The first night she asked whether she could pray as she used to do. They said: "Oh, yes!" So she knelt down and prayed as her mother had taught her; and when that was ended, she added a little prayer of her own: "O God, make these people as kind to me as father and mother were." The she paused and looked up, as if expecting the answer, and then added: "Of course you will." How sweetly simple was that little one's faith! She expected God to answer and "do," and "of course" she got her request, and that is the spirit in which God invites us to approach him.

In contrast to that incident is the story told of the quaint Yorkshire class leader, Daniel Quorm, who was visiting a friend. One forenoon he came to the friend and said, "I am sorry you have met with such a great disappointment."

"Why, no," said the man, "I have not met with any disappointment."

"Yes," said Daniel, "you were expecting something remarkable today."

"What do you mean?" said the friend.

"Why you prayed that you might be kept sweet and gentle all day long. And, by the way things have been going, I see you have been greatly disappointed."

"Oh," said the man, "I thought you meant something particular."

Prayer is mighty in its operations, and God never disappoints those who put their trust and confidence in him. They may have to wait long for the answer, and they may not live to see it, but the prayer of faith never misses its object.

"A friend of mine in Cincinnati had preached his sermon and sank back in his chair, when he felt impelled to make another appeal," says Dr. J. Wilbur Chapman.

> A boy at the back of the church lifted his hand. My friend left the pulpit and went down to him, and said, "Tell me about yourself." The boy said, "I live in New York. I am a prodigal. I have disgraced my father's name and broken my mother's heart. I ran away and told them I would never come back until I became a Christian or they brought me home dead." That night there went from Cincinnati a letter telling his father and mother that their boy had turned to God.
>
> Seven days later, in a black-bordered envelope, a reply came which read: "My dear boy, when I got the news that you had received Jesus Christ the sky was overcast; your father was dead." Then the letter went on to tell how the father had prayed for his prodigal boy with his last breath, and concluded, "You are a Christian tonight because your old father would not let you go."

A fourteen-year-old boy was given a task by his father. It so happened that a group of boys came along just then and wiled the boy away with them, and so the work went undone. But the father came home that evening and said,

"Frank, did you do the work that I gave you?" "Yes, sir," said Frank. He told an untruth, and his father knew it, but said nothing. It troubled the boy, but he went to bed as usual. Next morning his mother said to him, "Your father did not sleep all last night."

"Why didn't he sleep?" asked Frank.

His mother said, "He spent the whole night praying for you."

This sent the arrow into his heart. He was deeply convicted of his sin, and knew no rest until he had got right with God. Long afterward, when the boy became Bishop Warne, he said that his decision for Christ came from his father's prayer that night. He saw his father keeping his lonely and sorrowful vigil praying for his boy, and it broke his heart. Said he, "I can never be sufficiently grateful to him for that prayer."

An evangelist, much used of God, has put on record that he commenced a series of meetings in a little church of about twenty members who were very cold and dead, and much divided. A little prayer-meeting was kept up by two or three women. "I preached, and closed at eight o'clock," he says. "There was no one to speak or pray. The next evening one man spoke.

"The next morning I rode six miles to a minister's study, and kneeled in prayer. I went back, and said to the little church:

"'If you can make out enough to board me, I will stay until God opens the windows of heaven. God has promised to bless these means, and I believe he will.'

"Within ten days there were so many anxious souls that I met one hundred and fifty of them at a time in an inquiry meeting, while Christians were praying in another house of worship. Several hundred, I think, were converted. It is safe to believe God."

A mother asked the late John B. Gough to visit her son to win him to Christ. Gough found the young man's mind full of skeptical notions, and impervious to argument. Finally, the young man was asked to pray, just once, for light. He replied: "I do not know anything perfect to whom or to which I could pray." "How about your mother's love?" said the orator. "Isn't that perfect? Hasn't she always stood by you, and been ready to take you in, and care for you, when even your father had really kicked you out?" The young man choked with emotion, and said, "Y-e-s, sir; that is so." "Then pray to Love—it will help you. Will you promise?" He promised. That night the young man prayed in the privacy of his room. He kneeled down, closed his eyes, and struggling a moment uttered the words: "O Love." Instantly as by a flash of lightning, the old Bible text came to him: "God is love," and he said, brokenly, "O God!" Then another flash of divine truth, and a voice said, "God so loved the world, that he gave his only begotten Son,"—and there, instantly, he exclaimed, "O Christ, Thou incarnation of divinest love, show me light and truth." It was all over. He was in the light of the most perfect peace. He ran downstairs, adds the narrator of this incident, and told his mother that he was saved. That young man is today an eloquent minister of Jesus Christ.

A water famine was threatened in Hakodate, Japan. Miss Dickerson, of the Methodist Episcopal Girls' School, saw the water supply growing less daily, and in one of the fall months appealed to the Board in New York for help. There was no money on hand, and nothing was done. Miss Dickerson inquired the cost of putting down an artesian well, but found the expense too great to be undertaken. On the evening of December 31st, when the water was almost exhausted, the teachers and the older pupils met to pray for water, though they had no idea how their prayer was to be answered. A couple of days later a letter was received in the New York office which ran something like this: "Philadelphia, January 1st. It is six o'clock in the morning of New Year's Day. All the other members of the family are asleep, but I was awakened with a strange impression that some one, somewhere, is in need of money which the Lord wants me to supply." Enclosed was a check for an amount which just covered the cost of the artesian well and the piping of the water into the school buildings.

"I have seen God's hand stretched out to heal among the heathen in as mighty wonder-working power as in apostolic times," once said a well-known minister to the writer.

> I was preaching to two thousand famine orphan girls, at Kedgaum, India, at Ramabai's Mukti (salvation) Mission. A swarm of serpents as venomous and deadly as the reptile that smote Paul, suddenly raided the walled grounds, 'sent of Satan,' Ramabai said, and several of her most beautiful and faithful Christian girls were smitten by them, two of them bitten twice. I saw four of the very flower of her flock in convulsions at once, unconscious and apparently in the agonies of death.
>
> Ramabai believes the Bible with an implicit and obedient faith. There were three of us missionaries there. She said: "We will do just what the Bible says. I want you to minister for their healing according to James 5:14–18." She led the way into the dormitory where her girls were lying in spasms, and we laid our hands upon their heads and prayed, and anointed them with oil in the name of the Lord. Each of them was healed as soon as anointed and sat up and sang with faces shining. That miracle and marvel among the heathen mightily confirmed the word of the Lord, and was a profound and overpowering proclamation of God.

Some years ago, the record of a wonderful work of grace in connection with one of the stations of the China Inland Mission attracted a good deal of attention. Both the number and spiritual character of the converts had been far greater than at other stations where the consecration of the missionaries had been just as great as at the more fruitful place.

This rich harvest of souls remained a mystery until Hudson Taylor on a visit to England discovered the secret. At the close of one of his addresses a gentleman came forward to make his acquaintance. In the conversation which followed, Mr. Taylor was surprised at the accurate knowledge the man possessed concerning this inland China station. "But how is it," Mr. Taylor asked, "that you are so conversant with the conditions of that work?" "Oh!" he replied, "the missionary there and I are old college-mates; for years we have regularly corresponded; he has sent me names of inquirers and converts, and these I have daily taken to God in prayer."

At last the secret was found! A praying man at home, praying definitely, praying daily, for specific cases among the heathen. That is the real intercessory missionary.

Hudson Taylor himself, as all the world knows, was a man who knew how to pray and whose praying was blessed with fruitful answers. In the story of his life, told by Dr. and Mrs. Howard Taylor, we find page after page aglow with answered prayer. On his way out to China for the first time, in 1853, when he was only twenty-one years of age, he had a definite answer to prayer that was a great encouragement to his faith.

They had just come through the Dampier Strait, but were not yet out of sight of the islands. Usually a breeze would spring up after sunset and last until about dawn. The utmost use was made of it, but during the day they lay still with flapping sails, often drifting back and losing a good deal of the advantage gained at night.

This happened notably on one occasion when we were in dangerous proximity to the north of New Guinea. Saturday night had brought us to a point some thirty miles off the land, and during the Sunday morning service, which was held on deck, I could not fail to see that the Captain looked troubled and frequently went over to the side of the ship. When the service was ended I learnt from him the cause. A four-knot current was carrying us toward some sunken reefs, and we were already so near that it seemed improbable that we should go through the afternoon in safety. After dinner, the long boat was put out and all hands endeavored, without success, to turn the ship's head from the shore.

After standing together on the deck for some time in silence, the Captain said to me:

"Well, we have done everything that can be done. We can only await the result."

A thought occurred to me, and I replied: "No, there is one thing we have not done yet."

"What is that?" he queried.

"Four of us on board are Christians. Let us each retire to his own cabin, and in agreed prayer ask the Lord to give us immediately a breeze. He can as easily send it now as at sunset."

The Captain complied with this proposal. I went and spoke to the other two men, and after prayer with the carpenter, we all four retired to wait upon God. I had a good but very brief season in prayer, and then felt so satisfied that our request was granted that I could not continue asking, and very soon went up again on deck. The first officer, a godless man, was in charge. I went over and asked him to let down the clews or corners of the mainsail, which had been drawn up in order to lessen the useless flapping of the sail against the rigging.

"What would be the good of that?" he answered roughly.

I told him we had been asking a wind from God; that it was coming immediately; and we were so near the reef by this time that there was not a minute to lose.

With an oath and a look of contempt, he said he would rather see a wind than hear of it.

But while he was speaking I watched his eye, following it up to the royal, and there, sure enough, the corner of the topmost sail was beginning to tremble in the breeze.

"Don't you see the wind coming? Look at the royal!" I exclaimed.

"No, it is only a cat's paw," he rejoined (a mere puff of wind).

"Cat's paw or not," I cried, "pray let down the mainsail and give us the benefit."

This he was not slow to do. In another minute the heavy tread of the men on deck brought up the Captain from his cabin to see what was the matter. The breeze had indeed come! In a few minutes we were plowing our way at six or seven knots an hour through the water . . . and though the wind was sometimes unsteady, we did not altogether lose it until after passing the Pelew Islands.

Thus God encouraged me ere landing on China's shores to bring every variety of need to him in prayer, and to expect that he would honor the name of the Lord Jesus and give the help each emergency required.

In an address at Cambridge some time ago (reported in "The Life of Faith," April 3rd, 1912), Mr. S. D. Gordon told in his own inimitable way the story of a man in his own country, to illustrate from real life the fact of the reality of prayer, and that it is not mere talking.

"This man," said Mr. Gordon,

came of an old New England family, a bit farther back an English family. He was a giant in size, and a keen man mentally, and a university-trained man. He had gone out west to live, and represented a prominent district in our House of Congress, answering to your House of Commons. He was a prominent leader there. He was reared in a Christian family, but he was a skeptic, and used to lecture against Christianity. He told me he was fond, in his lectures, of proving, as he thought, conclusively, that there was no God. That was the type of his infidelity.

One day he told me he was sitting in the Lower House of Congress. It was at the time of a presidential election, and when party feeling ran high. One would have thought that was the last place where a man would be likely to think about spiritual things. He said: 'I was sitting in my seat in that crowded House and that heated atmosphere, when a feeling came to me that the God, whose existence I thought I could successfully disprove, was just there above me, looking down on me, and that he was displeased with me, and with the way I was doing. I said to myself, "This is ridiculous, I guess I've been working too hard. I'll go and get a good meal and take a long walk and shake myself, and see if that will take this feeling away." He got his extra meal, took a walk, and came back to his seat, but the impression would not be shaken off that God was there and was displeased with him. He went for a walk, day after day, but could never shake the feeling off. Then he went back to his constituency in his state, he said, to arrange matters there. He had the ambition to be the governor of his state, and his party was the dominant party in the state, and, as far as such things could be judged, he was in the line to become Governor there, in one of the most dominant States of our central west. He said: "I went home to fix that thing up as far as I could, and to get ready for it. But I had hardly reached home and exchanged greetings, when my wife, who was an earnest Christian woman, said to me that a few of them had made a little covenant of prayer that I might become a Christian." He did not want her to know the experience that he had just been going through, and so he said as carelessly as he could, "When did this thing begin, this praying of yours?" She named the date. Then he did some very quick thinking, and he knew, as he thought back, that it was the day on the calendar when that strange impression came to him for the first time.

He said to me: "I was tremendously shaken. I wanted to be honest. I was perfectly honest in not believing in God, and I thought I was right. But if what she said was true, then merely as a lawyer sifting his evidence in a case, it would be good evidence that there was really something in their prayer. I was terrifically shaken, and wanted to be honest, and did not know what to do. That same night I went to a little Methodist chapel, and if somebody had known how to talk with me, I think I should have accepted Christ that night." Then he said that the next night he went back again to that chapel, where meetings were being held each night, and there he kneeled at the altar, and yielded his great strong will to the will of God. Then he said, "I knew I was to preach," and he is preaching still in a western state. That is half of the story. I also talked with his wife—I wanted to put the two halves together, so as to get the bit of teaching in it all—and she told me this. She had been a Christian—what you call a nominal Christian—a strange confusion of terms. Then there came a time when she was led into a full surrender of her life to the Lord Jesus Christ. Then she said, "At once there came a great intensifying of desire that my husband might be a Christian, and we made that little compact to pray for him each day until he became a Christian. That night I was kneeling at my bedside before going to rest, praying for my husband, praying very earnestly and then a voice said to me, "Are you willing for the results that will come if your husband is converted?" The little message was so very distinct that she said she was frightened; she had never had such an experience. But she went on praying still more earnestly, and again there came the quiet voice, "Are you willing for the consequences?" And again there was a sense of being startled, frightened. But she still went on praying, and wondering what this meant, and a third time the quiet voice came more quietly than ever as she described it, "Are you willing for the consequences?"

Then she told me she said with great earnestness, "O God, I am willing for anything thou dost think good, if only my husband may know thee, and become a true Christian man." She said that instantly, when that prayer came from her lips, there came into her heart a wonderful sense of peace, a great peace that she could not explain, a 'peace that passeth understanding,' and from that moment—it was the very night of the covenant, the night when her husband had that first strange experience—the assurance never left her that he would accept Christ. But all those weeks she prayed with the firm assurance that the result was coming. What were the consequences? They were of a kind that I think no one would think small. She was the wife of a man in a very prominent political position; she was the wife of a man who was in the line of becoming the first official of his state, and she officially the first lady socially of that state, with all the honor that that social standing would imply. Now she is the wife of a Methodist preacher, with her home changed every two or three years, she going from this place to that, a very different social position, and having a very different income than she would otherwise have had. Yet I never met a woman who had more of the wonderful peace of God in her heart, and of the light of God in her face, than that woman.

And Mr. Gordon's comment on that incident is this: "Now, you can see at once that there was no change in the purpose of God through that prayer. The prayer worked out his purpose; it did not change it. But the woman's surrender gave the opportunity of working out the will that God wanted to work out. If we might give ourselves to him and learn his will, and use all our strength in learning his will and bending to his will, then we would begin to pray, and there is simply nothing that could resist the tremendous power of the prayer. Oh, for more men who will be simple enough to get in touch with God, and give him the mastery of the whole life, and learn his will, and then give themselves, as Jesus gave himself, to the sacred service of intercession!"

To the man or woman who is acquainted with God and who knows how to pray, there is nothing remarkable in the answers that come. They are sure of being heard, since they ask in accordance with what they know to be the mind and the will of God. Dr. William Burt, Bishop of Europe in the Methodist Episcopal church, tells that a few years ago, when he visited their Boys' School in Vienna, he found that although the year was not up, all available funds had been spent. He hesitated to make a special appeal to his friends in America. He counseled with the teachers. They took the matter to God in earnest and continued prayer, believing that he would grant their request. Ten days later Bishop Burt was in Rome, and there came to him a letter from a friend in New York, which read substantially thus: "As I went to my office on Broadway one morning [and the date was the very one on which the teachers were praying], a voice seemed to tell me that you were in need of funds for the Boys' School in Vienna. I very gladly enclose a check for the work." The check was for the amount needed. There had been no human communication between Vienna and New York. But while they were yet speaking God answered them.

Some time ago there appeared in an English religious weekly the report of an incident narrated by a well-known preacher in the course of an address to children. For the truth of the story he was able to vouch. A child lay sick in a country cottage, and her younger sister heard the doctor say, as he left the house, "Nothing but a miracle can save her." The little girl went to her money-box, took out the few coins it contained, and in perfect simplicity of heart went to shop after shop in the village street, asking, "Please, I want to buy a miracle." From each she came away disappointed. Even the local chemist had to say, "My dear, we don't sell miracles here." But outside his door two men were talking, and had overheard the child's request. One was a great doctor from a London hospital, and he asked her to explain what she wanted. When he understood the need, he hurried with her to the cottage, examined the sick girl, and said to the mother: "It is true—only a miracle can save her, and it must be performed at once." He got his instruments, performed the operation, and the patient's life was saved.

D. L. Moody gives this illustration of the power of prayer:

> While in Edinburgh, a man was pointed out to me by a friend, who said: "That man is chairman of the Edinburgh Infidel Club."
>
> I went and sat beside him and said, "My friend, I am glad to see you in our meeting. Are you concerned about your welfare?"
>
> "I do not believe in any hereafter."
>
> "Well, just get down on your knees and let me pray for you."
>
> "No, I do not believe in prayer."
>
> I knelt beside him as he sat, and prayed. He made a great deal of sport of it. A year after I met him again. I took him by the hand and said: "Hasn't God answered my prayer yet?"
>
> "There is no God. If you believe in one who answers prayer, try your hand on me."
>
> "Well, a great many are now praying for you, and God's time will come, and I believe you will be saved yet."
>
> Some time afterward I got a letter from a leading barrister in Edinburgh telling me that my infidel friend had come to Christ, and that seventeen of his club men had followed his example.
>
> I did not know *how* God would answer prayer, but I knew he would answer. Let us come boldly to God.

Robert Louis Stevenson tells a vivid story of a storm at sea. The passengers below were greatly alarmed, as the waves dashed over the vessel. At last one of them, against orders, crept to the deck, and came to the pilot, who was lashed to the wheel which he was turning without flinching. The pilot caught sight of the terror-stricken man, and gave him a reassuring smile. Below went the passenger, and comforted the others by saying, "I have seen the face of the pilot, and he smiled. All is well."

That is how we feel when through the gateway of prayer we find our way into the father's presence. We see his face, and we know that all is well, since his hand is on the helm of events, and "even the winds and the waves obey him." When we live in fellowship with him, we come with confidence into his presence, asking in the full confidence of receiving and meeting with the justification of our faith.

12

Prayer Undergirds Revivals

IT has been said that the history of revivals is the history of religion, and no one can study their history without being impressed with their mighty influence on the destiny of the race. To look back over the progress of the divine kingdom upon earth is to review revival periods which have come like refreshing showers upon dry and thirsty ground, making the desert to blossom as the rose, and bringing new eras of spiritual life and activity just when the church had fallen under the influence of the apathy of the times, and needed to be aroused to a new sense of her duty and responsibility. "From one point of view, and that not the least important," writes Principal Lindsay, in "The Church and the Ministry in the Early Centuries," "the history of the church flows on from one time of revival to another, and whether we take the awakenings in the old Catholic, the medieval, or the modern church, these have always been the work of men specially gifted with the power of seeing and declaring the secrets of the deepest Christian life, and the effect of their work has always been proportionate to the spiritual receptivity of the generation they have spoken to."

As God, from the beginning, has wrought prominently through revivals, there can be no denial of the fact that revivals are a part of the divine plan. The kingdom of our Lord has been advanced in large measure by special seasons of gracious and rapid accomplishment of the work of conversion, and it may be inferred, therefore, that the means through which God has worked in other times will be employed in our time to produce similar results. "The quiet conversion of one sinner after another, under the ordinary ministry of the gospel," says one writer on the subject,

> must always be regarded with feelings of satisfaction and gratitude by the ministers and disciples of Christ; but a periodical manifestation of the simultaneous conversion of thousands is also to be desired, because of its adaptation to afford a visible and impressive demonstration that God has made that same Jesus, who was rejected and crucified, both Lord and Christ; and that, in virtue of his divine mediatorship, he has assumed the royal scepter of universal supremacy, and "must reign till all his enemies be made his footstool.' It is, therefore, reasonable to expect that, from time to time, he will repeat that which on the day of Pentecost formed the conclusive and crowning evidence of his messiahship

and Sovereignty; and, by so doing, startle the slumbering souls of careless worldlings, gain the attentive ear of the unconverted, and, in a remarkable way, break in on those brilliant dreams of earthly glory, grandeur, wealth, power, and happiness, which the rebellious and God-forgetting multitude so fondly cherish. Such an outpouring of the Holy Spirit forms at once a demonstrative proof of the completeness and acceptance of his once offering of himself as a sacrifice for sin, and a prophetic "earnest" of the certainty that he "shall appear the second time without sin unto salvation," to judge the world in righteousness.

And that revivals are to be expected, proceeding, as they do, from the right use of the appropriate means, is a fact which needs not a little emphasis in these days, when the material is exalted at the expense of the spiritual, and when ethical standards are supposed to be supreme. That a revival is not a miracle was powerfully taught by Charles G. Finney. There might, he said, be a miracle among its antecedent causes, or there might not. The apostles employed miracles simply as a means by which they arrested attention to their message, and established its divine authority. "But the miracle was not the revival. The miracle was one thing; the revival that followed it was quite another thing. The revivals in the apostles' days were connected with miracles, but they were not miracles." All revivals are dependent on God, but in revivals, as in other things, he invites and requires the assistance of man, and the full result is obtained when there is cooperation between the divine and the human. In other words, to employ a familiar phrase, God alone can save the world, but God chooses not to save the world alone. God and man unite for the task, the response of the divine being invariably in proportion to the desire and the effort of the human.

This cooperation, then, being necessary, what is the duty which we, as co-workers with God, require to undertake? First of all, and most important of all—the point which we desire particularly to emphasize—we must give ourselves to prayer. "Revivals," as Dr. J. Wilbur Chapman reminds us, "are born in prayer. When Wesley prayed, England was revived; when Knox prayed, Scotland was refreshed; when the Sunday School teachers of Tannybrook prayed, 11,000 young people were added to the church in a year. Whole nights of prayer have always been succeeded by whole days of soul-winning."

When D. L. Moody's church in Chicago lay in ashes, he went over to England, in 1872, not to preach, but to listen to others preach while his new church was being built. One Sunday morning he was prevailed upon to preach in a London pulpit. But somehow the spiritual atmosphere was lacking. He confessed afterward that he never had such a hard time preaching in his life. Everything was perfectly dead, and, as he vainly tried to preach, he said to himself, "What a fool I was to consent to preach! I came here to listen, and here I am preaching." Then the awful thought came to him that he had to preach again at night, and only the fact that he had given the promise to do so kept him faithful to the engagement. But when Mr. Moody entered the pulpit at night, and faced the crowded congregation, he was conscious of a new atmosphere. "The powers of an unseen world seemed to have fallen upon the audience." As he drew toward the close of his sermon he became emboldened to give out an invitation, and as he concluded he said, "If there is a man or woman here who will tonight accept Jesus Christ, please stand up." At once about 500 people rose to their feet. Thinking that there must be some mistake, he asked the people to be seated, and then, in order that there might be no possible misunderstanding, he repeated the invitation, couching it in even more definite and difficult terms. Again the same number rose. Still thinking that something must be wrong, Mr. Moody, for the second time, asked the standing men and women to be seated, and then he invited all who really meant to accept Christ to pass into the vestry. Fully 500 people did as requested, and that was the beginning of a revival in that church and neighborhood, which brought Mr. Moody back from Dublin, a few days later, that he might assist the wonderful work of God.

The sequel, however, must be given, or our purpose in relating the incident will be defeated. When Mr. Moody preached at the morning service there was a woman in the congregation who had an invalid sister. On her return home she told the invalid that the preacher had been a Mr. Moody from Chicago, and on hearing this she turned pale. "What," she said, "Mr. Moody from Chicago! I read about him some time ago in an American paper, and I have been praying God to send him to London, and to our church. If I had known he was going to preach this morning I would have eaten no breakfast. I would have spent the whole time in prayer. Now, sister, go out of the room, lock the door, send me no dinner; no matter who comes, don't let them see me. I am going to spend the whole afternoon and evening in prayer." And so while Mr. Moody stood in the pulpit that had been like an ice-chamber in the morning, the bedridden saint was holding him up before God, and God, who ever delights to answer prayer, poured out his Spirit in mighty power.

The God of revivals who answered the prayer of his child for Mr. Moody, is willing to hear and to answer the faithful, believing prayers of his people today. Wherever God's conditions are met, there the revival is sure to fall. Professor Thomas Nicholson, of Cornell College, U.S.A., relates an experience on his first circuit that impresses anew the old lesson of the place of prayer in the work of God.

There had not been a revival on that circuit in years, and things were not spiritually hopeful. During more than four weeks the pastor had preached faithfully, visited from house to house, in stores, shops, and out-of-the-way places, and had done everything he could. The fifth Monday night saw *many of the official members at lodges,* but only a corporal's guard at the church.

From that meeting the pastor went home, cast down, but not in despair. He resolved to spend that night in prayer. "Locking the door, he took Bible and hymn book and began to inquire more diligently of the Lord, though the meetings had been the subject of hours of earnest prayer. Only God knows the anxiety and the faithful, prayerful study of that night. Near the dawn a great peace and a full assurance came that God would surely bless the plan which had been decided on, and a text was chosen which he felt sure was of the Lord. Dropping upon the bed, the pastor slept about two hours, then rose, hastily breakfasted, and went nine miles to the far side of the circuit to visit some sick people. All day the assurance increased.

> Toward night a pouring rain set in, the roads were heavy and we reached home, wet, supperless, and a little late, only to find no fire in the church, the lights unlit, and no signs of service. The janitor had concluded that the rain would prevent the service. We changed the order, rang the bell, and prepared for war. Three young men formed the congregation, but in that "full assurance" the pastor delivered the message which had been prayed out on the preceding night, as earnestly and as fully as if the house had been crowded, then made a personal appeal to each young man in turn. Two yielded, and testified before the meeting closed.
>
> The tired pastor went to a sweet rest, and next morning, rising a little later than usual, learned that one of the young men was going from store to store throughout the town telling of his wonderful deliverance, and exhorting the people to salvation. Night after night conversions occurred, until in two weeks we heard 144 people testify in forty-five minutes. All three points of that circuit saw a blaze of revival that winter, and family after family came into the church, until the membership was more than tripled.
>
> Out of that meeting one convert is a successful pastor in the Michigan Conference, another is the wife of one of the choicest of our pastors, and a third was in the ministry for a number of years, and then went to another denomination, where he is faithful unto this day. Probably none of the members ever knew of the pastor's night of prayer, but he verily believes that God somehow does for the man who thus prays, what he does not do for the man who does not pray, and he is certain that "more things are wrought by prayer than this world dreams of."

All the true revivals have been born in prayer. When God's people become so concerned about the state of religion that they lie on their faces day and night in earnest supplication, the blessing will be sure to fall.

It is the same all down the ages. Every revival of which we have any record has been bathed in prayer. Take, for example, the wonderful revival in Shotts (Scotland) in 1630. The fact that several of the then persecuted ministers would take a part in solemn convocation having become generally known, a vast concourse of godly persons assembled on this occasion from all quarters of the country, and *several days were spent in social prayer,* preparatory to the service. In the evening, instead of retiring to rest, the multitude divided themselves into little bands, and *spent the whole night in supplication and praise.* The Monday was consecrated to thanksgiving, a practice not then common, and proved the great day of the feast. After much entreaty, John Livingston, chaplain to the Countess of Wigtown, a young man and not ordained, agreed to preach. He *had spent the night in prayer* and conference—but as the hour of assembling approached his heart quailed at the thought of addressing so many aged and experienced saints, and he actually fled from the duty he had undertaken. But just as the kirk of Shotts was vanishing from his view, those words, "Was I ever a barren wilderness or a land of darkness?" were borne in upon his mind with such force as compelled him to return to the work. He took for his text Ezekiel 36:25, 26, and discoursed with great power for about two hours. *Five hundred conversions* were believed to have occurred under that one sermon, thus prefaced by prayer. "It was the sowing of a seed through Clydesdale, so that many of the most eminent Christians of that country could date their conversion, or some remarkable confirmation of their case, from that day."

Of Richard Baxter it has been said that "he stained his study walls with praying breath; and after becoming thus anointed with the unction of the Holy Spirit he sent a river of living water over Kidderminster." Whitfield once thus prayed, "O Lord, give me souls or take my soul." After much closet pleading, "he once went to the Devil's fair and took more than a thousand souls out of the paw of the lion in a single day."

Mr. Finney says: "I once knew a minister who had a revival fourteen winters in succession. I did not know how to account for it till I saw one of his members get up in a prayer meeting and make a confession. 'Brethren,' he said, 'I have been long in the habit of praying every Saturday night till after midnight for the descent of the Holy Spirit among us. And now, brethren (and he began to weep), I confess that I have neglected it for two or three weeks.' The secret was out. That minister had a praying church."

And so we might go on multiplying illustration upon illustration to show the place of prayer in revival and to demonstrate that every mighty movement of the Spirit of God has had its source in the prayer-chamber. The lesson of it all is this, that as workers together with God we must regard ourselves as in not a little measure responsible for the conditions which prevail around us today. Are we concerned about the coldness of the church? Do we grieve over the lack of conversions? Does our soul go out to God in midnight cries for the outpouring of his Spirit?

If not, part of the blame lies at our door. If we do our part, God will do his. Around us is a world lost in sin, above us is a God willing and able to save; it is ours to build the bridge that links heaven and earth, and prayer is the mighty instrument that does the work.

And so the old cry comes to us with insistent voice, "Pray, brethren, pray."

13

Christ Commanded Us to Pray

THE example of our Lord in the matter of prayer is one which his followers might well copy. Christ prayed much and he taught much about prayer. His life and his works, as well as his teaching, are illustrations of the nature and necessity of prayer. He lived and labored to answer prayer. But the necessity of importunity in prayer was the emphasized point in his teaching about prayer. He taught not only that men must pray, but also that they must persevere in prayer.

He taught in command and precept the idea of energy and earnestness in praying. He gives to our efforts gradation and climax. We are to ask, but to the asking we must add seeking, and seeking must pass into the full force of effort in knocking. The pleading soul must be aroused to effort by God's silence. Denial, instead of abating or abashing, must arouse its latent energies and kindle anew its highest ardor.

In the Sermon on the Mount, in which he lays down the cardinal duties of his religion, he not only gives prominence to prayer in general and secret prayer in particular, but he sets apart a distinct and different section to give weight to importunate prayer. To prevent any discouragement in praying he lays as a basic principle the fact of God's great fatherly willingness—that God's willingness to answer our prayers exceeds our willingness to give good and necessary things to our children, just as far as God's ability, goodness, and perfection exceed our infirmities and evil. As a further assurance and stimulant to prayer Christ gives the most positive and emphasized assurance of answer to prayers. He declares: "Ask and it shall be given you; seek and ye shall find; knock and it shall be opened unto you." And to make assurance doubly sure, he adds: "For every one that asketh, receiveth; and he that seeketh, findeth; and to him that knocketh it shall be opened."

Why does he unfold to us the father's loving readiness to answer the prayer of his children? Why does he assert so strongly that prayer will be answered? Why does he repeat that positive assertion six times? Why does Christ on two distinct occasions go over the same strong promises, emphases, and repetitions in regard to the certainty of prayer being answered? Because he knew that there would be delay in many an answer which would call for importunate pressing, and that if our faith did not have the strongest assurance of

God's willingness to answer, delay would break it down. And he knew that our spiritual sloth would come in, under the guise of submission and say it is not God's will to give what we ask, and so we cease praying and lose our case. After Christ had put God's willingness to answer prayer in a very clear and strong light, he then urges to importunity, and that every unanswered prayer, instead of abating our pressure should only increase intensity and energy. If asking does not get, let asking pass into the settled attitude and spirit of seeking. If seeking does not secure the answer, let seeking pass on to the more energetic and clamorous plea of knocking. We must persevere till we get it. No failure here if our faith does not break down.

As our great example in prayer, our Lord puts love as a primary condition—a love that has purified the heart from all the elements of hate, revenge, and ill will. Love is the supreme condition of prayer, a life inspired by love. The thirteenth chapter of First Corinthians is the law of prayer as well as the law of love. The law of love is the law of prayer, and to master this chapter from the epistle of Paul is to learn the first and fullest condition of prayer.

Christ taught us also to approach the father in his name. That is our passport. It is in his name that we are to make our petitions known. "Verily, verily, I say unto you, he that believeth on me, the works that I do shall he do also; and greater *works* than these shall he do; because I go unto the father. And whatsoever ye shall ask in my name, that will I do, that the father may be glorified in the son. If ye shall ask me anything in my name, that will I do."

How wide and comprehensive is that "whatsoever." There is no limit to the power of that name. "Whatsoever ye shall ask." That is the divine declaration, and it opens up to every praying child a vista of infinite resource and possibility.

And that is our heritage. All that Christ has may become ours if we obey the conditions. The one secret is prayer. The place of revealing and of equipment, of grace and of power, is the prayer-chamber, and as we meet there with God we shall not only win our triumphs but we shall also grow in the likeness of our Lord and become his living witnesses to men.

Without prayer the Christian life, robbed of its sweetness and its beauty, becomes cold and formal and dead; but rooted in the secret place where God meets and walks and talks with his own, it grows into such a testimony of divine power that all men will feel its influence and be touched by the warmth of its love. Thus, resembling our Lord and master, we shall be used for the glory of God and the salvation of our fellowmen.

And that, surely, is the purpose of all real prayer and the end of all true service.

BOOK

◆6◆

The Weapon of Prayer

1

God Says Prayer Is Essential

IT must never be forgotten that Almighty God rules this world. He is not an absentee God. His hand is ever on the throttle of human affairs. He is everywhere present in the concerns of time. His eyes behold, his eyelids try the children of men." He rules the world just as he rules the church by prayer. This lesson needs to be emphasized and stressed in the ears of men of modern times and brought to bear with cumulative force on the consciences of this generation whose eyes have no vision for the eternal things, whose ears are deaf toward God.

Nothing is more important to God than prayer in dealing with mankind. But it is likewise all-important to man to pray. Failure to pray is failure along the whole line of life. It is failure of duty, service, and spiritual progress. God must help man by prayer. He who does not pray, therefore, robs himself of God's help and places God where he cannot help man. Man must pray to God if love for God is to exist. Faith and hope, and patience and all the strong, beautiful, vital forces of piety are withered and dead in a prayerless life. The life of the individual believer, his personal salvation, and personal Christian graces have their being, bloom, and fruitage in prayer.

All this and much more can be said as to the necessity of prayer to the being, and culture of piety in the individual. But prayer has a larger sphere, a more obligated duty, a loftier inspiration. Prayer concerns God, whose purposes and plans are conditioned on prayer. His will and his glory are bound up in praying. The days of God's splendor and renown have always been the great days of prayer. God's great movements in this world have been conditioned on, continued and fashioned by prayer. God has put himself in these great movements just as men have prayed. Present, prevailing, conspicuous and mastering prayer has always brought God to be present. The real and obvious test of a genuine work of God is the prevalence of the spirit of prayer. God's mightiest forces surcharge and impregnate a movement when prayer's mightiest forces are there.

God's movement to bring Israel from Egyptian bondage had its inception in prayer. Thus early did God and the human race put the fact of prayer as one of the granite forces upon which his world movements were to be based.

Hannah's petition for a son began a great prayer movement for God in

369

Israel. Praying women, whose prayers like those of Hannah, can give to the cause of God men like Samuel, do more for the church and the world than all the politicians on earth. Men born of prayer are the saviors of the state, and men saturated with prayer give life and impetus to the church. Under God they are saviors and helpers of both church and state.

We must believe that the divine record of the facts about prayer and God are given in order that we might be constantly reminded of him, and be ever refreshed by the faith that God holds his church for the entire world, and that God's purpose will be fulfilled. His plans concerning the church will most assuredly and inevitably be carried out. That record of God has been given without doubt that we may be deeply impressed that the prayers of God's saints are a great factor, a supreme factor, in carrying forward God's work, with facility and in time. When the church is in the condition of prayer God's cause always flourishes and his kingdom on earth always triumphs. When the church fails to pray, God's cause decays and evil of every kind prevails. In other words, God works through the prayers of his people, and when they fail him at this point, decline and deadness ensue. It is according to the divine plans that spiritual prosperity comes through the prayer channel. Praying saints are God's agents for carrying on his saving and providential work on earth. If his agents fail him, neglecting to pray, then his work fails. Praying agents of the most high are always forerunners of spiritual prosperity.

The men of the church of all ages who have held the church for God have had in affluent fulness and richness the ministry of prayer. The rulers of the church which the scriptures reveal have had preeminence in prayer. Eminent, they may have been, in culture, in intellect and in all the natural or human forces; or they may have been lowly in physical attainments and native gifts; yet in each case prayer was the all-potent force in the rulership of the church. And this was so because God was with and in what they did, for prayer always carries us back to God. It recognizes God and brings God into the world to work and save and bless. The most efficient agents in disseminating the knowledge of God, in prosecuting his work upon the earth, and in standing as breakwater against the billows of evil, have been praying church leaders. God depends upon them, employs them, and blesses them.

Prayer cannot be retired as a secondary force in this world. To do so is to retire God from the movement. It is to make God secondary. The prayer ministry is an all-engaging force. It must be so, to be a force at all. Prayer is the sense of God's need and the call for God's help to supply that need. The esteem and place of prayer is the esteem and place of God. To give prayer the secondary place is to make God secondary in life's affairs. To substitute other forces for prayer, retires God and materializes the whole movement.

Prayer is an absolute necessity to the proper carrying on of God's work. God has made it so. This must have been the principal reason why in the early church, when the complaint that the widows of certain believers had been neglected in the daily administration of the church's benefits, that the twelve called the disciples together, and told them to look for seven men, "full of the Holy Ghost, and wisdom," whom they would appoint over that benevolent work, adding this important statement, "But we will give ourselves continually to prayer and to the ministry of the Word." They surely realized that the success of the Word and the progress of the church were dependent in a preeminent sense upon their "giving themselves to prayer." God could effectively work through them in proportion as they gave themselves fully to prayer.

The apostles were as dependent upon prayer as other folks. Sacred work—church activities—may so engage and absorb us as to hinder praying, and when this is the case, evil results always follow. It is better to let the work go by default than to let the praying go by neglect. Whatever affects the intensity of our praying affects the value of our work. "Too busy to pray" is not only the keynote to backsliding, but it mars even the work done. Nothing is well done without prayer for the simple reason that it leaves God out of the account. It is so easy to be seduced by the good to the neglect of the best, until both the good and the best perish. How easily may men, even leaders in Zion, be led by the insidious wiles of Satan to cut short our praying in the interests of the work! How easy to neglect prayer or abbreviate our praying simply by the plea that we have church work on our hands. Satan has effectively disarmed us when he can keep us too busy doing things to stop and pray.

"Give ourselves continually to prayer and the ministry of the word." The Revised Version has it, "We will continue steadfastly in prayer." The implication of the word used here means to be strong, steadfast, to be devoted to, to keep at it with constant care, to make a business out of it. We find the same word in Colossians 4:12, and in Romans 12:12, which is translated, "Continuing instant in prayer."

The apostles were under the law of prayer, which law recognizes God as God, and depends upon him to do for them what he would not do without prayer. They were under the necessity of prayer, just as all believers are, in every age and in every clime. They had to be devoted to prayer in order to make their ministry of the Word efficient. The business of preaching is worth very little unless it is in direct partnership with the business of praying. Apostolic preaching cannot be carried on unless there is apostolic praying. Alas, that this plain truth has been so easily forgotten by those who minister in holy things! Without in any way passing a criticism on the ministry, we feel it to be high time that somebody or other declared to its members that effective preaching is conditioned on effective praying. The preaching which is most successful is that ministry which has much of prayer in it. Perhaps one might go so far as to say that it is the only kind that is successful. God can mightily use the preacher who prays. He is God's chosen messenger for good, whom the Holy Spirit delights to honor, God's efficient agent in saving men and in edifying the saints.

In Acts 6:1–8 we have the record of how, long ago, the apostles felt that they were losing—had lost—in apostolic power because they did not have relief from certain duties in order that they might give themselves more to prayer. So they called a halt because they discovered to their regret that they were too deficient in praying. Doubtless they kept up the form of praying, but it was seriously defective in intensity and in point of the amount of time given to it. Their minds were too much preoccupied with the finances of the church. Today, too, we find in many places both laymen and ministers are so busily engaged in "serving tables," that they are glaringly deficient in praying. In fact, in present-day church affairs men are looked upon as religious because they give largely of their money to the church, and men are chosen for official positions not because they are men of prayer, but because they have the financial ability to run church finances and to get money for the church.

Now these apostles, when they looked into this matter, determined to put aside these hindrances growing out of church finances, and resolved to "give themselves to prayer." Not that these finances were to be ignored or set aside, but ordinary laymen, "full of faith and the Holy Spirit" could be found, really religious men, who could easily attend to this money business without in the least affecting their piety or their praying, thus giving them something to do in the church, and at the same time taking the burden from the apostles who would be able now to pray more, and praying more, to be blessed themselves in soul, and at the same time to more effectually do the work to which they had been called.

They realized, too, as they had not realized before, that they were being so pressed by attention to material things, things right in themselves, that they could not give to prayer that strength, ardor, and time which its nature and importance demanded. And so we will discover, under close scrutiny of ourselves sometimes, that things legitimate, things right in themselves, things commendable, may so engross our attention, so preoccupy our minds and so draw on our feelings, that prayer may be omitted, or at least very little time may be given to prayer. How easy to slip away from the closet! Even the apostles had to guard themselves at that point. How much do we need to watch ourselves at the same place! Things legitimate and right may become wrong when they take the place of prayer. Things right in themselves may become wrong things when they are allowed to fasten themselves inordinately upon our hearts. It is not only the sinful things which hurt prayer. It is not alone questionable things which are to be guarded against. It is things which are right in their places, but which are allowed to sidetrack prayer and shut the closet door, often with the self-comforting plea that "we are too busy to pray."

Possibly this has had as much to do with the breaking down of family prayer in this age as any other one cause. It is at this point that family religion has decayed, and just here is one cause of the decline of the prayer meeting.

Men and women are too busy with legitimate things to "give themselves to prayer." Other things are given the right of way. Prayer is set aside or made secondary. Business comes first. And this means not always that prayer is second, but that prayer is put entirely out. The apostles drove directly at this point, and determined that even church business should not affect their praying habits. Prayer must come first. Then would they be in deed and truth God's real agents in his world, through whom he could effectually work, because they were praying men, and thereby put themselves directly in line with his plans and purposes, which was that he works through praying men.

When the complaint came to their ears the apostles discovered that that which they had been doing did not fully serve the divine ends of peace, gratitude, and unity. Discontent, complainings, and division were the result of their work, which had far too little prayer in it. And so prayer was put prominently to the front.

Praying men are a necessity in carrying out the divine plan for the salvation of men. God has made it so. He it is who established prayer as a divine ordinance, and this implies men are to do the praying. So praying men are a necessity in the world. The fact that so often God has employed men of prayer to accomplish his ends clearly proves the proposition. It is altogether unnecessary to name all the instances where God used the prayers of righteous men to carry out his gracious designs. Time and space are too limited for the list. Yet one or two cases might be named. In the case of the golden calf, when God purposed to destroy the Israelites because of their great sin of idolatry, at the time when Moses was receiving the law at God's hands, the very being of Israel was imperilled, for Aaron had been swept away by the strong popular tide of unbelief and sin. All seemed lost but Moses and prayer, and prayer became more efficient and wonder-working in behalf of Israel than Aaron's magic rod. God was determined to destroy Israel and Aaron. His anger waxed hot. It was a fearful and a critical hour. But prayer was the levee which held back heaven's desolating fury. God's hand was held fast by the interceding of Moses, the mighty intercessor.

Moses was set on delivering Israel. It was with him a long and exhaustive struggle of praying for forty days and forty nights. Not for one moment did he relax his hold on God. Not for one moment did he quit his place at the feet of God, even for food. Not for one moment did he moderate his demand or ease his cry. Israel's existence was in the balance. Almighty God's wrath must be stayed. Israel must be saved at all hazards. And Israel was saved. Moses would not let God alone. And so, today, we can look back and give the credit of the present race of the Jews to the praying of Moses centuries ago.

Persevering prayer always wins; God yields to importunity and fidelity. He has no heart to say No to such praying as Moses did. Actually God's purpose to destroy Israel is changed by the praying of this man of God. It is but an illustration of how much just one praying man is worth in this world, and how much depends upon him.

When Daniel, in Babylon, refused to obey the decree of the king not to ask any petition of any god or man for thirty days, he shut his eyes to the decree which would shut him off from his praying room, and refused to be deterred from calling upon God for fear of the consequences. So he "kneeled upon his knees three times a day" and prayed as he had done before, leaving it all with God as to the consequences of thus disobeying the king.

There was nothing impersonal about Daniel's praying. It always had an objective, and was an appeal to a great God, who could do all things. There was no coddling of self, nor looking after subjective or reflex influences. In the face of the dreadful decree which is to precipitate him from place and power, into the lion's den, "he kneeled upon his knees three times a day, and gave thanks to God as aforetime." The gracious result was that prayer laid its hands upon an almighty arm, which interposed in that den of vicious, cruel lions and closed their mouths and preserved his servant Daniel, who had been true to him and who had called upon him for protection. Daniel's praying was an essential factor in defeating the king's decree and in discomfiting the wicked, envious rulers, who had set the trap for Daniel in order to destroy him and remove him from place and power in the kingdom.

2

Putting God to Work

THE assertion voiced in the title given this chapter is but another way of declaring that God has of his own motion placed himself under the law of prayer, and has obligated himself to answer the prayers of men. He has ordained prayer as a means whereby he will do things through men as they pray, which he would not otherwise do. Prayer is a specific divine appointment, an ordinance of heaven, whereby God purposes to carry out his gracious designs on earth and to execute and make efficient the plan of salvation.

When we say that prayer puts God to work, it is simply to say that man has it in his power by prayer to move God to work in his own way among men, in which way he would not work if prayer was not made. Thus while prayer moves God to work, at the same time God puts prayer to work. As God has ordained prayer, and as prayer has no existence separate from men, but involves men, then logically prayer is the one force which puts God to work in earth's affairs through men and their prayers.

Let these fundamental truths concerning God and prayer be kept in mind in all allusions to prayer, and in all our reading of the incidents of prayer in the Scriptures.

If prayer puts God to work on earth, then, by the same token, prayerlessness rules God out of the world's affairs, and prevents him from working. And if prayer moves God to work in this world's affairs, then prayerlessness excludes God from everything concerning men, and leaves man on earth the mere creature of circumstances, at the mercy of blind fate or without help of any kind from God. It leaves man in this world with its tremendous responsibilities and its difficult problems, and with all of its sorrows, burdens and afflictions, without any God at all. In reality the denial of prayer is a denial of God himself, for God and prayer are so inseparable that they can never be divorced.

Prayer affects three different spheres of existence—the divine, the angelic and the human. It puts God to work, it puts angels to work, and it puts man to work. It lays its hands upon God, angels and men. What a wonderful reach there is in prayer! It brings into play the forces of heaven and earth. God, angels and men are subjects of this wonderful law of prayer, and all these have to do with the possibilities and the results of prayer. God has so far

375

placed himself subject to prayer that by reason of his own appointment, he is induced to work among men in a way in which he does not work if men do not pray. Prayer lays hold upon God and influences him to work. This is the meaning of prayer as it concerns God. This is the doctrine of prayer, or else there is nothing whatever in prayer.

Prayer puts God to work in all things prayed for. While man in his weakness and poverty waits, trusts, and prays, God undertakes the work. "For from old men have not heard, nor perceived by the ear, neither hath the eye seen a God beside thee, which worketh for him that waiteth for thee."

Jesus Christ commits himself to the force of prayer. "Whatsoever ye ask in my name," he says, "that will I do, that the Father may be glorified in the Son. If ye shall ask anything in my name, I will do it." And again: "If ye abide in me, and my words abide in you, ye shall ask what ye will and it shall be done unto you."

To no other energy is the promise of God committed as to that of prayer. Upon no other force are the purposes of God so dependent as this one of prayer. The Word of God dilates on the results and necessity of prayer. The work of God stays or advances as prayer puts forth its strength. Prophets and apostles have urged the utility, force, and necessity of prayer. "I have set watchmen upon thy walls, O Jerusalem, which shall never hold their peace day nor night. Ye that make mention of the Lord, keep not silence, and give him no rest, till he establish, and till he make Jerusalem a praise in the earth."

Prayer, with its antecedents and attendants, is the one and only condition of the final triumph of the gospel. It is the one and only condition which honors the Father and glorifies the Son. Little and poor praying has weakened Christ's power on earth, postponed the glorious results of his reign, and retired God from his sovereignty.

Prayer puts God's work in his hands, and keeps it there. It looks to him constantly and depends on him implicitly to further his own cause. Prayer is but faith resting in, acting with, leaning on, and obeying God. This is why God loves it so well, why he puts all power into its hands, and why he so highly esteems men of prayer.

Every movement for the advancement of the gospel must be created by and inspired by prayer. In all these movements of God, prayer precedes and attends as an invariable and necessary condition.

In this relation, God makes prayer identical in force and power with himself, and says to those on earth who pray: "You are on the earth to carry on my cause. I am in heaven, the Lord of all, the maker of all, the Holy One of all. Now whatever you need for my cause, ask me and I will do it. Shape the future by your prayers, and all that you need for present supplies, command me. I made heaven and earth, and all things in them. Ask largely. Open thy mouth wide, and I will fill it. It is my work which you are doing. It concerns my cause. Be prompt and full in praying. Do not abate your asking, and I will not wince nor abate in my giving."

Everywhere in his Word God conditions his actions on prayer. Everywhere in his Word his actions and attitude are shaped by prayer. To quote all the Scriptural passages which prove the immediate, direct, and personal relation of prayer to God, would be to transfer whole pages of the Scripture to this study. Man has personal relations with God. Prayer is the divinely appointed means by which man comes into direct connection with God. By his own ordinance God holds himself bound to hear prayer. God bestows his great good on his children when they seek it along the avenue of prayer.

When Solomon closed his great prayer which he offered at the dedication of the temple, God appeared to him, approved him, and laid down the universal principles of his action. In 2 Chronicles 7:12–15 we read as follows:

> And the Lord appeared to Solomon by night and said unto him, I have heard thy prayer, and have chosen this place to myself, for a house of sacrifice.
> If I shut up heaven that there be no rain, or if I command the locusts to devour the land, or if I send pestilence among the people; if my people which are called by my name, shall humble themselves and pray, and seek my face, and turn from their wicked ways, then will I hear from heaven, and will forgive their sin, and will heal their land. Now my eyes shall be open, and my ears attentive to the prayer that is made in this place.

In his purposes concerning the Jews in the Babylonian captivity (Jer. 29:10–13) God asserts his unfailing principles:

> For thus saith the Lord, that after seventy years be accomplished, at Babylon, I will visit you, and perform my good word toward you, in causing you to return to this place. For I know the thoughts that I think toward you, saith the Lord, thoughts of peace, and not of evil, to give you an expected end. Then shall ye call upon me, and ye shall go and pray unto me, and I will hearken unto you. And ye shall seek me and find me, when ye shall search for me with all your heart.

In Bible terminology prayer means calling upon God for things we desire, asking things of God. Thus we read: "Call upon me and I will answer thee, and will show thee great and mighty things which thou knowest not" (Jer. 33:3). "Call upon me in the day of trouble, and I will deliver thee" (Ps. 50:15). "Then shalt thou call, and the Lord shall answer; thou shalt cry, and he shall say, Here I am" (Isa. 58:9).

Prayer is revealed as a direct application to God for some temporal or spiritual good. It is an appeal to God to intervene in life's affairs for the good of those for whom we pray. God is recognized as the source and fountain of all good, and prayer implies that all his good is held in his keeping for those who call upon him in truth.

That prayer is an application to God, communicating with God, and communion with God, comes out strongly and simply in the praying of Old Testament saints. Abraham's intercession for Sodom is a striking illustration of the nature of prayer, communicating with God, and showing the intercessory side of prayer. The declared purpose of God to destroy Sodom confronted Abraham, and his soul within him was greatly moved because of his great interest in that fated city. His nephew and family resided there. That purpose of God must be changed. God's decree for the destruction of this evil city's inhabitants must be revoked.

It was no small undertaking which faced Abraham when he conceived the idea of beseeching God to spare Sodom. Abraham sets himself to change God's purpose and to save Sodom with the other cities of the plain. It was certainly a most difficult and delicate work for him to undertake to throw his influence with God in favor of those doomed cities so as to save them.

He bases his plea on the simple fact of the number of righteous men who could be found in Sodom, and appeals to the infinite rectitude of God not to destroy the righteous with the wicked. "That be far from thee to slay the righteous with the wicked. Shall not the Judge of all the earth do right?" With what deep self-abasement and reverence does Abraham enter upon his high and divine work! He stood before God in solemn awe, and meditation, and then drew near to God and spoke. He advanced step by step in faith, in demand and urgency, and God granted every request which he made. It has been well said that "Abraham left off asking before God left off granting." It seems that Abraham had a kind of optimistic view of the piety of Sodom. He scarcely expected when he undertook this matter to have it end in failure. He was greatly in earnest, and had every encouragement to press his case. In his final request he surely thought that with Lot, his wife, his daughters, his sons, and his sons-in-law, he had his ten righteous persons for whose sake God would spare the city. But alas! The count failed when the final test came. There were not ten righteous people in that large population.

But this was true. If he did not save Sodom by his importunate praying, the purposes of God were stayed for a season, and possibly had not Abraham's goodness of heart overestimated the number of pious people in that devoted city, God might have saved it had Abraham reduced his figures still further.

This is a representative case illustrative of Old Testament praying, and disclosing God's mode of working through prayer. It shows further how God is moved to work in answer to prayer in this world even when it comes to changing his purposes concerning a sinful community. This praying of Abraham was no mere performance, no dull, lifeless ceremony, but an earnest plea, a strong advocacy, to secure a desired end, to have an influence, one person with another person.

How full of meaning is this series of remarkable intercessions made by Abraham! Here we have arguments designed to convince God, and pleas to persuade God to change his purpose. We see deep humility, but holy boldness as well, perseverance, and advances made based on victory in each petition. Here we have enlarged asking encouraged by enlarged answers. God stays and answers as long as Abraham stays and asks. To Abraham God is existent, approachable, and all powerful, but at the same time he defers to men, acts favorably on their desires, and grants them favors asked for. Not to pray is a denial of God, a denial of his existence, a denial of his nature, and a denial of his purposes toward mankind.

God has specifically to do with prayer promises in their breadth, certainty, and limitations. Jesus Christ presses us into the presence of God with these prayer promises, not only by the assurance that God will answer, but also that no other being but God can answer. He presses us to God because only in this way can we move God to take a hand in earth's affairs, and induce him to intervene in our behalf.

"All things whatsoever ye ask in prayer, believing, ye shall receive," says Jesus, and this all-comprehensive condition not only presses us to pray for all things, everything great and small, but it also sets us on and shuts us up to God, for who but God can cover the illimitable of universal things, and can assure us certainly of receiving the very thing for which we may ask in all the thesaurus of earthly and heavenly good?

It is Jesus Christ, the Son of God, who makes demands on us to pray, and it is he who puts himself and all he has so fully in the answer. He it is who puts himself at our service and answers our demands when we pray.

And just as he puts himself and the Father at our command in prayer, to come directly into our lives and to work for our good, so also does he engage to answer the demands of two or more believers who are agreed as touching any one thing. "If two of you shall agree on earth as touching anything, that they shall ask, it shall be done for them of my Father which is in heaven." None but God could put himself in a covenant so binding as that, for only God could fulfil such a promise and could reach to its exacting and all controlling demands. Only God can answer for the promises.

God needs prayer, and man needs prayer, too. It is indispensable to God's work in this world, and is essential to getting God to work in earth's affairs. So God binds men to pray by the most solemn obligations. God commands men to pray, and so not to pray is plain disobedience to an imperative command of Almighty God. Prayer is such a condition without which the graces, the salvation, and the good of God are not bestowed on men. Prayer is a high privilege, a royal prerogative. Manifold and eternal are the losses when we fail to exercise it. Prayer is the great, universal force to advance God's cause; the reverence which hallows God's name; the ability to do God's will, and the establishment of God's kingdom in the hearts of the children of men. These, and their coincidences and agencies, are created and affected by prayer.

One of the constitutional enforcements of the gospel is prayer. Without prayer, the gospel can neither be preached effectively, promulgated faithfully, experienced in the heart, nor be practiced in the life. And for the very simple reason that by leaving prayer out of the catalogue of religious duties, we leave God out, and his work cannot progress without him.

The movements which God purposed under Cyrus, king of Persia, prophesied about by Isaiah many years before Cyrus was born, are conditioned on prayer. God declares his purpose, power, independence, and defiance of obstacles in the way of him carrying out those purposes. His omnipotent and absolutely infinite power is set to encourage prayer. He has been ordering all events, directing all conditions, and creating all things, that he might answer prayer, and then turns himself over to his praying ones to be commanded. And then all the results and power he holds in his hands will be bestowed in lavish and unmeasured munificence to carry out prayers and to make prayer the mightiest energy in the world.

The passage in Isaiah (chap. 46) is too lengthy to be quoted in its entirety but it is well worth reading. It closes with such strong words as these, words about prayer, which are the climax of all which God has been saying concerning his purposes in connection with Cyrus:

> Thus saith the Lord, the Holy One of Israel, and his Maker: Ask me of things to come, concerning my sons, and concerning the work of my hands, command ye me. I have made the earth, and created man upon it; I, even my hands, have stretched out the heavens, and all their hosts have I commanded.

In the conclusion of the history of Job, we see how God intervenes in behalf of Job and calls upon his friends to present themselves before Job that he may pray for them. "My wrath is kindled against thee and against thy two friends," is God's statement, with the further words added, "My servant Job shall pray for you, for him will I accept," a striking illustration of God intervening to deliver Job's friends in answer to Job's prayer.

We have heretofore spoken of prayer affecting God, angels and men. Christ wrote nothing while living. Memoranda, notes, sermon writing, sermon making, were alien to him. Autobiography was not to his taste. The Revelation of John was his last utterance. In that book we have pictured the great importance, the priceless value, and the high position which prayer obtains in the movements, history, and unfolding progress of God's church in this world. We have this picture in Revelation 8:3, disclosing the interest the angels in heaven have in the prayers of the saints and in accomplishing the answers to those prayers:

> And another angel came and stood at the altar, having a golden censer, and there was given unto him much incense, that he should offer it with the prayers of all saints, upon the golden altar which was before the throne. And the smoke of the incense which came with the prayers of the saints, ascended up before God, out of the angel's hand. And the angel took the censer, and filled it with fire of the altar, cast it into the earth, and there were voices, and thunderings and lightnings and an earthquake.

Translated into the prose of everyday life, these words show how the capital stock by which heaven carries on the business of salvation under Christ, is made up of the prayers of God's saints on earth, and discloses how these prayers in flaming power come back to earth and produce its mighty commotions, influences, and revolutions.

Praying men are essential to Almighty God in all his plans and purposes. God's secrets, councils, and cause have never been committed to prayerless men. Neglect of prayer has always brought loss of faith, loss of love, and loss of prayer. Failure to pray has been the baneful, inevitable cause of backsliding and estrangement from God. Prayerless men have stood in the way of God fulfilling his Word and doing his will on earth. They tie the divine hands and interfere with God in his gracious designs. As praying men are a help to God, so prayerless men are a hindrance to him.

We press the Scriptural view of the necessity of prayer, even at the cost of repetition. The subject is too important for repetition to weaken or tire, too vital to be trite or tame. We must feel it anew. The fires of prayer have burned low. Ashes and not flames are on its altars.

No insistence in the Scriptures is more pressing than prayer. No exhortation is more often reiterated, none is more hearty, none is more solemn and stirring, than to pray. No principle is more strongly and broadly declared than that which urges us to prayer. There is no duty to which we are more strongly obliged than the obligation to pray. There is no command more imperative and insistent than that of praying. Art thou praying in everything without ceasing, in the closet, hidden from the eyes of men, and praying always and everywhere? That is the personal, pertinent, and all-important question for every soul.

Many instances occur in God's Word showing that God intervenes in this world in answer to prayer. Nothing is clearer when the Bible is consulted than that Almighty God is brought directly into the things of this world by the praying of his people. Jonah flees from duty and takes ship for a distant port. But God follows him, and by a strange providence this disobedient prophet is cast out of the vessel, and the God who sent him to Nineveh prepares a fish to swallow him. In the fish's belly he cries out to the God against whom he had sinned, and God intervenes and causes the fish to vomit Jonah out on dry land. Even the fishes of the great deep are subject to the law of prayer.

Likewise the birds of the air are brought into subjection to this same law. Elijah had foretold to Ahab the coming of that prolonged drought, and food and even water became scarce. God sent him to the brook Cherith, and said unto him, "It shall be that thou shalt drink of the brook, and I have commanded the ravens to feed thee there. And the ravens brought bread and flesh in the morning, and bread and flesh in the evening." Can anyone doubt that this man of God, who later on shut up and opened the rain clouds by prayer was not praying about this time, when so much was at stake? God interposed among the birds of the air this time and strangely moved them to take care of his servant so that he would not lack food and water.

David in an evil hour, instead of listening to the advice of Joab, his prime minister, yielded to the suggestion of Satan, and counted the people, which displeased God. So God told him to choose one of three evils as a retribution for his folly and sin. Pestilence came among the people in violent form, and David betakes himself to prayer.

> And David said unto God, Is it not I that commanded the people to be num-bered? Even I it is that hath sinned and done evil indeed. But as for these sheep, what have they done? Let thy hand, I pray thee, O Lord my God, be on me, and on my father's house; but not on thy people, that they should be plagued (1 Chron. 21:17).

And though God had been greatly grieved at David for numbering Israel, yet he could not resist this appeal of a penitent and prayerful spirit, and God was moved by prayer to put his hand on the springs of disease and stop the fearful plague. God was put to work by David's prayer.

Numbers of other cases could be named. These are sufficient. God seems to have taken great pains in his divine revelation to men to show how he interferes in earth's affairs in answer to the praying of his saints.

The question might arise just here in some overcritical minds who are not strong believers in prayer, as to the so-called "laws of nature," as if there was a conflict between what they call the "laws of nature" and the law of prayer. These people make nature a sort of imaginary god entirely separate of Almighty God. What is nature anyway? It is but the creation of God, the Maker of all things. And what are the "laws of nature" but the laws of God, through which he governs the material world. As the law of prayer is also the law of God, there cannot possibly be any conflict between the two sets of laws, but all must work in perfect harmony. Prayer does not violate any natu-ral law. God may set aside one law for the higher working of another law, and this he may do when he answers prayer. Or Almighty God may answer prayer working through the course of natural law. But whether or not we understand it, God is over and above all nature, and can and will answer prayer in a wise, intelligent, and just manner, even though man may not comprehend it. So in no sense is there any discord or conflict between God's several laws when God is induced to interfere with human affairs in answer to prayer.

In this connection another word might be said. We used the form of words to which there can be no objection, that prayer does certain things, but this of course implies not that prayer as a human means accomplishes anything, but that prayer only accomplishes things instrumentally. Prayer is the instrument, God is the efficient and active agent. So prayer in itself does not interfere in earth's affairs, but prayer in the hands of men moves God to intervene and do things, which he would not otherwise do if prayer was not used as the instru-ment.

It is as we say, "faith hath saved thee," by which is simply meant that God through the faith of the sinner saves him, faith being only the instrument used by the sinner which brings salvation to him.

3

The Necessity for Praying Men

ONE of the crying things of our day is for men whose faith, prayers, and study of the Word of God have been vitalized, and a transcript of that Word is written on their hearts, and who will give it forth as the incorruptible seed that lives and abides forever. Nothing more is needed to clear up the haze by which a critical unfaith has eclipsed the Word of God than the fidelity of the pulpit in its unwavering allegiance to the Bible and the fearless proclamation of its truth. Without this the standard-bearer fails, and wavering and confusion all along the ranks follow. The pulpit has wrought its mightiest work in the days of its unswerving loyalty to the Word of God.

In close connection with this, must we have men of prayer, men in high and low places who hold to and practice Scriptural praying. While the pulpit must hold to its unswerving loyalty to the Word of God, it must, at the same time, be loyal to the doctrine of prayer which that same Word illustrates and enforces upon mankind.

Schools, colleges, and education considered simply as such cannot be regarded as being leaders in carrying forward the work of God's kingdom in the world. They have neither the right, the will nor the power to do the work. This is to be accomplished by the preached Word, delivered in the power of the Holy Spirit sent down from heaven, sown with prayerful hands, and watered with the tears of praying hearts. This is the divine law, and so "nominated in the bond." We are shut up and sealed to it—we would follow the Lord.

Men are demanded for the great work of soul saving, and men must go. It is no angelic or impersonal force which is needed. Human hearts baptized with the spirit of prayer, must bear the burden of this message, and human tongues on fire as the result of earnest, persistent prayer, must declare the Word of God to dying men.

The church today needs praying men to execute her solemn and pressing responsibility to meet the fearful crisis which is facing her. The crying need of the times is for men, in increased numbers—God-fearing men, praying men, Holy-Spirit men, men who can endure hardness, who will count not their lives dear unto themselves, but count all things but dross for the excellency of the knowledge of Jesus Christ, the Savior. The men who are so greatly needed in this age of the church are those who have learned the business of praying—learned it on their knees, learned it in the need and agony of their own hearts.

Praying men are the one commanding need of this day, as of all other days, in which God is to have or make a showing. Men who pray are, in reality, the only religious men, and it takes a full-measured man to pray. Men of prayer are the only men who do or can represent God in this world. No cold, irreligious, prayerless man can claim the right. They misrepresent God in all his work, and all his plans. Praying men are the only men who have influence with God, the only kind of men to whom God commits himself and his gospel. Praying men are the only men in which the Holy Spirit dwells, for the Holy Spirit and prayer go hand-in-hand. The Holy Spirit never descends upon prayerless men. He never fills them, he never empowers them. There is nothing whatever in common between the Spirit of God and men who do not pray. The Spirit dwells only in a prayer atmosphere.

In doing God's work there is no substitute for praying. The men of prayer cannot be displaced with other kinds of men. Men of financial skill, men of education, men of worldly influence—none of these can possibly be put in substitution for the men of prayer. The life, the vigor, the motive-power of God's work is formed by praying men. A vitally diseased heart is not a more fearful symptom of approaching death than nonpraying men are of spiritual atrophy.

The men to whom Jesus Christ committed the fortunes and destiny of his church were men of prayer. To no other kind of men has God ever committed himself in this world. The apostles were preeminently men of prayer. They gave themselves to prayer. They made praying their chief business. It was first in point of importance and first in results. God never has, and he never will, commit the weighty interests of his kingdom to prayerless men, who do not make prayer a conspicuous and controlling factor in their lives. Men who do not pray never rise to any eminence of piety. Men of piety are always men of prayer. Men who are not preeminently men of prayer are never noted for the simplicity and strength of their faith. Piety flourishes nowhere so rapidly and so rankly as in the closet. The closet is the garden of faith.

The apostles allowed no duty, however sacred, to so engage them as to infringe upon their time and prevent them from making prayer the main thing. The Word of God was ministered by apostolic fidelity and zeal. It was spoken by men with apostolic commissions and whose heads the fiery tongues of Pentecost had baptized. The Word was pointless and powerless unless they were freshly endued with power by continuous and mighty prayer. The seed of God's Word must be saturated in prayer to make it germinate. It grows readier and roots deeper when it is prayer-soaked.

The apostles were praying men, themselves. They were teachers of prayer, and trained their disciples in the school of prayer. They urged prayer upon their disciples not only that they might attain to the loftiest eminence of faith, but also that they might be the most powerful factors in advancing God's kingdom.

Jesus Christ was the divinely appointed leader of God's people, and no one thing in his life proves his eminent fitness for that office so fully as his habit of prayer. Nothing is more suggestive of thought than Christ's continual praying, and nothing is more conspicuous about him than prayer. His campaigns were arranged, his victories gained, in the struggles and communion of his all-night praying. His praying rent the heavens. Moses and Elijah and the transfiguration glory waited on his praying. His miracles and his teaching had their force from the same source. Gethsemane's praying crimsoned Calvary with serenity and glory. His prayer makes the history and hastens the triumphs of his church. What an inspiration and command to prayer is Christ's life! What a comment on its worth! How he shames our lives by his praying!

Like all his followers who have drawn God nearer to the world and lifted the world nearer to God, Jesus was the man of prayer, made of God a leader and commander to his people. His leadership was one of prayer. A great leader he was, because he was great in prayer. All great leaders for God have fashioned their leadership in the wrestlings of their closets. Many great men have led and molded the church who have not been great in prayer, but they were great only in their plans, great for their opinions, great for their organization, great by natural gifts, by the force of genius or of character. However, they were not great for God. But Jesus Christ was a great leader for God. His was the great leadership of great praying. God was in his leadership greatly because prayer was in it greatly. We might just well express the wish that we be taught by him to pray, and to pray more and more.

Herein has been the secret of the men of prayer in the past history of the church. Their hearts were after God, their desires were on him, their prayers were addressed to him. They communed with him, sought nothing of the world, sought great things of God, wrestled with him, conquered all opposing forces, and opened up the channel of faith deep and broad between them and heaven. And all this was done by the use of prayer. Holy meditations, spiritual desires, heavenly drawings, swayed their intellects, enriched their emotions, and filled and enlarged their hearts. And all this was so because they were first of all men of prayer.

The men who have thus communed with God and who have sought after him with their whole hearts, have always risen to consecrated eminence, and no man has ever risen to this eminence whose flames of holy desire have not all been dead to the world and all aglow for God and heaven. Nor have they ever risen to the heights of the higher spiritual experiences unless prayer and the spirit of prayer have been conspicuous and controlling factors in their lives.

The entire consecration of many of God's children stands out distinctly like towering mountain peaks. Why is this? How did they ascend to these heights? What brought them so near to God? What made them so Christlike?

The answer is easy—prayer. They prayed much, prayed long, and drank deeper and deeper still. They asked, they sought, and they knocked, till heaven opened its richest inner treasures of grace to them. Prayer was the Jacob's ladder by which they scaled those holy and blessed heights, and the way by which the angels of God came down to and ministered to them.

The men of spiritual mold and might always value prayer. They took time to be alone with God. Their praying was no hurried performance. They had many serious wants to be relieved, and many weighty pleas they had to offer. Many large supplies they must secure. They had to do much silent waiting before God, and much patient emphasis to utter to him. Prayer was the only channel through which supplies came, and was the only way to utter pleas. The only acceptable waiting before God of which they knew anything was prayer. They valued praying. It was more precious to them than all jewels, more excellent than any good, more to be valued than the greatest good of earth. They esteemed it, valued it, prized it, and did it. They pressed it to its farthest limits, tested its greatest results, and secured its most glorious patrimony. To them prayer was the one great thing to be appreciated and used.

The apostles above everything else were praying men, and left the impress of their prayer example and teaching on the early church. But the apostles are dead, and times and men have changed. They have no successors by official heirship. And the times have no commission to make other apostles. Prayer is the requisite for spiritual and apostolic leadership. Unfortunately the times are not prayerful times. God's cause just now needs very greatly praying leaders. Other things may be needed, but above all else this is the crying demand of these times and the urgent first need of the church.

This is the day of great wealth in the church and of wonderful material resources. But unfortunately the affluence of material resources is a great enemy and a severe hindrance to strong spiritual forces. It is an invariable law that the presence of attractive and potent material forces creates a trust in them, and by the same inevitable law, creates distrust in the spiritual forces of the gospel. They are two masters which cannot be served at one and the same time. For just in proportion as the mind is fixed on one, will it be drawn away from the other. The days of great financial prosperity in the church have not been days of great religious prosperity. Moneyed men and praying men are not synonymous terms.

Paul in the second chapter of his First Epistle to Timothy, emphasizes the need of men to pray. Church leaders in his estimation are to be conspicuous for their praying. Prayer ought and must of necessity shape their characters, and must be one of their distinguishing characteristics. Prayer ought to be one of their most powerful elements, so much so that it cannot be hid. Prayer ought to make church leaders notable. Character, official duty, reputation and life, all should be shaped by prayer. The mighty forces of prayer lie in its praying leaders in a marked way. The standing obligation to pray rests in a peculiar sense on church leaders. Wise will the church be to discover this prime truth and give prominence to it.

It may be laid down as an axiom, that God needs, first of all, leaders in the church who will be first in prayer, men with whom prayer is habitual and characteristic, men who know the primacy of prayer. But even more than a habit of prayer, and more than prayer being characteristic of them, church leaders are to be *impregnated* with prayer—men whose lives are made and molded by prayer, whose heart and life are made up of prayer. These are the men—the only men—God can use in the furtherance of his kingdom and the implanting of his message in the hearts of men.

4

God's Need of Men Who Pray

WE proceed now to declare that it demands prayer-leadership to hold the church to God's aims, and to fit it for God's uses. Prayer-leadership preserves the spirituality of the church, just as prayerless leaders make for unspiritual conditions. The church is not spiritual simply by the mere fact of its existence, nor by its vocation. It is not held to its sacred vocation by generation, nor by succession. Like the new birth, "It is not of blood, neither of the flesh, nor of the will of man, but of God."

The church is not spiritual simply because it is concerned and deals in spiritual values. It may hold its confirmations by the thousand, it may multiply its baptisms, and administer its sacraments innumerable times, and yet be as far from fulfilling its true mission as human conditions can make it.

This present world's general attitude retires prayer to insignificance and obscurity. By it, salvation and eternal life are put in the background. It cannot be too often affirmed, therefore, that the prime need of the church is not men of money nor men of brains, but men of prayer. Leaders in the realm of religious activity are to be judged by their praying habits, and not by their money or social position. Those who must be placed in the forefront of the church's business, must be, first of all, men who know how to pray.

God does not conduct his work, solely, with men of education or of wealth or of business capacity. Neither can he carry on his work through men of large intellects or of great culture, nor yet through men of great social eminence and influence. All these can be made to count provided they are not regarded as being primary. These men, by the simple fact of these qualities and conditions, cannot lead in God's work nor control his cause. Men of prayer, before anything else, are indispensable to the furtherance of the kingdom of God on earth. No other sort will fit in the scheme or do the deed. Men, great and influential in other things, but small in prayer, cannot do the work Almighty God has set out for his church to do in this, his world.

Men who represent God and who stand here in his stead, men who are to build up his kingdom in this world, must be in an eminent sense men of prayer. Whatever else they may have, whatever else they may lack, they must be men of prayer. Having everything else and lacking prayer, they must fail. Having prayer and lacking all else, they can succeed. Prayer must be the most conspicuous and the most potent factor in the character and conduct of men who undertake divine commission. God's business requires men who are versed in the business of praying.

It must be kept in mind that the praying to which the disciples of Christ is called by Scriptural authority and enforcement, is a valorous calling, for many men. The men God wants and upon whom he depends, must work at prayer just as they work at their worldly calling. They must follow this business of praying *through,* just as they do their secular pursuits. Diligence, perseverance, heartiness, and courage, must all be in it if it is to succeed.

Everything secured by gospel promise, defined by gospel measure, and represented by gospel treasure is to be found in prayer. All heights are scaled by it, all doors are opened to it, all victories are gained through it, and all grace distils on it. Heaven has all its good and all its help for men who pray.

How marked and strong is the injunction of Christ that sends men from the parade of public giving and praying to the privacy of their closets, where with shut doors, and in encircling silence they are alone in prayer with God!

In all ages, those who have carried out the divine will on the earth, have been men of prayer. The days of prayer are God's halcyon days. His heart, his oath, and his glory are committed to one issuance—that every knee should bow to him. The day of the Lord, in a preeminent sense, will be a day of universal prayer.

God's cause does not suffer through lack of divine ability, but by reason of the lack of prayer-ability in man. God's action is just as much bound up in prayer at this time, as it was when he said to Abimelech, "Abraham shall pray for thee, and thou shalt live." So also it was when God said to Job's friends, "My servant Job shall pray for you, for him will I accept."

God's great plan for the redemption of mankind is as much bound up to prayer for its prosperity and success as when the decree creating the movement was issued from the Father, bearing on its frontage the imperative, universal and eternal condition, "Ask of me, and I will give thee the heathen for thy inheritance and the uttermost part of the earth for thy possession."

In many places an alarming state of things has come to pass, in that the many who are enrolled in our churches are not praying men and women. Many of those occupying prominent positions in church life are not praying men. It is greatly to be feared that much of the work of the church is being done by those who are perfect strangers to the closet. Small wonder that the work does not succeed.

While it may be true that many in the church say prayers, it is equally true that their praying is of the stereotyped order. Their prayers may be charged with sentiment, but they are tame, timid, and without fire or force. Even this sort of praying is done by a few straggling men to be found at prayer meetings. Those whose names are to be found bulking large in our great church assemblies are not men noted for their praying habits. Yet the entire fabric of the work in which they are engaged has, perforce, to depend on the adequacy of prayer. This fact is similar to the crisis which would be created were a country to have to admit in the face of an invading foe that it cannot fight and has no knowledge of the weapons whereby war is to be waged.

In all God's plans for human redemption, he proposes that men *pray.* The men are to pray in every place, in the church, in the closet, in the home, on sacred days and on secular days. All things and everything are dependent on the measure of men's praying.

Prayer is the genius and mainspring of life. We pray as we live; we live as we pray. Life will never be finer than the quality of the closet. The mercury of life will rise only by the warmth of the closet. Persistent nonpraying eventually will depress life below zero.

To measure and weigh the conditions of prayer, is readily to discover why men do not pray in larger numbers. The conditions are so perfect, so blessed, that it is a rare character who can meet them. A heart all love, a heart that holds even its enemies in loving contemplation and prayerful concern, a heart from which all bitterness, revenge, and envy are purged—how rare! Yet this is the only condition of mind and heart in which a man can expect to command the power of prayer.

There are certain conditions laid down for authentic praying. Men are to pray, "lifting up holy hands"; hands here being the symbol of life. Hands unsoiled by stains of evil doing are the emblem of a life unsoiled by sin. Thus are men to come into the presence of God, thus are they to approach the throne of the highest, where they can "obtain mercy and find grace to help in time of need." Here, then, is one reason why men do not pray. They are too worldly in heart and too secular in life to enter the closet; and even though they enter there, they cannot offer the "fervent, effectual prayer of the righteous man, which availeth much."

Again, "hands" are the symbols of supplication. Outstretched hands stand for an appeal for help. It is the silent yet eloquent attitude of a helpless soul standing before God, appealing for mercy and grace. "Hands," too, are symbols of activity, power, and conduct. Hands outstretched to God in prayer must be "holy hands," unstained hands. The word holy here means undefiled, unspotted, untainted, and religiously observing every obligation. How far remote is all this from the character of the sin-loving, worldly minded, fleshly disposed men, soiled by fleshly lusts, spotted by worldly indulgence, unholy in heart and conduct! "He who seeks equity must do equity," is the maxim of earthly courts. So he who seeks God's good gifts must practice God's good deeds. This is the maxim of heavenly courts.

Prayer is sensitive, and always affected by the character and conduct of him who prays. Water cannot rise above its own level, and a spotless prayer cannot flow from a spotted heart. Straight praying is never born of crooked conduct. The men, what men are, behind their praying, gives character to their supplication. The timid heart cannot do brave praying. Soiled men cannot make clean, pure supplication.

It is neither words, nor thoughts nor ideas, nor feelings, which shape pray-ing, but character and conduct. Men must walk in upright fashion in order to be able to pray well. Bad character and unrighteous living break down pray-ing until it becomes a mere shibboleth. Praying takes its tone and vigor from the life of the man or the woman exercising it. When character and conduct are at a low ebb, praying can but barely live, much less thrive.

The man of prayer, whether layman or preacher, is God's right-hand man. In the realm of spiritual affairs, he creates conditions, inaugurates move-ments, brings things to pass.

By the fact and condition of their creation and redemption, all men are under obligation to pray. Every man *can* pray, and every man *should* pray. But when it comes to the affairs of the kingdom, let it be said, at once, that a prayerless man in the church of God is like a paralyzed organ of the physical body. He is out of place in the communion of saints, out of harmony with God, and out of accord with his purposes for mankind. A prayerless man handicaps the vigor and life of the whole system like a demoralized soldier is a menace to the force of which he forms part, in the day of battle. The absence of prayer lessens all the life-forces of the soul, cripples faith, sets aside holy living, shuts out heaven. Between praying saints and nonpraying men, in Holy Scripture, the line is sharply drawn. Of Fletcher of Madeley—one of the praying saints—it is written that:

> He was far more abundant in his public labors than the greater part of his companions in the holy ministry. Yet these bore but little proportion to those internal exercises of prayer and supplication to which he was wholly given up in private, which were almost uninterruptedly maintained from hour to hour. He lived in the spirit of prayer, and whatever employment in which he was engaged, this spirit of prayer was constantly manifested through them all.
>
> Without this he neither formed any design, nor entered upon any duty. Without this he neither read nor conversed. Without this, he neither visited nor received a visitor. There have been seasons of supplications in which he appeared to be carried out far beyond the ordinary limits of devotion, when, like his Lord upon the Mount of Transfiguration, while he continued to pour out his mighty prayer, the fashion of his countenance has been changed, and his face has appeared as the face of an angel.

O God, raise up more men of praying like John Fletcher! How we do need, in this our day, men through whom God can work!

5

Prayerless Christians

THERE is great need in this day for Christian businessmen to infuse their mundane affairs with the spirit of prayer. There is a great army of successful merchants of almost every kind who are members of Christ's church and it is high time these men attended to this matter. This is but another version of the phrase, "putting God into business," the realization and restraint of his presence and of his fear in all the secularities of life. We need the atmosphere of the prayer closet to pervade our public salesrooms and counting houses. The sanctity of prayer is needed to impregnate business. We need the spirit of Sunday carried over to Monday and continued until Saturday. But this cannot be done by prayerless men, but by men of prayer. We need businessmen to go about their concerns with the same reverence and responsibility with which they enter the closet. Men are badly needed who are devoid of greed, but who, with all their hearts, carry God with them into the secular affairs of life.

Men of the world imagine prayer to be too impotent a thing to come into rivalry with business methods and worldly practices. Against such a misleading doctrine Paul sets the whole commands of God, the loyalty to Jesus Christ, the claims of pious character, and the demands of the salvation of the world. Men must pray, and put strength and heart into their praying. This is part of the primary business of life, and to it God has called men, first of all.

Praying men are God's agents on earth, the representatives of government of heaven, set to a specific task on the earth. While it is true that the Holy Spirit, the angels of God, are agents of God in carrying forward the redemption of the human race, yet among them there must also be praying men. For such men God has great use. He can make much of them, and in the past has done wonderful things through them. These are his instruments in carrying out God's great purposes on the earth. They are God's messengers, his watchmen, shepherds, workmen, who need not be ashamed. Fully equipped for the great work to which they are appointed, they honor God and bless the world.

Above all things beside, Christian men and women must, primarily, be leaders in prayer. No matter how conspicuous they may be in other activities, they fail if they are not conspicuous in prayer. They must give their brain and heart to prayer. Men who make and shape the program of Christ's church, who map out its line of activity, should, themselves, be shaped and made by prayer. Men controlling the church finances, her thought, her action—should all be men of prayer.

The progress to consummation of God's work in this world has two basic principles—God's ability to give and man's ability to ask. Failure in either one is fatal to the success of God's work on earth. God's inability to do or to give would put an end to redemption. Man's failure to pray would, just as surely, set a limit to the plan. But God's ability to do and to give has never failed and *cannot* fail; but man's ability to ask can fail, and often does. Therefore the slow progress which is being made toward the realization of a world won for Christ lies entirely with man's limited asking. There is need for the entire church of God, on the earth, to betake itself to prayer. The church on its knees would bring heaven on the earth.

The wonderful ability of God to do for us is thus expressed by Paul in one of his most comprehensive statements, "And God is able to make all grace abound toward you," he says, "that ye, always, having all sufficiency in all things, may abound to *every good work.*"

Study, I pray you, that remarkable statement—"God is able to make all grace abound." That is, he is able to give such sufficiency, that we may abound—overflow—to every good work. Why are we not more fully fashioned after this overflowing order? The answer is—lack of prayer-ability. "We have not because we ask not." We are feeble, weak and impoverished because of our failure to pray. God is restrained in doing because we are restrained by reason of our nonpraying. All failures in securing heaven are traceable to lack of prayer or misdirected petition.

Prayer must be broad in its scope—it must plead for others. Intercession for others is the hallmark of all true prayer. When prayer is confined to self and to the sphere of one's personal needs, it dies by reason of its littleness, narrowness, and selfishness. Prayer must be broad and unselfish or it will perish. Prayer is the soul of a man stirred to plead with God for men. In addition to being interested in the eternal interests of one's own soul it must, in its very nature, be concerned for the spiritual and eternal welfare of others. One's ability to pray for self, finds its climax in the compassion its concern expresses for others.

In 1 Timothy 1, the apostle Paul urges with singular and specific emphasis, that those who occupy positions of influence and places of authority, are to give themselves to prayer. "I will, therefore, that men pray everywhere." This is the high calling of the men of the church, and no calling is so engaging, so engrossing and so valuable that we can afford to relieve Christian men from the all-important vocation of secret prayer. Nothing whatever can take the place of prayer. Nothing whatever can atone for the neglect of praying. This is uppermost, first in point of importance and first in point of time. No man is so high in position, or in grace, to be exempt from an obligation to pray. No man is too big to pray, no matter who he is, nor what office he fills. The king on his throne is as much obligated to pray as the peasant in his cottage. None is so high and exalted in this world or so lowly and obscure as to be excused from praying. The help of every one is needed in prosecuting the work of God, and the prayer of each praying man helps to swell the aggregate. The leaders in place, in gifts and in authority are to be chiefs in prayer.

Civil and church rulers shape the affairs of this world. And so civil and church rulers themselves need to be shaped personally in spirit, heart, and conduct, in truth and righteousness, by the prayers of God's people. This is in direct line with Paul's words:

> I exhort therefore that, first of all, supplications, prayers, intercessions, and giving of thanks be made for all men, for rulers and all that are in authority.

It is a sad day for righteousness when church politics instead of holy praying, shape the administration of the kingdom and elevate men to place and power. Why pray for all men? Because God wills the salvation of all men. God's children on earth must link their prayers to God's will. Prayer is to carry out the will of God. God wills the salvation of all men. His heart is set on this one thing. Our prayers must be the creation and exponent of God's will. We are to grasp humanity in our praying as God grasps humanity in his love, his interest, and his plans to redeem humanity. Our sympathies, prayers, wrestling and ardent desires must run parallel with the will of God, broad, generous, worldwide, and Godlike. The Christian man must in all things, first of all, be conformed to the will of God, but nowhere shall this royal devotion be more evident than in the salvation of the race of men. This high partnership with God, as his deputies on earth, is to have its fullest, richest, and most efficient exercise in prayer for all men.

Men are to pray for all men, are to pray especially for rulers in church and state, "that we may lead a quiet and peaceable life in all godliness and honesty." Peace on the outside and peace on the inside. Praying calms disturbing forces, allays tormenting fears, brings conflict to an end. Prayer tends to do away with turmoil. But even if there be external conflicts, it is well to have deep peace within the citadel of the soul. "That we may lead a quiet and peaceable life." Prayer brings the inner calm and furnishes the outward tranquility. Praying rulers and praying subjects were they worldwide would allay turbulent forces, make wars to cease, and peace to reign.

Men must pray for all men that we may lead lives "in all godliness and honesty." That is, with godliness and gravity. Godliness is to be like God. It is to be godly, to have Godlikeness, having the image of God stamped upon the inner nature, and showing the same likeness in conduct and in temper. Almighty God is the very highest model, and to be like him is to possess the highest character. Prayer molds us into the image of God, and at the same time tends to mold others into the same image just in proportion as we pray for others. Prayer means to be Godlike, and to be Godlike is to love Christ and love God, to be one with the Father and the Son in spirit, character, and conduct. Prayer means to stay with God till you are like him. Prayer makes a godly man, and puts within him "the mind of Christ," the mind of humility, of self-surrender, of service, of pity, and of prayer. If we really pray, we will become more like God, or else we will quit praying.

"Men are to pray everywhere," in the closet, in the prayer meeting, about the family altar, and to do it, "lifting up holy hands, without wrath and doubting." Here is not only the obligation laid upon the men to pray, but instructions as to how they should pray. "Men must pray without wrath." That is, without bitterness against their neighbors or brethren; without the obstinacy and impertinence of a strong will, and hard feelings, without an evil desire or emotion kindled by nature's fires in the carnal nature. Praying is not to be done by these questionable things, nor in company with such evil feelings, but "without" them, aloof and entirely separate from them. This is the sort of praying the men are called upon to do, the sort which God hears and the kind which prevails with God and accomplishes things. Such praying in the hands of Christian men becomes divine agencies in God's hands for carrying on God's gracious purposes and executing his designs in redemption.

Prayer has a higher origin than man's nature. This is true whether man's nature as separate from the angelic nature, or man's carnal nature unrenewed and unchanged is meant. Prayer does not originate in the realms of the carnal mind. Such a nature is entirely foreign to prayer simply because "the carnal mind is enmity against God." It is by the new Spirit that we pray, the new spirit sweetened by the sugar of heaven perfumed with the fragrance of the upper world, and invigorated by a breath from the crystal sea. The "new spirit" is native to the skies, panting after the heavenly things, inspired by the breath of God. It is the praying temper from which all the old juices of the carnal, unregenerate nature have been expelled, and the fire of God has created the flame which has consumed worldly lusts, and the juices of the Spirit have been injected into the soul, and the praying is entirely divorced from wrath.

Men are also to pray "without doubting." The Revised Version puts it, "without disputings." Faith in God, belief in God's Word, they must have "without question." No doubting or disputing must be in the mind. There must be no opinions, nor hesitancy, no questioning, no reasoning, no intellectual quibbling, no rebellion, but a strict, steadfast loyalty of spirit to God, a life of loyalty in heart and intellect to God's Word.

God has much to do with believing men, who have a living, transforming faith in Jesus Christ. These are God's children. A father loves his children, supplies their needs, hears their cries and answers their requests. A child believes his father, loves him, trusts in him, and asks him for what he needs, believing without doubting that his father will hear his requests. God has everything to do with answering the prayer of his children. Their troubles concern him, and their prayers awaken him. Their voice is sweet to him. He loves to hear them pray, and he is never happier than to answer their prayers.

Prayer is intended for God's ear. It is not man, but God who hears and answers prayer. Prayer covers the whole range of man's need. Hence, "in everything, by prayer and supplication," are "requests to be made known unto God." Prayer includes the entire range of God's ability. Is anything too hard for God? Prayer belongs to no favored segment of man's need, but reaches to and embraces the entire circle of his wants, simply because God is the God of the whole man. God has pledged himself to supply the needs of the whole man, physical, intellectual, and spiritual. "But my God shall supply all your need according to his riches in glory by Christ Jesus." Prayer is the child of grace, and grace is for the whole man, and for every one of the children of men.

6

Praying Men Are at a Premium

No insistence in the Bible is more pressing than the injunction it lays on men to pray. No exhortation contained therein is more hearty, more solemn, and more stirring. No principle is more strongly inculcated than that "men ought always to pray and not to faint." In view of this enjoinder is it pertinent to inquire as to whether Christian people are praying men and women in anything like body and bulk? Is prayer a fixed course in the schools of the church? In the Sunday school, the home, the colleges have we any graduates in the school of prayer? Is the church producing those who have diplomas from the great university of prayer? This is what God requires, what he commands, and it is those who possess such qualifications that he must have to accomplish his purposes and to carry out the work of his kingdom on earth.

And it is earnest praying that needs to be done. Languid praying, without heart or strength, with neither fire nor tenacity, defeats its own avowed purpose. The prophet of olden times laments that in a day which needed strenuous praying there was no one who stirred up himself to take hold of God." Christ charges us "not to faint" in our praying. Laxity and indifference are great hindrances to prayer, both to the practice of praying and the process of receiving; it requires a brave, strong, fearless and insistent spirit to engage in successful prayer. Diffuseness, too, interferes with effectiveness. Too many petitions break tension and unity, and breed neglect. Prayers should be specific and urgent. Too many words, like too much width, breeds shallows and sandbars. A single objective which absorbs the whole being and inflames the entire man, is the properly constraining force in prayer.

It is easy to see how prayer was a decreed factor in the dispensations preceding the coming of Jesus, and how that their leaders had to be men of prayer; how that God's mightiest revelation of himself was a revelation made through prayer, and, finally, how that Jesus Christ, in his personal ministry, and in his relation to God, was great and constant in prayer. Jesus' labors and dispensation overflowed with fullness in proportion to his prayers. The possibilities of his praying were unlimited and the possibilities of his ministry were in keeping. The necessity of his praying was equalled only by the constancy with which he practiced it during his earthly life.

The dispensation of the Holy Spirit is a dispensation of prayer, in a preeminent sense. Here prayer has an essential and vital relation. Without depreciating the possibilities and necessities of prayer in all the preceding dispensations of God in the world, it must be declared that it is in this latter dispensation that the engagements and demands of prayer are given their greatest authority, their possibilities rendered unlimited, and their necessity insuperable.

These days of ours have sore need of a generation of praying men, a band of men and women through whom God can bring his great and his greatest movements more fully into the world. The Lord our God is not straitened within himself, but he *is* straitened in us, by reason of our little faith and weak praying. A breed of Christian is greatly needed who will seek tirelessly after God—who will give him no rest, day and night, until he hearkens to their cry. The times demand praying men who are all athirst for God's glory, who are broad and unselfish in their desires, quenchless for God, who seek him late and early, and who will give themselves no rest until the whole earth be filled with his glory.

Men and women are needed whose prayers will give to the world the utmost power of God; who will make his promises to blossom with rich and full results. God is waiting to hear us and challenges us to bring him to do this thing by our praying. He is asking us, today, as he did his ancient Israel, to "prove him now herewith." Behind God's Word is God himself, and we read: "Thus saith the Lord, the Holy One of Israel, his Maker: Ask of me of things to come and concerning my sons, and concerning the work of my hands, command ye me." It is as though God places himself in the hands and at the disposal of his people who pray—as indeed he does.

The dominant element of all praying is faith, that is conspicuous, cardinal, and emphatic. Without such faith it is impossible to please God, and equally impossible to pray.

There is a current conception of spiritual duties which tends to separate the pulpit and the pew, as though the pulpit bore the entire burden of spiritual concerns, and while the pew was concerned only with duties that relate to the lower sphere of the secular and worldly. Such a view needs drastic correction. God's cause, its obligations, efforts, and successes, lie with equal pressure on pulpit and pew.

But the man in the pew is not taxed with the burden of prayer as he ought to be, and as he *must* be, ere any new visitation of power come to the church. The church never will be wholly for God until the pews are filled with praying men. The church cannot be what God wants it to be until those of its members who are leaders in business, politics, law, and society, are leaders in prayer.

God began his early movements in the world with men of prayer. He chose such a man to be the father of that race who became his chosen people in the world for hundreds of years, to whom he committed his oracles, and from whom sprang the promised Messiah. Abraham, a leader of God's cause, was preeminently a praying man. When we consider his conduct and character, we readily see how prayer ruled and swayed this great leader of God's people in the wilderness. "Abraham planted a grove in Beersheba, and called there on the name of the Lord, the everlasting God," and it is an outstanding fact that wherever Abraham pitched his tent and camped for a season, with his household, there he erected the altar of sacrifice and of prayer. His was a personal and a family religion, in which prayer was a prominent and abiding factor.

Prayer is the medium of divine revelation. It is through prayer that God reveals himself to the spiritual soul today, just as in the Old Testament days he made his revelations to the men who prayed. God shows himself to the man who prays. "God is with thee in all that thou doest." This was the clear conviction of those who would fain make a covenant with Abraham, and the reason for this tribute was the belief commonly held concerning the patriarch that, not only was he a man of prayer, but a man whose prayers God would answer. This is the summary and secret of divine rule in the church. In all ages God has ruled the church by prayerful men. When prayer fails, the divine rulership fails. As we have seen, Abraham, the father of the faithful, was a prince and a priest in prayer. He had remarkable influence with God. God stays his vengeance while Abraham prays. His mercy is suspended and conditioned on Abraham's praying. His visitations of wrath are removed by the praying of this ruler in Israel. The movements of God are influenced by the prayers of Abraham, the friend of God. Abraham's righteous prayerfulness permits him to share the secrets of God's counsels, while the knowledge of these secrets draws out and intensifies his praying. With Abraham, the altar of sacrifice is hard by the altar of prayer. With him the altar of prayer sanctifies the altar of sacrifice. To Abimelech God said, "Abraham is a prophet, and he shall pray for thee, and thou shalt live."

Christian people *must* pray for men. On one occasion, Samuel said unto the people, "Moreover as for me, God forbid that I should sin against the Lord in ceasing to pray for you." Fortunate for these sinful people who had rejected God, and desired a human king, that they had in Israel a man of prayer. The royal way to enlarge personal grace is to pray for others. Intercessory prayer is a means of grace to those who exercise it. We enter the richest fields of spiritual growth and gather its priceless riches in the avenues of intercessory prayer. To pray for men is of divine nomination, and represents the highest form of Christian service.

Men must pray, and men must be prayed for. The Christian must pray for all things, of course, but prayers for men are infinitely more important, just as men are infinitely more important than things. So also prayers for men are far more important than prayers for things because men more deeply concern God's will and the work of Jesus Christ than things. Men are to be cared for, sympathized with and prayed for, because sympathy, pity, compassion, and care accompany and precede prayer for men, when they are not called out for things.

All this makes praying a real business, not child's play, not a secondary affair, nor a trivial matter but a serious business. The men who have made a success of praying have made a business of praying. It is a process demanding the time, thought, energy, and hearts of mankind. Prayer is business for time, business for eternity. It is a man's business to pray, transcending all other business and taking precedence over all other vocations, professions, or occupations. Our praying concerns ourselves, all men, their greatest interests, even the salvation of their immortal souls. Praying is a business which takes hold of eternity and the things beyond the grave. It is a business which involves earth and heaven. All worlds are touched and worlds are influenced by prayer. It has to do with God and men, angels and devils.

Jesus was preeminently a leader in prayer, and his praying is an incentive to prayer. How prominently prayer stands out in his life! The leading events of his earthly career are distinctly marked by prayer. The wonderful experience and glory of the transfiguration was preceded by prayer, and was the result of the praying of our Lord. What words he used as he prayed we know not, nor do we know for what he prayed. But doubtless it was night, and long into its hours the Master prayed. It was while he prayed the darkness fled, and his form was lit with unearthly splendor. Moses and Elijah came to yield to him not only the palm of law and prophecy, but the palm of praying. None other prayed as did Jesus nor had any such a glorious manifestation of the divine presence or heard so clearly the revealing voice of the Father, "This is my beloved Son; hear ye him." Happy disciples to be with Christ in the school of prayer!

How many of us have failed to come to this glorious Mount of Transfiguration because we were unacquainted with the transfiguring power of prayer! It is the going apart to pray, the long, intense seasons of prayer, in which we engage which makes the face to shine, transfigures the character, makes even dull, earthly garments to glisten with heavenly splendor. But more than this: it is real praying which makes eternal things real, close and tangible, and which brings the glorified visitors and the heavenly visions. Transfigured lives would not be so rare if there were more of this transfigured praying. These heavenly visits would not be so few if there was more of this transfigured praying.

How difficult it appears to be for the church to understand that the whole scheme of redemption depends upon men of prayer! The work of our Lord, while here on the earth, as well of the apostle Paul was, by teaching and example, to develop men of prayer, to whom the future of the church should be committed. How strange that instead of learning this simple and all-important lesson, the modern church has largely overlooked it! We have need to turn afresh to that wondrous leader of spiritual Israel, our Lord Jesus Christ, who by example and precept enjoins us to prayer and to the great apostle to the Gentiles, who by virtue of his praying habits and prayer lessons is a model and an example to God's people in every age and clime.

7

The Ministry and Prayer

PREACHERS are God's leaders. They are divinely called to their holy office and high purpose and, primarily, are responsible for the condition of the church. Just as Moses was called of God to lead Israel out of Egypt through the wilderness into the promised land, so, also, does God call his ministers to lead his spiritual Israel through this world unto the heavenly land. They are divinely commissioned to leadership, and are by precept and example to teach God's people what God would have them be. Paul's counsel to the young preacher Timothy is in point: "Let no man despise thy youth," he says, "but be thou an example of the believers, in word, conversation, in charity, in spirit, in faith, in purity."

God's ministers shape the church's character, and give tone and direction to its life. The prefacing sentence of the letter to each of the seven churches in Asia reads, "To the angel of the church," seeming to indicate that the angel—the minister—was in the same state of mind and condition of life as the membership and that these angels or ministers were largely responsible for the spiritual condition of things existing in each church. The "angel" in each case was the preacher, teacher, or leader. The first Christians knew full well and felt this responsibility. In their helplessness, consciously felt, they cried out, "And who is sufficient for things?" as the tremendous responsibility pressed upon their hearts and heads. The only reply to such a question was, "God only." So they were necessarily compelled to look beyond themselves for help and throw themselves on prayer to secure God. More and more as they prayed, did they feel their responsibility, and more and more by prayer did they get God's help. They realized that their sufficiency was of God.

Prayer belongs in a very high and important sense to the ministry. It takes vigor and elevation of character to administer the prayer office. Praying prophets have frequently been at a premium in the history of God's people. In every age the demand has been for leaders in Israel who pray. God's watchmen must always and everywhere be men of prayer.

It ought to be no surprise for ministers to be often found on their knees seeking divine help under the responsibility of their call. These are the true prophets of the Lord, and these are they who stand as mouthpieces of God to a generation of wicked and worldly minded men and women. Praying preachers are the boldest, the truest, and the swiftest ministers of God. They mount up highest and are nearest to him who has called them. They advance more rapidly and in Christian living are most like God.

In reading the record of the four evangelists, we cannot but be impressed by the supreme effort made by our Lord to rightly instruct the twelve apostles in the things which would properly qualify them for the tremendous tasks which would be theirs after he had gone back to the bosom of the Father. His solicitude was for the church that she should have men, holy in life and in heart, and who would know full well from whence came their strength and power in the work of the ministry. A large part of Christ's teaching was addressed to these chosen apostles, and the training of the twelve occupied much of his thought and consumed much of his time. In all that training, prayer was laid down as a basic principle.

We find the same thing to be true in the life and work of the apostle Paul. While he addressed himself to the edification of the churches to whom he ministered and wrote, it was in his mind and purpose to rightly instruct and prepare ministers to whom would be committed the interests of God's people. The two epistles to Timothy were addressed to a young preacher, while that to Titus was also written to a young minister. And Paul's design appears to have been to give to each of them such instruction as would be needed rightly to do the work of the ministry to which they had been called by the Spirit of God. Underlying these instructions was the foundation stone of prayer, since by no means would they be able to "show themselves approved unto God, workmen that needeth not to be ashamed, rightly dividing the word of truth," unless they were men of prayer.

The highest welfare of the church of God on earth depends largely upon the ministry, and so Almighty God has always been jealous of his watchmen—his preachers. His concern has been for the character of the men who minister at his altars in holy things. They must be men who lean upon him, who look to him, and who continually seek him for wisdom, help and power effectively to do the work of the ministry. And so he has designed men of prayer for the holy office, and has relied upon them successively to perform the tasks he has assigned them.

God's great works are to be done as Christ did them; are to be done, indeed, with increased power received from the ascended and exalted Christ. These works are to be done by prayer. Men must do God's work in God's way, and to God's glory, and prayer is a necessity to its successful accomplishment.

The thing far above all other things in the equipment of the preacher is prayer. Before everything else, he must be a man who makes a specialty of prayer. A prayerless preacher is a misnomer. He has either missed his calling, or has grievously failed God who called him into the ministry. God wants men who are not ignoramuses, who "study to show themselves approved." Preaching the Word is essential; social qualities are not to be underestimated, and education is good; but under and above all else, prayer must be the main plank in the platform of the man who goes forth to preach the unsearchable riches of Christ to a lost and hungry world. The one weak spot in our church institutions lies just here. Prayer is not regarded as being the primary factor in church life and activity, and other things, good in their places, are made primary. First things need to be put first, and the first thing in the equipment of a minister is prayer.

Our Lord is the pattern for all preachers, and, with him, prayer was the law of life. By it he lived. It was the inspiration of his toil, the source of his strength, the spring of his joy. With our Lord prayer was no sentimental episode, nor an afterthought, nor a pleasing, diverting prelude, nor an interlude, nor a parade or form. For Jesus, prayer was exacting, all-absorbing, paramount. It was the call of a sweet duty to him, the satisfying of a restless yearning, the preparation for heavy responsibilities, and the meeting of a vigorous need. This being so, the disciple must be as his lord, the servant as his master. As was the Lord himself, so also must be those whom he has called to be his disciples. Our Lord Jesus Christ chose his twelve apostles only after he had spent a night in praying; and we may rest assured that he sets the same high value on those he calls to his ministry, in this our own day and time.

No feeble or secondary place was given to prayer in the ministry of Jesus. It comes first—emphatic, conspicuous, controlling. Of prayerful habits, of a prayerful spirit, given to long solitary communion with God, Jesus was above all else, a man of prayer. The crux of his earthly history, in New Testament terminology, is condensed to a single statement, to be found in Hebrews 5:7:

> Who in the days of his flesh, when he had offered up prayers and supplications with strong crying and tears, unto him that was able to save him from death, and was heard in that he feared.

As was their lord and master, whose they are and whom they serve, so let his ministers be. Let him be their pattern, their example, their leader and teacher. Much reference is made in some quarters about "following Christ," but it is confined to the following of him in modes and ordinances, as if salvation were wrapped up in the specific way of doing a thing. "The path of prayer thyself hath trod," is the path along which we are to follow him, and in no other. Jesus was given as a leader to the people of God, and no leader ever exemplified more the worth and necessity of prayer. Equal in glory with the Father, anointed and sent on his special mission by the Holy Spirit, his incarnate birth, his high commission, his royal anointing—all these were his but they did not relieve him from the exacting claims of prayer. Rather did they tend to impose these claims upon him with greater authority. He did not ask to be excused from the burden of prayer; he gladly accepted it, acknowledged its claims, and voluntarily subjected himself to its demands.

His leadership was preeminent, and his praying was preeminent. Had it not been, his leadership had been neither preeminent nor divine. If, in true leadership, prayer had been dispensable, then certainly Jesus could have dispensed with it. But he did not, nor can any of his followers who desire effectiveness in Christian activity do other than follow their Lord.

While Jesus Christ practiced praying himself, being personally under the law of prayer, and while his parables and miracles were but exponents of prayer, he labored directly to teach his disciples the specific art of praying. He said little or nothing about how to preach or what to preach. But he spent his strength and time in teaching men how to speak to God, how to commune with him, and how to be with him. He knew full well that he who has learned the craft of talking to God, will be well versed in talking to men. We may turn aside for a moment to observe that this was the secret of the wonderful success of the early Methodist preachers, who were far from being learned men. But with all their limitations, they were men of prayer, and they did great things for God.

All ability to talk to men is measured by the ability with which a preacher can talk to God for men. He "who plows not in his closet, will never reap in his pulpit."

The fact must ever be kept in the forefront and emphasized that Jesus Christ trained his disciples to pray. This is the real meaning of that saying, "The training of the twelve." It must be kept in mind that Christ taught the world's preachers more about praying than he did about preaching. Prayer was the great factor in the spreading of his gospel. Prayer conserved and made efficient all other factors. Yet he did not discount preaching when he stressed praying, but rather taught the utter dependence of preaching on prayer.

"The Christian's trade is praying," declared Martin Luther. Every Jewish boy had to learn a trade. Jesus Christ learned two, the trade of a carpenter, and that of praying. The one trade served earthly uses; the other served his divine and higher purposes. Jewish custom committed Jesus when a boy to the trade of a carpenter; the law of God bound him to praying from his earliest years, and remained with him to the end.

Christ is the Christian's example, and every Christian must pattern after him. Every preacher must be like his lord and master, and must learn the trade of praying. He who learns well the trade of praying masters the secret of the Christian art, and becomes a skilled workman in God's workshop, one who needeth not to be ashamed, a worker together with his lord and master.

"Pray without ceasing," is the trumpet call to the preachers of our time. If the preachers will get their thoughts clothed with the atmosphere of prayer, if they will prepare their sermons on their knees, a gracious outpouring of God's Spirit will come upon the earth.

The one indispensable qualification for preaching is the gift of the Holy Spirit, and it was for the bestowal of this indispensable gift that the disciples were charged to tarry in Jerusalem. The absolute necessity there is for receiving this gift, if success is to attend the efforts of the ministry, is found in the command the first disciples had to stay in Jerusalem till they received it, and also with the instant and earnest prayerfulness with which they sought it. In obedience to their Lord's command to tarry in that city till they were endued with power from on high, they immediately, after he left them for heaven, entered on securing it by continued and earnest prayer. "These all with one accord, continued steadfastly in prayer, with the women, and Mary the mother of Jesus and with his brethren." To this same thing John refers in his First Epistle. "Ye have an unction from the Holy One," he says. It is this divine unction that preachers of the present day should sincerely desire, pray for, remaining unsatisfied till the blessed gift be richly bestowed.

Another allusion to this same important procedure is made by our Lord shortly after his resurrection, when he said to his disciples: "And ye shall receive power after that the Holy Spirit is come upon you." At the same time Jesus directed the attention of his disciples to the statement of John the Baptist concerning the Spirit, the identical thing for which he had commanded them to tarry in the city of Jerusalem—"power from on high." Alluding to John the Baptist's words Jesus said, "For John indeed baptized with water, but ye shall be baptized with the Holy Spirit not many days hence." Peter at a later date said of our Lord: "God anointed him with the Holy Spirit and with power."

These are the divine statements of the mission and ministry of the Holy Spirit to preachers of that day and the same divine statements apply with equal force to the preachers of *this* day. God's ideal minister is a God-called, divinely anointed, Spirit-touched man, separated unto God's work, set apart from secularities and questionable affairs, baptized from above, marked, sealed and owned by the Spirit, devoted to his Master and his ministry. These are the divinely appointed requisites for a preacher of the Word; without them, he is inadequate, and inevitably unfruitful.

Today, there is no dearth of preachers who deliver eloquent sermons on the need and nature of revival, and advance elaborate plans for the spread of the kingdom of God, but the praying preachers are far more rare and the greatest benefactor this age can have is a man who will bring the preachers, the church and the people back to the practice of real praying. The reformer needed just now is the praying reformer. The leader Israel requires is one who, with clarion voice, will call the ministers back to their knees.

There is considerable talk of the coming revival in the air, but we need to have the vision to see that the revival we need and the only one that can be worth having is one that is born of the Holy Spirit, which brings deep conviction for sin, and regeneration for those who seek God's face. Such a revival comes at the end of a season of real praying, and it is utter folly to talk about or expect a revival without the Holy Spirit operating in his peculiar office, conditioned on much earnest praying. Such a revival will begin in pulpit and pew alike, will be promoted by both preacher and layman working in harmony with God.

The heart is the lexicon of prayer; the life the best commentary on prayer, and the outward bearing its fullest expression. The character is made by prayer; the life is perfected by prayer. And this the ministry needs to learn as thoroughly as the laymen. There is but one rule for both.

So averse was the general body of Christ's disciples to prayer, having so little taste for it, and having so little sympathy with him in the deep things of prayer, and its mightier struggles, that the master had to select a circle of three more apt scholars—Peter, James, and John—who had more of sympathy, and relish for this divine work, and take them aside that they might learn the lesson of prayer. These men were nearer to Jesus, more full of sympathy, and more helpful to him because they were more prayerful.

Blessed, indeed, are those disciples whom Jesus Christ, in this day, calls into a more intimate fellowship with him, and who, readily responding to the call, are found much on their knees before him. Distressing, indeed, is the condition of those servants of Jesus who, in their hearts, are averse to the exercise of the ministry of prayer.

All the great eras of our Lord, historical and spiritual, were made or fashioned by his praying. In like manner his plans and great achievements were born in prayer and impregnated by the spirit thereof. As was the master, so also must his servant be; as his Lord did in the great eras of his life, so should the disciple do when faced by important crises. "To your knees, O Israel!" should be the clarion call to the ministry of this generation.

The highest form of religious life is attained by prayer. The richest revelations of God—Father, Son, and Spirit—are made, not to the learned, the great or the "noble" of earth, but men of prayer. "For ye see your calling, brethren, that not many wise men after the flesh, not many mighty, not many noble, are called," to whom God makes known the deep things of God, and reveals the higher things of his character, but to the lowly, inquiring, praying ones. And again must it be said this is as true of preachers as of laymen. It is the spiritual man who prays, and to praying ones God makes his revelations through the Holy Spirit.

Praying preachers have always brought the greater glory to God, have moved his gospel onward with its greatest, speediest rate, and power. A nonpraying preacher and a nonpraying church may flourish outwardly and advance in many aspects of their life. Both preacher and church may become synonyms for success, but unless it rest on a praying basis, all success will eventually crumble into deadened life and ultimate decay.

"Ye have not because ye ask not," is the solution of all spiritual weakness both in the personal life and in the pulpit. Either that or it is, "Ye ask and receive not because ye ask amiss." Real praying lies at the foundation of all real success of the ministry in the things of God. The stability, energy, and facility with which God's kingdom is established in this world are dependent upon prayer. God has made it so, and so God is anxious for men to pray. Especially is he concerned that his chosen ministers shall be men of prayer, and so gives that wonderful statement found in Matthew 6:9 to encourage his ministers to pray :

> But I say unto you, Ask, and it shall be given you; seek, and ye shall find; knock, and it shall be opened unto you. For every one that asketh, receiveth, and he that seeketh, findeth; and to him that knocketh, it shall be opened.

Thus both command and direct promise give accent to his concern that they shall pray. Pause and think on these familiar words. "Ask, and it shall be given you." That itself would seem to be enough to set us all, laymen and preachers, to praying, so direct, simple, and unlimited. These words open all the treasures of heaven to us, simply by asking for them.

If we have not studied the prayers of Paul, primarily a preacher to the Gentiles, we can have but a feeble view of the great necessity for prayer, and how much it is worth in the life and the work of a minister of the gospel. Furthermore, we shall have but a very limited view of the possibilities of the gospel to enrich and make strong and perfect Christian character, as well as to equip preachers for their high and holy task. Oh, when will we learn the simple yet all-important lesson that the one great thing needed in the life of a preacher to help him in his personal life, to keep his soul alive to God, and to give power to the Word preached by him, is real, constant prayer!

Paul with prayer uppermost in his mind, assures the Colossians that "Epaphras is always laboring fervently for you in prayers, that ye may stand complete and perfect in all the will of God." To this high state of grace, "complete in all the will of God," he prays they may come. So prayer was the force which was to bring them to that elevated, vigorous, and stable state of heart. This is in line with Paul's teaching to the Ephesians, "And he gave some pastors and teachers, for the perfecting of the saints, for the work of the ministry, for the edifying of the body of Christ," where it is evidently affirmed that the whole work of the ministry is not merely to induce sinners to repent, but it is also the "perfecting of the saints." And so Epaphras labored fervently in prayers for this thing. Certainly he was himself a praying man, in thus so earnestly praying for these early Christians.

The apostles put out their force in order that Christians should honor God by the purity and consistency of their outward lives. They were to reproduce the character of Jesus Christ. They were to perfect his image in themselves, imbibe his temper, and reflect his behavior in all their conduct. They were to be imitators of God as dear children, to be holy as he was holy. Thus even laymen were to preach by their conduct and character, just as the ministry preached with their mouths.

To elevate the followers of Christ to these exalted heights of Christian experience, they were in every way true in the ministry of God's Word, in the ministry of prayer, in holy consuming zeal, in burning exhortation, in rebuke and reproof. Added to all these, sanctifying all these, invigorating all these, and making all of them salutary, they centered and exercised constantly the force of mightiest praying. "Night and day praying exceedingly," that is, praying out of measure, with intense earnestness, superabundantly, beyond measure, exceeding abundantly.

> Night and day praying exceeding abundantly, that we might see your face, and might perfect that which is lacking in your faith. Now God himself, and our Father, and our Lord Jesus Christ, direct our way unto you.
> And the Lord make you to increase and abound in love one toward another, and toward all men, even as we do toward you; to the end he may establish your hearts unblamable in holiness before God, even our Father, at the coming of our Lord Jesus Christ with all his saints.

It was after this fashion that these apostles—the first preachers in the early church—labored in prayer. And only those who labor after the same fashion are the true successors of these apostles. This is the true, the Scriptural "apostolical succession," the succession of simple faith, earnest desire for holiness of heart and life, and zealous praying. These are the things today which make the ministry strong, faithful and efficient, "workmen who needeth not to be ashamed, rightly dividing the word of truth."

Jesus Christ, God's leader and commander of his people, lived and suffered under this law of prayer. All his personal conquests in his life on earth were won by obedience to this law, while the conquests which have been won by his representatives since he ascended to heaven, were gained only when this condition of prayer was heartily and fully met. Christ was under this one prayer condition. His apostles were under the same prayer condition. His saints are under it, and even his angels are under it. By every token, therefore, preachers are under the same prayer law. Not for one moment are they relieved or excused from obedience to the law of prayer. It is their very life, the source of their power, the secret of their religious experience and communion with God.

Christ could do nothing without prayer. Christ could do all things by prayer. The apostles were helpless without prayer—and were absolutely dependent upon it for success in defeating their spiritual foes. They could do all things by prayer.

8

Prayerlessness in the Pulpit

ALL God's saints came to their sainthood by the way of prayer. The saints could do nothing without prayer. We can go further and say that the angels in heaven can do nothing without prayer, but can do all things by praying. These messengers of the highest are largely dependent on the prayers of the saints for the sphere and power of their usefulness, which open avenues for angelic usefulness and create missions for them on the earth. And as it is with all the apostles, saints, and angels in heaven, so is it of preachers. "The angels of the churches" can do nothing without prayer which opens doors of usefulness and gives power and point to their words.

How can a preacher preach effectively, make impressions on hearts and minds, and have fruits to his ministry, who does not get his message firsthand from God? How can he deliver a rightful message without having his faith quickened, his vision cleared, and his heart warmed by his closeting with God?

It would be well for all of us, in this connection, to read again Isaiah's vision recorded in the sixth chapter of his prophecy when, as he waited, and confessed and prayed before the throne, the angel touched his lips with a live coal from God's altar:

> "Then flew one of the seraphims unto me," he says, "having a live coal in his hand, which he had taken with the tongs from off the altar; and he laid it upon my mouth, and said, Lo, this hath touched thy lips; and thine iniquity is taken away, and thy sin is purged."

Oh, the need there is for present-day preachers to have their lips touched with a live coal from the altar of God! This fire is brought to the mouths of those prophets who are of a prayerful spirit, and who wait in the secret place for the appointed angel to bring the living flame. Preachers of the same temper as Isaiah received visits from the angel who brings live coals to touch their lips. Prayer always brings the living flame to loosen tongues, to open doors of utterance, and to open great and effectual doors of doing good. This, above all else, is the great need of the prophets of God.

As far as the abiding interests of religion are concerned, a pulpit without a closet will always be a barren thing. Blessed is the preacher whose pulpit and closet are hard by each other, and who goes from the one into the other. To consecrate no place to prayer, is to make a beggarly showing, not only in praying, but in holy living, for secret prayer and holy living are so closely joined that they can never be severed. A preacher or a Christian may live a decent, religious life, without secret prayer, but decency and holiness are two widely different things. And the latter is attained only by secret prayer.

A preacher may preach in an official, entertaining, and learned way, without prayer, but between this kind of preaching and the sowing of God's precious seed there is distance not easily covered.

We cannot declare too often or too strongly that prayer, involving all of its elements, is the one prime condition of the success of Christ's kingdom, and that all else is secondary and incidental. Prayerful preachers, prayerful men, and prayerful women only can press this gospel with aggressive power. Only they can put in it conquering forces. Preachers may be sent out by the thousand, their equipments be ever so complete, but unless they be men skilled in the trade of prayer, trained to its martial and exhaustive exercise, their going will be lacking in power and effectiveness. Moreover, except the men and women who are behind these preachers, who furnish their equipment, are men and women in whose characters prayer has become serious labor, their outlay will be a vain and ineffective effort.

Prayer should be the inseparable accompaniment of all missionary effort, and must be the one equipment of the missionaries as they go out to their fields of labor, and enter upon their delicate and responsible tasks. Prayer and missions go hand in hand. A prayerless missionary is a failure before he goes out, while he is out, and when he returns to his native land. A prayerless board of missions, too, needs to learn the lesson of the necessity of prayer.

Prayer enthrones God as sovereign and elevates Jesus Christ to sit with him, and had Christian preachers used to its full the power of prayer, long ere this the "kingdoms of this world would have become the kingdom of God and of his Christ." Added to all the missionary addresses, the money raised for missions, to the scores being sent out to needy fields, is prayer. Missions have their root in prayer, must have prayer in all of its plans, and prayer must precede, go with, and follow all of its missionaries and laborers.

In the face of all difficulties which face the church in its great work on earth, and the almost superhuman and complex obstacles in the way of evangelizing the world, God encourages us by his strongest promises: "Call unto me and I will answer thee, and show great and mighty things which thou knowest not." The revelations of God to him who is of a prayerful spirit go far beyond the limits of the praying. God commits himself to answer the specific prayer, but he does not stop there. He says, "Ask of me things to come concerning my sons, and concerning the work of my hands, command ye me." Think over that remarkable engagement of God to those who pray. "Command ye me." He actually places himself at the command of praying preachers and a praying church. And this is a sufficient answer to all doubts, fears, and unbelief, and a wonderful inspiration to do God's work in his own way, which means by the way of prayer.

And as if to still fortify the faith of his ministry and of his church, to hedge about and fortify against any temptation to doubt or discouragement, he declares by the mouth of the great apostle to the Gentiles, "He is able to do exceeding abundantly above all that ye can ask or think."

It is unquestionably taught that preachers in going forward with their God-appointed tasks, in their prayers, can command God, which is to command his ability, his presence and his power. "Certainly I will be with thee," is the reply to every sincere inquiring minister of God. All of God's called men in the ministry are privileged to stretch their prayers into regions where neither words nor thought can go, and are permitted to expect from him beyond their praying, and for their praying, God himself, and then in addition, "great and mighty things which thou knowest not."

Real heart-praying, live-praying, praying by the power of the Spirit, direct, specific, ardent, simple praying—this is the kind of praying which legitimately belongs to the pulpit. This is the kind demanded just now by the men who stand in the pulpit. There is no school in which to learn to pray in public but in the closet. Preachers who have learned to pray in the closet have mastered the secret of pulpit praying. It is but a short step from secret praying to effectual, live, pulpit praying. Good pulpit praying follows from good secret praying. A closed closet with the preacher makes for cold, spiritless, formal praying in the pulpit. Study how to pray, O preacher, but not by studying the forms of prayer, but by attending the school of prayer on your knees before God. Here is where we learn not only to pray before God, but learn also how to pray in the presence of men. He who has learned the way to the closet has discovered the way to pray when he enters the pulpit.

How easily we become professional and mechanical in the most sacred undertakings! Henry Martyn learned the lesson so hard to learn, that the cultivation and perfection of personal righteousness was the great and prime factor in the preacher's true success. So likewise he that learns the lesson so hard to learn, that live, spiritual, effective pulpit praying is the outgrowth of regular secret praying, has learned his lesson well. Moreover: his work, as a preacher, will depend upon his praying.

The great need of the hour is for good pray-ers in the pulpit as well as good preachers. Just as live, spiritual preaching is the kind which impresses and moves men, so the same kind of pulpit praying moves and impresses God. Not only is the preacher called to preach well, but also he must be called to pray well. Not that he is called to pray after the fashion of the Pharisees, who love to stand in public and pray that they may be seen and heard of men. The right sort of pulpit praying is far removed from Pharisaical praying, as far distant as light is from darkness, as great as heat is from cold, as life is from death.

Where are we? What are we doing? Preaching is the very loftiest work possible for a man to do. And praying goes hand-in-hand with preaching. It is a mighty, a lofty work. Preaching is a life-giving work, sowing the seeds of eternal life. Oh, may we do it well, do it after God's order, do it successfully! May we do it divinely well, so that when the end comes, the solemn close of earthly probation, we may hear from the Great Judge of all the earth, "Well done, good and faithful servant, enter thou into the joy of thy Lord."

When we consider this great question of preaching, we are led to exclaim, "With what reverence, simplicity, and sincerity ought it to be done!" What truth in the inward parts is demanded in order that it be done acceptably to God and with profit to men! How real, true, and loyal those who practice it ought to be! How great the need to pray as Christ prayed, with strong cryings, and tears, with godly fear! Oh, may we as preachers do the real thing of preaching, with no sham, with no mere form of words, with no dull, cold, professional utterances, but give ourselves to prayerful preaching and prayerful praying! Preaching which gives life is born of praying which gives life. Preaching and praying always go together, like Siamese twins, and can never be separated without death to one or the other, or death to both.

This is not the time for kid-glove methods nor sugarcoated preaching. This is no time for playing the gentleman as a preacher nor for putting on the garb of the scholar in the pulpit, if we propose to disciple all nations, destroy idolatry, crush the rugged and defiant forces of Mohammedanism, and overcome and destroy the tremendous forces of evil now opposing the kingdom of God in this world. Brave men, true men, praying men—afraid of nothing but God, are the kind needed just now. There will be no smiting the forces of evil which now hold the world in thralldom, no lifting of the degraded hordes of paganism to light and eternal life, by any but praying men. All others are merely playing at religion, make-believe soldiers, with no armor and no ammunition, who are absolutely helpless in the face of a wicked and gainsaying world. None but soldiers and bond servants of Jesus Christ can possibly do this tremendous work. "Endure hardness as a good soldier of Jesus Christ," cries the great apostle. This is no time to think of self, to consult with dignity, to confer with flesh and blood, to think of ease, or to shrink from hardship, grief, and loss. This is the time for toil, suffering, and self-denial. We must lose all for Christ in order to gain all for Christ. Men are needed in the pulpit, as well as in the pew, who are "bold to take up, firm to sustain, the consecrated cross." Here is the sort of preachers God wants. And this sort are born of much praying. For no man is sufficient for these things who is a prayerless preacher. Praying preachers alone can meet the demand and will be equal to the emergency.

The gospel of Jesus has neither relish nor life in it when spoken by prayerless lips or handled by prayerless hands. Without prayer the doctrines of Christ degenerate into dead orthodoxy. Preaching them without the aid of the Spirit of God, who comes into the preacher's messages only by prayer, is nothing more than mere lecturing, with no life, no grip, no force in the preaching. It amounts to nothing more than live rationalism or sickly sentimentalism. "But we will give ourselves continually to prayer and to the ministry of the Word," was the settled and declared purpose of the apostolic ministry. The kingdom of God waits on prayer, and prayer puts wings on the gospel and power into it. By prayer the kingdom of God moves forward with conquering force and rapid advance.

If prayer be left out of account, the preacher rises to no higher level than the lecturer, the politician, or the secular teacher. That which distinguishes him from all other public speakers is the fact of prayer. And as prayer deals with God, this means that the preacher has God with him, while other speakers do not need God with them to make their public messages effective. The preacher above everything else is a spiritual man, a man of the Spirit, who deals with spiritual things. And this implies that he has to do with God in his pulpit work in a high and holy sense. This can be said of no other public speaker. And so prayer must necessarily go with the preacher and his preaching. Pure intellectuality is the only qualification for other public speakers. Spirituality which is born of prayer belongs to the preacher.

In the Sermon on the Mount Jesus Christ often speaks of prayer. It stands out prominently in his utterances on that occasion. The lesson of prayer which he taught was one of hallowing God's name, of pushing God's kingdom. We are to long for the coming of the kingdom of God. It is to be longed for, and must be first in our communicating with God. God's will must have its royal way in the hearts and wills of those who pray. The point of urgency is made by our Lord that men are to pray in earnest, by asking, seeking, knocking, in order to hallow God's name, bring his will to pass, and to forward his kingdom among men.

And let it be kept in mind that while this prayer lesson has to do with all men, it has a peculiar application to the ministry, for it was the twelve would-be preachers who made the request of our Lord Jesus Christ, "Lord, teach us to pray, as John also taught his disciples." So primarily these words were spoken first to twelve men just entering upon their work as ministers. Jesus was talking as Luke records it, to preachers. So he speaks to the preachers of this day. How he pressed these twelve men into the ministry of prayer! The present-day ministry needs the same lesson to be taught them, and needs the same urgency pressing them to prayer as their habit of life.

Notwithstanding all he may claim for himself, nor how many good things may be put down to his credit, a prayerless preacher will never learn well God's truth, which he is called upon to declare with all fidelity and plainness of speech. Blind and blinding still will he be if he lives a prayerless life. A prayerless ministry cannot know God's truth, and not knowing it, cannot teach it to ignorant men. He who teaches us the path of prayer, must first of all walk in the same path. A preacher cannot teach what he does not know. A blind leader of the blind will be the preacher who is a stranger to prayer.

Prayer opens the preacher's eyes, and keeps them open to the evil of sin, the peril of it, and the penalty it incurs. A blind leader leading the blind will be the vocation of him who is prayerless in his own life.

The best and the greatest offering which the church and the ministry can make to God is an offering of prayer. If the preachers of the twentieth century will learn well the lesson of prayer, and use it fully in all its exhaustless efficiency, the millennium will come to its noon ere the century closes.

The Bible preacher prays. He is filled with the Holy Spirit, filled with God's Word, and is filled with faith. He has faith in God, faith in God's only begotten Son, his personal Savior, and he has implicit faith in God's Word. He cannot do otherwise than pray. He cannot be other than a man of prayer. The breadth of his life and the pulsations of his heart are prayer. The Bible preacher lives by prayer, loves by prayer, and preaches by prayer. His bended knees in the place of secret prayer advertise what kind of preacher he is.

Preachers may lose faith in God, in Jesus Christ as their personal and present Savior, become devoid of the peace of God and let the joy of salvation go out of their hearts, and yet be unconscious of it. How needful for the preacher to be continually examining himself, and inquiring into his personal relations to God and into his religious state! The preachers, like the philosophers of old, may defer to a system, and earnestly contend for it after they have lost all faith in its great facts. Men may speak in the pulpit with hearts of unbelief, and minister at the altars of the church while alien to the most sacred and vital principles of the gospel.

It is a comparatively easy task for preachers to become so absorbed in the material and external affairs of the church as to lose sight of their own souls, forget the necessity of prayer so needful to keep their own souls alive to God, and lose the inward sweetness of a Christian experience.

The prayer which makes much of our preaching must itself be made much of. The character of our praying will determine the character of our preaching. Serious praying will give serious weight to preaching. Prayer makes preaching strong, gives it unction, and makes it stick. In every ministry, weighty for good, prayer has always been a serious business prophetic of good.

It cannot be said with too much emphasis, the preacher must be preeminently a man of prayer. He must learn to pray, and he must have such an esteem of prayer and its great worth that he feels he cannot afford to omit it from the catalogue of his private duties. His heart must be attuned to prayer, while he himself touches the highest note of prayer. Only in the school of prayer can the heart learn to preach. No gifts, no learning, no brain-force, can atone for the failure to pray. No earnestness, no diligence, no study, no amount of social service will supply its lack. Talking to men for God may be a great thing, and may be very commendable. But talking to God for men, is far more valuable and commendable.

The power of Bible preaching lies not simply or solely in superlative devotion to God's Word, and jealous passion for God's truth. All these are essential, valuable, helpful. But above all these things, there must be the sense of the divine presence, and the consciousness of the divine power of God's Spirit on the preacher and in him. He must have an anointing, an empowering, a sealing of the Holy Spirit, for the great work of preaching, making him akin to God's voice, and giving him the energy of God's right hand, so that this Bible preacher can say, "Thy words were found, and I did eat them; and thy word was unto me the joy and rejoicing of my heart. For I am called by thy name, O Lord of hosts."

9

Prayer Equipment for Preachers

ALMOST the last words uttered by our Lord before his ascension to heaven, were those addressed to the eleven disciples, words which, really, were spoken to, and having directly to do with, preachers, words which indicate very clearly the needed fitness which these men must have to preach the gospel, beginning at Jerusalem: "But tarry ye in the city of Jerusalem," says Jesus, "till ye be endued with power from on high."

Two things are very clearly set forth in these urgent directions. First, the power of the Holy Spirit for which they must tarry. This was to be received after their conversion, an indispensable requisite, equipping them for the great task set before them. Secondly, the "promise of the Father," this "power from on high," would come to them after they had waited in earnest, continuous prayer. A reference to Acts 1:14 will reveal that these same men, with the women, "continued with one accord in prayer and supplication," and so continued until the Day of Pentecost, when the power from on high descended upon them.

This "power from on high," as important to those early preachers as it is to present-day preachers, was not the force of a mighty intellect, holding in its grasp great truths, flooding them with light, and forming them into verbal shapeliness and beauty. Nor was it the acquisition of great learning, or the result of an address, faultless and complete by rule of rhetoric. None of these things. Nor was this spiritual power held then, nor is it held now, in the keeping of any earthly sources of power. The effect and energy of all human forces are essentially different in source and character, and do not at all result from this "power from on high." The transmission of such power is directly from God, a bestowal, in rich measure, of the force and energy which pertains only to God, and which is transmitted to his messengers only in answer to a longing, wrestling attitude of his soul before his Master, conscious of his own impotency and seeking the omnipotence of the Lord he serves, in order more fully to understand the given Word and to preach the same to his fellowmen.

The "power from on high" may be found in combination with all sources of human power, but is not to be confounded with them, is not dependent upon them, and must never be superseded by them. Whatever of human gift, talent, or force a preacher may possess it is not to be made paramount, or even conspicuous. It must be hidden, lost, overshadowed by this "power from on high." The forces of intellect and culture may all be present, but without this inward, heaven-given power, all spiritual effort is vain and unsuccessful. Even when lacking the other equipment but having this "power from on high," a preacher cannot but succeed. It is the one essential, all-important vital force which a messenger of God must possess to give wings to his message, to put life into his preaching, and to enable him to speak the word with acceptance and power.

A word is necessary here. Distinctions need to be kept in mind. We must think clearly upon this question. "Power from on high" means "the unction of the Holy One" resting on and abiding in the preacher. This is not so much a power which bears witness to a man being the child of God as it is a preparation for delivering the word to others. Unction must be distinguished from pathos. Pathos may exist in a sermon while unction is entirely absent. So also, may unction be present and pathos absent. Both may exist together; but they are not to be confused, nor be made to appear to be the same thing. Pathos promotes emotion, tender feeling, sometimes tears. Quite often it results from the relation of an affecting incident, or when the tender side is peculiarly appealed to. But pathos is neither the direct nor indirect result of the Holy Spirit resting upon the preacher as he preaches.

But unction is. Here we are given the evidence of the workings of an undefinable agency in the preacher, which results directly from the presence of this "power from on high," deep, conscious, life-giving, and carrying, giving power and point to the preached Word. It is the element in a sermon which arouses, stirs, convicts, and moves the souls of sinners and saints. This is what the preacher requires, the great equipment for which he should wait and pray. This "unction of the Holy One" delivers from dryness, saves from superficiality, and gives authority to preaching. It is the one quality which distinguishes the preacher of the gospel from other men who speak in public; it is that which makes a sermon unique, unlike the deliverance of any other public speaker.

Prayer is the language of a man burdened with a sense of need. It is the voice of the beggar, conscious of his poverty, asking of another the things he needs. It is not only the language of lack, but of *felt lack,* of lack consciously realized. "Blessed are the poor in spirit," means not only that the fact of poverty of spirit brings the blessing, but also that poverty of spirit is realized, known, and acknowledged. Prayer is the language of those who need something—something which they, themselves, cannot supply but which God has promised them, and for which they ask. In the end, poor praying and prayerlessness amount to the same thing, for poor praying proceeds from a lack of the sense of need, while prayerlessness has its origin in the same soil. Not to pray is not only to declare there is nothing needed, but also to admit to a nonrealization of that need. This is what aggravates the sin of prayerlessness. It represents an attempt at instituting an independence of God, a self-sufficient ruling of God out of the life. It is a declaration made to God that we do not need him, and hence do not pray to him.

This is the state in which the Holy Spirit, in his messages to the seven churches in Asia, found the Laodicean church and "the Laodicean state" has come to stand for one in which God is ruled out, expelled from the life, put out of the pulpit. The entire condemnation of this church is summed up in one expression: "Because thou sayest, I have need of nothing," the most alarming state into which a person, or church or preacher can come. Trusting in its riches, in its social position, in things outward and material, the church at Laodicea omitted God, leaving him out of their church plans and church work, and declared, by their acts and by their omission of prayer, "I have need of nothing."

No wonder the self-satisfied declaration brought forth its sentence of punishment—"Because thou art lukewarm, and neither cold nor hot, I will spue thee out of my mouth." The idea conveyed is that such a backslidden state of heart is as repulsive to God as an emetic is to the human stomach, and as the stomach expels that which is objectionable, so Almighty God threatens to "spue out of his mouth" these people who were in such a religious condition so repulsive to him. All of it was traceable to a prayerless state of heart, for no one can read this word of the Spirit to this Laodicean church and not see that the very core of their sin was prayerlessness. How could a church, given to prayer, openly and vauntingly declare, "I have need of nothing," in the face of the Spirit's assertion that it needed everything, "Thou knowest not that thou art wretched, and poor, and miserable, and blind, and naked"? In addition to their sin of self-sufficiency and of independence of God, the Laodiceans were spiritually blind. Oh, what dullness of sight, what blindness of soul! These people were prayerless, and knew not the import of such prayerlessness. They lacked everything which goes to make up spiritual life, and force, and self-denying piety, and vainly supposed themselves to need nothing but material wealth, thus making temporal possessions a substitute for spiritual wealth, leaving God entirely out of their activities, relying upon human and material resources to do the work only possible to the divine and supernatural, and secured alone by prayer.

Nor let it be forgotten that this letter (in common with the other six letters) was primarily addressed to the preacher in charge of the church. All this strengthens the impression that the angel of the church himself was in this lukewarm state. He himself was living a prayerless life, relying upon things other than God, practically saying, "I have need of nothing." For these words are the natural expression of the spirit of him who does not pray, who does not care for God, and who does not feel the need of him in his life, in his work and in his preaching. Furthermore, the words of the Spirit seem to indicate that the "angel of the church" at Laodicea was indirectly responsible for this sad condition into which the Laodicean church had fallen.

May not this sort of a church be found in modern times? Is it not likely that we could discover some preachers of modern times who fall under a similar condemnation to that passed upon the "angel of the church" of Laodicea?

Preachers of the present age excel those of the past in many, possibly in all, human elements of success. They are well abreast of the age in learning, research, and intellectual vigor. But these things neither insure "power from on high" nor guarantee a live, thriving religious experience, or righteous life. These purely human gifts do not bring with them an insight into the deep things of God, or strong faith in the Scriptures, or an intense loyalty to God's divine revelation.

The presence of these earthly talents even in the most commanding and impressive form, and richest measure do not in the least abate the necessity for the added endowment of the Holy Spirit. Herein lies the great danger menacing the pulpit of today. All around us we see a tendency to substitute human gifts and worldly attainments for that supernatural, inward power which comes from on high in answer to earnest prayer.

In many instances modern preaching seems to fail in the very thing which should create and distinguish true preaching, which is essential to its being, and which alone can make of it a divine and powerfully aggressive agency. It lacks, in short, "the power from on high" which alone can make it a living thing. It fails to become the channel through which God's saving power can be made to appeal to men's consciences and hearts.

Quite often modern preaching fails at this vital point, for lack of exercising a potent influence which disturbs men in their sleep of security, and awakens them to a sense of need and of peril. There is a growing need of an appeal which will quicken and arouse the conscience from its ignoble stupor and give it a sense of wrongdoing and a corresponding sense of repentance. There is need of a message which searches into the secret places of man's being, dividing, as it were, the joints and the marrow, and laying bare the mysterious depths before himself and his God. Much of our present day preaching is lacking in that quality which infuses new blood into the heart and veins of faith, that arms it with courage and skill for the battle with the powers of darkness, and secures it a victory over the forces of the world.

Such high and noble ends can never be accomplished by human qualifications, nor can these great results be secured by a pulpit clothed only with the human elements of power, however gracious, comfortable, and helpful they may be. The Holy Spirit is needed. He alone can equip the ministry for its difficult and responsible work in and out of the pulpit. Oh, that the present day ministry may come to see that its one great need is an enduing of "power from on high," and that this one need can be secured only by the use of God's appointed means of grace—the ministry of prayer.

Prayer is needed by the preacher so that his personal relations with God may be maintained and because there is no difference between him and any other kind of a man insofar as his personal salvation is concerned. This he must work out "with fear and trembling," just as all other men must do. Thus prayer is of vast importance to the preacher that he may possess a growing religious experience, and be enabled to live such a life that his character and conduct will back up his preaching and give force to his message.

A man *must* have prayer in his pulpit work, for no minister can preach effectively without prayer. He also has use for prayer in praying for others. Paul was a notable example of a preacher who constantly prayed for those to whom he ministered.

But we come, now, to another sphere of prayer, that of the people praying for the preacher. "Brethren, pray for us." This is the cry which Paul set in motion, and which has been the cry of spiritually minded preachers—those who know God and who know that value of prayer—in all succeeding ages. No condition of success or the reverse of it must abate the cry. No degree of culture, no abundance of talents must cause that cry to cease. The learned preacher, as well as the unlearned, has equal need to call out to the people he serves, "Withal, praying also for us." Such a cry voices the felt need of a preacher's heart who feels the need there is for sympathies of a people to be in harmony with its minister. It is but the expression of the inner soul of a preacher who feels his insufficiency for the tremendous responsibilities of the pulpit, who realizes his weakness and his need of the divine unction, and who throws himself upon the prayers of his congregation, and calls out to them, "Praying always with all prayer and supplication, in the Spirit, and for me, that utterance may be given me." It is the cry of deeply felt want in the heart of the preacher who feels he must have this prayer made specifically for him that he may do his work in God's own way.

When this request to a people to pray for the preacher is cold, formal, and official, it freezes instead of blossoms. To be ignorant of the necessity for the cry, is to be ignorant of the sources of spiritual success. To fail to stress the cry, and to fail to have responses to it, is to sap the sources of spiritual life. Preachers must sound out the cry to the church of God. Saints everywhere and of every kind, and of every faith speedily respond and pray for the preacher. The imperative need of the work demands it. "Pray for us," is the natural cry of the hearts of God's called men—faithful preachers of the Word.

Saintly praying in the early church helped apostolic preaching mightily, and rescued apostolic men from many dire straits. It can do the same thing today. It can open doors for apostolic labors and apostolic lips to utter bravely and truly the gospel message. Apostolic movements wait their ordering from prayer and avenues long closed are opened to apostolic entrance by and through the power of prayer. The messenger receives his message and is schooled as to how to carry and deliver the message by prayer. The forerunner of the gospel, and that which prepares the way, is prayer; not only by the praying of the messenger himself, but by the praying of the church of God.

Writing along this line in his Second Epistle to the Thessalonians, Paul is first general in his request and says, "Brethren, pray for us." Then he becomes more minute and particular:

> Finally, brethren, pray for us, that the word of the Lord may have free course and be glorified, even as it is with you. And that we may be delivered from unreasonable and wicked men; for all men have not faith.

The Revised Version has for "free course" the word "run." "The word" means doctrine, and the idea conveyed is that this doctrine of the gospel is rapidly propagated, a metaphor taken from the running of a race, and is an exhortation to exert one's self, to strive hard, to expend strength. Thus the prayer for the spread of the gospel gives the same energy to the Word of the Lord, as the greatest outlay of strength gives success to the racer. Prayer in the pew gives the preached word energy, facility, and success. Preaching without the backing of mighty praying is as limp and worthless an effort as can be imagined. Prayerlessness in the pew is a serious hindrance to the running of the Word of the Lord.

The preaching of the Word of the Lord fails to run and be glorified from many causes. The difficulty may lie with the preacher himself, should his outward conduct be out of harmony with the rule of the Scriptures and his own profession. The word *lived* must be in accord with the word *delivered;* the *life* must be in harmony with the *sermon.* The preacher's spirit and behavior *out* of the pulpit must run parallel with the Word of the Lord spoken *in* the pulpit. Otherwise, a man is an obstacle to the success of his own message.

Again, the Word of the Lord may fail to run, may be seriously encumbered and crippled by the inconsistent lives of those who are the hearers thereof. Bad living in the pew will seriously cripple the Word of the Lord as it attempts to run on its appointed course. Unrighteous lives among the laity heavily weights down the Word of the Lord and hampers the work of the ministry. Yet prayer will remove this burden which seriously handicaps the preached word. It will tend to do this in a direct way, or in an indirect manner. For just as you set laymen to praying, for the preacher or even for themselves, it awakens conscience, stirs the heart, tends to correct evil ways, and to promote good living. No man will pray long and continue in sin. Praying breaks up bad living, while bad living breaks down prayer. Praying goes into bankruptcy when a man goes to sinning. To obey the cry of the preacher, "Brethren, pray for us," sets men to doing that which will induce right living in them, and will tend to break them away from sin. So it comes about that it is worth no little to get the laity to pray for the ministry. Prayer helps the preacher, is an aid to the sermon, assists the hearer, and promotes right living in the pew.

Prayer also moves him who prays for the preacher and for the Word of the Lord, to use all his influence to remove any hindrance to that word which he may see and which lies in his power to remove.

But prayer reaches the preacher directly. God hears the praying of a church for its minister. Prayer for the preached word is a direct aid to it. Prayer for the preacher gives wings to the gospel, as well as feet. Prayer makes the Word of the Lord go forward strongly and rapidly. It takes the shackles off the message, and gives it a chance to run straight to the hearts of sinners and saints alike. It opens the way, clears the track, furnishes a free course. The failure of many a preacher may be found just here. He was hampered, hindered, crippled by a prayerless church. Nonpraying officials stood in the way of the word preached, and became veritable stumbling blocks in the way of the word, definitely preventing its reaching the hearts of the unsaved.

Unbelief and prayerlessness go together. It is written of our Lord in Matthew's gospel that when he entered into his own country, "he did not many mighty works there because of their unbelief." Mark puts it a little differently, but giving out the same idea: "And he could there do no mighty work, save that he laid his hands upon a few sick folks and healed them. And he marveled because of their unbelief." Unquestionably the unbelief of that people hindered our Lord in his gracious work and tied his hands. And if that be true, it requires no undue straining of the Scriptures when we say that the unbelief and prayerlessness of a church can tie the hands of its preacher, and prevent him from doing many great works in the salvation of souls and in edifying saints. Prayerlessness, therefore, as it concerns the preacher is a very serious matter. If it exists in the preacher himself, then he ties his own hands and makes the word as preached by him ineffective and void. If prayerless men be found in the pew, then it hurts the preacher, robs him of an invaluable help, and interferes seriously with the success of his work. How great the need of a praying church to help in the preaching of the Word of the Lord! Both pew and pulpit are jointly concerned in this preaching business. It is a copartnership. The two go hand in hand. One must help the other, one can hinder the other. Both must work in perfect accord or serious damage will result and God's plan concerning the preacher and the preached word be defeated.

10

The Preacher's Cry: "Pray for Us!"

How far does praying for the preacher help preaching? It helps him personally and officially. It helps him to maintain a righteous life, it helps him in preparing his message, and it helps the word preached by him to run to its appointed goal, unhindered and unhampered.

A praying church creates a spiritual atmosphere most favorable to preaching. What preacher knowing anything of the real work of preaching doubts the veracity of this statement? The spirit of prayer in a congregation begets an atmosphere surcharged with the Spirit of the highest, removes obstacles and gives the Word of the Lord right of way. The very attitude of such a congregation constitutes an environment most encouraging and favorable to preaching. It renders preaching an easy task; it enables the word to run quickly and without friction, helped on by the warmth of souls engaged in prayer.

Men in the pew given to praying for the preacher are like the poles which hold up the wires along which the electric current runs. They are not the power, neither are they the specific agents in making the Word of the Lord effective. But they hold up the wires, along which the divine power runs to the hearts of men. They give liberty to the preacher, exemption from being straitened, and keep him from "getting in the brush." They make conditions favorable for the preaching of the gospel. Preachers, not a few, who know God, have had large experience and are aware of the truth of these statements. Yet how hard have they found it to preach in some places! This was because they had no "door of utterance," and were hampered in their delivery, there appearing no response whatever to their appeals. On the other hand, at other times, thought flowed easily, words came freely, and there was no failure in utterance. The preacher "had liberty," as the old men used to declare.

The preaching of the word to a prayerless congregation falls at the very feet of the preacher. It has no traveling force; it stops because the atmosphere is cold, unsympathetic, unfavorable to its running to the hearts of men and women. Nothing is there to help it along. Just as some prayers never go above the head of him who prays, so the preaching of some preachers goes no farther than the front of the pulpit from which it is delivered. It takes prayer in the pulpit and prayer in the pew to make preaching arresting, life-giving, and soul-saving.

The Word of God is inseparably linked with prayer. The two are conjoined, twins from birth, and twins by life. The apostles found themselves absorbed by the sacred and pressing duty of distributing the alms of the church, till time was not left for them to pray. They directed that other men should be appointed to discharge this task, that they might be the better able to give themselves continually to prayer and to the ministry of the word.

So it might likewise be said that prayer for the preacher by the church is also inseparably joined to preaching. A praying church is an invaluable help to the faithful preacher. The Word of the Lord runs in such a church, "and is glorified" in the saving of sinners, in the reclamation of backsliders, and in the sanctifying of believers. Paul connects the Word of God closely in prayer in writing to Timothy:

> For every creature of God is good and nothing to be refused, if it be received with thanksgiving. For it is sanctified by the Word of God and prayer.

And so the Word of the Lord is dependent for its rapid spread and for its full, and most glorious success in prayer.

Paul indicates that prayer transmutes the ills which come to the preacher: "For I know that this shall turn to my salvation through your prayer, and the supply of the Spirit of Jesus Christ." It was "through their prayer" he declares these benefits would come to him. And so it is "through the prayer of a church" that the pastor will be the beneficiary of large spiritual things.

In the latter part of the Epistle to the Hebrews, we have Paul's request for prayer for himself addressed to the Hebrew Christians, basing his request on the grave and eternal responsibilities of the office of a preacher:

> Obey them that have the rule over you and submit yourselves; for they watch for your souls as they that must give account, that they may do it with joy, and not with grief; for that is unprofitable for you. Pray for us; for we trust we have a good conscience in all things willing to live honestly.

How little does the church understand the fearful responsibility attaching to the office and work of the ministry! "For they watch for your souls as they that must give account." God's appointed watchmen, to warn when danger is nigh; God's messengers sent to rebuke, reprove, and exhort with all long-suffering; ordained as shepherds to protect the sheep against devouring wolves. How responsible is their position! And they are to give account to God for their work, and are to face a day of reckoning. How much do such men need the prayers of those to whom they minister! And who should be more ready to do this praying than God's people, his own church, those presumably who are in heart sympathy with the minister and his all-important work, divine in its origin.

Among the last messages of Jesus to his disciples are those found in the fourteenth, fifteenth, and sixteenth chapters of John's gospel. In the fourteenth, as well as in the others, are some very specific teachings about prayer, designed for their help and encouragement in their future work. We must never lose sight of the fact that these last discourses of Jesus Christ were given to disciples *alone,* away from the busy crowds, and seem primarily intended for them in their public ministry. In reality, they were words spoken to preachers, for these eleven men were to be the first preachers of the new dispensation.

With this thought in mind, we are able to see the tremendous importance given to prayer by our Lord, and the high place he gave it in the lifework of preachers, both in this day and in that day.

First our Lord proposes that he will pray for these disciples, that the Father might send them another Comforter, even the Spirit of truth, whom the world could not receive. He preceded this statement by a direct command to them to pray, to pray for anything, with the assurance that they would receive what they asked for.

If, therefore, there was value in their own praying, and it was of great worth that our Lord should intercede for them, then of course it would be worthwhile that the people to whom they would minister should also pray for them. It is no wonder then that the apostle Paul should take the key from our Lord, and several times break out with the urgent exhortation, "Pray for us."

True praying done by the laymen helps in many ways, but in one particular way. It helps very materially the preacher to be brave and true. Read Paul's request to the Ephesians:

> Praying always with all prayer and supplication in the Spirit, and watching thereunto with all perseverance, and supplication for all saints; and for me, that utterance may be given unto me, that I may open my mouth boldly, to make known the mystery of the gospel; for which I am an ambassador in bonds, that therein I may speak as I ought to speak.

How much of the boldness and loyalty of Paul was dependent upon the prayers of the church, or rather how much he was helped at these two points, we may not know. But unquestionably there must have come to him through the prayers of the Christians at Ephesus, Colossæ, and Thessalonica much aid in preaching the word, of which he would have been deprived had these churches not prayed for him. And in like manner, in modern times, has the gift of ready and effective utterance in the preacher been bestowed upon a preacher through the prayers of a praying church.

The apostle Paul did not desire to fall short of that most important quality in a preacher of the gospel, namely, boldness. He was no coward, or time-server, or man-pleaser, but he needed prayer, in order that he might not, through any kind of timidity, fail to declare the whole truth of God, or through fear of men, declare it in an apologetic, hesitating way. He desired to remove himself as far as possible from an attitude of this kind. His constant desire and effort was to declare the gospel with consecrated boldness and with freedom. "That I may open my mouth boldly, to make known the mystery of the gospel, that I may speak boldly, as I ought to speak," seemed to be his great desire, and it would appear that, at times, he was really afraid that he might exhibit cowardice, or be affected by the fear of the face of man.

This is a day that has urgent need of men after the mold of the great apostle—men of courage, brave and true, who are swayed not by the fear of men, or reduced to silence or apology by the dread of consequences. And one way to secure them is for the pew to engage in earnest prayer for the preachers.

In Paul's word to the Ephesian elders given when on his way to Jerusalem, Paul absolves himself from the charge of blood guiltiness, in that he had not failed to declare the whole counsel of God to them. To his Philippian brethren, also, he says, that through their prayers, he would prove to be neither ashamed nor afraid.

Nothing, perhaps, can be more detrimental to the advancement of the kingdom of God among men than a timid or doubtful statement of revealed truth. The man who states only the half of what he believes, stands side by side with the man who fully declares what he only half believes. No coward can preach the gospel, and declare the whole counsel of God. To do that, a man must be in the battle attitude not from passion, but by reason of deep conviction, strong conscience, and full-orbed courage. Faith is in the custody of a gallant heart while timidity surrenders, always, to a brave spirit. Paul prayed, and prevailed on others to pray that he might be a man of resolute courage, brave enough to do everything but sin. The result of this mutual praying is that history has no finer instance of courage in a minister of Jesus Christ than that displayed in the life of the apostle Paul. He stands in the premier position as a fearless, uncompromising, God-fearing preacher of the gospel of his Lord.

God seems to have taken great pains with his prophets of old time to save them from fear while delivering his messages to mankind. He sought in every way to safeguard his spokesmen from the fear of man, and by means of command, reasoning, and encouragement sought to render them fearless and true to their high calling. One of the besetting temptations of a preacher is the "fear" of the face of man. Unfortunately, not a few surrender to this fear, and either remain silent at times when they should be boldly eloquent, or temper with smooth words the stern mandate it is theirs to deliver. "The fear of man bringeth a snare." With this sore temptation Satan often besets the preacher of the word and few there be who have not felt the force of this temptation. It is the duty of ministers of the gospel to face this temptation to fear the face of man with resolute courage and to steel themselves against it, and, if need be, trample it under foot. To this important end, the preacher should be prayed for by his church. He needs deliverance from fear, and prayer is the agency whereby it can be driven away and freedom from the bondage of fear given to his soul.

We have a striking picture of the preacher's need of prayer, and of what a people's prayers can do for him in the seventeenth chapter of the Book of Exodus. Israel and Amalek were in battle, and the contest was severe and close. Moses stood on top of the hill with his rod lifted up in his hands, the symbol of power and victory. As long as Moses held up the rod, Israel prevailed, but when he let down his hand with the rod, Amalek prevailed. While the contest was in the balance, Aaron and Hur came to the rescue, and when Moses' hands were heavy, these two men "stayed up his hands . . . until the going down of the sun. And Joshua discomfited Amalek and his people."

By common consent, this incident in the history of ancient Israel has been recognized as a striking illustration of how a people may sustain their preacher by prayer, and of how victory comes when the people pray for their preacher.

Some of the Lord's very best men in Old Testament times had to be encouraged against fear by Almighty God. Moses himself was not free from the fear which harasses and compromises a leader. God told him to go to Pharaoh, in these words: "Come now therefore, and I will send thee unto Pharaoh, that thou mayest bring forth my people, the children of Israel, out of Egypt." But Moses, largely through fear, began to offer objections and excuses for not going, until God became angry with him, and said, finally, that he would send Aaron with Moses to do the talking, as long as Moses insisted that he "was slow of speech and of slow tongue." But the fact was, Moses was afraid of the face of Pharaoh, and it took God some time to circumvent his fears and nerve him to face the Egyptian monarch and deliver God's message to him.

And Joshua, too, the successor of Moses, and a man seemingly courageous, must needs be fortified by God against fear, lest he shrink from duty, and be reduced to discouragement and timidity. "Be strong and of good courage," God commanded him. "Have I not commanded thee? Be not afraid, neither be thou dismayed, for the Lord thy God is with thee whithersoever thou goest."

As good and true a man as Jeremiah was sorely tempted to fear and had to be warned and strengthened lest he prove false to his charge. When God ordained him a prophet unto the nations, Jeremiah began to excuse himself on the ground that he could not speak, being but a child in that regard. So the Lord had to safeguard him from the temptation of fear, that he might not prove faithless: "Thou therefore, gird up thy loins, and arise, and speak unto them," God said to his servant, "all that I command thee; be not dismayed at their faces, lest I confound thee before them."

Since these great men of old time were so beset with this temptation, and disposed to shrink from duty we need not be surprised that preachers of our own day are to be found in similar case. The devil is the same in all ages; nor has human nature undergone any change. How needful, then, that we pray for the leaders of our Israel especially that they may receive the gift of boldness, and speak the Word of God with courage.

This was one reason why Paul insisted so vigorously that the brethren pray for him, so that a door of utterance might be given him, and that he might be delivered from the fear of man, and blessed with holy boldness in preaching the word.

The challenge and demand of the world in our own day is that Christianity be made practical; that its precepts be expressed in practice, and brought down from the realm of the ideal to the levels of everyday life. This can be done only by praying men, who being much in sympathy with their ministers will not cease to bear them up in their prayers before God.

A preacher of the gospel cannot meet the demands made upon him, alone, any more than the vine can bear grapes without branches. The men who sit in the pews are to be the fruit-bearing ones. They are to translate the "ideal" of the pulpit into the "real" of daily life and action. But they will not do it, they cannot do it, if they be not devoted to God and much given to prayer. Devotion to God and devotion to prayer are one and the same thing.

11

Modern Examples of Prayer

GOD has not confined himself to Bible days in showing what can be done through prayer. Today also he is seen to be the same prayer-hearing God as aforetime. Even in these latter days he has not left himself without witness. Religious biography and church history, alike, furnish us with many noble examples and striking illustrations of prayer, its necessity, its worth, and its fruits, all tending to the encouragement of the faith of God's saints and all urging them on to more and better praying. God has not confined himself to Old and New Testament times in employing praying men as his agents in furthering his cause on earth, and he has placed himself under obligation to answer their prayers just as much as he did the saints of old. A selection from these praying saints of modern times will show us how they valued prayer, what it meant to them, and what it meant to God.

Take for example, the instance of Samuel Rutherford, the Scottish preacher, exiled to the north of Scotland, forbidden to preach, and banished from his home and pastoral charge. Rutherford lived between 1600 and 1661. He was a member of the Westminster Assembly, Principal of New College, and Rector of St. Andrews' University. He is said to have been one of the most moving and affectionate preachers of his time, or, perhaps, in any age of the church. Men said of him, "He is always praying," and concerning his and his wife's praying, one wrote: "He who had heard either pray or speak, might have learned to bemoan his ignorance. Oh, how many times have I been convinced by observing them of the evil of insincerity before God and unsavoriness in discourse! He so prayed for his people that he himself says, 'There I wrestled with the Angel and prevailed.'"

He was ordered to appear before Parliament to answer the charge of high treason, although a man of scholarly attainments and rare genius. At times he was depressed and gloomy; especially was this the case when he was first banished and silenced from preaching, for there were many murmurings and charges against him. But his losses and crosses were so sanctified that Christ became more and more to him. Marvelous are the statements of his esteem of Christ. This devoted man of prayer wrote many letters during his exile to preachers, to state officers, to lords temporal and spiritual, to honorable and holy men, to honorable and holy women, all breathing an intense devotion to Christ, and all born of a life of great devotion to prayer.

Ardor and panting after God have been characteristics of great souls in all ages of the church and Samuel Rutherford was a striking example of this fact. He was a living example of the truth that he who prays always, will be enveloped in devotion and joined to Christ in bonds of holy union.

Then there was Henry Martyn, scholar, saint, missionary, and apostle to India. Martyn was born February 18, 1781, and sailed for India August 31, 1805. He died at Tokai, Persia, October 16, 1812. Here is part of what he said about himself while a missionary:

> What a knowledge of man and acquaintance with the Scriptures, and what communion with God and study of my own heart ought to prepare me for the awful work of a messenger from God on business of the soul.

Said one of this consecrated missionary:

> Oh, to be able to emulate his excellencies, his elevation of piety, his diligence, his superiority to the world, his love for souls, his anxiety to improve all occasions to do souls good, his insight into the mystery of Christ, and his heavenly temper! These are the secrets of the wonderful impression he made in India.

It is interesting and profitable to note some of the things which Martyn records in his diary. Here is an example:

> "The ways of wisdom appear more sweet and reasonable than ever," he says, "and the world more insipid and vexatious. The chief thing I mourn over is my want of power, and lack of fervor in secret prayer, especially when attempting to plead for the heathen. Warmth does not increase within me in proportion to my light."

If Henry Martyn, so devoted, ardent, and prayerful, lamented his lack of power and want of fervor in prayer, how ought our cold and feeble praying abase us in the very dust? Alas, how rare are such praying men in the church of our own day!

Again we quote a record from his diary. He had been quite ill, but had recovered and was filled with thankfulness because it had pleased God to restore him to life and health again.

> "Not that I have yet recovered my former strength but I consider myself sufficiently restored to prosecute my journey. My daily prayer is that my late chastisement may have its intended effect, and make me, all the rest of my days, more humble and less self-confident.
>
> Self-confidence has often led me down fearful lengths, and would, without God's gracious interference, prove my endless perdition. I seem to be made to

feel this evil of my heart more than any other at this time. In prayer, or when I write or converse on the subject, Christ appears to me my life and my strength; but at other times I am thoughtless and bold, as if I had all life and strength in myself. Such neglects on our part are a diminution of our joys."

Among the last entries in this consecrated missionary's journal we find the following:

I sat in the orchard and thought, with sweet comfort and peace, of my God, in solitude, my Company, my Friend, my Comforter. Oh, when shall time give place to eternity!

Note the words, "in solitude"—away from the busy haunts of men, in a lonely place, like his Lord, he went out to meditate and pray.

Brief as this summary is, it suffices to show how fully and faithfully Henry Martyn exercised his ministry of prayer. The following may well serve to end our portrayal of him:

By daily weighing the Scriptures, with prayer, he waxed riper and riper in his ministry. Prayer and the Holy Scriptures were those wells of salvation out of which he drew daily the living water for his thirsty immortal soul. Truly may it be said of him, he prayed always with all prayer and supplication, in the Spirit, and watched thereunto with all perseverance.

David Brainerd, the missionary to the Indians, is a remarkable example of a praying man of God. Robert Hale thus speaks of him:

Such invincible patience and self-denial; such profound humility, exquisite prudence, indefatigable industry; such devotedness to God, or rather such absorption of the whole soul in zeal for the divine glory and the salvation of men, is scarcely to be paralleled since the age of the Apostles. Such was the intense ardor of his mind that it seems to have diffused the spirit of a martyr over the common incidents of his life.

Dr. A. J. Gordon speaks thus of Brainerd:

In passing through Northampton, Mass., I went into the old cemetery, swept off the snow that lay on the top of the slab, and I read these simple words:

Sacred to the memory of David Brainerd, the faithful and devoted missionary to the Susquehanna, Delaware and Stockbridge Indians of America, who died in this town, October 8th, 1717.

That was all there was on the slab. Now that great man did his greatest work by prayer. He was in the depths of those forests alone, unable to speak the language of the Indians, but he spent whole days literally in prayer. What was he praying for? He knew he could not reach these savages, for he did not understand their language. If he wanted to speak at all, he must find somebody who could vaguely interpret his thought. Therefore he knew that anything he could do must be absolutely dependent upon God. So he spent whole days in praying, simply that the power of the Holy Spirit might come upon him so unmistakably that these people would not be able to stand before him.

What was his answer? Once he preached through a drunken interpreter, a man so intoxicated that he could hardly stand up. This was the best he could do. Yet scores were converted through that sermon. We can account for it only that it was the tremendous power of God behind him.

Now this man prayed in secret in the forest. A little while afterward, William Carey read his life, and by its impulse he went to India. Payson read it as a young man, over twenty years old, and he said that he had never been so impressed by anything in his life as by the story of Brainerd. Murray McCheyne read it, and he likewise was impressed by it.

But all I care is simply to enforce this thought, that the hidden life, a life whose days are spent in communion with God, in trying to reach the source of power, is the life that moves the world. Those living such lives may be soon forgotten. There may be no one to speak a eulogy over them when they are dead. The great world may take no account of them. But by and by, the great moving current of their lives will begin to tell, as in the case of this young man, who died at about thirty years of age. The missionary spirit of this nineteenth century is more due to the prayers and consecration of this one man than to any other one.

So I say. And yet that most remarkable thing is that Jonathan Edwards, who watched over him all those months while he was slowly dying of consumption, should also say: "I praise God that it was in his providence that he should die in my house, that I might hear his prayers, and that I might witness his consecration, and that I might be inspired by his example."

When Jonathan Edwards wrote that great appeal to Christendom to unite in prayer for the conversion of the world, which has been the trumpet call of modern missions, undoubtedly it was inspired by this dying missionary.

To David Brainerd's spirit, John Wesley bore this testimony:

I preached and afterward made a collection for the Indian schools in America. A large sum of money is now collected. But will money convert heathens? Find preachers of David Brainerd's spirit, and nothing can stand before them. But without this, what will gold or silver do? No more than lead or iron.

Some selections from Brainerd's diary will be of value as showing what manner of man he was:

My soul felt a pleasing yet painful concern lest I should spend some moments without God. Oh, may I always live to God! In the evening I was visited by some friends, and spent the time in prayer, and such conversation as tended to edification. It was a comfortable season to my soul. I felt an ardent desire to spend every moment with God. God is unspeakably gracious to me continually. In time past, He has given me inexpressible sweetness in the performance of duty. Frequently my soul has enjoyed much of God, but has been ready to say, "Lord, it is good to be here," and so indulge sloth while I have lived on the sweetness of my feelings. But of late God has been pleased to keep my soul hungry almost continually, so that I have been filled with a kind of pleasing pain. When I really enjoy God, I feel my desires of him the more insatiable, and my thirstings after holiness the more unquenchable.

Oh, that I may feel this continual hunger, and not be retarded, but rather animated by every cluster from Canaan, to reach forward in the narrow way, for the full enjoyment and possession of the heavenly inheritance! Oh, may I never loiter in my heavenly journey!

It seems as if such an unholy wretch as I never could arrive at that blessedness, to be holy as God is holy. At noon I longed for sanctification and conformity to God. Oh, that is the one thing, the all!

Toward night enjoyed much sweetness in secret prayer, so that my soul longed for an arrival in the heavenly country, the blessed paradise of God.

If inquiry be made as to the secret of David Brainerd's heavenly spirit, his deep consecration, and exalted spiritual state, the answer will be found in the last sentence quoted above. He was given to *much secret prayer,* and was so close to God in his life and spirit that prayer brought forth much sweetness to his inner soul.

We have cited the foregoing cases as illustrative of the great fundamental fact that God's great servants are men devoted to the ministry of prayer; that they are God's agents on earth who serve him in this way, and who carry on his work by this holy means.

Louis Harms was born in Hanover, in 1809, and then came a time when he was powerfully convicted of sin. Said he, "I have never known what fear was. But when I came to the knowledge of my sins, I quaked before the wrath of God, so that my limbs trembled." He was mightily converted to God by reading the Bible. Rationalism, a dead orthodoxy, and worldliness, held the multitudes round Hermansburgh, his native town. When his father, a Lutheran minister, died, Louis succeeded him.

He began with all the energy of his soul to work for Christ, and to develop a church of a pure, strong type. The fruit was soon evident. There was a quickening on every hand, attendance at public services increased, reverence for the Bible grew, conversation on sacred things revived, while infidelity, worldliness, and dead orthodoxy vanished like a passing cloud. Harms proclaimed a conscious and present Christ, the Comforter, in the full energy of his mission, the revival of apostolic piety and power. The entire neighborhood became regular attendants at church, the Sabbath was restored to its sanctity, and hallowed with strict devotion, family altars were erected in the homes, and when the noon bell sounded, every head was bowed in prayer. In a very short time the whole aspect of the country was entirely changed. The revival in Hermansburgh was essentially a prayer revival, brought about by prayer and yielding fruits of prayer in a rich and an abundant ingathering.

William Carvosso, an old-time Methodist class-leader, was one of the best examples which modern times has afforded of what was probably the religious life of Christians in the apostolic age. He was a prayer-leader, a class-leader, a steward, and a trustee, but never aspired to be a preacher. Yet a preacher he was of the very first quality, and a master in the art and science of soul-saving. He was a singular instance of a man learning the simplest rudiments late in life. He had up to the age of sixty-five years never written a single sentence, yet he wrote letters which would make volumes, and a book which was regarded as a spiritual classic in the great worldwide Methodist church.

Not a page nor a letter, it is believed, was ever written by him on any other subject but religion. Here are some of his brief utterances which give us an insight into his religious character. "I want to be more like Jesus." "My soul thirsteth for thee, O God." "I see nothing will do, O God, but being continually filled with thy presence and glory."

This was the continual outcrying of his inner soul, and this was the strong inward impulse which moved the outward man. At one time we hear him exclaiming, "Glory to God! This is a morning without a cloud." Cloudless days were native to his sunny religion and his gladsome spirit. Continual prayer and turning all conversation toward Christ in every company and in every home, was the inexorable law he followed, until he was gathered home.

On the anniversary of his spiritual birth when he was born again, in great joyousness of spirit he calls it to mind, and breaks forth: "Blessed be thy name, O God! The last has been the best of the whole. I may say with Bunyan, 'I have got into that land where the sun shines night and day.' I thank thee, O my God, for this heaven, this element of love and joy, in which my soul now lives."

Here is a sample of Carvosso's spiritual experiences, of which he had many:

> I have sometimes had seasons of remarkable visitation from the presence of the Lord. I well remember one night when in bed being so filled, so overpowered with the glory of God, that had there been a thousand suns shining at noonday, the brightness of that divine glory would have eclipsed the whole. I was constrained to shout aloud for joy. It was the overwhelming power of saving grace. Now it was that I again received the impress of the seal and the earnest of the Spirit in my heart. Beholding as in a glass the glory of the Lord I was changed into the same image from glory to glory by the Spirit of the Lord. Language fails in giving but a faint description of what I there experienced. I can never forget it in time nor to all eternity.
>
> Many years before I was sealed by the Spirit in a somewhat similar manner. While walking out one day, I was drawn to turn aside on the public road, and under the canopy of the skies, I was moved to kneel down to pray. I had not long been praying with God before I was so visited from him that I was overpowered by the divine glory, and I shouted till I could be heard at a distance. It was a weight of glory that I seemed incapable of bearing in the body, and therefore I cried out, perhaps unwisely, Lord, stay thy hand. In this glorious baptism

these words came to my heart with indescribable power: "I have sealed thee unto the day of redemption."

Oh, I long to be filled more with God! Lord, stir me up more in earnest. I want to be more like Jesus. I see that nothing will do but being continually filled with the divine presence and glory. I know all that thou hast is mine, but I want to feel a close union. Lord, increase my faith.

Such was William Carvosso—a man whose life was impregnated with the spirit of prayer, who lived on his knees, so to speak, and who belonged to that company of praying saints which has blessed the earth.

Jonathan Edwards must be placed among the praying saints—one whom God mightily used through the instrumentality of prayer. As in the instance of the great New Englander, purity of heart should be ingrained in the very foundation areas of every man who is a true leader of his fellows and a minister of the gospel of Christ and a constant practicer in the holy office of prayer. A sample of the utterances of this mighty man of God is here given in the shape of a resolution which he formed, and wrote down:

> Resolved to exercise myself in this all my life long, viz., with the greatest openness to declare my ways to God, and to lay my soul open to God—all my sins, temptations, difficulties, sorrows, fears, hopes, desires, and everything and every circumstance.

We are not surprised, therefore, that the result of such impassioned and honest praying was to lead him to record in his diary:

> It was my continual strife day and night, and my constant inquiry how I should be more holy, and live more holily. The heaven I desired was a heaven of holiness. I went on with my eager pursuit after more holiness and conformity to Christ.

The character and work of Jonathan Edwards were exemplifications of the great truth that the ministry of prayer is the efficient agency in every truly God-ordered work and life. He himself gives some particulars about his life when a boy. He might well be called the "Isaiah of the Christian dispensation." There was united in him great mental powers, ardent piety, and devotion to study, unequalled save by his devotion to God. Here is what he says about himself:

> When a boy I used to pray five times a day in secret, and to spend much time in religious conversation with other boys. I used to meet with them to pray together. So it is God's will through his wonderful grace, that the prayers of his saints should be one great and principal means of carrying on the designs of Christ's kingdom in the world. Pray much for the ministers and the church of God.

The great powers of Edwards's mind and heart were exercised to procure an agreed union in extraordinary prayer of God's people everywhere. His life, efforts, and character are an exemplification of his statement.

The heaven I desire is a heaven spent with God; an eternity spent in the presence of divine love, and in holy communion with Christ.

At another time he said:

The soul of a true Christian appears like a little white flower in the spring of the year, low and humble on the ground, opening its bosom to receive the pleasant beams of the sun's glory, rejoicing as it were in a calm rapture, diffusing around a sweet fragrance, standing peacefully and lovingly in the midst of other flowers.

Again he writes:

Once as I rode out in the woods for my health, having alighted from my horse in a retired place, as my manner has been to walk for divine contemplation and prayer, I had a view, that for me was extraordinary, of the glory of the Son of God as Mediator between God and man, and of his wonderful, great, full, pure, and sweet grace and love, and his meek and gentle condescension. This grace that seemed so calm and sweet, appeared also great above the heavens. The person of Christ appeared ineffably excellent with an excellency great enough to swallow up all thought and conception, which continued, as near as I can judge, about an hour. It kept me the greater part of the time in a flood of tears and weeping aloud. I felt an ardency of soul to be, what I know not otherwise how to express, emptied and annihilated, to lie in the dust to be full of Christ alone, to love Him with my whole heart.

As it was with Jonathan Edwards, so it is with all great intercessors. They come into that holy and elect condition of mind and heart by a thorough self-dedication to God, by periods of God's revelation to them, making distinct marked eras in their spiritual history, eras never to be forgotten, in which faith mounts up with wings as eagles, and has given it a new and fuller vision of God, a stronger grasp of faith, a sweeter, clearer vision of all things heavenly, and eternal, and a blessed intimacy with, and access to, God.

12

Modern Examples of Prayer
(Continued)

LADY MAXWELL was contemporary with John Wesley, and a fruit of Methodism in its earlier phases. She was a woman of refinement, of culture, and of deep piety. Separating herself entirely from the world, she sought and found the deepest religious experience, and was a woman fully set apart to God. Her life was one of prayer, of complete consecration to God, living to bless others. She was noted for her systematic habits of life, which entered into and controlled her religion. Her time was economized and ordered for God. She arose at four o'clock in the morning, and attended preaching at five o'clock. After breakfast she held a family service. Then, from eleven to twelve o'clock she observed a season of intercessory prayer. The rest of the day was given to reading, visiting, and acts of benevolence. Her evenings were spent in reading. At night, before retiring, religious services were held for the family and sometimes in praising God for his mercies.

Rarely has God been served with more intelligence, or out of a richer experience, a nobler ardor, a richer nobility of soul. Strongly, spiritually, and ardently attached to Wesley's doctrine of entire dedication, she sought it with persistency, and a never flagging zeal. She obtained it by faith and prayer, and illustrated it in a life as holy and as perfect as is given mortals to reach. If this great feature of Wesley's teaching had today models and teachers with the profound spiritual understanding and experience as had Fletcher of Madeley and Lady Maxwell of Edinburgh, it would not have been so misunderstood, but would have commended itself to the good and pure everywhere by holy lives, if not by its verbiage.

Lady Maxwell's diary yields some rich counsel for secret prayer, holy experience, and consecrated living. One of the entries runs as follows:

> Of late I feel painfully convinced that I do not pray enough. Lord, give me the spirit of prayer and of supplication. Oh, what a cause of thankfulness is it that we have a gracious God to whom to go on all occasions! Use and enjoy this privilege and you can never be miserable. Who gives thanks for this royal privilege? It puts God in everything, his wisdom, power, control and safety. Oh, what

an unspeakable privilege is prayer! Let us give thanks for it. I do not prove all the power of prayer that I wish.

Thus we see that the remedy for nonpraying is *praying*. The cure for little praying is more praying. Praying can procure all things necessary for our good.

For this excellent woman praying embraced all things and included everything. To one of her most intimate friends she writes:

> I wish I could provide you with a proper maid, but it is a difficult matter. You have my prayers for it, and if I hear of one I will let you know.

So small a matter as the want of a housemaid for a friend was with her an event not too small to take to God in prayer.

In the same letter, she tells her friend that she wants "more faith. Cry mightily for it, and stir up the gift of God that is in you."

Whether the need was a small secular thing as a servant, or a great spiritual grace, prayer was the means to attain that end and supply that want. "There is nothing," she writes to a dear correspondent, "so hurtful to the nervous system as anxiety. It preys upon the vitals and weakens the whole frame, and what is more than all, it grieves the Holy Spirit." Her remedy, again, for a common evil, was prayer.

How prayer disburdens us of care by bringing God in to relieve and possess and hold! The apostle Paul says:

> Be careful for nothing but in everything by prayer and supplication, with thanksgiving, let your requests be made known unto God. And the peace of God which passeth all understanding shall keep your hearts and minds through Christ Jesus.

The figure is that of a beleaguered and distressed garrison, unable to protect the fort from the enemies which assault it, into which strong reinforcements are poured. Into the heart oppressed, distracted and discouraged, true prayer brings God, who holds it in perfect peace and in perfect safety. This Lady Maxwell fully understood theoretically, but which was better, experimentally.

Christ Jesus is the only cure for undue care and over anxiety of soul, and we secure God, his presence and his peace by prayer. Care is so natural and so strong, that none but God can eject it. It takes God, the presence and personality of God himself, to oust the care and to enthrone quietness and peace. When Christ comes in with his peace, all tormenting fears are gone, trepidation and harrowing anxieties capitulate to the reign of peace, and all disturbing elements depart. Anxious thought and care assault the soul, and feebleness, faintness, and cowardice are within. Prayer reinforces with God's peace, and the heart is kept by him. "Thou wilt keep him in perfect peace whose mind is stayed on thee." All now is safety, quietness and assurance. "The work of righteousness is peace, and the effect of righteousness, quietness, and assurance forever."

But to ensure this great peace, prayer must pass into strenuous, insistent, personal supplication, and thanksgiving must bloom into full flower. Our exposed condition of heart must be brought to the knowledge of God, by prayer and supplication, with thanksgiving. The peace of God will keep the heart and thoughts, fixed and fearless. Peace, deep, exhaustless, wide, flowing like a river, will come in.

Referring again to Lady Maxwell, we hear her saying:

> God is daily teaching me more simplicity of spirit, and makes me willing to receive all as his unmerited gift, and to call on him for everything I need, as I need it, and he supplies my wants according to existing needs. But I have certainly felt more of it this last eighteen months than in former periods. I wish to pray without ceasing. I see the necessity of praying always, and not fainting.

Again we hear her declaring: "I wish to be much in prayer. I greatly need it. The prayer of faith shuts or opens heaven. Come, Lord, and turn my captivity." If we felt the need of prayer as this saintly woman did, we could bear her company in her saintly ascension. Prayer truly "shuts or opens heaven." Oh, for a quality of faith that would test to the uttermost the power of prayer!

Lady Maxwell utters a great truth when she says:

> When God is at work either among a people, or in the heart of an individual, the adversary of souls is peculiarly at work also. A belief of the former should prevent discouragement, and a fear of the latter should stir us up to much prayer. Oh, the power of faithful prayer! I live by prayer! May you prove its sovereign efficacy in every difficult case.

We find a record among Lady Maxwell's writings which shows us that in prayer and meditation she obtained enlarged views of the full salvation of God, and what is thus discovered, faith goes out after, and according to its strength are its returns.

> I daily feel the need of the precious blood of sprinkling and dwell continually under its influence, and most sensibly feel its sovereign efficacy. It is by momentary faith in this blood alone that I am saved from sin. Prayer is my chief employ.

If this last statement "prayer, the chief employ" had ever been true of God's people, this world would have been by this time quite another world, and God's glory, instead of being dim, and shadowy, and only in spots, would now shine with universal and unrivaled effulgence and power.

Here is another record of her ardent and faithful praying: "Lately, I have been favored with a more ardent spirit of praying than almost ever formerly."

We need to study these words—"favored with a more ardent spirit of pray-ing"—for they are pregnant words. The spirit of prayer, the ardent spirit of prayer and its increase, and the more ardent spirit of prayer—all these are of God. They are given in answer to prayer. The spirit of prayer and the more ardent spirit are the result of ardent, importunate, secret prayer.

At another time, Lady Maxwell declared that secret prayer was the means whereby she derived the greatest spiritual benefit.

> I do indeed prove it to be an especial privilege. I could not live without it, though I do not always find comfort in it. I still ardently desire an enlarged sphere of usefulness, and find it comfortable to embrace the opportunities afforded me.

An "enlarged sphere of usefulness" is certainly a proper theme of intense prayer, but that prayer must ever be accompanied by an improvement of the opportunities afforded by the present.

Many pages might be filled with extracts from Lady Maxwell's diary as to the vital importance of, and the nature of the ministry of prayer, but we must forbear. For many years she was in ardent supplication for an enlargement of her sphere of usefulness, but all these years of ardent praying may be con-densed into one statement:

> My whole soul has been thirsting after a larger sphere of action agreeable to the promises of a faithful God. For these few last weeks I have been led to plead earnestly for more holiness. Lord, give me both, that I may praise thee.

These two things, for which this godly woman prayed, must go together. They are one, and not to be separated. The desire for a larger field of work without the accompanying desire for an increase of consecration, is perilous, and may be supremely selfish, the offspring of spiritual pride.

John Fletcher, also a contemporary of John Wesley, was intimatele associat-ed with the founder of Methodism. He was a scholar of courtesy and refine-ment, a strong, original thinker, eloquent in simplicity and truth. That which qualified him as a spiritual leader was his exceedingly great faith in God, his nearness to God and his perfect assurance of dear unquestioned relationship to his Lord. Fletcher had profound convictions concerning the truth of God, a deep and perpetual communion with his Lord and Savior, and was profound and humble in his knowledge of God and Christian experience. He was a man of deep spiritual insight into the things of God, and his thorough earnestness, his truth, and his consecration, marked him as a man of God, well equipped by all these things to be a leader in Israel.

Unceasing prayer was the sign and secret of Fletcher's sainthood, its power and influence. His whole life was one of prayer. So intently was his mind fixed on God that he sometimes said, "I would not rise from my seat without lifting up my heart to God." A friend relates the fact that whenever they met, his first salute was, "Do I meet you praying?" If they were talking on theology, in the midst of it he would break off abruptly and say, "Where are our hearts now?" If the misconduct of any person who was absent was mentioned, he would say, "Let us pray for him."

The very walls of his room—so it was said—were "stained" by the breath of his prayers. Spiritually, Madeley was a dreary, desolate desert when he went to live there, but it was so revolutionized by his prayers that it bloomed and blossomed like the garden of the Lord. A friend of his writes thus of Fletcher:

> Many of us have at times gone with him aside, and there we would continue for two or three hours, wrestling like Jacob for the blessing, praying one after another. And I have seen him on these occasions so filled with the love of God that he could contain no more, but would cry out, "O my God, withhold thy hand or the vessel will burst!" His whole life was a life of prayer.

John Foster, a man of exalted piety and deep devotion to God, while on his deathbed, thus spoke concerning prayer when about to depart this life:

> Pray without ceasing has been the sentence repeating itself in my silent thoughts, and I am sure that it will be, it must be, my practice till the last conscious hour of my life. O why was it not my practice throughout that long, indolent, inanimate half century past! I often think mournfully of the difference it would have made in me. Now there remains so little time for a more genuine, effective spiritual life.

The Reformation of the fifteenth century owes its origin to prayer. In all his lifework, begun, continued, and ended, Martin Luther was instant in prayer. The secret of his extraordinary activity is found in this statement: "I have so much work to do that I cannot get along without giving three hours daily of my best time to prayer." Another of his sayings was, "It takes meditation and prayer to make a divine," while his everyday motto was, "He that has prayed well, has studied well."

At another time he thus confessed his lack: "I was short and superficial in prayer this morning," he says. How often is this the case with us! Let it be remembered that the source of decline in religion and the proof of decline in a Christian life is found just here, in "short and superficial praying." Such praying betokens and secures strangeness with God.

William Wilberforce once said of himself: "I have been keeping too late hours, and hence have had but a hurried half hour to myself. I am lean and cold and hard. I had better allow more time, say two hours, or an hour-and-a-half, daily to religious exercises."

He must be much skilled and accustomed to long praying whose short prayers are not superficial. Short prayers make shallow lives. Longer praying would work like magic in many a decayed spiritual life. A holy life would not be so difficult and rare a thing if our praying was not so brief, cold, and superficial.

George Muller, that remarkable man of such simple yet strong faith in God, a man of prayer and Bible reading, founder and promoter of the noted orphanage in England, which cared for hundreds of orphan children, conducted the institution solely by faith and prayer. He never asked a man for anything, but simply trusted in the providence of God, and it is a notorious fact that never did the residents of the home lack any good thing. From his paper he always excluded money matters, and financial difficulties found no place in it. Nor would he mention the sums which had been given him, nor the names of those who made contributions. He never spoke of his wants to others nor asked a donation. The story of his life and the history of this orphanage read like a chapter from the Scriptures. The secret of his success was found in this simple statement made by him: "I went to my God and prayed diligently, and received what I needed." That was the simple course which he pursued. There was nothing he insisted on with greater earnestness than that, be the expenses what they might be, let them increase ever so suddenly, he must not beg for anything. There was nothing in which he took more delight and showed more earnestness in telling than that he had prayed for every want which ever came to him in his great work. His was a work of continuous and most importunate praying, and he always confidently claimed that God had guided him throughout it all. A stronger proof of a divine providence, and of the power of simple faith and of answered prayer, cannot be found in church history or religious biography.

In writing to a friend at one time, John Wesley helps, urges, and prays, as we will see from the following from his own pen: "Have you received a gleam of light from above, a spark of faith? If you have, let it not go! Hold fast by his grace that earnest of your inheritance. Come just as you are, and come boldly to the throne of grace. You need not delay. Even now the bowels of Jesus yearn over you. What have you to do with tomorrow? I love you today. And how much more does he love you?"

> He pities still his wandering sheep,
> And longs to bring you to his fold.
>
> Today hear his voice,
> the voice of him that speaks
> as never man spake.

The seekings of Madame Guyon after God were sincere, and her yearnings were strong and earnest. She applied to a devout Franciscan friar for advice and comfort. She stated her convictions and told him of her long and fruitless seeking. After she had finished speaking to him, the friar remained silent for some time, in inward meditation and prayer. Then he said to her:

> Your efforts have been unsuccessful, because you have *sought without* what you can only *find within*. Accustom yourself to seek God in your heart, and you will not fail to find him.

"When God has specially promised the thing," said Charles G. Finney, "we are bound to believe we shall receive it when we pray for it. You have no right to put in an 'if,' and say, 'Lord, *if* it be thy will, give me thy Holy Spirit.' This is to insult God. To put an 'if' in God's promise when God has put none there, is tantamount to charging God with being insincere. It is like saying, 'O God, if thou art in earnest in making these promises, grant us the blessing we pray for.'"

We may fittingly conclude this chapter by quoting a word of Adoniram Judson, the noted missionary to Burma. Speaking of the prevailing power of prayer he said:

> "Nothing is impossible," said one of the seven sages of Greece, "to industry." Let us change the word, *industry,* to persevering prayer, and the motto will be more Christian and more worthy of universal adoption. God loves importunate prayer so much that he will not give us much blessing without it. God says, "Behold I will do a new thing; now it shall spring forth; shall ye not know it? I will even make a way in the wilderness and rivers in the desert. This people have I formed for myself; they shall shew forth my praise."

Power Through Prayer

1

Men of Prayer Are Needed

WE are constantly on a stretch, if not on a strain, to devise new methods, new plans, new organizations to advance the church and secure enlargement and efficiency for the gospel. This trend of the day has a tendency to lose sight of the man or sink the man in the plan or organization. God's plan is to make much of the man, far more of him than of anything else. Men are God's method. The church is looking for better methods; God is looking for better men. "There was a man sent from God whose name was John." The dispensation that heralded and prepared the way for Christ was bound up in that man John. "Unto us a child is born, unto us a son is given." The world's salvation comes out of that cradled son. When Paul appeals to the personal character of the men who rooted the gospel in the world, he solves the mystery of their success. The glory and efficiency of the gospel is staked on the men who proclaim it. When God declares that "the eyes of the Lord run to and fro throughout the whole earth, to show himself strong in the behalf of them whose heart is perfect toward him," he declares the necessity of men and his dependence on them as a channel through which to exert his power on the world. This vital, urgent truth is one that this age of machinery is apt to forget. The forgetting of it is as baneful on the work of God as would be the striking of the sun from his sphere. Darkness, confusion, and death would ensue.

What the church needs today is not more machinery or better, not new organizations or more and novel methods, but men whom the Holy Spirit can use—men of prayer, men mighty in prayer. The Holy Spirit does not flow through methods, but through men. He does not come on machinery, but on men. He does not anoint plans, but men—men of prayer.

An eminent historian has said that the accidents of personal character have more to do with the revolutions of nations than either philosophic historians or democratic politicians will allow. This truth has its application in full to the gospel of Christ, the character and conduct of the followers of Christ—Christianize the world, transfigure nations and individuals. Of the preachers of the gospel it is eminently true.

The character as well as the fortunes of the gospel is committed to the preacher. He makes or mars the message from God to man. The preacher is the golden pipe through which the divine oil flows. The pipe must not only be golden, but open and flawless, that the oil may have a full, unhindered, unwasted flow.

The man makes the preacher. God must make the man. The messenger is, if possible, more than the message. The preacher is more than the sermon. The preacher makes the sermon. As the life-giving milk from the mother's bosom is but the mother's life, so all the preacher says is tinctured, impregnated by what the preacher is. The treasure is in earthen vessels, and the taste of the vessel impregnates and may discolor. The man, the whole man, lies behind the sermon. Preaching is not the performance of an hour. It is the outflow of a life. It takes twenty years to make a sermon, because it takes twenty years to make the man. The true sermon is a thing of life. The sermon grows because the man grows. The sermon is forceful because the man is forceful. The sermon is holy because the man is holy. The sermon is full of the divine unction because the man is full of the divine unction.

Paul termed it "my gospel;" not that he had degraded it by his personal eccentricities or diverted it by selfish appropriation but the gospel was put into the heart and lifeblood of the man Paul as a personal trust to be executed by his Pauline traits, to be set aflame and empowered by the fiery energy of his fiery soul. Paul's sermons—what were they? Where are they? Skeletons, scattered fragments, afloat on the sea of inspiration! But the man Paul, greater than his sermons, lives forever, in full form, feature and stature, with his molding hand on the church. The preaching is but a voice. The voice in silence dies, the text is forgotten, the sermon fades from memory; the preacher lives.

The sermon cannot rise in its life-giving forces above the man. Dead men give out dead sermons, and dead sermons kill. Everything depends on the spiritual character of the preacher. Under the Jewish dispensation the high priest had inscribed in jeweled letters on a golden frontlet: "Holiness to the Lord." So every preacher in Christ's ministry must be molded into and mastered by this same holy motto. It is a crying shame for the Christian ministry to fall lower in holiness of character and holiness of aim than the Jewish priesthood. Jonathan Edwards said: "I went on with my eager pursuit after more holiness and conformity to Christ. The heaven I desired was a heaven of holiness." The gospel of Christ does not move by popular waves. It has no self-propagating power. It moves as the men who have charge of it move. The preacher must impersonate the gospel. Its divine, most distinctive features must be embodied in him. The constraining power of love must be in the preacher as a projecting, eccentric, an all-commanding, self-oblivious force. The energy of self-denial must be his being, his heart and blood and bones. He must go forth as a man among men, clothed with humility, abiding in meekness, wise as a serpent, harmless as a dove; the bonds of a servant with the spirit of a king, a king in high, royal, independent bearing, with the simplicity and sweetness of a child. The preacher must throw himself, with all the abandon of a perfect, self-emptying faith and a self-consuming zeal, into his work for the salvation of men. Hearty, heroic, compassionate, fearless martyrs must the men be who take hold of and shape a generation for God. If they be timid time servers, place seekers, if they be men pleasers or men fearers, if their faith has a weak hold on God or his Word, if their denial be broken by any phase of self or the world, they cannot take hold of the church nor the world for God.

The preacher's sharpest and strongest preaching should be to himself. His most difficult, delicate, laborious, and thorough work must be with himself. The training of the twelve was the great, difficult, and enduring work of Christ. Preachers are not sermon makers, but men makers and saint makers, and he only is well-trained for this business who has made himself a man and a saint. It is not great talents nor great learning nor great preachers that God needs, but men great in holiness, great in faith, great in love, great in fidelity, great for God—men always preaching by holy sermons in the pulpit, by holy lives out of it. These can mold a generation for God.

After this order, the early Christians were formed. Men they were of solid mold, preachers after the heavenly type—heroic, stalwart, soldierly, saintly. Preaching with them meant self-denying, self-crucifying, serious, toilsome, martyr business. They applied themselves to it in a way that told on their generation, and formed in its womb a generation yet unborn for God. The preaching man is to be the praying man. Prayer is the preacher's mightiest weapon. An almighty force in itself, it gives life and force to all.

The real sermon is made in the closet. The man—God's man—is made in the closet. His life and his profoundest convictions were born in his secret communion with God. The burdened and tearful agony of his spirit, his weightiest and sweetest messages were received when alone with God. Prayer makes the man: prayer makes the preacher; prayer makes the pastor. The pulpit of this day is weak in praying. The pride of learning is against the dependent humility of prayer. Prayer is with the pulpit too often only official—a performance for the routine of service. Prayer is not to the modern pulpit the mighty force it was in Paul's life or Paul's ministry. Every preacher who does not make prayer a mighty factor in his own life and ministry is weak as a factor in God's work and is powerless to project God's cause in this world.

2

Our Sufficiency Is of God

THE sweetest graces by a slight perversion may bear the bitterest fruit. The sun gives life, but sunstrokes are death. Preaching is to give life; it may kill. The preacher holds the keys; he may lock as well as unlock. Preaching is God's great institution for the planting and maturing of spiritual life. When properly executed, its benefits are untold; when wrongly executed, no evil can exceed its damaging results. It is an easy matter to destroy the flock if the shepherd be unwary or the pasture be destroyed, easy to capture the citadel if the watchmen be asleep or the food and water be poisoned. Invested with such gracious prerogatives, exposed to so great evils, involving so many grave responsibilities, it would be a parody on the shrewdness of the devil and a libel on his character and reputation if he did not bring his master influences to adulterate the preacher and the preaching. In face of all this, the exclamatory interrogatory of Paul, "Who is sufficient for these things?" is never out of order.

Paul says: "Our sufficiency is of God, who also hath made us able ministers of the new testament; not of the letter, but of the spirit: for the letter killeth, but the spirit giveth life." The true ministry is God-touched, God-enabled, and God-made. The Spirit of God is on the preacher in anointing power, the fruit of the Spirit is in his heart, the Spirit of God has vitalized the man and the word; his preaching gives life, gives life as the spring gives life; gives life as the resurrection gives life; gives ardent life as the summer gives ardent life; gives fruitful life as the autumn gives fruitful life. The life-giving preacher is a man of God, whose heart is ever athirst for God, whose soul is ever following hard after God, whose eye is single to God, and in whom by the power of God's Spirit the flesh and the world have been crucified and his ministry is like the generous flood of a life-giving river.

The preaching that kills is nonspiritual preaching. The ability of the preaching is not from God. Lower sources than God have given to it energy and stimulant. The Spirit is not evident in the preacher nor his preaching. Many kinds of forces may be projected and stimulated by preaching that kills, but they are not spiritual forces. They may resemble spiritual forces, but are only the shadow, the counterfeit; life they may seem to have, but the life is magnetized. The preaching that kills is the letter; shapely and orderly it may be, but it is the letter still, the dry, husky letter, the empty, bald shell. The letter may have the germ of life in it, but it has not breath of spring to evoke it; winter seeds they are, as hard as the winter's soil, as icy as the winter's air, not thawing nor germinating by them. This letter-preaching has the truth. But even divine truth has no life-giving energy alone; it must be energized by the Spirit, with all God's forces at its back. Truth unquickened by God's Spirit deadens as much as, or more than, error. It may be the truth without admixture; but without the Spirit its shade and touch are deadly, its truth error, its light darkness. The letter-preaching is unctionless, neither mellowed nor oiled by the Spirit. There may be tears, but tears cannot run God's machinery; tears may be but summer's breath on a snow-covered iceberg, nothing but surface slush. Feelings and earnestness there may be, but it is the emotion of the actor and the earnestness of the attorney. The preacher may feel from the kindling of his own sparks, be eloquent over his own exegesis, earnest in delivering the product of his own brain; the professor may usurp the place and imitate the fire of the apostle; brains and nerves may serve the place and feign the work of God's Spirit, and by these forces the letter may glow and sparkle like an illumined text, but the glow and sparkle will be as barren of life as the field sown with pearls. The death-dealing element lies back of the words, back of the sermon, back of the occasion, back of the manner, back of the action. The great hindrance is in the preacher himself. He has not in himself the mighty life-creating forces. There may be no discount on his orthodoxy, honesty, cleanness, or earnestness; but somehow the man, the inner man, in its secret places has never broken down and surrendered to God, his inner life is not a great highway for the transmission of God's message, God's power. Somehow self and not God rules in the holy of holies. Somewhere, all unconscious to himself, some spiritual nonconductor has touched his inner being, and the divine current has been arrested. His inner being has never felt its thorough spiritual bankruptcy, its utter powerlessness; he has never learned to cry out with an indescribable cry of self-despair and self-helplessness till God's power and God's fire comes in and fills, purifies, empowers. Self-esteem, self-ability in some pernicious shape has defamed and violated the temple which should be held sacred for God. Life-giving preaching costs the preacher much—death to self, crucifixion to the world, the travail of his own soul. Only crucified preaching can give life. Crucified preaching can come only from a crucified man.

3

The Letter Killeth

THE preaching that kills may be, and often is, orthodox—dogmatically, inviolably orthodox. We love orthodoxy. It is good. It is the best. It is the clean, clear-cut teaching of God's Word, the trophies won by truth in its conflict with error, the levees which faith has raised against the desolating floods of honest or reckless misbelief or unbelief; but orthodoxy, clear and hard as crystal, suspicious and militant, may be but the letter well-shaped, well-named, and well-learned, the letter which kills. Nothing is so dead as a dead orthodoxy, too dead to speculate, too dead to think, to study, or to pray.

The preaching that kills may have insight and grasp of principles, may be scholarly and critical in taste, may have every minutiæ of the derivation and grammar of the letter, may be able to trim the letter into its perfect pattern, and illume it as Plato and Cicero may be illumined, may study it as a lawyer studies his textbooks to form his brief or to defend his case, and yet be like a frost, a killing frost. Letter-preaching may be eloquent, enameled with poetry and rhetoric, sprinkled with prayer, spiced with sensation, illumined by genius, and yet these be but the massive or chaste, costly mountings, the rare and beautiful flowers which coffin the corpse. The preaching which kills may be without scholarship, unmarked by any freshness of thought or feeling, clothed in tasteless generalities or vapid specialties, with style irregular, slovenly, savoring neither of closet or study, graced neither by thought, expression, or prayer. Under such preaching how wide and utter the desolation! How profound the spiritual death!

This letter-preaching deals with the surface and shadow of things, and not the things themselves. It does not penetrate the inner part. It has no deep insight into, no strong grasp of, the hidden life of God's Word. It is true to the outside, but the outside is the hull which must be broken and penetrated for the kernel. The letter may be dressed so as to attract and be fashionable, but the attraction is not toward God nor is the fashion for heaven. The failure is in the preacher. God has not made him. He has never been in the hands of God like clay in the hands of the potter. He has been busy about the sermon, its thought and finish, its drawing and impressive forces; but the deep things of God have never been sought, studied, fathomed, experienced by him. He has never stood before "the throne high and lifted up," never heard the

452

seraphim song, never seen the vision nor felt the rush of that awful holiness, and cried out in utter abandon and despair under the sense of weakness and guilt, and had his life renewed, his heart touched, purged, inflamed by the live coal from God's altar. His ministry may draw people to him, to the church, to the form and ceremony; but no true drawings to God, no sweet, holy, divine communion induced. The church has been frescoed but not edified, pleased but not sanctified. Life is suppressed; a chill is on the summer air; the soil is baked. The city of our God becomes the city of the dead; the church a graveyard, not an embattled army. Praise and prayer are stifled; worship is dead. The preacher and the preaching have helped sin, not holiness; peopled hell, not heaven.

Preaching which kills is prayerless preaching. Without prayer the preacher creates death, and not life. The preacher who is feeble in prayer is feeble in life-giving forces. The preacher who has retired prayer as a conspicuous and largely prevailing element in his own character has shorn his preaching of its distinctive life-giving power. Professional praying there is and will be, but professional praying helps the preaching to its deadly work. Professional praying chills and kills both preaching and praying. Much of the lax devotion and lazy, irreverent attitudes in congregational praying are attributable to professional praying in the pulpit. Long, discursive, dry, and inane are the prayers in many pulpits. Without unction or heart, they fall like a killing frost on all the graces of worship. Death-dealing prayers they are. Every vestige of devotion has perished under their breath. The deader they are, the longer they grow. A plea for short praying, live praying, real heart praying, praying by the Holy Spirit—direct, specific, ardent, simple, unctuous in the pulpit—is in order. A school to teach preachers how to pray, as God counts praying, would be more beneficial to true piety, true worship, and true preaching than all theological schools.

Stop! Pause! Consider! Where are we? What are we doing? Preaching to kill? Praying to kill? Praying to God! the great God, the maker of all worlds, the judge of all men! What reverence! What simplicity! What sincerity! What truth in the inward parts is demanded! How real we must be! How hearty! Prayer to God is the noblest exercise, the loftiest effort of man, the most real thing! Shall we not discard forever accursed preaching that kills and prayer that kills, and do the real thing, the mightiest thing—prayerful praying, life-creating preaching, bring the mightiest force to bear on heaven and earth and draw on God's exhaustless and open treasure for the need and beggary of man?

4

Tendencies to Be Avoided

THERE are two extreme tendencies in the ministry. The one is to shut itself out from communicating with the people. The monk, the hermit were illustrations of this; they shut themselves out from men to be more with God. They failed, of course. Our being with God is of use only as we expend its priceless benefits on men. This age, neither with preacher nor with people, is much intent on God. Our hankering is not that way. We shut ourselves to our study, we become students, bookworms, Bible worms, sermon makers, noted for literature, thought, and sermons; but the people and God, where are they? Out of heart, out of mind. Preachers who are great thinkers, great students must be the greatest of prayers, or else they will be the greatest of backsliders, heartless professionals, rationalistic, less than the least of preachers in God's estimate.

The other tendency is to thoroughly popularize the ministry. He is no longer God's man, but a man of affairs, of the people. He prays not, because his mission is to the people. If he can move the people, create an interest, a sensation in favor of religion, an interest in church work—he is satisfied. His personal relation to God is no factor in his work. Prayer has little or no place in his plans. The disaster and ruin of such a ministry cannot be computed by earthly arithmetic. What the preacher is in prayer to God, for himself, for his people, so is his power for real good to men, so is his true fruitfulness, his true fidelity to God, to man, for time, for eternity.

It is impossible for the preacher to keep his spirit in harmony with the divine nature of his high calling without much prayer. That the preacher by dint of duty and laborious fidelity to the work and routine of the ministry can keep himself in trim and fitness is a serious mistake. Even sermon-making, incessant and taxing as an art, as a duty, as a work, or as a pleasure, will engross and harden, will estrange the heart, by neglect of prayer, from God. The scientist loses God in nature. The preacher may lose God in his sermon.

Prayer freshens the heart of the preacher, keeps it in tune with God and in sympathy with the people, lifts his ministry out of the chilly air of a profession, fructifies routine and moves every wheel with the facility and power of a divine unction.

Mr. Spurgeon says: "Of course the preacher is above all others distinguished as a man of prayer. He prays as an ordinary Christian, else he were a hypocrite. He prays more than ordinary Christians, else he were disqualified for the office he has undertaken. If you as ministers are not very prayerful, you are to be pitied. If you become lax in sacred devotion, not only will you need to be pitied but your people also, and the day cometh in which you shall be ashamed and confounded. All our libraries and studies are mere emptiness compared with our closets. Our seasons of fasting and prayer at the tabernacle have been high days indeed; never has heaven's gate stood wider; never have our hearts been nearer the central glory."

The praying which makes a prayerful ministry is not a little praying put in as we put flavor to give it a pleasant smack, but the praying must be in the body, and form the blood and bones. Prayer is no petty duty, put into a corner; no piecemeal performance made out of the fragments of time which have been snatched from business and other engagements of life; but it means that the best of our time, the heart of our time and strength must be given. It does not mean the closet absorbed in the study or swallowed up in the activities of ministerial duties; but it means the closet first, the study and activities second, both study and activities freshened and made efficient by the closet. Prayer that affects one's ministry must give tone to one's life. The praying which gives color and bent to character is no pleasant, hurried pastime. It must enter as strongly into the heart and life as Christ's "strong crying and tears" did; must draw out the soul into agony of desire as Paul's did; must be an inwrought fire and force like the "effectual, fervent prayer" of James; must be of that quality which, when put into the golden censer and incensed before God, works mighty spiritual throes and revolutions.

Prayer is not a little habit pinned on to us while we were tied to our mother's apron strings; neither is it a little decent quarter of a minute's grace said over an hour's dinner, but it is a most serious work of our most serious years. It engages more of time and appetite than our longest dinings or richest feasts. The prayer that makes much of our preaching must be made much of. The character of our praying will determine the character of our preaching. Light praying will make light preaching. Prayer makes preaching strong, gives it unction, and makes it stick. In every ministry weighty for good, prayer has always been a serious business.

The preacher must be preeminently a man of prayer. His heart must graduate in the school of prayer. In the school of prayer only can the heart learn to preach. No learning can make up for the failure to pray. No earnestness, no diligence, no study, no gifts will supply its lack.

Talking to men for God is a great thing, but talking to God for men is greater still. He will never talk well and with real success to men for God who has not learned well how to talk to God for men. More than this, prayerless words in the pulpit and out of it are deadening words.

5

Prayer, the Great Essential

PRAYER, in the preacher's life, in the preacher's study, in the preacher's pulpit, must be a conspicuous and an all-impregnating force and an all-coloring ingredient. It must play no secondary part, be no mere coating. To him it is given to be with his Lord "all night in prayer." The preacher, to train himself in self-denying prayer, is charged to look to his master, who, "rising up a great while before day, went out, and departed into a solitary place, and there prayed." The preacher's study ought to be a closet, a Bethel, an altar, a vision, and a ladder, that every thought might ascend heavenward ere it went manward; that every part of the sermon might be scented by the air of heaven and made serious, because God was in the study.

As the engine never moves until the fire is kindled, so preaching, with all its machinery, perfection, and polish, is at a dead standstill, as far as spiritual results are concerned, till prayer has kindled and created the steam. The texture, fineness, and strength of the sermon is as so much rubbish unless the mighty impulse of prayer is in it, through it, and behind it. The preacher must, by prayer, put God in the sermon. The preacher must, by prayer, move God toward the people before he can move the people to God by his words. The preacher must have had audience and ready access to God before he can have access to the people. An open way to God for the preacher is the surest pledge of an open way to the people.

It is necessary to stress and repeat that prayer, as a mere habit, as a performance gone through by routine or in a professional way, is a dead and rotten thing. Such praying has no connection with the praying for which we plead. We are stressing true praying, which engages and sets on fire every high element of the preacher's being—prayer which is born of vital oneness with Christ and the fullness of the Holy Spirit, which springs from the deep, overflowing fountains of tender compassion, deathless solicitude for man's eternal good; a consuming zeal for the glory of God; a thorough conviction of the preacher's difficult and delicate work and of the imperative need of God's mightiest help. Praying grounded on these solemn and profound convictions is the only true praying. Preaching backed by such praying is the only preaching which sows the seeds of eternal life in human hearts and builds men up for heaven.

It is true that there may be popular preaching, pleasant preaching, taking preaching, preaching of much intellectual, literary, and brainy force, with its measure and form of good with little or no praying; but the preaching which secures God's end in preaching must be born of prayer from text to introduction, delivered with the energy and spirit of prayer, followed and made to germinate, and kept in vital force in the hearts of the hearers by the preacher's prayers, long after the occasion has passed.

We may excuse the spiritual poverty of our preaching in many ways, but the true secret will be found in the lack of urgent prayer for God's presence in the power of the Holy Spirit. There are preachers innumerable who can deliver masterful sermons after their order; but the effects are short-lived and do not enter as a factor into the regions of the spirit where the fearful war between God and Satan, heaven and hell, is being waged because they are not made powerfully militant and spiritually victorious by prayer.

The preachers who gain mighty results for God are the men who have prevailed in their pleadings with God ere venturing to plead with men. The preachers who are the mightiest in their closets with God are the mightiest in their pulpits with men.

Preachers are human folks, and are exposed to and often caught by the strong driftings of human currents. Praying is spiritual work; and human nature does not like taxing, spiritual work. Human nature wants to sail to heaven under a favoring breeze, a full, smooth sea. Prayer is humbling work. it abases intellect and pride, crucifies vainglory, and signs our spiritual bankruptcy, and all these are hard for flesh and blood to bear. It is easier not to pray than to bear them. So we come to one of the crying evils of these times, maybe of all times—little or no praying. Of these two evils, perhaps little praying is worse than no praying. Little praying is a kind of make-believe, a salve for the conscience, a farce, and a delusion.

The little value we put on prayer is evident from the little time we give to it. The time given to prayer by the average preacher scarcely counts in the sum of the daily aggregate. Not infrequently the preacher's only praying is by his bedside, ready for bed and soon in it, with, perchance, the addition of a few hasty snatches of prayer ere he is dressed in the morning. How feeble, vain, and little is such praying compared with the time and energy devoted to praying by holy men in and out of the Bible! How poor and mean our petty, childish praying is beside the habits of the true men of God in all ages! To men who think praying their main business and devote time to it according to this high estimate of its importance does God commit the keys of his kingdom, and by them does he work his spiritual wonders in this world. Great praying is the sign and seal of God's great leaders and the earnest of the conquering forces with which God will crown their labors.

The preacher is commissioned to pray as well as to preach. His mission is incomplete if he does not do both well. The preacher may speak with all the eloquence of men and of angels; but unless he can pray with a faith which draws all heaven to his aid, his preaching will be "as sounding brass or a tinkling cymbal" for permanent God-honoring, soul-saving uses.

6

A Praying Ministry Is Successful

IT may be put down as a spiritual axiom that in every truly successful ministry prayer is an evident and controlling force—evident and controlling in the life of the preacher, evident and controlling in the deep spirituality of his work. A ministry may be a very thoughtful ministry without prayer; the preacher may secure fame and popularity without prayer; the whole machinery of the preacher's life and work may be run without the oil of prayer or with scarcely enough to grease one cog; but no ministry can be a spiritual one, securing holiness in the preacher and in his people without prayer being made an evident and controlling force.

The preacher that prays indeed puts God into the work. God does not come into the preacher's work as a matter of course or on general principles, but he comes by prayer and special urgency. That God will be found of us in the day that we seek him with the whole heart is as true of the preacher as of the penitent. A prayerful ministry is the only ministry that brings the preacher into sympathy with the people. Prayer as essentially unites to the human as it does to the divine. A prayerful ministry is the only ministry qualified for the high offices and responsibilities of the preacher. Colleges, learning, books, theology, preaching cannot make a preacher, but praying does. The apostles' commission to preach was a blank till filled up by the pentecost which praying brought. A prayerful minister has passed beyond the regions of the popular, beyond the man of mere affairs, of secularities, of pulpit attractiveness; passed beyond the ecclesiastical organizer or general into a sublimer and mightier region, the region of the spiritual. Holiness is the product of his work; transfigured hearts and lives emblazon the reality of his work, its trueness and substantial nature. God is with him. His ministry is not projected on worldly or surface principles. He is deeply stored with and deeply schooled in the things of God. His long, deep communings with God about his people and the agony of his wrestling spirit have crowned him as a prince in the things of God. The iciness of the mere professional has long since melted under the intensity of his praying.

The superficial results of many a ministry, the deadness of others, are to be found in the lack of praying. No ministry can succeed without much praying, and this praying must be fundamental, ever-abiding, ever-increasing. The text, the sermon, should be the result of prayer. The study should be bathed in prayer, all its duties impregnated with prayer, its whole spirit the spirit of prayer. "I am sorry that I have prayed so little," was the deathbed regret of one of God's chosen ones, a sad and remorseful regret for a preacher. "I want a life of greater, deeper, truer prayer," said the late Archbishop Tait. So may we all say, and this may we all secure.

God's true preachers have been distinguished by one great feature: they were men of prayer. Differing often in many things, they have always had a common center. They may have started from different points, and traveled by different roads, but they converged to one point: they were one in prayer. God to them was the center of attraction, and prayer was the path that led to God. These men prayed not occasionally, not a little at regular or at odd times; but they so prayed that their prayers entered into and shaped their characters; they so prayed as to affect their own lives and the lives of others; they so prayed as to make the history of the church and influence the current of the times. They spent much time in prayer, not because they marked the shadow on the dial or the hands on the clock, but because it was to them so momentous and engaging a business that they could scarcely give over.

Prayer was to them what it was to Paul, a striving with earnest effort of soul; what it was to Jacob, a wrestling and prevailing; what it was to Christ, "strong crying and tears." They "prayed always with all prayer and supplication in the Spirit, and watching thereunto with all perseverance." "The effectual, fervent prayer" has been the mightiest weapon of God's mightiest soldiers. The statement in regard to Elijah—that he "was a man subject to like passions as we are, and he prayed earnestly that it might not rain: and it rained not on the earth by the space of three years and six months. And he prayed again, the heaven gave rain, and the earth brought forth her fruit"—includes all prophets and preachers who have moved their generation for God, and shows the instrument by which they worked their wonders.

7

Much Time Should Be Given to Prayer

WHILE many private prayers, in the nature of things, must be short; while public prayers, as a rule, ought to be short and condensed; while there is ample room for and value put on ejaculatory prayer—yet in our private communions with God time is a feature essential to its value. Much time spent with God is the secret of all successful praying. Prayer which is felt as a mighty force is the immediate product of much time spent with God. Our short prayers owe their point and efficiency to the long ones that have preceded them. The short prevailing prayer cannot be prayed by one who has not prevailed with God in a mightier struggle of long continuance. Jacob's victory of faith could not have been gained without that all-night wrestling. God's acquaintance is not made by quick visits. God does not bestow his gifts on the casual or hasty comers and goers. Much time with God alone is the secret of knowing him and of influence with him. He yields to the persistency of a faith that knows him. He bestows his richest gifts on those who declare their desire for and appreciation of those gifts by the constancy as well as earnestness of their importunity. Christ, who in this as well as other things is our example, spent many whole nights in prayer. His custom was to pray much. He had his habitual place to pray. Many long seasons of praying make up his history and character. Paul prayed day and night. It took time from very important interests for Daniel to pray three times a day. David's morning, noon, and night praying were doubtless on many occasions very protracted. While we have no specific account of the time these Bible saints spent in prayer, yet the indications are that they consumed much time in prayer, and on some occasions long seasons of praying was their custom.

We would not have anyone think that the value of prayer is to be measured by the clock, but our purpose is to impress on our minds the necessity of being much alone with God; and that if this feature has not been produced by our faith, then our faith is of a feeble and surface type.

The men who have most fully illustrated Christ in their character, and have most powerfully affected the world for him, have been men who spent so much time with God as to make it a notable feature of their lives. Charles Simeon devoted the hours from four till eight in the morning to God. Mr. Wesley spent two hours daily in prayer. He began at four in the morning. Of him, one who knew him well wrote: "He thought prayer to be more his business than anything else, and I have seen him come out of his closet with a serenity of face next to shining." John Fletcher "stained the walls of his room by the breath of his prayers." Sometimes he would pray all night; always, frequently, and with great earnestness. His whole life was a life of prayer. "I would not rise from my seat," he said, "without lifting my heart to God." His greeting to a friend was always: "Do I meet you praying?" Luther said: "If I fail to spend two hours in prayer each morning, the devil gets the victory through the day. I have so much business I cannot get on without spending three hours daily in prayer." He had a motto: "He that has prayed well has studied well."

Archbishop Leighton was so much alone with God that he seemed to be in a perpetual meditation. "Prayer and praise were his business and his pleasure," says his biographer. Bishop Ken was so much with God that his soul was said to be God-enamored. He was with God before the clock struck three every morning. Bishop Asbury said: "I propose to rise at four o'clock as often as I can and spend two hours in prayer and meditation." Samuel Rutherford, the fragrance of whose piety is still rich, rose at three in the morning to meet God in prayer. Joseph Alleine arose at four o'clock for his business of praying till eight. If he heard other tradesmen plying their business before he was up, he would exclaim: "O how this shames me! Doth not my master deserve more than theirs?" He who has learned this trade well draws at will, on sight, and with acceptance of heaven's unfailing bank.

One of the holiest and among the most gifted of Scottish preachers says: "I ought to spend the best hours in communion with God. It is my noblest and most fruitful employment, and is not to be thrust into a corner. The morning hours, from six to eight, are the most uninterrupted and should be thus employed. After tea is my best hour, and that should be solemnly dedicated to God. I ought not to give up the good old habit of prayer before going to bed; but guard must be kept against sleep. When I awake in the night, I ought to rise and pray. A little time after breakfast might be given to intercession." This was the praying plan of Robert McCheyne. The memorable Methodist band in their praying shame us. "From four to five in the morning, private prayer; from five to six in the evening, private prayer."

8

Examples of Praying Men

Bishop Wilson says: "In H. Martyn's journal the spirit of prayer, the time he devoted to the duty, and his fervor in it are the first things which strike me."

Payson wore the hardwood boards into grooves where his knees pressed so often and so long. His biographer says:

> His continuing instant in prayer, be his circumstances what they might, is the most noticeable fact in his history, and points out the duty of all who would rival his eminency. To his ardent and persevering prayers must no doubt be ascribed in a great measure his distinguished and almost uninterrupted success.

The Marquis DeRenty, to whom Christ was most precious, ordered his servant to call him from his devotions at the end of half an hour. The servant at the time saw his face through an aperture. It was marked with such holiness that he hated to arouse him. His lips were moving, but he was perfectly silent. He waited until three half hours had passed; then he called to him. When he arose from his knees, he said that the half hour was so short when he was communing with Christ.

Brainerd said: "I love to be alone in my cottage, where I can spend much time in prayer."

William Bramwell is famous in Methodist annals for personal holiness and for his wonderful success in preaching and for the marvelous answers to his prayers. For hours at a time he would pray. He almost lived on his knees. He went over his circuits like a flame of fire. The fire was kindled by the time he spent in prayer. He often spent as much as four hours in a single season of prayer in retirement.

Bishop Andrewes spent the greatest part of five hours every day in prayer and devotion.

Sir Henry Havelock always spent the first two hours of each day alone with God. If the encampment was struck at 6 A.M., he would rise at four.

Earl Carins rose daily at six o'clock to secure an hour and a half for the study of the Bible and for prayer, before conducting family worship at a quarter to eight.

Dr. Judson's success in prayer is attributable to the fact that he gave much time to prayer. He says on this point: "Arrange thy affairs, if possible, so that thou canst leisurely devote two or three hours every day not merely to devotional exercises but to the very act of secret prayer and communion with God. Endeavor seven times a day to withdraw from business and company and lift up thy soul to God in private retirement. Begin the day by rising after midnight and devoting some time amid the silence and darkness of the night to this sacred work. Let the hour of opening dawn find thee at the same work. Let the hours of nine, twelve, three, six, and nine at night witness the same. Be resolute in his cause. Make all practicable sacrifices to maintain it. Consider that thy time is short, and that business and company must not be allowed to rob thee of thy God." Impossible, say we, fanatical directions! Dr. Judson impressed an empire for Christ and laid the foundations of God's kingdom with imperishable granite in the heart of Burma. He was successful, one of the few men who mightily impressed the world for Christ. Many men of greater gifts and genius and learning than he have made no such impression; their religious work is like footsteps in the sands, but he has engraven his work on the diamond. The secret of its profundity and endurance is found in the fact that he gave time to prayer. He kept the iron red-hot with prayer, and God's skill fashioned it with enduring power. No man can do a great and enduring work for God who is not a man of prayer, and no man can be a man of prayer who does not give much time to praying.

Is it true that prayer is simply the compliance with habit, dull and mechanical? A petty performance into which we are trained till tameness, shortness, superficiality are its chief elements? "Is it true that prayer is, as is assumed, little else than the half-passive play of sentiment which flows languidly on through the minutes or hours of easy reverie?" Canon Liddon continues:

> Let those who have really prayed give the answer. They sometimes describe prayer with the patriarch Jacob as a wrestling together with an unseen power which may last, not unfrequently in an earnest life, late into the night hours, or even to the break of day. Sometimes they refer to common intercession with Paul as a concerted struggle. They have, when praying, their eyes fixed on the great intercessor in Gethsemane, upon the drops of blood which fall to the ground in that agony of resignation and sacrifice. Importunity is of the essence of successful prayer. Importunity means not dreaminess but sustained work. It is through prayer especially that the kingdom of heaven suffereth violence and the violent take it by force. It was a saying of the late Bishop Hamilton that "No man is likely to do much good in prayer who does not begin by looking upon it in the light of a work to be prepared for and persevered in with all the earnestness which we bring to bear upon subjects which are in our opinion at once most interesting and most necessary."

9

Begin the Day with Prayer

THE men who have done the most for God in this world have been early on their knees. He who fritters away the early morning, its opportunity and freshness, in other pursuits than seeking God will make poor headway seeking him the rest of the day. If God is not first in our thoughts and efforts in the morning, he will be in the last place the remainder of the day.

Behind this early rising and early praying is the ardent desire which presses us into this pursuit after God. Morning listlessness is the index to a listless heart. The heart which is behindhand in seeking God in the morning has lost its relish for God. David's heart was ardent after God. He hungered and thirsted after God, and so he sought God early, before daylight. The bed and sleep could not chain his soul in its eagerness after God. Christ longed for communion with God; and so, rising a great while before day, he would go out into the mountain to pray. The disciples, when fully awake and ashamed of their indulgence, would know where to find him. We might go through the list of men who have mightily impressed the world for God, and we would find them early after God.

A desire for God which cannot break the chains of sleep is a weak thing and will do but little good for God after it has indulged itself fully. The desire for God that keeps so far behind the devil and the world at the beginning of the day will never catch up.

It is not simply the getting up that puts men to the front and makes them captain generals in God's hosts, but it is the ardent desire which stirs and breaks all self-indulgent chains. But the getting up gives vent, increase, and strength to the desire. If they had lain in bed and indulged themselves, the desire would have been quenched. The desire aroused them and put them on the stretch for God, and this heeding and acting on the call gave their faith its grasp on God and gave to their hearts the sweetest and fullest revelation of God, and this strength of faith and fullness of revelation made them saints by eminence, and the halo of their sainthood has come down to us, and we have entered the enjoyment of their conquests. But we take our fill in enjoyment, and not in productions. We build their tombs and write their epitaphs, but are careful not to follow their examples.

We need a generation of preachers who seek God and seek him early, who give the freshness and dew of effort to God, and secure in return the freshness and fullness of his power that he may be as the dew to them, full of gladness and strength, through all the heat and labor of the day. Our laziness after God is our crying sin. The children of this world are far wiser than we. They are at it early and late. We do not seek God with ardor and diligence. No man gets God who does not follow hard after him, and no soul follows hard after God who is not after him in early morn.

10

Prayer and Devotion United

NEVER was there greater need for saintly men and women; more imperative still is the call for saintly, God-devoted preachers. The world moves with gigantic strides. Satan has his hold and rule on the world, and labors to make all its movements subserve his ends. Religion must do its best work, present its most attractive and perfect models. By every means, modern sainthood must be inspired by the loftiest ideals and by the largest possibilities through the Spirit. Paul lived on his knees, that the Ephesian church might measure the heights, breadths, and depths of an unmeasurable saintliness, and "be filled with all the fullness of God." Epaphras laid himself out with the exhaustive toil and strenuous conflict of fervent prayer, that the Colossian church might "stand perfect and complete in all the will of God." Everywhere, everything in apostolic times was on the stretch that the people of God might each and "all come in the unity of the faith, and of the knowledge of the Son of God, unto a perfect man, unto the measure of the stature of the fullness of Christ." No premium was given to dwarfs; no encouragement to an old babyhood. The babies were to grow; the old, instead of feebleness and infirmities, were to bear fruit in old age, and be fat and flourishing. The divinest thing in religion is holy men and holy women.

No amount of money, genius, or culture can move things for God. Holiness energizing the soul, the whole man aflame with love, with desire for more faith, more prayer, more zeal, more consecration—this is the secret of power. These we need and must have, and men must be the incarnation of this God-inflamed devotedness. God's advance has been stayed, his cause crippled, his name dishonored for their lack. Genius (though the loftiest and most gifted), education (though the most learned and refined), position, dignity, place, honored names, high ecclesiastics cannot move this chariot of our God. It is a fiery one, and fiery forces only can move it. The genius of a Milton fails. The imperial strength of a Leo fails. Brainerd's spirit can move it. Brainerd's spirit was on fire for God, on fire for souls. Nothing earthly, worldly, selfish came in to abate in the least the intensity of this all-impelling and all-consuming force and flame.

Prayer is the creator as well as the channel of devotion. The spirit of devotion is the spirit of prayer. Prayer and devotion are united as soul and body are united, as life and the heart are united. There is no real prayer without devotion, no devotion without prayer. The preacher must be surrendered to God in the holiest devotion. He is not a professional man, his ministry is not a profession; it is a divine institution, a divine devotion. He is devoted to God. His aim, aspirations, ambition are for God and to God, and to such prayer is as essential as food is to life.

The preacher, above everything else, must be devoted to God. The preacher's relations to God are the insignia and credentials of his ministry. These must be clear, conclusive, unmistakable. No common, surface type of piety must be his. If he does not excel in grace, he does not excel at all. If he does not preach by life, character, conduct, he does not preach at all. If his piety be light, his preaching may be as soft and as sweet as music, as gifted as Apollo, yet its weight will be a feather's weight, visionary, fleeting as the morning cloud or the early dew. Devotion to God—there is no substitute for this in the preacher's character and conduct. Devotion to a church, to opinions, to an organization, to orthodoxy—these are paltry, misleading, and vain when they become the source of inspiration, the animus of a call. God must be the mainspring of the preacher's effort, the fountain and crown of all his toil. The name and honor of Jesus Christ, the advance of his cause, must be all in all. The preacher must have no inspiration but the name of Jesus Christ, no ambition but to have him glorified, no toil but for him. Then prayer will be a source of his illuminations, the means of perpetual advance, the gauge of his success. The perpetual aim, the only ambition, the preacher can cherish is to have God with him.

Never did the cause of God need perfect illustrations of the possibilities of prayer more than in this age. No age, no person, will be examples of the gospel power except the ages or persons of deep and earnest prayer. A prayerless age will have but scant models of divine power. Prayerless hearts will never rise to these alpine heights. The age may be a better age than the past, but there is an infinite distance between the betterment of an age by the force of an advancing civilization and its betterment by the increase of holiness and Christlikeness by the energy of prayer. The Jews were much better when Christ came than in the ages before. It was the golden age of their Pharisaic religion. Their golden religious age crucified Christ. Never more praying, never less praying; never more sacrifices, never less sacrifice; never less idolatry, never more idolatry; never more of temple worship, never less of God worship; never more of lip service, never less of heart service (God worshiped by lips whose hearts and hands crucified God's Son!); never more of churchgoers, never less of saints.

It is prayer-force which makes saints. Holy characters are formed by the power of real praying. The more of true saints the more of praying; the more of praying the more of true saints.

11

An Example of Devotion

GOD has now, and has had, many of these devoted, prayerful preachers—
men in whose lives prayer has been a mighty, controlling, conspicuous force.
The world has felt their power, God has felt and honored their power, God's
cause has moved mightily and swiftly by their prayers, holiness has shone out
in their characters with a divine effulgence.

God found one of the men he was looking for in David Brainerd, whose
work and name have gone into history. He was no ordinary man, but was
capable of shining in any company, the peer of the wise and gifted ones, eminently suited to fill the most attractive pulpits and to labor among the most
refined and the cultured, who were so anxious to secure him for their pastor.
President Edwards bears testimony that he was "a young man of distinguished talents, had extraordinary knowledge of men and things, had rare
conversational powers, excelled in his knowledge of theology, and was truly,
for one so young, an extraordinary divine, and especially in all matters relating to experimental religion. I never knew his equal of his age and standing
for clear and accurate notions of the nature and essence of true religion. His
manner in prayer was almost inimitable, such as I have very rarely known
equaled. His learning was very considerable, and he had extraordinary gifts
for the pulpit."

No sublimer story has been recorded in earthly annals than that of David
Brainerd; no miracle attests with diviner force the truth of Christianity than
the life and work of such a man. Alone in the savage wilds of America, struggling day and night with a mortal disease, unschooled in the care of souls, having access to the Indians for a large portion of time only through the bungling
medium of a pagan interpreter, with the Word of God in his heart and in his
hand, his soul fired with the divine flame, a place and time to pour out his
soul to God in prayer, he fully established the worship of God and secured all
its gracious results. The Indians were changed with a great change from the
lowest besetments of an ignorant and debased heathenism to pure, devout,
intelligent Christians; all vice reformed, the external duties of Christianity at
once embraced and acted on; family prayer set up; the Sabbath instituted and
religiously observed; the internal graces of religion exhibited with growing
sweetness and strength. The solution of these results is found in David

Brainerd himself, not in the conditions or accidents but in the man Brainerd. He was God's man, for God first and last and all the time. God could flow unhindered through him. The omnipotence of grace was neither arrested nor straightened by the conditions of his heart; the whole channel was broadened and cleaned out for God's fullest and most powerful passage, so that God with all his mighty forces could come down on the hopeless, savage wilderness, and transform it into his blooming and fruitful garden; for nothing is too hard for God to do if he can get the right kind of a man to do it with.

Brainerd lived the life of holiness and prayer. His diary is full and monotonous with the record of his seasons of fasting, meditation, and retirement. The time he spent in private prayer amounted to many hours daily. "When I return home," he said, "and give myself to meditation, prayer, and fasting, my soul longs for mortification, self-denial, humility, and divorcement from all things of the world." "I have nothing to do," he said, "with earth, but only to labor in it honestly for God. I do not desire to live one minute for anything which earth can afford." After this high order did he pray:

> Feeling somewhat of the sweetness of communion with God and the constraining force of his love, and how admirably it captivates the soul and makes all the desires and affections to center in God, I set apart this day for secret fasting and prayer, to entreat God to direct and bless me with regard to the great work which I have in view of preaching the gospel, and that the Lord would return to me and show me the light of his countenance. I had little life and power in the forenoon. Near the middle of the afternoon God enabled me to wrestle ardently in intercession for my absent friends, but just at night the Lord visited me marvelously in prayer. I think my soul was never in such agony before. I felt no restraint, for the treasures of divine grace were opened to me. I wrestled for absent friends, for the ingathering of souls, for multitudes of poor souls, and for many that I thought were the children of God, personally, in many distant places. I was in such agony from sun half an hour high till near dark that I was all over wet with sweat, but yet it seemed to me I had done nothing. O, my dear savior did sweat blood for poor souls! I longed for more compassion toward them. I felt still in a sweet frame, under a sense of divine love and grace, and went to bed in such a frame, with my heart set of God.

It was prayer which gave to his life and ministry their marvelous power.

The men of mighty prayer are men of spiritual might. Prayers never die. Brainerd's whole life was a life of prayer. By day and by night he prayed. Riding through the interminable solitudes of the forests he prayed. On his bed of straw he prayed. Retiring to the dense and lonely forests, he prayed. Hour by hour, day after day, early morn and late at night, he was praying and fasting, pouring out his soul, interceding, communing with God. He was with God mightily in prayer, and God was with him mightily, and by it he being dead yet speaketh and worketh, and will speak and work till the end comes, and among the glorious ones of that glorious day he will be with the first.

Jonathan Edwards says of him: "His life shows the right way to success in the works of the ministry. He sought it as the soldier seeks victory in a siege or battle, or as a man that runs a race for a great prize. Animated with love to Christ and souls, how did he labor? Always fervently. Not only in word and doctrine, in public and in private, but in prayers by day and night, wrestling with God in secret and travailing in birth with unutterable groans and agonies, until Christ was formed in the hearts of the people to whom he was sent. Like a true son of Jacob, he persevered in wrestling through all the darkness of the night, until the breaking of the day!"

12

Heart Preparation Is Necessary

PRAYER, with its manifold and many-sided forces, helps the mouth to utter the truth in its fullness and freedom. The preacher is to be prayed for, the preacher is made by prayer. The preacher's mouth is to be prayed for; his mouth is to be opened and filled by prayer. A holy mouth is made by praying, by much praying; a brave mouth is made by praying, by much praying. The church and the world, God and heaven, owe much to Paul's mouth; Paul's mouth owed its power to prayer.

How manifold, illimitable, valuable, and helpful prayer is to the preacher in so many ways, at so many points, in every way! One great value is, it helps his heart.

Praying makes the preacher a heart preacher. Prayer puts the preacher's heart into the preacher's sermon; prayer puts the preacher's sermon into the preacher's heart.

The heart makes the preacher. Men of great hearts are great preachers. Men of bad hearts may do a measure of good, but this is rare. The hireling and the stranger may help the sheep at some points, but it is the good shepherd with the good shepherd's heart who will bless the sheep and answer the full measure of the shepherd's place.

We have emphasized sermon preparation until we have lost sight of the important thing to be prepared—the heart. A prepared heart is much better than a prepared sermon. A prepared heart will make a prepared sermon.

Volumes have been written laying down the mechanics and taste of sermon-making, until we have become possessed with the idea that this scaffolding is the building. The young preacher has been taught to lay out all his strength on the form, taste, and beauty of his sermon as a mechanical and intellectual product. We have thereby cultivated a vicious taste among the people and raised the clamor for talent instead of grace, eloquence instead of piety, rhetoric instead of revelation, reputation and brilliancy instead of holiness. By it we have lost the true idea of preaching, lost preaching power, lost pungent conviction for sin, lost the rich experience and elevated Christian character, lost the authority over consciences and lives which always results from genuine preaching.

It would not do to say that preachers study too much. Some of them do not study at all; others do not study enough. Numbers do not study the right way to show themselves workmen approved of God. But our great lack is not in head culture, but in heart culture; not lack of knowledge but lack of holiness is our sad and telling defect—not that we know too much, but that we do not meditate on God and his word and watch and fast and pray enough. The heart is the great hindrance to our preaching. Words pregnant with divine truth find in our hearts nonconductors; arrested, they fall shorn and powerless.

Can ambition, that lusts after praise and place, preach the gospel of him who made himself of no reputation and took on him the form of a servant? Can the proud, the vain, the egotistical preach the gospel of him who was meek and lowly? Can the bad-tempered, passionate, selfish, hard, worldly man preach the system which teems with long-suffering, self-denial, tenderness, which imperatively demands separation from enmity and crucifixion to the world? Can the hireling official, heartless, perfunctory, preach the gospel which demands the shepherd to give his life for the sheep? Can the covetous man, who counts salary and money, preach the gospel till he has gleaned his heart and can say in the spirit of Christ and Paul in the words of Wesley: "I count it dung and dross; I trample it under my feet; I (yet not I, but the grace of God in me) esteem it just as the mire of the streets, I desire it not, I seek it not?" God's revelation does not need the light of human genius, the polish and strength of human culture, the brilliancy of human thought, the force of human brains to adorn or enforce it; but it does demand the simplicity, the docility, humility, and faith of a child's heart.

It was this surrender and subordination of intellect and genius to the divine and spiritual forces which made Paul peerless among the apostles. It was this which gave Wesley his power and rooted his labors in the history of humanity. This gave to Loyola the strength to arrest the retreating forces of Catholicism.

Our great need is heart-preparation. Luther held it as an axiom: "He who has prayed well has studied well." We do not say that men are not to think and use their intellects; but he will use his intellect best who cultivates his heart most. We do not say that preachers should not be students; but we do say that their great study should be the Bible, and he studies the Bible best who has kept his heart with diligence. We do not say that the preacher should not know men, but he will be the greater adept in human nature who has fathomed the depths and intricacies of his own heart. We do say that while the channel of preaching is the mind, its fountain is the heart; you may broaden and deepen the channel, but if you do not look well to the purity and depth of the fountain, you will have a dry or polluted channel. We do say that almost any man of common intelligence has sense enough to preach the gospel, but very few have grace enough to do so. We do say that he who has struggled with his own heart and conquered it; who has taught it humility, faith, love, truth, mercy, sympathy, courage; who can pour the rich treasures of the heart thus trained, through a manly intellect, all surcharged with the power of the gospel on the consciences of his hearers—such a one will be the truest, most successful preacher in the esteem of his Lord.

13

Grace from the Heart Rather than the Head

THE heart is the savior of the world. Heads do not save. Genius, brains, brilliancy, strength, natural gifts do not save. The gospel flows through hearts. All the mightiest forces are heart forces. All the sweetest and loveliest graces are heart graces. Great hearts make great characters; great hearts make divine characters. God is love. There is nothing greater than love, nothing greater than God. Hearts make heaven; heaven is love. There is nothing higher, nothing sweeter, than heaven. It is the heart and not the head which makes God's great preachers. The heart counts much every way in religion. The heart must speak from the pulpit. The heart must hear in the pew. In fact, we serve God with our hearts. Head homage does not pass current in heaven.

We believe that one of the serious and most popular errors of the modern pulpit is the putting of more thought than prayer, of more head than of heart in its sermons. Big hearts make big preachers; good hearts make good preachers. A theological school to enlarge and cultivate the heart is the golden desire of the gospel. The pastor binds his people to him and rules his people by his heart. They may admire his gifts, they may be proud of his ability, they may be affected for the time by his sermons; but the stronghold of his power is his heart. His scepter is love. The throne of his power is his heart.

The good shepherd gives his life for the sheep. Heads never make martyrs. It is the heart which surrenders the life to love and fidelity. It takes great courage to be a faithful pastor, but the heart alone can supply this courage. Gifts and genius may be brave, but it is the gifts and genius of the heart and not of the head.

It is easier to fill the head than it is to prepare the heart. It is easier to make a brain sermon than a heart sermon. It was heart that drew the Son of God from heaven. It is heart that will draw men to heaven. Men of heart is what the world needs to sympathize with its woe, to kiss away its sorrows, to pity its misery, and to alleviate its pain. Christ was eminently the man of sorrows, because he was preeminently the man of heart.

"Give me thy heart," is God's requisition of men. "Give me thy heart!" is man's demand of man.

A professional ministry is a heartless ministry. When salary plays a great part in the ministry, the heart plays little part. We may make preaching our business, and not put our hearts in the business. He who puts self to the front in his preaching puts heart to the rear. He who does not sow with his heart in his study will never reap a harvest for God. The closet is the heart's study. We will learn more about how to preach and what to preach there than we can learn in our libraries. "Jesus wept" is the shortest and biggest verse in the Bible. It is he who goes forth *weeping* (not preaching great sermons), bearing precious seed, who shall come again rejoicing, bringing his sheaves with him.

Praying gives sense, brings wisdom, broadens and strengthens the mind. The closet is a perfect school teacher and schoolhouse for the preacher. Thought is not only brightened and clarified in prayer, but thought is born in prayer. We can learn more in an hour praying, when praying indeed, than from many hours in the study. Books are in the closet which can be found and read nowhere else. Revelations are made in the closet which are made nowhere else.

14

Unction, a Necessity

ALEXANDER Knox, a Christian philosopher of the days of Wesley, not an adherent but a strong personal friend of Wesley, and with much spiritual sympathy with the Wesleyan movement, writes:

It is strange and lamentable, but I verily believe the fact to be that except among Methodists and Methodistical clergyman, there is not much interesting preaching in England. The clergy, too generally, have absolutely lost the art. There is, I conceive, in the great laws of the moral world a kind of secret understanding like the affinities in chemistry, between rightly promulgated religious truth and the deepest feelings of the human mind. Where the one is duly exhibited, the other will respond. Did not our hearts burn within us?—but to this devout feeling is indispensable in the speaker. Now, I am obliged to state from my own observation that this *onction*, as the French not unfitly term it, is beyond all comparison more likely to be found in England in a Methodist conventicle than in a parish church. This, and this alone, seems really to be that which fills the Methodist houses and thins the churches. I am, I verily think, no enthusiast; I am a most sincere and cordial churchman, a humble disciple of the School of Hale and Boyle, of Burnet and Leighton. Now I must aver that when I was in this country, two years ago, I did not hear a single preacher who taught me like my own great masters but such as are deemed Methodistical. And I now despair of getting an atom of heart-instruction from any other quarter. The Methodist preachers (however I may not always approve of all their expressions) do most assuredly diffuse this true religion and undefiled. I felt real pleasure last Sunday. I can bear witness that the preacher did at once speak the words of truth and soberness. There was no eloquence—the honest man never dreamed of such a thing—but there was far better: a cordial communication of vitalized truth. I say vitalized because what he declared to others it was impossible not to feel he lived on himself.

This unction is the art of preaching. The preacher who never had this unction never had the art of preaching. The preacher who has lost this unction has lost the art of preaching. Whatever other arts he may have and retain—the art of sermon-making, the art of eloquence, the art of great, clear thinking, the art of pleasing an audience—he has lost the divine art of preaching. This unction makes God's truth powerful and interesting, draws and attracts, edifies, convicts, saves.

This unction vitalizes God's revealed truth, makes it living and life-giving. Even God's truth spoken without this unction is light, dead, and deadening. Though abounding in truth, though weighty with thought, though sparkling with rhetoric, though pointed by logic, though powerful by earnestness, without this divine unction it issues in death and not in life. Mr. Spurgeon says:

> I wonder how long we might beat our brains before we could plainly put into word what is meant by preaching with unction. Yet he who preaches knows its presence, and he who hears soon detects its absence. Samaria, in famine, typifies a discourse without it. Jerusalem, with her feast of fat things full of marrow, may represent a sermon enriched with it. Every one knows what the freshness of the morning is when orient pearls abound on every blade of grass, but who can describe it, much less produce it of itself? Such is the mystery of spiritual anointing. We know, but we cannot tell to others what it is. It is as easy as it is foolish, to counterfeit it. Unction is a thing which you cannot manufacture, and its counterfeits are worse than worthless. Yet it is in itself, priceless, and beyond measure needful if you would edify believers and bring sinners to Christ.

15

Unction, the Mark
of True Gospel Preaching

UNCTION is that indefinable, indescribable something which an old, renowned Scotch preacher describes thus: "There is sometimes somewhat in preaching that cannot be ascribed either to matter or expression, and cannot be described what it is, or from whence it cometh, but with a sweet violence it pierceth into the heart and affections and comes immediately from the Lord; but if there be any way to obtain such a thing, it is by the heavenly disposition of the speaker."

We call it unction. It is this unction which makes the word of God "quick and powerful, and sharper than any two-edged sword, piercing even to the dividing asunder of soul and spirit, and of the joints and marrow, and a discerner of the thoughts and intents of the heart." It is this unction which gives the words of the preacher such point, sharpness, and power, and which creates such friction and stir in many a dead congregation. The same truths have been told in the strictness of the letter, smooth as human oil could make them; but no signs of life, not a pulse throb; all as peaceful as the grave and as dead. The same preacher in the meanwhile receives a baptism of this unction, the divine inspiration is on him, the letter of the Word has been embellished and fired by this mysterious power, and the throbbings of life begin—life which receives or life which resists. The unction pervades and convicts the conscience and breaks the heart.

This divine unction is the feature which separates and distinguishes true gospel preaching from all other methods of presenting the truth, and which creates a wide spiritual chasm between the preacher who has it and the one who has it not. It backs and impregnates revealed truth with all the energy of God. Unction is simply putting God in his own word and on his own preacher. By mighty and great prayerfulness and by continual prayerfulness, it is all potential and personal to the preacher; it inspires and clarifies his intellect, gives insight and grasp and projecting power; it gives to the preacher heart power, which is greater than head power; and tenderness, purity, force flow from the heart by it. Enlargement, freedom, fullness of thought, directness and simplicity of utterance are the fruits of this unction.

478

Often earnestness is mistaken for this unction. He who has the divine unction will be earnest in the very spiritual nature of things, but there may be a vast deal of earnestness without the least mixture of unction.

Earnestness and unction look alike from some points of view. Earnestness may be readily and without detection substituted or mistaken for unction. It requires a spiritual eye and a spiritual taste to discriminate.

Earnestness may be sincere, serious, ardent, and persevering. It goes at a thing with good will, pursues it with perseverance, and urges it with ardor; puts force in it. But all these forces do not rise higher than the mere human. The *man* is in it—the whole man, with all that he has of will and heart, of brain and genius, of planning and working and talking. He has set himself to some purpose which has mastered him, and he pursues to master it. There may be none of God in it. There may be little of God in it, because there is so much of the man in it. He may present pleas in advocacy of his earnest purpose which please or touch and move along earthly ways, being propelled by human forces only, its altar made by earthly hands and its fire kindled by earthly flames. It is said of a rather famous preacher of gifts, whose construction of Scripture was to his fancy or purpose, that he "grew very eloquent over his own exegesis." So men grow exceeding earnest over their own plans or movements. Earnestness may be selfishness simulated.

What of unction? It is the indefinable in preaching which makes it preaching. It is that which distinguishes and separates preaching from all mere human addresses. It is the divine in preaching. It makes the preaching sharp to those who need sharpness. It distills as the dew to those who need to be refreshed. It is well described as:

> A two-edged sword
> Of heavenly temper keen,
> And double were the wounds it made
> Where'er it glanced between.
> 'Twas death to sin; 'twas life
> To all who mourned for sin.
> It kindled and it silenced strife,
> Made war and peace within.

This unction comes to the preacher not in the study but in the closet. It is heaven's distillation in answer to prayer. It is the sweetest exhalation of the Holy Spirit. It impregnates, suffuses, softens, percolates, cuts, and soothes. It carries the Word like dynamite, like salt, like sugar; makes the Word a soother, an accuser, a revealer, a searcher; makes the hearer a culprit or a saint, makes him weep like a child and live like a giant; opens his heart and his purse as gently, yet as strongly as the spring opens the leaves. This unction is not the gift of genius. It is not found in the halls of learning. No eloquence can woo it. No industry can win it. No prelatical hands can confer it. It is the gift of God—the signet set to his own messengers. It is heaven's knighthood given to the chosen true and brave ones who have sought this anointed honor through many an hour of tearful, wrestling prayer.

Earnestness is good and impressive; genius is gifted and great. Thought kindles and inspires, but it takes a diviner endowment, a more powerful energy than earnestness or genius or thought to break the chains of sin, to win estranged and depraved hearts to God, to repair the breaches and restore the church to her old ways of purity and power. Nothing but this holy unction can do this.

16

Much Prayer Is the Price of Unction

IN the Christian system unction is the anointing of the Holy Spirit, separating unto God's work and qualifying for it. This unction is the one divine enablement by which the preacher accomplishes the peculiar and saving ends of preaching. Without this unction there are no true spiritual results accomplished; the results and forces in preaching do not rise above the results of unsanctified speech. Without unction the former is as potent as the pulpit.

This divine unction on the preacher generates through the Word of God the spiritual results that flow from the gospel; and without this unction, these results are not secured. Many pleasant impressions may be made, but these all fall far below the ends of gospel preaching. This unction may be simulated. There are many things that look like it, there are many results that resemble its effects; but they are foreign to its results and to its nature. The fervor or softness excited by a pathetic or emotional sermon may look like the movements of the divine unction, but they have no pungent, penetrating, heart-breaking force. No heart-healing balm is there in these surface, sympathetic, emotional movements; they are not radical, neither sin-searching nor sin-curing.

This divine unction is the one distinguishing feature that separates true gospel preaching from all other methods of presenting truth. It backs and interpenetrates the revealed truth with all the force of God. It illumines the Word and broadens and enriches the intellect and empowers it to grasp and apprehend the Word. It qualifies the preacher's heart, and brings it to that condition of tenderness, of purity, of force and light that are necessary to secure the highest results. This unction gives to the preacher liberty and enlargement of thought and soul—a freedom, fullness, and directness of utterance that can be secured by no other process.

Without this unction on the preacher the gospel has no more power to propagate itself than any other system of truth. This is the seal of its divinity. Unction in the preacher puts God in the gospel. Without the unction, God is absent, and the gospel is left to the low and unsatisfactory forces that the ingenuity, interest, or talents of men can devise to enforce and project its doctrines.

It is in this element that the pulpit oftener fails than in any other element. Just at this all-important point it lapses. Learning it may have, brilliancy and eloquence may delight and charm, sensation or less offensive methods may bring the populace in crowds, mental power may impress and enforce truth with all its resources; but without this unction, each and all these will be but as the fretful assault of the waters on a Gibraltar. Spray and foam may cover and spangle; but the rocks are there still, unimpressed and unimpressible. The human heart can no more be swept of its hardness and sin by these human forces than these rocks can be swept away by the ocean's ceaseless flow.

This unction is the consecration force, and its presence the continuous test of that consecration. It is this divine anointing on the preacher that secures his consecration to God and his work. Other forces and motives may call him to the work, but this only is consecration. A separation to God's work by the power of the Holy Spirit is the only consecration recognized by God as legitimate.

The unction, the divine unction, this heavenly anointing, is what the pulpit needs and must have. This divine and heavenly oil put on it by the imposition of God's hand must soften and lubricate the whole man—heart, head, spirit—until it separates him with a mighty separation from all earthly, secular, worldly, selfish motives and aims, separating him to everything that is pure and Godlike.

It is the presence of this unction on the preacher that creates the stir and friction in many a congregation. The same truths have been told in the strictness of the letter, but no ruffle has been seen, no pain or pulsation felt. All is quiet as a graveyard. Another preacher comes, and this mysterious influence is on him; the letter of the Word has been fired by the Spirit, the throes of a mighty movement are felt, it is the unction that pervades and stirs the conscience and breaks the heart. Unctionless preaching makes everything hard, dry, acrid, dead.

This unction is not a memory or an era of the past only; it is a present, realized, conscious fact. It belongs to the experience of the man as well as to his preaching. It is that which transforms him into the image of his divine master, as well as that by which he declares the truths of Christ with power. It is so much the power in the ministry as to make all else seem feeble and vain without it, and by its presence to atone for the absence of all other and feebler forces.

This unction is not an inalienable gift. It is a conditional gift, and its presence is perpetuated and increased by the same process by which it was at first secured; by unceasing prayer to God, by impassioned desires after God, by esteeming it, by seeking it with tireless ardor, by deeming all else loss and failure without it.

How and whence comes this unction? Direct from God in answer to prayer. Only praying hearts are the hearts filled with this holy oil; praying lips only are anointed with this divine unction.

Prayer, much prayer, is the price of preaching unction; prayer, much prayer, is the one, sole condition of keeping this unction. Without unceasing prayer the unction never comes to the preacher. Without perseverance in prayer, the unction, like the manna overkept, breeds worms.

17

Prayer Marks Spiritual Leadership

THE apostles knew the necessity and worth of prayer to their ministry. They knew that their high commission as apostles, instead of relieving them from the necessity of prayer, committed them to it by a more urgent need; so that they were exceedingly jealous else some other important work should exhaust their time and prevent their praying as they ought; so they appointed laymen to look after the delicate and engrossing duties of ministering to the poor, that they (the apostles) might, unhindered, "give themselves continually to prayer and to the ministry of the word." Prayer is put first, and their relation to prayer is put most strongly—"give themselves to it," making a business of it, surrendering themselves to praying, putting fervor, urgency, perseverance, and time in it.

How holy, apostolic men devoted themselves to this divine work of prayer! "Night and day praying exceedingly," says Paul. "We will give ourselves continually to prayer" is the consensus of apostolic devotion. How these New Testament preachers laid themselves out in prayer for God's people! How they put God in full force into their churches by their praying! These holy apostles did not vainly fancy that they had met their high and solemn duties by delivering faithfully God's word, but their preaching was made to stick and tell by the ardor and insistence of their praying. Apostolic praying was as taxing, toilsome, and imperative as apostolic preaching. They prayed mightily day and night to bring their people to the highest regions of faith and holiness. They prayed mightier still to hold them to this high spiritual altitude. The preacher who has never learned in the school of Christ the high and divine art of intercession for his people will never learn the art of preaching, though homiletics be poured into him by the ton, and though he be the most gifted genius in sermon-making and sermon-delivery.

The prayers of apostolic, saintly leaders do much in making saints of those who are not apostles. If the church leaders in after years had been as particular and fervent in praying for their people as the apostles were, the sad, dark times of worldliness and apostasy would not have marred the history and eclipsed the glory and arrested the advance of the church. Apostolic praying makes apostolic saints and keeps apostolic times of purity and power in the church.

What loftiness of soul, what purity and elevation of motive, what unselfishness, what self-sacrifice, what exhaustive toil, what ardor of spirit, what
divine tact are requisite to be an intercessor for men!

The preacher is to lay himself out in prayer for his people; not that they
might be saved, simply, but that they be mightily saved. The apostles laid
themselves out in prayer that their saints might be perfect; not that they
should have a little relish for the things of God, but that they "might be filled
with all the fullness of God." Paul did not rely on his apostolic preaching to
secure this end, but "for this cause he bowed his knees to the Father of our
Lord Jesus Christ." Paul's praying carried Paul's converts farther along the
highway of sainthood than Paul's preaching did. Epaphras did as much or
more by prayer for the Colossian saints than by his preaching. He labored fervently always in prayer for them that "they might stand perfect and complete
in all the will of God."

Preachers are preeminently God's leaders. They are primarily responsible
for the condition of the church. They shape its character, give tone and direction to its life.

Much depends on these leaders. They shape the times and the institutions.
The church is divine, the treasure it encases is heavenly, but it bears the
imprint of the human. The treasure is in earthen vessels, and it smacks of the
vessel. The church of God makes, or is made by, its leaders. Whether it makes
them or is made by them, it will be what its leaders are; spiritual if they are
so, secular if they are, conglomerate if its leaders are. Israel's kings gave character to Israel's piety. A church rarely revolts against or rises above the religion
of its leaders. Strongly spiritual leaders; men of holy might, at the lead, are
tokens of God's favor; disaster and weakness follow the wake of feeble or
worldly leaders. Israel had fallen low when God gave children to be their
princes and babes to rule over them. No happy state is predicted by the
prophets when children oppress God's Israel and women rule over them.
Times of spiritual leadership are times of great spiritual prosperity to the
church.

Prayer is one of the eminent characteristics of strong spiritual leadership.
Men of mighty prayer are men of might and mold things. Their power with
God has the conquering tread.

How can a man preach who does not get his message fresh from God in
the closet? How can he preach without having his faith quickened, his vision
cleared, and his heart warmed by his closeting with God? Alas, for the pulpit
lips which are untouched by this closet flame. Dry and unctionless they will
ever be, and truths divine will never come with power from such lips. As far
as the real interests of religion are concerned, a pulpit without a closet will
always be a barren thing.

A preacher may preach in an official, entertaining, or learned way without
prayer, but between this kind of preaching and sowing God's precious seed with
holy hands and prayerful, weeping hearts there is an immeasurable distance.

A prayerless minister is the undertaker for all God's truth and for God's church. He may have the most costly casket and the most beautiful flowers, but it is a funeral, notwithstanding the charmful array. A prayerless Christian will never learn God's truth; a prayerless ministry will never be able to teach God's truth. Ages of millennial glory have been lost by a prayerless church. The coming of our Lord has been postponed indefinitely by a prayerless church. Hell has enlarged herself and filled her dire caves in the presence of the dead service of a prayerless church.

The best, the greatest offering is an offering of prayer. If the preachers of the twentieth century will learn well the lesson of prayer, and use fully the power of prayer, the millennium will come to its noon ere the century closes. "Pray without ceasing" is the trumpet call to the preachers of the twentieth century. If the twentieth century will get their texts, their thoughts, their words, their sermons in their closets, the next century will find a new heaven and a new earth. The old sin-stained and sin-eclipsed heaven and earth will pass away under the power of a praying ministry.

18

Preachers Need the Prayers of the People

SOMEHOW the practice of praying in particular for the preacher has fallen into disuse or become discounted. Occasionally have we heard the practice arraigned as a disparagement of the ministry, being a public declaration by those who do it of the inefficiency of the ministry. It offends the pride of learning and self-sufficiency, perhaps, and these ought to be offended and rebuked in a ministry that is so derelict as to allow them to exist.

Prayer, to the preacher, is not simply the duty of his profession, a privilege, but it is a necessity. Air is not more necessary to the lungs than prayer is to the preacher. It is absolutely necessary for the preacher to pray. It is an absolute necessity that the preacher be prayed for. These two propositions are wedded into a union which ought never to know any divorce: *the preacher must pray; the preacher must be prayed for*. It will take all the praying he can do, and all the praying he can get done, to meet the fearful responsibilities and gain the largest, truest success in his great work. The true preacher, next to the cultivation of the spirit and fact of prayer in himself, in their most intense form, covets with a great covetousness the prayers of God's people.

The holier a man is, the more does he esteem prayer; the clearer does he see that God gives himself to the praying ones, and that the measure of God's revelation to the soul is the measure of the soul's longing, importunate prayer for God. Salvation never finds its way to a prayerless heart. The Holy Spirit never abides in a prayerless spirit. Preaching never edifies a prayerless soul. Christ knows nothing of prayerless Christians. The gospel cannot be projected by a prayerless preacher. Gifts, talents, education, eloquence, God's call, cannot abate the demand of prayer, but only intensify the necessity for the preacher to pray and to be prayed for. The more the preacher's eyes are opened to the nature, responsibility, and difficulties in his work, the more will he see, and if he be a true preacher the more will he feel, the necessity of prayer; not only the increasing demand to pray himself, but to call on others to help him by their prayers.

Paul is an illustration of this. If any man could project the gospel by dint of personal force, by brain power, by culture, by personal grace, by God's apostolic commission, God's extraordinary call, that man was Paul. That the preacher must be a man given to prayer, Paul is an eminent example. That the true apostolic preacher must have the prayers of other good people to give to his ministry its full quota of success, Paul is a preeminent example. He asks, he covets, he pleads in an impassioned way for the help of all God's saints. He knew that in the spiritual realm, as elsewhere, in union there is strength; that the concentration and aggregation of faith, desire, and prayer increased the volume of spiritual force until it became overwhelming and irresistible in its power. Units of prayer combined, like drops of water, make an ocean which defies resistance. So Paul, with his clear and full apprehension of spiritual dynamics, determined to make his ministry as impressive, as eternal, as irresistible as the ocean, by gathering all the scattered units of prayer and precipitating them on his ministry. May not the solution of Paul's preeminence in labors and results, and impress on the church and the world, be found in this fact that he was able to center on himself and his ministry more of prayer than others? To his brethren at Rome he wrote: "Now I beseech you, brethren, for the Lord Jesus Christ's sake, and for the love of the Spirit, that ye strive together with me in prayers to God for me." To the Ephesians he says: "Praying always with all prayer and supplication in the Spirit, and watching thereunto with all perseverance and supplication for all saints; and for me, that utterance may be given unto me, that I may open my mouth boldly, to make known the mystery of the gospel." To the Colossians he emphasizes: "Withal praying also for us, that God would open unto us a door of utterance, to speak the mystery of Christ, for which I am also in bonds: that I may make it manifest as I ought to speak." To the Thessalonians he says sharply, strongly: "Brethren, pray for us." Paul calls on the Corinthian church to help him: "Ye also helping together by prayer for us." This was to be part of their work. They were to lay to the helping hand of prayer. He in an additional and closing charge to the Thessalonian church about the importance and neccessity of their prayers says: "Finally, brethren, pray for us, that the word of the Lord may have free course, and be glorified, even as it is with you: and that we may be delivered from unreasonable and wicked men." He impresses the Philippians that all his trials and opposition can be made subservient to the spread of the gospel by the efficiency of their prayers for him. Philemon was to prepare a lodging for him, for through Philemon's prayer Paul was to be his guest.

Paul's attitude on this question illustrates his humility and his deep insight into the spiritual forces which project the gospel. More than this, it teaches a lesson for all times, that if Paul was so dependent on the prayers of God's saints to give his ministry success, how much greater the necessity that the prayers of God's saints be centered on the ministry of today!

Paul did not feel that this urgent plea for prayer was to lower his dignity, lessen his influence, or depreciate his piety. What if it did? Let dignity go, let influence be destroyed, let his reputation be marred—he must have their prayers. Called, commissioned, chief of the apostles as he was, all his equipment was imperfect without the prayers of his people. He wrote letters everywhere, urging them to pray for him. Do you pray for your preacher? Do you pray for him in secret? Public prayers are of little worth unless they are founded on or followed up by private praying. The praying ones are to the preacher as Aaron and Hur were to Moses. They hold up his hands and decide the issue that is so fiercely raging around them.

The plea and purpose of the apostles were to put the church to praying. They did not ignore the grace of cheerful giving. They were not ignorant of the place which religious activity and work occupied in the spiritual life; but not one nor all of these, in apostolic importance or urgency, could at all compare in necessity and importance with prayer. The most sacred and urgent pleas were used, the most fervent exhortations, the most comprehensive and arousing words were uttered to enforce the all-important obligation and necessity of prayer.

"Put the saints everywhere to praying" is the burden of the apostolic effort and the keynote of apostolic success. Jesus Christ had striven to do this in the days of his personal ministry. As he was moved by infinite compassion at the ripened fields of earth perishing for lack of laborers—and pausing in his own praying—he tries to awaken the stupid sensibilities of his disciples to the duty of prayer as he charges them, "Pray ye the Lord of the harvest that he will send forth laborers into his harvest." "And he spake a parable unto them to this end, that men ought always to pray and not to faint."

19

Deliberation Is Necessary
for Largest Results from Prayer

Our devotions are not measured by the clock, but time is of their essence. The ability to wait and stay and press belongs essentially to our communicating with God. Hurry, everywhere unseeming and damaging, is so to an alarming extent in the great business of communion with God. Short devotions are the bane of deep piety. Calmness, grasp, strength, are never the companions of hurry. Short devotions deplete spiritual vigor, arrest spiritual progress, sap spiritual foundations, blight the root and bloom of spiritual life. They are the prolific source of backsliding, the sure indication of a superficial piety; they deceive, blight, rot the seed, and impoverish the soil.

It is true that Bible prayers in word and print are short, but the praying men of the Bible were with God through many a sweet and holy wrestling hour. They won by few words but long waiting. The prayers Moses records may be short, but Moses prayed to God with fastings and mighty cryings forty days and nights.

The statement of Elijah's praying may be condensed to a few brief paragraphs, but doubtless Elijah, who when "Praying he prayed," spent many hours of fiery struggle and lofty communicating with God before he could, with assured boldness, say to Ahab, "There shall not be dew nor rain these years, but according to my word." The verbal brief of Paul's prayers is short, but Paul "prayed night and day exceedingly." The "Lord's Prayer" is a divine epitome for infant lips, but the man Christ Jesus prayed many an all-night ere his work was done; and his all-night and long-sustained devotions gave to his work its finish and perfection, and to his character the fullness and glory of its divinity.

Spiritual work is taxing work, and men are loath to do it. Praying, true praying, costs an outlay of serious attention and of time, which flesh and blood do not relish. Few persons are made of such strong fiber that they will make a costly outlay when surface work will pass as well in the market. We can habituate ourselves to our beggarly praying until it looks well to us, at least it keeps up a decent form and quiets conscience—the deadliest of opiates! We can slight our praying, and not realize the peril till the foundations are gone. Hurried devotions make weak faith, feeble convictions, questionable piety. To be little with God is to be little for God. To cut short the praying makes the whole religious character short, stingy, miserly, and slovenly.

It takes good time for the full flow of God into the spirit. Short devotions cut the pipe of God's full flow. It takes time in the secret places to get the full revelation of God. Little time and hurry mar the picture.

Henry Martyn laments that "want of private devotional reading and short-ness of prayer through incessant sermon-making had produced much strangeness between God and his soul." He judged that he had dedicated too much time to *public* ministrations and too little to *private* communion with God. He was much impressed to set apart times for fasting and to devote times for solemn prayer. Resulting from this he records: "Was assisted this morning to pray for two hours." Said William Wilberforce, the peer of kings: "I must secure more time for private devotions. I have been living far too pub-lic for me. The shortening of private devotions starves the soul; it grows lean and faint. I have been keeping too late hours." Of a failure in Parliament he says: "Let me record my grief and shame, and all, probably, from private devo-tions having been contracted, and so God let me stumble." More solitude and earlier hours was his remedy.

More time and early hours for prayer would act like magic to revive and invigorate many a decayed spiritual life. More time and early hours for prayer would be manifest in holy living. A holy life would not be so rare or so diffi-cult a thing if our devotions were not so short and hurried. A Christlike tem-per in its sweet and passionless fragrance would not be so alien and hopeless a heritage if our closet stay were lengthened and intensified. We live shabbily because we pray meanly. Plenty of time to feast in our closets will bring mar-row and fatness to our lives. Our ability to stay with God in our closet mea-sures our ability to stay with God out of the closet. Hasty closet visits are deceptive, defaulting. We are not only deluded by them, but we are losers by them in many ways and in many rich legacies. Tarrying in the closet instructs and wins. We are taught by it, and the greatest victories are often the results of great waiting—waiting till works and plans are exhausted, and silent and patient waiting gains the crown. Jesus Christ asks with an affronted emphasis, "Shall not God avenge his own elect which cry day and night unto him?"

To pray is the greatest thing we can do: and to do it well there must be calmness, time, and deliberation; otherwise it is degraded into the littlest and meanest of things. True praying has the largest results for good; and poor praying, the least. We cannot do too much of real praying; we cannot do too little of the sham. We must learn anew the worth of prayer, enter anew the school of prayer. There is nothing which it takes more time to learn. And if we would learn the wondrous art, we must not give a fragment here and there—"A little talk with Jesus," as the tiny saints sing—but we must demand and hold with iron grasp the best hours of the day for God and prayer, or there will be no praying worth the name.

This, however, is not a day of prayer. Few men there are who pray. Prayer is defamed by preacher and priest. In these days of hurry and bustle, of electricity and steam, men will not take time to pray. Preachers there are who "say prayers" as a part of their program, on regular or state occasions; but who "stirs himself up to take hold upon God?" Who prays as Jacob prayed—till he is crowned as a prevailing, princely intercessor? Who prays as Elijah prayed—till all the locked-up forces of nature were unsealed and a famine-stricken land bloomed as the garden of God? Who prayed as Jesus Christ prayed as out upon the mountain he "continued all night in prayer to God?" The apostles "gave themselves to prayer"—the most difficult thing to get men or even the preachers to do. Laymen there are who will give their money—some of them in rich abundance—but they will not "give themselves" to prayer, without which their money is but a curse. There are plenty of preachers who will preach and deliver great and eloquent addresses on the need of revival and the spread of the kingdom of God, but not many there are who will do that without which all preaching and organizing are worse than vain—pray. It is out of date, almost a lost art, and the greatest benefactor this age could have is the man who will bring the preachers and the church back to prayer.

20

A Praying Pulpit Begets
a Praying Pew

ONLY glimpses of the great importance of prayer could the apostles get before Pentecost. But the Spirit coming and filling on Pentecost elevated prayer to its vital and all-commanding position in the gospel of Christ. The call now of prayer to every saint is the Spirit's loudest and most exacting call. Sainthood's piety is made, refined, perfected, by prayer. The gospel moves with slow and timid pace when the saints are not at their prayers early and late and long.

Where are the Christlike leaders who can teach the modern saints how to pray and put them at it? Do we know we are raising up a prayerless set of saints? Where are the apostolic leaders who can put God's people to praying? Let them come to the front and do the work, and it will be the greatest work which can be done. An increase of educational facilities and a great increase of money force will be the direst curse to religion if they are not sanctified by more and better praying than we are doing. More praying will not come as a matter of course. The campaign for the twentieth- or thirtieth-century fund will not help our praying but hinder if we are not careful. Nothing but a specific effort from a praying leadership will avail. The chief ones must lead in the apostolic effort to establish the vital importance and *fact* of prayer in the heart and life of the church. None but praying leaders can have praying followers. Praying apostles will beget praying saints. A praying pulpit will beget praying pews. We do greatly need somebody who can set the saints to this business of praying. We are not a generation of praying saints. Nonpraying saints are a beggarly gang of saints who have neither the ardor nor the beauty nor the power of saints. Who will restore this breach? The greatest will he be of reformers and apostles, who can set the church to praying.

We put it as our most sober judgment that the great need of the church in this and all ages is men of such commanding faith, of such unsullied holiness, of such marked spiritual vigor and consuming zeal, that their prayers, faith, lives, and ministry will be of such a radical and aggressive form as to work spiritual revolutions which will form eras in individual and church life.

We do not mean men who get up sensational stirs by novel devices, nor those who attract by a pleasing entertainment; but men who can stir things, and work revolutions by the preaching of God's Word and by the power of the Holy Spirit, revolutions which change the whole current of things.

Natural ability and educational advantages do not figure as factors in this matter; but capacity for faith, the ability to pray, the power of thorough conse-cration, the ability of self-denigration, an absolute losing of one's self in God's glory, and an ever-present and insatiable yearning and seeking after all the fullness of God—men who can set the church ablaze for God; not in a noisy, showy way, but with an intense and quiet heat that melts and moves every-thing for God.

God can work wonders if he can get a suitable man. Men can work won-ders if they can get God to lead them. The full endowment of the spirit that turned the world upside down would be eminently useful in these latter days. Men who can stir things mightily for God, whose spiritual revolutions change the whole aspect of things, are the universal need of the church.

The church has never been without these men; they adorn its history; they are the standing miracles of the divinity of the church; their example and his-tory are an unfailing inspiration and blessing. An increase in their number and power should be our prayer.

That which has been done in spiritual matters can be done again, and be better done. This was Christ's view. He said "Verily, verily, I say unto you, he that believeth on me, the works that I do shall he do also; and greater works than these shall he do; because I go unto my Father." The past has not exhausted the possibilities nor the demands for doing great things for God. The church that is dependent on its past history for its miracles of power and grace is a fallen church.

God wants elect men—men out of whom self and the world have gone by a severe crucifixion, by a bankruptcy which has so totally ruined self and the world that there is neither hope nor desire of recovery; men who by this insolvency and crucifixion have turned toward God perfect hearts.

Let us pray ardently that God's promise to prayer may be more than realized.

BOOK

◆8◆

Prayer and Praying Men

1

Praying Saints of the Old Testament

OLD Testament history is filled with accounts of praying saints. The leaders of Israel in those early days were noted for their praying habits. Prayer is the one thing which stands out prominently in their lives.

To begin with, note the incident in Joshua 10 where the very heavenly bodies were made subject to prayer. A prolonged battle was on between the Israelites and their enemies, and when night was rapidly coming on, and it was discovered that a few more hours of daylight were needful to ensure victory for the Lord's hosts, Joshua, that sturdy man of God, stepped into the breach, with prayer. The sun was too rapidly declining in the west for God's people to reap the full fruits of a noted victory, and Joshua, seeing how much depended upon the occasion, cried out in the sight and in the hearing of Israel, "Sun, stand thou still upon Gibeon, and thou, Moon, in the valley of Ajalon." And the sun actually stood still and the moon stopped on her course at the command of this praying man of God, till the Lord's people had avenged themselves upon the Lord's enemies.

Jacob was not a strict pattern of righteousness, prior to his all-night praying. Yet he was a man of prayer and believed in the God of prayer. So we find him swift to call upon God in prayer when he was in trouble. He was fleeing from home fearing Esau, on his way to the home of Laban, a kinsman. As night came on, he lighted on a certain place to refresh himself with sleep, and as he slept he had a wonderful dream in which he saw the angels of God ascending and descending on a ladder which stretched from earth to heaven. It was no wonder when he awoke he was constrained to exclaim, "Surely the LORD is in this place and I knew it not."

Then it was he entered into a very definite covenant with Almighty God, and in prayer vowed a vow unto the Lord, saying, "If God will be with me, and will keep me in this way that I go, and will give me bread to eat and raiment to put on, so that I come again to my father's house in peace; then shall the LORD be my God, and this stone, which I have set for a pillar, shall be God's house; and of all that thou shalt give me I will surely give the tenth unto thee."

With a deep sense of his utter dependence upon God, and desiring above all the help of God, Jacob conditioned his prayer for protection, blessing and guidance by a solemn vow. Thus Jacob supported his prayer to God by a vow.

Twenty years had passed while Jacob tarried at the house of Laban, and he had married two of his daughters and God had given him children. He had increased largely in wealth, and he resolved to leave that place and return home to where he had been reared. Nearing home it occurred to him that he must meet his brother Esau, whose anger had not abated notwithstanding the passage of many years. God, however, had said to him, "Return to thy father's house and to thy kindred, and I will be with thee." In this dire emergency doubtless God's promise and his vow made long ago came to his mind, and he took himself to an all-night season of prayer. Here comes to our notice that strange, inexplicable incident of the angel struggling with Jacob all night long, till Jacob at last obtained the victory. "I will not let thee go except thou bless me." And then and there, in answer to his earnest, pressing and importunate praying, he was richly blessed personally and his name was changed. But even more than that, God went ahead of Jacob's desire, and strangely moved upon the angry nature of Esau; and lo and behold, when Jacob met him next day, Esau's anger had entirely abated, and he vied with Jacob in showing kindness to his brother who had wronged him. No explanation of this remarkable change in the heart of Esau is satisfactory which leaves out prayer.

Samuel, the mighty intercessor in Israel and a man of God, was the product of his mother's prayer. Hannah is a memorable example of the nature and benefits of importunate praying. No son had been born to her and she yearned for a man child. Her whole soul was in her desire. So she went to the house of worship, where Eli, the priest of God, was, and staggering under the weight of that which bore down on her heart she was beside herself and seemed to be really intoxicated. Her desires were too intense for articulation. "She poured out her soul in prayer before the Lord." Insuperable natural difficulties were in the way, but she "multiplied her praying," as the passage means, till her God-lightened heart and her bright face recorded the answer to her prayers, and Samuel was hers by a conscious faith and a nation was restored by faith.

Samuel was born in answer to the vowful prayer of Hannah, for the solemn covenant which she made with God if He would grant her request must not be left out of the account in investigating this incident of a praying woman and the answer she received. It is suggestive in James 5:15 that "The prayer of faith shall save the sick," the word translated means a vow. So that prayer in its highest form of faith is that prayer which carries the whole man as a sacrificial offering. Thus devoting the whole man himself, and his all, to God in a definite, intelligent vow, never to be broken, in a quenchless and impassioned desire for heaven—such an attitude of self-devotement to God mightily helps praying. Samson is somewhat of a paradox when we examine his religious character. But amid all his faults, which were grave in the extreme, he knew the God who hears prayer and he knew how to talk to God.

No farness to which Israel had gone, no depth to which Israel had fallen, no chains however iron with which Israel was bound but that their cry to God easily spanned the distance, fathomed the depths, and broke the chains. It was the lesson they were ever learning and always forgetting, that prayer always brought God to their deliverance, and that there was nothing too hard for God to do for His people. We find all of God's saints in straits at different times in some way or another. Their straits are, however, often the heralds of their great triumphs. But for whatever cause their straits come, or of what kind soever, there is no strait of any degree of direness or from any source whatsoever of any nature whatsoever, from which prayer could not extricate them. The great strength of Samson does not relieve him nor extricate him out of his straits. Read what the Scriptures say:

> And when he came unto Lehi, the Philistines shouted against him; and the Spirit of the Lord came mightily upon him, and the cords that were upon his arms became as flax that was burnt with fire, and his bands loosed from off his hands.
>
> And he found a new jawbone of an ass, and put forth his hand, and took it, and slew a thousand men therewith.
>
> And Samson said, "With the jawbone of an ass, heaps upon heaps, with the jawbone of an ass have I slain a thousand men."
>
> And it came to pass when he had made an end of speaking, that he cast away the jawbone out of his hand, and called that place Ramath-Lehi.
>
> And he was sore athirst, and called on the Lord, and said, "Thou hast given this great deliverance into the hand of thy servant, and now shall I die of thirst, and fall into the hand of the uncircumcised?"
>
> But God clave a hollow place that was in the jaw, and there came water thereout; and when he had drunk, his spirit came again and he revived.

We have another incident in the case of this strange Old Testament character, showing how, when in great straits, their minds involuntarily turned to God in prayer. However irregular in life they were, however far from God they departed, however sinful they might be when trouble came upon these men, they invariably called upon God for deliverance, and, as a rule, when they repented God heard their cries and granted their requests. This incident comes at the close of Samson's life, and shows us how his life ended.

Read the record as found in Judges 16. Samson had formed an alliance with Delilah, a heathen woman, and she, in connivance with the Philistines, sought to discover the source of his immense strength. Three successive times she failed, and at last by her persistence and womanly arts persuaded Samson to divulge to her the wonderful secret. So in an unsuspecting hour he disclosed to her the fact that the source of his strength was in his hair which had never been cut; and she deprived him of his great physical power by cutting off his hair. She called for the Philistines, and they came and put out his eyes and otherwise mistreated him.

On an occasion when the Philistines were gathered together to offer a great sacrifice to Dagon, their idol god, they called for Samson to make sport for them. And the following is the account as he stood there presumably the laughingstock of these enemies of his and of God.

> And Samson said unto the lad that held him by the hand, "Suffer me that I may feel the pillars whereupon the house standeth, that I may lean upon them."
>
> Now the house was full of men and women; and all the lords of the Philistines were there; and there were upon the roof about three thousand men and women, that beheld while Samson made sport.
>
> And Samson called unto the Lord and said, "O Lord God, remember me, I pray thee, and strengthen me, I pray thee, only this once, my God, that I may be at once avenged of the Philistines for my two eyes." And Samson took hold of the two middle pillars upon which the house stood, and on which it was borne up, of the one with his right hand and of the other with his left.
>
> And Samson said, "Let me die with the Philistines." And he bowed himself with all his might, and the house fell upon the lords, and upon all the people that were there within. So the dead which he slew at his death were more than they which he slew in his life.

2

Praying Saints of the Old Testament
(Continued)

JONAH, the man who prayed in the fish's belly, brings to view another remarkable instance of these Old Testament worthies who were given to prayer. This man Jonah, a prophet of the Lord, was a fugitive from God and from the place of duty. He had been sent on a mission of warning to wicked Nineveh, and had been commanded to cry out against them, "for their wickedness is come up before me," said God. But Jonah, through fear or otherwise, declined to obey God, and took passage on a ship for Tarshish, fleeing from God. He seems to have overlooked the plain fact that the same God who had sent him on that alarming mission had His eye upon him as he hid himself on board that vessel. A storm arose as the vessel was on its way to Tarshish, and it was decided to throw Jonah overboard in order to appease God and to avert the destruction of the boat and of all on board. But God was there as He had been with Jonah from the beginning. He had prepared a great fish to swallow Jonah, in order to arrest him, to defeat him in his flight from the post of duty, and to save Jonah that he might help to carry out the purposes of God.

It was Jonah who was in the fish's belly, in that great strait, and passing through a strange experience, who called upon God, who heard him and caused the fish to vomit him out on dry land. What possible force could rescue him from this fearful place? He seemed hopelessly lost, in "the belly of hell," as good as dead and damned. But he prays—what else can he do? And this is just what he had been accustomed to do when in trouble before.

> "I cried by reason of my affliction unto the Lord, and he heard me; out of the belly of hell cried I, and thou heardst my voice."
> And the Lord spake unto the fish, and it vomited out Jonah upon the dry land.

Like others he joined prayer to a vow he had made, for he says in his prayer, "But I will sacrifice unto thee with the voice of thanksgiving; I will pay that that I have vowed. Salvation is of the Lord."

Prayer was the mighty force which brought Jonah from "the belly of hell." Prayer, mighty prayer, has secured the end. Prayer brought God to the rescue of unfaithful Jonah, despite his sin of fleeing from duty, and God could not deny his prayer. Nothing is too hard for prayer because nothing is too hard for God.

That answered prayer of Jonah in the fish's belly in its mighty results became an Old Testament type of the miraculous power displayed in the resurrection of Jesus Christ from the dead. Our Lord puts his seal of truth upon the fact of Jonah's prayer and resurrection.

Nothing can be simpler than these cases of God's mighty deliverance. Nothing is plainer than that prayer has to do with God directly and simply. Nothing is clearer than that prayer has its only worth and significance in the great fact that God hears and answers prayer. This the Old Testament saints strongly believed. It is the one fact that stands out continuously and prominently in their lives. They were essentially men of prayer.

How greatly we need a school to teach the art of praying! This simplest of all arts and mightiest of all forces is ever in danger of being forgotten or depraved. The further we get away from our mother's knees, the further do we get away from the true art of praying. All our after-schooling and our after-teachers unteach us the lessons of prayer. Men prayed well in Old Testament times because they were simple men and lived in simple times. They were childlike, lived in childlike times and had childlike faith.

In citing the Old Testament saints noted for their praying habits, by no means must David be overlooked, a man who preeminently was a man of prayer. With him prayer was a habit, for we hear him say, "Evening and morning and at noon will I pray and cry aloud." Prayer with the sweet psalmist of Israel was no strange occupation. He knew the way to God and was often found in that way. It is no wonder we hear his call so clear and impressive, "O come, let us worship and bow down; let us kneel before the Lord our maker." He knew God as the one being who could answer prayer: "O thou that hearest prayer, to thee shall all flesh come."

When God smote the child born of Bathsheba, because David had by his grievous sins given occasion for the enemies of God to blaspheme, it is no surprise that we find him engaged in a week's praying, asking God for the life of the child. The habit of his life asserted itself in this great emergency in his home, and we find him fasting and praying for the child to recover. The fact that God denied his request does not at all affect the question of David's habit of praying. Even though he did not receive what he asked for, his faith in God was not in the least affected. The fact is that while God did not give him the life of that baby boy, He afterward gave him another son, even Solomon. So that possibly the latter son was a far greater blessing to him than would have been the child for whom he prayed.

In close connection with this season of prayer, we must not overlook David's penitential praying when Nathan, by command of God, uncovered

David's two great sins of adultery and murder. At once David acknowledged his wickedness, saying unto Nathan, "I have sinned." And as showing his deep grief over his sin, his heartbroken spirit, and his genuine repentance, it is necessary only to read Psalm 51 where confession of sin, deep humiliation and prayer are the chief ingredients of the Psalm.

David knew where to find a sin-pardoning God, and was received back again and had the joys of salvation restored to him by earnest, sincere, penitential praying. Thus are all sinners brought into the divine favor, thus do they find pardon, and thus do they find a new heart.

The entire Book of Psalms brings prayer to the front, and prayer fairly bristles before our eyes as we read this devotional book of the Scriptures.

Nor must even Solomon be overlooked in the famous catalogue of men who prayed in Old Testament times. Whatever their faults, they did not forget the God who hears prayer nor did they cease to seek the God of prayer. While this wise man in his later life departed from God, and his sun set under a cloud, we find him praying at the commencement of his reign.

Solomon went to Gibeon to offer sacrifice, which always meant that prayer went in close companionship with sacrifice, and while there, the Lord appeared to Solomon in a vision by night, saying unto him, "Ask what I shall give thee." The sequel shows the material out of which Solomon's character was formed. What was his request?

> O Lord my God, thou hast made thy servant king instead of my father; and I am but a little child; I know not how to go out or to come in.
>
> And thy servant is in the midst of thy people which thou hast chosen, a great people, that cannot be numbered nor counted for multitude.
>
> Give therefore thy servant an understanding heart to judge thy people, that I may discern between good and bad; for who is able to judge this thy so great a people?

We do not wonder that it is recorded as a result of such praying:

> And the speech pleased the Lord, that Solomon had asked this thing.
> And God said unto him, "Because thou hast asked this thing, and hast not asked for thyself long life; neither hast asked riches for thyself, nor hast asked the life of thy enemies, but has asked for thyself understanding to discern judgment;
>
> "Behold I have done according to thy word; Lo, I have given thee a wise and understanding heart; so that there was none like thee before thee, neither after thee shall any arise like unto thee.
>
> "Also I have given thee that which thou hast not asked, both riches and honor; so that there shall not be any among the kings like unto thee all thy days."

What praying was this! What self-deprecation and simplicity! "I am but a little child." How he specified the one thing needful! And see how much more he received than that for which he asked!

Take the remarkable prayer at the dedication of the temple. Possibly this is the longest recorded prayer in God's Word. How comprehensive, pointed, intensive, it is! Solomon could not afford to lay the foundations of God's house in anything else but in prayer. And God heard this prayer as he heard him before, "And when Solomon had made an end of his praying, the fire came down from heaven, and the glory of the Lord filled the house," thus God attested the acceptance of this house of worship and of Solomon, the praying king.

The list of these Old Testament saints given to prayer grows as we proceed, and is too long to notice at length all of them. But the name of Isaiah, the great evangelical prophet, and that of Jeremiah, the weeping prophet, must not be left out of the account. Still others might be mentioned. These are sufficient, and with their names we may close the list. Let careful readers of old Scripture keep the prayer question in mind, and they will see how great a place prayer occupied in the minds and lives of the men of those early days.

3

Abraham, the Man of Prayer

ABRAHAM, the friend of God, was a striking illustration of one of the Old Testament saints who believed strongly in prayer. Abraham was not a shadowy figure by any means. In the simplicity and dimness of the patriarchal dispensation, as illustrated by him, we learn the worth of prayer, as well as discover its antiquity. The fact is, prayer reaches back to the first ages of man on earth. We see how the energy of prayer is absolutely required in the simplest as well as in the most complex dispensations of God's grace. When we study Abraham's character, we find that after his call to go out into an unknown country, on his journey with his family and his household servants, wherever he tarried by the way for the night or longer, he always erected an altar, and "called upon the name of the Lord." And this man of faith and prayer was one of the first to erect a family altar, around which to gather his household and offer the sacrifices of worship, of praise and of prayer. These altars built by Abraham were, first of all, essentially altars about which he gathered his household, as distinguished from secret prayer.

As God's revelations became fuller and more perfect, Abraham's prayerfulness increased, and it was at one of these spiritual eras that "Abraham fell on his face and God talked with him." On still another occasion we find this man, "the father of the faithful," on his face before God, astonished almost to incredulity at the purposes and revelations of Almighty God to him in promising him a son in his old age, and the wonderful arrangements which God made concerning his promised son.

Even Ishmael's destiny is shaped by Abraham's prayer when he prayed, "O that Ishmael might live before thee!"

What a remarkable story is that of Abraham's standing before God repeating his intercessions for the wicked city of Sodom, the home of his nephew Lot, doomed by God's decision to destroy it! Sodom's fate was for a while stayed by Abraham's praying, and was almost entirely relieved by the humility and insistence of the praying of this man who believed strongly in prayer and who knew how to pray. No other recourse was opened to Abraham to save Sodom but prayer. Perhaps the failure to ultimately rescue Sodom from her doom of destruction was due to Abraham's optimistic view of the spiritual condition of things in that city. It might have been possible—who knows—that if Abraham had entreated God once more, and asked Him to spare the city if even one righteous man was found there, for Lot's sake, God might have heeded Abraham's request.

Note another instance in the life of Abraham as showing how he was a man of prayer and had power with God. Abraham had journeyed to and was sojourning in Gerar. Fearing that Abimelech might kill him and appropriate Sarah his wife to his own lustful uses, Abraham deceived Abimelech by claiming that Sarah was his sister. God appeared unto Abimelech in a dream and warned him not to touch Sarah, telling him that she was the wife of Abraham, and not his sister. Then he said unto Abimelech, "Now restore therefore the man his wife; for he is a prophet, and he shall pray for thee, and thou shalt live." And the conclusion of the incident is thus recorded: "So Abraham prayed unto God, and God healed Abimelech and his wife, and his maid servants, and they bare children. For the Lord had fast closed up all the wombs of the house of Abimelech because of Sarah, his wife."

This was a case somewhat on the line of that of Job at the close of his fearful experience and his terrible trials, when his friends, not understanding Job, neither comprehending God's dealings with this servant of His, falsely charged Job with being in sin as the cause of all his troubles. God said to these friends of Job, "My servant Job shall pray for you, for him will I accept. And the Lord turned the captivity of Job when he had prayed for his friends."

Almighty God knew his servant Job as a man of prayer, and he could afford to send these friends of Job to him to pray in order to carry out and fulfill his plans and purposes.

It was Abraham's rule to stand before the Lord in prayer. His life was surcharged with prayer and Abraham's dispensation was sanctified by prayer. For wherever he halted in his pilgrimage, prayer was his inseparable accompaniment. Side by side with the altar of sacrifice was the altar of prayer. He got up early in the morning to the place where he stood before the Lord in prayer.

4

Moses, the Mighty Intercessor

PRAYER unites with the purposes of God and lays itself out to secure those purposes. How often would the wise and benign will of God fail in its rich and beneficent ends by the sins of the people if prayer had not come in to arrest wrath and make the promise sure! Israel as a nation would have met their just destruction and their just fate after their apostasy with the golden calf had it not been for the interposition and unfainting importunity of Moses' forty days' and forty nights' praying!

Marvelous was the effect of the character of Moses by his marvelous praying. His near and sublime communication with God in the giving of the law worked no transfiguration of character like the tireless praying of those forty days in prayer with God. It was when he came down from that long struggle of prayer that his face shone with such dazzling brightness. Our mounts of transfiguration and the heavenly shining in character and conduct are born of seasons of wrestling prayer. All-night praying has changed many a Jacob, the supplanter, into Israel, a prince, who has power with God and with men.

No mission was more majestic in purpose and results than that of Moses, and none was more responsible, diligent, and difficult. In it we are taught the sublime ministry and rule of prayer. Not only is it the medium of supply and support, but it is a compassionate agency through which the pitying long-suffering of God has an outflow. Prayer is a medium to restrain God's wrath, that mercy might rejoice against judgment.

Moses himself and his mission were the creation of prayer. Thus it is recorded: "When Jacob was come into Egypt, and your fathers cried unto the Lord, then the Lord sent Moses and Aaron, who brought your fathers out of Egypt, and made them dwell in this place." This is the genesis of the great movement for the deliverance of the Hebrews from Egyptian bondage.

The great movements of God have had their origin and energy in and were shaped by prayers of men. Prayer has directly to deal with God. Other ends, collateral and incidental, are secured by prayer, but mainly, almost solely, prayer has to deal with God. He is pleased to order his policy, and base his action on the prayers of his saints. Prayer influences God greatly. Moses cannot do God's great work, though God-commissioned, without praying much. Moses cannot govern God's people and carry out the divine plans, without having his censer filled full of the incense of prayer. The work of God cannot be done without the fire and fragrance are always burning, ascending and perfuming.

Moses' prayers are often found relieving the terrible stroke of God's wrath. Four times were the prayers of Moses solicited by Pharaoh to relieve him of the fearful stroke of God's wrath. "Entreat the Lord," most earnestly begged Pharaoh of Moses, while the loathsome frogs were upon him. And "Moses cried unto the Lord because of the frogs which God had brought against the land of Egypt, and the Lord did according to the word of Moses." When the grievous plague of flies had corrupted the whole land, Pharaoh again piteously cried out to Moses, "Entreat for me." Moses went out from Pharaoh and entreated the Lord, and the Lord again did according to the word of Moses. The mighty thunderings and hail in their alarming and destructive fury extorted from this wicked king the very same earnest appeal to Moses, "Entreat the Lord." And Moses went out from the city into privacy, and alone with Almighty God, he "spread abroad his hands unto the Lord, and the thunderings and hail ceased, and the rain was not poured out upon the earth."

Though Moses was the man of law, yet with him prayer asserted its mighty force. With him, as in the more spiritual dispensation, it could have been said, "My house is the house of prayer."

Moses accepts at its full face value the foundation principle of praying that prayer has to do with God. With Abraham we saw this clearly and strongly enunciated. With Moses it is clearer and stronger still if possible. Moses declared that prayer affected God, that God was influenced in his conduct by prayer, and that God hears and answers prayer even when the hearing and answering might change his conduct and reverse his action. Stronger than all other laws, and more inflexible than any other decree, is the decree, "Call upon me and I will answer you."

Moses lived near God, and had the freest and most unhindered and boldest access to God, but this, instead of abating the necessity of prayer, made it more necessary, obvious and powerful. Familiarity and closeness to God gives relish, frequency, point, and potency to prayer. Those who know God the best are the richest and most powerful in prayer. Little acquaintance with God, and strangeness and coldness to him, make prayer a rare and feeble thing.

There were conditions of extremity to which Moses was reduced which prayer did not relieve, but there is no position of extremity which baffles God, when prayer puts God into the matter. Moses' mission was a divine one. It was ordered, directed, and planned by God. The more there is of God in a movement, the more there is of prayer, conspicuous and controlling. Moses' prayer rule of the church illustrates the necessity of courage and persistence in prayer. For forty days and forty nights was Moses pressing his prayer for the salvation of the Lord's people. So intense was his concern for them which accompanied his long season of praying, that bodily infirmities and appetites were retired. How strangely the prayers of a righteous man affect God is evident from the exclamation of God to Moses, "Now, therefore, let me alone, that my wrath may wax hot against them, that I may consume them; and I will make of thee a great nation." The presence of such an influence over God fills us with astonishment, awe and fear. How lofty, bold, and devoted must be such a pleader!

Read this from the divine record:

> And Moses returned unto the Lord, and said, "Oh, this people have sinned a great sin, and have made them gods of gold!
>
> "Yet now if thou wilt forgive their sin—and if not, blot me, I pray thee, out of thy book which thou hast written."
>
> And the Lord said unto Moses, "Whosoever hath sinned against me, him will I blot out of my book.
>
> "Therefore now go, and lead the people unto the place of which I have spoken unto thee. Behold my angel shall go before thee."

The rebellion of Korah was the occasion of God's anger flaming out against the whole congregation of Israel, who sympathized with these rebels. Again Moses appears on the stage of action, this time having Aaron to join him in intercession for these sinners against God. But it only shows that in a serious time like this Moses knew to whom to go for relief, and was encouraged to pray that God would stay his wrath and spare Israel. Here is what is said about the matter:

> "And the Lord spake unto Moses and Aaron, saying,
>
> "Separate yourselves from among this congregation, that I may consume them in a moment."
>
> And they fell on their faces, and said, "O God, the God of the spirits of all flesh, shall one man sin, and wilt thou be wroth with all the congregation?"

The assumption, pride and rebellion of Miriam, sister of Moses, in which she had the presence and sympathy of Aaron, put the praying and the spirit of Moses in the noblest and most amiable light. Because of her sin God smote her with leprosy. But Moses made tender and earnest intercession for his sister who had so grievously offended God, and his prayer saved her from the fearful and incurable malady.

The record is intensely interesting:

> And the anger of the Lord was kindled against them and the cloud departed from off the tabernacle and behold, Miriam became leprous, white as snow; and Aaron looked upon Miriam, and behold she was leprous.
>
> And Aaron said unto Moses, "Alas, my Lord, I beseech thee, lay not the sin unto us, wherein we have done foolishly, and wherein we have sinned.

"Let her not be as one dead, of whom the flesh is half consumed when he cometh out of his mother's womb."

And Moses cried unto the Lord, saying, "Heal her, O God, I beseech thee."

And the Lord said unto Moses, "If her father had but spit in her face, should she not be ashamed seven days? Let her be shut out from the camp seven days, and after that let her be received again."

The murmurings of the children of Israel furnished conditions which called into play the full forces of prayer. They impressively bring out the intercessory feature of prayer and disclose Moses in his great office as an intercessor before God in behalf of others. It was at Marah, where the waters were bitter and the people grievously murmured against Moses and God.

Here is the Scripture account:

And when they came to Marah, they could not drink of the waters of Marah; for they were bitter; therefore the name of it was called Marah.

And the people murmured against Moses, saying, "What shall we drink?"

And Moses cried unto the Lord; and the Lord showed him a tree, which when he had cast into the waters, the waters were made sweet; there he made for them a statute and an ordinance, and there he proved them.

How many of the bitter places of the earth have been sweetened by prayer the records of eternity alone will disclose.

Again at Taberah the people complained, and God became angry with them, and Moses came again to the front and stepped into the breach and prayed for them. Here is the brief account:

And when the people complained, it displeased the Lord; and the Lord heard it; and his anger was kindled; and the fire of the Lord burnt among them, and consumed them that were in the uttermost part of the camp.

And the people cried unto Moses, and when Moses prayed unto the Lord, the fire was quenched.

Moses got what he asked for. His praying was specific and God's answer was likewise specific. Always was he heard by Almighty God when he prayed, and always was he answered by God. Once the answer was not specific. He had prayed to go into Canaan. The answer came but not what he asked for. He was given a vision of the Promised Land, but he was not allowed to go over Jordan into that land of promise. It was a prayer on the order of Paul's when he prayed three times for the removal of the thorn in the flesh. But the thorn was not removed. Grace, however, was vouchsafed which made the thorn a blessing.

It must not be thought that because the 90th Psalm is incorporated with what is known as the "Psalms of David," that David was the author of it. By general consent it is attributed to Moses, and it gives us a sample of the praying of this giver of the law of God to the people. It is a prayer worth studying. It is sacred to us because it has been the requiem uttered over our dead for many years. It has blessed the grave of many a sleeping saint. But its very familiarity may cause us to lose its full meaning. Wise will we be if we digest it, not for the dead, but for the living, that it may teach us how to live, how to pray while living, and how to die. "So teach us to number our days that we may apply our hearts to wisdom. Establish thou the work of our hands, yea, the work of our hands establish thou it."

5

Elijah, the Praying Prophet

ELIJAH is preeminently the elder of the prophets. The crown, the throne and the scepter are his. His garments are white with flame. He seems exalted in his fiery and prayerful nature, as a being seemingly superhuman, but the New Testament places him alongside of us as man of like nature with us. Instead of placing himself outside the sphere of humanity, in the marvelous results of his praying, it points to him as an example to be imitated and as inspiration to stimulate us. To pray like Elijah, and to have results like Elijah, is the crying need of the times.

Elijah had learned the lesson of prayer, and had graduated in that divine school ere we know him. Somewhere in the secret places, on mountain or in plain, he had been alone with God, an intercessor against the debasing idolatry of Ahab. Mightily had his prayers prevailed with God. How confidently and well assured were the answers to his praying.

He had been talking with God about vengeance. He was the embodiment of his times. Those times were times of vengeance. The intercessor was not to be clothed with an olive branch with its fillet of wood, the symbol of a suppliant for mercy, but with fire, the symbol of justice and the messenger of wrath. How abruptly does he come before us in the presence of Ahab! Well assured and with holy boldness does he declare before the astonished, cowering king his message of fearful import, a message gained by his earnest praying, "in praying he prayed that it might not rain," and God did not deny his prayer. "As the Lord God of Israel liveth, before whom I stand, there shall not be dew nor rain these years but according to my word."

The secret of his praying and the character of the man are found in the words, "Before whom I stand." We are here reminded of Gabriel's words to Zacharias in informing this priest of the coming of a son to him and his wife in their old age: "I am Gabriel that standeth in the presence of God." The archangel Gabriel had scarcely more unflinching devotion, more courage, and more readiness of obedience, and more jealousy of God's honor, than Elijah. What projecting power do we see in his prayer! "And it rained not on the earth by the space of three years and six months." What omnipotent forces which can command the powers of nature! "Not dew nor rain." What man is this who dares utter such a claim or assert such a power? If his claim be false, he is a fanatic or a madman. If his claim be true, he has stayed the benevolent arm of Omnipotence, and put himself, by God's leave, in God's place. The accursed and burnt-up land and the fiery, rainless and dewless days and nights, attest to the truth of his saying, and prove the sternness, strength, firmness and passion of the man who holds back the clouds and stays the blessed visitation of the rain. Elijah is his name, and this attests the truth of that name, "My God is Jehovah."

His prayers have the power to stay the beneficial course of nature. He stands in God's stead in this matter. The sober, passionless, unimaginative James, the brother of our Lord, in his Epistle, says to us: "See what prayer can do, by Elijah! Pray as Elijah prayed. Let the righteous man put forth to its fullest extent the energy of prayer. Let saints and sinners, angels and devils, see and feel the mighty potencies of prayer. See how the prayer of a good man has power and influence, and avails with God!"

No sham praying was that of Elijah, no mere performance, no spiritless, soulless, official praying was it. Elijah was in Elijah's praying. The whole man, with all his fiery forces, was in it. Almighty God to him was real. Prayer to him was the means of projecting God in full force on the world, in order to vindicate his name, establish his own being, to avenge his blasphemed name and violated law, and to vindicate his servants.

Instead of "prayed earnestly," in James 5:17, the Revised Version has it, "In his prayer he prayed," or "with prayer he prayed." That is, with all the combined energies of prayer he prayed.

Elijah's praying was strong, insistent, and resistless in its elements of power. Feeble praying secures no results and brings neither glory to God nor good to man.

Elijah learned new and higher lessons of prayer while hidden away by God and with God when he was by the brook Cherith. He was doubtless communing with God while Ahab was searching all lands for him. After a while he was ordered to Sarepta, where God had commanded a widow to sustain him. He went there for the widow's good as well as for his own. A benefit to Elijah and a signal good to the widow were the results of Elijah's going. While this woman provided for him, he provided for the woman. Elijah's prayers did more for the woman than the woman's hospitality did for Elijah. Great trials awaited the widow and great sorrows too. Her widowhood and her poverty tell of her struggles and her sorrows. Elijah was there to relieve her poverty and to assuage her griefs.

Here is the interesting account:

> And it came to pass that after these things, the son of the woman, the mistress of the house, fell sick; and his sickness was sore, that there was no breath left in him.
>
> And she said unto Elijah, "What have I do to with thee, O thou man of God? Art thou come unto me to call my sin to remembrance and to slay my son?"
>
> And he said unto her, "Give me thy son." And he took him out of her

bosom, and carried him up into a loft, where he abode, and laid him upon his own bed.

And he cried unto the Lord, and said, "O Lord my God, hast thou also brought evil upon the widow with whom I sojourn by slaying her son?"

And he stretched himself upon the child three times, and cried unto the Lord, and said, "O Lord my God, I pray thee let this child's soul come into him again."

And the Lord heard the voice of Elijah, and the soul of the child came into him again, and he revived.

And Elijah took the child and brought him down out of the chamber into the house, and delivered him unto his mother. And Elijah said, "See, thy son liveth."

And the woman said to Elijah, "Now by this I know that thou art a man of God, and that the word of the Lord in thy mouth is truth."

Elijah's prayer enters regions where prayer had never gone before. The awful, mysterious and powerful regions of the dead are now invaded by the presence and demands of prayer. Jesus Christ refers to Elijah's going to this widow as mainly, if not solely, for her good. Elijah's presence and praying keep the woman from starving and bring her son back from death. Surely no sorrow is like the bitterness of the loss of an only son. With what assured confidence Elijah faces the conditions! There is no hesitancy in his actions, and there is no pause in his faith. He takes the dead son to his own room, and alone with God he makes the issue. In that room God meets him and the struggle is with God alone. The struggle is too intense and too sacred for companionship or for spectator. The prayer is made to God and the issue is with God. The child has been taken by God, and God rules in the realms of death. In his hands are the issues of life and death. Elijah believed that God had taken the child's spirit, and that God could as well restore that spirit. God answered Elijah's prayer. The answer was the proof of Elijah's mission from God, and of the truth of God's Word. The dead child brought to life was a sure conviction of this truth: "Now by this I know that thou art a man of God, and that the word of the Lord in thy mouth is truth." Answers to prayer are the evidences of the being of God and of the truth of his Word.

The immortal test of Elijah made in the presence of an apostate king, and in the face of a backslidden nation and an idolatrous priesthood on Mount Carmel, is a sublime exhibition of faith and prayer. In the contest the prophets of Baal had failed. No fire from heaven falls from heaven in answer to their frantic cries. Elijah, in great quietness of spirit and with confident assurance, calls Israel to him. He repairs the wasted altar of God, the altar of sacrifice and of prayer, and puts the pieces of the bullock in order on the altar. He then uses every preventive against any charge of deception. Everything is flooded with water. Then Elijah prays a model prayer, remarkable for its clearness, its simplicity and its utmost candor. It is noted for its brevity and its faith.

Read the account given in the Scriptures:

> And it came to pass at the time of the offering of the evening sacrifice, that Elijah the prophet came near and said, "Lord God of Abraham, Isaac and of Israel, let it be known this day that thou art God in Israel, and that I am thy servant, and that I have done all these things at thy word.
>
> "Hear me, O Lord, hear me, that this people may know that thou art the Lord God, and that thou hast turned their heart back again."
>
> Then the fire of the Lord fell, and consumed the burnt sacrifice, and the wood, and the stones, and the dust, and licked up the water that was in the trench.
>
> And when all the people saw it, they fell on their faces; and they said, "The Lord, he is God; The Lord, he is God."

Elijah had been dealing directly with God as before. True prayer always deals with God. This prayer of Elijah was to determine the existence of the true God, and the answer direct from God settles the question. The answer is also the credentials of Elijah's divine mission and the evidence that God deals with men. If we had more of Elijah's praying, marvels would not be the marvels that they are now to us. God would not be so strange, so far away in being and so feeble in action. Everything is tame and feeble because our praying is so tame and feeble.

God said to Elijah, "Go show thyself to Ahab, and I will send rain on the earth." Elijah acted promptly on the divine order, and showed himself to Ahab. He had made his issue with Ahab, Israel, and Baal. The whole current of national feeling had turned back to God. The day was fading into the evening shades. No rain had come. But Elijah did not fold his arms and say the promise had failed, but gave point and fulfilment to the promise.

Here is the Scripture record with the result given:

> And Elijah said unto Ahab, "Get thee up, eat and drink, for there is a sound of abundance of rain."
>
> So Ahab went up to eat and to drink. And Elijah went up to the top of Carmel. And he cast himself down upon the earth, and put his face between his knees.
>
> And said to his servant, "Go up now, look toward the sea." And he went up and looked, and said, "There is nothing." And he said, "Go again seven times."
>
> And it came to pass at the seventh time that he said, "Behold there riseth a little cloud out of the sea, like a man's hand." And he said, Go up, say unto Ahab, "Prepare thy chariot, and get thee down, that the rain stop thee not."
>
> And it came to pass in the meanwhile, that the heaven was black with clouds and wind, and there was a great rain. And Ahab rode and went to Jezreel.
>
> And the hand of the Lord was on Elijah.

Then it was, as James records, "And he prayed again, and the heaven gave rain, and the earth brought forth her fruit."

Elijah's importunate, fiery praying and God's promise brought the rain. Prayer carries the promise to its gracious fulfillment. It takes persistent and persevering prayer to give to the promise its largest and most gracious results. In this instance it was expectant prayer, watchful of results, looking for the answer. Elijah had the answer in the small cloud like a man's hand. He had the inward assurance of the answer even before he had the rain. How Elijah's praying shames our feeble praying! His praying brought things to pass. It vindicated the existence and being of God, brought conviction to dull and sluggish consciences, and proved that God was still God in the nation. Elijah's praying turned a whole nation back to God, ordered the moving of the clouds, and directed the falling of the rain. It called down fire from heaven to prove the existence of God or to destroy God's enemies.

The praying of the elder prophet of Israel was clothed in his robes of fire. The golden crown was on his head, and his censer was full and fragrant with the flame, the melody and the perfume of prayer. What wonderful power clothed him on this occasion! It was no wonder that Elisha cried out as he saw this fiery prophet of the Lord enter the chariot for his heavenly ride, "My father! My father! The chariot of Israel and the horsemen thereof!" But chariots and armies could not begin to do as much for Israel as did this praying Elijah. Prayers are omnipotent forces, world-wide and heaven-reaching.

Where are the praying ones of modern times of fiery faith who can incense Elijah's prayers? We need at this time rulers in the church who can add to the force, flame and fragrance of Elijah's praying by their own prayers.

Elijah could touch nothing but by prayer. God was with him mightily because he was mighty in prayer.

In the contest with the prophets of Baal, he makes the issue clearly and positively to determine the true God, as one to be made by prayer. Does God live? Is the Bible a revelation from him? How often in these days are those questions rising? How often do they need to be settled? An appeal by prayer is the only settlement to them. Where is the trouble? Not in God but in our praying. The proof of God and of his being is that he answers prayer. It takes the faith and prayer of Elijah to settle the question. Where are the Elijahs in the church of the present day? Where are the men of like passions as he, who can pray as he prayed? We have thousands of men of like passions, but where are the men of like praying as he was? Notice with what calm, assured confidence he stakes the issue and builds the altar. How calm and pointed is his prayer on that occasion!

Instead of such praying being out of the range of New Testament principles and moderation, this very praying of Elijah is pressed as an example to be imitated and as an illustration of what prayer is and what prayer can do when performed by the right men in the right way. Elijah's results could be secured if we had more Elijah men to do the praying.

Elijah prayed really, truly, and earnestly. How much of praying there is at the present time which is not real praying, but is a mere shell, shucks, and mere words! Much of it might well be termed non-praying. The world is full of such praying. It goes nowhere, it avails nothing, it brings no returns. In fact, no returns nor results are expected.

The requisites of true prayer are the requisites of scriptural, vital, personal religion. They are the requisites of real religious service in this life. Primary among these requisites is that in serving, we serve. So in praying, we must pray. Truth and heart reality, these are the core, the substance, the sum, the heart of prayer. There are no possibilities in prayer unless we really pray in all simplicity, reality, and trueness. Prayerless praying—how common, how popular, how delusive and vain!

6

Hezekiah, the Praying King

THE great religious reformation under King Hezekiah and the prophet Isaiah was thoroughly impregnated with prayer in its various stages. King Hezekiah, of Judah, will serve as an illustration of a praying elder of God's church, white-robed and gold-crowned. He had genius and strength, wisdom and piety. He was a statesman, a general, a poet and a religious reformer. He is a distinct surprise to us, not so much because of his strength and genius—they were to be expected—but in his piety, under all the circumstances connected with him. The rare statement, "He did that which was right in the sight of the Lord," is a glad and thrilling surprise when we consider all his antecedents and his environments. Where did he come from? Under what circumstances was his childhood life spent? Who were his parents and what was their religious character? Worldliness, half-heartedness, and utter apostasy marked the reign of his father, grandfather, and his great-grandfather. His home surroundings as he grew up were far from being favorable to godliness and faith in God. One thing, however, favored him. He was fortunate in having Isaiah for his friend and counselor when he assumed the crown of Judah. How much good there is in a ruler's having a God-fearing man for a counselor and an associate!

With what familiar and successful praying did he intercede with God is seen in the Passover feast, in which a number of the people were unfitted to participate. They had not prepared themselves by the required ceremonial cleansing, and it was important that they be allowed to eat the Passover feast with all the others.

Here is the brief account with special reference to the praying of Hezekiah and the result:

> For there were many in the congregation that were not sanctified; therefore the Levites had the charge of the killing of the passover for every one that was not clean, to sanctify them unto the Lord.
>
> For a multitude of the people had not cleansed themselves yet did they eat the passover otherwise than it was written. But Hezekiah prayed for them saying, "The Good Lord pardon every one. That prepareth his heart to seek God, the Lord God of his fathers, though he be not cleansed according to the purification of the sanctuary."
>
> And the Lord hearkened to Hezekiah, and healed the people.

So the Lord heard him as he prayed, and even the violation of the most sacred law of the Passover was forgiven in answer to the prayer of this praying, God-fearing king. Law must yield its scepter to prayer.

The strength, directness and foundation of his faith and prayer are found in his words to his army. Memorable words are they, stronger and mightier than all the hosts of Sennacherib:

> Be strong and courageous; be not afraid nor dismayed for the king of Assyria, nor for all the multitude that is with him; for there be more with us than with him.
>
> With him is an arm of flesh; but with us is the Lord our God to help us, and to fight our battles. And the people rested themselves upon the words of Hezekiah, king of Judah.

His defense against the mighty enemies of God was prayer. His enemies quailed and were destroyed by his prayers when his own armies were powerless. God's people were always safe when their princes were princes in prayer.

An occasion of serious import came to the people of God during his reign which was to test his faith in God and furnish opportunity to try the prayer agency to obtain deliverance. Judah was sorely pressed by the Assyrians, and, humanly speaking, defeat and captivity seemed imminent. The King of Assyria sent a commission to defy and blaspheme the name of God and to insult King Hezekiah, and they uttered their insults and blasphemy publicly. Note what Hezekiah immediately did without hesitation:

> And it came to pass when King Hezekiah heard it, that he rent his clothes and covered himself with sackcloth, and went into the house of the Lord.

His very first impression was to turn to God by going to the "house of prayer." God was in his thoughts, and prayer was the first thing to be done. And so he sent messengers to Isaiah to join him in prayer. In such an emergency God must not be left out of the account. God must be appealed to for deliverance from these blasphemous enemies of God and His people.

Just at this particular juncture the forces of the King of Assyria, which were besieging Hezekiah, were diverted from an immediate attack on Jerusalem. The King of Assyria, however, sent to Hezekiah a defaming and blasphemous letter.

For the second time, as he is insulted and beset by the forces of this heathen king, he enters the house of the Lord, the "house of prayer." Where else should he go? And to whom should he appeal but unto the God of Israel?

> And Hezekiah received the letter from the hand of the messengers, and read it; and Hezekiah went up to the house of the Lord, and spread it before the Lord.
>
> And Hezekiah prayed unto the Lord: "O Lord of hosts, the God of Israel that

dwellest between the cherubim, Thou art the God, even thou alone, of all the kingdoms of the earth. Thou hast made heaven and earth.

"Now, therefore, O Lord our God, save us from his hand, that all the kingdoms of the earth may know that thou art the Lord, even thou only."

And note the speedy answer and the marvelous results of such praying by this God-fearing king. First, Isaiah gave the king full assurance that he need fear nothing. God had heard the prayer, and would give a great deliverance.

Then secondly, the angel of the Lord came with swift wings and smote 185,000 Assyrians. The king was vindicated, God was honored, and the people of God were saved.

The united prayers of the praying king and of the praying prophet were almighty forces in bringing deliverance and destroying God's enemies. Armies lay at their mercy, defenseless; and angels, swift-winged and armed with almighty power and vengeance, were their allies.

Hezekiah had ministered in prayer in destroying idolatry and in reforming his kingdom. In meeting his enemies, prayer had been his chief weapon. He now comes to try its efficiency against the set and declared purposes of Almighty God. Will it avail in this new field of action? Let us see. Hezekiah was very sick, and God sends his own familiar friend and wise counselor and prophet, Isaiah, to warn him of his approaching end, and to tell him to arrange all his affairs for his final departure. This is the scriptural statement:

> In those days was Hezekiah sick unto death. And the Prophet Isaiah, the son of Amoz, came to him, and said unto him, "Thus saith the Lord: Set thy house in order, for thou shalt die and not live."

The decree came direct from God that he should die. What can set aside or reverse that divine decree of heaven? Hezekiah had never been in a condition so insuperable with a decree so direct and definite from God. Can prayer change the purposes of God? Can prayer snatch from the jaws of death one who has been decreed to die? Can prayer save a man from an incurable sickness? These were the questions with which his faith had now to deal. But his faith does not seem to pause one moment. His faith is not staggered one minute at the sudden and definite news conveyed to him by the Lord's prophet. No such questions which modern unbelief or disbelief would raise are started in his mind. At once he gives himself to prayer. Immediately without delay he applies to God who issued the edict. To whom else could he go? Cannot God change his own purposes if he chooses?

Note what Hezekiah did in this emergency, sorely pressed, and see the gracious result:

> Then he turned his face to the wall and prayed unto the Lord, saying,
> "I beseech thee, O Lord, remember now how I have walked before thee in truth and with a perfect heart, and have done that which is good in thy sight." And Hezekiah wept sore.

It was no self-righteous plea which he offered to God for recovery. He was only pleading his fidelity, just as Christ did in after years:

"Father, I have glorified thee on earth." He is the Lord's reminder, and is putting him in mind as to his sincerity, fidelity and service, which was in every way legitimate. This prayer was directly in line with that of David in Psalm 26:1, "Judge me, O Lord, for I have walked in my integrity." This is not a prayer test with Hezekiah, nor is it a faith cure, but it is a testing of God. It must be God's cure if a cure comes at all.

Hezekiah had hardly finished his prayer, and Isaiah was just about to go home when God gave him another message for Hezekiah, this time one more pleasant and encouraging. The mighty force of prayer had affected God, and had changed his edict and reversed him in his purpose concerning Hezekiah. What is that which prayer cannot do? What is it which a praying man cannot accomplish through prayer?

> And it came to pass before Isaiah had gone out into the middle court, that the word of the Lord came to him, saying,
> "Turn again, and tell Hezekiah, the captain of my people, 'Thus, saith the Lord, the God of David thy father, I have heard thy prayer; I have seen thy tears; Behold, I will heal thee; on the third day thou shalt go up to the house of the Lord. And I will add unto thy days fifteen years, and I will deliver thee and this city out of the hand of the King of Assyria; and I will defend this city for my own sake, and for David, my servant's sake.'"

The prayer was to God. It was that God should reconsider and change his mind. Doubtless Isaiah returned to his house with a lighter heart than he did when he delivered his original message. God had been prayed to by this sick king, and had been asked to revoke his decree, and God had condescended to grant the request. God sometimes changes his mind. He has a right to do so. The reasons for him to change his mind are strong reasons. His servant Hezekiah wants it done. Hezekiah had been a dutiful servant and had done much for God. Truth, perfection and goodness have been the elements of Hezekiah's service and the rule of his life. Hezekiah's tears and prayer are in the way of God's executing his decree to take away the life of his servant. Prayer and tears are mighty things with God. They are to him much more than consistency and much more to him than decrees. "I have heard thy prayer; I have seen thy tears; behold I will heal thee."

Sickness dies before prayer. Health comes in answer to prayer. God answered more than Hezekiah asked for. Hezekiah prayed only for his life, and God gave him life, and in addition promised him protection and security from his enemies.

But Isaiah had something to do with the recovery of this praying king.

There was something more than prayer in it. Isaiah's praying was changed into the skill of the physician. "And Isaiah said, Take a lump of figs. And they took and laid it on the boil, and he recovered."

God often uses remedies in answering prayer. It frequently takes a stronger faith to rise above means and not to trust in them, than it does to wholly reject all means. Here was a simple remedy that all might know that it did not cure the deadly disease, and only a means to aid or to test faith. But still more praying was to be done. Isaiah and Hezekiah could not do things without much praying:

> And Hezekiah said unto Isaiah, "What shall be the sign that the Lord will heal me, and that I shall go up into the house of the Lord the third day?"
>
> And Isaiah said, "This sign shalt thou have of the Lord, that the Lord will do the thing that he hath spoken: Shall the shadow go forward ten degrees, or go back ten degrees?"
>
> And Hezekiah answered, "It is a light thing for the shadow to go down ten degrees; nay, but let the shadow return backward ten degrees.
>
> And Isaiah the prophet cried unto the Lord, and he brought the shadow ten degrees backward, by which it had gone down in the dial of Ahaz.

Hezekiah meets the occasion and covers the answer to his prayer with thanksgiving. The fragrance of the sweet spices are there, and the melody of the harp also.

Four things let us ever keep in mind: God hears prayer, God heeds prayer, God answers prayer, and God delivers by prayer. These things cannot be too often repeated. Prayer breaks all bars, dissolves all chains, opens all prisons, and widens all straits by which God's saints have been held.

Life was sweet to Hezekiah and he desired to live, but what can bear God's decree? Nothing but the energy of faith. Hezekiah's heart was broken under the strain, and its waters flowed and added force and volume to his praying. He pleaded with great strivings and with strong arguments; and God heard Hezekiah praying, saw his tears, and changed his mind, and Hezekiah lived to praise God and to be an example of the power of mighty praying.

Like Hezekiah, the decent way of praying without soul did not suit Paul. He puts himself in the attitude of a wrestler, and charges his brethren to join him in the agony of a great conflict. "Brethren, I beseech you," he says, "for the Lord Jesus Christ's sake, and for the love of the Spirit, that ye strive together with me in your prayers to God for me." He was too much in earnest to touch the praying business genteelly or with gloved hands. He was in it as an agony, and he desired his brethren to be his partners in this conflict and wrestling of his soul. Epaphras was doing this same kind of praying for the Colossians: "Always laboring fervently for you in prayers, that ye may stand perfect and complete in all the will of God." An end worth agonizing for always. This kind of praying by these early pastors of the apostolic church was one secret of the purity, one source of the power of the church. And this was the kind of praying which was done by Hezekiah.

Here was prayer born in the fire of a great desire, and pursued through the deepest agony of conflict and opposition to success. Our spiritual cravings are not strong enough to give life to the mighty conflicts of prayer. They are not absorbing enough to stop business, arrest worldly pursuits, awaken us before day, and send us to the closet, to solitude, and to God; to conquer every opposing force and win our victories from the very jaws of hell. We want preachers and men and women who can illustrate the uses, the forces, the blessing, and the utmost limits of prayer.

Isaiah laments that there was no one who stirred himself up to take hold of God. Much praying was done, but it was too easy, indifferent, complacent. There were no mighty movements of the soul toward God, no array of all the sanctified energies to reach out and grapple God and draw out his treasures for spiritual uses. Forceless prayers have no power to overcome difficulties, no power to win marked results, or gain a complete and wonderful victory.

7

Ezra, the Praying Reformer

EZRA, the priest, and one of God's great reformers, comes before us in the Old Testament as a praying man, one who uses prayer to overcome difficulties and bring good things to pass. He had returned from Babylon under the patronage of the king of Babylon, who had been strangely moved toward Ezra and who favored him in many ways. Ezra had been in Jerusalem but a few days when the princes came to him with the distressing information that the people had not separated themselves from the people of that country, and were doing according to the abominations of the heathen nations about them. And that which was worse than all was that the princes and rulers in Israel had been chief in the trespass.

It was a sad state of affairs facing Ezra as he found the church almost hopelessly involved with the world. God demands of his church in all ages that it should be separated from the world, a separation so sharp that it amounts to an antagonism. To effect this very end, he put Israel in the promised land, and cut them off from other nations by mountains, deserts and seas, and straightway charged them that they should not form any relation with alien nations, neither marital, social, nor business.

But Ezra finds the church at Jerusalem, as he returns from Babylon, paralyzed and hopelessly and thoroughly prostrated by the violation of this principle. They had intermarried, and had formed the closest and most sacred ties in family, social, and business life, with the Gentile nations. All were involved in it: priests, Levites, princes, and people. The family, the business, and the religious life of the people was founded in this violation of God's law. What was to be done? What could be done? Here were the important questions which faced this leader in Israel, this man of God.

Everything appeared to be against the recovery of the church. Ezra could not preach to them, because the whole city would be inflamed, and would hound him out of the place. What force was there which could recover them to God so that they would dissolve business partnerships, divorce wives and husbands, cut acquaintances and dissolve friendships?

The first thing about Ezra which is worthy of remark was that he saw the situation and realized how serious it was. He was not a blind-eyed optimist who never sees anything wrong in the church. By the mouth of Isaiah God had propounded the very pertinent question, "Who is blind but my servant?"

But it could not possibly be made to apply to Ezra. Nor did he minimize the condition of things or seek to conceal the sins of the people or to minimize the enormity of their crimes. Their offense appeared in his eyes to be serious in the extreme. It is worth not a little to have leaders in Zion who have eyes to see the sins of the church as well as the evils of the times. One great need of the modern church is for leaders after the style of Ezra, who are not blind in their seeing department, who are willing to see the state of things in the church, and who are not reluctant to open their eyes to the real situation.

Very naturally, seeing these dreadful evils in the church and in the society of Jerusalem, he was distressed. The sad condition of things grieved him, so much so that he rent his garments, plucked his hair, and sat down astonished. All these things are evidences of his great distress of soul at the terrible state of affairs. Then it was in that frame of mind, concerned, solicitous, and troubled in soul, that he gave himself to prayer, to confession of the sins of the people, and to pleading for pardoning mercy at the hands of God. To whom should he go in a time like this but unto the God who hears prayer, who is ready to pardon and who can bring the unexpected thing to pass?

He was amazed beyond expression at the wicked conduct of the people, was deeply moved and began to fast and pray. Prayer and fasting always accomplish something. He prays with a broken heart, for there is naught else that he can do. He prays unto God, deeply burdened, prostrate on the ground and weeping, while the whole city unites with him in prayer.

Prayer was the only way to placate God, and Ezra became a great mover in a great work for God, with marvelous results. The whole work, its principles and its results, are summarized by just one verse in Ezra 10:1:

> Now when Ezra had prayed, and had confessed, weeping and casting himself down before the house of God, there assembled unto him out of Israel a very great congregation of men and women and children, for the people wept sore.

There had been mighty, simple and persevering prayer. Intense and prevailing prayer had accomplished its end. Ezra's praying had brought into being and brought forth results in a great work for God. It was mighty praying because it brought Almighty God to do his own work, which was absolutely hopeless from any other source save by prayer and by God. But nothing is hopeless to prayer because nothing is hopeless to God.

Again we must say that prayer has only to do with God, and is only resultful as it has to do with God. Whatever influence the praying of Ezra had upon himself, its chief, if not its only, results followed because it affected God, and moved him to do the work.

A great and general repentance followed this praying of Ezra, and there occurred a wonderful reformation in Israel. And Ezra's mourning and his praying were the great factors which had to do with bringing these great things to pass.

So thorough was the revival which occurred that as evidences of its genuineness it is noted that the leaders in Israel came to Ezra with these words:

> We have trespassed against our God, and have taken strange wives of the people of the land. Yet now there is hope in Israel concerning this thing.
>
> Now therefore let us make a covenant with our God to put away all the wives, and such as are born to them, according to the counsel of my lord, and of those that tremble at the commandment of our God; and let it be done according to the law.
>
> Arise, for this matter belongeth unto thee. We also will be with thee; be of good courage, and do it.

8

Nehemiah, the Praying Builder

In enumerating the praying saints of the Old Testament, we must not leave out of that sacred catalogue Nehemiah, the builder. He stands out on an equal footing with the others who have been considered. In the story of the reconstruction of Jerusalem after the captivity, he plays a prominent part, and prayer is prominent in his life during those years. He was a captive in Babylon, and had an important position in the palace of the king to whom he was cupbearer. There must have been considerable merit in him to cause the king to take a Hebrew captive and place him in such an office, where he really had the life of the king in his charge, because he was responsible for the wine which he drank.

It was while Nehemiah was in Babylon, in the king's palace, that one day his brethren came from Jerusalem, and very naturally Nehemiah desired news from the people there and information concerning the city itself. The distressing information was given him that the walls were broken down, the gates were burned with fire, and the remnant who were left there at the beginning of the captivity were in great affliction and reproach.

Just one verse gives the effect of this sad news upon this man of God:

> And it came to pass when I heard these words, that I sat down and wept, and mourned certain days and fasted, and prayed before the God of heaven.

Here was a man whose heart was in his own native land far away from where he now lived. He loved Israel, was concerned for the welfare of Zion, and was true to God. Deeply distressed by the information concerning his brethren at Jerusalem, he mourned and wept. How few the strong men in these days who can weep at the evils and abominations of the times! How rare those who, seeing the desolations of Zion, are sufficiently interested and concerned for the welfare of the church to mourn! Mourning and weeping over the decay of religion, the decline of revival power, and the fearful inroads of worldliness in the church are almost an unknown quantity. There is so much of so-called optimism that leaders have no eyes to see the breaking down of the walls of Zion and the low spiritual state of the Christians of the present day, and have less heart to mourn and cry about it: Nehemiah was a mourner in Zion. And possessing this state of heart, distressed beyond measure, he does that which other praying saints had done—he goes to God and makes it a subject of prayer. The prayer is recorded in Nehemiah, first chapter, and is a model after which to pattern our prayers. He begins with adoration, makes confession of the sins of his nation, pleads the promises of God, mentions former mercies, and begs for pardoning mercy. Then with an eye to the future—for unquestionably he had planned, the next time he was summoned into the king's presence, to ask permission to visit Jerusalem and to do there what was possible to remedy the distressing state of affairs—we hear him pray for something very special: "And prosper thy servant this day, I pray thee, and grant him mercy in the sight of this man. For," he adds by way of explanation, "I was the king's cupbearer."

It seemed all right to pray for his people, but how was a heathen king, with possibly no sympathy whatever for the sad condition of his city and his people in a captive land, and who had no interest in the matter, to be so favorably affected that he would consent to give up his faithful cupbearer and allow him to be gone for months? But Nehemiah believed in a God who could touch even the mind of a heathen ruler and move him favorably toward the request of his praying servant.

Nehemiah was summoned into the king's presence, and God used even the appearance of Nehemiah's countenance as an entering wedge to gain the consent of Artaxerxes. This started the inquiry of the king as to its cause, and the final result was that the king not only permitted Nehemiah to go back to Jerusalem but also furnished him with everything needful for the journey and for the success of the enterprise.

Nor did Nehemiah rest his case when he first prayed about this matter, but he stated this significant fact as he was talking to the king: "So I prayed unto the God of heaven" giving the impression that while the king was inquiring about his request and the length of time he would be gone, Nehemiah was then and there talking to God about the matter.

The intense, persistent praying of Nehemiah prevailed. God can even affect the mind of a heathen ruler, and this he can do in answer to prayer without in the least overturning his free agency or forcing his will. It was a parallel case with that of Esther when she called upon her people to fast and pray for her as she went uninvited into the king's presence. As a result, his mind at a very critical moment was touched by the Spirit of God, and he was favorably moved toward Esther and held out to her the golden scepter.

Nor did the praying of Nehemiah cease when he had succeeded thus far. In building the wall of Jerusalem, he met with great opposition from Sanballat and Tobiah, who ridiculed the efforts of the people to rebuild the city's walls. Unmoved by these revilings and the intense opposition of these wicked opponents of that which was for God's cause, he pursued the task which he had undertaken. But he mixes prayer with all he does: "Hear, O our God, for we are despised; and turn their reproach upon their own head, and give them for a prey in the land of our captivity." And in continuing the account he says, "Nevertheless we made our prayer unto our God."

All along in the accounts of the high and noble work he was doing, we find prayer comes out prominently to the front. Even after the walls were completed, these same enemies of his and of the people of God again opposed him in his task. But he renews his praying, and he himself records this significant prayer: "Now there, O God, strengthen my hands."

Still further on, when Sanballat and Tobiah had hired an emissary to frighten and hinder Nehemiah, we find him setting himself directly against this new attack, and then again he turns to God in prayer: "My God, think thou upon Tobiah and Sanballat according to these their works and on the prophetess Noadiah, and the rest of the prophets, that would have put me in fear." And God answered his faithful laborer, and defeated the counsels and the plans of these wicked opponents of Israel.

Nehemiah discovered to his dismay that the portions of the Levites had not been given them, and as a result the house of God was forsaken. He took steps to see that the lawful tithes were forthcoming so that God's house should be opened to all religious services, and appointed treasurers to give attention to this business. But prayer must not be overlooked, so we find his prayer recorded at this time: "Remember me, O my God, concerning this, and wipe not out my good deeds that I have done for the house of my God, and for the offices thereof."

Let it not be thought that this was the plea of self-righteousness as was that of the Pharisee in our Lord's time who professedly went up to the temple to pray, who paraded his self-righteous claims in God's sight. It was a prayer after the fashion of Hezekiah, who reminded God of his fidelity to him and of his heart's being right in his sight.

Once more Nehemiah finds evil among the people of God. Just as he corrected the evil which caused the closing of the house of God, he discovers practices of Sabbath breaking, and here he has not only to counsel the people and seek to correct them by mild means, but he also proposes to exercise his authority if they did not cease their buying and selling on the Sabbath Day. But he must close this part of his work also with prayer, and so he records his prayer on that occasion: "Remember me, O my God, concerning this also, and spare me according to the greatness of thy mercy."

Lastly, as a reformer, he discovers another great evil among the people. They had intermarried with the men and women of Ashdod, Ammon, and Moab. Contending with them, he caused them to reform in this matter, and the close of his record has a prayer in it: Remember me, O my God, because they have defiled the priesthood, and the covenant of the priesthood, and of the Levites.

Cleansing them from all strangers, he appointed the wards of the priests, and the Levites, and his recorded career closes with this brief prayer: "Remember me, O my God, for good."

Fortunate is that church whose leaders are men of prayer. Happy is that congregation who are contemplating the erection of a church to have leaders who will lay its foundations in prayer, and whose walls go up side by side with prayer. Prayer helps to build churches and to erect the walls of houses of worship. Prayer defeats the opponents of those who are prosecuting God's enterprises. Prayer touches favorably the minds even of those not connected with the church, and moves them toward church matters. Prayer helps mightily in all matters concerning God's cause and wonderfully aids and encourages the hearts of those who have his work in hand in this world.

9

Samuel, the Child of Prayer

SAMUEL came into this world and was given existence in direct answer to prayer. He was born of a praying mother, whose heart was full of earnest desire for a son. He came into life under prayer surroundings, and his first months in this world were spent in direct contact with a woman who knew how to pray. It was a prayer accompanied by a solemn vow that if he should be given, he should be "lent unto the Lord," and true to that vow, this praying mother put him directly in touch with the minister of the sanctuary and under the influence of "the house of prayer." It was no wonder he developed into a man of prayer. We could not have expected otherwise with such a beginning in life and with such early environments. Such surroundings always make impressions upon children and tend to make character and determine destiny.

He was in a favorable place to hear God when he spoke to him, and was in an atmosphere where it tended to his heeding the divine call which came to him. It was the most natural thing in the world when at the third call from heaven, when he recognized God's voice, that his childish heart responded so promptly, "Speak, Lord, thy servant heareth." Quickly was there a response from his boyish spirit, of submission, willingness, and prayer.

Had he been born of a different sort of mother, had he been placed under different surroundings, had he spent his early days in contact with different influences, does any one for one moment suppose he could have easily heard the voice of God calling him to his service, and that he would have so readily yielded his young life to the God who brought him into being? Would a worldly home, with worldly surroundings, separated from the church of God, with a worldly minded mother, have produced such a character as Samuel? It takes such influences and agencies in early life to produce such praying men as Samuel. Would you have your child called early into divine service and separated from the world unto God? Would you have him so situated that he will be called in childhood by the Spirit of God? Put him under prayer influences. Place him near to and directly under the influence of the Man of God and in close touch with that house which is called "the house of prayer."

Samuel knew God in boyhood. As a consequence he knew God in manhood. He recognized God in childhood, obeyed him and prayed unto him.

The result was that he recognized God in manhood, obeyed him, and prayed unto him. If more children were born of praying mothers, brought up in direct contact with "the house of prayer," and reared under prayer environments, more children would hear the voice of God's spirit speaking to them, and would more quickly respond to those divine calls to a religious life. Would we have praying men in our churches? We must have praying mothers to give them birth, praying homes to color their lives, and praying surroundings to impress their minds and to lay the foundations for praying lives. Praying Samuels come from praying Hannahs. Praying priests come from "the house of prayer." Praying leaders come from praying homes.

Israel for years had been under bondage to the Philistines and the ark was housed in the home of Abinadab, whose son Eleazer was appointed to keep this sacred testimony of God. The people had gone into idolatry and Samuel was disturbed about the religious condition of the nation. The ark of God was absent, the people were given to the worship of idols, and there had been a grievous departure from God. Calling upon them to put away their strange gods, he urged them to prepare their hearts unto the Lord and to begin again to serve him—promising them that the Lord would deliver them out of the hands of the Philistines. His preaching thus plainly to them, for with all else belonging to him, Samuel was a preacher of the times, made a deep impression and bore rich fruits as such preaching always does. "Then the children of Israel did put away Baalim and Ashtoreth, and served the Lord only."

But this was not enough. Prayer must be mixed with and must accompany their reformation. So Samuel, true to his convictions about prayer, says to the people, "Gather all Israel to Mizpeh, and I will pray for you unto the Lord." While Samuel was offering up prayer for these wicked Israelites, the Philistines drew near to battle against the nation, but the Lord intervened at the critical moment and thundered with a great thunder, and discomfited these enemies of Israel, "and they were smitten before Israel."

The nation fortunately had a man who could pray, who knew the place and the worth of prayer, and a leader who had the ear of God and who could influence God.

But Samuel's praying did not stop there. He judged Israel all the days of his life, and had occasion from year to year to go in circuit to Bethel, Gilgal, and Mizpeh. Then he returned home to Ramah, where he resided. "And there he built an altar unto the Lord." Here was an altar of sacrifice but as well was it an altar of prayer. And while it may have been for the benefit of the community where he lived, after the fashion of a town church, yet it must not be overlooked that it must have been a family altar, a place where the sacrifice for sin was offered but at the same time where his household gathered for worship, praise and prayer. Here Almighty God was acknowledged in the home, here was the advertisement of a religious home, and here father and mother called upon the name of the Lord, differentiating this home from all the worldly and idolatrous homes about them.

Here is an example of a religious home, the kind so greatly needed in this irreligious, godless age. Blessed is that home which has in it an altar of sacrifice and of prayer, where daily thanksgivings ascend to heaven and where morning and night praying is done.

Samuel was not only a praying priest, a praying leader and a praying teacher and leader, but he was a praying father. And any one who knows the situation so far as family religion is concerned knows full well that the great demand of these modern times is religious homes and praying fathers and mothers. Here is where the breakdown in religion occurs, where the religious life of a community first begins to decay, and where we must go first to beget praying men and women in the church of God. It is in the home that the revival must commence.

A crisis came in the history of this nation. The people were infatuated by the glory of a kingdom with a human king, and was prepared to reject God as their king, as he had always been. So they came to Samuel with the bold request, "Make us a king to judge us like all the nations." The thing displeased this man of God, who was jealous for the name, the honor and the pleasure of the Lord God. How could it be otherwise? Who would not have been likewise displeased if he were built after the pattern of Samuel? It grieved him in soul. The Lord, however, came to him just at that time with the comforting assurance so far as he was personally concerned in the transaction, that "they have not rejected thee, but they have rejected me, that I should not reign over them. Hearken unto the voice of the people, in all that they say unto thee."

Then it was that Samuel followed the bent of his mind, "And Samuel prayed unto the Lord." It seemed that in every matter concerning this people, with which Samuel was connected, he must pray over it. How much more now when there was to be an entire revolution in the form of government, and God was to be displaced as the ruler of the people, and a human king was to be set up? National affairs need to be prayed over. Praying men are demanded to carry to God in prayer the affairs of government. Lawmakers, law judges, and law executives need leaders in Israel to pray for them. How much fewer the mistakes if there was more praying done in civil matters?

But this was not to be the end of this matter. God must show so definitely and plainly His displeasure at such a request as had been made for a human king, that the people might know what a wicked thing they had done, even though God acceded to their request. They must know God still existed and had to do with this people, and with their king and the affairs of the government. So the prayers of Samuel must again be brought into play to carry out the divine purposes. So Samuel called upon the people to stand still, and he would show them what the Lord would do before their eyes. So he called upon God, and in answer God sent a tremendous storm of thunder and rain, which exceedingly terrified the people, and caused them to acknowledge their great sin in asking for a king. So afraid were the people that they hastily called upon Samuel to pray for them and to spare them from what seemed to be destruction. Samuel again prayed, and God heard and answered, and the thunder and rain ceased.

One more incident in the prayer life of Samuel is worth noticing. King Saul had been ordered to destroy all the Amalekites, root and branch, and all their stuff, but Saul, contrary to divine instructions, had spared King Agag and the best of the sheep and the cattle, and had justified it because he claimed that the people wanted it done.

God brought this message to Samuel at this time:

> It repenteth me that I have set up Saul to be king; for he is turned back from following me, and hath not performed my commandments. And it grieved Samuel, and he cried all night unto the Lord.

Such a sudden declaration was enough to produce grief of soul in a man like Samuel, who loved his nation, who was true to God, and who above everything else desired the prosperity of Zion. Such grief of soul over the evils of the church and at the sight of the abominations of the times always drives a man to his knees in prayer. Of course, Samuel carried the case to God. It was a time for prayer. The case was too serious for him not to be deeply moved to pray. So greatly was the inner soul of Samuel disturbed that he prayed all night about it. Too much was at stake for him to shut his eyes to the affair, to treat it indifferently, and to let it pass without taking God into the matter, for the future welfare of Israel was in the balance.

10

Daniel, the Praying Captive

THAT was a notable experience in the life of Daniel when he was ordered by the king while in Babylon not to ask any petition of any God or king for thirty days, under penalty of being cast into the lions' den. He paid no attention to the edict, for it is recorded, "Now when Daniel knew that the writing was signed, he went into his house, and his windows being opened in his chamber toward Jerusalem, he kneeled upon his knees three times a day, and prayed and gave thanks before his God, as he did aforetime." Do not forget that this was the regular habit of this man of God. "He kneeled upon his knees and prayed as he did aforetime." What was the result? Just as expected. God sent an angel into the den of lions with Daniel and locked their mouths so that not a hair on his head was touched, and he was wonderfully delivered. Even so today deliverance always come to God's saints who tread the path of prayer as the saints of old did.

Daniel did not forget his God while in a foreign land, away from the house of God and its religious services, and deprived as he was of many religious privileges. He was a striking illustration of a young man who was decidedly religious under the most unfavorable surroundings. He proved conclusively that one could be definitely a servant of God though his environments were anything else than religious. He was among heathens so far as a God-fearing nation was concerned. There was no temple worship, no Sabbath Day, no Word of God to be read. But he had one help there which remained with him, and of which he could not be deprived, and that was his secret prayers.

Purposing in his heart without debating the question one moment or compromising at any one point, that he would not eat of the king's meat nor drink the king's wine, he stood out in that ungodly country a striking illustration of a young man, fearing God first of all, and resolving to be religious, cost what it may. But he was not to have a flowery bed on which to rest nor a smooth road on which to travel. The whimsical, tyrannical, and unreasonable king, Nebuchadnezzar, was to put him to the test, and his praying qualities were to be proved. This king had a strange dream, the particular items of which passed from his memory, but the fact of the dream remained. So troubled was he about the dream, he called for all the soothsayers, astrologers and sorcerers to call the dream to mind, an impossible task, humanly speaking, and then to interpret it. He classed Daniel and his three companions, Shadrach, Meshach and Abednego, with these men, though there really was nothing in them in common with the two classes of men. Being informed that it was impossible to discover a dream like that, and at their saying if the king would tell the dream to them, they would interpret it, the king became very angry, and ordered them to be put to death. This sentence of death was against Daniel and his three companions.

But Daniel appeared upon the stage of action. At his suggestion the execution of the rash edict was held up, and he immediately called his three companions into counsel, and he urged them to unite with him in a concert of prayer that God would reveal to Daniel the dream with the interpretation thereof. In answer to this united praying, it is recorded: "Then was the secret revealed unto Daniel in a night vision. Then Daniel blessed the God of heaven." As a sequel to this incident of the praying of these four men, Daniel revealed to the king his dream and its interpretation, and as a final result the king acknowledged the God of Daniel and elevated to high positions Daniel and his three associates. And it all came about because there was a praying man there just at a critical time. Blessed is that nation which has praying men who can come to the help of civil rulers who are greatly perplexed and in great difficulties, and who can be depended upon to pray for rulers of state and church.

Years afterward, while still in a foreign land, he still had not forgotten the God of his fathers, and to him was given the noted vision of the "Ram and the He Goat." But Daniel did not comprehend this strange vision, and yet he knew it was from God and had a deep and future meaning for nations and people. So, of course, he followed the bent of his religious mind and prayed about it.

> And it came to pass when I, even I Daniel, had seen the vision, and sought for the meaning, then behold there stood before me as the appearance of a man. And I heard a man's voice which called, and said, Gabriel, make this man to understand the vision.

And so Gabriel made him understand the full meaning of this remarkable vision. But it came in answer to Daniel's praying. So puzzling questions may often find an answer in the closet. And as elsewhere, God employs angelic intelligences to convey information as to prayer answers. Angels have much to do with prayer. Praying men and the angels of heaven are in close touch with each other.

Some years thereafter, Daniel was studying the records of the nation, and he discovered that it was about time for the seventy years of captivity of his people to end. So he gave himself to prayer:

> And I set my face to seek by prayer and supplications, with fasting and sackcloth and ashes. And I prayed unto the Lord, and made confession.

Then follows the record in those Old Testament scriptures of Daniel's prayer, so full of meaning, so simple in its utterances, so earnest in its spirit, so direct in its confession and requests, worthy of being patterned after.

And it was while he was speaking in prayer that the same archangel Gabriel, who seemed to have a direct interest in the praying of this man of God, "being caused to fly swiftly, touched me about the time of the evening sacrifice, and he informed me and talked with me," and then gave him much desired information valuable to Daniel.

The angels of God are much nearer us in our seasons of prayer than we imagine. God employs these glorious heavenly intelligences in the blessed work of hearing and answering prayer, when the prayer, as in the case of Daniel on this occasion, has to do with the present and future welfare of his people.

One other incident on the prayer line in the life of this captive man in Babylon. Another revelation was made to Daniel, but the time of its fulfillment appeared to be far in the future. "In those days, I, Daniel was mourning three full weeks. I ate no pleasant bread, neither came flesh nor wine into my mouth till the three whole weeks were fulfilled."

It was then that he had a very strange experience and a still stranger revelation was made to him by some angelic being. It is worthwhile to read the Scripture account:

> And behold a hand touched me, which set me on my knees, and upon the palms of my hands. And he said unto me, "O Daniel, a man greatly beloved, understand the words that I speak unto thee, and stand upright, for unto thee am I now sent." And when he had spoken this word unto me, I stood trembling. Then he said unto me, "Fear not, Daniel; for from the first day that thou didst set thy heart to understand and to chasten thyself before thy God, thy words were heard, and I am come for thy words. But the Prince of the Kingdom of Persia withstood me one and twenty days; but lo, Michael, one of the chief princes, came to help me, and I remained there with the kings of Persia."

What all this means is difficult to comprehend, but enough appears on its face to lead us to believe that the angels in heaven are deeply interested in our praying, and are sent to tell us the answers to our prayers. Further, it is very clear that some unseen forces or invisible spirits are operating to hinder the answers to our prayers. Who the Prince of Persia was who withstood this great angelic being is not divulged, but enough is revealed to know that there must be a contest in the unseen world about us between those spirits sent to minister to us in answer to our prayers and the devil and his evil spirits who seek to defeat these good spirits.

The passage furthermore gives us some intimation as to the cause of delayed answers to prayer. For "three full weeks" Daniel mourned and prayed, and for "one and twenty days" the divinely appointed angel was opposed by the "Prince of the Kingdom of Persia."

Well was it for praying Daniel that he had the courage, fortitude, and determination to persist in his praying for three weeks while the fearful conflict between good and bad spirits was going on about him unseen by mortal eyes. Well will it be for us if we do not give up in our praying when God seems not to hear and the answer is not immediate. It takes time to pray, and it takes time to get the answer to prayer. Delays in answering prayer are not denials. Failure to receive an immediate answer is no evidence that God does not hear prayer. It takes not only courage and persistence to pray successfully, but it requires much patience. "Wait on the Lord and be of good courage; and he shall strengthen thy heart; wait, I say, on the Lord."

11

Faith of Sinners in Prayer

ONE of the peculiar features of prayer as we study the Old Testament on this subject is the faith of unrighteous and backslidden men in prayer, and the great confidence they had in the prayers of praying men of that day. They knew certain men as men of prayer, who believed in God, who were favored of God and who prayed unto God. They recognized these men as having influence with God in averting wrath and in giving deliverance from evil.

Frequently when in trouble, when God's wrath was threatened and even when there were visitations of evil upon them for their iniquities, they showed their faith in prayer by appealing to the men who prayed, to beg God to avert his displeasure and turn aside his wrath against them. Recognizing the value of prayer as a divine agency to save men, they made application to the men who prayed, to intercede with God for them.

It is one of the strange paradoxes of those early days that while people departed from God, and went into grievous sin, they did not become either atheists nor unbelievers when it came to the question of the existence of a prayer-answering God. Wicked men held fast to a belief in God's existence, and to faith in the power of prayer to secure pardon for sin and to deliver them from God's wrath. It is worth something as showing the influence of the church on sinners, when the latter believe in prayer and beg Christian people to pray for them. It is an item of interest and an event of importance when a sinner on a dying bed calls for a praying man to come to his bedside to pray for him. It means something when penitent sinners, under a sense of their guilt, feeling the displeasure of God, approach a church altar and say, "Pray for me, ye praying men and women." Little does the church understand its full import, and still less does the church appreciate and take in the full import of praying, especially for the unsaved men and women who ask them to pray for their immortal souls. If the church was fully alive to God and awake to the real peril of the unconverted all about it, and was in a thriving state, more sinners would be found seeking the altars of the church and crying out to praying people, "Pray for my soul."

Much so-called praying for sinners there may be, but it is cold, formal, official praying, which goes nowhere, never reaches God, and accomplishes nothing. Revivals begin when sinners seek the prayers of praying people.

Several things stand out in bold relief as we look at those Old Testament days:

First, the disposition of sinners against God to almost involuntarily turn to praying men for help and refuge when trouble draws near, and to invoke their prayers for relief and deliverance. "Pray for us" was their cry.

Second, the readiness with which those praying men responded to these appeals and prayed to God for those who desired this thing. Moreover, we are impressed with the fact that these praying men were always in the spirit of prayer and ready at any time to inquire of God. They were always keyed up on prayer.

Third, we note the wonderful influence these men of prayer had with God whenever they made their appeal to him. God nearly always quickly responded and heard their praying for others. So intercessory prayer predominated in those early days of the church. It is a question worthy of earnest consideration, how far the present-day church is responsible for the unbelief of sinners of these modern times in the value of prayer as an agency in averting God's wrath, in sparing barren lives and in giving deliverance. How far is the Church responsible for the precious few mourners in Zion in these times, who ignore your altar calls and treat with indifference your appeals to come and be prayed for?

The first illustration we notice as showing the faith of wicked men in prayer and their appeal for a man of God to intercede for them is the case of the fiery serpents sent upon the Israelites. They were journeying from Mount Hor by way of the Red Sea, seeking to compass the land of Edom, when they spoke against God and Moses, after this fashion:

> "Wherefore have ye brought us up out of Egypt to die in the wilderness? for there is no bread, neither is there any water; and our soul loatheth this light bread." The thing so sorely displeased God that He sent fiery serpents among the people, and many of the people of Israel died. Therefore the people came to Moses, and said, "We have sinned because we have spoken against the Lord, and against thee; pray unto the Lord, that He take away the serpents from us." And Moses prayed for the people.

As far as these people had departed from God, and as great as was their sin in complaining against God's dealings with them, they had not lost faith in prayer, neither did they forget that there was a leader in Israel who had influence with God in prayer, and who could by that means avert disaster and bring deliverance to them.

Jeroboam, first king of the ten tribes when the kingdom was divided, was another case in point. This was a most noted case because of the notoriety of his departure from God, which was often referred to in the after history of Israel, as "the sin of Jeroboam, the son of Nebat," and shows that despite his great wickedness in the sight of God, he did not lose his faith in the efficacy of prayer. This king on one occasion presumed to take the place of the high priest, and stood by the altar to burn incense. A man of God came out of Judah and cried against the altar and proclaimed, "Behold the altar shall be rent, and the ashes that are upon it shall be poured out." This angered Jeroboam, who saw that it was intended as a public rebuke for him, who had undertaken contrary to the Levitical law to assume the office of God's priest, and the king put forth his hand with the apparent purpose of arresting or doing violence to the man of God, saying, at the same time to those about him, "Lay hold upon him."

Immediately God smote the king with leprosy, so that he could not pull his hand back again, and at the same time the altar was rent. Astonished beyond measure at this sudden retribution for his sin, coming like lightning from heaven, and very much afraid, he cried out to the man of God, "Entreat now the face of the Lord thy God for me, that my hand may be restored again." And it is recorded that "the man of God besought the Lord, and the king's hand was restored him again, and became as it was before."

Let us keep in mind that we are not now considering the praying habits of the man of God nor the possibilities of prayer, though both face us here. But rather we are finding just here that a ruler in Israel, guilty of a grievous sin, and departing from God, when God's wrath falls upon him, he immediately calls upon a praying man to intercede with God in his behalf. It is but another case where a sinner against God showed his faith in the virtue of the prayers of a man of God. Sad is the day in a Christian land, not only where there is the decay of prayer in the church, but where sinners are so unaffected by the religion of the church that they have no faith in prayer and care little about the prayers of praying men.

Another illustration follows this case very quickly. The son of King Jeroboam fell sick, and was about to die. And this wicked, indifferent king, posted his wife off to Ahijah, the prophet of God, to ask him to say what would be the result of the illness of the child. She attempted to practice a deception upon the old prophet who was nearly blind, intending not to make herself known to him. But he had the vision of a prophet even though dim in sight, and immediately revealed to her that she was known to him. After telling her many things of vast importance concerning the kingdom and charging her husband that he had not kept God's commandments, but had gone into idolatry, he said to her: "Arise, therefore, and get thee down to thy house; and when thy feet enter into the city, the child shall die."

How natural for a father in trouble to appeal to a praying prophet for relief? And as in the first mentioned case, his sin did not blind his eyes to the value of having a man of God intercede for him. It availed nothing as was proved, but it did prove our contention that in Old Testament times sinners, while they were not themselves praying men, believed strongly in the prayers of praying men.

Take the instance of Johanan, just as the children of Israel began their life of captivity in Babylon. Johanan and Jeremiah, with a small company, had been left in their native land, and Ishmael had conspired against Gedaliah, the appointed governor of the country, and had slain him. Johanan came to the rescue and delivered the people from Ishmael who was taking them away from their land. But Johanan wanted to see down into Egypt, which was contrary to the divine plan. At this particular juncture of affairs, he assembled all the people, and they went to Jeremiah with the earnest appeal:

> We beseech thee, let our supplication be accepted before thee, and pray for us unto the Lord thy God, that the Lord thy God may show us the way wherein we may walk and the thing that we may do.

Like all other appeals to good men for prayer, Jeremiah interceded for these inquirers after the right way, and after ten days the answer came, and they were informed by Jeremiah what God would have them do. This was to the effect that they should not go down to Egypt, but remain in and about Jerusalem, but the people and Johanan played Jeremiah false, and refused to do as God had told them in answer to prayer. But it did not disprove the fact that they had faith in prayer and in praying men.

Another case may be noticed as showing the truth of our proposition that sinners had faith in prayer in the Old Testament dispensation, thus indirectly proving the preeminence of prayer in those days, for certainly prayer must have had a prominent place and its necessity must have received general recognition, when even sinners by their actions give endorsement to its virtue and necessity. Surely if sinners bore testimony to its worth, and at that time displayed their need of prayer, even by the prayers of someone else, church people of this day ought to have a deep sense of its need, and should have strong faith in prayer and its virtue. And certainly if the men of Old Testament times were such men of prayer, and had such a reputation as praying men, then in this favored day, Christian men should be so given to prayer that they also would have a wide reputation as praying men.

Zedekiah was king of Judah just as the captivity of God's people began. He was in charge of the kingdom when Jerusalem was besieged by the king of Babylon. And it was just about this time that Zedekiah sent two chosen men unto Jeremiah saying:

> Inquire, I pray thee, of the Lord for us; for Nebuchadnezzar, king of Babylon, maketh war against us; if so be that the Lord will deal with us according to all his wondrous works, that he may go up from us.

And God told Jeremiah in answer to this inquiry what to do, and what would occur, but as in another case, that of Johanan, Zedekiah proved false, and would not do as God instructed Jeremiah to tell him. At the same time it proved conclusively that Zedekiah had not lost his faith in prayer as a means of finding out the mind of God, nor did it affect him in his belief in the virtue of the prayers of a praying man.

Verily, prayer must have had a preeminent place in all Old Testament history when not only the men of God were noted for their praying habits, but even men who departed from God and proved false bore testimony to its virtue by appealing to the men of prayer to make intercessions for them. This is so notorious in Old Testament history that no careful reader of these old scriptures can fail to discover and notice it.

12

Paul, the Teacher of Prayer

How instant, strenuous, persistent, and pathetic was Paul's urgency of prayer upon those to whom he wrote and spoke! "I exhort," says he, writing to Timothy, "first of all, that supplications, prayers, intercessions, and giving of thanks be made for all men." This he meant was to be the prime deposit and truth for the church. First of all, before all things, to the front of all things, the church of Christ was to be a praying church, was to pray for men, was to pray for all men. He charged the Philippians to this effect: "Be careful for nothing, but in everything, by prayer and supplication, with thanksgiving, let your requests be made known unto God." The church must be anxious about nothing. In everything prayer must be made. Nothing was too small about which to pray. Nothing was too great for God to overcome.

Paul lays it down as a vital, all-essential injunction in writing to the church at Thessalonica, "Rejoice evermore. Pray without ceasing. In everything give thanks. For this is the will of God concerning you." The church must give itself to unceasing prayer. Never was prayer to cease in the church. This was the will of God concerning his church on earth.

Paul was not only given to prayer himself, but he continually and earnestly urged it in a way that showed its vital importance. He was not only insistent in urging prayer upon the church in his day, but he urged persistent praying. "Continue in prayer and watch in the same," was the keynote of all his exhortations on prayer. "Praying always with all prayer and supplication," was the way he pressed this important matter upon the people. "I will, therefore," I exhort, this is my desire, my mind upon this question, "that men pray everywhere, without wrath and doubting." As he prayed after this fashion himself, he could afford to press it upon those to whom he ministered.

Paul was a leader by appointment and by universal recognition and acceptance. He had many mighty forces in this ministry. His conversion, so conspicuous and radical, was a great force, a perfect magazine of aggressive and defensive warfare. His call to the apostleship was clear, luminous and convincing. But these forces were not the divinest energies which brought forth the largest results to his ministry. Paul's course was more distinctly shaped and his career rendered more powerfully successful by prayer than by any other force.

544

It is no surprise then that he should give such prominence to prayer in his preaching and writing. We could not expect it to be otherwise. As prayer was the highest exercise in his personal life, so also prayer assumed the same high place in his teaching. His example of prayer added force to his teaching on prayer. His practice and his teaching ran in parallel lines. There was no inconsistency in the two things.

Paul was the chief of the apostles as he was chief in prayer. If he was the first of the apostles, prayer conspired to that end. Hence he was all the better qualified to be a teacher on prayer. His praying fitted him to teach others what prayer was and what prayer could do. And for this reason he was competent to urge upon the people that they must not neglect prayer. Too much depended upon it.

He was first in prayer for this cause. For the reason that on him centered more saintly praying than on any one else, he became the first in apostleship. The crown of martyrdom was the highest crown in the royalty of heaven, but prayer put this crown of martyrdom on his head.

He who would teach the people to pray must first himself be given to prayer. He who urges prayer on others must first tread the path of prayer himself. And just in proportion as preachers pray, will they be disposed to urge prayer upon those to whom they preach. Moreover, just in proportion as preachers pray, will they be fitted to preach on prayer. If that course of reasoning be true, would it be legitimate to draw the conclusion that the reason why there is so little preaching on prayer in these modern times is because preachers are not praying men?

We might stake the whole question of the absolute necessity and the possibilities of prayer in this dispensation on Paul's attitude toward prayer. If personal force, if the energy of a strong will, if profound convictions, if personal culture and talents, and if the divine call and the divine empowerment—if any one of these, or all of them united, could direct the church of God without prayer, then logically prayer would be unnecessary. If profound piety and unswerving consecration to a high purpose, if impassioned loyalty to Jesus Christ, if any or all of these could exist without devoted prayer, or lift a church leader above the necessity of prayer, then Paul was above its use. But if the great and gifted, the favored and devoted Paul felt the necessity of unceasing prayer, and realized that it was urgent and pressing in regard to its claims and necessity, and if he felt that it was clamorous and insistent that the church should pray without ceasing, then he and his brethren in the apostolate should be aided by universal and mighty praying.

Paul's praying and his commands and the urgency with which he pressed upon the church to pray, is the most convincing proof of the absolute necessity of prayer as a great moral force in the world, an indispensable and inalienable factor in the progress and spread of the Gospel, and in the development of personal piety. In Paul's view, there was no church success without prayer, and no piety without prayer, in fact without much prayer. A church out of whose life streams prayer as the incense flames went out of the censer, and a leadership out of whose character, life and habits flames prayer as imposing, conspicuous and spontaneous as the fragrant incense flamed, this was the leadership for God.

To pray everywhere, to pray in everything, to continue instant in prayer, and to pray without ceasing, thus Paul spoke as a commentator on the divine uses and the nature of prayer.

Timothy was very dear to Paul, and the attachment was mutual and intensified by all their affinities. Paul found in Timothy those elements which fitted him to be his spiritual successor, at least the depository and the leader of the great spiritual principles and forces which were essential to the establishment and prosperity of the church. These primary and vital truths he would enforce on and radicate in Timothy. Paul regarded Timothy as one to whom fundamental and vital truths might be committed, who would preserve them truly, and who would commit them inviolate to the future. So he gives to Timothy this deposit of prayer for all ages as found in First Timothy 2:1.

Let it be noted before we go any further that Paul wrote directly under the superintendency of the Holy Spirit, who guarded Paul against error, and who suggested the truths which Paul taught. We hold definitely without compromise in the least to the plenary inspiration of the Scriptures, and as Paul's writings are part and parcel of those sacred writings, then Paul's epistles are portions of the Scriptures or the Word of God. This being true, the doctrine of prayer which Paul affirmed is the doctrine of the Holy Spirit. His epistles are of the Word of God, inspired, authentic and of divine authority. So that prayer as taught by Paul is the doctrine which Almighty God would have his church accept, believe, and practice.

These words to Timothy, therefore, were divinely inspired words. This section of Holy Writ is much more than merely suggestive, and is far more than a broad, bare outline on prayer. It is so instructive about prayer, about how men ought to pray, how businessmen should pray, and so forceful about the reasons why men ought to pray, that it needs to be strongly and insistently pressed.

Here are Paul's words to Timothy on prayer:

> I exhort, therefore, that, first of all, supplications, prayers, intercessions and giving of thanks, be made for all men; For kings and all that are in authority that we may lead a quiet and peaceable life in all godliness and honesty. For this is good and acceptable in the sight of God, our Saviour; Who will have all men to be saved and to come to the knowledge of the truth. For there is one God, and one mediator between God and men, the man Christ Jesus; Who gave himself a ransom for all, to be testified in due time. I will therefore that men pray everywhere, lifting up holy hands, without wrath and doubting.

In this prayer section we have set forth by Paul the inheritance and practice of every Christian in all ages. It is a manual in the great business of praying. It gives us a view of the energy and many-sidedness of prayer. First in point of time in all excellence of all duties is prayer. It must be first in all occupations. So exacting and imperative in its import and power is prayer that it stands first among spiritual values. He that prays not, is not at all. He is naught, less than naught. He is below zero, so far as Christ and God and heaven are concerned. Not simply among the first things does prayer stand on a level with other things, but first of the first, to the very forefront, does Paul put prayer with all his heart. "I exhort that first of all."

His teaching is that praying is the most important of all things on earth. All else must be restrained, retired, to give it primacy. Put it first, and keep its primacy. The conflict is about the primacy of prayer. Defeat and victory lie in this one thing. To make prayer secondary is to discrown it. It is to fetter and destroy prayer. If prayer is put first, then God is put first, and victory is assured. Prayer must either reign in the life or must abdicate. Which shall it be?

According to Paul, "supplications, prayers, intercessions, and giving of thanks" all these elements of prayer and forms of prayer are to be offered for men. Prayer is offered for things, for all things, for all temporal good, and for all spiritual good and grace, but in these directions Paul rises to the highest results and purposes of prayer. Men are to be affected by prayer. Their good, their character, conduct, and destiny are all involved in prayer. In this regard prayer moves along the highest way, and pursues its loftiest end. We are cognizant and consonant with things, with blessings, and bestowments, with matters and things which touch men, but men themselves are here set forth as the objects of prayer. This broadens and ennobles prayer. Men, through the whole sweep and range of their conditions, are to be held in the mighty grasp of prayer.

Paul's teaching is to the effect that prayer is essentially a thing of the inner nature. The spirit within us prays. So note Paul's directions: "I will therefore that men pray everywhere, without wrath." "Wrath" is a term which denotes the natural, internal motion of plants and fruits, swelling with juice. The natural juices are warmed into life, and rise by the warmth of spring. Man has in him natural juices which rise as does the sap. Warmth, heat, all stages of passions and desires, every degree of feeling, these spontaneously rise under provocation. Guard against and suppress them. Man cannot pray with these natural feelings rising in him, cultivated, cherished and continued there. Prayer is to be without these. "Without wrath." Higher, better, nobler inspiration are to lift prayer upward. "Wrath" depresses prayer, hinders it, suppresses it.

The word "without" means making no use of, having no association with, apart from, aloof from. The natural, unrenewed heart has no part in praying. Its heat and all its nature juices poison and destroy praying. The nature of prayer is deeper than nature. We cannot pray by nature, even by the kindliest and the best nature.

Prayer is the true test of character. Fidelity to our conditions and trueness to our relations are often evinced by our prayerfulness. Some conditions give birth to prayer. They are the soil which germinates and perfects prayer. To pray under some circumstances seems very fitting. Not to pray in some conditions seems heartless and discordant. The great storms of life, when we are helpless and without relief, or are devoid of assuagement, are the natural and providential conditions of prayer.

Widowhood is a great sorrow. It comes to saintly women as well as to others. True widows there are who are saintly. They are to be honored and their sorrow is divine. Their piety is aromatic and lightened by their bruised hearts. Here is Paul's description of such widows:

> Now she that is a widow indeed and desolate, trusteth in God, and continueth in supplications and prayers night and day. But she that liveth in pleasure is dead while she liveth.

Here is the striking contrast between two classes of women. One gives herself to supplications night and day. The other lives in pleasure and is spiritually dead. So Paul describes a true widow as being great in prayer. Her prayers, born of her faith and desolation, are a mighty force. Day and night her prayers go up to God unceasingly. The widowhood heart is a mighty appeal to God when that heart is found in the way of prayer, intense, unwearied prayer.

One of Paul's striking injunctions worthy of study is this one, "continuing instant in prayer," or as the Revised Version reads, "Continuing steadfast in prayer," which is his description of prayer. The term means to tarry, to remain, to be steadfast and faithful in prayer, to stick to it strong, to stay at it with strength to the end, to give attention to it with vigor, devotion and constancy, to give unremitting care to it.

Praying is a business, a lifelong business, one to be followed with diligence, fervor, and toil.

The Christian's business by way of preeminence is prayer. It is his most engaging, most heavenly, most lucrative business. Prayer is a business of such high and deserved dignity and import that it is to be followed "without ceasing." That is, with no let up nor break down, followed assiduously and without intermission. To prayer we are to give all strength. It must cover all things, be in every place, find itself in all seasons, and embrace everything, always, and everywhere.

In the remarkable prayer in Ephesians three, he is praying for wide reaches of religious experience. He is there bowing his knees unto God, in the name of Jesus Christ, and asking that God would grant that these Ephesian believers would in their experiences go far beyond the utmost stretches of past sainthood. "Filled with all the fullness of God," an experience so great and so glorious that it makes the head of the modern saint so dizzy that he is afraid to look up to those supernal heights or peer down into the fathomless depths.

Paul just passes us on to him, "who is able to do exceeding abundantly above all that we can ask or think." This is a specimen of his teaching on prayer.

In writing to the Philippian church, Paul recounts the situation, and shows the transmuting power of prayer as follows:

> Some indeed preach Christ of envy and strife; and some also of good will; The one preach Christ of contention, not sincerely, supposing to add affliction to my bonds; But the other of love, knowing that I am set for the defense of the Gospel. What then? Notwithstanding every way, whether in pretense or in truth, Christ is preached; and I therein do rejoice, yea, and will rejoice. For I know that this shall turn to my salvation through our prayer and the supply of the Spirit of Jesus Christ. According to my earnest expectation and my hope; that in nothing shall I be ashamed, but that with all boldness, as always, so now also Christ shall be magnified in my body, whether it be by life or death.

Boldness was to be secured by him and discomfiture and shame prevented by their prayers, and Christ was to be gloriously magnified by and through Paul, whether he lived or died.

It is to be remarked that in all these quotations in Corinthians, Ephesians or Philippians, the Revised Version gives us the most intense form of prayer, "supplications." It is the intense, personal, strenuous, persistent praying of the saints, that Paul requests, and they must give special strength, interest, time, and heart to their praying to make it bear its largest golden fruit.

The general direction about prayer to the Colossian Christians is made specific and is sharpened to the point of a personal appeal:

> Continue in prayer and watch in the same, with thanksgiving; withal praying also for us, that God would open unto us a door of utterance, to speak the mystery of Christ, for which I am also in bonds; that I make it manifest as I ought to speak.

Paul is accredited with the authorship of the Epistle to the Hebrews. We have it in a reference to the character of Christ's praying, which is illustrative, directory, and authentic as to the elements of true praying. How deep tones are his words! How heart-affecting and how sublime was his praying who prayed as never man prayed before, and yet prayed in order to teach man how to pray, "who in the days of his flesh, when he had offered prayers and supplications, with strong crying and tears, to Him that was able to save him from death, and was heard in that he feared." The praying of Jesus Christ drew on the mightiest forces of his being. His prayers were his sacrifices; which he offered before he offered himself on the cross for the sins of mankind. Prayer-sacrifice is the forerunner and pledge of self-sacrifice. We must die in our closets before we can die on the cross.

13

Paul and His Praying

HE who studies Paul's praying, both his prayers and his commands about prayer, will find what a wide, general, minute, and diversified area it covers. It will appear that these men like Wesley, Brainerd, Luther, and all their holy successors in the spiritual realms, were not guilty of fanaticism nor superstition when they ordered all things by prayer great and small, and committed all things, secular and religious, natural and spiritual, to God in prayer. In this they were but following the great exemplar and authority of the Apostle Paul.

To seek God as Paul did by prayer, to commune with God as Paul did, to supplicate Jesus Christ as Paul did, to seek the Holy Spirit by prayer as Paul did, to do this without ceasing, to be always a racer, and to win Christ as Paul did by prayer—all this makes a saint, an apostle, and a leader for God. This kind of a life engages, absorbs, enriches, and empowers with God and for God. Prayer, if successful, must always engage and absorb us. This kind of praying brings Pauline days and secures Pauline gifts. Pauline days are good, Pauline gifts are better, but Pauline praying is best of all, for it brings Pauline days, and secures Pauline gifts. Pauline praying costs much, is death to self, the flesh, and the world. Pauline praying is worth all it costs. Prayer which costs nothing gets nothing. It is beggarly business at best.

Paul's estimate of prayer is seen and enforced by the fact that Paul was a man of prayer. His high position in the church was not one of dignity and position to enjoy and luxuriate in. It was not one of officialism, nor was it one of arduous and exhaustless toil, for Paul was preeminently a praying man. He began his great career for Christ in the great struggle and school of prayer. God's convincing and wonderful argument to assure Ananias was, "Behold he prayeth." Three days was he without sight, neither eating nor drinking, but the lesson was learned well.

He went out on his first great missionary trip under the power of fasting and prayer, and they, Paul and Barnabas, established every church by the very same means, by fasting and prayer. He began his work in Philippi "where prayer was wont to be made." As "they went to prayer," the spirit of divination was cast out of the young woman. And when Paul and Silas were put in prison, at midnight they prayed and sang praises to God.

Paul made praying a habit, a business and a life. He literally gave himself to prayer. So with him praying was not an outer garb, a mere coloring, a paint, a polish. Praying made up the substance, the bone, the marrow, and the very being of his religious life. His conversion was a marvel of grace and power. His apostolic commission was full and royal. But he did not vainly expect to make full proof of his ministry, by the marvels of conditions and by wonderful results in the conversion, nor by the apostolic commission signed and sealed by divine authority, and carrying with it all highest gifts and apostolic enrichments, but by prayer, by ceaseless, wrestling, agonizing, and Holy Spirit praying. Thus did Paul work his work, and crown his work, his life and the death with martyr principles and with martyr glory.

Paul had a spiritual trait which was very marked and especially promised, and it was that of prayer. He had a profound conviction that prayer was a great as well as a solemn duty; that prayer was a royal privilege; that prayer was a mighty force; that prayer gauges piety, makes faith mighty and mightier; that much prayer was necessary to Christian success; that prayer was a great factor in the ongoing of God's kingdom on earth; and that God and heaven expected to pray.

Somehow we are dependent on prayer for great triumphs of holiness over sin, of heaven over hell, and of Christ over Satan. Paul took it for granted that men who knew God would pray; that men who lived for God would pray much, and that men could not live for God who did not pray. So Paul prayed much. He was in the habit of praying. He was used to praying, and that formed the habit of prayer. He estimated prayer so greatly that he fully knew its value, and that fastened the habit on him. Paul was in the habit of praying because he loved God, and such love in the heart always finds its expression in regular habits of prayer. He felt the need of much grace, and of more and more grace, and grace only comes through the channels of prayer, and only abounds more and more as prayer abounds more and more.

Paul was in the habit of praying, but he prayed not by mere force of habit. Man is such a creature of habit that he is always in danger of doing things simply by heart, in a routine, perfunctory manner. Paul's habit was regular and hearty. To the Romans he writes, "For God is my witness, that without ceasing, I make mention of you always in my prayers." Prison doors are opened and earthquakes take place by such praying as Paul did, even by such melodious Pauline praying. All things are opened to the kind of praying which was done by Paul and Silas. All things are opened by prayer. They could shut up Paul from preaching, but this could not shut him up from praying. And the Gospel could win its way by Paul's praying as well as by Paul's preaching. The apostle might be in prison, but the Word of God was free, and went like the mountain air, while the apostle is bound in prison and abounds in prayer.

How profound their joy in Jesus which expressed itself so happily and so sweetly in praise and prayer, under conditions so painful and so depressing!

Prayer brought them into full communion with God which made all things radiant with the divine presence which enabled them to "rejoice that they were counted worthy to suffer shame for His name, and to count it all joy when they fell into divers trials." Prayer sweetens all things and sanctifies all things. The prayerful saint will be a suffering saint. Suffering prayerfully he will be a sweet saint. A praying saint will be a praising saint. Praise is but prayer set to music and song.

After that notable charge to the elders at Ephesus, as he tarried there while on his way to Jerusalem, this characteristic record is made in Acts:

> And when he had thus spoken, he kneeled down and prayed with them. And they all wept sore, and fell on Paul's neck and kissed him.

"He kneeled down and prayed." Note those words. Kneeling in prayer was Paul's favorite attitude, the fitting posture of an earnest, humble suppliant. Humility and intensity are in such a position in prayer before Almighty God. It is the proper attitude of man before God, of a sinner before a Savior, and of a beggar before his benefactor. To seal his sacred and living charge to those Ephesian elders by prayer was that which made the charge efficient, beneficial and abiding.

Paul's religion was born in the throes of that three days' struggle of prayer, while he was in the house of Ananias, and there he received a divine impetus which never slackened till it brought him to the gates of the eternal city. That spiritual history and religious experience projected along the line of unceasing prayer, brought him to the highest spiritual altitudes and yields the largest spiritual results. Paul lived in the very atmosphere of prayer. His first missionary trip was projected by prayer. It was by prayer and fasting that he was called into the foreign missionary field, and by the same means the church at Antioch was moved to send forth Paul and Barnabas on their first missionary journey. Here is the Scripture record of it:

> Now there were in the church which was at Antioch certain prophets and teachers, as Barnabas and Simeon, that was called Niger; and Lucius of Cyrene, and Manean, which had been brought up with Herod the tetrarch, and Saul. And as they ministered to the Lord, and fasted, the Holy Ghost said, "Separate me Barnabas and Saul for the work whereunto I have called them." And when they had fasted and prayed, and had laid their hands on them, they sent them away.

Here is a model for all missionary outgoings, a presage of success. Here was the Holy Spirit directing a prayerful church obedient to the divine leadership, and this condition of things brought forth the very largest possible results in the mission of these two men of God. We may confidently assert that no church in which Paul was prominent would be a prayerless church. Paul lived, toiled, and suffered in an atmosphere of prayer. To him prayer was the very heart and life of religion, its bone and marrow, the motor of the Gospel, and the sign by which it conquered. We are not left in ignorance, for that spirit established churches, putting in them the everlasting requisite of self-denial, in the shape of fasting, and in the practice of prayer. Here is the divine record of Paul's work on this line:

> Confirming the souls of the disciples, and exhorting them to continue in the faith, and that we must through much tribulation enter into the kingdom of God. And when they had ordained them elders in every church, and had prayed with fasting, they commended them to the Lord, on whom they believed.

In obedience to a heavenly vision, Paul lands in Europe, and finds himself at Philippi. There is no synagogue, and few if any Jews are there. A few pious women, however, have a meeting place for prayer, and Paul is drawn by spiritual attraction and spiritual affinities to the place "where prayer is wont to be made." And Paul's first planting of the gospel in Europe is at that little prayer meeting. He is there the chief prayer and the leading talker. Lydia was the first convert at that prayer meeting. They protracted the meeting. They called it a meeting for prayer.

It was while they were going to that protracted prayer meeting that Paul performed the miracle of casting the devil of divination out of a poor demon-possessed girl, who had been made a source of gain by some covetous men, the results of which, by the magistrate's orders, were his scourging and imprisonment. The result by God's orders was the conversion of the jailer and his whole household. To the praying apostle no discouragements are allowed. A few praying women are enough for an apostolical field of labor.

In this last incident we have a picture of Paul at midnight. He is in the inner prison, dark and deadly. He has been severely and painfully scourged, his clothing is covered with blood, while there are blood clots on his gnashed and torn body. His feet are in the stocks, every nerve is feverish and swollen, sensitive and painful. But we find him under these very unfavorable and suffering conditions at his favorite pursuit. Paul is praying with Silas, his companion, in a joyous, triumphant strain.

> And at midnight, Paul and Silas prayed and sang praises unto God, and the prisoners heard them. And suddenly there was an earthquake, so that the foundation of the prison was shaken, and immediately all the doors were shaken; and every one's ban was loosed. And the keeper of the prison awaking out of his sleep, and seeing the prison doors opened, he drew out his sword, and would have killed himself, supposing that the prisoners had fled. But Paul cried out with a loud voice saying, "Do thyself no harm; for we are all here."

Never was prayer so beautiful, never more resultful. Paul was adept at prayer, a lover of prayer, a wondrous devotee of prayer, who could pursue it with such joyous strains, under such conditions of despondency and despair.

What a mighty weapon of defense was prayer to Paul! How songful! The angels doubtless stilled their highest and sweetest notes to listen to the music which bore those prayers to heaven. The earthquake trod along the path made by the mighty forces of Paul's praying. He did not go out when his chains were loosed, and the stocks fell off. His praying taught him that God had nobler purposes that night than his own individual freedom. His praying and the earthquake alarm were to bring salvation to that prison, freedom from the slavery and prison house of sin which was prefigured to him by his body emancipation. God's mighty providence had opened his prison door and had broken his prison bonds, not to give freedom, but to give freedom to the jailer. God's providential openings are often to test our ability to stay rather than to go. It tested Paul's ability to stay.

14

Paul and His Praying
(Continued)

THERE are two occasions with wonderful results where the statement is not explicit that Paul was in prayer, but the circumstances and the results, and Paul's universal and intense praying habit, make it most evident that the key to the results of both occasions is prayer. The first occasion is when Paul sailed away from Philippi and came to Troas, where he abode seven days. On the first day of the week, when the disciples came together to break bread, Paul preached unto them, expecting to depart on the morrow, and continued his preaching till late in the night.

There was sitting in the window a young man named Eutychus, who naturally fell asleep, and as Paul was rather long in speaking, the young man fell out of the high window, and was taken up for dead. Paul went down to the place where the young man had fallen, and embracing him, told the people about him that they need not be troubled, for life was still in the body. Paul returned to the upper room, where he had been preaching, and talked with the disciples till break of day. And the young man was brought alive, and as a consequence all were greatly comforted.

The very natural conclusion without the fact being specially stated is that Paul must have prayed for the young man when he embraced him, and his prayer was answered in the quick recovery of the young man.

The second occasion was in the perilous and protracted storm which overtook the vessel in which Paul was being carried as a prisoner to Rome. They were being exceedingly tossed about with the great tempest, and neither sun nor stars appeared as they were beset and struggled against wind and storm. All hope that they would be saved seemed gone. But after long abstinence, Paul stood in the midst of those on board, and speaking more particularly to the officers of the vessel, said,

"Sirs, ye should have hearkened unto me, and not have loosed from Crete, and to have gained this harm and loss. And now I exhort you, to be of good cheer, for there shall be no loss of any man's life among you, but of the ship. For there stood by this night the angel of God, whose I am and whom I serve, saying, Fear not, Paul; thou must be brought before Caesar, and lo, God hath given thee all them that sail with thee. Wherefore, sirs, be of good cheer; for I believe God, that it shall be even as God hath told me."

It requires no strained interpretation to read into this simple record the fact that Paul must have been praying when the angel appeared unto him with that message of encouragement and assurance of safety. Paul's habit of prayer and his strong belief in prayer must have driven him to his knees. Such an emergency with him would necessarily move him to pray under such crucial circumstances.

After the shipwreck, while on the island of Melita, we have another representation of Paul at prayer. He is at his work of praying for a very ill man. While a fire was being made, a deadly poisonous viper fastened itself on his hand, and the barbarians immediately concluded it was a case of retribution for some crime Paul had committed, but they soon discovered that Paul did not die, and changed their minds and concluded that he was a sort of god. In the same quarter at the time, was the father of Publius, who was very ill of a fever, and bloody flux, approaching seemingly his end. Paul went to him, and laid his hands upon him, and with simple confidence in God he prayed, and immediately the disease was rebuked, and the man was healed. When the natives of the island beheld this remarkable incident, they brought others to Paul, and they were healed, after the same fashion, by Paul's praying.

Turning back in Paul's life to the time he was at Ephesus on his way to Jerusalem, we find him stopping at Tyre after he departed from Ephesus. Before leaving Ephesus he had prayed with them all. But he did not trust in his words howsoever strong, fitting and solemn they might have been. God must be recognized, invoked and sought. Paul did not take it for granted, after he had done his best, that God as a matter of course would bless his efforts to do good, but he sought God. God does not do things in a matter-of-course sort of way. God must be invoked, sought unto, and put into things by prayer.

Following his visit to Ephesus, he arrived at Tyre, where he stopped a few days. Here he found some disciples, who begged Paul not to go to Jerusalem, saying through the Spirit that he should not go up to that city. But Paul adhered to his original purpose to go to Jerusalem. The account says:

> And when we had accomplished those days, we departed, and went our way; and they all brought us on our way with their wives and children, till we were out of the city; and we kneeled down on the shore and prayed.

What a sight to behold on that seashore. Here is a family picture of love and devotion where husbands, wives and even children are present, and prayer is made out in the open air. What an impression it must have made upon those children! The vessel was ready to depart, but prayer must cement their affections and sanctify wives and children, and bless their parting—a parting which was to be final so far as this world was concerned. The scene is beautiful and does honor to the head and heart of Paul, to his person and his piety, and shows the tender affection in which he was held. His devoted habit of sanctifying all things by prayer comes directly to the light. "We kneeled down on the shore and prayed." Never did sea strand see a grander picture or witness a lovelier sight—Paul on his knees on the sands of that shore, invoking God's blessing upon these men, women, and children.

When Paul was arraigned at Jerusalem, in making his public defense, he refers to two instances of his praying. One was when he was in the house of Judas, in Damascus, after he had been stricken to the earth and brought under conviction. He was there three days, and to him was Ananias sent, to lay his hand upon him, at the time of his blindness and darkness. It was during those three days of prayer. This is the scriptural record, and the words are those of Ananias addressed to him:

> And now why tarriest thou? Arise and be baptized, and wash away thy sins, calling on the name of the Lord.

The Lord had emboldened the timid Ananias to go and minister to Paul, by telling him, "Behold he prayeth." And so we have in this reference Paul's prayerfulness intensified by the exhortation of Ananias. Prayer precedes pardon of sins. Prayer becomes those who seek God. Prayer belongs to the earnest, sincere inquirer after God. Pardon of sin and acceptance with God always come at the end of earnest praying. The evidence of sincerity in a true seeker of religion is that it can be said of him, "Behold he prayeth."

The other reference in his defense lets us into the prayerful intenseness into which his whole religious life had been fashioned and shows us how in the absorbing ecstasy of prayer, the vision came and directions were received by which his toilsome life was to be guided. Also we see the familiar terms on which he stood and talked with his Lord:

> And it came to pass when I was come again to Jerusalem, even while I prayed in the temple, I was in a trance; And saw him saying unto me, "Make haste and get thee quickly out of Jerusalem, for they will not receive thy testimony concerning me."
>
> And I said, "Lord, they know that I imprisoned and beat in every synagogue them that believed on thee. And when the blood of thy martyr Stephen was shed, I also was standing by, and consenting to his death, and kept the raiment of them that slew him." And he said unto me, "Depart, for I will send thee far hence unto the Gentiles."

Prayer always brings directions from heaven as to what God would have us to do. If we prayed more and more directly, we should make fewer mistakes in life as to duty. God's will concerning us is revealed in answer to prayer. If we prayed more and prayed better and sweeter, then clearer and more entrancing visions would be given us, and our intercourse with God, would be of the most intimate, free, and bold order.

It is difficult to itemize or classify Paul's praying. It is so comprehensive, so discursive, and so minute, that it is no easy task to do so. Paul teaches much about prayer in his didactics. He specifically enforces the duty and necessity of prayer upon the church, but that which was better for Paul and better for us is that he himself prayed much and illustrated his own teaching. He practiced what he preached. He put to the test the exercise of prayer which he urged upon the people of his day.

To the church at Rome he plainly and specifically asserted with solemnity his habit of praying. This he wrote to those Roman believers:

> For God is my witness, whom I serve with my spirit in the Gospel of his Son, that without ceasing I make mention of you always in my prayers.

Paul not only prayed for himself. He also made a practice of praying for others. He was preeminently an intercessor. As he urged intercessory prayer on others, so he interceded himself for others beside himself.

He begins that remarkable Epistle to the Romans in the spirit of prayer. He closes it with this solemn charge: "Now I beseech you, brethren, for the Lord Jesus Christ's sake, and for the love of the Spirit, that ye strive with me in your prayers to God for me."

But this is not all. In the very heart of that epistle, he commands "Continuing instant in prayer." That is, give constant attention to prayer. Make it the business of life. Be devoted to it. Just what he did himself, for Paul was a standing example of the doctrine of prayer which he advocated and pressed upon the people.

In his epistles to the Thessalonians, how all inclusive and wonderful the praying! Says he in writing his first epistle to this church:

> We give thanks to God always for you, making mention of you in my prayers; remembering without ceasing your work of faith, and labor of love, and patience of hope.

Not to quote all he says, it is worthwhile to read his words to this same church of true believers further on:

> Night and day praying exceedingly that we might see your face, and might perfect that which is lacking in your faith. Now God himself direct our way unto you. And the Lord make you to increase and abound in love one toward another, even as we do toward you, to the end he may establish your hearts unblameable in holiness before God, even our Father.

And this sort of praying for these Thessalonian Christians is in direct line with that closing prayer for these same believers in this epistle, where he records that striking prayer for their entire sanctification:

> And the very God of peace sanctify you wholly; and I pray God your whole
> spirit, and soul and body be preserved blameless unto the coming of our Lord
> Jesus Christ.

How Paul did pray for those early Christians! They were in his mind and
on his heart, and he was continually at it, "night and day praying exceedingly." Oh, if we had a legion of preachers in these days of superficial piety and
these times of prayerlessness, who were given to praying for their churches as
Paul did for those to whom he ministered in his day! Praying men are needed.
Likewise praying preachers are demanded in this age.

At the conclusion of that remarkable prayer in the third chapter of
Ephesians, he declared that "God was able to do exceeding abundantly above
all that we could ask or think," now he declares he is praying exceeding
abundantly, striving after the most earnest order, to have his prayers run parallel with God's power, and that they may not limit that power nor exhaust
that power, but get all there is in it to bless and greatly enrich his church.

Paul and his companions prayed for the saints everywhere. It may be
referred to again. With what solemnity does Paul call the attention of the
Roman Christians to the important fact of praying for them, believers whom
he had never seen! "God is my witness that without ceasing, I make mention
of you in my prayers." To the churches he says, "Praying always for you."

Again on the same line, we hear him articulating clearly, "Always in every
prayer of mine for you all, making request with joy." Again he writes thus: "I
do not cease to pray for you." Once more we read the record, "Wherefore we
pray always for you." And again it is written, "Cease not to give thanks for
you, making mention of you in my prayers." And then he says,
"Remembrance of thee in my prayers night and day."

His declaration, "night and day praying exceedingly," is a condensed
record of the engrossing nature of the praying done by this praying apostle. It
shows conclusively how important prayer was in his estimate and in his ministry, and further shows how to him prayer was an agony of earnest striving in
seeking from God blessings which could be secured in no other way.

The unselfishness of his praying is seen in his writing to the Romans
where he tells them, "Making request if by any means I might have a prosperous journey to come to you. For I long to see you that I may impart to you
some spiritual gift to the end ye may be established." The object of his desire
to visit Rome was not for selfish gratification, the pleasure of a trip, or for
other reasons, but that he might be the means under God of "imparting to
them some spiritual gift," in order that they "might be established" in their
hearts, unblameably in love. It was that his visit might give to them some
spiritual gift which they had not received and that they might be established
at those points where they needed to be rooted, and grounded in faith, in
love, and in all that made up Christian life and character.

15

Paul and His Requests for Prayer

THE many requests of Paul for prayer for himself, made to those to whom he ministered, put prayer to the front in Paul's estimate of its possibilities. Paul prayed much himself, and tried hard to arouse Christians to the imperative importance of the work of prayer. He so deeply felt the need of prayer that he was given to the habit of personal praying. Realizing this for himself, he pressed this invaluable duty upon others. Intercessory prayer, or prayer for others, occupied a high place in his estimate of prayer. It is no surprise, therefore, when we find him throwing himself upon the prayers of the churches to whom he wrote.

By all their devotion to Jesus Christ, by all their interest in the advance of God's kingdom on earth, by all the ardor of their personal attachment to Jesus, he charges them to pray much, to pray unceasingly, to pray at all times, to pray in all things, and to make praying a business of praying. And then realizing his own dependence upon prayer for his arduous duties, his sore trials and his heavy responsibilities, he urges those to whom he wrote to pray especially for him.

The chief of the apostles needed prayer. He needed the prayers of others, for this he practically admitted in asking for their prayers. His call to the apostleship did not lift him above this need. He realized and acknowledged his dependence on prayer. He craved and prized the prayers of all good people. He was not ashamed to solicit prayers for himself nor to urge the brethren everywhere to pray for him.

In writing to the Hebrews, he bases his request for prayer on two reasons, his honesty and his anxiety to visit them. If he were insincere, he could lay no claim to their prayers. Praying for him, it would be a powerful agent in facilitating his visit to them. They would touch the secret place of the wind and the waves, and arrange all secondary agencies and make them minister to this end. Praying puts God in haste to do for us the things which we wish at his hands.

Paul's frequent request of his brethren was that they would "pray for him." We are to judge of the value of a thing by the frequency of asking for it, and by the special and urgent plea made for it. If that be true, then with Paul the prayers of the saints were among his greatest assets. By the urgency and repetition of the request, "Pray for me," Paul showed conclusively the great value he put upon prayer as a means of grace. Paul had no need so pressing as the need of prayer. There were no values so appreciated and appreciable as the prayers of the faithful.

Paul put the great factor of prayer as the great factor in his work. The most powerful and far-reaching energy in Paul's estimate is prayer. He covets it and hoards it as he seeks the prayers of God's people. The earnestness of his soul goes out in these requests. Hear him in this entreaty for prayer he is writing to the Romans:

> I beseech you, brethren, for the Lord Jesus Christ's sake, and for the love of the Spirit, that ye strive together with me in your prayers for me.

Prayers by others for Paul were valuable because they helped him. Great helpers are prayers. Nothing gives so much aid to us in our needs as real prayers. They supply needs and deliver from straits. Paul's faith, so he writes to the Corinthians, had been much tried, and he had been much helped and much strengthened by God's deliverance. "Ye also helping by prayer." What marvelous things has God done for his favored saints through the prayers of others! The saints can help the saints more by fervent praying than in any other way.

In the midst of envy and detraction, and in perils by false brethren, he writes thus to the Philippians:

> For I know that this shall turn to my salvation though your prayer, and the supply of the Spirit of Jesus Christ. According to my expectation, and my hope, that in nothing I shall be ashamed, but with all boldness as always, so now also Christ shall be magnified in my body, whether it be by life or death.

Shame was taken away, holy boldness secured, and life and death made glorious by the prayers of the saints at Philippi for Paul.

Paul had many mighty forces in his ministry. His remarkable conversion was a great force, a point of mighty projecting and propelling power, and yet he did not in his ministry secure its results by the force of his epochal conversion. His call to the apostleship was clear, luminous, and all convincing, but he did not depend on that for the largest results in his ministry.

Paul's course was more clearly marked out and his career rendered more powerfully successful by prayer than by any other force.

Paul urges the Roman Christians to pray for him that he may be delivered from unbelieving men. Prayer is a defense and protection against the malignity and machinations of evil men. It can affect men because God can affect them. Paul had not only unbelieving enemies with whom to contend, but many Christians were prejudiced against him to an extent which rendered it questionable whether they would accept any Christian service at his hands. Especially was this the case at Jerusalem, and so prayer, powerful prayer, must be used to remove the mighty and pernicious force of inflamed and deep-seated prejudice.

Prayer on their part for him must be used for his safety, and also that a prosperous journey and God's will might bring him speedily and surely to them, in order to bless and refresh mutually the Roman Christians.

These prayer requests of Paul are many-sided and all-comprehensive. How many things does his request to the Roman church include! The request for their prayers, like the church to whom it is directed, is cosmopolitan. He beseeches them, entreats them, a term indicating intensity and earnestness, "for the sake of Jesus Christ, to strive with him in their prayers for him." This he desires that he may be delivered from evil and designing men, who might hinder and embarrass him in his mission, then further that his service for the poor saints might be accepted by the saints, and that he might ultimately come unto them with joy that they might be refreshed.

How full of heart earnestness is his request! How tender and loving is his appeal! How touching and high is the motive to the highest and truest form of prayer, "for the Lord Jesus Christ's sake!" Also for the love we bear to the Spirit, or for the love which the Spirit bears to us; by the ties of the holy brotherhood. By these lofty and constraining motives does he urge them to pray for him and to "strive with him" in their mutual praying. Paul is in the great prayer struggle, a struggle in which the mightiest issues are involved and imperiled; and he is in the midst of this struggle. He is committed to it because Christ is in it. He needs help, help which comes alone through prayer. So he pleads with his brethren to pray for him and with him.

By prayer enemies are to be swept out of the way. By prayer prejudices are to be driven out of the hearts of good men. His way to Jerusalem would be cleared of difficulties, the success of his mission would be secured, and the will of God and the good of the saints would be accomplished. All these marvelous ends would be secured by marvelous praying. Wonderful and world-wide are the results to be gained by mighty praying. If all apostolic successors had prayed as Paul did, in all Christians in all these ages had been one with apostolical men in the mighty wrestlings of prayer, how marvelous and divine would have been the history of God's church! How unparalleled would have been its success! The glory of its millennium would have brightened and blessed the world ages ago.

We see in Paul's requests his estimate of the far-reaching power of prayer. Not that prayer has in it any talismanic force, nor that it is a fetish, but that it moves God to do things that it nominates. Prayer has no magic, potent charm in itself, but is only all potent because it gets the Omnipotent God to grant its request. A precedent basis in all prayer as expressed or understood by Paul is that "Ye strive together with me in your prayers for me." It is of the nature of a severe conflict in which Paul's soul is engaged, a wrestle, a hand-to-hand fight. The strain is severe and exhaustive to all the energies of the soul, and the issue is tossed in uncertainty. Paul in this prayer struggle needs reinforcements and divine help in his striving. He is in the midst of the struggle, and will bear the brunt, but he solicits and pleads for the help of others. Their prayers are just now needed. He needs help to offer intense prayers.

Prayer is not inaptly called "wrestling," because it is a most intense struggle. To prayer there are the greatest hindrances and the most inveterate foes. Mighty evil forces surge around the closets of prayer. Enemies strong and strongly entrenched are about the closets where praying is done. No feeble, listless act is this praying done by Paul. In this thing he has "put away childish things." The commonplace and the tame have been retired. Paul must do this praying mightily or not do it at all. Hell must stagger under the mightiness of his prayer stroke, or he strikes not at all. The strongest graces and the manliest efforts are requisite here. Strength is demanded in the praying done by Paul. Courage is at a premium in it. Timid touches and faint-hearted desires avail nothing in the mind of Paul which we are considering. Enemies are to be faced and routed and fields are to be won. The most unflagging and invincible bravery and the highest qualities of Christian soldierhood are demanded for prayer. It is a trumpet call to prayer, a chieftain's clarion note, sounded out for earnest, persistent prayer as the great spiritual conflict rages.

16

Paul and His Requests for Prayer
(Continued)

WE come to the request of Paul made to the church at Ephesus, found in the latter part of Ephesians six:

> Praying always with all prayer and supplication in the Spirit, and watching thereunto with all perseverance and supplication for all saints; And for me that utterance may be given unto me, that I may open my mouth boldly, to make known the mystery of the Gospel, For which I am an ambassador in bonds, that therein I may speak boldly as I ought to speak.

For this church he had labored and prayed night and day, with many watchings and tears, and much humility. As he drew a vivid picture of the Christian soldier, with his foes besetting him, he gave them this charge of praying specially for him.

To these Ephesian Christians he gave a comprehensive statement of the necessity, nature and special benefits of prayer. It was to be urgent, covering all times and embracing all manner of places. Supplication must give intensity, the Holy Spirit must be invoked, vigilance and perseverance must be added, and the whole family of saints were involved.

The force of his request for prayer centered on him, that he might be able to talk with force, fluency, directness and courage. Paul did not depend upon his natural gifts, but on those which came to him in answer to prayer. He was afraid he would be a coward, a dull, dry speaker, or a hesitating stammerer, and he urged these believers to pray that he might have courage, not only to speak clearly, but also freely and fully.

He desired them to pray that he might have boldness. No quality seems more important to the preacher than that of boldness. It is that positive quality which does not reckon consequences, but with freedom and fullness meets the crisis, faces a present danger, and discharges unawed a present duty. It was one of the marked characteristics of apostolic preachers and apostolic preaching. They were bold men, they were bold preachers. The reference to the manifestation of the principle by them is almost the record of their trials. It is the applause of their faith.

There are many chains which enslave the preacher. His very tenderness makes him weak. His attachments to the people tend to bring him into bondage. His personal intercourse, his obligations to his people, his love for them, all tend to hamper his freedom and restrain his pulpit deliverances. What great need to be continually praying for boldness to speak boldly as he ought to speak!

The prophets of old were charged not to be afraid of the faces of men. Unawed by the frowns of men, they were to declare the truth of God without apology, timidity, hesitancy or compromise. The warmth and freedom of conviction and of sincerity, the fearlessness of a vigorous faith, and above all the power of the Holy Spirit, are all wonderful helpers and elements of boldness. How all this should be coveted and sought with all earnestness by ministers of the Gospel in this day!

Meekness and humility are high virtues of the first importance in the preacher, but these qualities do not at all militate against boldness. This boldness is not the freedom of passionate utterances. It is not scolding nor rashness. It speaks the truth in love. Boldness is not rudeness. Roughness dishonors boldness. It is as gentle as a mother with a babe, but as fearless as a lion standing before a foe. Fear, in the mild and innocent form of timidity, or in the criminal form of cowardice, has no place in the true ministry. Humble but holy boldness is of the very first importance.

What hidden, mysterious mighty force can add courage to apostolic preaching, and give bolder utterances to apostolic lips? There is one answer, and it is that prayer can do the deed.

What force can so affect and dominate evil that the very results of evil will be changed into good? We have the answer in Paul's words again, in connection with prayers made for him:

> Who delivered us from so great a death, and doth deliver; in whom we trust that he will yet deliver us; Ye also helping together in prayer for us. What then? Notwithstanding every way, whether in pretense or in truth, Christ is preached, and therein I do rejoice, yea, and will rejoice.

We can see how the promises of God are made real and personal by prayer. "All things work together for good to them that love God." Here is a jeweled promise. Paul loved God, but he did not leave the promise alone, as a matter of course, to work out its blessed results. So he wrote to the Corinthians as we have before seen, "I am in trouble. I trust in God to deliver. Ye also helping together by prayer." Helping me by prayer, you help God to make the promise strong and rich in realization.

Paul's prayer requests embraced "supplication for all saints," but especially for apostolic courage for himself. How much he needed this courage just as all true preachers, called of God, need it! Prayer was to open doors for apostolic labors but at the same time it was to open apostolic lips to utter bravely and truly the apostolic message. Hear him as he speaks to the church at Colosse:

> Withal praying also for us, that God would open to us a door of utterance to speak the mystery of Christ, for which I am also in bonds; That I may make it manifest as I ought to speak.

How appropriate such a request to be made by a present-day preacher to his congregation! How great the need of those things by the present-day preacher which Paul desired for himself!

As in the request to the Ephesians, Paul wants a "door of utterance" given him, that he may preach with the liberty of the Spirit, be delivered from being straitened in thought or hampered in delivery. Furthermore, he desires the ability to make manifest in the clearest terms, without confusion of thought, and with force of utterance, the Gospel "as he ought to speak," and just as every preacher should speak. Happy that preacher who ministers to a people who pray thus for him! And happier still if he inwardly feels, as he faces his responsible task and realizes how much he needs these things to preach clearly, forcibly and effectively, that he has urged his people to pray for him!

Prayer transforms crosses, trials, and oppositions into blessings, and causes them to work together for good. "These shall turn to my salvation through your prayers," says Paul. Just as the same things today in the life of the preacher are transformed into gracious blessings in the end, "ye also helping together by prayer." Saintly praying mightily helped apostolic preaching and rescued apostolic men from many sore straits. So just such praying in these days will effect like results in faithful preaching done by brave, fearless ministers. Prayer for the preacher avails just as prayer by the preacher avails. Two things are always factors in the life and work of a true preacher: First when he prays constantly, fervently, and persistently for those to whom he preaches; and secondly, when those to whom he ministers pray for their preacher. Happy is the preacher so situated. Blessed is that congregation thus favored.

To the church at Thessalonica Paul sends this pressing request, pointed, clear, and forcible:

> Finally, brethren, pray for us, that the word of the Lord may have free course, and be glorified, even as it is with you; And that we may be delivered from wicked and unreasonable men.

He has in mind a racecourse, on which the racer is exerting himself to reach the goal. Hindrances are in the way of his success and must be removed, so that the racer may finally succeed and obtain the reward. The "Word of the Lord" is this racer, as preached by Paul. This Word is personified and there are serious impediments which hinder the running of the Word. It must have "free course." Everything in the way and opposing its running must be taken out of its roadway. These impediments in the way of the Word of the Lord "running and being glorified" are found in the preacher himself, in the church to whom he ministers, and in the sinners around him. The Word runs and is glorified when it has unobstructed access to the minds and hearts of those to whom it is preached, when sinners are convicted for sin, when they seriously consider the claims of God's Word on them, and when they are induced to pray for themselves, asking for pardoning mercy. It is glorified when saints are instructed in religious experience, corrected of errors of doctrine and mistakes in practice, and when they are led to seek for higher things and to pray for deeper experiences in the divine life.

Mark you. It is not when the preacher is glorified because of the wonderful success wrought by the Word. It is not when people praise him unduly, and make much of him because of his wonderful sermons, his great eloquence and his remarkable gifts. The preacher is kept in the background in all this work of glorification, even though he is foremost as being the object of all this praying.

Prayer is to do all these things. So Paul urges, entreats, insists, "Pray for us." And it is not so much prayer for Paul personally in his Christian life and religious experience. All this needed much prayer. It was really for him officially, prayer for him in the office and work of a gospel minister. His tongue must be unloosed in preaching, his mouth unstopped, and his mind set free. Prayer must help in his religious life not so much because it would help to "work out his own salvation," but rather because right living would give strength to the Word of the Lord, and would save him from being a hindrance to the Word which he preached. And as he desires that no hindrance should be in himself which would defeat his own preaching, so he wants all hindrances taken away from the churches to whom he ministers that church people may not stand in the way or weigh down the Word as it runs on the racecourse attempting to reach the goal, even the minds and hearts of the people. Furthermore, he wishes hindrances in the unsaved to be set aside that God's Word as preached by him may reach their hearts and be glorified in their salvation.

With all this before him, Paul sends this pressing request to these believers at Thessalonica, "Pray for us," because praying by true Christians would greatly help in the running of the Word of the Lord.

Wise that preacher who has the eyes to see these things, and who realizes that his success largely depends upon praying of this kind on the part of his people for him. How much do we need churches now who, having the preacher in mind and the preached Word on their hearts, pray for him that "the Word of the Lord may have free course, and be glorified."

One other item in this request is worth noting: "That we may be delivered from wicked and unreasonable men." Such men are hindrances in the way of the Word of the Lord. Few preachers but are harassed by them and need to be delivered from them. Prayer helps to bring such a deliverance to preachers from "unreasonable and wicked men." Paul was annoyed by such characters, and for this very reason he urged prayer for him that he might find deliverance from them.

Summing it all up, we find that Paul feels that the success of the Word, its liberty and largeness, are bound up in their prayers, and that their failure to pray would restrict its influence and its glory. His deliverance from unreasonable and wicked men as well as his safety, he asserts, are in some way dependent upon their prayers. These prayers, while they greatly helped him to preach, would at the same time protect his person from the cruel purposes of wicked and unreasonable men.

In Hebrews 13:9, Paul thus opens his heart to those Hebrew Christians in asking them to pray for him:

> Pray for us, for we trust we have a good conscience, in all things willing to live honestly.

In this prayer request, Paul's inward consciousness of his integrity of heart and his internal witness to his personal honesty come out and are a basic truth of his Christian character. No room for blame does he find in himself. "Pray for us." Your prayers for us will find in me honest integrity and honest execution and honest administration of all prayer results.

The request is intended to stir up the saints to more earnest praying, more devotion to prayer, and more urgency in prayer. Prayer must affect his visit to them, would hasten it and enlarge its beneficial results.

Paul is on the most cordial and freest terms with Philemon. He is anxious and expects to visit him at some future day and makes the appointment. He takes it for granted that Philemon is praying, for as this man had been converted under his ministry, it is assumed that he has been taught the Pauline lesson of prayer. He assumes also that prayer will open up the way for his visit, remove the hindrances, and bring them graciously together. So he requests Philemon to prepare a lodging place for him, adding, "I trust through your prayers I shall be given to you." Paul had the idea that his movements were hindered or helped by the prayers of his brethren.